Monetary Trends in the United States and the United Kingdom

A National Bureau
of Economic Research
Monograph

Monetary Trends in the United States and the United Kingdom

Their Relation to Income, Prices, and Interest Rates, 1867–1975

Milton Friedman and
Anna J. Schwartz

 The University of Chicago Press

Chicago and London

The University of Chicago Press, Chicago 60637
The University of Chicago Press, Ltd., London

Printed in the United States of America
89 88 87 86 85 84 83 5 4 3 2

Library of Congress Cataloging in Publication Data

Friedman, Milton, 1912—
    Monetary trends in the United States and the
United Kingdom, their relation to income, prices,
and interest rates, 1867–1975.

    (National Bureau of Economic Research monograph)
    Bibliography: p.
    Includes indexes.
    1. Money supply—United States—History.
2. Money supply—Great Britain—History.
3. United States—Economic conditions. 4. Great
Britain—Economic conditions. I. Schwartz, Anna
Jacobson. II. Title. III. Series.
HG501.F74   332.4'973   81–16273

ISBN 0-226-26409-2 (cloth)   AACR2
        0-226-26410-6 (paper)

Relation of the Directors to the
Work and Publications of the
National Bureau of Economic Research

1. The object of the National Bureau of Economic Research is to ascertain and to present to the public important economic facts and their interpretation in a scientific and impartial manner. The Board of Directors is charged with the reponsibility of ensuring that the work of the National Bureau is carried on in strict conformity with this object.

2. The President of the National Bureau shall submit to the Board of Directors, or to its Executive Committee, for their formal adoption all specific proposals for research to be instituted.

3. No research report shall be published by the National Bureau until the President has sent each member of the Board a notice that a manuscript is recommended for publication and that in the President's opinion it is suitable for publication in accordance with the principles of the National Bureau. Such notification will include an abstract or summary of the manuscript's content and a response form for use by those Directors who desire a copy of the manuscript for review. Each manuscript shall contain a summary drawing attention to the nature and treatment of the problem studied, the character of the data and their utilization in the report, and the main conclusions reached.

4. For each manuscript so submitted, a special committee of the Directors (including Directors Emeriti) shall be appointed by majority agreement of the President and Vice Presidents (or by the Executive Committee in case of inability to decide on the part of the President and Vice Presidents), consisting of three Directors selected as nearly as may be one from each general division of the Board. The names of the special manuscript committee shall be stated to each Director when notice of the proposed publication is submitted to him. It shall be the duty of each member of the special manuscript committee to read the manuscript. If each member of the manuscript committee signifies his approval within thirty days of the transmittal of the manuscript, the report may be published. If at the end of that period any member of the manuscript committee withholds his approval, the President shall then notify each member of the Board, requesting approval or disapproval of publication, and thirty days additional shall be granted for this purpose. The manuscript shall then not be published unless at least a majority of the entire Board who shall have voted on the proposal within the time fixed for the receipt of votes shall have approved.

5. No manuscript may be published, though approved by each member of the special manuscript committee, until forty-five days have elapsed from the transmittal of the report in manuscript form. The interval is allowed for the receipt of any memorandum of dissent or reservation, together with a brief statement of his reasons, that any member may wish to express; and such memorandum of dissent or reservation shall be published with the manuscript if he so desires. Publication does not, however, imply that each member of the Board has read the manuscript, or that either members of the Board in general or the special committee have passed on its validity in every detail.

6. Publications of the National Bureau issued for informational purposes concerning the work of the Bureau and its staff, or issued to inform the public of activities of Bureau staff, and volumes issued as a result of various conferences involving the National Bureau shall contain a specific disclaimer noting that such publication has not passed through the normal review procedures required in this resolution. The Executive Committee of the Board is charged with review of all such publications from time to time to ensure that they do not take on the character of formal research reports of the National Bureau, requiring formal Board approval.

7. Unless otherwise determined by the Board or exempted by the terms of paragraph 6, a copy of this resolution shall be printed in each National Bureau publication.

(Resolution adopted October 25, 1926, as revised through September 30, 1974)

What are large collections of facts for? To make theories *from*, says Bacon: to try ready-made theories *by*, says the history of discovery: it's all the same, says the idolater: nonsense, say we!

Augustus de Morgan, *A Budget of Paradoxes*

Contents

Charts

Tables

Preface

This preface is like the "synopsis" that appears at the head of each new chapter of a serialized novel, recounting the key events of earlier chapters so that the reader who has picked up the story for the first time can make sense out of the installment that follows. It is especially needed for this book because of the long interval that has elapsed between the earlier installments and this one—the fourth and last of a series of books that had their origin in new estimates of the quantity of money in the United States. For the benefit of new arrivals, this preface, like the standard "synopsis," touches on the highlights of some of the earlier books, repeating for the first two what was said in the preface of the third.

A Monetary History of the United States, 1867–1960, by Milton Friedman and Anna J. Schwartz, was the first in the series. "It traces changes in the stock of money for nearly a century, from just after the Civil War to 1960, examines the factors that accounted for the changes, and analyzes the reflex influence that the stock of money exerted on the course of events."[1]

Determinants and Effects of Changes in the Money Stock, 1875–1960, by Phillip Cagan, examines intensively the sources of changes in the stock of money and gives a detailed statistical analysis of the cyclical and secular behavior of each of the proximate determinants of the quantity of money: high-powered money, the ratio of deposits at banks to their reserves, and the ratio of the public's holdings of deposits to its holdings of currency.[2]

Monetary Statistics of the United States, by Friedman and Schwartz, describes in detail how the new estimates of the stock of money were

---

1. Princeton University Press for the National Bureau of Economic Research, 1963, p. 3.
2. National Bureau of Economic Research, 1965.

constructed and gives supplementary tables that, though by-products of the estimation process, are of interest in their own right.[3] Its title, unlike those of the earlier volumes, is not qualified by dates because *Monetary Statistics* also surveys earlier attempts to estimate the United States money stock and gives a comprehensive summary of earlier numerical estimates. Hence its temporal scope is roughly coterminous with that of the Republic. Finally, *Monetary Statistics* surveys the usage of the term *money* in economic literature, examines a number of attempts to settle on a particular definition of money on the basis of theoretical considerations, and presents the criteria and evidence that led us to the particular definition we have selected for the United States for the period covered by our estimates: currency held by the public plus all deposits adjusted of commercial banks.

Monetary Statistics "is for the monetary statistician who is interested in basic data on the quantity of money. It provides raw material for analysis but little economic analysis."[4]

The present book, like the first two in the series, attempts to provide such analysis. *A Monetary History* presented a chronological and largely qualitative analysis. *Determinants and Effects* presented both a historical and a statistical analysis of the supply of money. The special task of this book is to present a statistical and theoretical analysis of the relation between the quantity of money and other key economic magnitudes over periods longer than those dominated by cyclical fluctuations—hence the term *trends* in the title. Unlike the first three books, this one is not restricted to the United States but includes comparable data for the United Kingdom.

This book has been a long time in the making—indeed, a first draft of it was completed before any of the others in the series had been published. A second draft, more comparable to the present version in topics covered and statistical approach, was completed in 1966 and submitted tentatively to an NBER reading committee (Phillip Cagan, Solomon Fabricant, chairman, and Jack Guttentag). That draft was restricted entirely to the United States. The reading committee suggested that the book's value would be enhanced by broadening its coverage to include the United Kingdom and perhaps other countries so as to permit international comparisons. At the time the suggestion seemed to us eminently sensible, and we thought it could be implemented with a modest expenditure of time. We were clearly wrong. Getting comparable data for the United Kingdom, making parallel analyses, and consolidating the results for the two countries turned out to be far more difficult and time-consuming than we had expected. We underestimated how much of a start the earlier

3. National Bureau of Economic Research, 1970.
4. Ibid., p. 3

three volumes—all for the United States only—had given us for the United States analysis in this one, and how much of that background material we would have to duplicate for the United Kingdom. Other digressions and interruptions affecting both authors delayed us further, so that the book was not finished until a decade after the latest date at which we initially expected to complete it.

The delay enabled us to lengthen the period studied and to benefit from the flood of research on monetary matters during the past two decades. Needless to say, incorporating the new material added to the delay. Though no doubt the new material, the longer period covered, and the inclusion of the United Kingdom have all added to the value of the book, in retrospect we probably made a mistake in accepting the reading committee's suggestion. We doubt that the added contribution of the book adequately compensates for the additional effort and the long delay. We are somewhat comforted for the mistake—if mistake it was—by the fairly wide informal circulation that the original and subsequent drafts have had among scholars and the economic research that has been stimulated thereby, much of it through the Workshop in Money and Banking at the University of Chicago and through associates at the NBER. We in turn have been able to use the results of that research and have incorporated much of it herein.

In the preface to *Monetary Statistics* we wrote that we planned an additional book on monetary cycles. Much to our regret, that plan has proved another casualty to the unanticipated time it took us to complete this book. Our systematic published work on cycles will therefore be restricted to our earlier article, "Money and Business Cycles."[5] Perhaps it is pure rationalization, but we have been surprised to find how much of the material in this book has direct relevance to the topics frequently considered under the heading "cyclical fluctuations." Whether that is true or not, we shall have to leave to other hands a fuller study of monetary cycles. Similarly, we shall have to leave to other hands the extension of our study of monetary trends to countries other than the United States and the United Kingdom.[6]

5. *Review of Economics and Statistics* 45 (1, suppl.) (February 1963): 32–64; reprinted in M. Friedman, *The Optimum Quantity of Money* (Aldine, 1969), chap. 10.

6. Such an extension has already been made for some countries and some of the topics we cover. See David Meiselman, ed., *Varieties of Monetary Experience* (University of Chicago Press, 1970), which includes six studies of monetary phenomena: for a cross-section of forty-seven countries during the post–World War II period (Morris Perlman); for Canada from 1867 to 1965 (George Macesich); for Chile, from 1879 to 1955 (John Deaver); for South Korea from 1953 to 1961 and for Brazil from 1948 to 1965 (Colin Campbell); for Argentina from 1935 to 1962 (Adolfo Cesar Diz); and for Japan after World War II (Michael Keran). Other studies include: Allan H. Meltzer, "The Behavior of the French Money Supply: 1938–54, " *Journal of Political Economy* 67 (June 1959): 275–91; K. A. J. Hay, "Money and Cycles in Post Confederation Canada," *Journal of Political Economy* 75

Because this book has been such a long time in the making, we have accumulated intellectual debts to many persons. We apologize in advance to any that we fail to acknowledge because of the exponential decay of memory over time.

For a discussion of problems of measurement of the United Kingdom money stock before the 1900s, we are indebted to Shizuya Nishimura, David K. Sheppard, and Michael D. Bordo. Nishimura sent us an unpublished paper, referred to in chapter 4, that helped us to extend into the 1870s the series that Sheppard had constructed beginning 1880 and to revise some of Sheppard's estimates. Sheppard was most generous in extending his money series beyond 1966, the final year of his published estimates. Bordo's work on the nineteenth-century British monetary data was also helpful to us.

A revised and improved money stock series for the United Kingdom is likely to become available as part of a new study of United Kingdom monetary history now under way, under the direction of Brian Griffiths, at the Centre for Banking and International Finance of City University, London. Had that study been completed in time for us to use its results, our task would have been easier. Some of our findings may require revision if the new money series differs appreciably from the one we use.

Problems we encountered with estimates of the British income series before World War I led us to address a memorandum to a group of British economic statisticians concerning the data movements we found defective (see chap. 4 for the details). We acknowledge with thanks the courteous replies we received, especially those from C. H. Feinstein.

Among those who provided criticism, comments, and stimulation especially relevant to this book are the late Clark Warburton, Moses Abramovitz, Solomon Fabricant, Phillip Cagan, and participants in the Workshop on Money and Banking of the University of Chicago. Among those who assisted us in the statistical work of the earliest drafts of this book, dating back to the 1960s, are Lottie Boschan, Juanita Johnson, and Martha S. Lichtenstein; also Nadeschda Bohsack, Antonette Burgar, Marilyn McGirr, Esther D. Reichner, Selma Seligsohn, the late Hanna Stern, Mark L. Wehle, and Tom Teng-pin Yu. Successive drafts that we prepared in the 1970s benefited greatly from the devoted efforts of three

---

(June 1967): 262–73; Lars Jonung, "Money and Prices in Sweden, 1732–1972," in *Inflation in the World Economy*, ed. J. M. Parkin and G. Zis (Manchester: Manchester University Press, 1975); T. J. Courchene, "An Analysis of the Canadian Money Supply, 1925–34," *Journal of Political Economy* 77 (May/June 1969): 363–91. For Japan, a project at the Institute for Industrial Relations, Rikkyo University, has produced a major study, Kokishi Asakuri and Chiaki Nishiyama, eds., *A Monetary Analysis and History of the Japanese Economy, 1868–1970* (Tokyo: Sobunsha, 1974) [primarily in Japanese but with table titles and caption headings, and summary articles in English]. The extensive bibliography of this volume includes still other studies.

outstanding research assistants: Roy Andersen, Nurhan Helvacian, and Linda Dunn. We gratefully acknowledge their help.

We have also received helpful suggestions on the final draft from the NBER staff and directors' reading committees (Phillip Cagan, Stanley Fischer, and Robert J. Gordon; Walter F. Hoadley, Stephan F. Kaliski, and James Simler).

The National Bureau and its successive directors of research and presidents—Arthur F. Burns, Solomon Fabricant, Geoffrey H. Moore, John R. Meyer, and Martin Feldstein—have been incredibly patient and understanding in giving us their full support during the long period involved in completing this and the earlier studies in the series. In addition, we are most grateful to the Ford Foundation and the J. Howard Pew Freedom Trust for grants for the specific purpose of enabling us to complete this work.

All in all, it is with a sense of satisfaction and relief that we terminate our part in a scholarly venture that we started more than a quarter of a century ago.

Monetary Trends in the United States and the United Kingdom

Principal Empirical Findings

Note

Money throughout refers to currency plus adjusted demand and time deposits of commercial banks held by the public.

Income throughout refers to net national product.

Nominal money or income is money or income in dollars or pounds at current prices.

Real income or output refers to net national product at constant prices.

Prices refer to the implicit price index obtained by dividing national product at current prices by national product at constant prices.

Basic data are geometric averages of annual data for cycle phases (expansions or contractions) that average 2.0 years in length for the United States and 2.8 years for the United Kingdom.

Rates of change for a phase are generally the slopes of straight lines fitted to the logarithms of three successive phase averages (the phase in question, the prior phase, and the following phase).

Demand for Money

1. In the century from the mid-1870s to the mid-1970s, the quantity of money rose in the United States from the equivalent of eleven weeks' income to nearly thirty weeks' income but fell in the United Kingdom from more than thirty weeks' income to twenty-five weeks' income (table 5.2).

2. These contrasting results were produced by

    a) Increasing financial sophistication in the United States (particularly before World War I), reflected in a reduction in the fraction of money held as currency from 33 percent to 12 percent just before World War I and 11 percent in the mid-1920s (sec. 6.3).

    b) Rising real per capita incomes in both the United States and the United Kingdom. The rise in income raised money holdings in the United

States, expressed in terms of weeks on income, lowered them in the United Kingdom (see point 4).

c) A more rapid rise in nominal yields on financial and physical assets in the United Kingdom than in the United States. United States yields were higher than United Kingdom yields at the outset of the century but lower at the end (table 5.3).

3. Our data support the theoretical expectation that changes in population and prices would affect nominal aggregate money holding but not real per capita money holdings (sec. 6.5).

4. Rising real per capita income had opposite effects on money holdings expressed in terms of weeks of income in the United States and the United Kingdom. With other variables constant, a 1 percent increase in real per capita income on the average increases real per capita money holdings by about 1.1 percent in the United States, by about 0.9 percent in the United Kingdom (sec. 6.7). Hence rising income raised money holdings expressed in terms of weeks of income in the United States (i.e., lowered monetary velocity) but lowered them in the United Kingdom (i.e., raised monetary velocity).

5. Aside from the difference in real income elasticity and change in financial sophistication, not only was the real quantity of money demanded affected by the same variables in the two countries during the century we study, but also those variables had the same quantitative effect (sec. 6.7). The chief other variables that operated throughout the period were (1) the differential between the interest return on financial assets and the interest return on money; (2) the yield on physical assets (sec. 6.6). In addition, two factors had significant effects for part of the period in both countries: (3) a delayed adjustment to wartime disturbances; (4) an upward shift in demand during the Great Depression and the Second World War, produced, we conjecture, by greatly increased uncertainty (sec. 6.4).

7. On the average a one percentage point (*not* 1 percent) change in the difference between the yield on financial assets and on money produces something more than a 9 percent (not percentage point) change in the opposite direction in the quantity of money. We measured the yield on financial assets by the short-term interest rate, which in various tests proved a better variable than an alternative long-term rate. Nothing was gained by adding a long-term rate as well. However, theoretical considerations suggest that the entire term structure of yields should be relevant. An experiment with United States data supports the theory but does not increase predictive accuracy of the resulting demand equation (sec. 6.9).

8. As a proxy for the nominal yield on physical assets we have used the rate of change of aggregate nominal income. Both theoretical considerations and empirical tests (sec. 6.6.3; sec. 10.3) support the validity of the

proxy as possibly the best available approximation to the average yield on a broad range of physical assets (including not only those for which there are corresponding market instruments such as shares of stock or deeds of possession, but also human capital). On the average, a one percentage point change in our proxy produces something more than a 0.4 percent change in the quantity of money demanded in the opposite direction (sec. 6.6.3).

9. The single equation we estimate for the two countries combined leaves a residual variation to be explained by omitted variables or statistical error of about 5 percent for the level of money demanded, about 1.5 percentage points for the rate of change of the quantity of money demanded. The residual variation is approximately the same for the United States and for the United Kingdom.

10. The simplest of quantity theories, which supposes that the ratio of nominal money to nominal income is a numerical constant aside from independent random errors in money and income, supplemented for the United States by an adjustment for increasing financial sophistication before World War I, turns out to be an impressive first approximation, which accounts for well over half the variation in money (if income is viewed as the independent variable) or in income (if money is viewed as the independent variable). Allowing for an income elasticity differing from unity, shift variables, and yields does improve the results. It cuts the error remaining after allowing for the simple quantity theory by nearly three-quarters for the level of money (which means, cuts the variance by less than half) but by only one-quarter for the rates of change of money (chap. 6, tables 6.6 and 6.14 and equations 26 and 27).

11. For both levels and rates of change, allowing for an income elasticity differing from unity and for the shifts accounts for the bulk of the reduction in the residual error. Allowing in addition for yields reduces the residual error for levels by about one-fifth, and that for rates of change only trivially (chap. 6, tables 6.6 and 6.14 and equations 26 and 27).

Common Financial System

12. The level of velocity in the United States parallels that in the United Kingdom for most of the century our data cover; and the rates of change are nearly identical in the two countries (sec. 7.2; chart 7.1; table 7.2).

13. The high correlation between the two countries of velocity and its rate of change reflects the determination of the demand for money in the two countries by the same variables (point 5 above) plus the similar movements in these common determinants. If the movements of the common determinants had been uncorrelated between the two countries,

the variance of the differences between the two countries would have been doubled for levels of velocity and more than quadrupled for rates of change of velocity (sec. 7.3; table 7.3).

14. The common movements of velocity reflect a unified financial system in which monetary variables such as prices, interest rates, nominal income, and stocks of money are constrained to keep largely in step except as changes in exchange rates alter the number of units of one country's currency equivalent to one unit of the other country's currency. However, physical magnitudes are not so constrained. The highest correlation for the two countries is for prices; the lowest, for real per capita income (table 7.2).

15. Influence ran both ways across the Atlantic, though there is some evidence that real effects were stronger from the United States to the United Kingdom and price effects from the United Kingdom to the United States. Changes in each country affected both nominal income and prices in the other country (sec. 7.4.2).

16. For nominal income before 1914, the influence of each country on the other was manifested entirely through its influence on the other country's quantity of money—the classical specie-flow process. After 1914, that remains true for the United States but not for the United Kingdom. United Kingdom nominal income, for a given quantity of money in the United Kingdom, was also affected by changes in United States money and velocity. We conjecture that the channel of influence was interest rates. The difference between the United States and the United Kingdom in channels of influence is something of a puzzle, only partly explained by the far greater role of the United States after 1914 than before (sec. 7.4.2).

17. For prices throughout the period, the influence of each country on the other operates not only through effects on the other country's quantity of money but also more directly. To isolate this effect after 1914 requires allowing explicitly for changes in exchange rates (sec. 7.4.2). This is an expression of the "law of one price."

18. Evidence on how well the "law of one price" holds is provided by estimates of the purchasing-power-parity exchange rate—the number of United States dollars that has the same purchasing power as one British pound. If the "law of one price" held perfectly, the purchasing-power-parity exchange rate would equal the market rate. Our year-by-year estimates fluctuate around the market rate, much more closely before the early 1930s (between plus and minus 10 percent of the market rate) than afterward (between 10 percent below the market rate and 60 percent above). Government intervention in the exchange market since the 1930s has been more potent in disunifying the markets than improvements in transportation and communication have been in unifying them (sec. 6.8).

Relation between Nominal Money and Nominal Income

19. The level of nominal income parallels with great fidelity the level of the nominal quantity of money, and the rate of change of nominal income parallels the rate of change of the nominal quantity of money. That is true for both the United States and the United Kingdom and for the whole of the century our data cover. The largest discrepancies occur during and just after World War II (secs. 5.2, 5.3; charts 5.2 and 5.4). This parallelism is a manifestation of the stable demand curve for money plus the excellence of the simple quantity theory approximation.

20. The fluctuations about the trend tend to be greater in amplitude for nominal income than for nominal money—in conformance with an implication of the theoretical analysis of chapter 2 (sec. 5.2; table 5.5).

21. Both nominal money and nominal income are more variable after 1914 than before, and that is equally true for output and prices for both countries—which we interpret as resulting from the effective end of the international gold standard (table 5.5).

22. We estimate that measurement error (standard error) in the level of nominal income is between 2.5 and 4.5 percent; in the rate of change of nominal income between 0.5 and 0.75 of one percentage point, about the same for the two countries. We have no comparable estimates for nominal money or its rate of change (sec. 8.1).

23. Estimates of the temporal reaction pattern of income to a sustained change in the rate of monetary growth, though not firmly determined statistically, are in general conformance with the pattern suggested by the theoretical analysis of chapter 2. Generally the pattern involves an initial overshoot of nominal income, produced by transient effects, then a highly damped cyclical return to an equilibrium trend (chart 8.1). The effects take a considerable time, measured in phases, not quarters.

24. Our data are consistent with the theoretical expectation that the cumulative effect of a 1 percentage point change in monetary growth will be a 1 percentage point change in the same direction in the rate of nominal income growth (table 8.6).

The Division of Nominal Income Change between Prices and Output

25. The fraction of nominal income change accounted for by price change and output change varied greatly over the period. In both countries, prices had roughly a horizontal trend before 1914 and a generally rising trend after 1914 (interrupted most drastically by the Great Depression). There is no corresponding difference in output, which had a generally rising trend, at roughly the same rate, throughout the century. As a result price change accounted for a decidedly larger share of nominal income change after than before 1914 (table 5.5).

26. The average rate of output rise was greater throughout in the United States (3.1 percent per year) than in the United Kingdom (1.7 percent per year). The rate of price rise was greater in the United Kingdom (2.3 percent per year for the century, 3.0 percent after 1914) than in the United States (1.8 percent per year for the century, 2.1 percent after 1914) (table 5.5; chap. 9).

27. Throughout the period, the level of the nominal quantity of money per unit of output parallels with great fidelity the level of prices, and the rate of change of the nominal quantity of money per unit of output parallels the rate of change of prices. That is true for both the United States and the United Kingdom and for the whole of the century our data cover. The largest discrepancies occur during and after World War II (chap. 5; charts 5.3, panel 3, and 5.6, panel 3). This parallelism reflects the parallelism of nominal money and nominal income (point 19 above) plus the greater influence of monetary change on prices than on output.

28. Estimates of the temporal reaction patterns of prices and output to a sustained change in the rate of monetary growth, though not well determined statistically, are in general conformance with the pattern suggested by the theoretical analysis of chapter 2: generally, an initial overshoot of prices followed by a cyclical reaction pattern, and a cyclical reaction pattern in output. The price pattern deserves some confidence, the output pattern very little (chap. 9; chart 9.5).

29. It takes a considerable time, measured in phases, not months or quarters, before a change in the rate of monetary growth is fully reflected in prices (point 23 above and secs. 9.3 and 9.6).

30. For United Kingdom peacetime years, there is little if any effect of monetary change on output. The rate of change of output seems to be a random series from phase to phase (though not pure white noise because there is some serial dependence). Its variability is of the same order of magnitude as would be produced by measurement error (chap. 9, tables 9.10, 9.13, 9.14). The results are consistent with a simple quantity theory that regards price change as determined primarily by monetary change and output by independent other factors. A sustained 1 percentage point change in the rate of monetary growth ultimately produces a change of 1 percentage point in the same direction in the rate of price change, but initially is absorbed partly by a change in velocity in the opposite direction.

31. For the United States, roughly the same conclusions hold for the pre–World War I and post–World War II periods with two minor differences: (1) there is evidence of at least a transitory influence of monetary factors on output change; (2) output is more variable than prices, whereas the reverse is true for the United Kingdom (tables 9.10, 9.13, 9.14). However, the dominant influence and ultimately the whole influence of monetary change is on prices rather than output and, as for the United Kingdom, a sustained change of 1 percentage point in the rate of

monetary growth ultimately produces a 1 percentage point change in the same direction in the rate of price change.

32. For peacetime years for the United Kingdom, and for the United States excluding the interwar period, price change between cycle phases tends to be inversely related to output change, rather than positively related, as seems true within cycles and as is implicit in analysis along Phillips curve lines. Put differently, the Phillips curve, at least for cycle phases, seems, if anything, positively, rather than negatively, sloped (tables 9.1, 9.12; secs. 9.2, 9.7).

33. The interwar period for the United States is idiosyncratic—though for that very reason both important and instructive. It is the only peacetime period for either country in which (*a*) monetary change has a major influence on output change in the same direction (table 9.1; secs. 9.5, 9.7); (*b*) price change and output change are positively correlated (table 9.1); (*c*) most of nominal income change is absorbed by output change (table 9.6); (*d*) a Phillips curve is clearly negatively sloped (table 9.13).

34. The idiosyncrasy of the interwar period appears to arise from the importance of major economic contractions during the period (three in twenty years: 1920–21, 1929–33, 1937–38) and to reflect features common to such major contractions. Traces of the same phenomena appear in the pre–World War I period at times of major contractions (sec. 9.2). We concluded in *A Monetary History* that there is a one-to-one connection between severe monetary contractions and severe economic contractions, and that connection seems to dominate the United States interwar period.

35. The rate of price change (i.e., inflation), given the rate of monetary change, depends systematically on the prior rate of inflation, not at all (except for the United States interwar period) on the ratio of output to capacity (sec. 9.7; table 9.13). We use the rate of prior inflation as a proxy for expectations of inflation.

Interest Rates

36. For the century our data cover taken as a whole, the nominal yield on short-term nominal assets averaged 4.2 percent for the United States, 3.5 percent for the United Kingdom. The corresponding averages for long-term assets were 4.8 percent for the United States, 4.2 percent for the United Kingdom, or a trifle higher than for short-term assets, reflecting the rather small price that borrowers had to pay on the average to get lenders to sacrifice liquidity (table 10.1).

37. The corresponding real yield on nominal assets, obtained by subtracting the rate of inflation from the nominal yield, averaged for short-term assets, 2.6 percent for the United States, 0.9 percent for the United Kingdom; for long-term assets, 3.3 percent for the United States, 1.7 percent for the United Kingdom (table 10.1).

38. On the average for the century as a whole, the yield on physical assets (as proxied by the rate of change of income) was between the short-term and long-term yields on nominal assets: nominal yields of 4.5 percent for the United States, 4.2 percent for the United Kingdom; real yields of 3.0 percent for the United States, 1.6 percent for the United Kingdom (table 10.1). Apparently, for the century as a whole, there was effective arbitrage between the yields on nominal and physical assets.

39. For both nominal and real yields, the United States yields are higher than those in the United Kingdom: by about 0.7 percentage points for nominal yields, by about twice as much for real yields. The smaller differential for nominal than for real yields reflects the higher average inflation in the United Kingdom (table 10.1).

40. For the period as a whole, short- and long-term rates on nominal assets are highly correlated (correlation coefficient about 0.9 or higher). In view of the high correlation, and the problem of identifying the holding period corresponding to long-term yields on nominal assets, our more detailed analysis of yields on nominal assets is restricted to short rates only (sec. 10.3). Neither the short- nor the long-term rate on nominal assets is highly correlated with the yield on physical assets (table 10.1).

41. The rough equality of yields on nominal and physical assets for the century as a whole does not hold for subperiods classified by the behavior of prices. The yield on physical assets tends to exceed the yield on nominal assets in periods of rising prices, to be less than the yield on nominal assets in periods of falling prices.

42. The data for all subperiods before World War II behave as if prices were expected to be stable and both inflation and deflation were unanticipated: nominal yields on nominal assets average much the same in periods of rising and falling prices; real yields on nominal assets are low in periods of rising prices and high in periods of falling prices. On the other hand, nominal yields on physical assets are high in periods of rising prices, low in periods of falling prices; real yields on physical assets are much the same in periods of falling and rising prices. These results for physical assets do not represent successful prediction of inflation. Rather, the receipts from the use of physical assets and the costs of operating them adjust more or less automatically to the contemporaneous rate of inflation or deflation, and hence produce the equivalent of automatic indexing in respect of their yields (table 10.3).

43. The failure of the nominal yield on nominal assets to adjust to inflation or deflation before World War II confirms the general conception that inflation benefits debtors and harms creditors, whereas deflation benefits creditors and harms debtors. However, the evidence does not confirm a related conception: that such transfers of wealth make deflation adverse to growth and inflation favorable to growth. The clearest comparison is between the period of falling prices before 1896 and of rising

prices from 1896 to World War I. For both the United States and the United Kingdom, output grew somewhat more rapidly in the earlier period of deflation than in the later period of inflation (sec. 10.4.2).

44. After World War II, the financial markets began to behave differently. Beginning in the 1960s, there is a gradual shift, in both the United States and the United Kingdom, from the prior pattern to one involving anticipation of inflation: interest rates start to parallel rates of inflation, so nominal returns on nominal assets become more variable, and real returns on nominal assets become less variable.

45. We estimate from the subperiod data for both countries that, on the average, asset holders preferred physical to nominal assets, being willing to accept a 1.25 percentage point lower yield on physical than on nominal assets (sec. 10.4.2).

46. The differential between United States and United Kingdom yields on nominal assets also varies considerably among subperiods. (a) It was highest before 1896, when the fear of inflation, despite the fact of deflation, kept United States rates high (they averaged 2.5 percentage points higher than United Kingdom rates). (b) The differential was about one percentage point lower from 1896 to 1914, when confidence in the stability of the currency kept United States rates low despite the fact of inflation. (c) It declined another percentage point (to about 0.5 percentage points) from the pre–World War I period to the interwar period as a result of a decline of about that magnitude in the excess of the yield on physical capital in the United States over the yield in the United Kingdom. (d) It fell another two percentage points (to −1.5 percentage points) from the interwar to the post–World War II period as a result of greater inflation in the United Kingdom than in the United States and an accompanying depreciation of the pound sterling (table 10.4; sec. 10.4.1).

47. Our results strongly support the doubts expressed by Frederick Macaulay more than forty years ago about the universality of the "Gibson paradox"—a positive correlation between interest rates and price *levels* (not rates of price change). Such a correlation does hold for the United States and the United Kingdom before World War I; it does not hold over periods witnessing a substantial shift in the price level; it holds in much-muted form between the wars; it is hardly evident at all for the period after World War II (chart 10.18; table 10.6; sec. 10.6).

48. The more restricted "Gibson phenomenon" (hardly a "paradox") can plausibly be explained along the lines suggested by Irving Fisher: a relation between interest rates and the anticipated rate of price change, where anticipations are formed by extrapolating a fairly long series of past price changes, plus allowance for such episodic phenomena as the free silver movement in the United States in the 1880s and the 1890s (sec. 10.7.1).

49. Our estimate of the period of price change entering into the formation of price anticipations is some six to nine years, distinctly shorter than the period estimated by Fisher and others (table 10.8; sec. 10.7.1).

50. Our data reject the Wicksell-Keynes explanation that the positive correlation between interest rates and the price level reflects fluctuations in the real yield on capital, transmitted to both prices and nominal interest rates through commercial banks, which delay the impact of changes in real yields on nominal rates by altering the quantity of money (sec. 10.7.2).

Long Swings

51. For the United States, the long swings in money, nominal income, and real income that remain after lengthening the period used to compute rates of change from three successive phases to nine phases are members of the same species as those studied by Kuznets, Burns, Abramovitz, and others. For the United Kingdom, it is dubious that there are any long swings in our series except those that reflect the smoothing of the two wars, plus possibly a post–World War II upsurge. This corresponds with the difficulty that investigators of long swings have had in demonstrating their existence in the United Kingdom (sec. 11.1; chart 11.1).

52. For the United States, the swings in money and nominal income are decidedly larger in amplitude than in real income. Yet the extensive literature on long swings hardly mentions money.

53. The evidence from our data suggests (*a*) that money has played a major role in the United States long swings identified in the long-swing literature; (*b*) that wars and major deep depressions have been the major source of wide variability in money, nominal income, prices, and real income. These findings suggest that the empirically observed swings reflect not a self-generating cyclical process but rather episodic phenomena smoothed both by the economic reaction to them and by the statistical treatment of the economic data. This episodic interpretation is consistent with the apparent absence of long swings in the United Kingdom, since the absence can be explained by the relative unimportance of deep depressions in the United Kingdom.

1   Scope of the Study

This book analyzes the relation between the longer-term movements in the quantity of money in the United States and the United Kingdom and such other key economic magnitudes as income, prices, output, and interest rates. It starts from the broad theoretical framework that guided our earlier study of United States monetary history but was not explicitly spelled out in that book (chap. 2) and proceeds to elaborate, test, and give numerical content to some of the elements and hypotheses embedded in that framework as well as some of the generalizations suggested by *A Monetary History*.

In order to isolate the longer-term relations that are our primary concern, we have converted our basic data, which are annual, into a form designed to be free from the shorter-term movements that are called business cycles. These are brief in duration by comparison with the length of our series. For the United States, the nearly eleven decades from 1867 to 1975 for which we have continuous data contain twenty-six full reference cycles running from trough to trough, according to the NBER chronology. For the United Kingdom, the century from 1874 to 1975 for which we have continuous data contains eighteen and one-half reference cycles. Though brief, the cyclical fluctuations are often large relative to the more gradual long-period changes. Hence, comparisons between dates separated even by decades can be seriously distorted if the initial and terminal dates refer to different stages of the business cycle.

The device we have used to free the data from cyclical fluctuations is to take as our basic observation an average of annual observations over a cycle phase—that is, our basic observation is an average for either an expansion from cyclical trough to cyclical peak or a contraction from cyclical peak to cyclical trough, sometimes referred to as half-cycles. Chapter 3 discusses this device and the various statistical measures we have constructed from the phase averages. Chapter 4 discusses our basic data; its appendix gives our annual series, and the appendix to chapter 5 gives the phase averages constructed from them.

Our substantive analysis begins in chapter 5 with a comparison of the long-term movements in nominal income and nominal money and their ratio (velocity), both within each country and between the United States and the United Kingdom. The movements in the nominal magnitudes can be regarded as resulting from changes in three elements: population, prices, and the real magnitude per capita. We proceed to decompose trends and fluctuations in nominal income and money into these elements. Throughout, we analyze both the levels of the various series and their rates of change. The rates of change provide a sensitive way to allow for trends and thereby to isolate the movements intermediate between the brief business cycles and the really long-term secular trends.

The most striking feature of the charts and tables is the extraordinary parallelism displayed by the movements in nominal income and money within each country and in velocity as between the two countries, combined with considerable apparent differences between the two countries in the decomposition of the movements in the nominal magnitudes.

These results, which are highly consistent with the general quantity-theory framework that underlies our analysis, suggest that there must have been a relatively stable demand function for money over the period of our data that had characteristics common to both the United States and the United Kingdom. Accordingly, chapter 6 explores the determinants of velocity, which is to say of the demand for money in the sense of a function relating the quantity of money demanded to a small number of other variables. Chapter 7 explores the interrelations between the movements in velocity in the two countries.

Chapter 8 goes on to study the way the demand function identified in chapter 6 accounts for the parallelism between the temporal movements in nominal income and nominal money, taking up one of the themes of chapter 5 and exploring in particular the dynamic process presented in abstract form in chapter 2, whereby changes in the quantity of money are reflected in current and subsequent changes in income.

Chapter 9 takes up another theme from chapter 5: the apparent difference between the two countries in the decomposition of nominal movements in money and income between prices and output. What determines this decomposition is one of the major unsettled questions in monetary theory; it has been the source of much of the dispute about the role of money in recent decades and is a key to the controversy between the quantity-theory framework and the Keynesian income-expenditure framework. It is the issue that generated the Phillips curve and all the opposing views that have peppered the economic literature. We do not, of course, settle these hotly debated issues, but we believe our data greatly clarify them.

The relation between money and interest rates is another topic of long standing in the literature of monetary theory. Chapter 10 examines it at great length, on both a theoretical and an empirical level, with special reference to the reconciliation of the so-called Gibson paradox with both the theory and the evidence.

The final substantive chapter, chapter 11, is something of a digression. It deals with the relevance of our findings to the extensive work that has been done by economic historians and statisticians on long swings in economic activity. Though brief and a by-product of our main concern, this chapter settles the issue it deals with more definitively and with clearer implications for the corresponding body of research than do any of our other chapters.

Chapter 12 summarizes our main conclusions about the role of money.

2   The General Theoretical Framework

As is so pungently stated in the quotation from de Morgan that we use as the epigraph of this book, every empirical study rests on a theoretical framework,[1] on a set of tentative hypotheses that the evidence is designed to test or to adumbrate. It may help the reader if we set out explicitly the general theoretical framework that underlies this and our earlier volumes.[2]

The words *general* and *framework* are included in this statement of the purpose of this chapter to make clear its limits. The chapter does not present a fully developed theory that has as implications all the empirical regularities that those of us studying monetary phenomena have isolated. A fully developed theory is much to be desired, but it would require an entire treatise. It is not something that can readily be done in an introductory chapter of an empirical study concerned with only one aspect of monetary relations. Further, the chapter makes no attempt to present a comprehensive doctrinal history of the development of either the quantity theory or Keynesian theory. References to earlier writers are simply expository devices to illuminate analytical points. Finally, this chapter

---

1. The first five sections of this chapter draw heavily on Milton Friedman, "Money: Quantity Theory," *International Encyclopedia of the Social Sciences* (New York: Macmillan and Free Press, 1968).

2. Several reviewers of *A Monetary History* criticized us for not making explicit the theoretical framework employed in that book. This chapter is largely a response to that criticism. See John M. Culbertson, "United States Monetary History: Its Implications for Monetary Theory," *National Banking Review* 1 (March 1964): 372–75; Allan H. Meltzer, "Monetary Theory and Monetary History," *Schweizerische Zeitschrift für Volkswirtschaft und Statistik* 101, no. 4 (1965): 409–22; James Tobin, "The Monetary Interpretation of History," *American Economic Review* 55 (June 1965): 464–85.

supplements, rather than replaces, others of our writings on issues in monetary theory.[3]

Our theoretical framework is the quantity theory of money—a theory that has taken many different forms and traces back to the very beginning of systematic thinking about economic matters. It has probably been "tested" with quantitative data more extensively than any other set of propositions in formal economics—unless it be the negatively sloping demand curve. Nonetheless, the quantity theory has been a continual bone of contention. Until the mid-1930s, it was generally supported by serious students of economics, those whom today we would term professional economists, and rejected by laymen. However, the success of the Keynesian revolution led to its rejection by many, perhaps most, professional economists. Only in the past two decades has it experienced a revival so that it once again commands the adherence of many professional economists. Its initial acceptance, its rejection, and its recent revival have all been grounded basically on judgments about empirical regularities.

2.1 The Quantity Theory:
Nominal versus Real Quantity of Money

In all its versions, the quantity theory rests on a distinction between the *nominal* quantity of money and the *real* quantity of money. The nominal quantity of money is the quantity expressed in whatever units are used to designate money—talents, shekels, pounds, francs, liras, drachmas, dollars, and so on. The real quantity of money is the quantity expressed in terms of the volume of goods and services the money will purchase.

There is no unique way to express the real quantity of money. One way to express it is in terms of a specified standard basket of goods and services. That is what is done implicitly when the real quantity of money is calculated by dividing the nominal quantity of money by a price index. The standard basket is then the basket whose components are used as weights in computing the price index—generally, the basket purchased by some representative group in a base year.

A different way to express the real quantity of money is in terms of the time durations of the flows of goods and services the money could purchase. For a household, for example, the real quantity of money can be expressed in terms of the number of weeks of the household's average level of consumption it could finance with its money balances or, alternatively, in terms of the number of weeks of its average income to which its

---

3. These caveats are occasioned by the reaction to an earlier version of this chapter published separately. See Robert J. Gordon, ed., *Milton Friedman's Monetary Framework: A Debate with His Critics* (University of Chicago Press, 1974).

money balances are equal. For a business enterprise, the real quantity of money it holds can be expressed in terms of the number of weeks of its average purchases, or of its average sales, or of its average expenditures on final productive services (net value added) to which its money balances are equal. For the community as a whole, the real quantity of money can be expressed in terms of the number of weeks of aggregate transactions of the community, or aggregate net output of the community, to which its money balances are equal.

The reciprocal of any of this latter class of measures of the real quantity of money is a velocity of circulation for the corresponding unit or group of units. For example, the ratio of the annual transactions of the community to its stock of money is the "transactions velocity of circulation of money," since it gives the number of times the stock of money would have to "turn over" in a year to accomplish all transactions. Similarly, the ratio of annual income to the stock of money is termed "income velocity." In every case, the real quantity of money or velocity is calculated at the set of prices prevailing at the date to which the calculation refers. These prices are the bridge between the nominal and the real quantity of money.

The quantity theory of money takes for granted first, that what ultimately matters to holders of money is the real quantity rather than the nominal quantity they hold and, second, that there is a fairly definite real quantity of money that people wish to hold in any given circumstances. Suppose that the nominal quantity that people hold at a particular moment of time happens to correspond at current prices to a real quantity larger than the quantity that they wish to hold. Individuals will then seek to dispose of what they regard as their excess money balances; they will try to pay out a larger sum for the purchase of securities, goods, and services, for the repayment of debts, and as gifts than they are receiving from the corresponding sources. However, they cannot as a group succeed. One man's expenditures are another's receipts. One man can reduce his nominal money balances only by persuading someone else to increase his. The community as a whole cannot in general spend more than it receives.

The attempt to do so will nonetheless have important effects. If prices and income are free to change, the attempt to spend more will raise expenditures and receipts, expressed in nominal units, which will lead to a bidding up of prices and perhaps also to an increase in output. If prices are fixed by custom or by government edict, the attempt to spend more will either be matched by an increase in goods and services or produce "shortages" and "queues." These in turn will raise the effective price and are likely sooner or later to force changes in customary or official prices.

The initial excess of nominal balances will therefore tend to be eliminated, even though there is no change in the nominal quantity of money, by either a reduction in the real quantity available to hold through price rises or an increase in the real quantity desired through output increases. And conversely for an initial deficiency of nominal balances.

It is clear from this discussion that changes in prices and nominal income can be produced either by changes in the real balances that people wish to hold or by changes in the nominal balances available for them to hold. Indeed, it is a tautology, summarized in the famous quantity equation, that all changes in nominal income can be attributed to one or the other—just as a change in the price of any good can always be attributed to a change in either demand or supply. The quantity theory is not, however, this tautology. On an analytical level, it is an analysis of the factors determining what quantity of money the community wishes to hold; on an empirical level, it is the generalization that changes in desired real balances (in the demand for money) tend to proceed slowly and gradually or to be the result of events set in train by prior changes in supply, whereas, in contrast, substantial changes in the supply of nominal balances can and frequently do occur independently of any changes in demand. The conclusion is that substantial changes in prices or nominal income are almost invariably the result of changes in the nominal supply of money.

2.2 Quantity Equations

The tautology embodied in the quantity equation is a useful device for classifying the variables stressed in the quantity theory. The quantity equation has taken different forms as quantity theorists have stressed different variables.

2.2.1 Transactions Equation

The most famous version of the quantity equation is doubtless the transactions version popularized by Irving Fisher:[4]

(1) $$MV = PT,$$
or
(2) $$MV + M'V' = PT.$$

In this version the elementary event is a transaction—an exchange in which one economic actor transfers goods or services or securities to another economic actor and receives a transfer of money in return. The right-hand side of the equations corresponds to the transfer of goods, services, or securities; the left-hand side, to the matching transfer of money.

---

4. See Irving Fisher, *The Purchasing Power of Money* (New York: Macmillan, 1911; rev. ed. 1920; 2d rev. ed. 1922; reprinted New York: Kelly, 1963), pp. 24–54.

Each transfer of goods, services, or securities is regarded as the product of a price and a quantity: wage per week times number of weeks, price of a good times number of units of the good, dividend per share times number of shares, price per share times number of shares, and so on. The right-hand side of equations (1) and (2) is the aggregate of such payments during some interval, with P a suitably chosen *average* of the prices and T a suitably chosen *aggregate* of the quantities during that interval, so that PT is the total nominal value of the payments during the interval in question. The units of P are dollars per unit of quantity; the units of T are number of unit quantities per period of time. We can convert the equation from an expression applying to an *interval* of time to one applying to a *point* in time by the usual limiting process of letting the interval for which we aggregate payments approach zero, and expressing T not as an aggregate but as a rate of flow (that is, the limit of the ratio of aggregate quantities to the length of the interval as the length of the interval approaches zero). The magnitude T then has the dimension of quantity per unit time; the product of P and T, of dollars per unit time.

Because the right-hand side is intended to summarize a continuing process, a flow of physical goods and services, the physical item transferred (good, service, or security) is treated as if it disappeared from economic circulation once transferred. If, for example, a single item— say, a house—were transferred three times in the course of the time interval for which PT is measured, it would enter into T as three houses for that interval. Further, only those physical items that enter into transactions are explicitly included in T. Houses that exist but are not bought or sold during the time interval are omitted, though if they are rented the rental values of their services are included in PT and the number of dwelling-unit years per year are included in T. Clearly, T is a rather special kind of index of quantities: it includes service flows (man-hours) and also physical capital items yielding flows (houses, electric-generating plants) and securities representing such capital items as well as such intangible capital items as "goodwill." Each of the capital items or securities is weighted by the number of times it enters into transactions (its "velocity of circulation," in strict analogy with the "velocity of circulation" of money). Similarly, P is a rather special kind of price index.

The monetary transfer analyzed on the left-hand side of equations (1) and (2) is treated very differently. The money that changes hands is treated as retaining its identity, and all money, whether used in transactions during the time interval in question or not, is explicitly accounted for. Money is treated as a stock, not as a flow or a mixture of a flow and a stock. For a single transaction, the breakdown into M and V is trivial: the cash that is transferred is turned over once, or $V = 1$. For all transactions during an interval of time, we can, in principle, classify the existing stock of dollars of money according as each dollar entered into 0, 1, 2, . . .

transactions—that is, according as each dollar "turned over" 0, 1, 2, . . . times. The weighted average of these numbers of turnover, weighted by the number of dollars that turned over that number of times, is the conceptual equivalent of V. The dimensions of M are dollars; of V, number of turnovers per unit time; so, of the product, dollars per unit time.[5]

Equation (2) differs from equation (1) by dividing payments into two categories: those effected by the transfer of hand-to-hand currency (including coin) and those effected by the transfer of deposits. In equation (2) M stands solely for the volume of currency and V for the velocity of currency, M' for the volume of deposits, and V' for the velocity of deposits.

One reason for the emphasis on this particular division was the persistent dispute about whether the term *money* should include only currency or deposits as well.[6] Another reason was the direct availability of data on $M'V'$ from bank records of clearings or of debits to deposit accounts. These data make it possible to calculate V' in a way that is not possible for V.[7]

Equations (1) and (2), like the other quantity equations we shall discuss, are intended to be identities—a special application of double-entry bookkeeping, with each transaction simultaneously recorded on both sides of the equation. However, as with the national income identities with which we are all familiar, when the two sides, or the separate elements on the two sides, are estimated from independent sources of data, many differences between them emerge.[8] This statistical defect has been less obvious for the quantity equations than for the national income identities—with their standard entry "statistical discrepancy"—because of the difficulty of calculating V directly. As a result, V in equation (1) and V and V' in equation (2) have generally been calculated as the numbers

---

5. A common criticism of the quantity equation is that it takes account of the velocity of circulation of money but not of the velocity of circulation of goods. As the preceding two paragraphs make clear, this criticism, though not literally valid, makes a real point. The velocity of circulation of money is explicit; the velocity of circulation of goods is implicit. It might well make the right-hand side of equations (1) and (2) more meaningful to make it the sum of two components—one, the total value of transactions involving continuing flows, the other, the value of transfers of existing items of wealth—and to express the second component as a price times a velocity times a stock. In effect, the shift to the income version of the equation resolves the issue by completely neglecting transfers of existing items of wealth.

6. See Milton Friedman and Anna J. Schwartz, *Monetary Statistics of the United States* (New York: Columbia University Press for NBER, 1970), chap. 2.

7. For an extremely ingenious indirect calculation of V, not only for currency as a whole but for particular denominations of currency, see Robert Laurent, "Currency Transfers by Denominations," Ph.D. diss., University of Chicago, 1969.

8. See Wesley C. Mitchell, *Business Cycles* (New York: NBER, 1927), pp. 128–39.

having the property that they render the equations correct. These calculated numbers therefore embody the whole of the counterpart to the "statistical discrepancy."

Just as the left-hand side of equation (1) can be divided into several components, as in equation (2), so also can the right-hand side. The emphasis on transactions reflected in this version of the quantity equation suggests dividing total transactions into categories of payments for which payment periods or practices differ: for example, into capital transactions, purchases of final goods and services, purchases of intermediate goods, and payments for the use of resources, perhaps separated into wage and salary payments and other payments. The observed value of V might well be a function of the distribution of total payments among categories. Alternatively, if the quantity equation is interpreted not as an identity but as a functional relation expressing desired velocity as a function of other variables, the distribution of payments may well be an important set of variables.

2.2.2 The Income Form of the Quantity Equation

Despite the large amount of empirical work done on the transactions equations, notably by Irving Fisher and Carl Snyder,[9] the ambiguities of the concepts of "transactions" and the "general price level"—particularly those arising from the mixture of current and capital transactions—have never been satisfactorily resolved. The more recent development of national or social accounting has stressed income transactions rather than gross transactions and has explicitly if not wholly satisfactorily dealt with the conceptual and statistical problems involved in distinguishing between changes in prices and changes in quantities. As a result, the quantity equation has more recently tended to be expressed in terms of income transactions rather than of gross transactions. Let $Y =$ nominal national income, $P =$ the price index implicit in estimating national income at constant prices, $N =$ the number of persons in the population, $y =$ per capita national income in constant prices, and $y' = Ny =$ national income at constant prices, so that

$$(3) \qquad Y = PNy = Py'.$$

Let M represent, as before, the stock of money; but define V as the average number of times per unit time that the money stock is used in making *income* transactions (that is, payments for final productive services or, alternatively, for final goods and services) rather than all transactions. We can then write the quantity equation in income form as

9. See Irving Fisher, *Purchasing Power of Money*, pp. 280–318; Irving Fisher, "Money, Prices, Credit and Banking," *American Economic Review* 9 (June 1919): 407–9; and Carl Snyder, "On the Statistical Relation of Trade, Credit and Prices," *Review of International Statistical Institute* 2 (October 1934): 278–91.

(4) $MV = PNy = Py'$,

or, if we desire to distinguish currency from deposit transactions, as

(5) $MV + M'V' = PNy$.

Although the symbols P, V, and V' are used both in equations (4) and (5) and in equations (1) and (2), they stand for different concepts in each pair of equations.

Equations (4) and (5) are conceptually and empirically more satisfactory than equations (1) and (2). However, they have the disadvantage that they completely neglect the ratio of intermediate to final transactions and transactions in existing capital assets.

In the transactions version of the quantity equation, each intermediate transaction—that is, purchase by one enterprise from another—is included at the total value of the transaction, so that the value of wheat, for example, is included once when it is sold by the farmer to the mill, a second time when the mill sells flour to the baker, a third time when the baker sells bread to the grocer, a fourth time when the grocer sells bread to the consumer. In the income version, only the net value added by each of these transactions is included. To put it differently, in the transactions version the elementary event is an isolated exchange of a physical item for money—an actual, clearly observable event. In the income version, the elementary event is a hypothetical event that can be inferred from observation but is not directly observable. It is a complete series of transactions involving the exchange of productive services for final goods, via a sequence of money payments, with all the intermediate transactions in this income circuit netted out. The total value of all transactions is therefore a multiple of the value of income transactions only.

For a given flow of productive services or, alternatively, of final products (two of the multiple faces of income), the volume of transactions will be affected by vertical integration or disintegration of enterprises, which reduces or increases the number of transactions involved in a single income circuit, or by technological changes that lengthen or shorten the process of transforming productive services into final products. The volume of income will not be thus affected.

Similarly, the transactions version includes the purchase of an existing asset—a house or a piece of land or a share of equity stock—precisely on a par with an intermediate or final transaction. The income version excludes such transactions completely.

Are these differences an advantage or disadvantage of the income version? That clearly depends on what it is that determines the amount of money people want to hold. Do changes of the kind considered in the preceding paragraphs, changes that alter the ratio of intermediate and capital transactions to income, also alter in the same direction and by the same proportion the amount of money people want to hold? Or do they tend to leave this amount unaltered? Or do they have a more complex effect?

Clearly, the transactions and income versions of the quantity theory involve very different conceptions of the role of money. For the transactions version, the most important thing about money is that it is transferred. For the income version, the most important thing is that it is held. This difference is even more obvious from the Cambridge cash-balances version of the quantity equation. Indeed, the income version can perhaps best be regarded as a way station between the Fisher and the Cambridge versions.

2.2.3   Cambridge Cash-Balances Approach

The essential feature of a money economy is that it enables the act of purchase to be separated from the act of sale. An individual who has something to exchange need not seek out the double coincidence— someone who both wants what he has and offers in exchange what he wants. He need only find someone who wants what he has, sell it to him for general purchasing power, and then find someone who has what he wants and buy it with general purchasing power.

For the act of purchase to be separated from the act of sale, there must be something that everybody will accept in exchange as "general purchasing power"—this aspect of money is emphasized in the transactions approach. But also there must be something that can serve as a temporary abode of purchasing power in the interim between sale and purchase. This aspect of money is emphasized in the cash-balances approach.

How much money will people or enterprises want to hold as a temporary abode of purchasing power? As a first approximation, it has generally been supposed that the amount bears some relation to income, on the assumption that income affects the volume of potential purchases for which the individual or enterprise wishes to hold cash balances. We can therefore write

(6) $M = kPNy = kPy'$,

where M, N, P, y, and y' are defined as in equation (4) and k is the ratio of money stock to income—either the observed ratio so calculated as to make equation (6) an identity or the "desired" ratio so that M is the "desired" amount of money, which need not be equal to the actual amount. In either case, k is numerically equal to the reciprocal of the V in equation (4), the V being interpreted in one case as measured velocity and in the other as desired velocity.

Although equation (6) is simply a mathematical transformation of equation (4), it brings out much more sharply the difference between the aspect of money stressed by the transactions approach and that stressed by the cash-balances approach. This difference makes different definitions of money seem natural and leads to placing emphasis on different variables and analytical techniques.

The transactions approach makes it natural to define money in terms of whatever serves as the medium of exchange in discharging obligations. By stressing the function of money as a temporary abode of purchasing power, the cash-balances approach makes it seem entirely appropriate to include in addition such stores of value as demand and time deposits not transferable by check, although the cash-balances approach clearly does not require their inclusion.[10]

Similarly, the transactions approach leads to emphasis on such variables as payments practices, the financial and economic arrangements for effecting transactions, and the speed of communication and transportation as it affects the time required to make a payment—essentially, that is, to emphasis on the mechanical aspect of the payments process. The cash-balances approach, on the other hand, leads to emphasis on variables affecting the usefulness of money as an asset: the costs and returns from holding money instead of other assets, the uncertainty of the future, and so on—essentially, that is, to emphasis on the role of cash in a portfolio.

Of course, neither approach enforces the exclusion of the variables stressed by the other—and the more sophisticated economists have had broader conceptions than the particular approach they adopted. Portfolio considerations enter into the costs of effecting transactions and hence affect the most efficient payment arrangements; mechanical considerations enter into the returns from holding cash and hence affect the usefulness of cash in a portfolio.

Finally, with regard to analytical techniques, the cash-balances approach fits in much more readily with the general Marshallian demand-supply apparatus than does the transactions approach. Equation (6) can be regarded as a demand function for money, with P, N, and y on the right-hand side being three of the variables on which demand for money depends and k symbolizing all the other variables, so that k is to be regarded not as a numerical constant but as itself a function of still other variables. For completion, the analysis requires another equation showing the supply of money as a function of other variables. The price level or the level of nominal income is then the resultant of the interaction of the demand and supply functions.

The quantity theory in its cash-balances version thus suggests organizing an analysis of monetary phenomena in terms of (1) the factors determining the nominal quantity of money to be held—the conditions determining supply; (2) the factors determining the real quantity of money the community wishes to hold—the conditions determining de-

10. Friedman and Schwartz, *Monetary Statistics*, chap. 3.

mand; and (3) the reconciliation of demand with supply—the conditions determining how changes in demand or supply work themselves out through prices and quantities.

2.2.4   The Transmission Mechanism: Money to Income, Prices, Output

A frequent criticism of the quantity theory and the quantity equations concerns the third of these items—the mechanism whereby a change in the nominal quantity of money is transmitted to prices and quantities. The criticism is that the transmission mechanism is not specified, that the proponents of the quantity theory rely on a black box connecting the input—the nominal quantity of money—and the output—effects on prices and quantities.

On one level this criticism is not justified; on another it points to an important element in the unfinished agenda of research—an element to which some of the later chapters of this book make, we trust, a contribution.

The criticism is not justified insofar as it implies that there is a fundamental difference between the adjustment mechanism implicit or explicit in the quantity equation and in a demand-supply analysis for a particular product—shoes, or copper, or haircuts. In both cases the demand function for the community as a whole is an aggregation of demand functions for individual consumer or producer units, and the separate demand functions are determined by the tastes and opportunities of the units. In both cases, supply functions depend on production possibilities, institutional arrangements for organizing production, and the conditions of supply of resources. In both cases a shift in supply or in demand introduces a discrepancy between the amounts demanded and supplied *at the preexisting price*. In both cases any discrepancy can be eliminated only by either a price change or some alternative rationing mechanism, explicit or implicit.

On this level, two features of the demand-supply adjustment for money have concealed the parallelism. One is that demand-supply analysis for particular products typically deals with flows—number of pairs of shoes or number of haircuts per year—whereas the quantity equations deal with the stock of money at a point in time. In this respect the analogy is with the demand for, say, land, which, like money, derives its value from the flow of services it renders but has a purchase price and not merely a rental value. The second is the widespread tendency to confuse "money" and "credit," which has produced misunderstanding about the relevant price variable. The "price" of money is the quantity of goods and services that must be given up to acquire a unit of money—the inverse of the price level. This is the price that is analogous to the price of land or of copper or of haircuts. The "price" of money is not the interest rate, which is the "price" of credit. The interest rate connects stocks with flows—the rental value of land with the price of land, the value of the service flow from a unit of money with the price of money. Of course, the interest rate may affect the quantity of money demanded—just as it may affect the quantity of land demanded—but so may a host of other variables.

On a more sophisticated level, the criticism about the transmission mechanism applies equally to money and to other goods and services. In all cases it is desirable to go beyond equality of demand and supply as defining a stationary equilibrium position and examine the variables that affect the quantities demanded and supplied and the dynamic temporal process whereby actual or potential discrepancies are eliminated. For money, an examination of the variables affecting demand and supply has been carried very far—farther than for most other economic goods or services, as sections 2.3 and 2.4 and the references contained therein, indicate. But for both money and most other goods and services, there is as yet no satisfactory and widely accepted description, in precise quantifiable terms, of the dynamic temporal process of adjustment—though in recent decades much research has been devoted to this question. It remains a challenging subject for research. Section 2.6 discusses a particular hypothesis about the adjustment mechanism, and chapters 8 and 9 explore some of the issues empirically.

2.2.5   The International Transmission Mechanism

From its very earliest days, the quantity theory was intimately connected with the analysis of the adjustment mechanism in international trade. A commodity standard, in which money was specie or its equivalent, was taken as the norm. Under such a standard, the supply of money in any one country is determined by the links between that country and other countries that use the same commodity as money. Under such a standard, the same theory explains links among money and prices and nominal income in various parts of a single country—money, prices, and nominal income in Illinois and money, prices, and nominal income in the rest of the United States—and the corresponding links among various countries. The differences between interregional adjustment and international adjustment are empirical: greater mobility of people, goods, and capital among regions than among countries, and hence a more rapid adjustment.

The specie-flow mechanism developed by Hume and elaborated by Ricardo and his successors analyzed the links among countries primarily in terms of the effect of a disequilibrium stock of money on prices and thereby the balance of payments. "Too" high a money stock in country A tends to make prices in A high relative to prices in the rest of the world, encouraging imports and discouraging exports. The resulting deficit in the balance of trade will be met by shipments of specie, which reduces the quantity of money in country A and raises it in the rest of the world. The changes in the quantity of money will tend to reduce prices in country A and raise them in the rest of the world, correcting the original disequilibrium. The process will continue until price levels in all countries are at a level at which balances of payments are in equilibrium (which may, of course, mean a continuing movement of specie, for example, from gold- or silver-producing countries to non-gold- or silver-producing countries, or between countries growing at different secular rates).

Another strand of the classical analysis has recently been revived under the title "the monetary theory of the balance of payments." This theory is logically equivalent to the specie-flow mechanism except that it makes different assumptions about the speed of adjustment of the several variables. The specie-flow mechanism implicitly assumes that prices are slow to adjust and do so only in response to changes in the quantity of money produced by specie flows. However, there can be only a single price for goods traded internationally if the markets are efficient and transportation costs are neglected. Speculation tends to assure this result for the prices of traded goods expressed in a common currency. Internally, competition between traded and nontraded goods tends to keep their relative prices in a relation determined by relative costs. If these adjustments are rapid, prices will always be in equilibrium among countries ("the law of one price"). If the money stock is not distributed among countries in such a way as to be consistent with these prices, the excess demands and supplies of money will lead to specie flows. If the quantity of money in a country is "too" low, domestic nominal demand will not be adequate to absorb a total value of domestic goods plus imports equal to the value of domestic output. Export of the excess will produce a balance of payments surplus for that country, which will raise the quantity of money. Specie flows are still the adjusting mechanism, but they are produced not by discrepancies in prices but by differences between demand for output in nominal terms and the supply of output at world prices. Putative, not actual, price differences are the spur to adjustment. This description is a highly over simplified picture, primarily because it omits the important role assigned to short- and long-term capital flows by all theorists—those who stress the specie-flow mechanism and even more those who stress the single-price mechanism.[11]

In practice, few countries have had pure commodity standards. Most have had a mixture of commodity and fiduciary standards. Changes in the

---

11. For a fuller discussion, see: Jacob A. Frenkel, "Adjustment Mechanisms and the Monetary Approach to the Balance of Payments," in *Recent Issues in International Monetary Economics*, ed. E. Claassen and P. Salin (Amsterdam: North-Holland, 1976); Jacob A. Frenkel and Harry G. Johnson, "The Monetary Approach to the Balance of Payments: Essential Concepts and Historical Origins," in *The Monetary Approach to the Balance of Payments*, ed. J. Frenkel and H. Johnson (Toronto: University of Toronto Press 1976), pp. 21–45.

fiduciary component of the stock of money can replace specie flows as a means of adjusting the quantity of money.

The situation is more complex for countries that do not share a unified currency, that is, a currency in which only the name assigned to a unit of currency differs among countries. Changes in the rates of exchange between national currencies then serve to keep prices in various countries in the appropriate relation when expressed in a common currency. Exchange rate adjustments replace specie flows or changes in the quantity of domestically created money. And exchange rate changes too may be produced by actual or putative price differences or by short- or long-term capital flows.

And, of course, there are all kinds of mixtures of commodity and fiduciary standards. The most important in recent decades have been currencies linked by rates of exchange fixed, at least temporarily, by governments rather than by the commodity content of the different currencies. Though superficially similar to a unified currency, such fixed rates are fundamentally different since they contain no automatic mechanism for equilibrating adjustment. The adjustments often have taken the form of direct controls over foreign exchange transactions, subsidies to exports, and obstacles to imports, sometimes giving rise to an implicit multiple exchange rate system, sometimes effected through an explicit multiple rate system; government borrowing to finance balance-of-payment deficits, or governmental lending to offset surpluses; and, ultimately, exchange rate adjustments.[12]

For the purposes of this chapter, we shall neglect these complications and proceed throughout as if we are dealing with a closed economy or, equivalently, with a set of national economies using a unified currency. We shall return to the problem of the international transmission mechanism on an empirical level in chapter 7, where we consider the interrelations between the United States and the United Kingdom during the century that our study covers.

2.2.6 First-Round Effects

Another frequent criticism of the quantity equations is that they neglect any effect the source of change in the quantity of money may have on the outcome—in Tobin's words, the question is whether "the genesis of new money makes a difference," in particular, whether "an increase in the quantity of money has the same effect whether it is issued to purchase goods or to purchase bonds."[13]

---

12. M. Connolly and D. Taylor, "Adjustment to Devaluation with Money and Non-traded Goods," *Journal of International Economics* 6 (August 1976): 289–98; and idem, "Testing the Monetary Approach to Devaluation in Developing Countries," *Journal of Political Economy* 84, part 1 (August 1976): 849–59.

13. James Tobin, in Gordon, *Milton Friedman's Monetary Framework*, p. 87.

This criticism too is invalid on a purely theoretical level, but it raises an important question for research. On a theoretical level, there is no difficulty in allowing for the source of the change in the quantity of money by including the appropriate variables in the demand (or supply) function (e.g., the ratio of interest-bearing government debt to total wealth).

On an empirical level, the basic issue is ancient—whether the "first-round effect" of a change in the quantity of money largely determines the ultimate effect. As John Stuart Mill put a view very much like Tobin's in 1844, "The issues of a *Government* paper, even when not permanent, will raise prices; because Governments usually issue their paper in purchases for consumption. If issued to pay off a portion of the national debt, we believe they would have no effect."[14]

Ludwig von Mises in his theory of the cycle implicitly accepted a similar empirical judgment. For example, Lionel Robbins, in his Misean analysis of the Great Depression, says, "In normal times, expansion and contraction of the money supply comes, not *via* the printing press and government decree, but *via* an expansion of credit through the banks. . . . This involves a mode of diffusion of new money radically different from the case we have just examined—a mode of diffusion which may have important effects."[15]

Of course, Mill, von Mises, and Tobin are right that the way the quantity of money is increased will affect the outcome in some measure or other. If one group of individuals receives the money on the first round, they will likely use it for different purposes than another group of individuals. If the newly printed money is spent on the first round for goods and services, it adds directly at that point to the demand for such goods and services, whereas if it is spent on purchasing debt it has no such immediate effect on the demand for goods and services. Effects on the demand for goods and services come later as the initial recipients of the "new" money themselves dispose of it. Clearly, also, as the "new" money spreads through the economy, any first-round effects will tend to be dissipated. The "new" money will be merged with the old and will be distributed in much the same way.

One way to characterize the Keynesian approach (sec. 2.5) is that it gives almost exclusive importance to the first-round effect. This leads to emphasis primarily on flows of spending rather than on stocks of assets. Similarly, one way to characterize the quantity-theory approach is to say that it gives almost no importance to first-round effects.

The empirical question is how important the first-round effects are compared with the ultimate effects. Theory cannot answer that question.

14. See John Stuart Mill, "Review of Books by Thomas Tooke and R. Torrens," *Westminster Review* 41 (June 1844): 579–93; quotation, p. 589.
15. See Lionel Robbins, *The Great Depression* (London: Macmillan, 1934), pp. 35–36.

The answer depends on how different are the reactions of the recipients of cash via alternative routes, on how rapidly a larger money stock is distributed through the economy, on how long it stays at each point in the economy, on how much the demand for money depends on the structure of government liabilities, and so on. Casual empiricism yields no decisive answer. Tobin can say, "The monetization of commercial loans . . . seems to me to be alchemy of much deeper significance than semi-monetization of Treasury bills."[16] But we could answer, "True, but remember that the transactions velocity of money may well be twenty-five to thirty or more times a year, to judge from the turnover of bank deposits. So the first round covers at most a two-week period, whereas the money continues circulating indefinitely." Maybe the first-round effect is so strong that it dominates later effects; but maybe it is highly transitory. We shall have to examine empirical evidence systematically to find out.

Despite repeated assertions by various authors that the first-round effect is significant in this sense, none, so far as we know, has presented any systematic empirical evidence to support that assertion. The apparently similar response of income to changes in the quantity of money at widely separated dates in different countries and under diverse monetary systems seems to us to establish something of a presumption that the first-round effect is not highly significant. More recently, several empirical studies designed explicitly to test the importance of the first-round effect have supported this presumption.[17]

Perhaps other studies will reverse this tentative conclusion. In any event, the importance of the first-round effect will be provided by empirical evidence, not by argumentation or theory.[18]

16. See James Tobin, "The Monetary Interpretation of History," *American Economic Review* 55 (June 1965): 464–85; quotation, p. 467.

17. Cagan investigated the first-round effect on interest rates. He was able to identify the existence of such an effect, but it was of minor quantitative importance. Auerbach found no evidence of a first-round effect on nominal income of the division of the change in the quantity of money between high-powered money and bank credit, or the division of high-powered money between financing current government expenses and debt redemption. Bordo, in a thesis dealing with the pre–World War I period for the United States, found at best very limited traces of the first-round effect. See Robert Auerbach, "The Income Effects of the Government Deficit," Ph.D. diss., University of Chicago, 1969; Phillip Cagan, *The Channels of Monetary Effects on Interest Rates* (New York: NBER, 1972); Michael Bordo, "The Effects of the Sources of Change in the Money Supply on the Level of Economic Activity," Ph.D. diss., University of Chicago, 1972.

18. In a more recent article, "Monetary Policies and the Economy: The Transmission Mechanism," James Tobin, on the basis of his approach, which stresses the role in the transmission process of the credit markets and of the ratio of the market value to the replacement value of physical capital, again concludes that "the effects of an expansion of monetary aggregates depends on how it is brought about," and that "inside money is . . . more powerful stuff than outside money." The only empirical evidence cited refers to the influence of the ratio of the market to the replacement value of investment. However, there

2.3   Supply of Money in Nominal Units

The factors determining the nominal quantity of money available to be held depend critically on the monetary system. For systems like those that have prevailed in the United States and in the United Kingdom during the past century, they can usefully be analyzed under the three main headings that we have termed the proximate determinants of the money stock: (1) the amount of high-powered money—determined for a country that has a fiduciary standard by the monetary authorities, for any one country under an international commodity standard through the balance of payments; (2) the ratio of bank deposits to bank holdings of high-powered money—determined by the banking system subject to any requirements that are imposed on them by law or the monetary authorities; and (3) the ratio of the public's deposits to its currency holdings—determined by the public subject to any controls on interest rates imposed by law or the monetary authorities.[19]

These factors determine the *nominal*, but not the *real* quantity of money. The *real* quantity of money is determined by the interaction between the nominal quantity supplied and the *real* quantity demanded and, in our view, ultimately by demand rather than supply. In the process, changes in demand for real balances have feedback effects on the variables determining the nominal quantity supplied, and changes in nominal supply have feedback effects on the variables determining the real quantity demanded. In our judgment, these feedback effects are for the most part relatively minor, so that the *nominal* supply can generally be regarded as determined by a set of variables distinct from those that affect the quantity of *real* balances demanded. In this sense the nominal quantity can be regarded as determined primarily by supply; the real quantity, by demand. Whether or not this judgment is correct, any discussion of the interrelation between demand and supply that neglects

---

is many a slip between that empirical result and his quoted conclusions, if those conclusions are regarded as referring to the effect of changes in monetary aggregates on nominal income, prices, and output. Tobin does not refer to any empirical evidence to support such an interpretation of his conclusions. His thoughtful and sophisticated analysis is concerned almost wholly with the effect of credit institutions on the composition of output and the structure of interest rates. *Southern Economic Journal* 44 (January 1978): 421–31; quotations, p. 431.

19. High-powered money consists of specie and obligations of the monetary authorities that are used either as currency by the public or as reserves by the banks. The monetary authorities are the central bank and the Treasury. See Friedman and Schwartz, *A Monetary History*, pp. 776–98 and note 59, p. 50, for use of the term high-powered money as early as the 1930s by Federal Reserve research personnel; for analysis of the proximate determinants, see also Phillip Cagan, *Determinants and Effects of Changes in the Stock of Money, 1875–1960* (New York: Columbia University Press for NBER, 1965).

the distinction between the nominal and the real quantity of money is necessarily incomplete and misleading.[20]

The preceding paragraph is another way of stating that part of our description of the quantity theory that asserts that "substantial changes in the supply of nominal balances can and frequently do occur independently of any change in demand." If this generalization were not valid, that is, if (a) the quantity of money supplied were a function of the same variables as the quantity demanded and (b) the supply function were as stable over time and place as the demand function, observed data on the quantity of money, nomimal and real, and on the variables affecting the quantities of money supplied and demanded, would simply record random perturbations about the intersection of the stable demand and supply functions. A function calculated from such data could not then be regarded as an estimate of a demand function—in the jargon of econometrics, the demand function would not have been identified.[21]

20. This paragraph was stimulated by the criticism of the analysis of the Great Depression in our *Monetary History* by Peter Temin, *Did Monetary Forces Cause the Great Depression?* (New York: Norton, 1976), esp. pp. 14–27. Temin's analysis is basically flawed by his failure to make this distinction.

Consider, for example, one statement from his discussion of our analysis, in which we have inserted in brackets words to make clear the confusion between nominal and real in Temin's analysis: "There is nothing in the narrative in Chapter 7 of the *Monetary History* to refute the following story: Income [real or nominal?] and production fell from 1929 to 1933 for nonmonetary reasons. Since the demand for [real] money [balances] is a function of [real] income, the demand for [real] money [balances] fell also. To equilibrate the money market [i.e., credit market], either interest rates, the [nominal or real?] stock of money, or both, had to fall. And since the [nominal] supply of money was partly a function of the [nominal] interest rate, this movement down along the supply curve of [nominal] money meant a decrease in both [interest rates and the (nominal or real?) stock of money]" (ibid., p. 27).

Omit the bracketed words, and the statement seems eminently reasonable—but only because of the implicit identification of nominal and real magnitudes, and the confusion between the interest rate, which is the price of credit, and the inverse of the price level, which is the price of money. According to his story, what explains the sharp decline in prices? If production fell for independent reasons, and this led to a movement down the nominal supply curve of money, so that demand and supply were continuously equated, why should prices have fallen? How does a decline in the demand for real balances produce a decline in nominal supply? Would it not instead, in the first instance, lead to *upward* pressure on prices, so that on Temin's alternative story, prices should have risen rather than fallen?

Temin has succumbed to the Keynesian assumption that the price level is an institutional datum discussed in greater detail in section 2.5 below.

For a fuller examination of Temin's analysis, see Arthur E. Gandolfi and James Lothian, "Did Monetary Forces Cause the Great Depression?" *Journal of Money, Credit and Banking* 9 (November 1977), 679–91; and Anna J. Schwartz, "Understanding 1929–1933," in *The Great Depression Revisited*, ed. Karl Brunner (Boston: Martinus Nijhoff, 1981).

21. For one of the earliest and still pertinent discussions of this point, see E. J. Working, "What Do Statistical 'Demand Curves' Show?" *Quarterly Journal of Economics* 41 (Febru-

Our rejection of points *a* and *b* is of course an empirical finding, not something that can be justified by theoretical considerations alone. With respect to point *a*, theory suggests many possible links between the quantity of money supplied and both real income and interest rates. Changes in real income affect imports and exports, both directly and by altering domestic prices for given monetary growth. Under international financial arrangements embodying fixed exchange rates, these effects disturb the balance of payments unless offset by the appropriate changes in the quantity of money. Under a fiduciary or fiat standard embodying flexible exchange rates, changes in real income may affect systematically the behavior of the monetary authorities. Under both standards, changes in real income affect the reserve ratios desired by banks and the currency-deposit ratios desired by money holders; changes in interest rates similarly alter international capital flows, the behavior of monetary authorities, and reserve and currency ratios. However, these numerous effects by no means all run in the same direction. For example, under an international commodity standard, a higher rate of real growth adds directly to imports, which tends to reduce the rate of monetary growth. On the other hand, higher real growth has a downward effect on prices, which raises exports, tending to increase the rate of monetary growth; and higher real growth may produce either capital outflows or capital inflows. Changes in rates of interest similarly have effects in both directions. Moreover, time lags enter on both the demand and the supply side, and there is no reason to expect them to be the same. Hence, even if the same named variables were to enter importantly into the demand and the supply functions, the economically relevant variables might differ because differently dated.

With respect to point *b*, theoretical considerations suggest that the supply function depends on the financial structure—for example, will be different for a commodity standard and a fiduciary standard. Financial institutions have undergone major changes in the century our data cover and have differed in important respects between the United States and the United Kingdom, introducing changes in supply. However, many elements in the financial structure remained the same throughout the period and have been common to both countries. There is no way in principle to judge whether the changes over time and the differences between countries had major or minor effects on the supply function.

The findings of chapters 6 and 7 are indirect empirical evidence that neither point *a* nor point *b* can be accepted. A much larger body of

---

ary 1927): 212–35. A classic statement of the problem is given in T. C. Koopmans, "Identification Problems in Economic Model Construction," in *Studies in Econometric Method*, ed. W. C. Hood and T. C. Koopmans, Cowles Commission Monograph no. 14 (New York: Wiley, 1953). For a more elaborate statement, see Franklin M. Fisher, *The Identification Problem in Econometrics* (New York: McGraw-Hill, 1966).

evidence justifying the same conclusion is contained in our *Monetary History*, in Phillip Cagan's companion volume, *Determinants and Effects of Changes in the Stock of Money, 1875–1960*, and in studies of the supply of money by other scholars.[22] These studies have concluded that neither interest rates nor real income have a consistent and sizable influence on the nominal quantity of money supplied. The same result is implicit in the evidence we have summarized elsewhere that supports the conclusion that the cyclical relation between money and income reflects primarily an influence running from money to income, which dominates the reflex influence running the other way.[23] This prior body of evidence explains why we do not in this book explore systematically the supply function of money. We shall for the most part take it for granted that the nominal quantity of money available to be held is largely independent of the variables entering into the demand function—that, in the jargon of econometrics, it can be treated as an exogenous variable entering into the determination of such endogenous vari-

22. For the United States, in addition to Cagan, see Albert E. Burger, *The Money Supply Process* (Belmont, Calif.: Wadsworth, 1971), and idem, "Money Stock Control," in *Controlling Monetary Aggregate II: The Implementation*, pp. 33–55, Conference Series no. 9 (Boston: Federal Reserve Bank of Boston, Feb. 1973); David I. Fand, "Some Implications of Money Supply Analysis," *American Economic Review Papers and Proceedings* 57 (May 1967): 380–400; J. R. Zecher, "An Evaluation of Four Econometric Models of the Financial Sector," *Federal Reserve Bank of Cleveland, Economic Papers* Dissertation Series no. 1, (January 1970); Robert H. Rasche, "A Review of Empirical Studies of the Money Supply Mechanism," *Federal Reserve Bank of Saint Louis Review* 54 (July 1972): 11–19.

For the United Kingdom, see A. R. Nobay, "A Model of the United Kingdom Monetary Authorities' Behaviour 1959–1969," paper presented at the February 1972 Money Study Group Conference; D. Fisher, "The Instruments of Monetary Policy and the Generalized Tradeoff Function for Britain, 1955–1968," *Manchester School of Economics and Social Studies* 38 (September 1970): 209–22; R. L. Crouch, "A Model of the United Kingdom Monetary Sector," *Econometrica* 35 (July–October 1967): 398–418. See also Harry G. Johnson and associates, eds., *Readings in British Monetary Economics*, (Oxford: Clarendon Press, 1972), sec. 3, "The Supply of Money," pp. 203–77; and Harold Black, "The Relative Importance of Determinants of the Money Supply: The British Case," *Journal of Monetary Economics* 1 (April 1975): 251–64.

23. "The Monetary Studies of the National Bureau," in *The National Bureau Enters Its Forty-Fifth Year* (44th Annual Report, 1964), pp. 7–25 (reprinted in Milton Friedman, *The Optimum Quantity of Money and Other Essays* [Chicago: Aldine, 1969], pp. 261–84).

See also Donald P. Tucker, "Dynamic Income Adjustment to Money-Supply Changes," *American Economic Review* 56 (June 1966): 433–49; Christopher A. Sims, "Money, Income, and Causality," *American Economic Review* 62 (September 1972): 540–52; E. L. Feige and D. K. Pearce, "The Casual Relationship between Money and Income: Some Caveats for Time Series Analysis," *Review of Economics and Statistics* 61 (November 1979): 521–33: David Laidler, "Monetarism: An Interpretation and an Assessment," University of Western Ontario Centre for the Study of International Economic Relations, Working Paper no. 8010 (July 1980).

ables as nominal income, prices, interest rates, and real income.[24] However, nothing essential would be altered if the nominal quantity of money supplied were expressed as a function of other variables, comparable to the demand function, provided that, insofar as the same variables enter the supply and demand functions, the functional relation between them and the quantity of money is different. For example, the supply function is frequently written as:

(6a) $M^s = h(R, Y)$,

where R is an interest rate or set of interest rates, either actual or anticipated, and Y is nominal income or NPy. In the special case of M^s strictly exogenous, the supply function reduces to

(6b) $M^s = M_o$.

The simple quantity theory then specifies that

(6c) $M^D = M^s$,

where M^D is defined by equation (6), and M^s by either equation (6a) or equation (6b), and where, in the long run, the variable that equates demand and supply is the price level, though, in the short run, in so-called transition periods, other variables may also be affected.

24. Of course, that does not mean that the nominal quantity of money is not an endogenous variable from a different point of view. It simply means that the variables determining it are largely independent of the variables we are seeking to analyze. To put the matter differently, there is no "first cause." Whatever is taken for granted at one level of analysis itself requires explanation at a different level. The quantity of money is what it is at any time because antecedent circumstances have made it that amount rather than something else. These antecedent circumstances are a valid subject for examination. In such an examination the quantity of money would be treated as endogenous, and some other variables affecting it as exogenous—variables such as the balance of payments, the identity of the members of the Federal Open Market Committee, the operating procedures of the New York Federal Reserve Bank, and so on in endless variety. At a still deeper level of analysis, these other variables would be treated as endogenous, and so on in infinite regress.

A basic scientific problem is how to carve up a broad question into narrower sectors for investigation. The desideratum is to have sectors that are orthogonal to one another, in the sense that there is a minimum of interaction between them, so that the analysis of each can proceed independently. In terms of "endogeneity" and "exogeneity," this means that variables that are treated as exogenous for one sector should be determined in another sector by variables other than those regarded as endogenous in the first sector. The "recursive" systems analyzed extensively by Herman Wold are a particular example of systems satisfying this requirement. See Herman Wold, "Statistical Estimation of Economic Relationships," *Econometrica* 17, suppl. (July 1949): 1–22; also Herman Wold and R. H. Strotz, "Recursive vs. Non-Recursive Systems: An Attempt at Synthesis," *Econometrica* 28 (April 1960): 417–27.

2.4   The Demand for Money

J. M. Keynes's liquidity preference analysis (discussed further in sec. 2.5) reinforced the shift of emphasis from mechanical aspects of the payments process to the qualities of money as an asset. Keynes's analysis, though strictly in the Cambridge cash-balances tradition, was much more explicit in stressing the role of money as one among many assets, and of interest rates as the relevant cost of holding money.

More recent work has gone still further in this direction, treating the demand for money as part of capital or wealth theory, concerned with the composition of the balance sheet or portfolio of assets.[25]

From this point of view, it is important to distinguish between ultimate wealth holders, to whom money is one form in which they choose to hold their wealth, and enterprises, to whom money is a producer's good like machinery or inventories.[26]

2.4.1   Demand by Ultimate Wealth Holders

For ultimate wealth holders the demand for money, in real terms, may be expected to be a function primarily of the following variables:

1. *Total wealth.* This is the analogue of the budget constraint in the usual theory of consumer choice. It is the total that must be divided among various forms of assets. In practice, estimates of total wealth are

---

25. Much attention has been devoted in the past decade or so to the so-called micro-foundations of money (see Robert J. Barro and Stanley Fischer, "Recent Developments in Monetary Theory," *Journal of Monetary Economics* 2, April 1976: 151–55). The aim has been to provide a deeper theoretical underpinning for the kind of demand functions we develop in this section (or an alternative to such functions) in terms of a general equilibrium analysis of individual utility maximizing choices. The aim is admirable but, like Walrasian general equilibrium analysis for the most part, we suspect that the return will be primarily in improving our "analytical filing box" rather than in generating substantive hypotheses about economic phenomena (see M. Friedman, "Leon Walras and His Economic System" *American Economic Review* 45 [December 1955]: 900–909).

Much of the work along this line is summarized and an extensive bibliography is provided in *Models of Monetary Economies*, Federal Reserve Bank of Minneapolis, 1980, containing the proceedings of a conference held in December 1978.

One particular theoretical construction for which its authors made extravagant claims is the attempt to base the theory of money on an overlapping generations model (see papers by Wallace; and by Cass, Okuno and Zilcha in ibid.). We share the view expressed by James Tobin in his cogent comments on these papers (ibid., pp. 83–90) that, as it has been developed so far at least, this model is *not* "the key to the theory of money." On the contrary, in our view this ingenious and subtle model abstracts from what we regard as the essential role of money. What is left may be of interest in other contexts but not for the theory of money.

26. See Milton Friedman, "The Quantity Theory of Money—A Restatement," in *Studies in the Quantity Theory of Money*, ed. M. Friedman (Chicago: University of Chicago Press, 1956); reprinted in *The Optimum Quantity of Money* (Chicago: Aldine, 1969).

seldom available. Instead, income may serve as an index of wealth. However, it should be recognized that income as measured by statisticians may be a defective index of wealth because it is subject to erratic year-to-year fluctuations, and a longer-term concept, like the concept of permanent income developed in connection with the theory of consumption, may be more useful.[27]

The emphasis on income as a surrogate for wealth, rather than as a measure of the "work" to be done by money, is conceptually perhaps the basic difference between the more recent analyses of the demand for money and the earlier versions of the quantity theory.

2. *The division of wealth between human and nonhuman forms.* The major asset of most wealth holders is personal earning capacity. However, the conversion of human into nonhuman wealth or the reverse is subject to narrow limits because of institutional constraints. It can be done by using current earnings to purchase nonhuman wealth or by using nonhuman wealth to finance the acquisition of skills, but not by purchase or sale of human wealth and to only a limited extent by borrowing on the collateral of earning power. Hence, the fraction of total wealth that is in the form of nonhuman wealth may be an additional important variable.

3. *The expected rates of return on money and other assets.* These rates of return are the counterparts to the prices of a commodity and its substitutes and complements in the usual theory of consumer demand. The nominal rate of return on money may be zero, as it generally is on currency, or negative, as it sometimes is on demand deposits subject to net service charges, or positive, as it sometimes is on demand deposits on which interest is paid and generally is on time deposits. The nominal rate of return on other assets consists of two parts: first, any currently paid yield or cost, such as interest on bonds, dividends on equities, and storage costs on physical assets, and, second, a change in the nominal price of the asset. The second part will, of course, be especially important under conditions of inflation or deflation.

4. *Other variables determining the utility attached to the services rendered by money relative to those rendered by other assets—in Keynesian terminology, determining the value attached to liquidity proper.* One such variable may be one already considered—namely, real wealth or income, since the services rendered by money may, in principle, be regarded by

27. See M. Friedman, *A Theory of the Consumption Function* (Princeton: Princeton University Press for NBER, 1957); idem "The Demand for Money: Some Theoretical and Empirical Results," *Journal of Political Economy* 67 (August 1959): 327–51, reprinted as Occasional Paper no. 68 (New York: NBER), and in *The Optimum Quantity of Money* (Chicago: Aldine, 1969); Karl Brunner and Allan H. Meltzer, "Predicting Velocity: Implications for Theory and Policy," *Journal of Finance* 18 (May 1963): 319–54; Allan H. Meltzer, "The Demand for Money: The Evidence from the Time Series," *Journal of Political Economy* 71 (June 1963): 219–46.

wealth holders as a "necessity," like bread, the consumption of which increases less than in proportion to any increase in income, or as a "luxury," like recreation, the consumption of which increases more than in proportion.

Another variable that is likely to be important empirically is the degree of economic stability expected to prevail in the future. Wealth holders are likely to attach considerably more value to liquidity when they expect economic conditions to be unstable than when they expect them to be highly stable. This variable is likely to be difficult to express quantitatively even though the direction of change may be clear from qualitative information. For example, the outbreak of war clearly produces expectations of instability, which is one reason war is often accompanied by a notable increase in real balances—that is, a notable decline in velocity.

The rate of inflation enters under item 3 as a factor affecting the cost of holding various assets, particularly currency. The variability of inflation enters here, as a major factor affecting the usefulness of money balances. Empirically, variability of inflation tends to increase with the level of inflation, reinforcing the negative effect of higher inflation on the quantity of money demanded.

Still another variable may be the volume of capital transfers relative to income—of trading in existing capital goods by ultimate wealth holders. The higher the turnover of capital assets, the higher the fraction of total assets people may find it useful to hold as cash. This variable corresponds to the class of transactions neglected in going from the transactions version of the quantity equation to the income version.

We can symbolize this analysis in terms of the following demand function for money for an individual wealth holder:

(7) $$M/P = f(y, w; R_M{}^*, R_B{}^*, R_E{}^*, g_p{}^*; u),$$

where M, P, and y have the same meaning as in equation (6) except that they relate to a single wealth holder (for whom $y = y'$); w is the fraction of wealth in nonhuman form (or, alternatively, the fraction of income derived from property): an asterisk denotes an expected value, so $R_M{}^*$ is the expected nominal rate of return on money; $R_B{}^*$ is the expected nominal rate of return on fixed-value securities, including expected changes in their prices; $R_E{}^*$ is the expected nominal rate of return on equities, including expected changes in their prices; $g_P{}^* = (1/P) (dP/dt)^*$ is the expected rate of change of prices of goods and hence the expected nominal rate of return on physical assets in addition to any direct income they yield (or storage costs they impose);[28] and u is a portmanteau symbol standing for whatever variables other than income may affect the utility

---

28. See also the discussion in section 6.6.3. We use the term physical assets in contrast to nominal assets to refer to all sources of permanent income, whether they are tangible assets,

attached to the services of money. Each of the four rates of return stands, of course, for a set of rates of return, and for some purposes it may be important to classify assets still more finely—for example, to distinguish currency from deposits, long-term from short-term fixed-value securities, risky from relatively safe equities, and one kind of physical assets from another.[29]

The usual problems of aggregation arise in passing from equation (7) to a corresponding equation for the economy as a whole—in particular, from the possibility that the amount of money demanded may depend on the distribution among individuals of such variables as y and w and not merely on their aggregate or average value. If we neglect these distributional effects, equation (7) can be regarded as applying to the community as a whole, with M and y referring to per capita money holdings and per capita real income, respectively, and w to the fraction of aggregate wealth in nonhuman form.

The major problems that arise in practice in applying equation (7) are the precise definitions of y and w, the estimation of *expected* rates of return as contrasted with actual rates of return, and the quantitative specification of the variables designated by u.

2.4.2 Demand by Business Enterprises

Business enterprises are not subject to a constraint comparable to that imposed by the total wealth of the ultimate wealth holder. The total amount of capital embodied in productive assets, including money, is a variable that an enterprise can determine to maximize returns, since it can acquire additional capital through the capital market. Hence there is no reason on this ground to include total wealth, or y as a surrogate for total wealth, as a variable in the business demand function for money.

It may, however, be desirable to include, on different grounds, a somewhat similar variable defining the "scale" of the enterprise—namely, as an index of the productive value of different quantities of money to the enterprise, in line with the earlier transactions approach emphasizing the "work" to be done by money. It is by no means clear

---

such as factories, buildings, or the like; or intangible assets such as goodwill or the productive capacities of human beings.

We shall use g to refer to the percentage rate of change of the variable designated by a subscript.

29. Under some assumed conditions, the four rates of return may not be independent. For example, in a special case considered in Friedman, "The Quantity Theory of Money—a Restatement," pp. 9–10,

$$R_B = R_E.$$

Note that R_E is here defined differently than r_e was in the source here cited; r_e there referred to the real, not nominal, return on equities.

what the appropriate variable is: for example, total transactions, net value added, net income, total capital in nonmoney form, or net worth. The lack of data has meant that much less empirical work has been done on the business demand for money than on an aggregate demand curve encompassing both ultimate wealth holders and business enterprises. As a result there are as yet only faint indications about the best variable to use.

The division of wealth between human and nonhuman form has no special relevance to business enterprises, since they are likely to buy the services of both forms on the market.

Rates of return on money and on alternative assets are, of course, highly relevant to business enterprises. These rates determine the net cost to them of holding the money balances. However, the particular rates that are relevant may be quite different from those that are relevant for ultimate wealth holders. For example, the rates banks charge on loans are of minor importance for wealth holders yet may be extremely important for businesses, since bank loans may be a way in which they can acquire the capital embodied in money balances.

The counterpart for business enterprises of the variable u in equation (7) is the set of variables other than scale affecting the productivity of money balances. At least one subset of such variables—namely, expectations about economic stability and the variability of inflation—is likely to be common to business enterprises and ultimate wealth holders.

With these interpretations of the variables, equation (7), with w excluded, can be regarded as symbolizing the business demand for money and, as it stands, symbolizing aggregate demand for money, although with even more serious qualifications about the ambiguities introduced by aggregation.

2.5 The Keynesian Challenge to the Quantity Theory

The income-expenditure analysis developed by John Maynard Keynes offered an alternative approach to the interpretation of changes in nominal income that emphasized the relation between nominal income and investment or autonomous expenditures rather than the relation between nominal income and the stock of money.[30]

Keynes's basic challenge to the reigning theory can be summarized in three propositions that he set forth:

1. As a purely *theoretical* matter, *a long-run equilibrium* position characterized by "full employment" of resources need not exist, even if all prices are flexible.

---

30. *The General Theory of Employment, Interest and Money* (London: Macmillan, 1936).

2. As an *empirical* matter, prices can be regarded as rigid—an institutional datum—for *short-run economic fluctuations*; that is, the distinction between real and nominal magnitudes that is at the heart of the quantity theory is not important for such fluctuations.

3. The demand function for money has a particular empirical form—corresponding to absolute liquidity preference—that makes velocity highly unstable much of the time, so that, in the main, changes in the quantity of money frequently produce offsetting changes in *V*. This proposition is critical for the other two, though the reasons for absolute liquidity preference are different in the long run and in the short run. Absolute liquidity preference at an interest rate approaching zero is a necessary though not a sufficient condition for proposition 1. Absolute liquidity preference at the "conventional" interest rate explains why Keynes regarded the quantity equation, though perfectly valid as an identity, as largely useless for policy or for predicting short-run fluctuations in nominal and real income (identical by proposition 2). In its place, Keynes put the income identity supplemented by a stable propensity to consume.

2.5.1 Long-Run Equilibrium

Though this book is about monetary trends, and hence the first proposition about long-run equilibrium is particularly relevant, that proposition can be treated summarily because it has been demonstrated to be false. Keynes's error consisted in neglecting the role of wealth in the consumption function—or, stated differently, in neglecting the existence of a desired stock of wealth as a goal motivating savings.[31] All sorts of frictions and rigidities may interfere with the attainment of a hypothetical long-run equilibrium position at full employment; dynamic changes in technology, resources, and social and economic institutions may continually change the characteristics of that equilibrium position; but there is no fundamental "flaw in the price system" that makes unemployment a natural outcome of a fully operative market mechanism.

This proposition played a large role in gaining for Keynes the adherence of many noneconomists, particularly the large band of reformers,

31. Keynes, of course, verbally recognized this point, but it was not incorporated in his formal model of the economy. Its key role was pointed out first by Gottfried Haberler, *Prosperity and Depression* 3d ed. (Geneva: League of Nations, 1941), pp. 242, 389, 403, 491–503; and subsequently by Arthur C. Pigou, "Economic Progress in a Stable Environment," *Economica*, n.s., 14 (August 1947): 180–88; James Tobin, "Money Wage Rates and Employment," in *The New Economics*, ed. Seymour Harris (New York: Knopf, 1947); Don Patinkin, "Price Flexibility and Full Employment," in *Readings in Monetary Theory*, ed. F. A. Lutz and L. W. Mints (Homewood, Ill.: Irwin, 1951), a revised version of an article that appeared in *American Economic Review* 38 (September 1948): 543–64; Harry G. Johnson, "*The General Theory* after Twenty-Five Years," *American Economic Association Papers and Proceedings* 51 (May 1961): 1–17.

social critics, and radicals who were persuaded that there was something fundamentally wrong with the capitalist "system." There is a long history, going back at least to Malthus, of attempts, some highly sophisticated, to demonstrate that there is a "flaw in the price system."[32] In modern times, one of the most popular and persistent attempts is the "social credit" doctrine of Major C. H. Douglas, which even spawned a political party in Canada that in 1935 captured control of the government of the Canadian province of Alberta and attempted to implement some of Major Douglas's doctrines. This policy ran into legal obstacles and had to be abandoned. The successor party controlled Alberta until 1971, when it gave way to the Progressive Conservative Party; it controlled British Columbia for most of the period from 1952 to the present (1980). However, while retaining the name the successor party rejected the basic social-credit doctrine. Before Keynes these attempts had been made primarily by persons outside the mainstream of the economics profession, and professional economists had little trouble demonstrating their theoretical flaws and inadequacies.

Keynes's attempt was therefore greeted with enthusiasm. It came from a professional economist of the very highest repute, regarded—and properly so—by his fellow economists as one of the great economists of all time. The analytical system was sophisticated and complex, yet, once mastered, appeared highly mechanical and capable of yielding far-reaching and important conclusions with a minimum of input; and these conclusions were, besides, highly congenial to the opponents of the market system.

Needless to say, the demonstration that this proposition of Keynes's is false, and even the acceptance of this demonstration by economists who regard themselves as disciples of the Keynes of *The General Theory*, has not prevented the noneconomist opponents of the market system from continuing to believe that Keynes proved the proposition and continuing to cite his authority for it.

2.5.2 Short-Run Price Rigidity

Alfred Marshall's distinction among market equilibrium, short-period equilibrium, and long-period equilibrium was a device for analyzing the dynamic adjustment in a particular market to a change in demand or supply.[33] This device had two key characteristics. One, the less important

---

32. The title of one such attempt by P. W. Martin, *The Flaw in the Price System* (London: King, 1924).

33. We are indebted to a brilliant book by Axel Leijonhufvud, *On Keynesian Economics and the Economics of Keynes* (London: Oxford University Press, 1968), for a full appreciation of the importance of this proposition in the Keynesian system. This subsection and the one that follows, on the liquidity preference function, owe much to Leijonhufvud's penetrating analysis.

for our purposes, is that it replaced the continuous process by a series of discrete steps—comparable to approximating a continuous function by a set of straight-line segments. The second is the assumption that prices adjust more rapidly than quantities, indeed, so rapidly that the price adjustment can be regarded as instantaneous. An increase in demand (a shift to the right of the long-run demand curve) will produce a new market equilibrium involving a higher price but the same quantity. The higher price will, in the short run, encourage existing producers to produce more with their existing plants, thus raising quantity and bringing prices back down toward their original level. In the long run, it will attract new producers and encourage existing producers to expand their plants, still further raising quantities and lowering prices. Throughout the process, it takes time for output to adjust but no time for prices to do so. This assumption has no effect on the final equilibrium position, but it is vital for the path to equilibrium.

This Marshallian assumption about the price of a particular product became widely accepted and tended to be carried over unthinkingly to the price level in analyzing the dynamic adjustment to a change in the demand for or supply of money. As noted above, the Cambridge cash-balances equation lends itself to a demand-supply interpretation along Marshallian lines.[34] So interpreted, a change in the nominal quantity of money (a once-for-all shift in the supply schedule) will require a change in one or more of the variables on the right-hand side of equation (6)—k, or P or N, or y—in order to reconcile demand and supply. In the final full equilibrium, the adjustment will, in general, be entirely in P, since the change in the nominal quantity of money need not alter any of the "real" factors on which k, N, and y ultimately depend.[35] As in the Marshallian case, the final position is not affected by relative speeds of adjustment.

There is nothing in the logic of the quantity theory that specifies the dynamic path of adjustment, nothing that requires the whole initial adjustment (Marshall's market equilibrium) to take place through P rather than through k or y (it clearly is unlikely to affect N in any short period). It was widely recognized that the adjustment during what Fisher, for example, called "transition periods" would in practice be partly in k and y as well as in P. Yet this recognition was not incorporated in formal theoretical analysis. The formal analysis simply took over Marshall's assumption. In this sense the quantity theorists can be validly criticized for having "assumed" price flexibility—just as Keynes can be validly criticized for "assuming" that consumption is independent of wealth,

34. Pigou, "Economic Progress."

35. The "in general" is inserted to warn the reader that this is a complex question, requiring for a full analysis a much more careful statement of just how the quantity of money is increased. However, these more sophisticated issues are not relevant to the point under discussion and so are bypassed.

even though he recognized in his asides that wealth has an effect on consumption.[36]

Keynes was a true Marshallian in method. He followed Marshall in taking the demand-supply analysis as his framework. He followed Marshall in replacing the continuous adjustment by a series of discrete steps

36. In an article, "On the Short-Run Non-Neutrality of Money in the Quantity Theory," *Banca Nazionale del Lavoro Quarterly Review* 100 (March 1972): 3–22, Don Patinkin cites evidence that he regards as decisively contradicting the interpretation that Fisher and quantity theorists "simply took over Marshall's assumption" that "prices adjust more rapidly than quantities" (as contended in Friedman, "A Theoretical Framework for Monetary Analysis," *Journal of Political Economy* 78 [March/April 1970]: 207–8, and Gordon, *Milton Friedman's Monetary Framework*, p. 17). Yet we regard the evidence Patinkin cites as strikingly confirming our interpretation. One sample of his evidence will do:

"The sequence of effects visualized by Fisher" after an increase in the quantity of money is as follows:

"1. Prices rise.

"2. Velocities of circulation (V and V') increase; the rate of interest rises, but not sufficiently.

"3. Profits increase, loans expand, and the Q's [i.e., the real volume of trade] increase.

"4. Deposit currency (M') expands relatively to money (M).

"5. Prices continue to rise; that is, phenomenon No. 1 is repeated. Then No. 2 is repeated, and so on."

Is not Fisher's sequence precisely the counterpart for the aggregate to Marshall's analysis for a particular product summarized in the second paragraph before the one to which this footnote is attached?

Further proof is that just before listing the five steps that Patinkin quotes, Fisher states that "an increase in currency cannot, even temporarily, very greatly increase trade. . . . almost the entire effect of an increase of deposits must be seen in a change of prices" (Fisher, *Purchasing Power of Money*, pp. 62–63).

Consider how a Keynesian would describe the effects of an increase in the quantity of money. It would go:

1. Interest rates fall.

2. Investment increases.

3. Output and real income increases.

4. Consumption increases.

It is not clear when he would come to the statement "prices rise," but it would surely be late in his list. Moreover, his step 1 implies that velocity falls, but he would be most unlikely ever to refer to that phenomenon.

Is this not precisely the contrast that we draw between the quantity theorists and the Keynesians when we say that Keynes "deviated from Marshall . . . in reversing the roles assigned to price and quantity"? References in Patinkin's article to statements by Pigou, Keynes, Robertson, Lavington, and Chicago economists, all equally strike us as confirming our interpretation.

Patinkin also criticizes our assertion that "this recognition was not incorporated in formal theoretical analysis," asserting, "The facts of the case, however, are quite different," and giving as evidence that "Fisher wrote incomparably more on his monetary proposals for mitigating the cyclical problems of the 'transition period' than on the long-run proportionality of prices to money. This concentration on short-run analysis was even more true for the policy-oriented Chicago quantity-theory school of the 1930s and 1940s."

However, there can be a great difference between what is implied by or contained in a formal theory, what proponents of the theory may believe it implies or contains, and what

and so analyzing a dynamic process in terms of a series of shifts between static equilibrium positions. Even his steps were essentially Marshall's, his short-run being distinguished from his long-run by the fixity of the aggregate capital stock. However, he tended to merge the market period and the short-run period, and, true to his own misleading dictum, "in the long run we are all dead," he concentrated almost exclusively on the short run.[37]

Keynes also followed Marshall in assuming that one variable adjusted so quickly that the adjustment could be regarded as instantaneous, while the other variable adjusted slowly. Where he deviated from Marshall, and it was a momentous deviation, was in reversing the roles assigned to price and quantity. He assumed that, at least for changes in aggregate demand, quantity was the variable that adjusted rapidly, while price was the variable that adjusted slowly, at least downward.[38] Keynes embodied this assumption in his formal model by expressing all variables in wage

---

they write about. Of course Fisher, the Chicago monetary economists, and the host of other economists who studied business cycles wrote a great deal about short-run movements and constructed many ingenious theories about business cycles that have much to teach us. In particular, Fisher's distinction between nominal and real interest rates, which dates back to some of his earliest writing, remains a seminal and penetrating insight. Yet, so far as we know, none of this voluminous writing and none of these theories provide a formal theoretical extension of the quantity theory to explain the division of changes in nominal income between changes in prices and in output or of changes in the quantity of money between changes in velocity, in prices, and in output, just as none of Keynes's extensive discussion of changes in money-wage rates before the point of full employment provides a formal theoretical analysis of such changes.

37. This famous quoted remark is from Keynes, *A Tract on Monetary Reform* (London: Macmillan, 1923), reprinted as volume 4 of *The Collected Works of John Maynard Keynes* (London: Macmillan, 1971), p. 65. See the full quotation in context in chapter 6, note 11, below.

38. The reference to "quantity," not "output," is based on the conjecture that Keynes, if pressed to distinguish the market from the short-run period, would have done so by regarding quantity available to purchase as adjusting rapidly in the market period largely through changes in inventories, and in the short-run period through changes in output.

The statement that Keynes assumed prices rigid is an oversimplification, since he distinguished between the price level of products and the wage rate and allowed for a change in the ratio of prices to wages, even before the point of full employment. However, this change in prices in wage-units plays no important role in the aspects of his theory that are relevant to our purposes, so we have simplified our analysis of Keynes's theory by regarding prices as well as wages as rigid—a simplification that has been widely used. (Explicit reference to this simplification should have been made in M. Friedman, "Theoretical Framework for Monetary Analysis." We are indebted to an unpublished paper by Paul Davidson for recognition that the exposition on this point in that source may have been misleading.)

Keynes himself minimized the importance of changes in prices relative to wages, noting that, "This policy [of maintaining the money wage level as a whole as stable as possible] will result in a fair degree of stability in the price-level. . . . Apart from 'administered' or monopoly prices, the price-level will only change in the short period in response to the extent that changes in the volume of employment affect marginal prime costs; whilst in the

units, so that his formal analysis—aside from a few passing references to a situation of "true" inflation—dealt with "real" magnitudes, not "nominal" magnitudes.[39] He rationalized the assumption in terms of wage rigidity arising partly from money illusion, partly from the strength of trade unions. And, at a still deeper level, he rationalized wage rigidity by proposition 1: under conditions when there was no full-employment equilibrium, there was also no equilibrium nominal price level; something had to be brought in from outside to fix the price level; it might as well be institutional wage rigidity. Put differently, flexible nominal wages in such circumstances had no economic function to perform; hence nominal wages might as well be made rigid.

However rationalized, the basic reason for the assumption was undoubtedly the lack of concordance between observed phenomena and the implications of a literal application of Marshall's assumption to aggregate magnitudes. Such a literal application implied that economic fluctuations would take the form wholly of fluctuations in prices with continuous full employment of men and resources. Clearly, experience did not correspond. If anything, at least in the decade and a half between the end of World War I and the writing of *The General Theory*, economic fluctuations were manifested to a greater degree in output and employment than in prices. It therefore seemed highly plausible that, at least for aggregate phenomena, relative speeds of adjustment were just the reverse of those assumed by Marshall.[40]

---

long period they will only change in response to changes in the cost of production due to new technique and new or increased equipment" (*General Theory*, p. 270).

Leijonhufvud, in response to criticism by Herschel I. Grossman, has retracted his initial position on Keynes's assumptions, writing, "it is *not* correct to attribute to Keynes a general reversal of the Marshallian ranking of relative price and quantity adjustment velocities. In the 'shortest run' for which system behavior can be defined in Keynes' model, output-prices *must* be treated as perfectly flexible." See Grossman, "Was Keynes a 'Keynesian'? A Review Article," *Journal of Economic Literature* 10 (March 1972): 26–30; Leijonhufvud, "Keynes' Employment Function," *History of Political Economy* 6 (1974): 158–70; quotation from p. 169.

Leijonhufvud's textual exegesis is correct, and relevant to Keynes's employment function, but it does not alter the role that the reversal of the Marshallian ranking of relative price and quantity adjustments played in Keynes's theory. In the "shortest run" that Leijonhufvud refers to, the elasticity of demand for labor is high, so that, as Keynes noted, prices in wage-units will be highly stable.

And, whatever may be true for Keynes himself, there is no doubt that his followers who shaped much of economic thinking since *The General Theory* appeared, took product prices as well as wages as determined by forces outside those dealt with in Keynesian theory (see footnotes 43 and 45 below).

39. Keynes, *General Theory*, pp. 119, 301, 303.

40. Marshall's assumption is clearly not always the best one for particular markets. On the contrary, one of the significant advances in recent years in relative price theory is the development of more sophisticated price adjustment models that allow the rates of adjust-

Keynes explored this penetrating insight by carrying it to the extreme: all adjustment in quantity, none in price. He qualified this statement by assuming it to apply only to conditions of underemployment. At "full" employment, he shifted to the quantity-theory model and asserted that all adjustment would be in price—he designated such a situation one of "true inflation." However, Keynes paid no more than lip service to this possibility, and his disciples have done the same; so it does not misrepresent the body of his analysis largely to neglect the qualification.

Given this assumption, a change in the nominal quantity of money means a change in the real quantity of money. In equation (6) we can divide through by P, making the left-hand side the real quantity of money. A change in the (nominal and real) quantity of money will then be matched by a change in k, N, or y.

Nothing up to this point seems to prevent Keynes from having a purely monetary theory of economic fluctuations, with changes in M being reflected entirely in y'. However, a purely monetary theory conflicted with Keynes's interpretation of the Great Depression, which he regarded, we believe erroneously, as showing that expansionary monetary policy was ineffective in stemming a decline.[41] Hence he was inclined to interpret changes in M as reflected in k rather more than in y'. This is where his proposition 3 about liquidity preference enters in.

Indeed, in the most extreme, and we are tempted to say purest, form of his analysis, Keynes supposes that the whole of the adjustment will be in k. And, interestingly enough, this result can also be regarded as a direct consequence of his assumption about the relative speed of adjustment of price and quantity. For k is not a numerical constant but a function of other variables. It embodies liquidity preference. In Keynes's system, the main variable it depends on is the interest rate. This too is a price. Hence it was natural for Keynes to regard the interest rate as slow to adjust and to take, as the variable that responds, the real quantity of money people desire to hold.

If changes in M do not produce changes in y', what does? Keynes's answer is the need to reconcile investment, the amount some people want to add to the stock of productive capital, with savings, the amount the community wants to add to its stock of wealth. Hence Keynes puts at the center of his analysis the distinction between investment and consumption, or more fundamentally between spending that is largely independent of current income and spending linked closely to current income.

---

ment of both price and quantity to vary continuously between instantaneous and very slow adjustment. However, these developments are not directly relevant to the present discussion, although they partly inspire section 2.6 below.

41. See Milton Friedman, "The Monetary Theory and Policy of Henry Simons," *Journal of Law and Economics* 10 (October 1967): 1–13; reprinted in *Optimum Quantity of Money*, pp. 81–93.

As a result of both experience and further theoretical analysis, hardly an economist today accepts Keynes's conclusion about the strictly passive character of k, or the accompanying conclusion that money (in the sense of the quantity of money) does not matter, or will explicitly assert that P is "really" an institutional datum that will be completely unaffected, even in short periods, by changes in M.[42]

Yet Keynes's assumption about the relative speed of adjustment of price and quantity remains a key to the difference in approach and analysis between those economists who regard themselves as Keynesians and those who do not. Whatever the first group may say in their asides and in their qualifications, they treat the price level as an institutional datum in their formal theoretical analysis. They continue to regard changes in the nominal quantity of money as equivalent to changes in the real quantity of money and hence as having to be reflected in k and y'. And they continue to regard the initial effect as being on k. The difference is that they no longer regard interest rates as institutional data, as Keynes in considerable measure did. Instead, they regard the change in k as requiring a change in interest rates that in turn produces a change in y'. Hence they attribute more significance to changes in the quantity of money than Keynes and his disciples did in the first several decades after the appearance of *The General Theory*.

The statement that Keynes and his followers "treat the price level as an institutional datum in their formal theoretical analysis" does not mean they assert that prices and wages are in fact constant, or even that in their empirical work they do not introduce relations designed to predict the movements of prices and wages. Treating the price level or the wage level as an institutional datum, or, as Keynes did, as the "numeraire," is not equivalent to asserting that wages or prices are constant. It means, rather, that the theory in question has nothing to say about what determines the wage level; that the forces determining the wage level are forces abstracted from in the theory. This assumption is reflected in the kind of ad hoc relations Keynesians introduce into their empirical work to predict prices and wages.[43]

---

42. Milton Friedman, "Money: Quantity Theory," *International Encyclopedia of the Social Sciences*; *The Counter-Revolution in Monetary Theory*, Institute of Economic Affairs for the Wincott Foundation, Occasional Paper 33 (London: Tonbridge, 1970).

43. The price equations generally simply link prices to costs, mainly wages. This equation can be regarded as derivable from Keynes's system. But the wage equations are either purely ad hoc or, insofar as they are derivable from any theoretical system, it is the pre-Keynesian classical system rather than Keynes's. For example, Patinkin (Gordon, *Milton Friedman's Monetary Framework*, p. 128) refers approvingly to Lawrence Klein's comment that "the main reasoning behind this equation is that of the law of supply and demand. Money wage rates move in response to excess demand on the labor market." The "law of supply and demand" is hardly Keynesian! More important, Klein misapplies it. The "classical law," *as taken over by Keynes*, connects *real-wage rates*, not *money-wage rates*,

It is important to distinguish between the logical implications of a theory and the statements about observable phenomena that a professed adherent of the theory may make. As Keynes says, "We can keep 'at the back of our heads' the necessary reserves and qualifications and the adjustments which we shall have to make later on."[44] Of course, both the Keynesians and Keynes himself recognize that, as a factual matter, changes in income are partly in prices and partly in output; and, of course, both have instructive ideas and insights about the factors that determine the division in particular cases. But Keynes's formal theory has nothing to say about what determines the absolute price or wage level, though it does have some implications for the behavior of prices relative to wages.[45]

---

with excess supply or demand. Klein's inclusion of the rate of change of prices in the equation, which Patinkin cites, is a move toward the correct classical inclusion of real wages, but if it went wholly in that direction it would leave money wages and money prices either undetermined or a simple inheritance from past history—which is precisely what we say Keynes's system assumes.

44. Keynes, *General Theory*, p. 297.

45. For a fuller discussion of this point, see Gordon, *Milton Friedman's Monetary Framework*, pp. 79–80, 93–94, 127–29, 143, 155–57, 176–77.

A striking illustration of the Keynesian tendency to treat the price level as an institutional datum is provided in Cowles Foundation Monograph 21, *Financial Markets and Economic Activity* (New York: Wiley 1967). A key essay in that book presents a comparative static analysis of the general equilibrium adjustment of stocks of assets (W. C. Brainard and J. Tobin, "Financial Intermediaries and the Effectiveness of Monetary Controls," ibid., pp. 55–93). Yet the distinction between nominal and real magnitudes is not even discussed. The entire analysis is valid only on the implicit assumption that nominal prices of goods and services are completely rigid, although interest rates and real magnitudes are flexible.

A specific example documenting this statement is that Tobin and Brainard explicitly assume that central banks can determine the ratio of currency (or high-powered money) to total wealth including real assets (pp. 61–62). If prices are flexible, the central bank can determine only nominal magnitudes, not such a real ratio.

Other papers in Monograph 21, notably the paper by Brainard, "Financial Institutions and a Theory of Monetary Control" (ibid., pp. 94–141), make the same implicit assumptions. The word "prices" does not appear in the cumulative subject index of this monograph and of two companion volumes, Monographs 19 and 20.

Still another example is a paper by the same authors, "Pitfalls in Financial Model Building" (*American Economic Association Papers and Proceedings* 58 (May 1968): 99–122), in which they present a simulation of a "fictitious economy of our construction." In this economy the replacement value of physical assets is used as the numeraire of the system, and all prices are expressed relative to the replacement value. The result is that the system—intended to illuminate the problems of monetary analysis—takes the absolute price level as determined outside the system. The Central Bank is implicitly assumed to be able to determine the *real* and not merely the *nominal* volume of bank reserves.

Another striking example is Lyle Gramley and Samuel B. Chase, "Time Deposits in Monetary Analysis," *Federal Reserve Bulletin* 51 (October 1965): 1380–1406, reprinted in Karl Brunner, ed., *Targets and Indicators of Monetary Policy* (San Francisco: Chandler, 1969), pp. 219–49. In this article the assumption about price rigidity is explicit and presented

The NBER series of monetary studies, including this volume, illustrates the other side of the coin—the approach of those of us who do not regard ourselves as Keynesians. Many of the questions discussed in these monographs would not have appeared to be open questions, and large parts of those monographs would never have been written, had we, implicitly or explicitly, accepted Keynes's assumption that prices are an institutional datum.

2.5.3   Absolute Liquidity Preference

Keynes gave a highly specific form to equation (6) or (7). The quantity of money demanded, he argued, could be treated as if it were divided into two parts, one part, M_1, "held to satisfy the transactions- and precautionary-motives," the other M_2, "held to satisfy the speculative motive."[46] He regarded M_1 as a roughly constant fraction of income. He regarded the (short-run) demand for M_2 as arising from "*uncertainty* as to the future of the rate of interest" and the amount demanded as depending on the relation between current rates of interest and the rates of interest expected to prevail in the future.[47] Keynes, of course, emphasized that there was a whole complex of interest rates. However, for simplicity, he spoke in terms of the "rate of interest," usually meaning by that the rate on long-term securities that involved minimal risks of default—for example, government bonds. The key distinction to Keynes was between short-term and long-term securities, not between securities that were fixed in nominal value and those that were not. The latter distinction was rendered irrelevant by his assumption that prices were rigid.

The distinction between short-term and long-term securities was important to Keynes because it corresponded to a difference in risk of capital gain or loss as a result of a change in the interest rate. The capital value of short-term securities is not much affected by a change in the interest rate; the capital value of long-term securities is. Leijonhufvud

---

as if it were only a tentative assumption made for convenience of analysis. Yet the empirical significance Gramley and Chase attach to their results belies this profession.

See also the econometric study by Stephen M. Goldfeld, *Commercial Bank Behavior and Economic Activity* (Amsterdam: North-Holland, 1966), which concentrates on real forms of the functions estimated because of "the superiority of the deflated version" (p. 166).

Evidence for a somewhat earlier period is provided by Franklyn D. Holzman and Martin Bronfenbrenner, "Survey of Inflation Theory," *American Economic Review* 53 (September 1963): 593–661. Theories of inflation stemming from the Keynesian approach stress institutional, not monetary, factors.

An even more striking example is Peter Temin's attack on our interpretation of the Great Depression. His central criticism is marred precisely by the implicit identification of nominal and real magnitudes (see footnote 20 above).

46. *General Theory*, p. 199.
47. Ibid., p. 168; italics in original.

has argued, we believe correctly, that Keynes used the term "money" as referring not only to currency and deposits narrowly defined but to the whole range of short-term assets that provide "liquidity" in the sense of security against capital loss arising from a change in the interest rate.[48] Needless to say, Keynes also regarded other kinds of risks, such as risks of default, as highly relevant, but, consistent with his proposition 2, he almost entirely disregarded risks arising from a change in the price level of goods and services.[49]

It is therefore somewhat misleading to regard Keynes, as most of the literature does, as distinguishing between "money" and "bonds." Nonetheless, we shall continue to follow current practice and use that terminology. One justification for doing so is that Keynes did treat the short-term assets he labeled "money" as yielding no interest return. (It is well to recall that he was writing at a time when short-term interest rates were extremely low both absolutely and relative to long-term rates. His procedure would seem highly unrealistic today.)

To formalize Keynes's analysis in terms of the symbols we have used so far, we can write his demand function as

$$(8) \qquad M/P = M_1/P + M_2/P = k_1 y' + f(R - R^*, R^*),$$

where R is the current rate of interest, R^* is the rate of interest expected to prevail, and k_1, the analogue to the inverse of income velocity of circulation of money, is treated as determined by payment practices and hence as a constant at least in the short run.[50] The current interest rate, R, is an observed magnitude. Hence it will be the same for all holders of money, if, like Keynes, we abstract from the existence of a complex of interest rates. The expected rate, R^*, is not observable. It may differ from one holder to another and, for each holder separately, is to be interpreted as the mean value of a probability distribution, not as a single value anticipated with certainty. For an aggregate function, R^* should strictly speaking be interpreted as a vector, not a number. Though we have introduced P into the equation for consistency with our earlier equations, Keynes omitted it because of his proposition 2, which meant that P or, more precisely, the wage rate, was taken to be a constant.

---

48. In this respect the Radcliffe Committee was faithful to Keynes in treating "liquidity" broadly defined as the relevant monetary aggregate rather than "money" narrowly defined. (Radcliffe) Committee on the Working of the Monetary System, 1959. *Report*. Cmd. 827.

49. Leijonhufvud, *On Keynesian Economics*, chap. 2.

50. Later writers in this tradition have argued that k_1 too should be regarded as a function of interest rates. See W. J. Baumol, "The Transactions Demand for Cash: An Inventory Theoretic Approach," *Quarterly Journal of Economics* 66 (November 1952): 545–56; James Tobin, "The Interest-Elasticity of Transactions Demand for Cash," *Review of Economics and Statistics* 38 (August 1956): 241–47. However, this issue is not relevant to the present discussion.

In a "given state of expectations," that is, for a given value of R^*, the higher the current rate of interest, the lower will be the amount of money people would want to hold for speculative motives. The cost of holding money instead of securities would be greater in two ways: first, a larger amount of current earnings would be sacrificed; second, it would be more likely that interest rates would fall, and hence security prices rise, and so a larger amount of capital gains would be sacrificed.

Although expectations about interest rates are given great prominence in developing the liquidity function expressing the demand for M_2, Keynes and his followers generally did not explicitly introduce an expected interest rate into that function, as we have done. For the most part, Keynes and his followers in practice treated the amount of M_2 demanded simply as a function of the current interest rate, the emphasis on expectations serving only as a reason for their attributing instability to the liquidity function.[51]

The reason for the omission of the expected interest rate is their concentration on the short-run demand function. For that function they regarded R^* as fixed, so that the speculative demand was a function of R alone. We have introduced R^* to distinguish between the different reasons that are implicit in Keynes's analysis for absolute liquidity preference in the short run and the long run.

Keynes's special twist was less expressing the demand function in the general form described by equation (8) than the particular form he gave to the function $f(R - R^*, R^*)$. For given R^*, he believed that this function was highly elastic at $R = R^*$, the degree of elasticity at an observed numerical value of R depending on how homogeneous the expectations of different holders of money are and how firmly they are held.[52] Let there be a substantial body of holders of money who have the same expectation and let them hold that expectation firmly, and the function f would become perfectly elastic at that current interest rate. Money and bonds would become perfect substitutes; liquidity preference would become absolute. The monetary authorities would find it impossible to change the interest rate because speculators holding these firm expectations would frustrate them.

An attempt by the monetary authorities to increase the amount of money by buying bonds tends to raise bond prices and lower the rate of return. Even the slightest lowering would, Keynes argued, lead specula-

51. A notable exception is James Tobin, "Liquidity Preference as Behavior towards Risk," *Review of Economic Studies* 25 (February 1958): 65–86.

52. Tobin, "Liquidity Preference," presents an excellent and illuminating analysis of this case. Because he assumes that shifts into or out of securities involve commitments for a finite period equal to the unit of time in terms of which the interest rate is expressed, his critical value is not $R = R^*$ but $R = R^*/(1 + R^*)$, current income on the securities compensating for an expected capital loss.

tors with firm expectations to absorb the additional money balances and sell any bonds demanded by the initial holders of the additional money. The result would simply be that the community as a whole would be willing to hold the increased quantity of money at an essentially unchanged interest rate; k would be higher and V lower. Conversely, an attempt by the monetary authorities to decrease the amount of money by selling bonds would tend to raise the rate of interest, and even the slightest rise would induce the speculators to absorb the bonds offered.[53]

Or, again, suppose there is an increase in nominal income for whatever reason. That will require an increase in M_1, which can come out of M_2 without any further effects. Conversely, any decline in M_1 can be added to M_2 without any further effects. The conclusion is that in circumstances of absolute liquidity preference, income can change without a change in M or in interest rates and M can change without a change in income or in interest rates. The holders of money are in metastable equilibrium, like a tumbler on its side on a flat surface; they will be satisfied with whatever the amount of money happens to be.

For the long-run demand schedule, the reason for absolute liquidity preference is different. In long-run equilibrium, R must equal R^*, so $f(R - R^*, R^*)$ reduces to a function of R^* alone. Let there be a deficiency of investment opportunities, the kind of situation envisaged in Keynes's proposition 1, so that R^* becomes very low. The lower the rate, the lower the returns from capital assets other than money—whether these be bonds, equities, or physical assets (recall that because of the assumption that the price level is rigid, Keynes did not regard the distinction among these assets as important). Accordingly, the lower R^*, the lower the cost of holding money. At a sufficiently low, yet finite rate, the extra return from holding nonmoney assets would only just compensate for the extra risks involved. Hence at that rate liquidity preference would be absolute. The "market rate" of interest could not be indefinitely low; a bottom limit was set by the widespread desire to substitute money for other assets at low interest rates.

This conclusion was a key element in Keynes's proposition 1. One way to summarize his argument for that proposition is in terms of a possible conflict between the "market" and the "equilibrium" rate of interest. If investment opportunities were sparse, yet the public's desire to save were strong, the "equilibrium" rate of interest, he argued, might have to be very low or even negative to equate investment and saving. But there was a floor to the "market rate" set by liquidity preference. If this floor exceeded the "equilibrium rate," he argued, there was a conflict that

53. In Keynes's analysis, the result would be the same if the amount of money were increased or decreased by operations that added to or subtracted from total wealth, rather than by substituting one form of wealth for another, because he assumed that wealth had no direct effect on spending.

could be resolved only by unemployment that frustrated the public's thriftiness. The fallacy in this argument is that the introduction of money not only introduces a floor to the "market rate"; it also sets a floor to the "equilibrium rate." And, in the long run, the two floors are identical. This is the essence of the so-called Pigou effect.[54]

Neither Keynes himself nor most of his followers distinguished as sharply as we have between the short-run and long-run liquidity traps. They tended to merge the two and, in line with the general emphasis on the short run, to stress the elasticity of the demand for money with respect to current, not expected, interest rates.[55]

Keynes regarded absolute liquidity preference as a strictly "limiting case" of which, though it "might become practically important in future," he knew "of no example . . . hitherto." However, he treated velocity as if in practice its behavior frequently approximated that which would prevail in this limiting case.[56]

Economists no longer explicitly avow absolute liquidity preference. The failure of repeated attempts by central banks to peg interest rates at low levels has made that proposition untenable. No Keynesian can any-more say, as Keynes did in the sentence immediately following that quoted in the preceding paragraph, "Indeed, owing to the unwillingness of most monetary authorities to deal boldly in debts of long term, there has not been much opportunity for a test [of absolute liquidity preference]."[57] Yet, like absolutely rigid prices, absolute liquidity prefer-ence still plays an important role in the theorizing of many an economist. It is implicit in the tendency to regard k or velocity as passively adjusting to changes in the quantity of money. It is explicit in the tendency to regard the demand for money as "highly" elastic with respect to interest rates.

Consider again equation (6). Let there be a change in M. Economists in the Keynesian tradition continue, as we noted earlier, to regard P as an institutional datum and so unaffected. They must therefore regard the change in M as affecting k or N or y. With absolute liquidity preference, k can absorb the impact without any change in the interest rate. Since they take the interest rate as the only link between monetary change and real income, the whole of the change would then be absorbed in k with no

54. See Milton Friedman, *Price Theory* (Chicago: Aldine, 1962), pp. 262–63; (2d ed., Chicago: Aldine, 1976), pp. 313–15.

55. Tobin makes an explicit distinction of this kind, though not in connection with a liquidity trap as such.

56. *General Theory*, p. 207.

In his criticism of an earlier version of this chapter, Patinkin objects to the key role we assign to absolute liquidity preference in our interpretation of Keynes, citing as evidence solely the quotation in the prior sentence of the text. Friedman's reply cites thirteen quotations from *The General Theory* supporting our interpretation. Gordon, *Milton Fried-man's Monetary Framework*, pp. 129–30, 168–70, 175–76.

57. *General Theory*, p. 207.

effect on N or y. If liquidity preference is not absolute, k can change only through a change in the interest rate. But a change in the interest rate affects Ny through investment spending. The more elastic is the demand for money, the less interest rates will have to change. The more inelastic are investment spending and saving with respect to the interest rate, the less will any given change in the interest rate affect y'. Hence the tendency for these economists to regard k as absorbing the main impact of changes in M means that implicitly or explicitly they regard the demand for money as highly elastic with respect to the interest rate and investment spending and saving as highly inelastic.

The tendency on the part of many economists to assume implicitly that prices are an institutional datum and that the demand for money is highly elastic with respect to the interest rate underlies some of the criticisms that have been directed against our earlier work and that of some of our associates. We have been interpreted, wrongly, we believe, as saying that k is completely independent of interest rates.[58] In that case, changes in M need not be reflected at all in k. If, also, P is taken as an institutional datum, all of the effect will be on y'. This is the implicit source of the criticism leveled against us, that we regard the quantity of money as determining the level of economic activity. Not only, say our critics, do we believe that money matters, we believe that money is all that matters.[59] If P is not regarded as an institutional datum, and we have not so regarded it, then even if we supposed k to be completely insensitive to interest rates and to anything else that might be affected by changes in M (such as the rate of change in P or in y') and so to be an absolute constant, aside from random disturbances, something other than the quantity of money would have to be brought into the analysis to explain how much of the change in M would be reflected in P and how much in y' (see sec. 2.6).

We have always tried to qualify our statements about the importance of changes in M by referring to their effect on *nominal* income. But this qualification appeared meaningless to economists who implicitly identified nominal with real magnitudes. Hence they have misunderstood our conclusions.

We have accepted the quantity-theory presumption and have thought it supported by the evidence we examined, that changes in the quantity of money as such have a negligible effect *in the long run* on real income, so that nonmonetary forces are "all that matter" for changes in real income over the decades and money "does not matter." On the other hand, we

58. See M. Friedman, "Interest Rates and the Demand for Money," *Journal of Law and Economics* 9 (October 1966): 71–85; reprinted in M. Friedman, *Optimum Quantity of Money*, pp. 141–55.
59. See Arthur M. Okun, "Money and Business Cycles: A Comment," *Review of Economics and Statistics* 45 suppl. (1), part 2 (February 1963): 72–77; Tobin, "Monetary Interpretation of History," p. 481.

have regarded the quantity of money, plus the other variables (including real income itself) that affect k as essentially "all that matter" for the long-run determination of nominal income. The price level is then a joint outcome of the monetary forces determining nominal income and the real forces determining real income.[60]

For shorter periods of time, we have argued that changes in M will be reflected in all variables on the right-hand side of equation (6): k, P, N, and y. But we have argued that the effect on k is empirically not to absorb the change in M, as the Keynesian analysis implies, but often to reinforce it, changes in M and k frequently affecting income in the same rather than opposite directions. Hence we have emphasized that changes in M are a major factor, though even then not the only factor, accounting for short-run changes in both nominal income and the real level of activity(y'). We regard the description of our position as "money is all that matters for changes in *nominal* income and for *short-run* changes in real income" as an exaggeration, but one that gives the right flavor of our conclusions. We regard the statement that "money is all that matters," period, as a basic misrepresentation of our conclusions.[61]

Another, more subtle difference between the approach of economists in the Keynesian tradition and the approach we have adopted has also contributed to much misunderstanding. This difference is in the transmission mechanism that is assumed to connect a change in the quantity of money with a change in total nominal income (= total spending). The Keynesians regard a change in the quantity of money as affecting in the first instance "the" interest rate, interpreted as a market rate on a fairly narrow class of financial liabilities. They regard spending as affected only "indirectly" as the changed interest rate alters the profitability and amount of investment spending, again interpreted fairly narrowly, and as investment spending, through the multiplier, affects total spending. Hence the emphasis they give in their analysis to the interest elasticities of the demand for money and of investment spending. We, on the other hand, stress a much broader and more "direct" impact on spending, saying, as in section 2.1, that individuals seeking "to dispose of what they regard as their excess money balances . . . will try to pay out a larger sum

---

60. See Milton Friedman, "The Supply of Money and Changes in Prices and Output," in United States Congress, Joint Economic Committee, Compendium, *The Relationship of Prices to Economic Stability and Growth* (1952), pp. 242–46; reprinted in M. Friedman, *Optimum Quantity of Money*, pp. 171–87; M. Friedman and A. J. Schwartz, *A Monetary History of the United States, 1867–1960* (Princeton: Princeton University Press for NBER, 1963), p. 695.

61. Friedman, "Supply of Money and Changes in Prices and Output," pp. 246–51; Friedman and Schwartz, *Monetary History*, pp. 678, 695; idem, "Money and Business Cycles," *Reivew of Economics and Statistics*, 45, suppl. (1), part 2 (February 1963): 38–39, 45–46, 55–64; reprinted in Friedman, *Optimum Quantity of Money*, pp. 189–235.

for the purchase of securities, goods, and services, for the repayment of debts, and as gifts than they are receiving from the corresponding sources."[62]

The two approaches can be readily reconciled on a formal level. The transmission mechanism we have stressed can be described as operating "through" the balance sheet and "through" changes in interest rates. The attempt by holders of money to restore or attain a desired balance sheet after an unexpected increase in the quantity of money will tend to raise the prices of assets and reduce interest rates, which will encourage spending to produce new assets and also spending on current services rather than on purchasing existing assets. This is how an initial effect on balance sheets gets translated into an effect on income and spending.

The difference between us and the Keynesians is less in the nature of the process than in the range of assets considered. The Keynesians tend to concentrate on a narrow range of marketable assets and recorded interest rates. We insist that a far wider range of assets and interest rates must be taken into account—such assets as durable and semi-durable consumer goods, structures, and other real property. As a result, we regard the market rates stressed by the Keynesians as only a small part of the total spectrum of rates that are relevant.[63]

This difference in the assumed transmission mechanism is largely a by-product of the different assumptions about price. The rejection of absolute liquidity preference forced Keynes's followers to let the interest rate be flexible. This chink in the key assumption that prices are an institutional datum was minimized by interpreting the "interest rate" narrowly, and market institutions made it easy to do so. After all, it is most unusual to quote the "interest rate" implicit in the sales and rental prices of houses and automobiles, let alone furniture, household appliances, clothes, and so on. Hence the prices of these items continued to be regarded as an institutional datum, which forced the transmission process to go through an extremely narrow channel. On our side there was no such inhibition. Since we regarded prices as flexible, though not "perfectly" flexible, it was natural for us to interpret the transmission mechanism in terms of relative price adjustments over a broad area rather than in terms of narrowly defined interest rates.

62. We have put "indirectly" and "direct" in quotes because this distinction, tirelessly repeated, is purely semantic and has no substantive content. What is regarded as "indirect" or "direct" depends simply on the theoretical structure that is found most convenient. For example, start with the quantity theory equations, and the effect of a change in the quantity of money on desired spending is "direct," the effect on interest rates "indirect," since it will be described as arising via the change in desired spending (as in the quotation to which this note is attached). Start with the Keynesian structure and the situation is reversed: the effect on interest rates is "direct," the effect on desired spending is "indirect."

63. See Milton Friedman, "The Lag in Effect of Monetary Policy," *Journal of Political Economy* 69 (October 1961): 461–63; Milton Friedman and David Meiselman, "The Relative Stability of Monetary Velocity and the Investment Multiplier in the United States,

2.6   The Adjustment Process

In an earlier publication preliminary to this chapter, we outlined the elements common to simple quantity theory and Keynesian models, noting that these common elements form an incomplete system with one equation missing and that the key difference between the two theories is the assumption adopted to fill the gap. For the simple quantity theory, the assumption is that aggregate real income is determined outside the system; for the Keynesian theory, the assumption is that the nominal wage (and hence price) level is determined outside the system. We also sketched a third possibility, the assumption that the elasticity of demand for real balances with respect to real income is unity plus the twin assumptions that speculators determine the interest rate in accord with firmly held anticipations, and that the difference between the permanent real interest rate and the secular growth of output can be taken as a constant for short-period fluctuations. We called the third possibility a theory of nominal income, since it defines only the path of nominal income, not of prices and output separately.

Though we regard the third approach as distinctly superior to the other two, all three have the basic defect that they say nothing about the factors that determine the proportions in which a change in nominal income will, in the short run, be divided between price change and output change. In addition, the simple quantity and Keynesian approaches have nothing to say about the adjustment process and leave little room for anticipations to play a role. The monetary theory of nominal income is less unsatisfactory in these respects but shares with the other two the absence of a satisfactory link between short-run change and long-run adjustment.

To remedy the defects common to all three theories, the key is a theory that will explain (a) the short-run division of a change in nominal income between prices and output; (b) the short-run adjustment of nominal income to a change in autonomous variables; and (c) the transition between the short-run situation and a long-run equilibrium.[64]

The central idea we shall use in sketching the direction in which such a theory might be developed is the distinction between actual and anticipated magnitudes or, to use a terminology that need not be identical but that we shall treat for this purpose as if it is, between measured and permanent magnitudes. At a long-run equilibrium position, all anticipa-

---

1897–1958," in *Stabilization Policies* ed. Commission on Money and Credit (Englewood Cliffs, N.J.: Prentice-Hall, 1963), pp. 217–22; Friedman and Schwartz, "Money and Business Cycles," pp. 59–63; M. Friedman, *Counter-Revolution in Monetary Theory*, pp. 24–25; Karl Brunner, "The 'Monetarist Revolution' in Monetary Theory," *Weltwirtschaftliches Archiv* 105, no. 1 (1970): 3–5.

64. Still other parts of the theoretical framework are developed more fully in the course of the analysis of specific issues in later chapters of this book.

tions are realized, so that actual and anticipated magnitudes, or measured and permanent magnitudes, are equal.[65]

We shall regard long-run equilibrium as determined by the Walrasian equations of general equilibrium, which determine the real variables, plus the quantity theory, which, for the given real variables, determines the price level.

We shall regard short-run equilibrium as determined by an adjustment process in which the rate of adjustment in a variable is a function of the discrepancy between the measured and the anticipated values of that variable or its rate of change, as well as, perhaps, of other variables or their rates of change. Finally, we shall let at least some anticipated variables be determined by a feedback process from past observed values.

2.6.1 Division of a Change in Nominal Income between Prices and Output

It seems plausible that the division of a change in nominal income between prices and output depends on two major factors: anticipations about the behavior of prices—this is the inertia factor stressed by Keynes—and the current level of output or employment compared with the full-employment (permanent) level of output or employment—this is the supply-demand response stressed by quantity theorists. We can express this in general form as:

(9) $$g_P = f[g_Y, g_P^*, g_{y'}^*, y', y'^*]$$

(10) $$g_{y'} = j[g_Y, g_P^*, g_{y'}^*, y', y'^*],$$

where an asterisk attached to a variable denotes the anticipated value of that variable and where the form of equations (9) and (10) must be consistent with the identity

(11) $$Y = Py',$$

so that only one of equations (9) and (10) is independent.

To illustrate, a specific linearized version of equations (9) and (10) might be

(12) $$g_P = g_P^* + \eta(g_Y - g_Y^*) + \xi(\log y' - \log y'^*);$$

(13) $$g_{y'} = g_{y'}^* + (1 - \eta)(g_Y - g_Y^*) - \xi(\log y' - \log y'^*).$$

---

65. Note that the equality of actual and anticipated magnitudes is a necessary but not a sufficient condition for a long-run equilibrium position. In principle, actual and anticipated magnitudes could be equal along an adjustment path between one equilibrium position and another. The corresponding proposition is more complicated for measured and permanent magnitudes and depends on the precise definition of these terms. However, since we shall be considering a special case in which the stated condition is treated as both necessary and sufficient for long-run equilibrium, these complications will be bypassed.

The sum of equations (12) and (13) is exactly the logarithm of equation (11), differentiated with respect to time, provided the anticipated variables also satisfy a corresponding identity,[66] so the equations satisfy the specified conditions.

The extreme quantity theory assumption that all the change in income is in prices, and that output is always at its permanent level, is obtained by setting $\eta = 1$ and $\xi = \infty$. An infinite value of ξ corresponds to "perfectly flexible prices" and assures that $y' = y'^*$. The unit value of η assures that prices absorb any change in nominal income, so that real income grows at its long-term rate of growth.[67]

The extreme Keynesian assumption, that all the change in income is in output, so long as there is unemployment, and all in prices, once there is full employment, is obtained by setting $g_P^* = 0$, and $\eta = \xi = 0$ for $y' < y'^*$, and then shifting to the quantity theory specification of $\eta = 1, \xi = \infty$ for $y' \geq y'^*$. The zero value of g_P^* assures that anticipations are for stable prices and, combined with the zero values of η and ξ, that $g_P = 0$. It would be somewhat more general, and perhaps more consistent with the spirit rather than the letter of Keynes's analysis, and even more that of his modern followers, to let g_P^* differ from zero while keeping $\eta = \xi = 0$ for $y' < y'^*$. This would introduce the kind of price rigidity relevant to Keynes's short-period analysis, yet it could be regarded as capturing the phenomenon that his modern followers have emphasized as cost-push inflation.[68]

Equations (12) and (13) do not by themselves specify the path of prices or output beginning with any initial position. In addition, we need to know how anticipated values are formed. Presumably anticipations are affected by the course of events so that, in response to a disturbance that produces a discrepancy between actual and anticipated values of the variables, there is a feedback effect that brings the actual and anticipated variables together again (see below). If this feedback process proceeds rapidly, then the transitory adjustments defined by equations (12) and (13) are of little significance. The relevant analysis is the analysis that connects the asterisked variables.

Chapter 9 explores empirically the adjustment mechanism both to evaluate the relative importance of anticipations and rate of capacity

66. This also explains why $g_{y'}^*$ does not appear explicitly in equation (12), or $g_{\hat{p}}^*$ in equation (13), as they do in equations (9) and (10). They are implicitly included in g_Y^*.

67. With ξ infinity, and $\log y' = \log y'^*$, the final expression in equations (12) and (13) is $\infty \cdot 0$, or technically indeterminate. The product can be taken to be zero in general, except possibly for a few isolated points at which $\log y'$ deviates from $\log y'^*$, a deviation closed instantaneously by infinite rates of change in $\log P$ and $\log y'$.

68. The simple monetary theory of nominal income developed in Gordon, *Milton Friedman's Monetary Framework*, pp. 34–48, is of course consistent with these equations in their general form since it does not specify anything about the division of a change in nominal income between prices and output.

utilization and to examine the time path of adjustment. In the process, we develop approximations to these abstract differential equations that can be estimated empirically (see especially sec. 9.10).

2.6.2 Short-Run Adjustment of Nominal Income

For monetary theory, the key question is the process of adjustment to a discrepancy between the nominal quantity of money demanded and the nominal quantity supplied. Such a discrepancy could arise from either a change in the supply of money (a shift in the supply function) or a change in the demand for money (a shift in the demand function). The key insight of the quantity-theory approach is that such a discrepancy will be manifested primarily in attempted spending, and through that route in the rate of change in nominal income. Put differently, money holders cannot determine the nominal quantity of money (though their reactions may introduce feedback effects that will affect the nominal quantity of money), but they can make velocity anything they wish.

What, on this view, will cause the rate of change in nominal income to depart from its permanent value? Anything that produces a discrepancy between the nominal quantity of money demanded and the quantity supplied, or between the two rates of change of money demanded and money supplied. In general form

$$(14) \qquad g_Y = f\,[g_Y^*, g_{M^S}, g_{M^D}, M^S, M^D],$$

where M^S refers to money supplied, M^D refers to money demanded, and the two symbols are used to indicate that the two are not necessarily equal. That is, equation (21) replaces the adjustment equation (6c), $M^D = M^S$, common to all the simple models.

To illustrate, a particular linearized version of equation (14) would be

$$(15) \qquad g_Y = g_Y^* + \Psi(g_{M^S} - g_{M^D}) + \phi(\log M^S - \log M^D).$$

Unlike equations (12) and (13), the two final adjustment terms on the right-hand side do not explicitly include any asterisked magnitudes. But implicitly they do. The amount of money demanded will depend on anticipated or permanent income and prices as well as on the anticipated rate of change in prices.[69]

---

69. The three simple models considered in Gordon, *Milton Friedman's Monetary Framework*, pp. 34–46 all require setting $\Phi = \infty$ in our equation (15) to assure that $M^S = M^D$. However, once this is done, the rest of the equation provides no information on the adjustment process, since the final term, which is then of the form $\infty \cdot 0$ is indeterminate. Hence, even though $M^S = M^D$ implies that

$$(a) \qquad g_{M^S} = g_{M^D}$$

so that the second term on the right-hand side of equation (15) is zero for any finite value of Ψ, it does not follow that

In its general form, equation (15) allows for changes in both supply of money and demand for money. It also implicitly allows for the forces emphasized by Keynes, shifts in investment or other autonomous expenditures, through the effect of such changes on M^S and M^D. For example, an autonomous rise in investment demand will tend to raise interest rates. The rise in interest rates will tend to reduce M^D, introducing a discrepancy in one or both of the bracketed expressions on the right-hand side of equation (15), which will cause g_Y to exceed g_Y^*.

Chapter 8 explores empirically, for time units spanning a phase, the adjustment of nominal income to current and prior monetary change, developing empirically manageable approximations to equation (14). See especially sec. 8.4.

2.6.3 Money Demand and Supply Functions

To complete the theory of the adjustment process, it is necessary to specify the functions connecting M^D and M^S with other variables in the system, and also to provide relations determining any additional variables—such as interest rates—entering into these functions. Sections 2.3 and 2.4 discuss the demand and supply functions for money that we regard as relevant for this purpose, so only a few brief supplementary comments are required for present purposes.

First, for reasons discussed in section 2.3, we have taken M^S itself as an autonomous variable in much of our empirical work and have not incorporated in the analysis any feedback from other adjustments.

(b) $g_Y = g_Y^*.$

The requirement (a) leads to the equation

(c) $g_Y = g_M$

for the simple quantity theory, since, with real income and the interest rate fixed, the quantity of money demanded is proportional to prices and hence to nominal income. This equation says that a change in money supply is reflected immediately and proportionately in nominal income.

For the simple Keynesian theory, equation (a) leads, from the equation for the LM curve (equation 22 in Gordon, p. 33) to

(d) $g_M = [\dfrac{\partial \log \ell}{\partial \log Y} + \dfrac{\partial \log \ell}{\partial R} \dfrac{dR}{d \log Y}] g_Y$

where $dR/d \log Y$ is to be calculated from the equation for the IS curve (equation [21] in Gordon, (p. 33). In the special case of absolute liquidity preference $\partial \log \ell/\partial R = \infty$; in the special case of completely inelastic investment and saving functions, $dR/d \log Y = \infty$. In either of these cases, equation (d) implies that g_M finite, $g_Y = 0$; that is, a change in the supply of money has no influence on nominal income. In the more general case, equation (d) says that a change in money supply is reflected immediately, but not necessarily proportionately, in nominal income.

For the monetary theory of nominal income, equation (a) implies equation (41), in Gordon, p. 42, which allows for a delayed adjustment of permanent income to measured income, but not for any discrepancy between M^S and M^D.

Second, the function specifying M^D might in principle include a transitory component. That is, the theory here sketched is entirely consistent with distinguishing between a short-run and a long-run demand for money, as some writers have done.[70]

Chapter 6 explores this and other issues empirically. We there find it possible to estimate a single demand equation fitting all our data: that is, a single demand equation for the United States and the United Kingdom for a century, confirming in a rather remarkable way the initial insight of the quantity theory approach on the stability of the demand for money.

2.6.4   Determination of Interest Rates

Given that interest rates enter into the demand function for money (equation 7) and also, possibly, into the supply function (equation 6a), a complete model must specify the factors determining them. Our long-run model determines their permanent values. So what is needed is an analysis of the adjustment process for interest rates comparable with that for prices and nominal income discussed above—provided, as seems reasonable, that measured as well as permanent values of interest rates enter into the money demand and supply functions.

The pure theory of this adjustment process is outlined in the initial section of chapter 10. The components of the adjustment include an initial liquidity and loanable funds effect, a subsequent income effect, and a still more delayed price anticipation effect. The rest of chapter 10 explores these adjustments empirically, giving special attention to the adjustment process via the anticipated rate of price change incorporated in the monetary theory of nominal income.

In some of our empirical work, particularly in chapters 6 through 9, we have treated interest rates as exogenous.

2.6.5   Determination of Anticipated Values

The transition between the short-run adjustment process and long-run equilibrium is produced by a revision of anticipated values in response to measured values in such a way that, for a stable system, a single disturbance sets up discrepancies that are in the course of time eliminated. To put this in general terms, we must have

$$(16) \qquad g_P^*(t) = f\left[g_P(T)\right]$$

$$(17) \qquad g_Y^*(t) = h\left[g_Y(T)\right]$$

70. See H. Robert Heller, "The Demand for Money: The Evidence from the Short-Run Data," *Quarterly Journal of Economics* 79 (May 1965): 291–30; Gregory C. Chow, "On the Long-Run and Short-Run Demand for Money," *Journal of Political Economy* 74 (April 1966): 111–31; H. Konig, "Demand Function, Short-Run and Long-Run Function, and the Distributed Lag," *Zeitschrift für die Gesamte Staatswissenschaft* (February 1968): 124 ff.; J. Carr and M. R. Darby, "The Role of Money Supply Shocks in the Short-Run Demand for Money," *Journal of Monetary Economics* 8 (September 1981): 183–99.

(18) $y'^*(t) = j\,[y'(T)]$

(19) $P^*(t) = k\,[P(T)],$

where t stands for a particular point in time and T for a vector of all dates before t.

A disturbance of long-term equilibrium, let us say, introduces discrepancies in the two final terms in parentheses on the right-hand side of equation (15). These discrepancies cause the rate of change in nominal income to deviate from its permanent value, which through equations (12) and (13) produce similar discrepancies between the rates of price and output change and their permanent values. These may in turn reenter equation (15), but whether they do or not, through equations (16)–(19) they produce revisions in the anticipated values that, sooner or later and perhaps after a cyclical reaction process, eliminate the discrepancies between measured and permanent values.

These anticipation equations are in one sense very general, in another, very special. They require that anticipations be determined entirely by the history of the particular variable in question, not by other history or other currently observed phenomena. They thereby deny any "autonomous" role to anticipations.

One response to this potential defect has been the theory of rational expectations that has recently received much attention.[71] This theory asserts that economic agents should be treated as if their anticipations fully incorporate both currently available information about the state of the world and a correct theory of the interrelationships among the variables. Anticipations formed in this way will on the average tend to be correct (a statement whose simplicity conceals fundamental problems of interpretation, as we point out in sec. 10.7). The theory of rational expectations has been extremely fruitful on an analytic level but as yet is in a preliminary stage as a source of empirically testable hypotheses about the formation of expectations.

In our own empirical work, we have relied primarily on expectation models of the general type described by equations (16)–(19) and on simple adaptive expectations models, in which an anticipated value is revised at a rate proportional to the discrepancy between the actual and anticipated value. However, this area is attracting much research attention, so rapid progress in the development of specific models can be expected.[72]

71. Robert J. Shiller, "Rational Expectations and the Dynamic Structure of Macroeconomic Models: A Critical Review," *Journal of Monetary Economics* 4 (January 1978): 1–44; J. J. Sijben, *Rational Expectations and Monetary Policy* (Germantown, Md.: Sijthoff and Noordhoff, 1980).

72. See Brian Kantor, "Rational Expectations and Economic Thought," *Journal of Economic Literature* 17 (December 1979): 1422–41. Studies that use a weighted average of past values to obtain expected values have been criticized in the rational expectations

One subtle problem in this kind of a structure, in which the absence of a discrepancy between actual and anticipated values defines long-period equilibrium, is to assure that the feedback relations defined by equations (16)–(19), as well as the other functions, are consistent with the expanded system of Walrasian equations that specify the long-term equilibrium values. At least some values are implicitly determined in two ways: by a feedback relation such as equations (16)–(19) and by the system of long-run equilibrium equations. The problem is to assure that at long-run equilibrium these two determinations do not conflict.

2.7   An Illustration

It may help to clarify the general nature of this theoretical approach if we apply it to a hypothetical monetary disturbance.[73]

Let us start with a situation of full equilibrium with stable prices and full employment and with output growing at, say, 3 percent per year. For simplicity, assume that the income elasticity of demand for money is unity, so that the quantity of money is also growing at the rate of 3 percent per year. Assume also that money is wholly noninterest-bearing fiat money and that its quantity can be taken as autonomous.

Assume that there is a shift at time $t = t_0$ in the rate of growth of the quantity of money from 3 percent per year to, say, 8 percent per year and that this new rate of growth is maintained indefinitely. Chart 2.1 shows the time path of the money stock before and after time t_0. The lines are not drawn strictly to scale. For emphasis, they exaggerate the difference in the slopes of the lines before and after t_0.

2.7.1   Long-Run Equilibrium

Let us first ask what the long-run equilibrium solution will be. Clearly, after full adjustment, nominal income will be rising at 8 percent per year. If, for the moment, we neglect any effect of this monetary change on real output and the rate of growth of output, prices would be rising at 5 percent per year. It might therefore seem as if the equilibrium path of nominal income would duplicate that of the quantity of money in chart 2.1 (redrawn as the solid plus dashed lines in chart 2.2). But this is not the

---

literature. Benjamin Friedman has defended distributed lags not just as an acceptable procedure but an optimal means of forecasting. See his "Optimal Expectations and the Extreme Information Assumptions of 'Rational Expectations' Macromodels," *Journal of Monetary Economics* 5 (January 1979): 23–42. Karl Brunner, Alex Cukierman, and Allan H. Meltzer also defend adaptive expectations as rational in "Stagflation, Persistent Unemployment, and the Permanence of Economic Shocks," *Journal of Monetary Economics* 6 (October 1980): 467–92.

73. For an application to quarterly data for 1952–70, see Dean Taylor, "Friedman's Dynamic Models: Empirical Tests," *Journal of Monetary Economics* 2 (November 1976): 531–38.

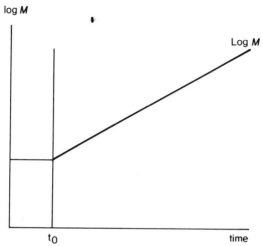

Chart 2.1   Time path of money stock before and after time t_0.

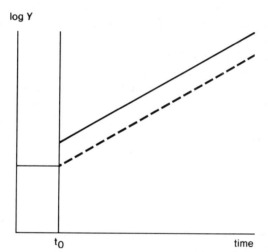

Chart 2.2   Equilibrium path of nominal income before and after time t_0.

case. With prices rising at the rate of 5 percent per year and, at equilibrium, with this price rise fully anticipated by everyone, it is now more
costly to hold money. As a result, equation (7) would indicate a decline in
the real quantity of money demanded relative to income, that is, a rise in
desired velocity. This rise would be achieved by a rise in nominal income
above that required to match the rise in the nominal quantity of money.
The equilibrium path of nominal income would be like the solid line in
chart 2.2 rather than the dashed line.

    If equilibrium real output and the rate of growth of real output were
unaffected by the monetary change, as we have so far assumed, the

equilibrium path of prices would be the same as that of nominal income, except that it would have a slope of 3 percent per year less, to allow for the growth in real income. However, equilibrium real output will not be unaffected by this monetary change. The exact effect depends on just how real output is measured, in particular whether it includes or excludes the nonpecuniary services of money. If it includes them, as in principle it should, then the level of real output will be lower after the monetary change than before. It will be lower for two reasons: first, the higher cost of holding cash balances will lead producers to substitute other resources for cash, which will lower productive efficiency; second, the flow of nonpecuniary services from money will be reduced.[74] For both reasons, the price level of output will have to rise more than nominal income—a solid line and a dashed line like those for nominal income in chart 2.2 would be farther apart vertically for prices of final products than for nominal income.

It is harder to be precise about the equilibrium rate of growth, since that depends on the particular growth model. What is clear is that the aggregate stock of nonhuman capital, including money, will be lower relative to human capital, but that the aggregate stock of physical (non-money) capital will be higher, so that the real yield on capital will be lower. The nominal interest rate(the R_B of equation 7) will equal this real yield plus the rate of change in prices, so it will be higher. If these changes have any effect on the rate of growth of real output, they will tend to reduce it, so that the equilibrium price level of final products not only will be higher relative to its initial value than the equilibrium level of nominal income, but also may rise more rapidly.[75] For simplicity, we shall neglect this possibility and assume that the equilibrium rate of rise in prices is 5 percent per year.

2.7.2   The Adjustment Process

So much for the equilibrium position. What of the adjustment process? This description of the equilibrium position already tells us one thing about the adjustment process. To produce the shift in the equilibrium path of nominal income from the dashed to the solid line, nominal income and prices must rise over some period at a faster rate than the final equilibrium rate—at a faster rate than 8 percent per year for nominal

74. See M. Friedman, *Optimum Quantity of Money*, pp. 14–15.

75. See Jerome L. Stein, "Money and Capacity Growth," *Journal of Political Economy* 74 (October 1966): 451–65; Harry G. Johnson, "The Neo-Classical One-Sector Growth Model: A Geometrical Exposition and Extension to a Monetary Economy," in *Essays in Monetary Economics* (London: Allen and Unwin, 1967); idem, "Neutrality of Money in Growth Models: A Reply," *Economica*, n.s., 34 (February 1967): 73–74; Alvin Marty, "The Optimal Rate of Growth of Money," *Journal of Political Economy*, 76, part 2 (July/August 1968): 860–73.

income and 5 percent per year for prices. There must, that is, be a cyclical reaction, an overshooting, in the rate of change in nominal income and prices, though not necessarily in their levels.

How will this adjustment process be reflected in our theoretical sketch of the adjustment process? The shift in g_{MS} at time t_0 from 3 percent to 8 percent introduces a discrepancy of positive sign into the second term on the right-hand side of equation (15), while initially leaving the third term unchanged. As a result, g_Y will increase, exceeding g_Y^*, which, viewed in this transitional process as an anticipated value rather than as a long-run equilibrium value, is unchanged from the prior long-run equilibrium value. How rapidly the rate of growth of nominal income rises depends partly on the value of Ψ, the coefficient indicating speed of adjustment, and partly on the demand function for money. If the latter depends only on anticipated values [that is, if all the variables in equation (7) have asterisks], g_{MD} will initially be unchanged, so everything will depend on Ψ, which might have any value, from zero, meaning no adjustment, to a value higher than unity, meaning that nominal income would rise initially by more than 8 percent per year.[76]

Whatever the rate of rise in nominal income, it will be divided into a rise in prices and a rise in output, in accordance with equations (12) and (13). If η is less than unity, both real output and prices will start rising, their relative rates depending on the size of η.

The rising prices and nominal income will start affecting anticipated rates of change, through equations (16)–(19), feeding back into equations (15) and (12) and (13).

All of this is so at time t_0, with no effect on the levels of any of the variables. As the process continues, however, the levels start being affected. In equation (15), log M^S comes to exceed log M^D, so the final term of equation (15) adds to the upward pressure on g_Y, making for a speeding up in the expansion of nominal income. In equations (12) and (13), log y' comes to exceed log y'^*, thus increasing the fraction of income increase absorbed by prices and reducing the fraction absorbed by output. The changed levels of y' and P feed into equations (18) and (19) and so start altering y'^* and P^*.

The changes in all of the variables now start affecting the demand functions for money, both directly, as these variables enter the demand functions, and indirectly, as they affect other variables, such as interest rates, that in turn enter the demand functions. As a result g_{MD} and log M^D in equation (15) start to change. The process will, of course, finally be completed when the relevant measured variables are all equal to their permanent counterparts and these are equal to the long-run equilibrium values discussed above.

76. The model briefly sketched in the final two paragraphs of M. Friedman, "Demand for Money," implicitly has an initial value of Ψ that is mugh higher than unity.

It is impossible to carry much further this verbal statement of the solution of an incompletely specified system of simultaneous differential equations. The precise adjustment path depends on how the missing elements of the system are specified and on the numerical values of the parameters, but perhaps this sketch suffices to give the flavor of the kind of adjustment process they generate and to indicate why the process is necessarily cyclical.

What is the reflection in these equations of the point made in the first paragraph of this subsection, namely, that g_Y and g_P must, during the transition, average higher than their final long-term equilibrium values? Consider equation (15). Suppose that over a period the *average* value of g_Y and g_P had been 8 percent per year and 5 percent per year, respectively. Suppose the anticipation functions (16)–(19) were such that this was fully reflected in anticipated values. Then, as we have seen, though M^S would have risen at the rate of 8 percent per year, M^D would not have; so the final term in equation (15) would not be zero, even though the middle term on the right-hand side might be. Hence, g_Y would exceed g_Y^*, which by assumption is at its long-run equilibrium value; so full equilibrium would not have been attained.

Chart 2.3 summarizes various possible adjustment paths of g_Y consistent with the theory sketched. The one common feature of all of them is that the area above the 8 percent line must exceed the area below. In principle, of course, still other paths are possible. For example, it is conceptually possible for the adjustment to be explosive rather than damped. Restricting ourselves to damped paths is an empirical judgment.

2.8   Conclusion

The climate of professional opinion has changed greatly since the first draft of this chapter was written. Many issues about which controversy then raged now seem outdated. Defending the quantity theory approach and adopting the kind of framework outlined in this chapter no longer seem idiosyncratic and reactionary. On the contrary, they are more nearly in the mainstream, though still not without vigorous critics. Theoretical controversy today is less about Keynes and the classics than about rational expectations and "supply-side" economics, or about the microfoundations of macroeconomics.

This change in the climate of theoretical opinion has not been produced by the persuasiveness or lack thereof of the arguments adduced by economic theorists. Just as the emergence of the Keynesian revolution was a reaction to the brute facts of depression, so the resurgence of the quantity theory (renamed undescriptively "monetarism") and the rejection of simple Keynesianism have been a reaction to the emergence of inflation and stagflation. Theoretical analysis has an essential role to play

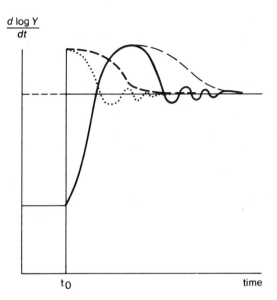

Chart 2.3   Possible adjustment paths of rate of change of nominal income.

in guiding and organizing research, in interpreting empirical evidence, in providing compact ways to summarize masses of generalizations, and in avoiding errors. But in our opinion the basic differences among economists are not theoretical, but empirical.

The controversy about the role of money in economic affairs that raged for so long and has by no means died down even yet reflects different implicit and explicit answers to empirical questions such as those considered in the later chapters of this book: Is the demand function for money stable? What variables are most important in determining the quantity of money demanded? How elastic is the response of the quantity of money demanded to interest rates (chap. 6)? What are the channels whereby changes in one country influence another, and how important are those influences (chap. 7)? When changes in the demand or supply produce discrepancies between the quantity of money the public holds and the quantity it desires to hold, how rapidly do these discrepancies tend to be eliminated? Is the impact on nominal income asymptotic or cyclical (chap. 8)? What about the separate adjustment of prices and output? Do the reactions of prices depend more on price anticipations or on the level of output relative to capacity? How are anticipations formed (chap. 9)? What about the effects on interest rates? Does the distinction between "nominal" and "real" interest rates play a key role? Or is that purely a theoretical construct of little practical importance (chap. 10)?

The reason differences about such empirical questions have been able to persevere is that adjustment to monetary disturbances takes a long time and affects many economic magnitudes (chaps. 8 and 9). If adjustment were swift, immediate, and mechanical, as some earlier quantity theorists may have believed or, more likely, as was attributed to them by their critics, the role of money would be clearly and sharply etched even in the imperfect figures that have been available. But if the adjustment is slow, delayed, and sophisticated, then crude evidence may be misleading, and a more subtle examination of the record may be needed to disentangle what is systematic from what is random and erratic. That, not the elaboration of the theory, is the primary aim of this book as well as of the other monetary studies of the NBER.

3   The General Statistical Framework

An analysis of the long-period movements that are the subject of this volume requires freeing the data so far as possible from the effects of the shorter-term movements we call business cycles. These are brief compared to the more than a century covered by our data, averaging about four years in length for the twenty-six full reference cycles (from peak to peak) in the United States, about five years for the nineteen full reference cycles in the United Kingdom. Yet, though brief, the cyclical fluctuations are often large relative to the more gradual long-period changes. Hence temporal comparisons can be seriously distorted if the initial and terminal dates refer to different stages of the business cycle, even though the dates are separated by decades.

The method generally followed in cyclical studies of the NBER is to use the average value of a series over a full specific or reference cycle as the elementary unit of observation in studying secular movements.[1] That method gives two sets of secular observations: one constructed from trough-to-trough cycles—that is, the period between successive specific or reference cycle troughs—the other, from peak-to-peak cycles—that is, the period between successive specific or reference cycle peaks.

3.1   The Reference Phase Base as the Unit of Observation

The method we use is a slight variant: instead of a full cycle as the basic unit, we use a cycle phase. There are two kinds of phases: an expansion

---

1. Arthur F. Burns and Wesley C. Mitchell, in *Measuring Business Cycles* (New York: NBER, 1946), pp. 28, 141–44, use specific-cycle bases as the elementary unit of observation in studying secular movements. Moses Abramovitz uses reference-cycle bases (for sources, see chap. 11, note 1). R. C. Bird, M. J. Desai, J. J. Enzler, and P. J. Taubman find specific-cycle bases superior to reference cycle bases for accurately determining long-cycle turning points (" 'Kuznets Cycles' in Growth Rates: The Meaning," *International Economic Review* 6 [May 1965]: 237–39).

phase running from a cycle trough to a cycle peak; and a contraction phase running from a cycle peak to a cycle trough. For regularly recurring cycles, the average over a cycle phase is clearly as free from cyclical effects as is the average over a full cycle composed of two successive phases. In practice, of course, neither is entirely free from cyclical effects: there is no way of eliminating by simple averaging the effects of an unusually large cyclical movement like the great contraction from 1929 to 1933.

We use the phase base rather than the cycle base because it gives us a larger number of observations on secular movements and greater flexibility. A two-period moving average of phase bases, weighted by the duration of the phases, gives the more usual cycle bases, trough-to-trough bases alternating with peak-to-peak bases.

As between specific and reference cycle phases, we have chosen to use the reference phases. The reason is that we want to compare different series with one another, and it is much easier to do so if the same chronology is used for all.

3.1.1 Phase Reference Dates

For the United States, we adopted the NBER's annual reference cycle chronology, which currently ends with a trough in 1975,[2] except that for our purposes we added turns in 1966 (peak) and 1967 (trough) that are not recognized in the official NBER chronology.[3]

For the United Kingdom, after reexamining the evidence, we revised some of the turning dates listed in the NBER reference chronology available through 1938.[4] We also extended the chronology through 1975 by examining a small collection of economic indicators as well as the turning points selected by others.[5]

2. A list of the dates ending with a trough in 1970 is given in United States Bureau of Economic Analysis, *Long-Term Economic Growth, 1860–1970* (Washington, D.C.: Government Printing Office, 1973), p. 64. G. H. Moore, *Business Cycles, Inflation, and Forecasting* (Cambridge, Mass.: Ballinger for NBER 1980), table A-1, pp. 438–39, gives monthly, quarterly, and calendar year dates ending with a trough in 1975.

Since this study was completed, the NBER has added a monthly reference cycle peak in January 1980 and a trough in July 1980, corresponding to an annual peak in 1979 and a trough in 1980.

3. See the discussion of the "pause" of 1966–67 in Solomon Fabricant, "The 'Recession' of 1969–1970," in *The Business Cycle Today*, ed. Victor Zarnowitz, NBER Fiftieth Anniversary Colloquium (New York: NBER, 1972), pp. 116–17.

4. Burns and Mitchell, *Measuring Business Cycles*, p. 79. The revisions through 1938 were to omit 1901 (trough) and 1903 (peak), and shift the 1917 peak to 1918.

5. Monthly turns in British business for the 1950s in C. Drakatos, "Leading Indicators for the British Economy," *National Institute Economic Review*, no. 24 (May 1963), p. 43, confirm our selection. Monthly turns in British growth cycles are given in Phillip A. Klein, "Postwar Growth Cycles in the United Kingdom: An Interim Report," *Explorations in Economic Research* 3, no. 1 (winter 1976): 110. The United Kingdom Central Statistical

Table 3.1 gives for each phase the initial and terminal years, the midpoint date, the duration of the phase in years, and the kind of phase (E for expansion, C for contraction)—in part 1 for the United States, in part 2 for the United Kingdom. Each phase is numbered consecutively to permit easy identification of subperiods that we use later. The phase numbered 1 for each country is the first phase for which data on the money stock are available (see chap. 4). For the United Kingdom a preceding phase numbered 0 is also shown, since we use data for some other series for that phase.

3.1.2 Computation of Phase Base

We follow standard NBER procedure in computing the phase base as a weighted average of all the observations during the phase, including both the initial and terminal turning points. The initial and terminal turning point observations are weighted one-half, the intervening observations, unity. (See equation 1 below.) Since each turning point observation is included in two successive phases, it would be given undue weight if weighted as heavily as the intermediate observations.

The inclusion of the same observation in two successive phases introduces serial correlation between successive phase bases that is considered further below.

Throughout, we use logarithms of money, income, and prices and construct phase bases by averaging logarithms, not absolute values. The reason is both economic and statistical: economically, relative changes are the main subject of interest; statistically, the logarithms are more nearly homoskedastic over time than the absolute values; that is, they have more nearly a random variability that is the same size over time. For interest rates, we construct phase bases by averaging the absolute values.

3.1.3 Weighting of Phase Bases in Statistical Computations

Because phases differ in length, the bases are averages of different numbers of observations. Hence, if the initial observations are statistically homogeneous in the sense that all are subject to the same error of measurement, the bases will not be. This feature alone would be allowed for by weighting each phase base by the number of observations from

---

Office has published monthly growth cycle turns for dates since 1958 in *Economic Trends*, no. 257 (March 1975), pp. 95–109; no. 271 (May 1976), pp. 70–80; no. 282 (April 1977), pp. 66–68. D. J. O'Dea, *Cyclical Indicators for the Postwar British Economy* (Cambridge: Cambridge University Press for NIESR, 1975), p. 39, also gives monthly turning points, 1951–72. Edward Shapiro, "Fluctuations in Prices and Output in the United Kingdom, 1921–71," *Economic Journal* 86 (December 1976): 746–58, gives quarterly turning points, 1921–38 and 1952–72. For the first period, the turns are for "classical" cycles, for the second period, for "growth" cycles.

Table 3.1 Phase Reference Dates for the United States and the United Kingdom

Part 1: United States

Phase Number	Phase Reference Years	Midpoint[a] Date	Duration of Phase (Years)	Kind of Phase[b]	Phase Number	Phase Reference Years	Midpoint[a] Date	Duration of Phase (Years)	Kind of Phase[b]
1	1867–69	1868.5	2	E	27	1919–20	1920.0	1	E
2	1869–70	1870.0	1	C	28	1920–21	1921.0	1	C
3	1870–73	1872.0	3	E	29	1921–23	1922.5	2	E
4	1873–78	1876.0	5	C	30	1923–24	1924.0	1	C
5	1878–82	1880.5	4	E	31	1924–26	1925.5	2	E
6	1882–85	1884.0	3	C	32	1926–27	1927.0	1	C
7	1885–87	1886.5	2	E	33	1927–29	1928.5	2	E
8	1887–88	1888.0	1	C	34	1929–32	1931.0	3	C
9	1888–90	1889.5	2	E	35	1932–37	1935.0	5	E
10	1890–91	1891.0	1	C	36	1937–38	1938.0	1	C
11	1891–92	1892.0	1	E	37	1938–44	1941.5	6	E
12	1892–94	1893.5	2	C	38	1944–46	1945.5	2	C
13	1894–95	1895.0	1	E	39	1946–48	1947.5	2	E
14	1895–96	1896.0	1	C	40	1948–49	1949.0	1	C
15	1896–99	1898.0	3	E	41	1949–53	1951.5	4	E
16	1899–1900	1900.0	1	C	42	1953–54	1954.0	1	C
17	1900–1903	1902.0	3	E	43	1954–57	1956.0	3	E
18	1903–4	1904.0	1	C	44	1957–58	1958.0	1	C
19	1904–7	1906.0	3	E	45	1958–60	1959.5	2	E
20	1907–8	1908.0	1	C	46	1960–61	1961.0	1	C
21	1908–10	1909.5	2	E	47	1961–66	1964.0	5	E
22	1910–11	1911.0	1	C	48	1966–67	1967.0	1	C
23	1911–13	1912.5	2	E	49	1967–69	1968.5	2	E

Phase Number	Phase Reference Years	Midpoint[a] Date	Duration of Phase (Years)	Kind of Phase[b]
24	1913–14	1914.0	1	C
25	1914–18	1916.5	4	E
26	1918–19	1919.0	1	C

Phase Number	Phase Reference Years	Midpoint[a] Date	Duration of Phase (Years)	Kind of Phase[b]
50	1969–70	1970.0	1	C
51	1970–73	1972.0	3	E
52	1973–75	1974.5	2	C

Part 2: United Kingdom

Phase Number	Phase Reference Years	Midpoint[a] Date	Duration of Phase (Years)	Kind of Phase[b]
0	1868–74	1871.5	6	E
1	1874–79	1877.0	5	C
2	1879–83	1881.5	4	E
3	1883–86	1885.0	3	C
4	1886–90	1888.5	4	E
5	1890–93	1892.0	3	C
6	1893–1900	1897.0	7	E
7	1900–1904	1902.5	4	C
8	1904–7	1906.0	3	E
9	1907–8	1908.0	1	C
10	1908–13	1911.0	5	E
11	1913–14	1914.0	1	C
12	1914–18	1916.5	4	E
13	1918–19	1919.0	1	C
14	1919–20	1920.0	1	E
15	1920–21	1921.0	1	C
16	1921–24	1923.0	3	E
17	1924–26	1925.5	2	C
18	1926–27	1927.0	1	E

Phase Number	Phase Reference Years	Midpoint[a] Date	Duration of Phase (Years)	Kind of Phase[b]
19	1927–28	1928.0	1	C
20	1928–29	1929.0	1	E
21	1929–32	1931.0	3	C
22	1932–37	1935.0	5	E
23	1937–38	1938.0	1	C
24	1938–44	1941.5	6	E
25	1944–46	1945.5	2	C
26	1946–51	1949.0	5	E
27	1951–52	1952.0	1	C
28	1952–55	1954.0	3	E
29	1955–58	1957.0	3	C
30	1958–60	1959.5	2	E
31	1960–62	1961.5	2	C
32	1962–65	1964.0	3	E
33	1965–66	1966.0	1	C
34	1966–68	1967.5	2	E
35	1968–71	1970.0	3	C
36	1971–73	1972.5	2	E
37	1973–75	1974.5	2	C

[a]Read .5 as 30 June; .0 as 1 January.
[b]E = expansion; C = contraction.

which it is computed. However, the differential weighting of the initial and terminal observations introduces an additional complication.

Let

n = duration of phase, where unit of time is interval between observations (i.e., n is number of years for annual data, number of quarters for quarterly data, etc.).

X_i $(i = 1, \ldots, n + 1)$ = observations entering into phase average, where X_1 is observation at initial turning point and X_{n+1}, at terminal turning point.

Y = phase average.

σ^2 = variance of variable indicated by subscript.

We then have

(1) $$Y = \frac{\frac{1}{2} X_1 + \sum_{i=2}^{n} X_i + \frac{1}{2} X_{n+1}}{n}$$

by the definition of the phase average. Assume that the X_i's can be regarded as statistically independent, and as all having the same variance equal to σ_X^2. We then have

(2) $$\sigma_Y^2 = \frac{1}{n^2} \ [\frac{1}{4} \sigma_X^2 + \sum_{i=2}^{n} \sigma_X^2 + \frac{1}{4} \sigma_X^2] \ = \frac{\sigma_X^2}{n^2} \ [n - \frac{1}{2}]$$

$$= \frac{2n-1}{2n^2} \ \sigma_X^2.$$

Since the appropriate weight is inversely proportional to the variance, we take as the weight of the phase:

(3) $$w = \frac{2n^2}{2n-1} .$$

The chief question about this derivation is the assumption of statistical independence. This assumption is less stringent than it may at first appear. Given the purpose for which we use the phase averages, namely, to average out cyclical movements, the dependence that is relevant is that which remains after we eliminate the cyclical effect. Most of the observed fairly high serial correlation in annual data, which might be taken as evidence against the assumption of independence, reflects the cyclical movement. The serial correlation between deviations from the cyclical pattern must be very much lower and, for annual data, may even be negligible. Low serial correlation will not introduce much error into the weights.

We have neglected the serial correlation because evidence on the question is lacking and because it would be different for different series, whereas it is a great convenience to use the same weights for all series.

3.1.4   Possible Difficulties with Reference Phase Bases

Three major questions arise about this procedure of using reference phase bases as the unit of observation. (1) If there are important systematic differences between the cyclical timing of a series and the reference dates, the phase bases may have a residual cyclical element. The brevity of the phases may (2) leave too much random variation and (3) introduce substantial serial correlation.

Residual Cyclical Element

The problem here is suggested by chart 3.1, which shows a regularly recurring cycle that lags in timing behind the reference cycle by one-quarter of a cycle. No problem arises for specific phase bases.

For the reference phase bases we use, however, there clearly is a problem: reference contraction bases would tend to be larger, and refer-

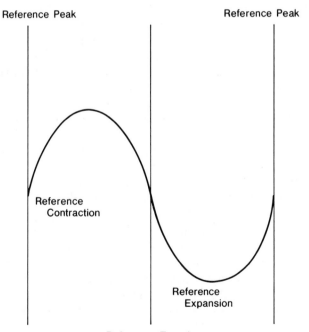

Chart 3.1   Illustration of a one-quarter specific cycle lag behind the reference cycle.

ence expansion bases smaller, than the relevant cycle-free average. Conversely, if the series leads in time, relevant contraction bases would tend to be smaller, and reference expansion bases larger, than the relevant cycle-free averages.

A lead or lag of one-quarter cycle maximizes the residual cyclical element, but clearly a lesser error of the same kind is introduced by a shorter systematic lead or lag.

One mitigating circumstance is that most of the series we use are annual and tend to be fairly synchronous with the cycle (nominal income, output, prices), so that any leads or lags are likely to be small relative to the time unit of observation.

We have made a number of tests to be sure that the residual cyclical element is negligible.

1. In the simple trend-free case pictured, each contraction base would be higher than each expansion base. In the presence of trends, this relation need not hold. To allow for trend, we have computed the average value of deviations from trend for all expansion bases and all contraction bases separately for a period chosen to begin and end with the same type of phase, which is a further protection against contamination by trend. The average values and standard deviations are shown in table 3.2. The final column gives the ratio of the mean difference to its standard error. Only one series for the United States, and only two for the United Kingdom have mean differences that are even as large as the relevant standard error, and no difference approaches statistical significance. It is interesting that the largest differences relative to their standard error are for interest rates, which are known in general to lag. As expected, the average for these series is larger for contractions than for expansions—as tends also to be true for the other series—but even for these the difference between expansion and contraction phases is clearly small enough to be neglected for any but the most refined analysis.

Note that the consistent difference in sign between the means for expansions and contractions (fifteen out of sixteen means negative for expansions and positive for contractions) is not relevant evidence of a systematic difference because the observations are not independent. All the means are calculated for precisely the same set of contractions and expansions. Given the high conformity among the series within cycles, if the expansions happen to yield negative deviations and the contractions positive deviations for one series, that is likely to be true also for others. For the same reason, the entries in the final column of table 3.2 do not provide sixteen independent bits of information, but a much smaller number.

2. A different test is to compute the rate of change between successive phases. If these are dominated by the cyclical element, they should

display a negative serial correlation—in the hypothetical case pictured, being alternatively positive and negative. Any constant percentage trend will tend to show up in the average value and not affect the serial correlation. The serial correlations obtained in this way are given in table 3.3 both for the period as a whole and for subperiods that we use in our subsequent analysis. For the United States, thirty-nine out of the fifty serial correlations are positive; for the United Kingdom, thirty-two out of forty are positive, indicating that any residual cyclical element is dwarfed by the long swings about the trends that show up in the phase bases. The negative correlations are almost all for short-term interest rates, which are highly volatile. Of these, only the postwar correlations differ significantly from zero, even at a .10 percent confidence level. So even here there is no evidence of a significant cyclical residual, only of the absence of long swings of the kind that characterize the other series.

3. On a less formal basis, we have examined the series to see whether they show many sawtooth sequences of ups and downs such as the residual cyclical element might produce. Needless to say, such sequences occasionally occur, but not frequently enough to give an impression of a significant residual cyclical, which is why we have not formalized this test.

All in all, we conclude that our phase bases do eliminate the bulk of the systematic cyclical fluctuation.

Brevity of Phases

Individual phases are often very brief. This is particularly serious for annual data. According to the annual reference dates,[6] nearly half of all phases in the United States since 1867 and more than one-quarter of all phases in the United Kingdom since 1874 have been only a year in duration (table 3.4). Phase averages for short phases do not average out much of the random movement. In addition, successive phase averages have substantial serial correlation because turning-point observations enter more than one phase.[7]

The effect of the turning-point observation is, of course, greater for annual than for monthly or quarterly data. Hence one test of the seriousness of this problem is to compare phase bases for the same series from monthly, quarterly, and annual data. For the periods for which our data permit such a comparison, the differences are always minor and mostly

---

6. The NBER has estimated separate sets of dates for data reported for different time units: for annual calendar year data, annual fiscal year data, quarterly data, and monthly data. See *Business Cycle Indicators*, ed. G. H. Moore, 1:670.

7. If the observations are annual, and the phase one year in length, there are no intervening observations; hence the phase average is based on values for only two years, and each of these values is used also in computing another phase average.

Table 3.2   **Average and Standard Deviations of Deviations from Trends: Expansion and Contraction Phases, for Period Beginning and Ending with Contraction**

	Expansion		Contraction		Difference		
Series	Mean	Standard Deviation	Mean	Standard Deviation	Mean (Contraction Minus Expansion)	Standard Error[c]	Ratio of Mean Difference to Standard Error
			United States (1873–1975)[a]				
1. Log nominal income	−.0151	.2705	.0274	.2055	.0425	.069	0.62
2. Log real income	.0096	.1044	.0016	.0733	−.0080	.026	−0.31
3. Log prices	−.0246	.2084	.0257	.2041	.0503	.059	0.85
4. Log money	−.0006	.1955	.0220	.1406	.0226	.049	0.46
5. Log velocity	−.0144	.2035	.0053	.1789	.0197	.055	0.36
Interest rates							
6. Call money	−.0012	.0193	.0027	.0172	.0039	.0052	0.75
7. Commercial paper	−.0019	.0177	.0037	.0170	.0056	.0049	1.14
8. Basic yield	−.0013	.0110	.0015	.0111	.0028	.0032	0.88
9. Bond rate	−.0013	.0127	.0017	.0124	.0030	.0036	0.83

United Kingdom (1874–1975)[b]

1. Log nominal income	−.0307	.2791	.0432	.2842	.0739	.093	0.79
2. Log real income	−.0012	.0945	−.0037	.0748	−.0025	.028	−0.09
3. Log prices	−.0295	.2580	.0469	.2654	.0764	.086	0.89
4. Log money	−.0273	.2063	.0314	.2235	.0587	.071	0.83
5. Log velocity	−.0035	.1900	.0119	.1430	.0154	.056	0.28
Interest rates							
6. Short-term rate	−.0028	.0196	.0053	.0193	.0081	.0064	1.27
7. Consol rate	−.0024	.0133	.0037	.0177	.0061	.0051	1.20

[a]Twenty-four expansions and twenty-five contractions.
[b]Eighteen expansions and nineteen contractions.
[c]Standard error is calculated as follows:

$$SE = \sqrt{\frac{\sigma_E^2}{n_E} + \frac{\sigma_C^2}{n_C}}$$

where n_E = number of expansions; n_C = number of contractions. See chapter 4 for a description of the series.

Table 3.3   Serial Correlations of Rates of Change between Successive Phase Bases: United States, 1869–1975; United Kingdom, 1874–1975

Series	Full Period	Peacetime Phases	Pre–World War I	Interwar	Post–World War II
United States					
Nominal income	.42	.44	.31	.33	.57
Real income	.19	.18	.10	.24	.20
Prices	.65	.61	.51	.15	.86
Money	.52	.52	.40	.37	.80
Velocity	.30	.44	.08	.11	.74
Population	.87	.94	.72	.90	.95
Call money rate	− .13	− .20	− .36	.02	− .70
Commercial paper rate	− .28	− .35	− .63	− .24	− .58
Basic yield	.55	.55	.47	− .37	.28
Bond rate	.48	.46	.04	− .29	.23
United Kingdom					
Nominal income	.62	.67	.48	.38	.81
Real income	.52	.08	− .45	.14	.36
Prices	.66	.69	.51	.33	.93
Money	.72	.80	.63	.33	.94
Velocity	.44	.59	− .37	.40	.86
Population	.76	.88	.67	.75	.71
Short rate	− .18	− .26	.05	− .47	− .71
Consol rate	.29	.28	.76	− .53	− .03

Note: Basic observations correlated are first differences of phase bases divided by interval between successive bases. See chapter 4 below for a description of the series. See chapter 5, note 34 for designation of wartime phases.

negligible, indicating that this effect of the overlap is not serious even for annual data.[8]

Serial Correlation

The serial correlation introduced by overlap can be readily estimated theoretically. Combining equation (10) below, which gives the covar-

8. For example, the average value of the United States money stock is as follows during the four United States reference phases, 1908–14, based on:

United States Phase Number	Annual Reference Dates: Annual Data	Quarterly Reference Dates: Quarterly Data	Monthly Reference Dates: Monthly Data
		(billions of dollars)	
21	12.52	12.40	12.42
22	13.72	13.77	13.79
23	15.02	15.15	15.20
24	16.06	16.08	16.08

The monthly and quarterly data are given in Friedman and Schwartz, *Monetary Statistics of the United States*, pp. 9–15, 65–66. For the annual data, see the appendix to chapter 4.

Table 3.4   **Distribution of Annual Reference Phases in the United States from 1867 to 1975 and in the United Kingdom from 1874 to 1975**

Duration (in Years)	United States			United Kingdom		
	Number of Expansions	Number of Contractions	Total	Number of Expansions	Number of Contractions	Total
1	3	20	23	3	7	10
2	11	3	14	3	5	8
3	6	2	8	4	5	9
4	3	0	3	3	1	4
4 +	3	1	4	5	1	6
Total	26	26	52	18	19	37
Mean duration	2.73	1.42	4.15	3.39	2.11	5.50

iance of successive phase bases, with equation (2) above, which gives the variance of a phase base, we have

$$(4) \qquad r_{12} = \frac{1}{2} \frac{1}{(2n_1 - 1)^{1/2}(2n_2 - 1)^{1/2}} \, ,$$

where r_{12} is the serial correlation between successive phase bases that would be produced by overlapping if the bases were otherwise statistically independent, n_1 is the duration of one of the two phases, and n_2 is the duration of the other. Some idea of the possible significance of this effect can be gained by tabulating the value of r for a number of special cases:

n_1	n_2	r_{12}
1	1	0.50
1	2	0.29
1	3	0.22
1	4	0.19
2	2	0.17

For the United States data, out of fifty-one successive pairs of phases, only four have $n_1 = n_2 = 1$, and another twenty have $n_1 = 1$, $n_2 = 2$ or $n_1 = 2$, $n_2 = 1$. Hence, while the problem of serial correlation as a result of overlap is clearly present, equally clearly it is not of major moment: a correlation coefficient of 0.29 means that only 9 percent of the variance of one phase is accounted for by its correlation with the prior phase.

3.2   Rates of Change Computed from Phase Bases

To examine in greater detail the movements in the various series over periods that are short relative to the whole period covered, though longer than the cycle phase, it is helpful to eliminate long-period trends. One way to do this is to compute trend lines and direct attention to the undulations about the trends (see charts 5.1 and 5.2). A different and frequently preferable technique is to compute rates of change between successive observations. This technique has the advantage that (1) it does not require choosing the period to cover or a specific mathematical form for the trend; (2) the observations for any one period do not depend on the far distant observations for other periods that affect fitted trends; and (3) the series can be extended either backward or forward without either recomputing or extrapolating trends. It has the disadvantages that it gives full play to measurement errors and it introduces negative serial correlation.[9]

For phase bases, the importance of measurement errors is reduced by the averaging of observations in constructing the phase average. However, as noted earlier, for annual data often only a few observations are averaged, and the overlap between successive phases introduces positive serial correlation. To reduce the measurement error, we calculate rates of change from groups of three successive phase bases. For each triplet, we calculate the slope of a least squares line, weighting each observation inversely to its variance (sec. 3.1.3). We treat this slope as the rate of change at the midpoint of the central phase of the three phases covered. It turns out that this procedure is arithmetically nearly the same as computing rates of change from overlapping cycle bases (see sec. 3.2.2).

Since a phase for the United States is on the average about 2 years in duration, and for the United Kingdom, about 2.8 years, our rates of change on the average refer to a time span of about 4 years for the United States from the midpoint of the initial phase to the midpoint of the third, and about 5.6 years for the United Kingdom. Of course the actual time span varies from date to date—from a minimum of 2 years for the United States for the triplet of phases centered on the expansion of 1919–20, to a maximum of 8.5 years for the triplet centered on the contraction of 1873–78; and from a minimum of 2 years for the United Kingdom for the triplet of phases centered on the expansion of 1919–20 or the contraction

9. Let $Y_1, Y_2, \ldots Y_n, \ldots$ be observations at time $t_1, t_2, \ldots t_n, \ldots.$ Rates of change between successive observations are then given by

$$\frac{Y_2 - Y_1}{t_2 - t_1}, \frac{Y_3 - Y_2}{t_3 - t_2}, \frac{Y_4 - Y_3}{t_4 - t_3}, \ldots.$$

If the random components of the Y_i are independent of one another, then the variance of the random component of the first difference will be the sum of the variance of the random components of the two observations differenced. As the first two sample observations show, Y_2 enters positively into the first, negatively into the second; hence the random components of the two will have a negative correlation, and similarly with the second and third. However, the serial correlation will be zero under these assumptions for observations separated by one or more other observations (e.g., first and third, etc.)

of 1927–28, to a maximum of 10.5 years for the triplet centered on the expansion of 1893–1900.

A slightly different procedure has been used extensively by Moses Abramovitz (see footnote 1, above) in his studies of long swings. He has generally computed rates of change between successive trough-to-trough cycles and also between successive peak-to-peak cycles, and then has interwoven the two sets of rates of change into a single series. His method makes each rate of change depend on four successive phases. After some experimentation, we concluded that our method gives greater sensitivity in tracing the movements in our series, with little if any loss in reliability.

3.2.1   Weights for Rates of Change

The statistical error associated with a rate of change computed in this way clearly depends on the length of the phases entering into its computation. To allow for this effect, we have weighted the rates of change in regression and similar calculations. The derivation of the weights follows.

Let

$$n_i = \text{duration of phase } i,$$
$$Y_i = \text{average value of phase } i,$$
$$w_i = \text{weight given by equation (3) for phase } i.$$

For rates of change computed from successive triplets of phases, i will take the values 1, 2, and 3. The time coordinates for the three phases measured from the midpoint of the first observation in phase 1 are

$$T_1 = \frac{n_1}{2} \, ,$$

$$(5) \qquad T_2 = n_1 + \frac{n_2}{2} \, ,$$

$$T_3 = n_1 + n_2 + \frac{n_3}{2} \, .$$

Using the weights from equation (3), we have the mean time as

$$(6) \qquad \bar{T} = \frac{\Sigma \, w_i T_i}{\Sigma \, w_i} \, ,$$

where the sums run throughout from $i = 1$ to $i = 3$. The slope of the regression fitted to the three phase averages, which we interpret as the rate of change at time T_2, is

$$(7) \qquad b = \frac{\Sigma \, w_i Y_i (T_i - \bar{T})}{\Sigma \, w_i (T_i - \bar{T})^2} \, .$$

The variance of this slope is given by

$$
(8) \qquad \sigma_b^2 = \frac{1}{[\Sigma\, w_i(T_i - \bar{T})^2]^2} \Big[\Sigma\, w_i^2(T_i - \bar{T})^2 \sigma_{Y_i}^2 \\
+ \sum_{i \neq j} \Sigma\, w_i w_j (T_i - \bar{T})(T_j - \bar{T}) \sigma_{Y_i Y_j} \Big] .
$$

By the definition of the weights

$$
(9) \qquad \sigma_{Y_i}^2 = \frac{\sigma_X^2}{w_i} .
$$

Under the assumption that the X's are independent, the covariance of the Ys differs from zero only because of common elements. Y_1 and Y_2 share the common element $\frac{1}{2} X_{n_1 + 1}$, Y_2 and Y_3 the common element $\frac{1}{2} X_{n_1 + n_2 + 1}$, and Y_1 and Y_3 have no common element. It follows that

$$
(10) \qquad \sigma_{Y_1 Y_2} = \frac{1}{4 n_1 n_2}\, \sigma_X^2
$$

$$
(11) \qquad \sigma_{Y_2 Y_3} = \frac{1}{4 n_2 n_3}\, \sigma_X^2
$$

$$
(12) \qquad \sigma_{Y_1 Y_3} = 0.
$$

Substituting equations (9), (10), (11), and (12) in equation (8), we have

$$
(13) \qquad \sigma_b^2 = \frac{\sigma_X^2}{\Sigma\, w_i(T_i - \bar{T})^2} \Big\{ 1 + \frac{w_2(T_2 - \bar{T})}{4 n_2 \Sigma\, w_i\, (T_i - \bar{T})^2} \\
\Big[\frac{w_1}{n_1}(T_1 - \bar{T}) + \frac{w_3}{n_3}\, (T_3 - \bar{T}]\Big\} .
$$

If $n_1 = n_3$, then $T_2 = \bar{T}$, and the term in the curly brackets is unity. For simplicity, we proceed as if this were the case, and so take as our weights for the rate of change:

$$
(14) \qquad w_b = \Sigma\, w_i(T_i - \bar{T})^2 .
$$

For any given ratio $\frac{n_3}{n_1} > 1$, the error made by setting the curly bracket equal to unity will be greatest for $n_1 = n_2 = 1$, and for these values of n_1 and n_2, it will increase with n_3; and the error for any triplet of n's is the same if n_1 and n_3 are interchanged. Accordingly, we can get some idea of the maximum possible error by calculations for a few cases, as follows:

n_1	n_2	n_3	*Error in Weight* *(percentage)*
1	1	1	0
1	1	2	2.0
1	1	3	4.8
1	1	4	7.1
1	1	5	9.0

For our United States data, there is only one triplet for which the n's are $1, 1, 3$, and no other triplet with so large a ratio of n_3 to n_1 (or n_1 to n_3). For our United Kingdom data, there is only one triplet for which the n's are $4, 1, 1$, and no other triplet with so large a ratio of n_1 to n_3 (or n_3 to n_1). Hence the maximum error made for the United States by setting the curly bracket equal to unity is 5 percent, and for the United Kingdom, 7 percent. This may well be less than the error involved in assuming the original observations independent. In any event the error is negligible compared with the variation in the weights computed from equation (14), which have a range of almost 37 to 1 (i.e., the largest weight is nearly 37 times the smallest) for the United States and more than 56 to 1 for the United Kingdom.

The special case of $n_1 = n_3$, for which the calculated weights are correct, has some other features of interest. In that special case, the mean time, $\bar{T}$, equals the middate of the second phase, the calculated slope is

$$(15) \qquad b(n_1 = n_3) = \frac{Y_3 - Y_1}{n_1 + n_2},$$

that is, the difference between the first and third phase divided by the time interval between them. The weight for the slope is given by

$$(16) \qquad w_b(n_1 = n_3) = \frac{n_1^2(n_1 + n_2)^2}{2n_1 - 1}.$$

3.2.2 Relation between Rates of Change Computed from Successive Triplets of Phase Averages and from Overlapping Cycle Bases

Let Z_1 and Z_2 be two successive overlapping cycle bases. Then, by definition,

$$(17) \qquad Z_1 = \frac{n_1 Y_1 + n_2 Y_2}{n_1 + n_2},$$

$$(18) \qquad Z_2 = \frac{n_2 Y_2 + n_3 Y_3}{n_2 + n_3},$$

where, if phase 1 is an expansion phase, Z_1 will run from trough to trough, and Z_2 from peak to peak, whereas, if phase 1 is a contraction phase, Z_1 will run from peak to peak and Z_2 from trough to trough.

The time coordinates of these two cycle bases measured from the midpoint of the first observation in phase 1 are:

(19)
$$T(Z_1) = \frac{n_1 + n_2}{2} ,$$

$$T(Z_2) = n_1 + \frac{n_2 + n_3}{2} ,$$

so the difference between the two time coordinates is

(20)
$$T(Z_2) - T(Z_1) = \frac{n_1}{2} + \frac{n_3}{2} .$$

Hence the rate of change between them is

(21)
$$\frac{Z_2 - Z_1}{T(Z_2) - T(Z_1)} = \frac{\dfrac{n_2 Y_2 + n_3 Y_3}{n_2 + n_3} - \dfrac{n_1 Y_1 + n_2 Y_2}{n_1 + n_2}}{\dfrac{n_1 + n_3}{2}} ,$$

which can be reduced to

(22)
$$2 \; \frac{-n_1(n_2 + n_3)Y_1 + n_2(n_1 - n_3)Y_2 + n_3(n_1 + n_2)Y_3}{(n_1 + n_2)(n_2 + n_3)(n_1 + n_3)} .$$

Consider now the slope of a least squares line fitted to Y_1, Y_2, and Y_3, where the phase averages are weighted by n_i instead of w_i, as given by equation (3). This would be the correct weight if successive phase averages had no items in common but were constructed as a straight average of the relevant number of observations rather than by giving half-weight to the initial and terminal observations.

The slope of such a regression would be given by

(23)
$$b' = \frac{\Sigma \, n_i Y_i (T_i - \bar{T}')}{\Sigma \, n_i (T_i - \bar{T}')^2} ,$$

where T_i are given by equation (5), and

(24)
$$\bar{T}' = \frac{\Sigma \, n_i T_i}{\Sigma \, n_i} = \frac{n_1 + n_2 + n_3}{2} ,$$

so that

$$T_1 - \bar{T}' = - \frac{n_2 + n_3}{2} ,$$

(25) $$T_2 - \bar{T}' = \frac{n_1 - n_3}{2} \, ,$$

$$T_3 - \bar{T}' = \frac{n_1 + n_2}{2} \, .$$

Substituting equations (25) in equation (23) and simplifying gives

(26) $$b' = 2 \, \frac{-n_1(n_2 + n_3)Y_1 + n_2(n_1 - n_3)Y_2 + n_3(n_1 + n_2)Y_3}{(n_1 + n_2)(n_2 + n_3)(n_1 + n_3)} \, ,$$

which is identical with equation (22).

It follows that the rates of change we compute would be identical with the rates of change computed from two overlapping cycle bases if we used n_i instead of w_i as weights.

3.2.3   Possible Difficulties with Rates of Change Computed from Phase Bases

The same difficulties that were considered for the phase bases are relevant for the rates of change. It turns out that a residual cyclical element is a less serious problem, while spurious serial correlation may be a more serious one.

Residual Cyclical Element

The rates of change can be divided into two classes: those computed from a contraction, an expansion, and a contraction (CEC rates) and those computed from an expansion, a contraction, and an expansion (ECE rates). Even if the original phases have a residual cyclical element, the rates of change should reflect this residual cyclical element in greatly diluted form. For example, if $n_1 = n_3$, then the rate of change depends only on the two end phases, both of which are the same kind and hence subject to the same bias, if any. That is not completely true when $n_1 \neq n_3$, but presumably is largely so.

However, to make sure that this conclusion is correct, we compared CEC and ECE rates for a considerable number of our series. For eighteen United States series and sixteen United Kingdom series, we classified the rates according to whether they were above ($+$) or below ($-$) the mean. The results, for all series combined, are as shown in table 3.5

The chi-square value for the United States contingency table is .004, for the United Kingdom table, .35. The United States value would be exceeded by chance over 95 percent of the time, the United Kingdom value, over 40 percent of the time.

Similar tables for smaller groups of series yielded the same result.

Table 3.5   Number of Rates of Change above or below the Mean, by Kind of Rate, for Selected Series

Kind of Rate	United States Number of Rates			United Kingdom Number of Rates		
	+	−	Total	+	−	Total
CEC	221	229	450	126	162	288
ECE	229	213	442	133	147	280
Total	450	442	892	259	309	568

In addition, we calculated t tests for the difference between the means of the CEC and ECE rates for individual series. These were uniformly not statistically significant.

Accordingly, we have concluded that our rates of change are not affected by the kind of triplet of phases from which they are computed.

Spurious Serial Correlation

The possibility of spurious serial correlation arises from two sources: (1) the serial correlation between successive phase bases arising from the turning-point observation common to them; (2) the phase bases common to different rates of change. Two consecutive rates of change are based on triplets of phases that have two phases in common; two nonconsecutive rates of change separated by one rate are based on triplets that have one phase in common. Only every third rate is based on nonoverlapping triplets, and even that is contaminated by effect 1 arising from the turning point common to the terminal phase of the first triplet and the initial phase of the second triplet.

A full examination of the size of these spurious correlations would be inordinately complex. However, we can gain an impression of their possible magnitude by considering the special case examined earlier, that in which $n_1 = n_3$. For that case, it is reasonably straightforward to derive mathematically the spurious serial correlation.

We shall consider separately three cases: (1) consecutive rates of change; (2) rates of change separated by one rate; (3) rates of change separated by two rates. More distant rates should be independent of any spurious correlation arising from common elements. We shall then (4) present some empirical evidence on the actual serial correlations in our computed rates of change.

1. *Consecutive rates of change.* Let

b_{13} = rate of change computed from phases 1, 2, and 3,
b_{24} = rate of change computed from phases 2, 3, and 4.

Assume that

(27) $$n_1 = n_3 \, ,$$

(28) $$n_2 = n_4 \, ,$$

so that from equation (15)

(29) $$b_{13} = \frac{Y_3 - Y_1}{n_1 + n_2} \, ,$$

(30) $$b_{24} = \frac{Y_4 - Y_2}{n_1 + n_2} \, .$$

We have that

(31) $$r_{b_{13}b_{24}} = \frac{Eb_{13}'b_{24}'}{\sigma_{b_{13}}\sigma_{b_{24}}} \, ,$$

where primes represent deviations of the slopes from their mean values, and E stands for expected value. The standard deviations are given by the square root of the reciprocal of w_b times σ_x or, by equation (16), by

(32) $$\sigma_{b_{13}} = \frac{\sqrt{2n_1 - 1}}{n_1(n_1 + n_2)} \, \sigma_x \, ,$$

(33) $$\sigma_{b_{24}} = \frac{\sqrt{2n_2 - 1}}{n_2(n_2 + n_3)} \, \sigma_x \, .$$

To estimate the covariance of the slope, multiply b'_{13} by b'_{24}, and take expected values. This gives

(34) $$Eb_{13}'b_{24}' = \frac{EY_3'Y_4' - EY_3'Y_2' - EY_1'Y_4' + EY_1'Y_2'}{(n_1 + n_2)(n_2 + n_3)} \, .$$

Equations (10) and (11) plus the counterpart of equation (10) for phases 3 and 4 and of equation (12) for phases 1 and 4 give the covariances. Substituting, and using equations (27) and (28), we get

(35) $$Eb_{13}'b_{24}' = \frac{\dfrac{1}{4n_1 n_2}}{(n_1 + n_2)(n_2 + n_3)} \, \sigma_x^2 .$$

Substituting equations (32), (33), and (35) into equation (31), we have

(36) $$r_{b_{13}b_{24}} = \frac{1}{4 \, \sqrt{2n_1 - 1} \, \sqrt{2n_2 - 1}} \, .$$

This correlation reaches its maximum value for $n_1 = 1$, $n_2 = 1$, or, by equations (27) and (28), for four successive phases all one year in length. For that extreme case, of which there is none in either our United States or United Kingdom record, the serial correlation is 0.25. For $n_1 = 1$ and $n_2 = 2$, or four phases lasting 1, 2, 1, 2 years respectively, the serial correlation is 0.14. There are three such quadruplets of phases in the United States record, none in the United Kingdom record. All other quadruplets involve more uneven numbers. We conclude that this source of serial correlation can readily be neglected.

2. *Nonconsecutive rates of change separated by one rate.* For our special case, for which

$$(37) \qquad (n_1 = n_3 = n_5) \, ,$$

the slopes are given by

$$(29) \qquad b_{13} = \frac{Y_3 - Y_1}{n_1 + n_2} \, ,$$

and

$$(38) \qquad b_{35} = \frac{Y_5 - Y_3}{n_1 + n_4} \, .$$

If the initial X's are all statistically independent, then so are Y_1, Y_3, and Y_5, since they contain no common elements. The slopes are not, however, statistically independent, since Y_3 enters positively into one and negatively into the other. The correlation between b_{13} and b_{35} will be precisely the same as that between successive first differences of a series of statistically independent observations, which is well known to be

$$(39)^{10} \qquad r_{b_{13}b_{35}} = -\frac{1}{2} \, .$$

10. A formal proof for this special case is readily given. We have

$$Eb'_{13}b'_{35} = \frac{E(Y'_3 - Y'_1)(Y'_5 - Y'_3)}{(n_1 + n_2)(n_1 + n_4)}$$

$$(a) \qquad = \frac{-EY'^2_3}{(n_1 + n_2)(n_1 + n_4)} = \frac{-\left(\dfrac{2n_1 - 1}{2n_1^2}\right)}{(n_1 + n_2)(n_1 + n_4)} \sigma_x^2$$

by equations (2), (12), and (37). The standard deviations are given by equation (32), and a comparable equation for b_{35}, so

$$(b) \qquad r_{b_{13}b_{35}} = \frac{-\dfrac{-(2n_1 - 1)}{2n_1^2(n_1 + n_2)(n_1 + n_4)} \sigma_x^2}{\dfrac{\sqrt{2n_1 - 1}}{n_1(n_1 + n_2)} \dfrac{\sqrt{2n_1 - 1}}{n_1(n_1 + n_4)} \sigma_x^2} = -\frac{1}{2}.$$

A serial correlation so large in absolute value clearly presents a potentially troublesome problem. While it does not bias correlation results between different series, it does introduce serial correlation of residuals and affects the validity of tests of statistical significance. How serious such a serial correlation is in practice depends on the size of the random element in the variability compared with the systematic element. The spurious negative correlation introduced into the rates of change contaminates our results less than a similar correlation would for first differences between temporally consecutive items for a number of reasons. First, it affects only alternate items. Second, the items affected are separated more widely in time—the average interval between two alternate rates of change is four years for the United States and five and a half years for the United Kingdom, which raises the importance of the systematic component relative to the random component.

3. *Nonconsecutive rates of change separated by two rates.* The relevant slopes for this case are given by

$$(29) \qquad b_{13} = \frac{Y_3 - Y_1}{n_1 + n_2} ,$$

and

$$(40) \qquad b_{46} = \frac{Y_6 - Y_4}{n_4 + n_5} .$$

The only source of serial correlation is the turning-point observation common to Y_3 and Y_4. We have that

$$(41) \qquad Eb'_{13}b'_{46} = \frac{EY'_3Y'_6 - EY'_3Y'_4 - EY'_1Y'_6 + EY'_1Y'_4}{(n_1 + n_2)(n_4 + n_5)} .$$

Of the terms in the numerator, all are zero (on the assumption that the original X's are statistically independent) except for $EY'_3Y'_4$ which, by equation (10), has the value $\dfrac{1}{4n_3n_4} \sigma_x^2$. It follows that, using the relevant counterparts of equations (31), (32), and (33) and the assumption $n_1 = n_3$,

$$r_{b_{13}b_{46}} = \frac{- \dfrac{1}{4n_3n_4(n_3 + n_2)(n_4 + n_5)} \sigma_x^2}{\dfrac{\sqrt{2n_3 - 1}}{n_3(n_3 + n_2)} \dfrac{\sqrt{2n_4 - 1}}{n_4(n_4 + n_5)} \sigma_x^2}$$

$$(42) \qquad = - \frac{1}{4 \sqrt{2n_3 - 1} \sqrt{2n_4 - 1}} .$$

Table 3.6   Serial Correlations* of Rates of Change for the United States and the United Kingdom

| | United States | | | | United Kingdom | | | |
| | Consecutive Rates 3–50[a] | Rates Separated by | | | Consecutive Rates 2–35 | Rates Separated by | | |
Series		One 3–49	Two 3–48	Three 3–47		One 2–34	Two 2–33	Three 2–32
Nominal income	.585	−.019	−.237	−.054	.668	.101	−.161	−.078
Real income	.356	−.384	−.481	−.139	.538	.034	−.200	−.185
Prices	.747	.276	−.022	−.032	.675	.140	−.180	−.220
Money	.652	.022	−.365	−.357	.735	.191	−.208	−.357
Velocity	.489	−.035	.020	.294	.632	.125	−.019	.063
Population	.915	.764	.605	.428	.830	.548	.333	.221
Short-term rate	.406	−.155	−.263	−.093	.210	−.007	.150	.057
Short-term rate	.450	−.024	−.099	.101				
Long-term rate	.744	.427	.336	.398	.744	.599	.413	.269
Long-term rate	.740	.425	.314	.332				
Number of observations	48	47	46	45	34	33	32	31

*Value of correlation coefficient that would be exceeded less than one time in 20:

.28	.28	.28	.29	.33	.33	.34	.34

[a]Initial phase numbers.

This correlation is clearly a maximum when $n_3 = n_4 = 1$, when it has the value -0.25. This correlation is opposite in sign but numerically equal to that for successive rates of change involving the same duration of the phases with the overlapping turning point. As for that case, it seems clear that this source of serial correlation is so trivial that it can readily be neglected.

4. *Some empirical evidence on serial correlation.* Table 3.6 gives serial correlations for rates of change of our main United States and United Kingdom annual series. If the spurious correlation were the only source of correlation, we would observe positive correlations for consecutive rates, all less than .25 and generally much less so; for rates separated by one, we would observe negative correlations, all around $-.5$; for rates separated by two, we would observe negative correlations, all less than .25 in absolute value and generally much less so; for rates separated by three, we would observe serial correlations of zero. Clearly, the serial correlations in table 3.6 do not correspond to this picture, either in detail or in general, except for the substantial number of insignificant correlations for rates separated by three. Any spurious correlation has apparently been eliminated by the systematic relations between the rates of change, a relation that reflects the existence of the long swings that have by now been so widely recognized, and that we analyze in chapter 11.

It is worth emphasizing that serial correlations do not introduce any bias into correlations among statistically independent series. They do affect the precise validity of tests of statistical significance, and they do affect the serial independence of residuals. On the whole, both the theoretical analysis and the empirical evidence in table 3.6 justify the conclusion that the "noise" introduced by the serial correlations is sufficiently small relative to the systematic variation we are trying to describe that it can for the most part be neglected.

4   The Basic Data

Our basic data are annual time series for (*a*) money, (*b*) income in current and constant prices, (*c*) prices, (*d*) short- and long-term interest rates, and (*e*) population. The United States money series before 1947 are our own estimates; the remaining time series are the work of other investigators, though we have occasionally revised their estimates for years for which they appeared defective. And, of course, we have supplemented the basic series with other data in analyzing particular problems. The basic series as well as a series for high-powered money are given in the appendix to this chapter (sec. 4.4), which also gives detailed references to sources. This chapter describes the series in general terms.

Since this book is about trends in money, the availability of the money series determined our starting point—1867 for the United States, 1871 for the United Kingdom. The United States income and implicit price series are available only since 1869; the time series for all the other basic data cover a longer period, so that in studying some relations not directly involving money we have been able to start earlier than 1867 for the United States and 1871 for the United Kingdom. We have taken 1975 as the terminal year for both countries.

Many historical time series decline in accuracy the further they extend into the past, but by no means all. When underlying statistics are adequate for early years, the margin of error of the final estimates may be no greater for those years than for later years. The difference in reliability between estimates for the nineteenth and twentieth centuries for a particular variable may well be less than between estimates for different variables—for example, estimates for interest rates and prices may well differ more in quality than the earlier and later segments of each series.

The rest of this chapter describes the salient features of each time series used, first for the United States, then for the United Kingdom, and finally for the United States and United Kingdom combined.

4.1   United States Data

4.1.1   Money

Our series is an annual average of the sum of currency and adjusted deposits, both demand and time, held by the public, excluding large negotiable certificates of deposit from 1961 on. Terms like "the stock of money" and "the quantity of money," without additional modifiers, refer to this total. We have explained why we chose this definition in an earlier volume, which also explains in detail how the estimates were constructed.[1] The estimates are our own from 1867 through 1946 for deposits, 1942 for currency; Federal Reserve estimates are used thereafter. The annual estimates are averages of quarterly estimates before May 1907 and of monthly estimates thereafter, all seasonally adjusted. The basic quarterly estimates are single-day figures for the end-of-month; so are the basic monthly estimates through 1946; they are monthly averages of daily figures thereafter. All annual averages are centered on 30 June.

4.1.2   Income

Income, here and throughout this study unless otherwise specified, refers to annual estimates of net national product, variant III, component method, computed by Simon Kuznets, in current and 1929 prices, 1869–1947,[2] as revised by us for 1869–1909, 1917–19, and 1942–45. For 1948 and later years we used, for income in current prices, Department of Commerce net national product estimates multiplied by the ratio of the Kuznets estimates for 1947 to the Commerce estimates for that year, in order to adjust the Commerce series to the lower level of Kuznets's net national product, current prices. For income in constant prices for 1948 and later years, we deflated the adjusted Commerce net national product estimates, 1948–75, by the Commerce price deflator implicit in net national product on a 1972 base, shifted to the base 1929, and then multiplied by the ratio of Kuznets's implicit price deflator for 1947 to the Commerce deflator for that year to adjust to the level of the Kuznets series. We refer to net national product in current prices as nominal income; in 1929 prices, as real income or output.

In *A Monetary History*, we expressed agreement with Kuznets's own reservations about the accuracy of his estimates for the initial decade he covered. Our doubts derived from the anomalous behavior of the nominal income estimates relative to the money stock estimates.[3] Since then,

---

1. M. Friedman and A. J. Schwartz, *Monetary Statistics of the United States*, chaps. 1 and 4.

2. From unpublished worksheets underlying his *Capital in the American Economy: Its Formation and Financing* (Princeton: Princeton University Press for NBER, 1961).

3. pp. 36–41.

Robert E. Gallman has produced revised estimates of some components of Kuznets's estimates of gross national product in current prices as a by-product of work undertaken principally to extend Kuznets's estimates backward to 1834–59.[4] Kuznets offers three statistical variants that differ in the size of the various flows to consumers. We adopted variant III, which ties in with Commerce commodity flow and service estimates in 1929. Gallman, however, worked only with variant I, which reflects the basic Kuznets estimates for 1869–1909.

One reason Kuznets was doubtful about the accuracy of the early estimates was that he feared that deficiencies of the 1869 Manufacturing Census made his 1869 GNP estimate too low and gave the rate of change of the series an upward bias. Gallman, however, concludes that the deficiencies of the ninth (1869) and tenth (1879) manufacturing censuses had insignificant effects on the aggregates. He made minor adjustments to the estimates of final flows of manufactured and unmanufactured commodities, which necessitated changes in estimates of services flowing to consumers (the estimates are based on benchmark ratios of consumer expenditures on services to consumer expenditures on commodities). He also revised Kuznets's estimates of manufactured producer durables and gross new construction. Gallman's gross new construction estimate differs markedly from Kuznets's figure in 1869 and less markedly in later benchmark years. He did not revise Kuznets's estimate of changes in claims against foreigners or changes in inventories, although he expressed the view that revision would be desirable. He did not comment on or revise Kuznets's estimate of capital consumption, since he confined his study to GNP.

Using Gallman's revised components and the Kuznets components Gallman left unrevised, we compiled revised net national product estimates, 1869–1909, in current and 1929 prices.[5] We have substituted these estimates for Kuznets's, though they are clearly interim revisions, subject to further improvement as the remaining unrevised components are reviewed by investigators.

For wartime periods, 1917–19 and 1942–45, we revised Kuznets's estimates because they are misleading for our purpose. He estimated the value of government services to consumers as equal to the amount of direct taxes paid, and he treated any excess of government spending over

4. Robert E. Gallman, "Gross National Product in the United States, 1834–1909," in *Output, Employment, and Productivity in the United States after 1800*, Studies in Income and Wealth, vol. 30 (Princeton: Princeton University Press for NBER, 1966), pp. 3–76. Gallman also presents estimates in 1860 prices.

5. We are grateful to Professor Gallman for making available to us his unpublished revised annual estimates, 1834–59 and 1869–1909. In addition to revised components in current prices, he also made available to us his estimates of flows of goods and services to consumers in 1929 prices. We deflated the remaining components in current prices, revised and unrevised, by the appropriate Kuznets implicit price deflators.

direct taxes plus government capital formation as measuring intermediate services already incorporated in the value of marketable output. However good or bad an approximation this may be in peacetime to the puzzling problem of how to classify government expenditures, it seems clearly inappropriate for wartime. Its effect is to omit wartime spending from the national income on the specious ground that the services rendered are included elsewhere. John W. Kendrick adjusted Kuznets's estimates from 1889 on by adding national security outlays to obtain what he calls the "national security version" of net national product.[6] We used Kendrick's "national security version" in current prices as an interpolator of Kuznets's estimates. Values of Kuznets's net national product, current prices, were interpolated along a logarithmic straight line connecting the estimates for 1916 and 1920 and also along a logarithmic straight line connecting the estimates for 1941 and 1946. To these trend values for 1917, 1918, and 1919 and for 1942, 1943, 1944, and 1945, we added the difference betweeen the logarithms of actual values of Kendrick's national security version and the corresponding trend values for Kendrick's series. The antilogs are the revised estimates in current prices. For 1916–20 these estimates were deflated by Kuznets's implicit price deflator for wartime years to get estimates in 1929 prices. For 1943–46 we deflated the estimates by a revised version of Kuznets's implicit price deflator described below in the section 4.1.3, on prices.

4.1.3   Prices

In order to have a consistent triplet of income in current prices, income in constant prices, and prices, we use the implicit price index obtained by dividing national product in current prices by national product in 1929 prices. These series are described in the preceding section.

The behavior of measured prices in the United States during World War II and also from 1971 to 1974 is distorted by the effects of price control, since price control meant that price increases took indirect and concealed forms not recorded in the indexes. The large rise in price indexes when price control was repealed in 1946 consisted largely of an unveiling of the earlier concealed increases. Hence the recorded price indexes understate the price rise during the war and overstate the price rise after the war. This defect is reflected in the national income estimates in an overestimate of the wartime rise in income in constant prices, and hence an underestimate of the wartime rise in the implicit price index. Similar defects are present in the recorded indexes for 1971 to 1974.

---

6. See his *Productivity Trends in the United States* (Princeton: Princeton University Press for NBER, 1961), 235 ff. His table A-1, col. 7, pp. 290–92, shows the national security version in 1929 dollars; we obtained figures in current dollars from Kendrick's unpublished worksheets.

To correct, at least to some extent, for this distortion, we made independent estimates of the implicit price index for the four years 1943 through 1946 and for the period from the third quarter of 1971 to the second quarter of 1974 by interpolating between prior and succeeding values primarily on the basis of movements in nominal income. We use these estimates throughout this book, though we fully recognize that they are at best a crude approximation.

We have used this procedure because other indirect techniques for correcting the distortion that we experimented with, particularly for the United States for World War II, proved notably unsuccessful.[7] Accordingly, we decided instead to interpolate price indexes for the period in question by using a related series and the method of interpolation developed in constructing our money series.[8] Nominal income is the obvious candidate for the related series, since changes in the logarithm of nominal income equal the change in the logarithm of prices plus the change in the logarithm of output, so there must be a close relation between movements in nominal income and in prices. This procedure has the defect that the measures of nominal income are also affected by price control. The concealment of transactions at above legal prices and the omission of black market transactions presumably produced underestimates of nominal income during the years of price control that varied in size from year to year. However, the error in nominal income is presumably smaller than in the reported price index. We describe separately the estimates for the wartime period and the postwar period.

World War II

The procedure involves first interpolating both the logarithm of nominal income and the logarithm of the implicit price index along a straight line between their reported values for 1942 and 1947, then computing the deviation of the logarithm of nominal income from the interpolated values for 1943 through 1946, multiplying the deviations by factors designed to convert them to estimates of the deviation of the logarithm of the price index, adding the price deviations to the interpolated values for prices, and finally taking antilogs of the sum.

To estimate the conversion factors, we used the relation between such deviations from trend for 1914-42 and 1947-65, when price control was

7. One indirect technique that initially seemed promising was to use the average denomination of currency or the average denomination of checks as a proxy for the price level. However, exploration of this technique gave disappointing results. See John J. Klein, "German Money and Prices, 1932–44," in *Studies in the Quantity Theory of Money*, ed. M. Friedman (Chicago: University of Chicago Press, 1956), pp. 142–46; "Price-Level and Money-Denomination Movements," *Journal of Political Economy* 68 (August 1960): 369–78.

8. M. Friedman, *The Interpolation of Time Series by Related Series*, Technical Paper 16 (New York: NBER, 1962).

not in effect. For overlapping five-year intervals (to correspond to the five-year interval, 1942–47), 1914–19, 1915–20, 1916–21, through 1934–39; and 1947–52, 1948–53, through 1960–65, we computed the difference between the logarithms of implicit prices and the logarithm obtained by linear interpolation between the initial and terminal year of each five-year interval. We computed a similar set of logarithmic differences for nominal income.

We thus had pairs of deviations from trend values for implicit prices and nominal income for each of the four central years of each overlapping five-year interval. We then computed two sets of regressions of the deviations of prices on the deviations of nominal income, one for the prewar years and one for the postwar years. Each set consisted of separate regressions for the first, second, third, and fourth of the four central years, for the pooled first and fourth of the four central years (since each of the deviations was only one year distant from an actual value), and for the pooled second and third of the four central years (since each of those years was two years distant from an actual value). Table 4.1 records the slopes of the regressions and adjusted R^2.

There is a considerable difference between the pre- and postwar price regressions. The postwar correlations are lower because there is much

Table 4.1   **Statistics from Regressions of United States Prices (P) on Nominal Income (Y) Expressed as Deviations from Five-Year Trends, by Groups of Ordered Years within Trend Periods: World War I and Interwar, Post–World War II, and Full Period (Standard Errors in Parentheses)**

Group Number	1914–39 Adjusted R^2	1914–39 b	1947–65 Adjusted R^2	1947–65 b	1914–65 Adjusted R^2	1914–65 b
1	.66	.4473 (.071)	.37	.2697 (.092)	.65	.4342 (.054)
2	.72	.4131 (.008)	.38	.2715 (.090)	.71	.4095 (.044)
3	.75	.3992 (.010)	.29	.2507 (.100)	.74	.3980 (.040)
4	.68	.4203 (.007)	− .02	.0820 (.092)	.67	.4133 (.050)
Pooled Groups						
1, 4	.68	.4325 (.006)	.27	.2147 (.065)	.66	.4240 (.036)
2, 3	.74	.4062 (.010)	.37	.2630 (.064)	.73	.4037 (.030)
1, 2, 3, 4	.72	.4150 (.028)	.34	.2432 (.045)	.71	.4105 (.022)

less variability. As a result, the two regression coefficients of price on nominal income and nominal income on price differ much more for the postwar period than for the prewar period. A scatter diagram of the price deviations on the nominal income deviations for the two middle years of the overlapping five year intervals shows that the postwar points are concentrated around the origin and are not out of line with the points for the earlier period (see chart 4.1). Because the postwar points are limited in variability, they give little information on the slope. If the prewar and postwar periods are pooled, the slopes are not much changed from the prewar figures (table 4.1). Moreover, the deviations for 1943–46 that are to be interpolated are all outside the range of the post-1947 observations.

We therefore concluded that the slopes for the prewar period are more relevant to the years to be interpolated than the slopes for the postwar period, and that pooling the data for both periods would not change the estimates much but would make them less reliable. As anticipated, the slopes for groups 1 and 4 do not differ significantly, and neither do the slopes for groups 2 and 3, whereas the slope for the pooled group 1 and 4 is on the borderline of differing significantly from the slope for the pooled group 2 and 3. Accordingly, we used the pooled slopes for these two groups from the period 1914–39 as our conversion factors. Table 4.2 shows the final estimates and how they were computed and compares them with the reported price figures. The adjustment clearly makes an appreciable difference.

Because of our reservations about the adjusted price series as well as the different economic circumstances during World Wars I and II, we frequently present separate results excluding the wartime and immediately postwar years.

United States 1971–74

One further episode of price control in the United States occurred during the nine quarters from 1971:3 through 1973:3. To correct for the resulting understatement of price movements, we initially corrected the quarterly Commerce net national product implicit deflator on a 1972 base that is the counterpart of the annual series underlying our post-1947 data. We started with 1971:2, the quarter before price controls were introduced, and ended with 1974:3, to allow for the unwinding of the effects of controls, Since 1974:1, 1974:2, and 1974:3 were also affected by the OPEC price rise, we decided provisionally to eliminate that influence on the price level so that only price decontrol effects would be present. On the assumption that the OPEC price hike was equivalent to a 1.5 percent decrease in real GNP—this being the amount of the extra cost of imported oil—and that the effect was produced evenly during the first three quarters of 1974, we adjusted the reported price indexes for 1974:1 by dividing by 1.005, for 1974:2 by dividing by 1.010, and for 1974:3 by dividing by 1.015.

We then applied our usual method of interpolation, first obtaining the deviations of the logs of reported nominal net national product from the straight-line values interpolated between the 1971:2 and 1974:3 logs of nominal net national product, and multiplying the deviations by .41, the conversion factor shown in table 4.2, column 4, for central years. We then added the deviations so adjusted to the straight-line trend values interpolated between the 1971:2 log of the price index and the 1974:3 adjusted log. After obtaining the antilogs, we multiplied the result for 1974:1 by 1.005, for 1974:2, by 1.010, and for 1974:3, by 1.015, to restore the effect of the OPEC price rise. To obtain quarterly corrected real income estimates, we subtracted the logs of the corrected price indexes from the logs of reported nominal net national product. Table 4.3 shows the reported and corrected price and real income figures.

We corrected our annual estimates of the price deflator and real income by multiplying the reported figures by the respective annual averages of the quarterly ratios of the corrected to the reported data. Table 4.4 shows the original and the corrected annual estimates.[9]

4.1.4   Interest Rates

Our interest rate series include two short-term rates (the commercial paper rate and the call money rate) and two long-term yields on corporate bonds (the basic yield on high-grade corporate bonds and the yield on high-grade industrial bonds).

---

9. Different investigators of this episode of United States price controls disagree on its impact on the rate on inflation. Using different estimating techniques and different price indexes to evaluate the effects of controls, Barro, McGuire, and Feige and Pearce present findings that the inflation rate was no different than it would have been in the absence of controls; Darby and R. J. Gordon present contrary findings. See *The Economics of Price and Wage Controls*, Carnegie-Rochester Conference Series on Public Policy, vol. 2 (Amsterdam: North-Holland, 1976), for the papers by Darby, Feige and Pearce, and McGuire; also, R. J. Gordon, "Alternative Responses of Policy to External Supply Shocks," *Brookings Papers on Economic Activity* 6, no. 1 (1975): 183–204, and R. J. Barro, "Unanticipated Money, Output, and the Price Level in the United States," *Journal of Political Economy* 86 (August 1978): 549–80.

To test our corrections, we compared reported and corrected real income changes with reported employment changes, 1971–74. The correlations between quarter-to-quarter changes in payroll employment and in real NNP, as reported and as corrected by the ratio of our corrected to the original price index, are as follows for 1971:2 to 1974:3:

Reported NNP	.77
Corrected NNP	.81

The minor improvement in the correlation coefficient is weak evidence in favor of our correction.

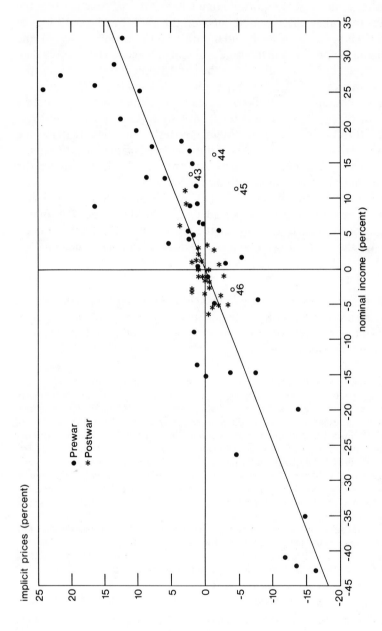

Chart 4.1 Deviations from trend of overlapping five-year periods of United States implicit prices and nominal income: scatter diagram of deviations of two central years of each period before and after World War II.

Table 4.2   Estimated United States Price Index, 1943–46

Five-Year Interval	Logarithm of Nominal Income Col. 1 (1)	Straight-Line Trend Values, Col. 1 (2)	Col. 1 Minus Col. 2 (3)	Con-version Factor (4)	Col. 3 Times Col. 4 (5)	Logarithm of Implicit Prices (6)	Straight-Line Trend Values, Col. 6 (7)	Col. 7 Plus Col. 5 (8)	Estimated Price Index (Antilog Col. 8) (9)	Kuznets Reported Price Index (10)
					(Natural Logarithms)					
1942	25.58546					−.01308				98.7
1. 1943	25.78274	25.64659	.13615	.4325	.05888		.05192	.11080	111.7	107.6
2. 1944	25.86789	25.70773	.16016	.4062	.06506		.11693	.18199	120.0	110.8
3. 1945	25.87662	25.76886	.10776	.4062	.04377		.18193	.22570	125.3	114.1
4. 1946	25.80163	25.82999	−.02836	.4325	−.01227		.24693	.23466	126.4	122.2
1947	25.89115					.31189				136.6

Table 4.3   Correction for United States Price Controls,
             Third Quarter, 1971, through Second Quarter, 1974

Year and Quarter		NNP Deflator (1972 = 100)		Real Income (Billions of 1972 $)	
		Reported	Corrected	Reported	Corrected
1971	1	94.3		994.9	
	2	95.6		1002.4	
	3	96.4	96.7	1009.1	1006.2
	4	97.2	97.9	1017.4	1010.8
1972	1	98.8	99.8	1037.7	1027.1
	2	99.4	101.3	1055.9	1036.1
	3	100.3	102.9	1073.2	1045.7
	4	101.4	104.8	1096.2	1060.1
1973	1	102.9	107.0	1120.9	1078.1
	2	104.7	108.3	1119.7	1082.8
	3	106.6	109.8	1124.4	1091.2
	4	109.1	111.6	1128.2	1102.5
1974	1	111.3	112.6	1114.9	1095.8
	2	114.2	114.1	1108.1	1098.6
	3	117.3		1099.3	
	4	120.8		1080.9	

Table 4.4   United States Price and Real Income Annual Estimates: As
             Reported and Corrected for Price Controls, 1971–74

Year	Implicit Price Deflator (1929 = 100)		Real Net National Product (Billions of 1929 $)	
	Reported (1)	Corrected (2)	Reported (3)	Corrected (4)
1971	262.5	263.2	305.248	304.546
1972	273.7	279.8	323.440	316.389
1973	289.7	298.9	340.885	330.352
1974	318.4	321.7	332.751	330.621

Each short-term rate by itself presents problems. Commercial paper refers to promissory notes issued by firms and offered on the open market. It is similar to the bill of exchange in the United Kingdom as a form of short-term business debt. However, commercial paper has changed in composition since the nineteenth century. Formerly, it consisted of trade notes received by manufacturers, wholesalers, or jobbers in payment for shipments to other firms. Denominations were in odd amounts related to the value of particular shipments. Dealers who bought the notes in turn sold them to banks. In recent decades, commercial paper has been issued in round denominations, unrelated to shipments of goods, usually by a finance company. As a result, the level of commercial paper rates before World War I is not continuous with the level since. The pre–World War I rates were raised by both high transactions costs and more than nominal default risk premiums. By contrast, neither affected the call money rate, our alternative short-term interest rate. Since World War I, both transactions costs and risk premiums have dwindled. In addition, the eligibility of commercial paper for rediscount at Federal Reserve banks under the Federal Reserve Act of 1913 presumably also lowered commercial paper rates relative to other short-term rates. The series we use is an annual average of monthly rates on sixty- to ninety-day commercial paper through 1923, thereafter four- to six-month commercial paper in New York City, based on weekly figures of dealers' offering rates until 1944 and on daily figures thereafter.

Our alternative short-term rate is for call loans at the New York Stock Exchange with securities as collateral. Call loans are made for an indefinite period but are subject to call on twenty-four hours' notice, the rate of interest varying from day to day. In the 1930s, placing call loans on account of "others" by the New York money market banks was prohibited, and the banks terminated the practice of borrowing at call to relend in the stock market because payment of interest on demand deposits was prohibited. These developments drastically changed the character of the call loan market. The call money rate, which used to be posted daily at the Stock Exchange Money Desk, has since been posted by the money market banks. It is the rate on stock exchange collateral for loans to brokers, who in turn lend to customers, usually at higher rates. Such loans are rarely called by the banks, though before the mid-1930s banks called loans to adjust reserve positions, and "others" called loans to obtain cash. The call money rate in recent decades has been relatively sticky, remaining unchanged in months when other short-term rates have fluctuated. Until 1923, the monthly averages underlying the annual averages were based on weekly renewal rates (rather than rates on new loans, which were discontinued in 1957); thereafter they depended on daily renewal rates.

The basic yield on high-grade corporate bonds to thirty years' maturity, one of our long-term interest rates series, was initially constructed as an annual series by David Durand for the period 1900–1947 and has been continued by other hands. It estimates the yield prevailing in the first quarter of each year on the highest grade corporate issues, classified by term to maturity. For each year, the yields to maturity of outstanding bonds—including practically every high-grade, seasoned, nonconvertible corporate bond not subject to special influences for which quotations were available during the period covered—were plotted by term to maturity on a scatter diagram. The basic yield curve for each year is a free-hand curve so fitted that it passes below most of the yields on the chart except for a few isolated low ones. Basic yields for each maturity are read from the curve. In the absence of fifty- or sixty-year corporate bonds in recent years, the thirty-year term to maturity is the longest maturity for which reliable basic yield estimates are available as a continuous series. We extended the series into the nineteenth century by linking it with an annual average of monthly yields on American railroad bonds constructed by F. R. Macaulay for the period beginning 1857.[10] During those years of the nineteenth century, the railroad industry had a higher credit rating than any other industry. The Macaulay series is available before and after adjustment to eliminate economic drift arising from secular changes in the quality of bonds included. We used the series adjusted for economic drift and raised its level to that of the basic yield segment by adding the average difference between the basic yield and the railroad yield for the overlapping years 1900–1902. The Macaulay series is based on yields for thirteen bonds in 1857, rising to thirty-seven in 1900, all with maturities of ten years or more. Yields for individual bonds were based on arithmetic averages of monthly high and low sale prices; the series is a chain index number based on the individual bond yields.

The other alternative long-term series we use is the yield on high-grade industrial bonds. We included it to check whether the first-quarter or February date of the annual basic yield series introduced a significant error, since all other annual series are dated at midyear. For the period from 1900 on, we use Standard and Poor's yield on high-grade industrial bonds, which before 1929 was an arithmetic average of the yield to maturity of fifteen bonds, based on the mean of monthly high-low prices. Beginning 1929, the series is an average of the four or five weekly figures for the month, the number of bonds and the average maturity varying slightly because of changes in rating or approaching maturity. In recent years only seven bonds with an average term to maturity of twenty-six years have been included. For the years before 1900, we used the same series based on railroad bonds that we used to extend the basic yield series, once again linking the two segments by adding to the earlier series the average excess of the later for the overlapping years 1900–1902.

10. Table 6.17 below gives estimates of yields on thirty-year-term-to-maturity railroad bonds from 1873 to 1899 that we constructed from Macaulay's tables of individual railroad bond yields (see pp. 294–95 for details of the construction of the estimates). At the time we assembled our basic United States data set, we did not anticipate making such estimates. Accordingly, our basic yield series was extended for years before 1900 in the way described in the text. As might be expected, the movements of the two series are essentially identical, but the estimates in table 6.17 tend to be higher than those in table 4.8 by an amount that tends to increase, the earlier the date to which the estimates relate. The largest difference is for 1875, for which the series in table 4.8 is 5.57, in table 6.17, 6.26. Fortunately, most of the differences are much smaller, so we have not regarded it as worth recomputing our results to use the more recent and, we believe, slightly preferable series for the early years.

4.1.5 Population

The population series is the total population residing in the United States except for 1917–19 and since 1940, when it also includes the Armed Forces overseas.

4.2 United Kingdom Data

4.2.1 Money

The United Kingdom money series is compiled from figures for gross deposits at London and country joint stock and private banks (later, London clearing banks and other domestic deposit banks and, since 1968, the National Giro) and at Scottish and Irish banks, less interbank and transit items, plus private deposits at the Bank of England and currency held by the public. We shifted gross deposits for 31 December to 30 June dates by a two-year moving average; the other components are 30 June estimates.

A published series of the United Kingdom money stock is available for 1880–1966.[11] The estimates we use revise the deposit component of this series for 1880–96 and the currency component for 1880–1910. In addition, we have extended the revised series back to 1871 on the basis of unpublished gross deposit estimates for 1870–80 in an unpublished paper.[12] For 1897–1966, we use Sheppard's underlying deposit components, and for 1911–60 we use his currency component. For 1967–68, Sheppard kindly furnished us with unpublished figures extending the money stock estimates in his book. We used them after substituting for those years and years back to 1960 revised official estimates of currency held by the public. The money estimates we use for 1969–75 were derived from Bank of England figures and linked to Sheppard's 1968 estimates.

We discuss the deposit estimates before 1891, the currency estimates before 1910, and the Bank of England figures for 1969–75 that we linked to Sheppard's 1968 estimate.

Deposits

Before 1891, reports of condition are not available for all joint stock and private banks in operation in England and Wales. Sheppard's figures beginning in 1880 make an inadequate allowance for the incomplete coverage of his statistics. His series is the sum of data from the balance sheets of banks published in the banking supplements of the *Economist*. Since private banks did not publish their balance sheets for 1880–90,

11. David K. Sheppard, *The Growth and Role of U.K. Financial Institutions, 1880–1962* (London: Methuen, 1971).
12. Shizuya Nishimura, "The Growth of the Stock of Money in the U.K., 1870–1913," unpublished paper, Hosei University, Tokyo, 1973.

Sheppard multiplied total deposits at joint stock banks (the coverage of which was not 100 percent), by a splicing factor ($= 1.135$) to obtain total deposits at all banks. The splicing factor was derived from the ratio of deposits at reporting joint stock and private banks in 1891, when the *Economist* first published private bank balance sheets, to reported joint stock deposits. Sheppard's deposit estimates for 1880–90 are clearly an underestimate, both because of undercoverage of joint stock banks and because he used too low a multiplier to adjust for private banks.

For 1870–80, Nishimura constructed a new deposit series from more comprehensive data in parliamentary sources, *Bankers Magazine*, and the *Banking Almanac*. He estimated separately deposits at London and country private banks by multiplying the number of offices of each class by the average deposits per branch of London and country joint stock banks, respectively. For joint stock banks, less estimation was required. All London-based joint stock banks reported a total of deposits plus acceptances. For eight of the nine London-based joint stock banks, data on acceptances were available; for the ninth, he obtained an estimate based on the ratio of acceptances to deposits plus acceptances in 1879–80. For country joint stock banks, he applied a multiplier representing the ratio of deposits and acceptances at all banks to reported deposits and acceptances and subtracted data on acceptances he obtained from the *Economist* banking supplements.

Sheppard regards Nishimura's procedure as questionable, since in his judgment many of the private bank offices were merely shops to settle debts between farmers, operated, for example, in pubs, and were not engaged in deposit business at the start of the period covered by Nishimura. He believes that only by 1891 were the private bank offices doing the same type of business as the head office.

To link the Nishimura gross deposit estimates to Sheppard's while taking account of the latter's criticisms of the estimates for 1870–80, we proceeded as follows. Assuming that Sheppard's series for 1891 eliminated underestimation of private bank deposits, we fitted a straight-line trend to the logarithms of the ratio of private to joint stock bank deposits for 1891–1914 and extrapolated the trend back to 1870. Similarly, using Nishimura's estimates, we fitted a straight-line trend to the logarithms of ratios of private to joint stock bank deposits for 1870–80 and obtained the deviation of each year's ratio from the corresponding trend value. For 1870–80, we added the deviation to the trend values obtained from the 1891–1914 regression and multiplied Nishimura's estimates of joint stock bank deposits for each year by the antilog. For 1881–90, we multiplied adjusted joint stock deposits (to be described below) by the antilog of the trend values obtained from the 1891–1914 regression. In this way we derived a new set of declining private bank deposits that keyed into Sheppard's figure in 1891.

In 1880, Nishimura's estimated joint stock bank deposits was 1.09 times Sheppard's estimate. We raised the level of Sheppard's estimate by this ratio in 1880 and by successively smaller ratios, declining arithmetically until 1896, when we set the ratio at 1.00. These are the adjusted joint stock bank deposits referred to in the preceding paragraph.

The sums of private and joint stock bank deposit estimates were shifted from year-end to midyear dates. The average of 31 December 1870 and 31 December 1871, dated 30 June 1871, is our initial estimate. We deducted an estimate of annual average interbank deposits obtained by multiplying our estimates of gross deposits for 1871–90 by the ratio of interbank to gross deposits in 1890–91. We then added an estimate of private deposits at the Bank of England obtained by allocating an aggregate of the deposits of private holders and branch offices of banks between private and other deposits in the same way that Sheppard had done for later years. The net result of these operations is total deposits adjusted for cash items.

Currency

The currency series is a residual after subtracting currency held by banks from total currency outstanding. Total currency outstanding is a sum of coin and notes outstanding. Notes outstanding of the Bank of England, Scottish, Irish, and other banks are reported figures, in compliance with the requirements of the Banking Acts of 1833 and 1844–45. Coin outstanding, consisting mainly of gold, but including also lesser amounts of silver and negligible amounts of bronze coin, was estimated before 1914. The gold coin estimates depend crucially on the validity of selected benchmark estimates. Sheppard used such estimates from published sources and from private communications from the Mint. Some of the estimates he used impart erratic movements into the estimates of gold outstanding, 1883–1905.

To construct the gold coin series for the decade for which Nishimura provides deposit estimates, we use an 1868 benchmark figure attributable to Jevons.[13] The first benchmark date thereafter that we regard as usable is the figure for 1888 that Sheppard obtained privately from the Mint. Later benchmark estimates for 1892, 1895, 1899, 1903, and the final one in 1910 seem unexceptionable.

Sheppard interpolated yearly estimates between the benchmark figures by constructing a total net change series, summing the net gold coin issued by the Mint and net imports of gold coin, adding or subtracting the net change series from the benchmark figure, starting anew with each benchmark year. The initial benchmark plus yearly cumulated net change yielded an estimate higher than the next benchmark figure.

---

13. *Investigations in Currency and Finance*, p. 269.

Sheppard then reduced the interbenchmark estimates by the ratio of the terminal original benchmark figure to the cumulated net change benchmark estimate. Nishimura experimented with a linear regression of gold coin on silver coin, 1905–13, and estimated gold coin for 1895–1904 from the regression coefficients.

We use an alternative interpolator. We converted annual estimates, 1868–1910, of the world monetary gold stock in ounces into dollars, and subtracted estimates given in the same source of the United States gold stock in millions of dollars.[14] We interpolated the ratio of the United Kingdom benchmark figures converted to dollars to the gold stock outside the United States along a straight line between the benchmark ratios. We multiplied the interpolated ratios by the stock outside the United States and converted dollars to pounds sterling. The new gold estimates were added to the remaining components of currency outstanding.

Currency held by banks was estimated by Sheppard, 1880–1920, and is a reported series thereafter. Our estimates for 1871–79 were constructed on the assumption that the 1880–85 average ratio of coins and notes held by the banks to bankers' balances at the Bank of England, which was approximately equal to one, was the same in the preceding decade.[15]

Bank of England Estimates, 1969–75

From 1963 to September 1971, the Bank of England published estimates of a number of monetary aggregates, including M_2, which corresponds to the concept we use for 1968 and earlier dates. It then discontinued the M_2 estimates but has continued to publish estimates of M_1 and M_3. For 1969 and later years, we used a two-year moving average of the Bank of England 31 December M_3 estimates, adjusted to the lower level of the M_2 estimates, by multiplying the later estimates by the ratio of our 1968 estimate to the centered Bank of England M_3 estimate for that year.

4.2.2   Income

The United Kingdom income series in current prices, 1868–1949, is C. H. Feinstein's GNP at factor incomes minus capital consumption.[16] These estimates key precisely into the official estimates of net national product, 1950–75 (described as "national income" in the Blue Books) since they are constructed in the same way.

Feinstein does not provide a table in constant prices matching the factor incomes table in current prices. Instead, he gives estimates of GNP from the expenditure side in current prices and of GNP and NNP in

14. G. F. Warren and F. A. Pearson, *Prices* (New York: Wiley, 1933), pp. 85–86.

15. See M. D. Bordo, "The U.K. Money Supply 1870–1914," *Research in Economic History* 6 (1981): 107–25, who used this procedure.

16. C. H. Feinstein, *National Income, Expenditure, and Output of the United Kingdom, 1855–1965* (Cambridge: Cambridge University Press, 1972).

constant prices, for 1870–1913, at 1900 prices; for 1913–48, at 1938 prices, and 1948 and later years, at 1958 prices.[17] We first derived NNP in current prices by deducting current price capital consumption from the GNP series in current prices. We then divided current price NNP by constant price NNP, both expenditure-based, and shifted the price deflators implicit in the NNP estimates to the base 1929. Finally, we divided net national product in current prices from the income side by the 1929-based price deflator.

Since we had a current price series from the income side back to 1868 but no constant price series in Feinstein's work for 1868–69, we derived an implicit price deflator for those years to apply to the current price series. The deflator was derived as follows. As shown in the source notes to table 4.9, column 4, GNP, calculated from the expenditure side, is available for the two years in question in both current and 1900 prices. To get net national product estimates, we subtracted Feinstein's current price capital consumption from the GNP figures. An estimate of net total fixed capital formation in current and 1900 prices is also available in another source. We used the deflator implicit in net total fixed capital formation to deflate capital consumption in current prices. Capital consumption in 1900 prices was then substracted from GNP in 1900 prices to get NNP in 1900 prices. The procedure thereafter is the same as described in the last two sentences of the preceding paragraph.

The Blue Books give constant net national product in 1970 prices for 1950–75. For these years also we shifted the implicit price deflator to a 1929 base and deflated nominal income by the 1929-based implicit price deflator.

4.2.3 Prices

Price controls were in effect in the United Kingdom not only during World War II but also during World War I.[18] In World War I, controls were imposed mainly on food, 1917–18, and were rapidly dismantled in the following three years. The price rise 1914–16, before controls, was 25

17. For this reason, we initially adopted the expenditure-based series for our data set. Subsequent work with that series in constant prices, particularly in real per capita income form, convinced us that the series was defective. The pre–World War I trend was so much higher than the trend of post–World War I years that the gap was never closed in all the subsequent period. We therefore discarded the expenditure-based series and adopted the income-based current price series, deflating it by the price index implicit in the expenditure-based series. The trend problem that persuaded us that the expenditure-based real series is defective does not affect the income-based real series.

18. On World War I controls, see Sidney Pollard, *The Development of the British Economy, 1914–1950* (London: E. Arnold, 1962), pp. 48–53; A. C. Pigou, "Government Controls in War and Peace," *Economic Journal* 28 (December 1918): 363–73; R. H. Tawney, "The Abolition of Economic Controls, 1918–21," *Economic History Review* 13, nos. 1–2 (1943): 1–30.

percent; 1916–18, during controls, 45 percent. In addition, as chart 5.5, panel 3, for the United Kingdom demonstrates, the rate of change of money stock per unit of output and the rate of reported prices show nearly identical movements during World War I. Accordingly, we made no attempt to correct for possible understatement of true price behavior during 1917–18.

Price controls during World War II, though not comprehensive, were much more extensive than during World War I. They remained in effect for some items until 1953 or so, though most items were decontrolled in 1949–50.[19] We initially considered correcting the price deflator for the years 1940 through 1952 (a fourteen-year trend period from 1939 to 1953). However, a scatter diagram we prepared for the United Kingdom covering deviations from fourteen-year trends for nonoverlapping years, including 1940–52, comparable to chart 4.1 for the United States, showed that the observations after 1946 were closer to the main cluster of points for the full period than the observations for 1940–46, which were outliers. We therefore corrected the price index for price control only for the seven years 1940 through 1946 (an eight-year trend period from 1939 to 1947).

Table 4.5 presents statistics from regressions of United Kingdom prices on nominal income, both prices and income expressed as deviations from eight-year trends, and the deviations classified by their order within the eight-year trend periods. Separate regressions were calculated for pre–World War I, interwar, post–World War II ending 1971, and the combined periods. Chart 4.2 is a scatter diagram of overlapping observations. Table 4.6 gives the estimated United Kingdom price index, 1940–46, based on the full period conversion factors.[20]

19. J. C. R. Dow, *The Management of the British Economy, 1945–60* (Cambridge: University Press, 1964), pp. 162–77.

20. In our final revision and checking of this manuscript, we discovered that an error in a figure used in the calculations had affected slightly these results. The effect is too small to justify the expense of the extensive recomputations that would have been required to incorporate the necessary revision in all our later work. However, for those who may want to use these data for other purposes, we note here the revised estimates that would supersede those in table 4.6 and in table 4.9:

1940	114.7	1944	145.7
1941	127.4	1945	146.2
1942	134.8	1946	150.0
1943	142.0		

One further qualification to our estimates: We made the estimates in table 4.6 before we decided to correct also the figures from 1966 to 1974 for statutory price controls. Hence we use the original uncorrected figures in the regressions in table 4.5. The omission of these years, or the substitution of the corrected figures, would almost certainly have a negligible quantitative effect on the final estimates.

Table 4.5 Statistics from Regressions of United Kingdom Prices (P) on Nominal Income (Y) Expressed as Deviations from Eight-Year Trends, by Groups of Ordered Years within Trend Periods: Pre–World War I, Interwar, Post–World War II, and Full Period (Standard Errors in Parentheses)

Pooled Groups	1870–1914 Adjusted R^2	1870–1914 b	1921–38 Adjusted R^2	1921–38 b	1947–71 Adjusted R^2	1947–71 b	1870–1971 Adjusted R^2	1870–1971 b
1, 7	.47	.4291 (.053)	.38	.4223 (.1188)	.43	.7887 (.1537)	.45	.4609 (.0454)
2, 6	.59	.5391 (.0523)	.32	.3386 (.1076)	.40	.7919 (.166)	.47	.4727 (.0440)
3, 4, 5	.74	.5863 (.0329)	.32	.2688 (.0703)	.27	.6728 (.1508)	.54	.4580 (.0303)
1–7	.66	.5508 (.0245)	.34	.3089 (.0507)	.36	.7409 (.0902)	.51	.4625 (.0215)

implicit prices (percent)

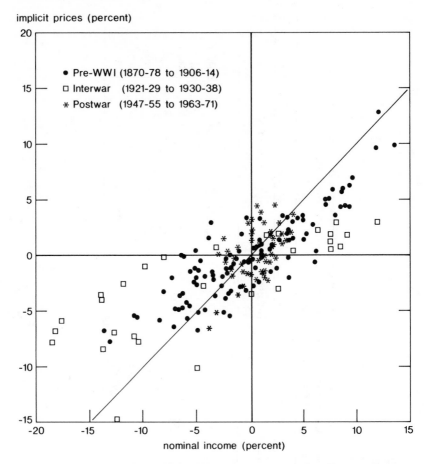

Chart 4.2   Deviations from trend of overlapping eight-year periods of United Kingdom implicit prices and nominal income: scatter diagram of deviations of three central years of the pre–World War I, interwar, and post-World War II periods.

The estimated index exceeded the reported index during the central years of price control by between 8 and 10 percent in the United States, by between 2 and 8 percent in the United Kingdom. One possible explanation is that the price controls were under less pressure in the United Kingdom than in the United States because the quantity of money rose decidedly less relative to output (see chart 5.6). A second is that controls were evaded less in the United Kingdom than in the United States. A third is that the United Kingdom nominal income estimates were biased by price control more than the United States estimates. We have not been able to assess the validity or relative importance of these

Table 4.6   Reported United Kingdom Price Index, 1940–46, and Index
                   Corrected for Effect of Price Control

Year	Price Index (1929 = 100)	
	Reported	Corrected
1939	99.9	—
1940	109.0	114.4
1941	118.4	125.8
1942	126.6	133.4
1943	131.4	140.5
1944	139.0	144.6
1945	143.3	145.7
1946	145.6	149.9
1947	158.5	—

possibilities, though the first must have played some role, and the second conforms to the casual impression of greater law obedience in Britain than in the United States.

As in the case of the United States, because of our reservations about the United Kingdom adjusted price series, we frequently present separate results excluding the wartime and immediately postwar years.

So-called voluntary price controls were imposed in Britain at various times from 1950 through mid-1966; statutory controls were imposed from July 1966 through February 1974.[21] We have not attempted a correction for the earlier period of voluntary controls, but we have done so for the later period of statutory controls.

Table 4.7 gives the results of our correction. Our procedure is similar to that used for the wartime period except that we did not use the same conversion factor. Instead, we used a conversion factor of .8342, calculated as the ratio of the change from 1965 to 1975 in the log of prices to the change over the same period in the log of nominal income. The corrected price series exhibits higher rates of annual price change than the reported series in the years from 1966 through 1970 and in 1973, and lower rates of change in other years. The corrected real income series rises throughout the period, failing to show the decline in 1975 of the reported series.[22]

21. See S. Brittan and P. Lilley, *The Delusion of Incomes Policy* (London: M. T. Smith, 1977), table 6, pp. 154–55, for a summary of United Kingdom incomes policies, 1948–76. See also *OECD Economic Surveys: United Kingdom* (November 1970), pp. 24–25; (March 1975), pp. 10–13; and F. T. Blackaby, "Incomes Policy," in *British Economic Policy 1960–74* (Cambridge: Cambridge University Press for NIESR, 1978), pp. 399–401.

22. We have tested our correction by comparing the reported and corrected price series with earlier monetary aggregates and the reported and corrected real income series with contemporaneous movements in employment and industrial production. The evidence is

Table 4.7   Reported and Corrected United Kingdom Price and
Real Income Series, 1965–75

Year	Implicit Prices (1929 = 100)		Real Income (Millions of 1929 Pounds Sterling)	
	Reported	Corrected	Reported	Corrected
1965	315.9		9,113	
1966	328.3	330.5	9,255	9,195
1967	338.2	345.2	9,467	9,275
1968	350.0	364.7	9,772	9,377
1969	362.5	381.3	9,951	9,460
1970	391.0	412.2	10,128	9,607
1971	431.3	454.1	10,313	9,794
1972	475.1	498.1	10,460	9,976
1973	515.3	566.1	11,243	10,233
1974	595.6	635.2	11,169	10,470
1975	765.6		10,866	

4.2.4 Interest Rates

For short-term United Kingdom interest rates, we use the open market rates on three-month bankers' bills. This series is continuous over two centuries. The level and fluctuations in the rate on bankers' bills during post–World War II years have been similar to those of the rate on three-month Treasury bills, while the call money rate has tended to be lower than both.

For long-term rates, we use the yield on the perpetual funded government debt known as consols.[23] This is also a continuous series over two centuries, but it is less representative of the long-term market since World War I than it was earlier. Until World War I, the United Kingdom national debt consisted largely of consols. Since then, the government has floated many issues with limited maturities. Consol yields tend to be at the lower end of the band of yields on long-term government issues. The yield series we use is an annual average based on the mean of opening and closing prices each day, excluding gross accrued interest, of 3 percent consols until 1888; 2.75 percent consols until July 1903; and thereafter 2.5 percent consols.

---

less clear-cut than that cited in footnote 9 above for the 1971–74 United States corrections, but seemed to us on the whole to support the corrected series as less inaccurate than the standard ones.

23. No comparable United States series exists, which explains why we use the United States corporate bond yield instead. Before 1917, many United States government securities bore the circulation privilege, which affected their yield; from 1917 to 1941, many United States government bonds were partially tax exempt; and, for some years, no long-term government bonds were outstanding.

4.2.5   Population

The United Kingdom population figures are midyear estimates. Except for the years 1915–20 and 1940–50, the figures refer to the population at home, that is, actually in the country. The figures for 1915–20 and 1940–50 are for the total population including the armed forces serving overseas but excluding Commonwealth and foreign forces in the United Kingdom.

4.2.6   Exclusion of Southern Ireland

The data for money, income, prices, and population in the appendix (sec. 4.4) show overlapping estimates for 1920, including and excluding Southern Ireland. (The Irish Free State was officially constituted a British dominion on 15 January 1922.) We used the percentage difference in 1920 to estimate figures excluding Southern Ireland in 1919 and including Southern Ireland in 1921. We were thus able to construct phase bases 1–15 including Southern Ireland, and from 14 to 37 excluding Southern Ireland. We adjusted the level of the bases 1–14 to the level of the later segment. We made no adjustments to the rates of change computed from triplets of the original phase bases. The triplet centered on 1919–20 (phase bases 13–15) includes Southern Ireland; the triplet centered on 1920–21 (phase bases 14–16) excludes Southern Ireland. Rates of change are not materially different for the two geographical entities, although the levels of the phase bases are affected by the exclusion of Southern Ireland.

4.3   Combined United States and United Kingdom Data

In some contexts, further discussed in the chapters that follow, we view the United States and the United Kingdom as a single economy. It is simple to add the populations. However, nominal magnitudes are expressed in United Kingdom pounds and United States dollars. One way we have combined the data is to convert United Kingdom nominal values (money stock, income in current prices) from pounds to dollars by multiplying by the annual exchange rate for pounds in dollars. The shortcomings of this procedure are discussed in chapter 6. National income in constant prices was converted to dollars by multiplying by the 1929 exchange rate. An implicit price deflator for the combined countries was derived by dividing the current price by the constant price income series. We did not combine the interest rate series for the two countries.

4.4   Appendix: Basic Annual Data

The appendix gives the annual data for the basic series discussed in this chapter and the source notes for each series (see table 4.8 for the United States data, table 4.9 for the United Kingdom data).

Table 4.8

Year	Money Stock (Billion $) (1)	Nominal Income (Billion $) (2)	Real Income (Billion 1929 $) (3)	Implicit Price Deflator 1929 = 100 (4)	Population (Millions) (5)	Short-Term Commercial Paper Rate (6)	Short-Term Call Money Rate (7)	Long-Term Yields on High-Grade Corporate Bonds (8)	Long-Term Yields on High-Grade Industrial Bonds (9)	High-Powered Money (Billion $) (10)
1867	1.28				37.376	7.33	6.22	6.44	7.90	0.820
1868	1.27				38.213	7.26	7.36	6.37	7.83	0.769
1869	1.28	7.242	9.959	72.7	39.051	9.66	10.45	6.64	8.10	0.760
1870	1.35	6.960	10.133	68.7	39.905	7.25	5.67	6.52	7.99	0.766
1871	1.50	6.946	9.956	69.8	40.938	6.98	5.40	6.46	7.92	0.778
1872	1.61	8.127	12.251	66.3	41.972	8.63	8.07	6.30	7.76	0.782
1873	1.62	8.074	12.319	65.5	43.006	10.31	14.41	6.33	7.79	0.789
1874	1.65	7.776	12.000	64.8	44.040	5.98	3.49	6.02	7.48	0.795
1875	1.72	7.665	12.104	63.3	45.073	5.44	3.13	5.57	7.04	0.773
1876	1.68	7.820	12.942	60.4	46.107	5.13	3.31	5.28	6.75	0.754
1877	1.65	8.062	13.859	58.2	47.141	5.18	3.81	5.29	6.76	0.758
1878	1.58	7.993	14.840	53.9	48.174	4.80	4.08	5.22	6.68	0.763
1879	1.66	8.509	16.367	52.0	49.208	5.06	5.60	4.88	6.34	0.801
1880	2.03	10.770	18.765	57.4	50.262	5.23	4.68	4.58	6.05	0.949
1881	2.44	10.762	19.130	56.3	51.542	5.20	5.88	4.26	5.72	1.077
1882	2.63	11.595	19.940	58.1	52.821	5.64	4.87	4.31	5.78	1.140
1883	2.80	11.228	19.578	57.4	54.100	5.62	3.68	4.33	5.80	1.186
1884	2.80	10.889	20.015	54.4	55.379	5.20	3.03	4.28	5.74	1.204
1885	2.87	10.127	19.954	50.8	56.658	4.06	1.54	4.08	5.54	1.233
1886	3.10	10.521	21.015	50.1	57.938	4.76	3.86	3.81	5.27	1.213

1887	3.31	10.887	21.530	50.6	59.217	5.75	5.23	3.87	5.34	1.271
1888	3.40	10.717	20.801	51.5	60.496	4.89	2.52	3.80	5.26	1.318
1889	3.60	11.093	21.422	51.8	61.775	4.86	4.32	3.66	5.12	1.342
1890	3.92	11.752	23.131	50.8	63.056	5.62	5.94	3.78	5.25	1.390
1891	4.08	12.112	24.074	50.3	64.361	5.39	3.47	3.95	5.41	1.461
1892	4.43	12.691	26.289	48.3	65.666	4.11	2.90	3.83	5.30	1.533
1893	4.26	12.497	25.266	49.5	66.970	6.79	4.57	3.93	5.40	1.561
1894	4.28	11.005	23.734	46.4	68.275	3.04	1.10	3.72	5.18	1.582
1895	4.43	12.089	26.470	45.7	69.580	3.67	1.85	3.59	5.05	1.499
1896	4.35	11.445	25.795	44.4	70.885	5.81	4.18	3.63	5.10	1.451
1897	4.64	12.613	28.277	44.6	72.189	3.50	1.80	3.44	4.90	1.554
1898	5.26	13.195	28.774	45.9	73.494	3.82	2.26	3.38	4.84	1.682
1899	6.09	15.136	32.114	47.1	74.799	4.15	4.95	3.24	4.71	1.812
1900	6.60	16.447	33.171	49.6	76.094	4.38	2.84	3.30	4.86	1.954
1901	7.48	18.254	37.030	49.3	77.584	4.28	4.20	3.25	4.78	2.096
1902	8.17	18.870	36.969	51.0	79.163	4.92	5.31	3.30	4.71	2.168
1903	8.68	19.910	38.628	51.5	80.632	5.47	3.71	3.45	4.88	2.278
1904	9.24	19.765	37.799	52.3	82.166	4.20	1.76	3.60	4.87	2.423
1905	10.24	21.794	40.809	53.4	83.822	4.40	3.97	3.50	4.53	2.489
1906	11.08	25.185	46.239	54.5	85.450	5.68	6.38	3.55	4.58	2.646
1907	11.60	26.479	46.628	56.8	87.008	6.34	6.57	3.80	4.98	2.833
1908	11.44	23.564	41.588	56.7	88.710	4.37	1.94	3.95	5.07	3.093
1909	12.68	27.780	47.294	58.7	90.490	3.98	2.70	3.77	4.76	3.122
1910	13.34	28.974	48.105	60.2	92.407	5.01	3.09	3.80	4.83	3.174
1911	14.12	29.233	48.939	59.7	93.863	4.03	2.67	3.90	4.78	3.276
1912	15.13	32.093	51.534	62.3	95.335	4.74	3.54	3.90	4.81	3.343
1913	15.73	33.758	53.942	62.6	97.225	5.58	3.18	4.00	4.99	3.417
1914	16.39	30.871	48.636	63.5	99.111	4.79	3.39	4.10	4.93	3.532
1915	17.59	32.847	50.121	65.5	100.546	3.45	1.94	4.15	4.97	3.669
1916	20.85	43.525	58.817	74.0	101.961	3.42	2.59	4.05	4.89	4.178

Table 4.8 (Continued)

Year	Money Stock (Billion $) (1)	Nominal Income (Billion $) (2)	Real Income (Billion 1929 $) (3)	Implicit Price Deflator 1929 = 100 (4)	Population (Millions) (5)	Short-Term		Long-Term		High-Powered Money (Billion $) (10)
						Commercial Paper Rate (6)	Call Money Rate (7)	Yields on High-Grade Corporate Bonds (8)	Yields on High-Grade Industrial Bonds (9)	
1917	24.37	52.344	57.269	91.4	103.268	4.74	3.40	4.05	5.09	5.096
1918	26.73	66.124	62.915	105.1	103.208	5.87	5.30	4.75	5.45	6.190
1919	31.01	69.864	65.477	106.7	104.514	5.42	6.47	4.75	5.40	6.770
1920	34.80	75.707	62.208	121.7	106.461	7.37	7.79	5.10	6.01	7.368
1921	32.85	61.793	59.567	103.7	108.538	6.53	6.00	5.17	5.96	6.679
1922	33.72	62.996	63.859	98.6	110.049	4.42	4.29	4.71	5.21	6.358
1923	36.60	74.095	73.460	100.9	111.947	4.97	4.86	4.61	5.26	6.726
1924	38.58	75.235	75.559	99.6	114.109	3.90	3.05	4.66	5.21	6.913
1925	42.05	78.602	77.343	101.6	115.829	4.00	4.18	4.50	5.06	7.098
1926	43.68	84.566	82.807	102.1	117.397	4.23	4.50	4.40	4.91	7.182
1927	44.73	83.104	83.623	99.4	119.035	4.02	4.06	4.30	4.83	7.214
1928	46.42	84.980	84.918	100.1	120.509	4.84	6.01	4.05	4.88	7.169
1929	46.60	90.320	90.308	100.0	121.767	5.78	7.67	4.42	5.04	7.159
1930	45.73	76.862	80.483	95.5	123.077	3.55	2.97	4.40	4.87	6.949
1931	42.69	61.733	73.508	84.0	124.040	2.63	1.77	4.10	4.79	7.302
1932	36.05	44.773	60.285	74.3	124.840	2.72	2.05	4.70	5.58	7.777
1933	32.22	42.650	58.205	73.3	125.579	1.67	1.16	4.15	4.98	8.151
1934	34.36	50.341	64.420	78.1	126.374	0.88	1.00	3.99	4.28	9.086
1935	39.07	58.165	75.393	77.1	127.250	0.75	0.56	3.50	3.73	10.644
1936	43.48	68.257	84.965	80.3	128.053	0.75	0.91	3.20	3.34	12.175

Year										
1937	45.68	75.070	92.717	81.0	128.825	0.94	1.00	3.08	3.16	13.426
1938	45.51	68.793	85.391	80.6	129.825	0.86	1.00	3.00	2.82	14.537
1939	49.27	73.848	92.268	80.0	130.880	0.72	1.00	2.75	2.64	17.501
1940	55.20	81.843	101.176	80.9	132.122	0.81	1.00	2.70	2.57	21.358
1941	62.51	98.958	113.348	87.3	133.402	0.70	1.00	2.65	2.50	23.341
1942	71.16	129.275	130.978	98.7	134.860	0.69	1.00	2.65	2.54	25.427
1943	89.91	157.521	141.021	111.7	136.739	0.72	1.00	2.65	2.54	30.181
1944	106.82	171.503	142.919	120.0	138.397	0.75	1.00	2.60	2.58	35.788
1945	126.63	172.983	138.055	125.3	139.928	0.75	1.00	2.55	2.50	41.851
1946	138.73	160.465	126.950	126.4	141.389	0.81	1.16	2.43	2.44	44.241
1947	146.00	179.049	131.075	136.6	144.126	1.03	1.38	2.50	2.52	45.026
1948	148.11	198.360	136.236	145.6	146.631	1.44	1.55	2.80	2.70	46.166
1949	147.46	196.072	136.445	143.7	149.188	1.49	1.63	2.74	2.52	45.396
1950	150.81	217.891	148.731	146.5	151.684	1.45	1.63	2.58	2.48	43.642
1951	156.45	251.358	161.024	156.1	154.287	2.16	2.17	2.67	2.72	47.165
1952	164.92	263.775	166.946	158.0	156.954	2.33	2.48	3.00	2.87	49.485
1953	171.19	277.847	173.221	160.4	159.565	2.52	3.06	3.15	3.08	50.201
1954	177.16	276.755	170.206	162.6	162.391	1.58	3.05	3.00	2.74	49.380
1955	183.69	302.321	182.011	166.1	165.275	2.18	3.20	3.04	2.97	49.160
1956	186.87	317.153	185.687	170.8	168.221	3.31	4.09	3.09	3.34	49.720
1957	191.82	332.880	188.494	176.6	171.274	3.81	4.50	3.68	3.80	50.069
1958	201.12	336.242	187.845	179.0	174.141	2.46	3.72	3.61	3.65	49.859
1959	210.49	365.775	199.768	183.1	177.830	3.97	4.22	4.10	4.25	50.490
1960	212.56	380.651	204.212	186.4	180.671	3.85	4.99	4.55	4.26	50.000
1961	223.68	393.912	209.194	188.3	183.691	2.97	4.50	4.22	4.20	49.273
1962	236.67	426.376	221.840	192.2	186.538	3.26	4.50	4.42	4.18	50.920
1963	251.97	450.620	230.850	195.2	189.242	3.55	4.50	4.16	4.12	52.420
1964	267.82	482.756	243.202	198.5	191.889	3.97	4.50	4.33	4.26	55.173
1965	289.25	523.820	257.785	203.2	194.303	4.38	4.69	4.35	4.39	58.100
1966	311.89	574.186	273.552	209.9	196.560	5.55	5.78	4.75	5.09	61.530

Table 4.8 (Continued)

Year	Money Stock (Billion $) (1)	Nominal Income (Billion $) (2)	Real Income (Billion 1929 $) (3)	Implicit Price Deflator 1929 = 100 (4)	Population (Millions) (5)	Interest Rates (Annual Percentage)				High-Powered Money (Billion $) (10)
						Short-Term		Long-Term		
						Commercial Paper Rate (6)	Call Money Rate (7)	Yields on High-Grade Corporate Bonds (8)	Yields on High-Grade Industrial Bonds (9)	
1967	335.88	605.779	280.194	216.2	198.712	5.10	5.66	4.95	5.47	64.628
1968	366.02	660.090	292.334	225.8	200.706	5.90	6.33	5.93	6.12	69.362
1969	389.82	708.573	299.228	236.8	202.677	7.83	7.96	6.54	6.92	73.625
1970	405.96	740.587	296.591	249.7	204.878	7.71	7.95	7.60	7.76	77.530
1971	453.12	801.277	304.546	263.2	207.053	5.11	5.73	7.12	7.16	83.227
1972	500.94	885.254	316.389	279.8	208.846	4.69	5.16	7.01	7.09	89.052
1973	549.12	987.543	330.352	298.9	210.410	8.15	8.25	7.20	7.37	94.478
1974	595.35	1059.479	330.621	321.7	211.901	9.84	10.98	7.80	8.04	103.592
1975	640.96	1125.473	324.812	346.5	213.540	6.32	8.02	8.35	8.43	108.439

Source, by Column

Column 1, United States Money Stock

These are annual averages, centered on 30 June, of quarterly figures 1867–1907, end-of-month data, 1908–46, and monthly averages of daily figures thereafter. Sums of currency held by the public plus adjusted deposits at all commercial banks, less large negotiable CDs since 1961.

1867–1946:   M. Friedman and A. J. Schwartz, *Monetary Statistics of the United States*, pp. 61–65 and 9–37.

1947–58:   *Federal Reserve Bulletin*, December 1970, p. 898.

1959–75:   Banking Section of the Federal Reserve Board's Division of Research and Statistics, Statistical Release (22 February 1977).

Column 2, United States Nominal Income

1869–1909:   Based on unpublished estimates provided by Robert E. Gallman, and worksheets underlying Simon Kuznets, *Capital in the American Economy: Its Formation and Financing*. See text.

1910–16,
1920–41,
1946–47:   Worksheets underlying Kuznets, *Capital in the American Economy*.

1917–19,
1942–45:   Values of Kuznets's nominal income for each year were interpolated arithmetically along a straight line connecting the estimates for the terminal years; these trend values were multiplied by the ratios to corresponding trend values of Kendrick's national security version (J. W. Kendrick, *Productivity Trends in the United States*).

1948–75:   Commerce NNP estimates, multiplied by the ratio of Kuznets's figure to Commerce NNP in 1947. Department of Commerce, *The National Income and Product Accounts of the United States 1929–1974*, pp. 23–24, and *Survey of Current Business*, July 1976, p. 27.

Column 3, United States Real Income in 1929 Dollars

1869–1909:   Based on unpublished estimates provided by Robert E. Gallman, and worksheets underlying Kuznets, *Capital in the American Economy*. See text.

1910–16,
1920–41,
1947:   Worksheets underlying Kuznets, *Capital in the American Economy*.

1917–19,
1942–46:   Column 2 divided by Kuznets's implicit price deflator including correction of price deflator, 1943–46, for effect of price controls. See text.

1948–75:   Column 2 divided by Commerce price deflator implicit in net national product, shifted to base 1929, as described in source notes for that series, and corrected for effect of price controls, 1971–74. See text.

Column 4, United States Implicit Price Deflator (1929 = 100)

1869–1947:   Column 2 divided by column 3. For estimates, 1943–46, see text and tables 4.1 and 4.2.

1947–75: Price deflator implicit in Department of Commerce NNP was shifted from 1970 to 1929 base (by multiplying by 2.994) and then adjusted to level of Kuznets's 1947 figure by multiplying by 0.9143. See *The National Income and Product Accounts of the United States, 1929–1974*, pp. 276–77, and *Survey of Current Business*, July 1976, table 7.6, p. 60. For estimates, 1971–74, see text and tables 4.3 and 4.4.

Column 5, United States Population

These are midyear figures of the resident population except for 1917–19 and since 1940, when the armed forces overseas are also included.

1867–1900: United States Bureau of the Census, *Historical Statistics of the United States to 1957* (Washington, D.C.), p. 7.

1900–1939: *Population Estimates*, P-25, no. 521 (May 1974).

1940–75: *Economic Report of the President*, February 1975, p. 275; February 1977, p. 217.

Column 6, United States Short-Term Interest Rate: Prime Commercial Paper Rate

These are annual averages of monthly rates on sixty-to-ninety-day, through 1923, since four-to-six-month commercial paper in New York City, based on weekly figures of dealers' offering rates until 1944, thereafter, on daily figures.

1869–Jan. 1937: F. R. Macaulay, *The Movements of Interest Rates, Bond Yields and Stock Prices in the United States since 1856*, pp. A145–A161.

Feb. 1937–44: *Bank and Quotation Record of the Commercial and Financial Chronicle, 1937–45*.

1945–63: Board of Governors of the Federal Reserve System, *Supplement to Banking and Monetary Statistics*, sec. 12, Money Rates and Securities Markets (January 1966) p. 37.

1964–75: Council of Economic Advisers, *Economic Indicators*, December 1971, p. 33; June 1977, p. 30.

Column 7, United States Short-Term Interest Rate: Call Money Rate

These are annual averages of monthly rates, based on weekly renewal rates until 1923; thereafter, daily renewal rates.

1869–1937: Macaulay, *Movements of Interest Rates, Bond Yields and Stock Prices in the United States since 1856*, pp. A145–A161.

1938–41: Board of Governors of Federal Reserve System, *Banking and Monetary Statistics*, 1943, p. 451.

1942–63: Board of Governors of Federal Reserve System, *Supplement to Banking and Monetary Statistics*, sec. 12, Money Rates and Securities Markets, (January 1966) p. 37.

1964–75: Federal Reserve System, Statistical Release, G13.

Column 8, United States Long-Term Interest Rate: Yields on High-Grade Corporate Bonds

1869–99: Annual average of monthly yields on railroad bonds adjusted for economic drift, Macaulay, *Movements of Interest Rates, Bond Yields and Stock Prices in the United States since 1856*, pp. A145–A152, col. 5, plus 0.114 percentage points to raise averages to level of following segment.

1900–1975: Basic yield on corporate bonds to thirty-year maturity (first quarter or February data). United States Bureau of the Census, *Historical Statistics of the United States, Colonial Times to 1970, Bicentennial Edition, Part 2*, (Washington, D.C., 1975), series X-491; United States Bureau of the Census, *Statistical Abstract of the United States: 1976 (97)* (Washington, D.C., 1976), p. 495.

Column 9, United States Long-Term Interest Rate: Yields on High-Grade Industrial Bonds

1869–99: Same as column 8, except that 1.468 percentage points is added to raise averages to level of following segment.

1900–1975: An arithmetic mean of yield to maturity based on mean of monthly high-low prices before 1929, thereafter, an average of four or five weekly prices for the month. Standard and Poor, *Trade and Securities Statistics: Security Price Index Record*, 1972 ed., p. 205; *Trade and Securities Statistics: Current Statistics*, January 1973, p. 36; *Security Price Index Record*, 1974 ed., p. 221; *Trade and Securities Statistics: Current Statistics*, January 1976, pp. 41–42.

Column 10, United States High-Powered Money

These are annual averages, centered on 30 June, of quarterly figures, 1867–1907, and of monthly data thereafter. Sums of (*a*) currency held by the public; and (*b*) bank vault cash, 1867–October 1914, thereafter including also (*c*) member bank deposits and (*d*) nonmember clearing account at Federal Reserve Banks.

1867–1907 II: (*a*) and (*b*) M. Friedman and A. J. Schwartz, *Monetary Statistics of the United States*, pp. 344–50.

1907–42: (*a*) and (*b*) ibid., pp. 8–34, 380–93; (*c*) *Annual Report*, Federal Reserve Board, 1914–21; *Banking and Monetary Statistics, 1914–1941*, pp. 378–94; *Federal Reserve Bulletin*, monthly issues; (*d*) *Annual Reports*, Federal Reserve Board and Board of Governors of the Federal Reserve System, 1914–21, 1926–42.

1943–75: (*a*) *Monetary Statistics*, pp. 34–52; Banking Section of the Federal Reserve Board's Division of Research and Statistics; (*b*) *A Monetary History*, pp. 741–44; Banking Section of the Federal Reserve Board's Division of Research and Statistics; (*c*) *Banking and Monetary Statistics, 1941–1970*, pp. 558–89; *Federal Reserve Bulletin*, monthly issues; (*d*) *Annual Report*, Board of Governors of the Federal Reserve System, 1943, 1945–75.

Table 4.9

Year	Money Stock (Million £) (1)	Nominal Income (Million £) (2)	Real Income (Million 1929 £) (3)	Implicit Price Deflator (1929 = 100) (4)	Population (Millions) (5)	Interest Rates (Annual Percentage) Short-Term Rates on Three-Month Bills (6)	Long-Term Yields on Consols (7)	Exchange Rate for £ in U.S. $ (8)	High-Powered Money (Million £) (9)
				Including Southern Ireland					
1868		805	1,346	59.8	30.690	2.46	3.20	6.8624	
1869		833	1,419	58.7	30.918	3.37	3.23	6.5045	
1870		899	1,597	56.3	31.257	3.28	3.24	5.6120	
1871	502	972	1,682	57.8	31.556	2.89	3.23	5.4858	159
1872	551	1,037	1,689	61.4	31.874	4.08	3.24	5.5094	162
1873	583	1,111	1,750	63.5	32.177	4.70	3.24	5.5203	163
1874	605	1,084	1,763	61.5	32.501	3.56	3.24	5.4482	164
1875	618	1,072	1,811	59.2	32.839	3.14	3.20	5.6169	170
1876	619	1,056	1,827	57.8	33.200	2.26	3.16	5.4586	173
1877	615	1,047	1,863	56.2	33.576	2.62	3.15	5.1059	172
1878	591	1,015	1,839	55.2	33.932	3.59	3.15	4.9141	174
1879	573	994	1,883	52.8	34.304	2.14	3.08	4.8556	179
1880	581	1,037	1,885	55.0	34.623	2.53	3.05	4.8490	170
1881	591	1,076	2,000	53.8	34.935	3.05	3.00	4.8460	167
1882	605	1,116	2,044	54.6	35.206	3.55	2.99	4.8757	166
1883	616	1,102	2,041	54.0	35.450	3.22	2.97	4.8543	164
1884	629	1,073	2,044	52.5	35.724	2.57	2.97	4.8590	164
1885	636	1,058	2,070	51.1	36.015	2.40	3.02	4.8597	166
1886	634	1,082	2,151	50.3	36.313	2.33	2.98	4.8682	163

Year								
1887	632	1,127	2,232	50.5	36.598	2.65	2.95	4.8617	162
1888	648	1,204	2,384	50.5	36.881	2.53	2.97	4.8826	163
1889	676	1,296	2,531	51.2	37.178	2.85	2.81	4.8812	169
1890	698	1,326	2,545	52.1	37.485	3.88	2.67	4.8703	173
1891	726	1,307	2,518	51.9	37.802	2.77	2.70	4.8677	182
1892	743	1,268	2,448	51.8	38.134	1.76	2.65	4.8777	184
1893	748	1,274	2,474	51.5	38.490	2.32	2.61	4.8704	187
1894	752	1,362	2,692	50.6	38.859	1.18	2.52	4.8819	192
1895	793	1,395	2,796	49.9	39.221	0.96	2.39	4.8944	198
1896	840	1,431	2,879	49.7	39.599	1.56	2.28	4.8774	211
1897	847	1,481	2,950	50.2	39.987	1.92	2.25	4.8673	203
1898	865	1,563	3,095	50.5	40.381	2.62	2.28	4.8536	202
1899	895	1,649	3,221	51.2	40.773	3.35	2.36	4.8715	205
1900	919	1,695	3,104	54.6	41.155	3.70	2.54	4.8717	209
1901	927	1,668	3,077	54.2	41.538	3.17	2.67	4.8786	210
1902	929	1,687	3,165	53.3	41.893	2.97	2.66	4.8764	212
1903	935	1,661	3,122	53.2	42.246	3.38	2.75	4.8682	213
1904	924	1,647	3,090	53.3	42.611	2.68	2.83	4.8717	211
1905	942	1,725	3,218	53.6	42.981	2.62	2.78	4.8663	216
1906	971	1,827	3,383	54.0	43.361	3.97	2.83	4.8573	218
1907	992	1,921	3,499	54.9	43.737	4.49	2.97	4.8667	223
1908	1,000	1,831	3,323	55.1	44.124	2.29	2.90	4.8684	223
1909	1,019	1,861	3,390	54.9	44.520	2.28	2.98	4.8760	226
1910	1,047	1,943	3,520	55.2	44.916	3.16	3.08	4.8676	226
1911	1,078	2,025	3,623	55.9	45.268	2.90	3.15	4.8660	226
1912	1,119	2,132	3,708	57.5	45.436	3.62	3.28	4.8701	233
1913	1,160	2,206	3,810	57.9	45.649	4.36	3.39	4.8689	244
1914	1,263	2,231	3,833	58.2	46.049	2.90	3.46	4.9296	327
1915	1,404	2,517	3,951	63.7	46.340	3.66	3.82	4.7570	367
1916	1,559	2,985	4,095	72.9	46.514	5.20	4.31	4.7660	437

Table 4.9 (Continued)

Year	Money Stock (Million £) (1)	Nominal Income (Million £) (2)	Real Income (Million 1929 £) (3)	Implicit Price Deflator (1929 = 100) (4)	Population (Millions) (5)	Interest Rates (Annual Percentage) Short-Term Rates on Three-Month Bills (6)	Long-Term Yields on Consols (7)	Exchange Rate for £ in U.S. $ (8)	High-Powered Money (Million £) (9)
1917	1,867	3,722	4,059	91.7	46.614	4.78	4.58	4.7644	513
1918	2,223	4,506	4,172	108.0	46.575	3.56	4.40	4.7651	634
1919	2,600	4,671	3,681	126.9	46.534	3.92	4.62	4.4258	732
1920	2,886	5,223	3,389	154.1	46.821				728
Excluding Southern Ireland									
1920	2,831	5,077	3,288	154.4	43.718	6.40	5.32	3.6643	711
1921	2,768	4,249	3,099	137.1	44.072	5.16	5.21	3.8490	684
1922	2,676	3,713	3,218	115.4	44.372	2.64	4.43	4.4292	638
1923	2,561	3,542	3,342	106.0	44.596	2.72	4.31	4.5748	614
1924	2,520	3,677	3,499	105.1	44.915	3.46	4.39	4.4171	610
1925	2,500	3,959	3,742	105.8	45.059	4.14	4.43	4.8289	610
1926	2,509	3,747	3,599	104.1	45.232	4.48	4.55	4.8582	597
1927	2,546	3,983	3,928	101.4	45.389	4.26	4.56	4.8610	589
1928	2,600	3,996	3,980	100.4	45.578	4.16	4.47	4.8662	584
1929	2,616	4,127	4,127	100.0	45.672	5.26	4.60	4.8569	572
1930	2,638	4,065	4,098	99.2	45.866	2.57	4.46	4.8621	566
1931	2,606	3,658	3,810	96.0	46.074	3.61	4.53	4.5350	561
1932	2,666	3,550	3,838	92.5	46.335	1.86	3.76	3.5061	569
1933	2,804	3,650	4,007	91.1	46.520	0.69	3.38	4.2368	605

Year									
1934	2,812	3,910	4,325	90.4	46.666	0.82	3.08	5.0393	612
1935	2,912	4,078	4,471	91.2	46.868	0.58	2.89	4.9018	624
1936	3,100	4,308	4,703	91.6	47.081	0.61	2.94	4.9709	663
1937	3,244	4,556	4,786	95.2	47.289	0.58	3.28	4.9440	715
1938	3,228	4,754	4,876	97.5	47.494	0.64	3.38	4.8894	731
1939	3,272	4,907	4,912	99.9	47.761	1.23	3.72	4.4354	758
1940	3,607	5,530	4,834	114.4	48.226	1.04	3.40	3.8300	855
1941	4,155	6,720	5,342	125.8	48.216	1.03	3.13	4.0318	970
1942	4,788	7,449	5,584	133.4	48.400	1.03	3.03	4.0350	1,157
1943	5,376	7,918	5,636	140.5	48.789	1.03	3.10	4.0350	1,362
1944	6,082	8,114	5,611	144.6	49.016	1.03	3.14	4.0350	1,571
1945	6,698	8,227	5,647	145.7	49.182	0.93	2.92	4.0302	1,761
1946	7,396	8,165	5,447	149.9	49.217	0.53	2.60	4.0328	1,878
1947	8,035	8,688	5,481	158.5	49.519	0.53	2.76	4.0286	1,982
1948	8,173	9,621	5,633	170.8	50.014	0.56	3.21	4.0313	1,873
1949	8,300	10,311	5,859	176.0	50.312	0.63	3.30	3.6872	1,897
1950	8,382	10,823	6,091	177.7	50.565	0.69	3.55	2.8007	1,904
1951	8,457	11,837	6,210	190.6	50.290	0.91	3.79	2.7996	1,962
1952	8,584	12,729	6,170	206.3	50.431	2.71	4.23	2.7926	2,028
1953	8,849	13,518	6,355	212.7	50.593	2.77	4.08	2.8127	2,130
1954	9,189	14,437	6,629	217.8	50.765	1.84	3.76	2.8087	2,239
1955	9,246	15,480	6,874	225.2	50.946	3.75	4.17	2.7913	2,354
1956	9,175	16,606	6,939	239.3	51.184	5.05	4.74	2.7957	2,464
1957	9,373	17,477	7,016	249.1	51.430	4.98	4.98	2.7932	2,557
1958	9,704	18,222	6,987	260.8	51.652	4.74	4.98	2.8098	2,633
1959	10,122	19,253	7,246	265.7	51.956	3.49	4.82	2.8088	2,717
1960	10,495	20,959	7,745	270.6	52.372	5.05	5.42	2.8076	2,843
1961	10,722	22,145	7,920	279.6	52.807	5.32	6.20	2.8022	2,962
1962	10,925	23,203	8,029	289.0	53.274	4.41	5.98	2.8078	2,986
1963	11,448	24,759	8,376	295.6	53.552	3.82	5.58	2.8000	3,060

Table 4.9 (Continued)

Year	Money Stock (Million £) (1)	Nominal Income (Million £) (2)	Real Income (Million 1929 £) (3)	Implicit Price Deflator (1929 = 100) (4)	Population (Millions) (5)	Interest Rates (Annual Percentage) Short-Term Rates on Three-Month Bills (6)	Interest Rates (Annual Percentage) Long-Term Yields on Consols (7)	Exchange Rate for £ in U.S. $ (8)	High-Powered Money (Million £) (9)
1964	12,010	26,772	8,836	303.0	53.885	4.81	6.03	2.7921	3,232
1965	12,702	28,787	9,113	315.9	54.218	6.29	6.42	2.7959	3,429
1966	13,219	30,385	9,195	330.5	54.500	6.43	6.80	2.7930	3,623
1967	13,796	32,017	9,275	345.2	54.800	6.08	6.69	2.7504	3,728
1968	14,780	34,201	9,377	364.7	55.049	7.42	7.39	2.3935	3,936
1969	15,538	36,073	9,460	381.3	55.263	8.48	8.88	2.3901	4,085
1970	16,528	39,600	9,607	412.2	55.421	8.26	9.16	2.3959	4,245
1971	18,405	44,479	9,794	454.1	55.610	6.41	9.05	2.4442	4,589
1972	22,002	49,696	9,976	498.1	55.793	6.11	9.11	2.5008	4,951
1973	27,841	57,933	10,233	566.1	55.933	10.43	10.85	2.4510	6,401
1974	33,175	66,512	10,470	635.2	55.965	13.06	14.95	2.3403	7,213
1975	36,480	83,188	10,866	765.6	55.943	10.62	14.66	2.2216	8,057

Source, by Column

Column 1, United Kingdom Money Stock

This series is the sum of gross deposits at London and country joint stock and private banks (later, London clearing banks and other domestic deposit banks and, since 1968, the National Giro) and at Scottish and Irish banks, less interbank and transit items, plus private deposits at the Bank of England and currency held by the public.

1871–80:   See text. Based on Shizuya Nishimura, "The Growth of the Stock of Money in the U.K., 1870–1913."

1881-96: See text. Based on David K. Sheppard, *The Growth and Role of U.K. Financial Institutions, 1880–1962*, table (A)1.1, col. 4, pp. 116–17; table (A) 3.3, col. 3, pp. 182–83.

1897-1966: Based on Sheppard's deposit components and his currency components for 1911–60. Thereafter currency held by the public is from *Annual Abstract of Statistics*, 1976 (no. 113), table 415.

1967-68: Unpublished estimates of deposits provided by Sheppard combined with currency obtained from source listed above.

1969-75: Bank of England, *Statistical Release*, October 1976. Bank of England M3 estimates linked to Sheppard's 1968 estimates.

Column 2, United Kingdom Nominal Income

This series is an estimate of net national product from the income side.

1868-1949: C. H. Feinstein, *National Income, Expenditure and Output of the United Kingdom, 1855–1965*, table 1, col. 13.

1950-75: Central Statistical Office, *National Income and Expenditure*, 1962–72; 1963–73; 1964–74; 1965–75 issues, table 1.1, national income plus or minus residual error (reference number 25 plus or minus reference number 21).

Column 3, United Kingdom Real Income in 1929 Pounds Sterling

1868-1975: Column 2 divided by column 4.

Column 4, United Kingdom Implicit Price Deflator (1929 = 100)

This series is the deflator implicit in net national product from the expenditure side obtained by dividing the series in current prices by the series in constant prices on various bases and then shifted to the 1929 base.

1868-69: The current price series is the one for 1870–1949, cited below. The constant price series was derived as follows: GNP, calculated from the expenditure side, is available for these years in both current and 1900 prices (Phyllis Deane, "New Estimates of Gross National Product for the United Kingdom, 1830–1914," pp. 104–7). To get net national product we subtracted an estimate of capital consumption from the GNP figures. The current price estimate is from Feinstein (table 1, col. 12). An estimate of net total fixed capital formation in current and 1900 prices is available (B. R. Mitchell and P. Deane, *Abstract of British Historical Statistics*, pp. 373–74). We used the deflator implicit in net total fixed capital formation to deflate capital consumption in current prices. Capital consumption in 1900 prices was then subtracted from GNP in 1900 prices to get NNP in 1900 prices.

1870–1939, 1947–49:	The current price series is in Feinstein, *National Income*, table 2, column 10, minus table 1, column 12 (pp. T4-T9). The constant price series on various bases is in ibid., table 5, column 15 (pp. T14-T16).
1940–46:	As above, and then adjusted for correction of reported implicit prices during period of price controls. See text and tables 4.5 and 4.6.
1950–65, 1975:	The current price series is from table 1.1 (reference number 25), the constant price series on a 1970 base, from table 2.1 (reference number 25), in Central Statistical Office, *National Income and Expenditure*, 1962–72; 1963–73; 1964–74; 1965–75 issues.
1966–74:	As above, and then adjusted for correction of reported implicit prices during period of price controls. See text and table 4.7.

Column 5, United Kingdom Population

1868–1951:	Feinstein, *National Income*, table 55 (pp. T120-T121).
1952–74:	C.S.O., *Annual Abstract of Statistics*, 1974, no. 111 and 1976, no. 113, table 6, p. 7.
1975:	C.S.O., *Monthly Digest of Statistics*, May 1977, table 2.2, p. 14.

Column 6, United Kingdom Short-Term Interest Rate: Rates for Three-Month Bankers' Bills

1868–1938:	These are annual averages of monthly figures. Mitchell and Deane, *Abstract of British Historical Statistics*, p. 460.
1939–75:	C.S.O. *Annual Abstract of Statistics*, nos. 84, 88, 96, 102, 111, 113.

Column 7, United Kingdom Long-Term Interest Rate: Annual Average Yield on Consols

1868–1959:	Sidney Homer, *A History of Interest Rates*, pp. 196–97, 409–410.
1960–73:	C.S.O. *Annual Abstract of Statistics*, 1965, no. 102, table 351; 1974, no. 111, table 388.
1974–75:	*Monthly Digest of Statistics* (May 1977) table 16.16, p. 147.

Column 8, United Kingdom Exchange Rates on the United States Dollar

These are annual averages of monthly data that are averages of daily rates, except for 1868–78, which are annual averages of quarterly data.

1868–78: $4.8665 times premium or discount on gold bills, from L. E. Davis and J. R. T. Hughes, "A Dollar-Sterling Exchange, 1803–95," table A-2, column headed "Macaulay," and times United States gold premium, from W. C. Mitchell, *Gold, Prices, and Wages under the Greenbacks Standard*, p. 4.

1879–1912: A time series in NBER files, compiled from *The Economist*, except 1899–1908, for which data are given in National Monetary Commission, *Statistics for Great Britain, Germany, and France, 1867–1909*, pp. 70–74.

1913–41: *Banking and Monetary Statistics*, p. 681.

1942–60: *Supplement to Banking and Monetary Statistics*, section 15, p. 92.

1961–75: *Federal Reserve Bulletin*, p. A-75.

Column 9, United Kingdom High-Powered Money

Sums of currency outside banks, currency held by banks, bankers' deposits, special deposits, and private deposits at the Bank of England.

1871–1968: See sources listed for column 1.

1969–75: Bank of England *Quarterly Bulletin*, and Bank of England *Report and Accounts for the Year Ended 28 February, 1969–76*.

5 Movements of Money, Income, and Prices

Table 5.1 summarizes the changes that have occurred in the United States and the United Kingdom over the longest period for which we have data on money and income for both the United States and the United Kingdom. As it happens, both the initial and the terminal phases for this common period are contraction phases for both countries: the initial phase is 1873–78 for the United States, 1874–79 for the United Kingdom; the terminal phase is 1973–75 for both. The interval between the midpoints of the initial and terminal phases is just short of a century: 98.5 years for the United States, 97.5 for the United Kingdom.

Though our United States data on money are available for three additional early phases (1867–69, 1869–70, and 1870–73), and on income for two, we shall generally treat 1873–78 as if it were the initial phase for the United States in order to maintain comparability with the United Kingdom.[1]

5.1 United States and United Kingdom Money Balances at the Beginning and End of a Century

In the 1873–78 phase, the quantity of money in the United States was $1.7 billion, or $36 for each of its nearly 46 million residents. In the roughly contemporaneous United Kingdom phase, 1874–79, the quantity of money in the United Kingdom was £0.6 billion or £19 for each of the more than 31 million residents. This cyclical phase is centered two years before the resumption of gold payments by the United States at the

---

1. We have consistently made computations for the longer period parallel to these for the shorter period to assure ourselves that we are not biasing the results by omitting the first two or three United States phases.

prewar parity, so that the market rate of exchange between the dollar and the pound sterling had not yet reached $4.8665, the parity rate that prevailed from 1 January 1879 until the outbreak of World War I in August 1914. The exchange rate averaged $5.242 for the United Kingdom phase 1874–79, so cash balances per capita in the United Kingdom were the market equivalent of $100, or nearly three times as large as in the United States.

This difference reflects primarily the greater financial sophistication of the United Kingdom at the time, not greater affluence. Per capita income in the United States was $173, in the United Kingdom almost exactly the same, $171, at the market rate of exchange.

In 1776 Adam Smith was able to write, "England is certainly, in the present times, a much richer country than any part of North America. The wages of labour, however, are much higher in North America than in any part of England. . . . But though North America is not yet so rich as England, it is much more thriving, and advancing with much greater rapidity to the further acquisition of riches."[2]

A century later, at the beginning of the period we study, the part of North America that had become the United States had a population 46 percent larger than the United Kingdom. Wages remained much higher than in England,[3] and the United States remained "much more thriving." In Adam Smith's time, the higher *wages* in North America may not have produced a higher *income* per capita because of the much larger capital accumulation in England. A century later, as just noted, our data indicate that per capita income was almost identical in the two countries. Aggregate United States income at the beginning of our period was therefore nearly 1.5 times aggregate United Kingdom income.[4]

2. Adam Smith, *The Wealth of Nations* (1776), Cannan ed. (London: Methuen, 1930), pp. 71–72.

3. According to Lebergott, average annual earnings of United States nonfarm employees (when employed) was $466 in 1873 (United States Bureau of the Census, *Historical Statistics of the United States, Colonial Times to 1970*, bicentennial edition, part 1 (Washington, D.C., 1975, series D-735). According to Feinstein, United Kingdom aggregate income from employment was £547 million in 1874, or £38 per capita working population, or $217 at the exchange rate current that year (C. H. Feinstein, *National Income, Expenditure and Output of the United Kingdom, 1855–1965* (Cambridge: Cambridge University Press, 1972), table 21 for income, table 57 for working population, and table 4.9, above, for exchange rate.

4. A caveat is in order that the market exchange rate is not wholly satisfactory for converting United Kingdom incomes to comparable United States incomes. The United Kingdom was at the time a capital exporter, the United States, a capital importer. On this score, domestic prices might be expected to be higher relative to international prices in the United States than in the United Kingdom. On the other side, the United Kingdom had much capital already invested abroad and was receiving a large income as return on capital and other "invisibles"; the United States was in the reverse position. This would work in the opposite direction: that is, a net capital *exporter* tends to have domestic prices that are low in relation to international prices while a *creditor* country tends to have domestic prices that

Table 5.1   **Secular Changes in Money Stock, Income, Velocity, Prices, and Population, United States (1873–1975) and United Kingdom (1874–1975)**

	United States (All Monetary Items in Dollars)				
	Average Value		Ratio of	Rate of Change (Annual Percentage) from	Slope of
	Initial Reference Phase (1873–78) (1)	Terminal Reference Phase (1973–75) (2)	Terminal to Initial Value (3)	Initial to Terminal Phase (4)	Semilog Trend (1873–1975) (5)
1. Nominal income (billions of dollars or pounds per year)	7.870	1056.9	134.3	4.97	4.91
2. Money stock (billions of dollars or pounds)	1.660	594.31	358.0	5.97	5.87
3. Velocity of money (ratio per year)	4.742	1.778	.375	−1.00	−0.96
4. Implicit price deflator (1929 = 100)	61.18	321.15	5.25	1.68	1.77
5. Real income (billions of 1929 dollars or pounds per year)	12.864	329.09	25.58	3.29	3.14
6. Population (millions)	45.564	211.935	4.65	1.56	1.50
7. Per capita nominal income (dollars or pounds per year)	172.7	4987.	28.9	3.41	3.41
8. Per capita real income (1929 dollars or pounds per year)	282.3	1553.	5.50	1.73	1.64
9. Per capita nominal balances (dollars or pounds)	36.4	2804.	77.03	4.41	4.37
10. Per capita real money balances (1929 dollars or pounds)	59.6	873.	14.65	2.72	2.60

Source: Lines 1, 2, 4–6: See source notes to table 4.8 and 4.9. Line 3 is line 1 divided by line 2. Line 7 is line 1 divided by line 6. Line 8 is line 5 divided by line 6. Line 9 is line 2 divided by line 6. Line 10 is line 9 divided by line 4.

United Kingdom (All Monetary Items in Pounds Sterling)				
Average Value		Ratio of	Rate of Change (Annual Percentage)	Slope
Initial Reference Phase (1874–79) (6)	Terminal Reference Phase (1973–75) (7)	Terminal to Initial Value (8)	from Initial to Terminal Phase (9)	of Semilog Trend (1874–1975) (10)
1.016	67.914	66.84	4.31	4.04
.594	32.515	54.74	4.10	3.97
1.709	2.089	1.22	0.21	0.068
57.16	646.67	11.31	2.49	2.34
1.778	10.502	5.91	1.82	1.69
31.172	55.952	1.795	0.60	0.575
32.6	1213.8	37.23	3.71	3.46
57.0	187.7	3.29	1.22	1.12
19.1	581.1	30.42	3.50	3.39
33.3	89.9	2.69	1.02	1.05

Allowing for the difference in per capita income increases a trifle the difference in money-holding propensities: the average United States resident held cash equal to not quite eleven weeks' income (see table 5.2); the average United Kingdom resident held cash equal to more than thirty weeks' income—striking testimony to the importance of the financial and economic structure for the demand for money. It produces here a nearly three to one difference in velocity.

Like money in total, the amount held as currency rather than deposits was also much greater relative to income in the United Kingdom than in the United States, 7.0 versus 3.6 weeks' income. However, the greater financial sophistication of the United Kingdom meant that the difference in currency holdings was less than in money in total—two to one rather than three to one—so that currency was a decidedly higher percentage of the money stock in the United States than in the United Kingdom.

The next century brought vast changes to both countries, but much greater changes to the United States. The population of the United States nearly quintupled; the population of the United Kingdom less than doubled. United States per capita income was destined to pass United Kingdom income decisively in a very few years, and to remain higher, except briefly during the United States Great Depression of the 1890s. United States per capita income in dollars multiplied twenty-nine-fold— or at the rate of 3.4 percent per year; United Kingdom per capita income in pounds multiplied thirty-seven-fold but, converted into dollars, seventeen-fold—or at the rate of 2.9 percent per year—because in 1973–75 the now floating exchange rate of the pound sterling averaged $2.34 rather than $5.24. By this measure, per capita income in comparable terms rose 1.76 times as much in the United States as in the United Kingdom, a difference produced by a half of one percentage point higher annual rate of growth through the miracle of compound interest. At the end of the

---

are high in relation to international prices. The two would just offset if the foreign yield on capital just equaled net export of capital; that is, if on balance all foreign income were reinvested abroad. In this case the trade account would balance.

Some indication of the margin of error is given by converting directly computed real per capita incomes in the two countries in 1929 prices (line 3 in table 5.2) into the same currency at the 1929 exchange rate (which was the same as the 1879 rate). This gives essentially the same result at the beginning of our period as the comparison of nominal incomes—roughly equal incomes in the two countries, implying that Britain's creditor status roughly balanced its status as a capital exporter. However, the same problems bedevil the calculation at the 1929 exchange rate. In addition, real income series constructed over such a long period are neither strictly comparable nor without significant error. Indeed, the closeness of the two estimates is rather surprising.

Jacob Viner's analysis of the role of changes in relative price levels in the mechanism of adjustment of international balances of indebtedness is the classic source on this subject. See *Canada's Balance of International Indebtedness, 1900–1913* (Cambridge: Harvard University Press, 1924), pp. 145–46, 191–255; also Paul Wonnacott, *The Canadian Dollar, 1948–1962* (Toronto: University of Toronto Press, 1965), p. 44.

Table 5.2 Money-Holding Propensities in the United States and United Kingdom over a Century (All United Kingdom Nominal Figures Converted to Dollars at Prevailing Exchange Rates; United Kingdom Real Figures Converted to Dollars at 1929 Exchange Rate)

Per Capita	Initial Phase		Terminal Phase		Annual Percentage Change, Initial to Terminal Phase	
	United States 1873–78	United Kingdom 1874–79	United States 1973–75	United Kingdom 1973–75	United States	United Kingdom
1. Nominal money balances	36.4	100.1	2804.	1358.0	4.41	2.67
2. Nominal income	172.7	170.9	4987.	2836.7	3.41	2.88
3. Real income	282.3	277.1	1553.	912.6	1.73	1.22
4. Number of weeks' income in the form of money	10.96	30.47	29.24	24.89	0.996	−.21
5. Number of weeks' income in the form of currency	3.57	7.01	3.19	3.57	−.11	−.69
6. Number of weeks' currency as a percentage of money	32.54	23.01	10.91	14.34	−1.11	−.49

period, United States per capita income was 76 percent higher than United Kingdom per capita income at the exchange rate than prevailing.[5]

The quantity of money in the United States rose much more than nominal income—to 358 instead of 134 times its level in 1873–78. This is the counterpart of the long-term downward trend in velocity so often noted. In the United Kingdom, on the other hand, the rise in money was less than the rise in income: fifty-five fold compared with sixty-seven-fold.

These divergent trends show up sharply in table 5.2. About 1876, the average United States resident held just under eleven weeks of income in money, the average United Kingdom resident just over thirty weeks; by 1974 the order was reversed, over twenty-nine weeks in the United States, under twenty-five weeks in the United Kingdom—a change in the United Kingdom–United States ratio by a factor of more than three to one.

Four items presumably explain the reversal in the recorded figures: differential changes in statistical errors, financial sophistication, real income, and cost of holding money.

5.1.1 Statistical Errors

The recorded figures overstate the size of the change that has occurred in the relative money-holding propensities of residents of the two countries. In both countries, the figures on the quantity of money (1) include domestic money held by foreigners as well as by residents, and (2) exclude foreign money held by residents.

Defect 1 makes all the recorded money figures too high. However, sterling was internationally held in the 1870s to a far greater extent than dollars were, whereas the reverse is almost surely true for recent years, so the overstatement on this score has risen for the United States and declined for the United Kingdom.

---

5. All rates of change cited throughout the book assume continuous compounding. The entries in columns 4 and 9 of table 5.1 are equal to 100 times the difference between natural logarithms of variables at terminal and initial dates divided by the number of years separating those dates. These continuously compounded rates of change are directly comparable (except for interest rates) to the rates of change computed from triplets of phases, since they are calculated from the slope of a least-squares line fitted to natural logarithms. The reason we make an exception for interest rates is discussed in section 6.6.1.

Note that the change in the exchange rate over the period is slightly greater than the difference in the movement of the price indexes used to deflate nominal income. As a result, the directly measured changes in real income differ a trifle less between the United Kingdom and the United States. Per capita real income, as measured directly, rose 5.5-fold in the United States from 1873–78 to 1973–75, or at the annual rate of 1.7 percent, and 3.3-fold in the United Kingdom between the corresponding phases, or at the annual rate of 1.2 percent. As a result, real income per capita in 1929 prices, converted to a common currency at the 1929 exchange rate, was only 1.70 times as high in the United States as in the United Kingdom, rather than the 1.76 times at the market exchange rate.

Defect 2 makes all the recorded money figures too low. However, United States residents undoubtedly held currency other than dollars (particularly of course sterling) in the 1870s to a far greater extent than United Kingdom residents held currency other than sterling, whereas the reverse is almost surely true for recent years, so the understatement on this score has declined for the United States and increased for the United Kingdom. Hence both defects make the recorded figures exaggerate the rise in United States money holdings relative to United Kingdom money holdings. We have no evidence on the precise size of this statistical error, but it can hardly account for more than a minor part of the major shift in the recorded figures.

5.1.2   Financial Sophistication

In the 1870s the United Kingdom was the world's financial center. It had the most sophisticated and well-developed financial institutions and was the world's banker. The world was said to be on a gold standard; it could better have been described as on a sterling standard. The United Kingdom was largely industrialized, and its agriculture was highly commercial. Only a bit over one-sixth of the male working force and one-eighth of the total working force, both male and female, was recorded as in agricultural occupations.[6] The "money economy" had spread widely if not yet to its outer limits.[7]

6. For percentage of males in agriculture in 1871, see B. R. Mitchell and Phyllis Deane, *Abstract of British Historical Statistics* (Cambridge: Cambridge University Press, 1962), p. 60; for percentage of labor force in agriculture in 1871, see Phyllis Deane and W. A. Cole, *British Economic Growth, 1888–1959: Trends and Structure* (Cambridge: Cambridge University Press, 1962), table 30, p. 142.

7. See Anand G. Chandavarkar, "Monetization of Developing Economies," *IMF Staff Papers* 34, no. 3 (November 1977): 665–721, for an extensive discussion of the role of monetization in the process of economic development, and for a survey of the literature and the empirical evidence on the subject.

Unfortunately, he devotes little attention to the aspect of monetization that is of primary interest for our purposes, namely, its effect on the demand for money. He devotes only one paragraph and one chart to the subject. In that paragraph, he fails to distinguish changes in the nominal quantity of money from changes in the real quantity of money, even though the paragraph is headed "Ratio of Money Supply to Nominal Income," and he dismisses the subject by asserting, "There is, in fact, no systematic observed relationship between money supply and the levels and rates of monetization or of development and national income. Thus, there is a valid distinction between an increase in the quantity of money and an enlargement of the sphere of money transactions" (p. 677). The second sentence is certainly correct, but its validity does not depend on the first, which is itself an ambiguous statement—though the accompanying chart does record the ratio of money supply to gross national product rather than simply money supply. In any event, the subject deserves much more careful study, which allows simultaneously for the effect of monetization and other variables and is careful to assure the comparability among countries of the aggregates labeled money supply.

It seems clear, on purely theoretical grounds, that, the relevant other things the same, in particular, the efficiency of the items included in "money" in rendering monetary services, the extension of the money economy will increase the real quantity of money demanded.

The United States, by contrast, though wealthier and more populous, was still financially backward, conducting its international trade largely in sterling. Nearly three-quarters of the population was classified as residing in rural areas, and half the working force (male and female) was still in agriculture.[8] Production for own use was widespread, and the "money economy" was still limited in scope.

These differences meant a much higher demand for money relative to income by United Kingdom than by United States residents.

By the 1970s the situation was very different. New York had become the financial capital of the world, and while the world had moved from what was said to be a gold exchange standard to what was said to be a regime of floating exchange rates, it could almost as well, and perhaps better, be described as on a dollar standard. London was still an extremely important financial center, but it had declined greatly in importance. The sterling area was a pale and rapidly disappearing reflection of the nineteenth-century British Empire.

Industrialization and the money economy had swept the United States. Only a quarter of the population was classified as residing in rural areas, and less than 5 percent of the working force was in agriculture.[9]

The changes in the United States raised the demand for money, perhaps substantially. The effects of the changes in the United Kingdom are less clear. As noted, the alteration in its international position clearly lowered demand—at least as reflected in the kind of figures we have available. But domestically the remaining pockets of nonmoney activity must have shrunk, and the banking system continued to spread—by the 1970s there were five times as many bank branches as in the 1870s.[10]

The changing relative financial sophistication of the United States and the United Kingdom must have had its major effect during the first part of the century our data cover. World War I was a major watershed. The United States banking system had been growing rapidly before World War I. The war added a further fillip and in addition produced a major expansion in the role of the United States in the world's financial system. From 1880 to 1910, United States population nearly doubled, but the number of banks multiplied more than sevenfold.[11] The fraction of the population residing in rural areas had declined from over two-thirds to only a bit over one-half; the fraction of the work force in agriculture had

8. *Historical Statistics*, ser. A-57, A-69, D-167, D-170.

9. *Historical Statistics*, ser. A-57, A-69; United States Bureau of the Census, *Statistical Abstract*, 100th ed. (1979), p. 403.

10. Estimate for 1870s based on sources for column 1, table 4.9 above; for 1970s, see *Britain 1979: An Official Handbook*, Central Office of Information (London: HMSO, 1979), p. 344.

11. Number of United States banks in 1880 was 3,355; in 1910, 25,151 (*Historical Statistics*, ser. X-580, pp. 1019–20).

declined from one-half to less than one-third.[12] The United States was still far less urbanized and far more rural than the United Kingdom—which by 1911 had only 8 percent of its working force in agriculture[13]—but the difference was much smaller than in the 1870s.

This judgment is supported by the behavior of velocity in the United Kingdom and the United States over the century—plotted in Chart 5.2 and discussed at greater length in section 5.2. The wide difference in velocity in the 1870s was largely erased by 1905, and thereafter velocity is not very different in the two countries until after World War II. Put in the terms we have been using, in the cycle phase 1904–7, which is dated the same in the two countries, money balances amounted to 23.6 weeks' income in the United States, to 28.3 weeks in the United Kingdom—far closer together than thirty years earlier. In the cycle phase 1920–21, after the end of World War I, the difference was much the same: 25.7 weeks' income in the United States, 31.3 in the United Kingdom.

In both 1906 and 1920, real income in the United States was higher than in the United Kingdom. One would expect on this score that real balances expressed in weeks of income would be higher in the United States than in the United Kingdom if financial sophistication were the same, since most of the evidence suggests that the elasticity of demand for money with respect to real per capita income in the United States has been greater than unity. In 1906 interest rates were decidedly higher in the United States than in the United Kingdom, which would tend to offset the effect of higher income, but in 1920 there was not much difference in interest rates. The lower cash balances in the United States than in the United Kingdom, both in 1906 and 1920, even if by nothing like so much as in 1880, presumably means that there was still some residual difference in financial sophistication between the two countries.

Nonetheless, the more than doubling of real balances expressed in weeks of income in the United States in the course of the three decades from 1876 to 1906, during which United Kingdom balances fell by 7 percent, suggests that the change in relative financial sophistication of the United Kingdom and the United States from 1880 to 1906 was probably by all odds the single most important factor accounting for the divergent trends in real balances.

5.1.3 Real Income

Our earlier research indicates that the real quantity of money demanded generally rises in greater proportion than real income—the income elasticity of demand for money is greater than unity—and this conclusion is on the whole confirmed for the United States by the analysis

12. See footnote 8, above.

13. Deane and Cole, *British Economic Growth*, p. 142; Feinstein, *National Income*, table 60, p. T131, gives figures for 1911 that amount to 11 percent in agriculture.

in chapter 6 below, though not for the United Kingdom. If this is so, the rise in per capita real income in both countries should have raised the level of money balances relative to income in the United States but not in the United Kingdom.

5.1.4   Cost of Holding Money

The cost of holding money instead of holding other assets expressed in nominal terms tends to be higher, the higher are interest rates on such other assets. Here there is a sharp contrast between the United States and the United Kingdom, itself one of the consequences of changes discussed in section 5.1.2. In 1876 the United States was a debtor and borrowing country and the United Kingdom was a creditor and lending country; accordingly, interest rates were relatively high in the United States and relatively low in the United Kingdom. In 1974 the situation was reversed. Figures extracted from tables 5.7 and 5.8 for the initial and terminal phases (table 5.3) highlight this contrast. Interest rates were two to four percentage points higher in the United States in the initial phase than in the United Kingdom, two to six percentage points lower in the terminal phase. Interest rates were higher in both countries at the terminal than at the initial phase, but the difference was far greater in the United Kingdom than in the United States.[14]

These interest rate changes presumably lowered the level of money balances demanded relative to income in both countries, but more so in the United Kingdom than in the United States. The interest rate changes therefore reinforced the effect of differential changes in statistical errors, financial sophistication, and real income. All four factors worked to raise United States real money balances relative to United Kingdom real money balances.

This comparison between the United States and the United Kingdom and this interpretation of their differential experience helps resolve a major problem that has arisen about the interpretation of the secular decline in velocity in the United States: how much of that decline, if any, to attribute to the corresponding rise in real income, and how much to

14. These results indicate that the change in the international position of the two countries was more important than their different price experiences. In 1876 the United States had experienced a much sharper price fall in the preceding fifteen years than the United Kingdom, and in 1974, a slower rate of price rise in the preceding two decades. Hence at both dates the expected rate of price rise might have been expected to have been lower in the United States than in the United Kingdom. By itself this would be expected to make interest rates lower in the United States at both dates, whereas they were decidedly higher in 1880. Of course, the change in the international position of the two countries reflects partly a change in the internal productivity of capital. In 1876 the real yield of capital in the United States was presumably very high, much higher than the United Kingdom at the time and probably higher than in the United States in 1974.

For a more detailed analysis of the relation between United States and United Kingdom interest rates before 1914, see section 10.4.

Table 5.3   **United States and United Kingdom Interest Rates in Initial and Terminal Phases**

	United States				United Kingdom	
Phase	Call Money Rate	Commercial Paper Rate	Basic Yield on Long-Term Bonds	Yield on High-Grade Corporate Bonds	Rate on Three-Month Bank Bills	Yield on Consols
Initial phase[a]	4.60	5.86	5.59	7.05	2.89	3.16
Terminal phase[b]	9.56	8.54	7.79	7.97	11.79	13.85

(spanning header: *Interest Rates* over United States and United Kingdom)

[a]1873–78 for United States; 1874–79 for United Kingdom.
[b]1973–75 for both United States and United Kingdom.

attribute to the changing financial structure. In the absence of any quantitative estimate of the latter effect, we have tended to attribute the decline in velocity to the rise in income.[15] But this interpretation yields elasticities of demand for money with respect to real per capita income for the earlier decades that are higher than for later decades and that are generally higher than the values obtained for other countries or from cross-sectional data.[16]

The comparison with the United Kingdom suggests that our earlier work overestimates the income elasticity for the earlier periods because we did not allow for the effect of the changing financial structure of the economy.[17]

In chapter 6 we explore the effect of increasing financial sophistication in more detail and devise a procedure for adjusting our money estimates for the United States for this effect. The adjusted money stock figures are given in table 5.7, though for the balance of this chapter we use the unadjusted figures.

The magnitude of the effect can be seen by a comparison of real per capita money balances on an unadjusted and adjusted basis in the 1873–78 phase with the single estimate for 1973–75:

Period	Real per Capita Money Balances	
	Unadjusted	Adjusted
1873–78	$60	$118
1973–75	$873	
Percent per year change	2.72	2.03

15. M. Friedman, *The Demand for Money: Some Theoretical and Empirical Results*, NBER Occasional Paper 68 (New York: NBER, 1959), p. 3 (reprinted from *Journal of Political Economy* 67 (August 1959):327–51; reprinted in *The Optimum Quantity of Money* (Chicago: Aldine, 1969), pp. 111–39; M. Friedman and A. J. Schwartz, "Money and Business Cycles," *Review of Economics and Statistics* 45, suppl. (February 1963): 44; idem, *A Monetary History of the United States, 1867–1960* (Princeton: Princeton University Press for NBER, 1963), pp. 679, 682.

16. E. L. Feige, *The Demand for Liquid Assets: A Temporal Cross Section Analysis* (Englewood Cliffs, N.J.: Prentice-Hall, 1964); idem, "Alternative Temporal Cross-Section Specifications of the Demand for Demand Deposits," in *Issues in Monetary Economics*, ed. H.G. Johnson and A. R. Nobay (London: Oxford University Press, 1974); D. Laidler, "The Influence of Money on Economic Activity: A Survey of Some Current Problems," in *Monetary Theory and Policy in the 1970s*, ed. G. Clayton, J.C. Gilbert, and R. Sedgwick (London: Oxford University Press, 1971), pp. 75–135; J. V. Deaver, "The Chilean Inflation and the Demand for Money," in *Varieties of Monetary Experience*, ed. D. Meiselman (Chicago: University of Chicago Press, 1970), pp. 16–21. See also M. D. Bordo and L. Jonung, "The Long-Run Behavior of Money in Five Advanced Countries, 1870–1975," *Economic Inquiry* 19 (January 1981): 96–116.

17. This suggestion has been made before by a number of reviewers of our *Monetary History*. In particular, see the comment by James Tobin, "The Monetary Interpretation of History," *American Economic Review* 55 (June 1965): 464–85.

About one-quarter of the annual rate of change over a century can apparently be accounted for by an improvement in financial sophistication over roughly the first quarter of that century—since we have not adjusted our monetary estimates after 1903. Clearly, improved financial sophistication was of major significance.

One minor but rather interesting feature brought out by table 5.2 is the divergent behavior of currency. In both the United Kingdom and the United States, the ratio of currency to the stock of money declined, but the decline was much sharper in the United States than in the United Kingdom—in the United States, from 33 percent in 1873–78 to 11 percent in 1973–75; in the United Kingdom, from 23 percent in 1874–79 to 14 percent in 1973–75. In the United States, the decline was produced primarily by a rapid increase in deposits relative to income. The amount of currency expressed in weeks of income declined only slightly from 3.6 weeks' income to 3.2. In the United Kingdom, by contrast, the amount of currency declined substantially, from 7.0 weeks to 3.6 weeks.

The sharper decline in the ratio of currency to money in the United States than in the United Kingdom is presumably another aspect of the growing financial sophistication of the United States relative to the United Kingdom. The spread of banking in the United States, the greater accessibility of banks, and the greater familiarity with their use enabled the public to satisfy its increased money-holding propensities entirely with deposits. This development reached its zenith in 1929, when currency had fallen to 2.4 weeks' income. The subsequent bank failures, and then the war, caused a return to wider use of currency until currency rose to nearly 8 weeks' income at the end of World War II, nearly twice the highest level ever attained before 1929. Currency holdings then declined back to 3.2 weeks' income by 1973–75.

A more puzzling feature is that both at the beginning and the end of the period, the use of currency was higher in the United Kingdom than in the United States—nearly twice as high at the beginning, 12 percent higher at the end. The lower interest rates in the United Kingdom than in the United States at the beginning of the period would make for higher currency holdings, but if this were the whole of the explanation the higher interest rates in the United Kingdom than in the United States at the end of the period should have produced the opposite result. The changing interest rates may explain why the differential between the United States and the United Kingdom narrowed; it cannot explain the consistently higher level in the United Kingdom.

This subject needs much more attention than we have given it. Our offhand inclination is to attribute the difference between the United Kingdom and the United States to two major factors: (1) the greater social stratification in the United Kingdom than in the United States, which produces a corresponding stratification of individuals having and using checking accounts; (2) different legal arrangements that make the penalty for writing a "bad" check less stringent and sure in the United Kingdom.[18]

So far we have compared the state of affairs in the two countries at the beginning and end of the century we cover. Another way to summarize the developments during that period is in terms of average rates of change as measured by the slopes of semilog trends fitted to the phase averages.

We can use the framework of the quantity equation for this purpose, as expanded by expressing real income as the product of population and real income per capita, or, to repeat equation (4) of chapter 2,

(1) $$MV = PNy ,$$

where M is the aggregate nominal amount of money; V is velocity; P, the price level; N, population; and y, real income per capita.

Taking logarithms of both sides of equation (1) gives

(2) $$\log M + \log V = \log P + \log N + \log y.$$

Differentiate with respect to time:

(3) $$\frac{1}{M}\frac{dM}{dt} + \frac{1}{V}\frac{dV}{dt} = \frac{1}{P}\frac{dP}{dt} + \frac{1}{N}\frac{dN}{dt} + \frac{1}{y}\frac{dy}{dt} ,$$

or in the notation introduced in chapter 2,

$$g_M + g_V = g_P + g_N + g_y .$$

We thus add rates of change, instead of multiplying levels. In these terms we have

---

18. We have observed that there is a fairly clear demarcation between countries in which checks are and countries in which checks are not widely used by people in many walks of life. This demarcation is not by stage of economic development. For example, checks are little used in Greece and Japan, widely used in Thailand, Israel, and Taiwan. One conjecture that we have formed is that the difference reflects a different legal situation with respect to "bad" checks. In the United States, trying to "pass" a "bad" check is a criminal offense. This encourages the widespread use of checks since, in effect, it reduces the risk and cost of collection. In countries like Greece, passing a bad check is a civil offense. The writer of the check can be sued for damages but is not liable to criminal prosecution. This discourages the use of checks and encourages the use of cash.

Our impression is that the legal situation in the United Kingdom is closer to that described as applying to Greece than to that in the United States. But whether this be the explanation or not, it is clear that checks are much less widely used in the United Kingdom than in the United States. In 1978 fewer than half of United Kingdom adults had any kind of account at a commercial bank; in the United States, 75 percent had checking accounts in 1970. George Katona et al., *1970 Survey of Consumer Finances*, University of Michigan Survey Research Center, Institute for Social Research, table 6-1, p. 98; article by Robert D. Hershey, Jr., *New York Times*, 28 January 1978.

Percent per year change in	*United States*	*United Kingdom*
M	5.87	3.97
V	− 0.96	+ 0.07
Y = nominal income	4.91	4.04
P	1.77	2.34
N	1.50	0.58
y	1.64	1.12

In both countries, the change in the quantity of money clearly domi-nated the change in nominal income—exceeding the income change in the United States because of the sizable decline in velocity; differing trivially in the United Kingdom because of the trivial change in velocity. Both money change and income change were decidedly higher in the United States than in the United Kingdom.

On the other side of the quantity equation, the similar rate of change of prices reflects the international linkage between the two countries and the constant rate of exchange for about half of the period (1879–1914, 1925–31). The faster rise in the United Kingdom than in the United States is the counterpart of the depreciation of the pound sterling relative to the dollar after 1931, and then again after World War II. Both population and real income grew less rapidly in the United Kingdom, much more than offsetting the more rapid rate of price rise, so nominal income rose only four-fifths as fast—4.0 compared with 4.9 percent.

As noted, the differential behavior of velocity reinforced the effect of the slower rate of rise in nominal income in the United Kingdom, so that the quantity of money rose only two-thirds as rapidly (instead of four-fifths, like income) in the United Kingdom as in the United States.

The changes we have summarized in this section did not of course proceed evenly. Section 5.2 describes the fluctuations of the levels of the various series around their trends, and section 5.3, of the rates of change.

5.2 Long Swings in the Levels of Money, Income, and Prices

Chart 5.1 plots the phase values of the nominal money stock at the middates of the corresponding phases for the United States and the United Kingdom. (The numerical values except for the United States money stock before 1902 are given in tables 5.7 and 5.8, sec. 5.5.)

For both countries, the phase values for the nominal money stock show long undulating movements about the semilog straight-line trends plotted on the chart.

U.S. billions of dollars
U.K. billions of pounds sterling

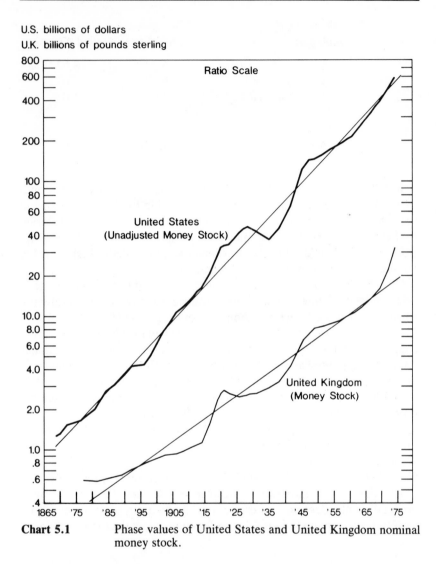

Chart 5.1   Phase values of United States and United Kingdom nominal
money stock.

For the United States, we have discussed in detail in *A Monetary History* the proximate reasons for these movements in the stock of money: the initial relatively slow rate of growth and the speeding up around 1880 reflect preparation for resumption and then the aftermath of resumption; the sharp retardation in the 1890s reflects the monetary disturbances associated with the agitation for free silver; the subsequent acceleration beginning around 1895 is partly a reaction to these disturbances, partly a result of the worldwide expansion in gold supplies following new discoveries and the practical application of the cyanide process in extracting gold from low-grade ore; the mild retardation after about 1905 reflects the end of the reaction to the earlier stagnation in an environment in which gold production continued at a fairly rapid rate; the rapid acceleration after 1913 and then sharp retardation reflect World War I monetary expansion and the postwar tight money policy that the Federal Reserve System imposed in 1920; the absolute decline after 1928 reflects the monetary collapse associated with the Great Contraction that terminated in the banking holiday of 1933; the subsequent rapid rate of growth was speeded up even more by the financing of World War II, which was followed by a distinct slowing up until about 1960, when monetary expansion accelerated.

It is a striking sign of the close financial links among major countries that the United States and United Kingdom figures show such similar patterns. World Wars I and II and their postwar aftermaths leave a similar imprint on the charts for the two countries and produce undulations that have a close family resemblance. Yet there are also important differences that mirror the different internal experiences of the two countries.

1. The sharp retardation of growth in the United States money stock in the 1890s has no counterpart in the United Kingdom data, just as the agitation for free silver that produced the United States retardation had no counterpart in the United Kingdom.

2. Despite the worldwide expansion of gold production after the 1890s, United Kingdom monetary growth slows down in the early 1900s and only starts accelerating after about 1907. This reversal of the United States pattern is almost certainly a consequence of that pattern, though it very likely was reinforced by the effect of the Boer War on the United Kingdom balance of payments. As the rapid United States expansion generated balance of payments surpluses and attracted gold, the United Kingdom had to surrender gold—or, more accurately, was able to attract an inordinately small share of newly mined gold. The resulting retardation in United Kingdom monetary growth is the other side of the acceleration in United States monetary growth. Then, as the United States experienced retardation, the United Kingdom was able to join the worldwide acceleration.

3. In World War I, the money stock rose slightly less in the United States than in the United Kingdom—from the phase centered on 1914 to the phase centered on 1920 the stock of money rose 105 percent in the United States and 126 percent in the United Kingdom. There was no corresponding difference in the growth of nominal income, which rose 125 percent in the United States and 123 percent in the United Kingdom. However, the further breakdown between prices and output was very different. In the United States, prices rose 81 percent and output rose 25

percent; in the United Kingdom, prices rose 141 percent, while output actually fell by 8 percent.

4. The much greater rise in United Kingdom than in United States prices plus the determination of the United Kingdom to return to gold at the prewar parity produced a striking difference in the postwar behavior of the money supply. After a mild retardation attributable to the immediate postwar deflation, the United States money stock continued to rise at roughly its long period trend rate until the onset of the Great Depression. The United Kingdom money stock declined sharply until 1925 as part of the deflationary policy that preceded Britain's return to gold. It then started to rise, though at a very slow rate, until 1930.

This pattern in the United Kingdom reproduces, though on a condensed time scale and about a much flatter trend, the behavior of the United States money stock after the Civil War. The decline relative to trend in the United States money stock from 1865 to 1879,[19] when the United States returned to gold at the pre–Civil War parity, is the counterpart of the absolute decline in the United Kingdom money stock from 1920 to 1925, when the United Kingdom returned to gold at the pre–World War I parity. The acceleration of monetary growth in the United States after 1879 is the counterpart of the slower acceleration in the United Kingdom after 1925.

5. The United States money stock falls sharply from the phase centered on 1928.5 to the phase centered on 1935.0. The United Kingdom money stock accelerates its rate of growth after the phase centered on 1931. The reason is clearly that the United Kingdom departed from gold in September 1931 and the United States not until March 1933. As a result, the contraction came to an end in the United Kingdom earlier than in the United States and was nothing like so severe (as we shall see below, the behavior of income parallels that of the money stock in both countries).

6. In World War II, the money stock rose more rapidly in the United States than in the United Kingdom—the opposite of the relation in World War I. From the phase centered on 1938 to the phase centered on 1949, the money stock rose 224 percent in the United States and only 152 percent in the United Kingdom. Nominal income shows a parallel difference, rising by 174 percent in the United States and by 111 percent in the United Kingdom. This time the whole of the difference in the rise in nominal income is accounted for by a different behavior of real income, and none by prices. In both countries, prices rose by nearly 80 percent, but this price rise was accompanied by a more than 50 percent increase in

19. Though we have reasonably accurate estimates only from 1869 on, other evidence suggests that the decline dates from 1865.

output in the United States and by less than a 20 percent increase in the United Kingdom.

7. The most fascinating feature about the post–World War II behavior is the close similarity in the rate and pattern of monetary growth, except for the much sharper acceleration in the final phases in the United Kingdom than in the United States. In both countries, monetary growth accelerated slightly in the early fifties during the Korean War, then slowed down, then speeded up appreciably after 1960. For a time this final acceleration was more marked in the United States than in the United Kingdom, but then the United Kingdom took the lead—if that is the right word—with a decisive spurt at a rate comparable to the prior record in World War I.

The main postwar pattern in both countries, as table 5.4 brings out, is an acceleration in money in the double sense of a rising rate of growth and also a shortening of the length of the successive step-ups in growth, though the first step does average out the acceleration and retardation associated with the Korean War. In both countries, nominal income at first rose more rapidly than money—the counterpart of the postwar rebound in velocity—but then, in the third period, the reverse occurred as velocity fell. The result was a less rapid acceleration in nominal income growth than in money growth, but a decided acceleration nonetheless, except only between the first two periods for the United Kingdom.

The most interesting feature of the postwar experience is the division of the nominal change between prices and output. The percentage absorbed by prices was consistently higher in the United Kingdom. In both countries it was roughly the same in the first two periods, but it rose even more sharply in the final period than did the rate of growth of nominal income, with the result that while output growth rose between the first two periods, it fell between the second and third. This is the much discussed postwar shift in the empirical Phillips curve, to which we shall return in chapter 9.[20]

Given the appreciable differences between the two countries in the long-term movement of the nominal money stock, do these differences leave their imprint on the long-term movements of nominal income? Panel 1 of chart 5.2 gives a clear affirmative answer. The striking feature of this chart is that the movements in nominal income differ between the two countries in the same way as the movements in money. In each country separately the undulations in nominal income mirror to a re- markable degree the undulations in the stock of money.

In the United States, the trend in money is steeper than in income; in the United Kingdom they are roughly the same. However, this apparent

20. M. Friedman, "Inflation and Unemployment" (Nobel Lecture), *Journal of Political Economy* 85 (June 1977): 451–72.

Table 5.4   Rates of Change of Money, Income, Prices, and Output in Three Post–World War II Periods, United States and United Kingdom

Period	Duration (in Years)	Rate of Change (Annual Percentage)				Percentage of Nominal Income Change Accounted for by Price Change
		Money g_M	Nominal Income g_Y	Price Level g_P	Output $g_{y'}$	
United States						
1948-60	12	3.62	5.90	2.20	3.71	37.3
1960-69	9	6.96	7.20	2.73	4.47	37.9
1969-75	6	8.39	7.92	5.80	2.12	73.2
United Kingdom						
1951-60	9	2.12	6.42	4.05	2.37	63.1
1960-68	8	4.39	6.37	3.72	2.65	58.4
1968-75	7	12.31	10.87	8.95	1.92	82.3

U.S. billions of dollars
U.K. billions of pounds sterling

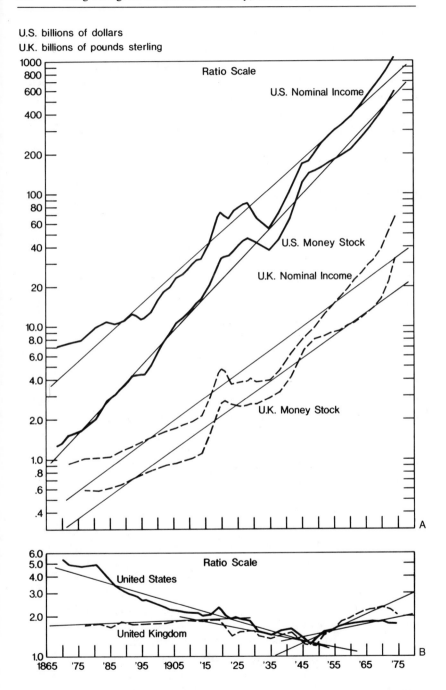

Chart 5.2   Phase values of United States and United Kingdom nominal income and nominal money stock and velocity.

difference conceals a similarity. In both countries, the trend in money is steeper than that in income from World War I to the end of World War II, and much less steep thereafter. This is the phenomenon discussed in section 5.1; it is reflected in the downward trend in United States velocity to the end of World War II, and the upward trend thereafter (panel 2 of chart 5.2), and in the roughly horizontal trend in United Kingdom velocity to World War I, the downward trend to the end of World War II, and the upward trend thereafter.

The undulations about the trends are, however, common to money and income, as is clear from the greater steadiness of the velocity series in each country than of either the money or the income series. In neither country does either the money or the income series have an appreciable movement that does not have a counterpart in the other—with one possible exception, already referred to, which interestingly enough is the same for the two countries. That exception is for roughly the decade of the 1950s. In both countries, income rose decidedly faster during the 1950s than money—that is, velocity rose sharply rather than falling as it had for most of the prior seven decades in the United States and rather than remaining stable or falling as it had for the prior eight decades in the United Kingdom. But this exception is temporary. In the decade of the sixties, money and income resumed their parallel movement in the United States and came much closer to parallelism in the United Kingdom.

The velocity series highlights the discrepancies between the undulations in the money and income series. One fascinating feature of the velocity series for the two countries is their extraordinary similarity, especially after 1905, when the sharp fall in United States velocity relative to United Kingdom velocity came to an end (see panel 2 of chart 5.2).

From 1905 on, a single description will suffice for both countries: velocity rose in the later stages of the World War I period, then declined, recovering slightly in the 1920s; velocity fell sharply in the Great Contraction, rose again at the beginning of World War II, fell sharply during the war, rose sharply thereafter to the middle or late sixties, then fell moderately. The only major difference after 1905 is the greater amplitude of the post–World War II movements in the United Kingdom than in the United States.

The two war periods are especially intriguing—in the first, velocity rose and in the second velocity fell, alike in the two countries. Presumably, this reversal must have reflected other differences that were also common to the two countries. Similarly, velocity rose sharply after World War II in both countries. One explanation offered for the United States has been the rapid growth of shares in savings and loan associations, which nearly quadrupled between 1950 and 1960, going from a total equal to about 9 percent of the money stock to nearly 30 percent.[21] The United Kingdom experienced a similar phenomenon: building societies' shares and deposits roughly tripled over the corresponding period, rising from a total equal to 14 percent of the money stock to 35 percent.[22] This common rapid expansion may have had different sources in the two countries (e.g., there was no development in the United Kingdom comparable to the extension in the United States in 1950 to savings and loan shares of insurance provisions identical with those for commercial bank deposits), but the occurrence of the same phenomenon in both, along with a similar behavior of velocity, adds to the evidence that this explanation has merit. We analyze these features of the behavior of velocity in greater detail in chapters 6 and 7 below.

The changes in the money and income series in chart 5.2 can be regarded as the composite of changes in prices and in real magnitudes, and the latter, in turn, of changes in population and per capita real magnitudes. Of these three components, population behaves most smoothly (see chart 5.3 and table 5.5). For both countries, population accounts for an appreciable part of the trend in the aggregate series but for a trivial part of the undulations about the trend.

The trend of prices is very different before and after 1914. The period before 1914, taken as a whole, is a period of roughly stable prices in both countries, though of course with considerable variation about the trend. The period after 1914, on the other hand, is a period of rising prices in both countries, interrupted only during the interwar period. For the post-1914 period as a whole, the rate of rise averages over 2 percent in the United States, 3 percent in the United Kingdom. This post-1914 price trend accounts for less than 40 percent of the total trend in nominal income and the nominal money stock in the United States, but for more than 60 percent in the United Kingdom, the steeper United Kingdom price trend being reinforced by a flatter trend in both population and per capita real magnitudes.

The different trend in prices before and after 1914 is not matched by any corresponding difference in the trend of real output per capita. In both the United Kingdom and the United States, per capita output has a slightly higher trend rate after 1914 than before: in the United States, 1.8 versus 1.6; in the United Kingdom, 1.5 versus 1.2. Because population grew more slowly in both countries after 1914, the slightly more rapid trend rate of growth in per capita output is converted into a slower rate of growth in total output in both countries after 1914 than before. The most

21. M. Friedman and A. J. Schwartz, *Monetary Statistics of the United States*, table 1, cols. 7 and 10, pp. 40–47.

22. D. K. Sheppard, *The Growth and Role of U.K. Financial Institutions, 1880–1962* (London: Methuen, 1971), table (A)2.4, p. 151, and table 4.9, above.

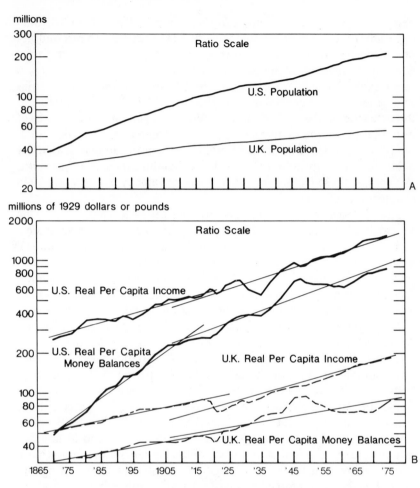

Chart 5.3   Phase values of United States and United Kingdom population, per capita real income and money, and prices and money stock per unit of output.

interesting feature of chart 5.3 and table 5.5, however, is what they say about the variability of various magnitudes about the trend.

Most important, nominal money is, with one exception (pre-1914 for the United Kingdom), less variable than nominal income, though per capita real money is uniformly more variable than per capita real income. This apparent contradiction is in fact wholly consistent with the theoretical analysis of chapter 2—as reflected for example in chart 2.3. That analysis suggests that a maintained change in the rate of change of money will ultimately produce an equal maintained change in the rate of change of nominal income and prices, but that, in the transition, the rate of

index 1929=100

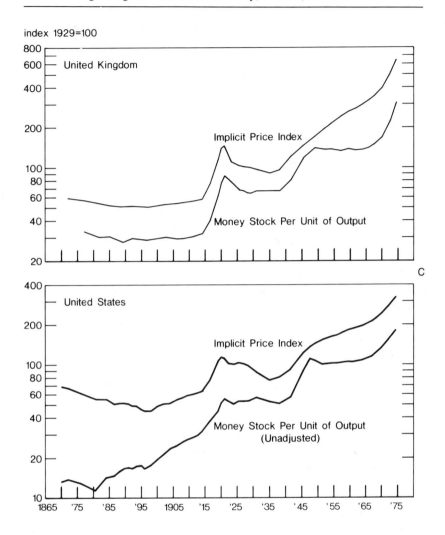

change of both nominal income and prices must overshoot in order to raise nominal income and prices to new levels consistent with an altered desired velocity—a higher rate of monetary growth raising desired velocity, a lower rate lowering desired velocity.

The effect is to produce a wider amplitude of movement in nominal income and prices than in nominal money—which is precisely what table 5.5 shows, with two minor exceptions (the lower variability of income than of money in the United Kingdom pre-1914 and of prices than of money in the United States after 1914). The wider fluctuations in prices than in money produce a negative relation between fluctuations in nominal balances and real balances—which is precisely what is required for the standard deviation of the fluctuations about the trend to be smaller for the logarithm of money than for one or more of its components, the logarithm of real balances and the logarithm of prices.[23] Because they can be reflected positively in nominal income as well as negatively in real income, the wider fluctuations in prices than in money need not produce as numerically large a negative correlation between the fluctuations in prices and output as between fluctuations in nominal and real balances, and may even be consistent with a positive correlation between prices and output; hence the standard deviation of the nominal income fluctuations can be larger than in any of its components, as it is except for the United Kingdom before 1914. Finally, the same reasoning explains why real balances uniformly fluctuate more widely about trend than output.

Another striking feature of the measures of variability in table 5.5 is that every magnitude is more variable for both countries after 1914 than before. This feature is closely related to the preceding. First, price fluctuations play a dominant role in the long-period undulations of the nominal magnitudes about trend. Population and output are constrained by physical limits. There are no such limits for prices—as has been demonstrated most dramatically in hyperinflations when prices have risen astronomically. That is why commodity standards such as gold or silver standards have emerged or been adopted—to provide physical limits to the stock of money. Second, price fluctuations have indirect effects that infect real magnitudes, both real balances, for reasons already indicated, and output, because wider price fluctuations increase uncertainty and instability. Third, from 1879 to 1914, the gold standard operated largely unchecked in both the United States and the United Kingdom. It limited the range of fluctuations in prices and hence in all magnitudes in table 5.5—though even then prices varied more than either real balances or output per capita. The widest fluctuations in prices in both the United States and the United Kingdom occurred when the physical limit imposed by a gold standard was absent or relatively ineffective—the sharp collapse in prices in in the United States from the Civil War to 1879 and the major rises in both countries during the two world wars, and in the United Kingdom after World War II. The post-1914 period is more variable than the pre-1914 period because it is the period when commodity standards were replaced by fiduciary or fiat standards and no effective substitute developed for the physical limits imposed by a commodity standard.

23. Recall that

$$\sigma_{X+Y}^2 = \sigma_X^2 + \sigma_Y^2 + 2r_{XY}\sigma_X\sigma_Y,$$

so that unless r_{XY} is negative, σ_{X+Y}^2 must be larger than either σ_x^2 or σ_Y^2 ; and it may be larger even though r_{XY} is negative, provided the absolute value of the correlation is low enough.

Insofar as the quantity of money demanded is negatively affected by the variability of prices (see sec. 2.4.1, point 4), the shift from a commodity to a fiduciary or fiat standard presumably was a factor tending to raise velocity in both countries, but it clearly was not a dominant factor, at least between the two wars.

The importance of prices for the long-period undulations in nominal magnitudes is of great significance for the understanding of economic developments. In particular, it means that the long swings in monetary magnitudes to which so much attention has been devoted are largely a price phenomenon, which has important implications for their explanation. We shall return to this matter in chapter 11.

Chart 5.3 contains one series not so far discussed; money stock per unit of output, a ratio of money stock to real income in 1929 dollars. If the quantity theory held in its most rigid and extreme form, so that the velocity of money was numerically an unchanging constant, prices and the quantity of money per unit of output would be strictly proportional to one another, the proportionality factor being the reciprocal of the velocity of money.[24] Except for the differences in the trend of prices and of the quantity of money per unit of output, the rigid relation comes very close indeed to being realized for both countries. The movements in the two series about their trends mirror one another faithfully, except for the one episode referred to earlier—the decade of the 1950s, when the sharply rising velocity in both countries is reflected in the opening up of a widening gap between prices and money per unit of output.

5.3 Rates of Change of Money, Income, and Prices

As we noted in chapter 3, rates of change provide an alternative, and frequently superior, way to isolate fluctuations about trends.

Chart 5.4 is the counterpart of chart 5.2, except that it plots rates of change rather than absolute levels. (Except for the United States money stock and velocity before 1902, the numerical values are given in tables 5.9 and 5.10.) It brings out even more strikingly the high degree of consilience between the movements in the quantity of money and in nominal income we remarked on in discussing chart 5.2. Rates of change are notoriously erratic. Yet there is scarcely a movement of any size in the money series that does not have its counterpart in the income series, and conversely. Out of forty-eight successive movements in the rates of

---

24. From equation (4) in chapter 2,

$$\frac{M}{y'} = \frac{1}{V}\,P,$$

where $\frac{M}{y'}$ is the quantity of money per unit of output.

Table 5.5   **Components of Trends and Fluctuations about Trend in Money Stock and Income**
United States: 1873–1975, 1873–1914, and 1914–75
United Kingdom: 1874–1975, 1874–1914, and 1914–75

	Trend					
	United States Annual Percentage					
	1873–1975		1873–1914		1914–75	
Component	Money	Income	Money	Income	Money	Income
1. Population	1.50		2.01		1.29	
2. Real magnitude per capita	2.60	1.64	4.01	1.57	2.07	1.83
3. Prices	1.77		0.039		2.08	
4. Nominal aggregate	5.87	4.91	6.06	3.62	5.44	5.20

	Fluctuations about Trend					
	United States Standard Deviation of Deviations from Trend (Percentage)					
	1873–1975		1873–1914		1914–75	
	Money	Income	Money	Income	Money	Income
5. Population	5.20		1.16		2.30	
6. Real magnitude per capita	16.34	8.60	6.50	5.78	11.76	9.31
7. Prices	20.78		10.47		18.60	
8. Interaction among components	[−20.86]	[6.79]	[−9.46]	[3.59]	[−11.08]	[16.13]
9. Nominal aggregate	17.05	24.06	7.98	12.54	19.15	26.42

Sources:
Lines 1, 2, 3, 4: Slopes of semilogarithmic trends fitted to indicated magnitudes.
Lines 5, 6, 7, 9: Standard deviations of the deviations of the logarithms of the magnitudes in question from a semilogarithmic trend.
Line 8: If $U = X + Y + Z$ (e.g., log money = log population + log per capita real money + log prices), then

$$\sigma_U = [\sigma_X^2 + \sigma_Y^2 + \sigma_Z^2 + 2r_{XY}\sigma_X\sigma_Y + 2r_{XZ}\sigma_X\sigma_Z + 2r_{YZ}\sigma_Y\sigma_Z]^{1/2}.$$

change for the United States and thirty-four for the United Kingdom, forty-one in the United States and twenty-five in the United Kingdom are in the same direction in both series, some of the exceptions involve movements that are small in magnitude, five of the seven exceptions for the United States and five of the nine exceptions for the United Kingdom are during World War II and the early postwar period, and two of the remaining four exceptions for the United Kingdom are connected with

Trend					
United Kingdom Annual Percentage					
1874–1975		1874–1914		1914–75	
Money	Income	Money	Income	Money	Income
0.58		0.87		0.45	
1.05	1.12	0.97	1.16	0.98	1.50
2.34		0.049		3.00	
3.97	4.04	1.90	2.08	4.42	4.95

Fluctuations about Trend					
United Kingdom Standard Deviation of Deviations from Trend (Percentage)					
1874–1975		1874–1914		1914–75	
Money	Income	Money	Income	Money	Income
2.85		0.29		0.49	
11.65	9.30	4.08	3.22	14.23	7.53
26.50		4.80		23.11	
[−19.31]	[3.46]	[−4.51]	[−4.31]	[−20.17]	[6.86]
21.75	28.44	4.41	3.86	18.17	25.26

Because the sum in the bracket is based on a sum of squares, it must be positive. The square root of that sum (times 100) is given in line 9. Similarly, the first three terms in the bracket must also be positive, and their square roots are given in lines 5, 6, and 7. However, the remaining terms may be positive or negative, and so may their sum. Strictly speaking, when it is, its square root is imaginary. Instead, in order to indicate the size and the direction of the interaction, we have changed the sign of such negative sums, extracted the square root, and then designated the square root by a minus sign. That is why we have entered the numbers in the table in brackets.

World War I. In both countries, once the wartime readjustments were completed, the relation returned to its prewar closeness.

For the United States, the first sizable discrepancy in movement is from the triplet of phases centered on 1878–82 to the triplet centered on 1882–85, when the money series rises and the income series declines. We are inclined to attribute this discrepancy to the effect of resumption which, by linking the dollar to gold, presumably raised the demand for

percent per year

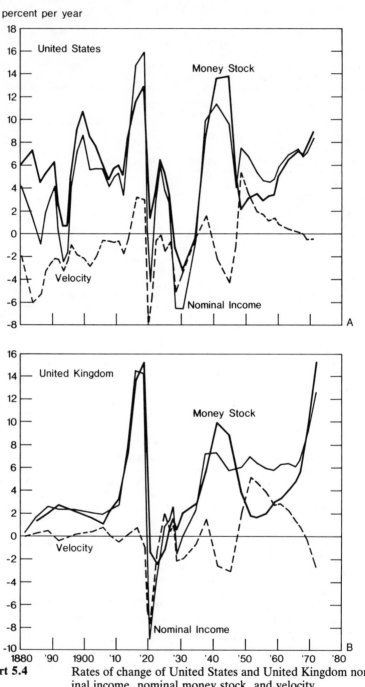

Chart 5.4   Rates of change of United States and United Kingdom nominal income, nominal money stock, and velocity.

dollars, in particular by leading to the substitution of dollars for foreign currencies by persons and firms engaged in foreign trade. For nearly a half-century thereafter there is no appreciable discrepancy, only one minor difference in direction (from the triplet centered on 1892–94 to that centered on 1894–95), though there are some sizable differences in amplitude of movement associated with World War I. The second sizable discrepancy in amplitude, though not in direction of movement, occurs in the period of the Great Contraction, when the rate of change in income fell to much lower levels than the rate of change in money. We are inclined to believe that the widespread bank failures in 1931, 1932, and early 1933 made this deviation smaller than might have been anticipated. The bank failures reduced the attractiveness of money as an asset and so moderated the sharp reduction in velocity that might have been expected as a result of the rapid rate of fall of prices, the decline in interest rates, and the great uncertainty about future economic developments. It is noteworthy that velocity fell much more sharply in Canada, where there were no bank failures, than in the United States, although economic conditions were otherwise very similar.[25] The remaining discrepancies all come during and after World War II, the opposite movements in the rate of rise in money and in income reflecting first the wartime decline in velocity and then the postwar reaction of velocity.

For the United Kingdom, the first sizable discrepancy is between the triplet of phases centered on 1888.5 and the second succeeding triplet centered on 1897, when the rate of rise of nominal income first decreases then increases slightly, while that of money first increases then decreases.

During and after World War I, there are two discrepancies in the direction of movement of the rates of change of money and income, one minor, the other appreciable. The larger discrepancy reflects the postwar reaction to the wartime rise in velocity, which produced a larger decline in income than in money—essentially the same pattern as in the United States.

The remaining discrepancies in movement are all for the World War II period, which again duplicates the United States pattern: the rate of change of money first overshoots the rate of change of income, then declines substantially below the rate of change of income, then closes the gap as the two rates of change come together. The only difference in the patterns for the two countries is that it took longer in the United Kingdom than in the United States for the rates of change of money and income to come back together. In the United States, the discrepancy is largely eliminated by the early 1960s; in the United Kingdom, not until the later 1960s.

This difference may well have reflected a phenomenon for the United Kingdom the reverse of that which we noted for the resumption period

---

25. See *A Monetary History*, p. 352.

for the United States: the replacement of the pound by the dollar as the preferred international currency. The changes in the exchange rate of the pound relative to the dollar, interpreted as due to United Kingdom, not United States, instability, reduced the quantity of pounds demanded. The end of the Bretton Woods system in 1971 presumably had a similar effect on the dollar, but that came too late in our period to show up in our rate of change series.

The wartime deviations offer a fascinating puzzle: they are essentially identical in the two countries in each war, but in both countries the pattern in World War I is the reverse of the pattern in World War II. In World War I, income is more volatile than money (velocity first rises and then declines); in World War II, money is more volatile than income (velocity first declines and then rises). In our *Monetary History*, we explained the World War II decline in velocity in the United States by price controls, the unavailability of consumer durable goods, and the expectation of a postwar contraction accompanied by declining prices. "World War I," we wrote, "differed markedly from World War II with respect to both the availability of goods and expectations about the postwar behavior of prices and incomes. 'Shortages' and 'controls' in World War I were nowhere nearly so sweeping as in World War II, and no major branch of civilian production suspended output entirely. World War I came after nearly two decades of generally rising prices, when the climate of opinion was characterized by belief in unlimited future potentialities rather than by fear of secular stagnation."[26]

Both wars involved much more serious economic dislocations for longer periods in the United Kingdom than in the United States—which is presumably why the return to normal took longer in the United Kingdom after both wars. But the contrast between the two wars in price controls, availability of goods, and public expectations was much the same in the United Kingdom as in the United States.

The financial policy of the two countries is an additional factor, not sufficiently stressed in our *Monetary History*, that was common to the two countries but different between the two wars and that may have contributed to the reversal in the behavior of velocity. In both countries, interest rates rose fairly sharply during World War I but fell during World War II. Partly, this different movement of interest rates reflected the different economic circumstances before the outbreak of war. Mostly it reflected a deliberate government policy of keeping interest rates low during World War II. The effect on velocity was reinforced by the much more extensive and effective official control of prices during World War II in both countries than during World War I. In an interesting dissertation on repressed inflation, Juan Toribio, adducing both theoretical considerations and empirical evidence, argues persuasively that repres-

26. *A Monetary History*, p. 560.

sion of inflation leads to a highly interest-elastic demand curve for money.[27] If this is so, the low controlled interest rates may have induced the public to hold in the form of money an unusually large fraction of the liquid assets they accumulated for the other reasons cited.

These discrepancies do not belie the close similarity between the rate-of-change series in each country for money and income. Indeed, the money and income series show such a remarkable similarity that it seems worth emphasizing that, so far as we are aware, the basic data on money and income from which they are derived are completely independent measurements that have no arithmetically common elements. The money data come primarily from the records of government monetary authorities and of banks; the income data, from a great variety of sources of which monetary authorities and banks contribute at most only that mite that corresponds to their expenditures for factor services. The similarity between the two series in each country does not reflect any spurious correlation arising from reliance on common data. It rather occurs despite independent errors of measurement in the data underlying the two series, and despite the brevity of many phases that limits averaging out of such errors in computing phase averages. The similarity records an economic phenomenon that must be explained in economic terms.

The similarity of movement says nothing in and of itself about direction of influence. It is consistent with changes in money producing corresponding changes in income, or with changes in income producing changes in money, or with changes in both money and income being the common consequence of changes in still other variables.

One quantitative measure of the similarity in the movements of the rates of change in money and income is the correlation coefficient between them, which, for the period as a whole is 0.86 for the United States, 0.84 for the United Kingdom (table 5.6, line 1). This means that at least 74 percent for the United States and at least 71 percent for the United Kingdom of the variation in each series can be accounted for by the systematic element it has in common with the other series. If the nonsys-

---

27. The essence of his theoretical argument is that, if some goods are rationed at controlled prices, all substitution has to take place among the unrationed goods, which raises the cross-price elasticities among them. Given the extensiveness of rationing at controlled prices in the United Kingdom during World War II, he concludes that, "A British holder of liquid assets had practically closed all possibility of choice except the alternative of buying bonds or keeping his cash balances." He goes on to say that, "In the extreme case, if all goods other than money and securities were rationed, it is conceivable that a liquidity trap might appear in the money market." His empirical evidence consists of relating velocity to interest rates for so-called free market periods and the repressed inflation period 1940–49. He finds small, often statistically insignificant interest elasticities for "free-market" periods, much larger, and statistically significant, elasticities for the repressed inflation period. Juan Toribio, "On the Monetary Effects of Repressed Inflation," Ph.D. diss., University of Chicago, 1970, especially pp. 118–31; quotation from p. 122.

Table 5.6   Rates of Change of Money, Income, and Velocity: Standard Deviations and Correlations

	Period and Country									
	Full Period		Pre–World War I		Post–World War I		Peacetime Years			
							Ex-War		Post–World War I	
Correlation Coefficient	United States 1873–1975	United Kingdom 1874–1975	United States 1873–1914	United Kingdom 1874–1914	United States 1914–75	United Kingdom 1914–75	United States 1873–1914, 1921–38, 1949–75	United Kingdom 1874–1914, 1921–38, 1951–75	United States 1921–38, 1949–75	United Kingdom 1921–38, 1951–75
1. g_M and g_Y	0.8612	0.8408	0.7296	0.9016	0.8960	0.7657	0.8571	0.8502	0.9497	0.8250
2. g_V and g_M	−0.0223	−0.3627	−0.0828	−0.4341	0.0037	−0.4280	0.0455	−0.2170	0.5956	−0.3037
3. g_V and g_Y	0.4889	0.1994	0.6212	−0.0016	0.4474	0.2535	0.5536	0.3294	0.8172	0.2879
Standard deviations										
4. σ_{g_M}	4.4456	3.4968	1.9890	0.8128	5.2772	4.0824	3.6119	2.4382	3.9381	4.0898
5. σ_{g_Y}	5.0949	3.3256	2.5295	0.7322	5.9008	3.8143	4.3327	2.5207	5.4883	4.0689
6. σ_{g_V}	2.5900	1.9316	1.7358	0.3517	2.6207	2.7143	2.2343	1.3594	2.1393	2.4134
Maximum residual variation										
7. $\sigma_{g_M \cdot g_Y}$	2.2595	1.8930	1.3602	0.3516	2.3434	2.6258	1.8607	1.2836	1.2333	2.3113
8. $\sigma_{g_Y \cdot g_M}$	2.5896	1.8003	1.7299	0.3167	2.6203	2.4533	2.2320	1.3270	1.7187	2.2995
Standard deviation of nonsystematic component										
9. g_M	1.6562	1.3952	1.0343	0.2550	1.7018	1.9761	1.3654	0.9437	0.8832	1.7109
10. g_Y	1.8982	1.3269	1.3153	0.2297	1.9029	1.8463	1.6378	0.9756	1.2309	1.7021

tematic element were equally important for money and for income, the correlation coefficients themselves would measure the fraction of variability that money and income have in common—or 86 percent for the United States, 84 percent for the United Kingdom.[28]

28. The usual way of describing the squared coefficient of correlation (r^2) between two series, say M (for the rate of change in money) and Y (for rate of change of income) is to describe it as giving "the fraction of the variation in Y accounted for by M," or, alternatively, "the fraction of the variation in M accounted for by Y." But this description is highly special, really a limiting description. Only one of these two statements can be correct—they are alternatives, not simultaneously valid statements. In the usual statistical jargon: the first assumes M to be fixed or exogenous or measured without error; the second assumes Y to be.

A more meaningful description is the one given in the text—that r^2 is the *minimum* fraction of the variation in Y and in M accounted for by the systematic element they have in common. To see that this is a valid description, we may use the permanent-transitory approach of Milton Friedman, *A Theory of the Consumption Function*. Let us assume that we can regard both M and Y as the sum of a systematic element which is common to the two and a nonsystematic element— these being the counterpart here to the "permanent" and "transitory" components of income and consumption. For simplicity we may assume that all variables are measured as deviations from their means so all average zero. Let

(a) $\qquad\qquad M = M_p + M_t$

(b) $\qquad\qquad Y = Y_p + Y_t$

define the division of each into a systematic component, designated by subscript p, and nonsystematic component, designated by t. As in the consumption counterpart, assume that M_t and M_p, and also Y_p and Y_t, and M_t and Y_t are uncorrelated, and that

(c) $\qquad\qquad Y_p = k M_p$

expressing the idea that these are the systematic elements that the two variables have in common except for a scale factor. We then have that

(d) $\qquad\qquad \sigma_M^2 = \sigma_{M_p}^2 + \sigma_{M_t}^2$

(e) $\qquad\qquad \sigma_Y^2 = \sigma_{Y_p}^2 + \sigma_{Y_t}^2,$

and

(f) $\qquad\qquad r_{MY}^2 \;=\; \dfrac{\sigma_{M_p}^2}{\sigma_M^2}\;\dfrac{\sigma_{Y_p}^2}{\sigma_Y^2},$

or $\qquad\qquad r_{MY}^2 = P_M P_Y,$

where P_M is the fraction of the variance of M, and P_Y, the fraction of the variance of Y, contributed by the systematic or permanent component. (This is the notation of *A Theory of the Consumption Function*, which is why we use it here despite possible confusion with our use of P to refer to price.)

In the usual description in which, for example, M is the fixed variable or measured without error, P_M is taken to be unity, and so r^2 is described as the fraction of the variance of Y accounted for by M, and conversely if Y is taken as the fixed variable. It is now clear why these cannot both simultaneously be valid. However, they are lower limits, since P_Y and P_M must both be less than unity, and hence each separately must be between unity and r^2.

If $P_M = P_Y$, then the correlation coefficient itself can be described as the "fraction of their variability the two variables have in common," but this too is a highly special case, since there is no reason in general why the unsystematic element should be the same fraction of the total variability for the two variables. Note that the unsystematic element includes pure

The slightly higher correlation for the United States than for the United Kingdom is somewhat misleading. The correlation is higher only because there is more variation in both money and income in the United States than in the United Kingdom, not because there is a closer relation between money and income. It has long been noted that economic fluctuations in the United States have both a greater frequency and a greater amplitude than in the United Kingdom. This is reflected in the consistently and substantially higher standard deviations of the rates of change for both money and income for the United States than for the United Kingdom (table 5.6, lines 4 and 5; the only exception is for post–World War I peacetime years for money). Hence there is more variation to be accounted for in the United States.

The comparative closeness of the relation between money and income in the two countries can be judged better by comparing standard errors of estimate: the variation in the rate of change in income when allowance is made for the concomitant systematic variation in the rate of change of money, and, conversely, the variation in the rate of change of money when allowance is made for the concomitant systematic variation of income. Lines 7 and 8 of table 5.6 give upper limits to the size of this residual variability. Lines 9 and 10 give an estimate of the residual variability on the assumption that the nonsystematic element is equally important for money and for income.[29] Despite the lower correlation for the United Kingdom, these estimates of the nonsystematic variability, like the initial variability, are smaller in the United Kingdom than in the United States for the period as a whole, though of course the difference is less for the nonsystematic than for the initial variability. The lower

---

error of measurement. For the United States, for example, our judgment is that such errors of measurement account for a larger fraction of the variance of Y than of M.

The statement that M and Y have a systematic component in common says nothing about direction of influence. It might be that the influence runs either way or both ways or that both systematic components are the common consequences of still other variables.

29. To continue with the preceding note, the standard error of estimate of Y given M, which is usually described as the variation in Y not accounted for by M, is obtained by assuming that $P_M = 1$; and similarly $\sigma_{M \cdot Y}$ by assuming that $P_Y = 1$. Both these assumptions cannot be simultaneously valid, hence both of these "residual" standard errors cannot be simultaneously valid. A better interpretation is that each is the maximum unsystematic error, obtained by assuming that all unsystematic variation is in the particular variable in question.

If $P_M = P_Y$, then the variance of the nonsystematic component is given by $(1 - r)$ rather than $(1 - r^2)$ times the variance of the measured variable. This assumption has been used in computing the entries in lines 9 and 10 of table 5.6.

If $P_M > P_Y$, then the corresponding standard deviation for M would be smaller and for Y larger, and conversely if $P_M < P_Y$.

Despite their unconventionality, we believe that the numbers computed on the assumption that $P_M = P_Y$ give a less biased indication of the size of the nonsystematic component than the maximum estimates in lines 7 and 8.

variability for the United Kingdom for the period as a whole is produced by the pre-1914 period.

The residual or nonsystematic variability consists of two very different elements: pure errors of measurement—these might be called the stochastic statistical element; and variability in income and money attributable to variables that do not affect them alike—this might be called the stochastic economic element. For the United Kingdom, for the period before 1914, the extensive use of interpolation particularly for the income data, probably produces a negative correlation between the statistical and the economic elements, and so biases sharply downward both the initial and the residual variation. Though we suspect, on historical grounds, that the nonsystematic variability was decidedly greater in the United States during this period than in the United Kingdom, we also suspect that the very wide difference recorded in table 5.6 overestimates the difference between the two countries, because of the difference in the statistical characteristics of the United Kingdom and the United States estimates.

For the entire period after 1914, for which the statistical difficulties are less serious, the residual variation is greater for the United Kingdom than for the United States for money but less for income, but both differences are small and not statistically significant. However, this equality too is misleading, reflecting primarily the greater impact of the two wars on the United Kingdom. For post–World War I peacetime years, the nonsystematic variation in the rates of change of money and income are both significantly larger (at the .05 level or a more stringent significance level) for the United Kingdom than for the United States, the reverse of the earlier relation, but again not inconsistent with the historical impression that, in recent decades, the United Kingdom has become the less stable economy.

The velocity series plotted in chart 5.4 is, by definition, the vertical difference between the other two series.[30] The high correlation between the rates of change of money and income implies that the rate of change of velocity has a smaller amplitude of fluctuation than either of them—as it uniformly does (see lines 4, 5, and 6 in table 5.6). Indeed, the reader's first impression may well be, as ours was, that the fluctuations in velocity are surprisingly large in view of the similarity of movements of the money

---

30. Since $V = Y/M$,

$$\log V = \log Y - \log M,$$

so

$$\frac{\Delta \log V}{\Delta t} = \frac{\Delta \log Y}{\Delta t} - \frac{\Delta \log M}{\Delta t}.$$

Our rates of change assume continuous compounding and hence are equal to these rates of change in the (natural) logarithms.

and income series. The reason is partly that the velocity series fluctuates most at those periods when the other two series are fluctuating most, so the larger differences between the other two series are overshadowed by their common violent movement, and partly that the velocity series reflects the nonsystematic components of both the other series. There is clearly much variation in velocity requiring attention—but clearly also the rigid quantity theory assumption of a strictly constant velocity is not a bad first approximation for movements lasting more than two or three years.

Any measurement error or nonsystematic fluctuation in the rate of change of income enters with the same sign into the rate of change of velocity and hence will tend to produce a positive correlation between the income and velocity series. Conversely, any error or fluctuation in the rate of change of money enters with the opposite sign into the rate of change of velocity and hence will tend to produce a negative correlation between the money and velocity series. These expectations are fulfilled in sixteen of the twenty correlations in table 5.6. Two of the exceptions are trivial (United Kingdom, pre–World War I, and United States, post–World War I). The substantial positive correlation between the rate of change of velocity and of money for United States peacetime years, after World War I, reflects the much larger variation in the income than in the money series, so that its fluctuations dominate the velocity correlations.[31]

31. It is easy to show that

$$r_{VY} = \frac{\sigma_Y - r_{YM}\sigma_M}{\sigma_V},$$

$$r_{VM} = \frac{r_{YM}\sigma_Y - \sigma_M}{\sigma_V}$$

so that

$$r_{VY} \gtrless 0$$

according as

$$\frac{\sigma_Y}{\sigma_M} \gtrless r_{YM}$$

and

$$r_{VM} \gtrless 0$$

according as

$$\frac{\sigma_Y}{\sigma_M} \gtrless \frac{1}{r_{YM}}.$$

For r_{VY} to be positive and r_{VM} negative, the requisite condition is that both $\frac{\sigma_M}{\sigma_Y}$ and $\frac{\sigma_Y}{\sigma_M}$ be greater than r_{YM}, which generally is the case in table 5.6.

Perhaps the most remarkable feature about the rate of change of velocity, as about its level, is the extraordinary similarity of movement in the two countries. Chart 5.5 superimposes the two separate levels of velocity series from chart 5.2 and the two rates of change of velocity series from chart 5.4. The parallelism for levels and the near identity for rates of change is striking. The rate-of-change series for the two countries are almost duplicates, except for the early period. The loose relation before World War I may reflect statistical defects, particularly the role of interpolation in the United Kingdom figures that produce such a stable rate of change of velocity, or looser links between the two countries than they were destined to become. Thereafter, the only notable discrepancy comes after World War II, when the peak rate of rise of velocity came later in the United Kingdom than in the United States and remained higher until 1970. The obvious explanation is the more severe economic impact of both wars in the United Kingdom than in the United States and hence a sharper and longer reaction.

This striking similarity in the movement of velocity in the two countries is of the greatest importance. It means that no explanation of these movements is acceptable that depends on conditions special to each country separately. The two countries have clearly been part of a single monetary order in which major velocity movements have reflected influences common to the two countries.

Chart 5.6, the counterpart of chart 5.3, shows rates of change for the components of the money and income series of chart 5.4. Population clearly accounts for only a minor part of the fluctuation in the money and income series. For the United States, only World War I, the Great Contraction, and the post–World War II baby boom leave an appreciable impress on the rates of change of population when they are plotted on the same scale as the other series; for the United Kingdom, only World War I, the twenties, and recent years do.

The next two panels for each country, each containing a pair of series, real income per capita, and real money per capita in panel B, and prices and money stock per unit of output in panel C, are derived from the aggregate money and income series by deflating both by the same variables—population and prices, in panel B, and aggregate real income, in panel C. Hence, in each panel the difference between the two series is precisely equal to the difference between the money and income series of chart 5.4, which is to say, equal to the velocity series of that chart.

The elimination of price and population movements leaves much variability in the rates of change in money and income, though for both countries the real magnitudes in chart 5.6, panel B, are much less variable than the original nominal magnitudes in chart 5.4, and also than the nominal series in chart 5.6, panel C, which relate prices to the money stock per unit of output. In addition, for both countries the two series in

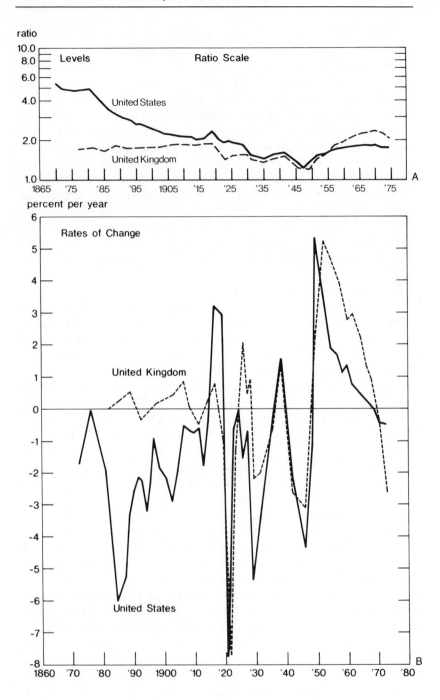

Chart 5.5   United States and United Kingdom velocity: levels and rates of change.

percent per year

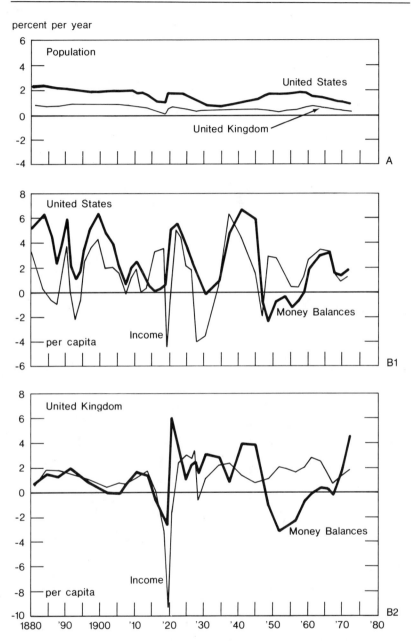

Chart 5.6   Rates of change of United States and United Kingdom population, per capita real income and money, and prices and money
stock per unit of output.

percent per year

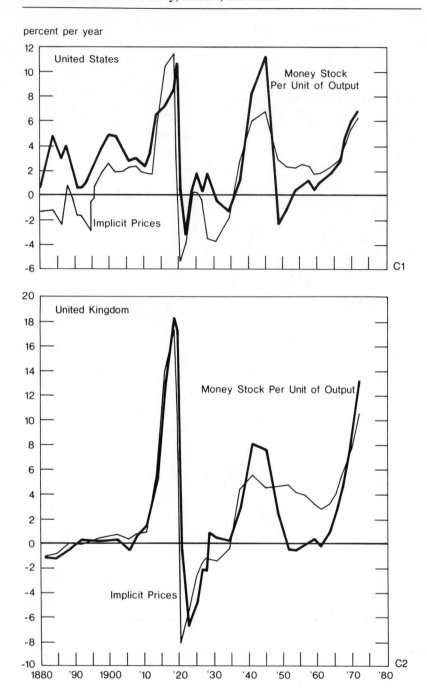

panel C are more highly correlated than the two in panel B. The chart thus illustrates our earlier conclusion that the common fluctuations in the rates of change of the stock of money and of nominal income are largely a price phenomenon. However, the chart also underlines the no less interesting fact that the common fluctuations are not solely a price phenomenon. For the United States in particular, the real magnitudes in panel B and not only the nominal magnitudes in panel C move together. For the United Kingdom, there may be some tendency in this direction, but it is much more muted.

This important issue can be examined more clearly in chart 5.7, which plots the rate of change of money (reproduced from chart 5.4) against the rate of change of prices and of real income (reproduced from chart 5.6), the two components of the nominal income series plotted in chart 5.4.

For the United States, it is striking how closely the movements in the stock of money series parallel the movements in real income; indeed, in terms of short-term movements there seems to be, if anything, a closer relation between the movements in money and in real income than between the movements in money and prices. Note, for example, how the bulge in the money series for the triplet of phases centered on 1910–11 (plotted at 1 January 1911) is matched by a corresponding bulge in the output series, but not in the price series,[32] and how much closer the parallelism between money and output is from 1923 to 1939 than between money and prices. The reason the correlation coefficient between money and real income (.620 for the period as a whole) is nonetheless lower than between money and prices (.785) is the failure of the real income series to follow the longer period and larger shifts in the money series as closely as the price series does. For example, when the money series shifts from one level before 1896 to another level thereafter, the price series follows the shift, whereas the real income series does not. Precisely the same difference emerges after World War I when the money series shifts to a lower level. As we noted in *A Monetary History*, longer-period movements in rates of change of money are paralleled mainly by corresponding movements in prices, not in real output.[33] However, chart 5.7 makes it clear that at least for the United States the periods over which rates of change of money and real output move together are of considerably longer duration than individual business cycles.

32. This particular parallelism is so striking that it seemed worth checking to be sure that it did not simply reflect an error in deflation, which recorded what was in fact a variation in prices as variation in output. Accordingly, we computed rates of change, 1869–1914, for two indexes constructed by Edwin Frickey (*Production in the United States, 1860–1914* [Cambridge: Harvard University Press, 1947], pp. 54, 127), both based on physical-quantity data, measuring production for manufacture and industrial and commercial production. The rate of change movements in the two series parallel those in real income after 1890, and show the same distinctive bulge for the triplet of phases centered on 1910–11.

33. Pp. 242–44, 677, 678.

percent per year

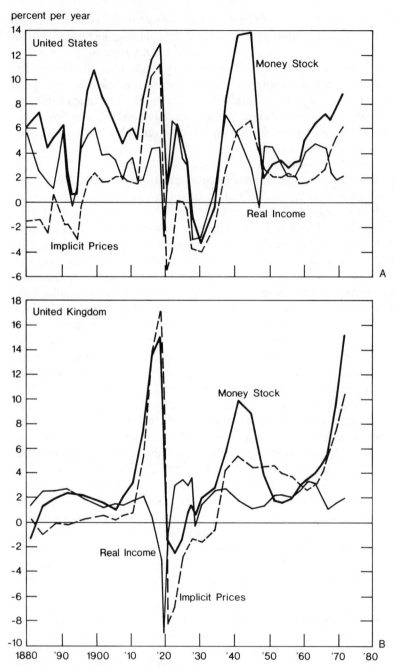

Chart 5.7   Rates of change of United States and United Kingdom money, prices, and real income.

The United Kingdom chart is more difficult to read than the United States chart, but when its story is extracted it turns out to be very much the same. The key difficulty in reading the chart is the greater violence done by two world wars to the United Kingdom than to the United States economy. Consider first the period before World War I. For that period, the money line nearly duplicates the real income series except for the early years. Consider next the period between the two wars. For that period, all three curves are remarkably parallel; but again, as for the United States, if anything, the real income and money series are more closely related, except for the sharp drop from before to after 1928 in the level of the real income curve that makes the computed correlation between the money rates of change and real income rates of change negative ($-.308$).

Consider next the two world wars. Both countries show very much the same pattern in rates of growth of money and prices: in World War I, sharp and parallel rises of almost the same amount and a subsequent very sharp fall; in World War II, a rise and subsequent fall in money and prices but a much sharper rise and fall in money than in prices, and with the fall in the rate of price change spread over a longer period in the United Kingdom. The behavior of real income differs much more between the countries: in the United States, an initial rise, then decline in both wars; in the United Kingdom, decline throughout the wars. For both countries, the relation between money and real income is much looser for these wartime periods than for the other periods. However, these wartime movements are much larger in amplitude compared with the peacetime movements for the United Kingdom than for the United States. Hence they dominate our first impression of the charts—and also computed correlation coefficients—for the United Kingdom far more than for the United States. For the United States, as noted, the correlation between the rates of change of money and real income is positive for the period as a whole (.620); for the United Kingdom it is negative ($-.294$). However, if the war periods are excluded, the correlation is positive though negligible for the United Kingdom (.027) and significantly higher for the United States (.802).

The economic relations that prevailed during the war years—and particularly World War II—were no doubt very different than during other times. Price controls, physical rationing and unavailability of goods, the direction of so large a fraction of resources to military use, the widespread expectations of a very different future than present—all no doubt altered the impact of monetary change on real output and prices. However, in addition to such real differences in economic relations, we have great doubts about the accuracy of our series during this period, particularly our price series. Price control meant that price increases took indirect and concealed forms not recorded in the indexes; the large rise in price indexes when price control was repealed consisted largely of an unveiling of the earlier concealed increases. Hence the price indexes understate the price rise during the war and overstate the price rise after the war. Similarly, price controls in the United States from 1971 to 1973 and in the United Kingdom from 1966 to 1974 distort the reported price indexes.

We have attempted to adjust our price series during World War II and during post–World War II peacetime years for these defects (see secs. 4.1.3 and 4.2.3), but we are far from certain that our adjustments are adequate. We suspect that wartime controls produced errors in the nominal income series and not only in its division into prices and output—this surely was the case insofar as controls stimulated black market and other unrecorded transactions. Hence, in many of the sections that follow we shall present separate results excluding the wartime and immediately postwar years.[34]

The relation between money and real income is considered in much greater detail in chapter 9. We there find that the relation is rather different than might appear given the preceding summary of this chapter. Not only the wars but also the great contractions turn out to produce something of an optical illusion.

5.4 Conclusion

The broad descriptions of the secular movements in money, income, prices, and velocity in the earlier sections of this chapter bring out sharply three phenomena that require further interpretation: first, the common movement of nominal money and nominal income; second, the largely common movement in velocity in the United States and in the United Kingdom; third, the rather different relations in the two countries be-

---

34. Level observations excluding wars omit the following phases in each war for each country:

World War I				World War II			
United States		United Kingdom		United States		United Kingdom	
Phase		Phase		Phase		Phase	
Number	Dates	Number	Dates	Number	Dates	Number	Dates
25	1914–18	12	1914–18	37	1938–44	24	1938–44
26	1918–19	13	1918–19	38	1944–46	25	1944–46
27	1919–20	14	1919–20	39	1946–48	26	1946–51

Rate of exchange observations exclude in addition to those listed above the preceding and following phases:

24	1913–14	11	1913–14	36	1937–38	23	1937–38
28	1920–21	15	1920–21	40	1948–49	27	1951–52

The reason for including the additional phases is that the rate of change triplet centered, for example, on 1914–18 is based on 1913–14, 1914–18, and 1918–19.

tween movements in money, on the one hand, and real income and prices on the other. Succeeding chapters explore these phenomena more fully.

5.5 Appendix: Basic Phase Data

Tables 5.7 and 5.8 give phase average values for our basic data set for the United States and the United Kingdom. Tables 5.9 and 5.10 give the rates of change computed from triplets of the phase average values.

Table 5.7 Average Value of Selected Nominal and Real Magnitudes during Reference Phases: United States, 1867–1975

Phase Number	Mid-phase Dates	Nominal Income Y (Billion $ per Year)	Money Stock M (Billion $ per Year)	Velocity V (Ratio per Year)	Implicit Price Deflator P (1929 = 100)	Real Income y' (Billion $ per Year)	Population N (Millions)	Per Capita Nominal Income Py ($ per Year)	Per Capita Real Income y (1929 $ per Year)	Per Capita Nominal Money Balances Pm ($ per Year)	Per Capita Real Money Balances m (1929 $ per Year)
1	1868.5		3.058				38.209			80	112
2	1870.0	7.100	3.037	2.337	68.79	10.046	39.476	180	254	77	120
3	1872.0	7.508	3.360	2.235	67.72	11.087	41.443	181	268	81	118
4	1876.0	7.870	3.300	2.384	61.18	12.864	45.564	173	282	72	118
5	1880.5	9.871	3.596	2.745	55.36	17.830	50.357	196	354	71	129
6	1884.0	10.983	4.530	2.424	55.34	19.846	54.726	201	363	83	150
7	1886.5	10.511	4.728	2.223	50.36	20.870	57.931	181	360	82	162
8	1888.0	10.802	4.942	2.185	51.04	21.162	59.853	180	354	83	162
9	1889.5	11.158	5.144	2.169	51.47	21.677	61.769	181	351	83	162
10	1891.0	11.931	5.466	2.183	50.56	23.598	63.705	187	370	86	170
11	1892.0	12.398	5.667	2.188	49.28	25.157	65.010	191	387	87	177

171	83	375	182	66.964	25.122	48.38	2.197	5.530	12.153	1893.5	12
170	78	364	167	68.924	25.065	46.02	2.142	5.385	11.534	1895.0	13
168	75	372	167	70.229	26.130	45.02	2.221	5.295	11.763	1896.0	14
174	79	393	178	72.831	28.610	45.39	2.260	5.746	12.987	1898.0	15
190	92	433	209	75.444	32.638	48.34	2.280	6.920	15.778	1900.0	16
204	103	467	235	78.356	36.594	50.29	2.292	8.029	18.404	1902.0	17
212	110	469	244	81.395	38.211	51.91	2.215	8.956	19.837	1904.0	18
230	125	508	275	84.605	42.948	54.12	2.203	10.551	23.243	1906.0	19
231	131	501	284	87.855	44.036	56.72	2.168	11.520	24.979	1908.0	20
236	138	508	298	90.514	45.993	58.58	2.153	12.516	26.942	1909.5	21
246	147	521	313	93.132	48.520	59.98	2.121	13.724	29.103	1911.0	22
255	157	539	333	95.432	51.457	61.71	2.115	15.016	31.752	1912.5	23
259	164	522	329	98.163	51.220	63.03	2.011	16.057	32.282	1914.0	24
264	204	543	422	101.724	55.281	77.57	2.062	20.797	42.881	1916.5	25
262	277	618	654	103.859	64.183	105.90	2.361	28.790	67.969	1919.0	26
273	311	605	690	105.483	63.822	113.95	2.214	32.850	72.727	1920.0	27
280	315	566	636	107.494	60.873	112.36	2.023	33.811	68.397	1921.0	28
309	311	590	593	110.139	64.994	100.45	1.909	34.194	65.289	1922.5	29
332	332	659	661	113.023	74.502	100.22	1.987	37.577	74.663	1924.0	30
354	359	676	684	115.786	78.217	101.23	1.906	41.547	79.181	1925.5	31
371	374	704	709	118.213	83.214	100.74	1.897	44.202	83.832	1927.0	32
383	382	713	712	120.451	85.903	99.88	1.864	46.036	85.805	1928.5	33
395	349	614	543	123.469	75.858	88.42	1.557	43.091	67.072	1931.0	34

Table 5.7 (Continued)

Phase Number	Mid-phase Dates	Nominal Income Y (Billion $ per Year)	Money Stock M (Billion $ per Year)	Velocity V (Ratio per Year)	Implicit Price Deflator P (1929 = 100)	Real Income y' (Billion $ per Year)	Population N (Millions)	Per Capita Nominal Income Py ($ per Year)	Per Capita Real Income y (1929 $ per Year)	Per Capita Nominal Money Balances Pm ($ per Year)	Per Capita Real Money Balances m (1929 $ per Year)
35	1935.0	54.800	37.716	1.453	77.26	70.932	126.811	432	559	297	385
36	1938.0	71.863	45.595	1.576	80.76	88.978	129.324	556	688	353	436
37	1941.5	104.774	65.060	1.610	92.16	113.686	133.660	784	851	487	528
38	1945.5	169.400	124.158	1.364	124.22	136.366	139.906	1211	975	887	714
39	1947.5	178.728	144.665	1.235	136.13	131.293	144.056	1241	911	1004	738
40	1949.0	197.213	147.784	1.334	144.65	136.340	147.903	1333	922	999	691
41	1951.5	240.973	157.684	1.528	153.04	157.457	154.292	1562	1020	1022	668
42	1954.0	277.301	174.149	1.592	161.50	171.706	160.972	1723	1067	1082	670
43	1956.0	307.592	184.963	1.663	168.77	182.251	166.752	1845	1093	1109	657
44	1958.0	334.556	196.414	1.703	177.80	188.170	172.701	1937	1090	1137	640
45	1959.5	361.743	208.618	1.734	182.88	197.803	177.603	2037	1114	1175	642
46	1961.0	387.224	218.050	1.776	187.35	206.689	182.175	2126	1135	1197	639
47	1964.0	470.701	261.385	1.801	197.55	238.272	190.380	2472	1252	1373	695
48	1967.0	589.771	323.663	1.822	213.03	276.852	197.633	2984	1401	1638	769
49	1968.5	657.625	363.927	1.807	226.03	290.942	200.696	3277	1450	1813	802
50	1970.0	724.400	397.810	1.821	243.16	297.908	203.774	3555	1462	1952	803
51	1972.0	846.520	474.995	1.782	271.95	311.274	207.840	4073	1498	2285	840
52	1974.5	1056.867	594.306	1.778	321.15	329.091	211.935	4987	1553	2804	873

Phase Number	Annual Percentage				High-Powered Money H (Billion $ per Year)	Money Stock per Unit of Output M/y' (Ratio Times 100)	Weight W
	Call Money Rate $R_{S'}$	Commercial Paper Rate R_S	Yield on Corporate Bonds $R_{L'}$	R_L			
1	7.85	7.88	6.46	7.92	.779	30.23	2.7
2	8.06	8.46	6.58	8.05	.763	30.30	2.0
3	7.84	8.13	6.40	7.86	.779	25.66	3.6
4	4.60	5.86	5.59	7.05	.771	20.17	5.6
5	5.16	5.18	4.62	6.09	.935	22.83	4.6
6	3.31	5.22	4.27	5.73	1.191	22.65	3.6
7	3.62	4.83	3.89	5.36	1.232	23.36	2.7
8	3.88	5.32	3.84	5.30	1.294	23.73	2.0
9	4.28	5.06	3.73	5.19	1.348	23.16	2.7
10	4.71	5.51	3.87	5.33	1.425	22.53	2.0
11	3.19	4.75	3.89	5.36	1.497	22.01	2.0
12	3.29	5.18	3.85	5.32	1.559	21.49	2.7
13	1.48	3.36	3.66	5.12	1.540	20.26	2.0
14	3.02	4.74	3.61	5.08	1.475	20.09	2.0
15	2.88	4.10	3.42	4.88	1.618	21.20	3.6
16	3.90	4.27	3.27	4.79	1.882	21.94	2.0
17	4.26	4.71	3.31	4.79	2.124	23.44	3.6
18	2.74	4.84	3.53	4.88	2.349	24.57	2.0
19	4.84	5.12	3.58	4.68	2.584	26.16	3.6
20	4.26	5.36	3.88	5.03	2.960	27.21	2.0
21	2.61	4.34	3.82	4.86	3.128	28.29	2.7
22	2.88	4.52	3.85	4.81	3.225	29.18	2.0
23	3.23	4.77	3.93	4.85	3.344		2.7

Table 5.7 (Continued)

Phase Number	Annual Percentage				High-Powered Money H (Billion \$ per Year)	Money Stock per Unit of Output M/y' (Ratio Times 100)	Weight W
	Call Money Rate R_S	Commercial Paper Rate R_S	Yield on Corporate Bonds				
			$R_{L'}$	R_L			
24	3.29	5.19	4.05	4.96	3.474	31.35	2.0
25	3.07	4.24	4.17	5.04	4.372	37.62	4.6
26	5.89	5.65	4.75	5.43	6.473	44.86	2.0
27	7.13	6.40	4.93	5.71	7.063	51.47	2.0
28	6.90	6.95	5.14	5.99	7.015	55.54	2.0
29	4.86	5.09	4.80	5.41	6.528	52.61	2.7
30	3.96	4.44	4.64	5.24	6.819	50.44	2.0
31	3.98	4.03	4.52	5.06	7.062	53.12	2.7
32	4.28	4.13	4.35	4.87	7.198	53.12	2.0
33	5.94	4.87	4.21	4.91	7.178	53.59	2.7
34	3.20	3.48	4.35	4.99	7.234	56.80	3.6
35	1.03	1.18	3.75	4.14	9.961	53.17	5.6
36	1.00	0.90	3.04	2.99	13.970	51.24	2.0
37	1.00	0.74	2.70	2.58	23.119	57.23	6.5
38	1.04	0.77	2.53	2.51	40.808	91.05	2.7
39	1.37	1.08	2.56	2.55	45.110	110.18	2.7

40	1.59	1.47	2.77	2.61	45.779	108.39	2.0
41	2.16	1.99	2.80	2.72	46.959	100.14	4.6
42	3.06	2.05	3.08	2.91	49.789	101.42	2.0
43	3.69	2.73	3.16	3.19	49.534	101.49	3.6
44	4.11	3.14	3.65	3.73	49.964	104.38	2.0
45	4.29	3.56	4.09	4.10	50.209	105.47	2.7
46	4.75	3.41	4.39	4.23	49.635	105.50	2.0
47	4.67	3.88	4.35	4.32	54.278	109.70	5.6
48	5.72	5.33	4.85	5.28	63.060	116.91	2.0
49	6.57	6.18	5.84	6.16	69.170	125.09	2.7
50	7.96	7.77	7.07	7.34	75.552	133.54	2.0
51	6.33	5.91	7.18	7.27	85.922	152.60	3.6
52	9.56	8.54	7.79	7.97	102.398	180.59	2.7

Note: Midphase dates ending .5 are as of 30 June; ending .0, as of 1 January. Entries in table are antilogs of reference phase averages for all variables except interest rates, computed from logarithms of original data. Interest rates are in original decimal units.

Source: See table 4.8 for annual data underlying phase averages for nominal income, money stock, implicit price deflator, real income, population, interest rates. High-powered money is the sum of commercial bank reserves and currency outstanding (from the sources used in deriving the money stock). United States money stock has been adjusted for the effect of changing financial sophistication relative to that of the United Kingdom, 1867–1902, as described in section 6.3. Remaining variables in the table were derived from the logs of the phase averages:

Velocity is the antilog of the log of nominal income minus the log of the money stock.

Per capita nominal (real) income is the antilog of the log of nominal (real) income minus the log of population.

Per capita nominal (real) money balances is the antilog of the log of money minus the log of population (and the log of the price deflator).

Money stock per unit of output is 100 times the antilog of the log of money stock minus the log of real income.

For the derivation of the column of weights, see section 3.1.3.

Table 5.8 Average Value of Selected Nominal and Real Magnitudes during Reference Phases: United Kingdom, 1868–1975

Phase Number	Mid-phase Dates	Nominal Income Y (Billion £ per Year)	Money Stock M (Billion £ per Year)	Velocity V (Ratio per Year)	Implicit Price Deflator P (1929 = 100)	Real Income y' (Billion £ per Year)	Population N (Millions)	Per Capita Nominal Income Py (£ per Year)	Per Capita Real Income y (1929 £ per Year)	Per Capita Nominal Money Balances Pm (£ per Year)	Per Capita Real Money Balances m (1929 £ per Year)
0	1871.5	.933			59.78	1.561	29.476	32	53		
1	1877.0	1.016	.594	1.709	57.16	1.778	31.172	33	57	19	33
2	1881.5	1.039	.581	1.786	54.29	1.913	32.594	32	59	18	33
3	1885.0	1.044	.618	1.689	51.99	2.008	33.494	31	60	18	36
4	1888.5	1.171	.642	1.823	50.94	2.299	34.442	34	67	19	37
5	1892.0	1.255	.716	1.752	51.92	2.418	35.456	35	68	20	39
6	1897.0	1.434	.815	1.761	50.81	2.823	37.160	39	76	22	43
7	1902.5	1.625	.911	1.784	53.76	3.023	39.111	41	77	23	43
8	1906.0	1.727	.939	1.840	53.99	3.198	40.309	43	79	23	43
9	1908.0	1.823	.977	1.866	55.10	3.309	41.018	44	81	24	43
10	1911.0	1.936	1.047	1.849	56.09	3.452	42.019	46	82	25	44
11	1914.0	2.156	1.188	1.816	58.15	3.708	42.810	50	87	28	48
12	1916.5	2.983	1.587	1.879	76.36	3.906	43.366	69	90	37	48
13	1919.0	4.459	2.359	1.891	117.28	3.802	43.469	103	87	54	46

14	1920.0	4.801	2.688	1.786	140.09	3.427	43.583	110	79	62	44
15	1921.0	4.645	2.799	1.659	145.50	3.192	43.895	106	73	64	44
16	1923.0	3.732	2.626	1.421	113.66	3.284	44.486	84	74	59	52
17	1925.5	3.833	2.507	1.529	105.20	3.644	45.066	85	81	56	53
18	1927.0	3.990	2.527	1.529	102.74	3.760	45.310	85	83	56	54
19	1928.0	4.061	2.573	1.551	100.90	3.954	45.483	88	87	57	56
20	1929.0	3.847	2.608	1.557	100.20	4.053	45.625	89	89	57	57
21	1931.0	3.988	2.628	1.464	97.11	3.961	45.981	84	86	57	59
22	1935.0	4.654	2.912	1.369	91.62	4.352	46.789	85	93	62	68
23	1938.0		3.236	1.438	96.34	4.831	47.391	98	102	68	71
24	1941.5	6.370	4.213	1.512	121.39	5.247	48.273	132	109	87	72
25	1945.5	8.183	6.702	1.221	146.46	5.587	49.149	166	114	136	93
26	1949.0	9.828	8.158	1.205	170.27	5.772	50.031	196	115	163	96
27	1952.0	12.274	8.520	1.441	198.29	6.190	50.360	244	123	169	85
28	1954.0	13.992	8.981	1.558	215.34	6.498	50.682	276	128	177	82
29	1957.0	16.955	9.339	1.815	243.55	6.962	51.304	330	136	182	75
30	1959.5	19.397	10.102	1.920	265.68	7.301	51.983	373	140	194	73
31	1961.5	22.099	10.715	2.062	279.62	7.903	52.814	418	150	203	73
32	1964.0	25.779	11.744	2.195	300.23	8.586	53.727	480	160	219	73
33	1966.0	29.508	12.958	2.277	323.12	9.132	54.359	543	168	238	74
34	1967.5	31.869	13.887	2.295	346.19	9.206	54.787	582	168	253	73
35	1970.0	38.170	16.180	2.359	399.92	9.544	55.337	690	172	292	73
36	1972.5	50.378	22.317	2.257	502.54	10.025	55.782	903	180	400	80
37	1974.5	67.914	32.515	2.089	646.67	10.502	55.952	1214	188	581	90

Table 5.8 (Continued)

| Phase Number | Annual Percentage | | High-Powered Money H (Billion £ per Year) | Money Stock per Unit of Output M/y' (Ratio Times 100) | Exchange Rate EX £ in U.S. $ | Weight W |
	Short-Term Rate R_S	Long-Term Rate R_L				
0	3.56	3.23	.168	33.44	5.779	5.6
1	2.89	3.16	.164	30.39	5.242	4.6
2	2.95	3.02	.161	30.79	4.856	3.6
3	2.58	2.99	.162	27.95	4.860	4.6
4	2.78	2.89	.178	29.64	4.874	3.6
5	2.54	2.66	.196	28.86	4.872	3.6
6	2.09	2.38	.206	30.13	4.874	7.5
7	3.18	2.69	.212	29.35	4.874	4.6
8	3.39	2.84	.218	29.53	4.864	3.6
9	3.39	2.94	.224	30.33	4.868	2.0
10	3.06	3.13	.275	32.02	4.870	5.6
11	3.63	3.43	.430	40.63	4.899	2.0
12	4.22	4.16	.665	62.03	4.783	4.6
13	3.74	4.51	.713	78.42	4.592	2.0
14	5.16	4.97	.697	87.68	4.027	2.0
15	5.78	5.27	.632	79.96	3.756	2.0
16	3.22	4.51	.607	68.81	4.372	3.6
17	4.06	4.45	.593	67.21	4.730	2.7
18	4.37	4.56	.586	65.06	4.860	2.0
19	4.21	4.52			4.864	2.0

20	4.71	4.54	.578	64.35	4.862	2.0
21	3.25	4.39	.566	66.35	4.498	3.6
22	0.78	3.16	.628	66.90	4.647	5.6
23	0.61	3.33	.723	66.99	4.917	2.0
24	1.03	3.27	1.010	80.29	4.129	6.5
25	.86	2.90	1.739	119.95	4.032	2.7
26	.63	3.20	1.915	141.34	3.550	5.6
27	1.81	4.01	1.995	137.64	2.796	2.0
28	2.61	4.01	2.184	138.22	2.804	3.6
29	4.76	4.77	2.503	134.15	2.796	3.6
30	4.19	5.01	2.726	138.36	2.809	2.7
31	5.03	5.95	2.938	135.58	2.805	2.7
32	4.66	5.94	3.163	136.78	2.798	3.6
33	6.36	6.61	3.525	141.90	2.794	2.0
34	6.50	6.89	3.752	150.85	2.667	2.7
35	7.89	8.75	4.193	169.52	2.402	3.6
36	7.27	9.53	5.180	222.62	2.474	2.7
37	11.79	13.85	7.197	309.61	2.337	2.7

Note: Midphase dates ending .5 are as of 30 June; ending .0, as of 1 January. Entries in table are antilogs of reference phase averages for all variables except interest rates, computed from logarithms of original data. Interest rates are in original decimal units.

Source: See table 4.9 for annual data underlying phase averages for nominal income, money stock, implicit price deflator, real income, population, interest rates, and the United Kingdom exchange rate in dollars. High-powered money is the sum of commercial bank reserves and currency outstanding (from the sources used in deriving the money stock). Remaining variables in the table were derived from the logs of the phase averages:

Velocity is the antilog of the log of nominal income minus the log of the money stock.

Per capita nominal (real) income is the antilog of the log of nominal (real) income minus the log of population.

Per capita nominal (real) money balances is the antilog of the log of money minus the log of population (and the log of the price deflator).

Money stock per unit of output is 100 times the antilog of the log of money stock minus the log of real income.

For the derivation of the column of weights, see section 3.1.3.

Table 5.9   Rates of Change Computed from Triplets of Reference Phase Averages (Annual Percentage): United States, 1869–1975.

Number	Central Phase of Triplet Midpoint	Nominal Income g_Y	Money Stock g_M	Velocity g_V	Implicit Price Deflator g_P	Real Income $g_{y'}$	Population g_N	Per Capita Nominal Income g_{Py}	Per Capita Real Income g_y	Per Capita Nominal Money Balances g_{Pm}
2	1870.0		2.873	0.785			2.331			0.542
3	1872.0	1.528	0.743	2.474	-2.452	3.980	2.383	-0.855	1.597	-1.640
4	1876.0	3.358	0.884	0.581	-2.359	5.717	2.287	1.071	3.430	-1.403
5	1880.5	4.278	3.697	-3.522	-1.376	5.654	2.282	1.996	3.372	1.415
6	1884.0	1.383	4.905	-2.781	-1.314	2.697	2.343	-0.960	0.354	2.562
7	1886.5	-0.701	2.080	-0.816	-2.394	1.693	2.249	-2.950	-0.556	-0.169
8	1888.0	2.000	2.816	-0.041	0.735	1.265	2.142	-0.142	-0.877	0.674
9	1889.5	3.323	3.364	0.363	-0.312	3.635	2.086	1.237	1.549	1.278
10	1891.0	4.259	3.896	0.271	-1.673	5.932	2.062	2.197	3.870	1.834
11	1892.0	0.495	0.224	-0.708	-1.699	2.194	2.006	-1.511	0.188	-1.782
12	1893.5	-2.395	-1.687	0.173	-2.278	-0.117	1.956	-4.351	-2.073	-3.643
13	1895.0	-1.553	-1.726	1.591	-2.928	1.375	1.914	-3.467	-0.539	-3.640
14	1896.0	4.170	2.579	0.651	-0.272	4.442	1.836	2.334	2.606	0.743
15	1898.0	7.347	6.696	0.352	1.779	5.568	1.796	5.551	3.772	4.900
16	1900.0	8.717	8.365	-0.725	2.559	6.158	1.829	6.888	4.329	6.536
17	1902.0	5.731	6.456	-0.993	1.785	3.946	1.903	3.828	2.043	4.553
18	1904.0	5.842	6.835	-0.525	1.834	4.008	1.921	3.921	2.087	4.914
19	1906.0	5.775	6.300	-0.671	2.211	3.564	1.915	3.860	1.649	4.385
20	1908.0	4.177	4.848	-0.736	2.269	1.908	1.929	2.248	-0.021	2.919
21	1909.5	5.108	5.844	-0.589	1.862	3.246	1.952	3.156	1.294	3.892
22	1911.0	5.486	6.075		1.729	3.757	1.767	3.719	1.990	4.308

23	1912.5	3.464	5.240	−1.776	1.640	1.824	1.768	1.696	0.056	3.472
24	1914.0	8.055	8.454	−0.399	6.075	1.980	1.575	6.480	0.405	6.879
25	1916.5	14.884	11.678	3.206	10.370	4.514	1.134	13.750	3.380	10.544
26	1919.0	15.981	13.038	2.943	11.363	4.618	0.989	14.992	3.629	12.049
27	1920.0	0.348	8.075	−7.727	2.973	−2.256	1.733	−1.385	−4.358	6.342
28	1921.0	−4.106	1.533	−5.639	−5.329	1.223	1.727	−5.833	−0.504	−0.194
29	1922.5	2.963	3.541	−0.578	−3.798	6.761	1.680	1.283	5.081	1.861
30	1924.0	6.465	6.506	−0.041	0.260	6.205	1.677	4.788	4.528	4.829
31	1925.5	3.896	5.418	−1.522	0.173	3.723	1.509	2.387	2.214	3.909
32	1927.0	2.723	3.416	−0.693	−0.421	3.144	1.330	1.393	1.814	2.086
33	1928.5	−6.437	−1.069	−5.368	−3.597	−2.840	1.069	−7.506	−3.909	−2.138
34	1931.0	−6.476	−3.121	−3.355	−3.814	−2.662	0.766	−7.242	−3.428	−3.887
35	1935.0	−0.473	−0.192	−0.281	−1.797	1.324	0.665	−1.138	0.659	−0.857
36	1938.0	9.990	8.432	1.558	2.741	7.249	0.815	9.175	6.434	7.617
37	1941.5	11.516	13.726	−2.210	5.974	5.542	1.059	10.457	4.483	12.667
38	1945.5	9.640	13.986	−4.346	6.731	2.909	1.228	8.412	1.681	12.758
39	1947.5	4.163	5.306	−1.143	4.379	−0.216	1.582	2.581	−1.798	3.724
40	1949.0	7.574	2.237	5.337	2.839	4.735	1.716	5.858	3.019	0.521
41	1951.5	6.825	3.279	3.546	2.233	4.592	1.703	5.122	2.889	1.576
42	1954.0	5.436	3.575	1.861	2.178	3.258	1.736	3.700	1.522	1.839
43	1956.0	4.705	2.999	1.706	2.413	2.292	1.769	2.936	0.523	1.230
44	1958.0	4.586	3.461	1.125	2.273	2.313	1.817	2.769	0.496	1.644
45	1959.5	4.846	3.502	1.344	1.687	3.159	1.802	3.044	1.357	1.700
46	1961.0	5.969	5.205	0.764	1.722	4.247	1.529	4.440	2.718	3.676
47	1964.0	7.010	6.576	0.434	2.127	4.883	1.367	5.643	3.516	5.209
48	1967.0	7.442	7.306	0.136	2.897	4.545	1.192	6.250	3.353	6.114
49	1968.5	6.858	6.901	−0.043	4.384	2.474	1.047	5.811	1.427	5.854
50	1970.0	7.268	7.716	−0.448	5.293	1.975	1.018	6.250	0.957	6.698
51	1972.0	8.448	8.940	−0.492	6.217	2.231	0.869	7.579	1.362	8.017

Table 5.9 (Continued)

Number	Per Capita Real Money Balances g_m	Call Money Rate $DR_{S'}$	Commercial Paper Rate DR_S	Yield on Corporate Bonds $DR_{L'}$	DR_L	High-Powered Money g_H	Money Stock per Unit of Output $g_{M/y'}$	Weight g_w
2		-0.012	0.053	-0.023	-0.023	0.085		19.2
3	0.812	-0.659	-0.48	-0.178	-0.178	0.022	-3.237	67.1
4	0.956	-0.281	-0.332	-0.209	-0.209	2.306	-4.833	147.4
5	2.791	-0.125	-0.088	-0.171	-0.171	5.295	-1.957	145.4
6	3.876	-0.302	-0.046	-0.118	-0.118	4.998	2.208	64.6
7	2.225	0.139	-0.014	-0.117	-0.117	1.909	0.387	22.6
8	-0.061	0.218	0.075	-0.056	-0.056	2.993	1.551	12.0
9	1.590	0.277	0.062	0.010	0.010	3.212	-0.271	9.0
10	3.507	-0.348	-0.072	0.069	0.070	4.137	-2.036	7.4
11	-0.083	-0.491	-0.078	-0.007	0.006	3.501	-1.970	7.4
12	-1.365	-0.570	-0.465	-0.078	-0.080	0.960	-1.570	9.0
13	-0.712	-0.241	-0.304	-0.101	-0.103	-2.039	-3.101	7.4
14	1.015	0.352	0.127	-0.082	-0.082	2.298	-1.863	12.8
15	3.121	0.220	-0.119	-0.085	-0.072	6.094	1.128	16.0
16	3.977	0.346	0.152	-0.027	-0.024	6.804	2.207	28.8
17	2.768	-0.290	0.142	0.064	0.023	5.555	2.510	16.0

18	3.080	0.144	0.102	0.069	−0.027	4.903	2.827	28.8
19	2.174	0.380	0.130	0.088	0.038	5.780	2.736	16.0
20	0.650	−0.609	−0.196	0.075	0.060	5.568	2.940	19.2
21	2.030	−0.458	−0.278	−0.008	−0.073	2.869	2.598	9.0
22	2.579	0.208	0.146	0.034	−0.002	2.239	2.318	12.0
23	1.832	0.135	0.221	0.067	0.052	2.498	3.416	9.0
24	0.804	−0.047	−0.169	0.059	0.044	7.052	6.474	28.6
25	0.174	0.520	0.092	0.140	0.093	12.448	7.164	25.0
26	0.686	1.151	0.602	0.220	0.182	14.249	8.420	20.2
27	3.369	0.505	0.653	0.193	0.280	4.053	10.700	4.0
28	5.135	−0.958	−0.611	−0.071	−0.150	−3.323	0.310	7.4
29	5.659	−0.977	−0.837	−0.166	−0.250	−0.932	−3.22	9.0
30	4.569	−0.293	−0.351	−0.094	−0.117	2.631	0.301	12.0
31	3.736	0.108	−0.103	−0.095	−0.121	1.810	1.695	9.0
32	2.507	0.650	0.279	−0.103	−0.051	0.553	0.272	12.0
33	1.459	−0.446	−0.246	0.013	0.031	0.172	1.771	22.7
34	−0.073	−0.707	−0.570	−0.089	−0.139	5.706	−0.459	85.1
35	0.940	−0.369	−0.418	−0.179	−0.268	9.066	−1.516	69.3
36	4.876	−0.005	−0.066	−0.159	−0.237	12.987	1.183	127.4
37	6.693	0.006	−0.015	−0.064	−0.059	14.288	8.184	66.0
38	6.027	0.049	0.044	−0.028	−0.009	11.856	11.077	78.9
39	−0.655	0.158	0.195	0.061	0.029	3.492	5.522	14.4
40	−2.318	0.201	0.224	0.053	0.043	1.037	−2.498	28.6

Table 5.9 (Continued)

Number	Per Capita Real Money Balances g_m	Call Money Rate $DR_{S'}$	Commercial Paper Rate DR_S	Yield on Corporate Bonds		High-Powered Money g_H	Money Stock per Unit of Output $g_{M/y'}$	Weight g_w
				$DR_{L'}$	DR_L			
41	-0.657	0.293	0.117	0.061	0.060	1.686	-1.313	25.0
42	-0.339	0.341	0.158	0.081	0.104	1.242	0.317	41.2
43	-1.183	0.264	0.271	0.142	0.204	0.098	0.707	16.0
44	-0.629	0.174	0.235	0.264	0.260	0.428	1.148	19.2
45	-0.013	0.212	0.091	0.247	0.168	-0.173	0.343	9.0
46	1.954	0.064	0.087	0.045	0.045	1.974	0.958	40.4
47	3.082	0.162	0.319	0.077	0.175	4.004	1.693	36.0
48	3.217	0.409	0.505	0.300	0.392	5.320	2.761	40.3
49	1.470	0.745	0.815	0.740	0.686	5.990	4.427	9.0
50	1.405	-0.128	-0.146	0.346	0.289	6.209	5.741	19.2
51	1.854	0.470	0.278	0.170	0.157	6.791	6.709	23.8

Notes: Interest rates in percent per year.

Source: Table 5.7. Rates of change are slopes of least-squares line of successive triplets of logarithmic phase averages, weighted inversely to their variances. For derivation of rate-of-change weights shown in the final column of this table, see section 3.2.1.

To derive rates of change of unadjusted United States money stock and velocity, for phases 2–16, add 2.5 percent to each entry for money, and subtract 2.5 percent from each entry for velocity. For phase 17, add (or subtract) 2.185 percent; phase 18, 0.936 percent. The effect of the adjustment for financial sophistication disappears by phase 19. See the discussion in section 6.3.

Table 5.10 Rates of Change Computed from Triplets of Reference Phase Averages (Annual Percentage): United Kingdom, 1870–1975

Central Phase of Triplet		Nominal Income g_Y	Money Stock g_M	Velocity g_V	Implicit Price Deflator g_P	Real Income $g_{y'}$	Population g_N	Per Capita Nominal Income g_{Py}	Per Capita Real Income g_y	Per Capita Nominal Money Balances g_{Pm}
Number	Midpoint									
1	1877.0	1.118			−0.948	2.066	1.007	0.111	1.059	
2	1881.5	0.358	0.366	−0.008	−1.179	1.537	0.910	−0.552	0.627	−0.544
3	1885.0	1.715	1.427	0.288	−0.911	2.626	0.788	0.927	1.838	0.639
4	1888.5	2.631	2.107	0.524	−0.019	2.650	0.813	1.818	1.837	1.294
5	1892.0	2.421	2.770	−0.349	−0.076	2.497	0.900	1.521	1.597	1.870
6	1897.0	2.443	2.264	0.179	0.388	2.055	0.937	1.506	1.118	1.327
7	1902.5	2.104	1.669	0.435	0.748	1.356	0.911	1.193	0.445	0.758
8	1906.0	1.989	1.158	0.831	0.352	1.637	0.867	1.122	0.770	0.291
9	1908.0	2.269	2.206	0.063	0.746	1.523	0.825	1.444	0.698	1.381
10	1911.0	2.803	3.254	−0.451	0.899	1.904	0.716	2.087	1.188	2.538
11	1914.0	7.711	7.444	0.267	5.458	2.253	0.583	7.128	1.670	6.861
12	1916.5	14.526	13.723	0.803	14.013	0.513	0.328	14.198	0.185	13.395
13	1919.0	14.272	15.270	−0.998	17.267	−2.995	0.135	14.137	−3.130	15.135
14	1920.0	2.039	8.588	−6.549	10.765	−8.726	0.531	1.508	−9.257	8.057
15	1921.0	−8.936	−1.292	−7.644	−8.114	−0.822	0.681	−9.617	−1.503	−1.973
16	1923.0	−3.614	−2.371	−1.243	−6.705	3.091	0.577	−4.191	2.514	−2.948
17	1925.5	0.908	−1.147	2.055	−2.647	3.555	0.472	0.436	3.083	−1.619
18	1927.0	1.465	0.967	0.498	−1.657	3.122	0.369	1.096	2.753	0.598
19	1928.0	2.502	1.575	0.927	−1.252	3.754	0.350	2.152	3.404	1.225
20	1929.0	−1.530	0.646	−2.176	−1.337	−0.193	0.369	−1.899	−0.562	0.277
21	1931.0	0.119	2.092	−1.973	−1.479	1.598	0.425	−0.306	1.173	1.667
22	1935.0	2.282	2.875	−0.593	−0.438	2.720	0.433	1.849	2.287	2.442

Table 5.10 (Continued)

Central Phase of Triplet		Nominal Income g_Y	Money Stock g_M	Velocity g_V	Implicit Price Deflator g_P	Real Income $g_{y'}$	Population g_N	Per Capita Nominal Income g_{Py}	Per Capita Real Income g_y	Per Capita Nominal Money Balances g_{Pm}
Number	Midpoint									
23	1938.0	7.250	5.729	1.521	4.384	2.866	0.482	6.768	2.384	5.247
24	1941.5	7.362	9.955	−2.593	5.469	1.893	0.482	6.880	1.411	9.473
25	1945.5	5.797	8.891	−3.094	4.517	1.280	0.477	5.320	0.803	8.414
26	1949.0	6.112	3.941	2.171	4.615	1.497	0.393	5.719	1.104	3.548
27	1952.0	7.097	1.881	5.216	4.730	2.367	0.256	6.841	2.111	1.625
28	1954.0	6.449	1.718	4.731	4.108	2.341	0.382	6.067	1.959	1.336
29	1957.0	5.986	2.061	3.925	3.845	2.141	0.458	5.528	1.683	1.603
30	1959.5	5.848	3.065	2.783	3.103	2.745	0.636	5.212	2.109	2.429
31	1961.5	6.311	3.382	2.929	2.727	3.584	0.731	5.580	2.853	2.651
32	1964.0	6.399	4.165	2.234	3.164	3.235	0.649	5.750	2.586	3.516
33	1966.0	6.129	4.815	1.314	4.034	2.095	0.571	5.558	1.524	4.244
34	1967.5	6.617	5.677	0.940	5.422	1.195	0.445	6.172	0.750	5.232
35	1970.0	9.163	9.491	−0.328	7.447	1.716	0.368	8.795	1.348	9.123
36	1972.5	12.665	15.279	−2.614	10.538	2.127	0.256	12.409	1.871	15.023

Number	Per Capita Real Money Balances g_m	Short-Term Interest Rate DR_S	Long-Term Interest Rate DR_L	High-Powered Money g_H	Money Stock per Unit of Output $g_{M/y'}$	Weight g_w
1		-0.066	-0.021		-1.171	276.3
2	0.635	-0.032	-0.023	-0.562	-1.199	145.4
3	1.550	-0.024	-0.018	-0.243	-0.543	112.0
4	1.313	-0.005	-0.046	1.471	0.273	88.2
5	1.946	-0.083	-0.060	2.256	0.209	214.5
6	0.939	0.072	0.007	1.367	0.313	225.1
7	0.010	0.156	0.052	0.857	-0.479	219.1
8	-0.061	0.045	0.043	0.924	0.683	49.9
9	0.635	-0.071	0.059	1.064	1.350	56.4
10	1.639	0.040	0.082	3.918	5.191	36.0
11	1.403	0.210	0.185	11.709	13.210	76.3
12	-0.618	0.022	0.217	17.635	18.265	25.0
13	-2.132	0.144	0.206	15.286	17.314	20.2
14	-2.708	1.020	0.378	2.380	-0.470	4.0
15	6.141	-0.780	-0.200	-4.192	-5.462	12.8
16	3.757	-0.296	-0.162	-2.925	-4.702	23.8
17	1.028	0.296	0.003	-1.617	-2.155	22.6
19	2.255	0.080	0.031	-1.372	-2.179	7.4
20	2.477	0.170	-0.010	-1.294	0.494	4.0
21	3.146	-0.641	-0.256	1.817	0.155	67.1
22	2.880	-0.434	-0.189	3.293		69.3

Table 5.10 (Continued)

Number	Per Capita Real Money Balances g_m	Short-Term Interest Rate DR_S	Long-Term Interest Rate DR_L	High-Powered Money g_H	Money Stock per Unit of Output $g_{M/y'}$	Weight g_w
23	0.863	0.040	0.016	7.362	2.863	127.4
24	4.004	0.023	-0.063	11.943	8.062	66.0
25	3.897	-0.054	-0.012	8.678	7.611	169.7
26	-1.067	0.120	0.161	2.195	2.444	49.6
27	-3.105	0.397	0.172	2.521	-0.486	56.4
28	-2.772	0.618	0.173	4.544	-0.623	35.4
29	-2.242	0.328	0.188	4.083	-0.080	47.3
30	-0.674	0.035	0.248	3.549	0.320	31.7
31	-0.076	0.082	0.187	3.278	-0.202	31.7
32	0.352	0.243	0.128	3.921	0.930	23.8
33	0.210	0.552	0.278	4.93	2.720	19.2
34	-0.190	0.417	0.579	4.363	4.482	22.7
35	1.676	0.153	0.528	6.453	7.775	33.4
36	4.485	0.77	1.059	11.703	13.152	31.7

Note: Interest rates in percent per year per year.
Source: Table 5.8. Rates of change are slopes of least-squares line of successive triplets of logarithmic phase averages, weighted inversely to their variances. For derivation of rate-of-change weights shown in the final column of this table, see section 3.2.1.

6   Velocity and the Demand For Money

The most intriguing finding in the preceding chapter is the extraordinary parallelism of velocity in the United States and the United Kingdom, especially since 1905 (see chart 5.5). We have attributed the deviations before 1903 primarily to the growing financial sophistication of the United States, but they may also reflect the greater inaccuracy of the earlier data for both the United States and the United Kingdom.

The parallelism presumably reflects both similar money-holding propensities in the United States and the United Kingdom for more than two-thirds of a century and a largely common set of factors determining the number of weeks of income that residents of the United States and the United Kingdom chose to hold as money. The alternative is to attribute the parallelism to an accidental offsetting of differences in propensities by differences in the factors affecting the amount of money held. The parallelism therefore suggests that we can use the data for the two countries as if they came from a single parent universe in trying to identify the factors determining the behavior of velocity. That is the task of the present chapter. The parallelism also suggests that it is worthwhile exploring the influences connecting the two countries. That is the task of chapter 7.

An analysis of the behavior of velocity is an analysis of the demand for money. As we noted in chapter 2, we can express the "real" quantity of money in various ways: most directly, as a quantity of money divided by a price index (as in equation 7 in chap. 2) or, as is frequently more meaningful in comparing different countries or widely separated periods, by the device used in chapter 5, as the number of weeks of income or consumption to which the quantity of money is equivalent. The income velocity of circulation is simply the reciprocal of the number of weeks of income held as money, which is why an analysis of velocity is equivalent to an analysis of the demand for money. Velocity is usually expressed per year rather than per week and hence, as usually expressed, is equal to the reciprocal of the number of weeks of income held as money times fifty-two. But that is simply a question of units. The percentage rate of change of weeks-of-income held as money is equal in numerical value but opposite in sign to the rate of change of velocity.

If velocity is viewed in terms of the demand for money, we must, as in any demand study, distinguish "desired" or "demanded" quantities from actual quantities and actual quantities from measured quantities. Desired and actual quantities may differ because the demand function in question involves a different level or stage of adjustment—a different Marshallian period—than corresponds to the observed quantity; because, that is, we admit that demanders may be "off" their demand curve of the kind in question. And actual quantities may differ from measured quantities because of errors of measurement.

The simplest explanation of measured velocity and its movements is that velocity is the ratio of two independent magnitudes, each determined by a separate set of forces. This explanation is consistent with the view that (1) there does not exist a stable demand for money as a function of a small number of variables; or (2) there exists a stable function but it has a special form, for example, Keynesian absolute liquidity preference, so that velocity adapts passively to the separate movements in income and money; or (3) the errors of measurement of numerator and denominator dominate the fluctuations of velocity. Section 6.1 demonstrates that our data are inconsistent with this explanation.

At the opposite extreme doctrinally is the explanation that desired velocity is a numerical constant—a simple-minded quantity theory rather than Keynesian theory. On this explanation, observed deviations from constancy reflect either errors of observation or differences between actual and desired velocity. This extreme quantity theory must be rejected. Yet it is impressive how far it carries us in explaining (1) the movements of aggregate income, if the quantity of money is regarded as exogenous; or (2) the movements of aggregate quantity of money, if income is regarded as exogenous and the quantity of money as demand-determined (i.e., an adaptive supply) (sec. 6.2).

To go beyond these simple theories, we must investigate the effect of other variables on the quantity of money demanded. In view of the findings of the previous chapter, one variable that we must allow for in some way or another is the changing financial sophistication in the United States—which we regard as the chief explanation for the difference between the United States and the United Kingdom in the level and trend of velocity before 1902 (sec. 6.3). Beyond this, we consider the possible influence of real per capita income (sec. 6.4), of population and prices (sec. 6.5), and of the cost of holding money (sec. 6.6). Finally in section 6.7, we consider the joint influence of these variables.

6.1   Velocity: A Will-o'-the Wisp?

As we indicated in chapter 2, much recent literature deriving its inspiration, though not always its details, from Keynes's *General Theory* treats nominal income as if it were determined by forces largely independent of the quantity of money, so that velocity adjusts passively.[1] Carried to its limits, this interpretation makes velocity—and its reciprocal—the ratio of two statistically independent magnitudes.[2] In that extreme case, the correlation between income and money would be zero and the variance of the logarithm of weeks of income held as money would be equal to the sum of the variances of the logarithms of income and money, and hence larger than either.

This interpretation is clearly not valid for *levels* of income, money, and weeks of income. The simple correlation between the logarithms of income and money is .992 for the United States and .991 for the United Kingdom for the period as a whole, and its lowest value for separate periods before and after 1914 is .980. As a result, the variance or standard deviation of the logarithm of weeks of income is much less than the variance or standard deviation of the logarithms of either money or income.

However, few if any proponents of this interpretation would apply it to the levels of income, money, and velocity for a long period. They grant that in the long run the desired ratio of money to income is not indefinitely malleable, that it would be impossible to multiply nominal income manyfold without something like a corresponding rise in the quantity of money. They view velocity as malleable over shorter periods—perhaps over periods even shorter than the phases that are our units of observation.

1. See J. G. Gurley and E. S. Shaw, *Money in a Theory of Finance*, Washington, D. C.: Brookings Institution, 1959; (Radcliffe) Committee on the Working of the Monetary System, *Report*, Cmd. 827, London: HMSO, 1959; R. S. Sayers, "Monetary Thought and Monetary Policy in England," *Economic Journal* 70 (December 1960): 710–24.

2. For example, Alvin Hansen, the leading American disciple of Keynes, wrote in 1957 (*The American Economy*, p. 50): "I think we should do well to eliminate once and for all, the phrase 'velocity of circulation' from our vocabulary. Instead, we should simply speak of the ratio of money to aggregate spending. The phrase 'velocity of circulation' is, I feel, unfortunate because those who employ it tend to make an independent entity out of it and imbue it with a soul. This little manikin is placed on the stage, and the audience is led to believe that it is endowed with the power of making decisions directing and controlling the flow of aggregate spending. In fact it is nothing of the sort. It is a mere residual. We should get on much better if we substitute the word 'ratio.' The little manikin would then be forced back into oblivion, where it properly belongs."

A more relevant application is therefore to the rates of change of money, income, and weeks of income. It could be that there is a fairly well determined relation between the trends of money and income but that deviations from the trends are largely attributable to forces affecting money and income separately, so that deviations of weeks of income from its trend are a largely passive consequence.[3] However, this application too is contradicted by the standard deviations and correlation coefficients in table 5.6. For the period as a whole, including and excluding war years, for two subperiods, and for both the United States and the United Kingdom, the correlations between the rates of change of income and money range from .73 to .95, and the rate of change of weeks of income fluctuates less than the rates of change of both nominal income and money.[4]

Taken as a whole, the evidence is decisive that movements in the rate of change of money are accompanied by sufficiently closely correlated movements in the same direction in the rate of change of income to make the rate of change of weeks of income or of velocity decidedly more stable than either of its components. Velocity is not simply or even mainly a will-o'-the-wisp, over either periods measured in decades or periods measured in phases.

6.2   Velocity: A Numerical Constant?

Velocity, as measured, is clearly not a numerical constant. However, measured velocity differs from "true," "permanent," or "desired" velocity for two reasons: errors of measurement, and deviations between actual and "desired" velocity. May these deviations not explain the failure of measured velocity to be a numerical constant?

In terms of the demand for money, this interpretation taken literally says that the demand function has a special form:

$$(1) \qquad M = kY,$$

where M is the nominal quantity of money, Y is nominal income, both measured accurately, and k is a numerical constant equal to the recipro-

---

3. The world "largely" is required in this statement because there must be some mechanism to bring the various series back to the trend lines, hence the deviations from trend cannot be wholly random. However, for short periods, the independent transitory elements in money and income could dominate the related systematic elements.

4. A positive correlation does not alone guarantee this result:

$$g_V = g_Y - g_M$$

$$\sigma_{g_V} = \sqrt{\sigma_{g_Y}^2 + \sigma_{g_M}^2 - 2r_{g_Y g_M} \sigma_{g_Y} \sigma_{g_M}}$$

If $\sigma_{g_Y} = \sigma_{g_M}$, then $r_{g_Y g_M}$ must exceed 0.5 for σ_{g_V} to be less than both σ_{g_Y} and σ_{g_M}. If $\sigma_{g_Y} \neq \sigma_{g_M}$, r must exceed half the ratio of the larger to the smaller to assure that σ_{g_V} is less than both σ_{g_M} and σ_{g_Y}.

cal of velocity. It says that if M can be regarded as exogenous, and money-holders are always on the demand curve defined by equation (1), then nominal income at time T will be $\frac{1}{k} M(T)$. Alternatively, if nominal income is regarded as exogenous, and the quantity of money as passively adapting to the quantity demanded, then the nominal quantity of money at time T will be $kY(T)$. Note that equation (1), as the preceding sentence indicates, is itself completely neutral about the much discussed question of "direction of influence" or "causal significance." It simply says that if equation (1) is the demand function for money and if money-holders are on their demand function and if M and Y are measured accurately, then M and Y will move together in fixed proportion. The observation that M and Y do move together would leave entirely open the question which is the "cause" and which the "effect," or whether both are the common "effect" of still other variables.

The significant time trends in velocity for long periods for the United States and the United Kingdom (e.g., for the period before World War I, the United States regression has a slope of $-.024$ with a standard error of $.0014$; the United Kingdom regression has a slope of $+.0018$ with a standard error of $.0006$) is alone sufficient to rule out this simple version. Presumably, trends average out both statistical errors and deviations between actual and desired balances.

A more sophisticated version, like the more sophisticated will-o'-the-wisp explanation, allows for time trends, regarding the demand equation as

(2) $M(T) = k(T) Y(T),$

where T is time and $k(T)$ is some simple function of time (such as a semilog trend), since if $k(T)$ were left completely free, equation (2) could be regarded as an identity defining $k(T)$.[5]

This version too can be rejected out of hand. A sufficient basis for rejecting it is the close parallelism of the deviations of velocity about trends in the United States and the United Kingdom for over two-thirds

5. J. P. Gould and C. R. Nelson, "The Stochastic Structure of the Velocity of Money," *American Economic Review* 65 (June 1974): 405–18, assert that there is no significant trend in our velocity series for the United States from 1869 to 1960—that, on the contrary, it can be regarded as a random walk without drift. On their interpretation, the data are consistent with equation (1) plus stochastic disturbances. Houston H. Stokes and Hugh Neuberger, "A Note on the Stochastic Structure of the Velocity of Money: Some Reservations," *American Economist* 23 (fall 1979): 62–64, demonstrate that the Gould-Nelson result is produced by combining nonhomogeneous periods and that for the period 1879–1940 the trend is significant, and the series is not a random walk with drift, that is, neither equation (1) nor equation (2) plus stochastic disturbances is acceptable. The next paragraph of our text, plus the rest of this chapter, provides additional and in our view decisive evidence contradicting the Gould-Nelson interpretation.

of a century, and also, of the rates of change of velocity, which can be regarded as incorporating a sensitive adjustment for trend. Since the statistical bases of the estimates are completely independent for the two countries, and in each country, for money and income, errors of measurement cannot account for the parallelism. Similarly, the obvious link between the two countries—the balance of payments—seems more likely to have produced inverse than parallel deviations in the two countries between measured and desired velocity. A surplus for one country tended to be accompanied by a deficit for the other country, so whatever the effect of the balance of payments on velocity, it would be in opposite directions in the two countries.[6] We know of no links that work in the other direction.

Though we have treated the constant-velocity explanation and the will-o'-the-wisp explanation as if they were opposite extremes, it is worth noting that they have much in common. Insofar as variations in velocity reflect errors of measurement—which they undoubtedly do to some extent—such variations are consistent with both explanations. Moreover, as in all analysis involving a distinction between actual and desired, or between permanent and transitory, it is generally impossible to separate the part of the transitory component of the measured variable that is attributable to errors of measurement from the part that is attributable to other forces. Hence, at least some part of the variability of velocity attributable to deviations between measured and desired velocity is also consistent with both explanations.

Though a numerically constant velocity must be rejected as a full explanation of the relation between money and income, it should not be dismissed without recording how far it takes us. For any lengthy period, equation (1)—the simplest and most rigid form of the constant-velocity view—accounts for the great bulk of the variation in nominal income (if the nominal quantity of money is regarded as exogenous and income as adapting to the quantity of money) or in nominal quantity of money (if nominal income is regarded as exogenous and the quantity of money as adapting to income).

This is demonstrated in table 6.1. For the century as a whole, or the more than eighty years excluding phases we have designated as war

---

6. Under fixed exchange rates, a surplus that arises from forces independent of the nominal income of the country with the surplus would tend to lower measured velocity below desired velocity in the interval between its effect on the quantity of money and the effect of the changed quantity of money on income. If the surplus arose from an autonomous rise in income that raised measured velocity above desired velocity (the sequence generally envisioned in the monetary theory of the balance of payments), it would reduce measured velocity to bring it back to desired velocity. In either case the surplus would be accompanied by a decline in velocity, though in the first there is no reason to expect it to be preceded by a rise in measured velocity; in the second there is.

phases, for the United States or the United Kingdom separately, or for the two combined, equation (1), with V set simply equal to its (geometric) average value over the period and for the country or countries in question, accounts for at least 94.5 percent of the variability in money or, alternatively, income.[7] For three separate peacetime periods the corresponding percentage exceeds 90 in nine out of eighteen observations, and 50 in fourteen out of eighteen observations.[8] The remaining four, one of which is negative and the other three between 30 and 40, are all for the briefest (eighteen years) and most turbulent subperiod—that between the wars. The most striking result is for the two countries together, for which the money and income observations have been pooled by the crude device of simply converting figures in pounds sterling to dollars at the ruling rate of exchange. Here, more than 95 percent of the variability is accounted for by equation (1) except for the pre–World War I period, where the sharp difference between the trends of velocity in the United States and the United Kingdom reduces the percentage accounted for to 61 for income and 66 for money.

The major upward trends in income and money in both countries play an important role in producing these results. The absence of wide differ-

7. Taking logs of equation (1), we have

(a) $$\log M = \log k + \log Y.$$

If this equation were satisfied precisely, the variables could stand equally for observed or predicted values. In fact, it will not be satisfied precisely, so we must distinguish between observed and predicted values of M, k, and Y. Let the variables as written in equation (a) stand for observed values, $\hat{M}$ and $\hat{Y}$ for predicted values of M and Y, and $\overline{\log k}$ for the mean value of the observed values of $\log k$ (so its antilog is the geometric mean of the observed values of k, and the reciprocal of its antilog, the geometric mean of the observed values of velocity, or V). Then assuming Y exogenous,

(b) $$\log \hat{M} = \overline{\log k} + \log Y,$$

and the error of prediction is

(c) $$\log M - \log \hat{M} = \log M - \log Y - \overline{\log k}$$
(d) $$= \log k - \overline{\log k}.$$

Hence the root-mean-square error in the logs is equal to the standard deviation of $\log k$, and, since $\log k = -\log V$, is also the standard deviation of $\log V$.

If M is assumed exogenous, we have

(e) $$\log \hat{Y} = \log M - \overline{\log k},$$
(f) $$\log Y - \log \hat{Y} = \log Y - \log M + \overline{\log k}$$
(g) $$= \log V - \overline{\log V},$$

so the root-mean-square error is again the standard deviation of $\log V$. As noted in footnote b of table 6.1, these estimates are maxima because neither $\log Y$ nor $\log M$ is measured without error. See also footnote 28 of chapter 5.

8. For reasons which will become apparent later in this chapter, we shift our periodization of nonwar phases for the rest of the book from the pre–World War I/ post–World War I dichotomy of chapter 5 to the trichotomy pre–World War I/ interwar/ post–World War II.

Table 6.1   Variability in Money and Income Accounted for by Constant-Velocity Demand Curves

	Phase Numbers		Total			Maximum[b] Residual after Allowing for Constant Velocity[c]			Minimum Fraction of Total Variance[d] Accounted for by Constant Velocity		
Period	U.S.	U.K.	U.S. (1)	U.K. (2)	U.S. and U.K. (3)	U.S. (4)	U.K. (5)	U.S. and U.K. (6)	U.S. (7)	U.K. (8)	U.S. and U.K. (9)
Level of Money: Income Assumed Exogenous											
Full period	4–52	1–37	172.6	117.1	148.6	34.0	16.7	29.2	96.1	98.0	96.1
Full period ex-wars			182.8	125.1	156.9	34.4	14.8	29.2	96.5	98.6	96.5
Pre–World War I	4–24	1–11	71.7	23.5	56.6	29.6	3.1	33.0	83.0	98.3	66.0
Interwar	28–36	15–23	11.4	7.7	61.0	13.3	6.0	12.9	–36.1	39.3	95.5
Post–World War II	40–52	27–37	44.4	40.6	109.3	8.4	16.0	14.8	96.4	84.5	98.2
Level of Income: Money Assumed Exogenous											
Full period	4–52	1–37	145.6	120.4	137.9	34.0	16.7	29.2	94.6	98.1	95.5
Full period ex-wars			155.3	131.4	146.4	34.4	14.8	29.2	95.1	98.7	96.0
Pre–World War I	4–24	1–11	44.3	25.7	53.1	29.6	3.1	33.0	55.4	98.6	61.4
Interwar	28–36	15–23	16.4	7.2	69.3	13.3	6.0	12.9	34.2	30.6	96.5
Post–World War II	40–52	27–37	50.6	51.9	105.1	8.4	16.0	14.8	97.2	90.5	98.0

Variation (Percent or Percentage Points)[a]

Rate of Change of Money: Rate of Change of Income Assumed Exogenous

Full period	5–51	2–36	4.45	3.50	4.05	2.79	1.91	2.28	70.0	67.1	69.1
Full period ex-wars			3.61	2.44	3.09	2.64	1.37	1.94	62.8	70.4	65.0
Pre–World War I	5–23	2–10	1.99	0.81	2.44	3.12	0.36	1.69	−52.1	75.7	−1.2
Interwar	29–35	16–22	3.13	1.95	2.69	2.74	1.53	2.24	63.9	41.5	64.5
Post–World War II	41–51	28–36	2.05	4.51	3.39	1.45	2.96	2.33	51.0	−67.1	−63.9

Rate of Change of Income: Rate of Change of Money Assumed Exogenous

Full period	5–51	2–36	5.09	3.33	4.10	2.79	1.91	2.28	60.7	70.2	68.3
Full period ex-wars			4.33	2.52	3.28	2.64	1.37	1.94	46.5	68.5	60.6
Pre–World War I	5–23	2–10	2.53	0.73	1.68	3.12	0.36	1.69	−145.8	80.2	52.0
Interwar	29–35	16–22	4.56	2.00	3.76	2.74	1.53	2.24	23.4	38.4	30.7
Post–World War II	41–51	28–36	1.18	2.29	1.82	1.45	2.96	2.33	50.0	56.9	52.8

Note: Based on unadjusted money and velocity for the United States.

[a]For levels, figures given are standard deviations of natural logarithms multiplied by 100, which can be regarded as estimates of the coefficients of variation of the original observations, expressed as a percentage. For rates of change, figures are standard deviations of the rates of change expressed as percentages, hence are in percentage points.

[b]"Maximum" residual because these are computed without allowing for errors of measurement of variable assumed exogenous, hence the reported residual includes such errors of measurement as part of the nonexplained part of dependent variable (see chap. 5, notes 28 and 29).

[c]For levels, equal to standard deviation of velocity; for rates of change, to the root-mean-square of the rate of change of velocity, that is, to the square root of the sum of the variance and the square of the mean rate of change. (See notes 7 and 10, pp. 211, 214.)

[d]Computed as unity minus square of ratio of residual standard deviation to total standard deviation. "Minimum" for reason explained in note b above.

[e]For the United States and United Kingdom combined by converting United Kingdom figure in pounds to dollars at contemporaneous rate of exchange. For rates of change, data for both United States and United Kingdom are pure numbers per unit time, hence can be combined without adjustment.

ences between the trend rates of growth in money and income is consistent with equation (1), but it provides, as it were, only a single observation that receives a heavy weight in the percentages cited in the preceding paragraph.

Yet even if we eliminate trends, equation (1) carries us a long way. As noted, rates of change are a sensitive way of allowing for trends.[9] Equation (1) implies that the rate of change of money should equal the rate of change of income, that is, that the rate of change of velocity should be zero. Hence, the root-mean-square value of the rate of change of velocity is an upper limit of the residual variability of rates of change of income or money not accounted for by equation (1) (upper limit because it includes errors of observation in both M and Y).[10]

Using this estimate gives a *minimum* estimate of the fraction of variation accounted for by equation (1). As columns 7, 8, and 9 of table 6.1 show, this *minimum* estimate ranges from 46 to 69 percent for the full period, including or excluding war phases. For other periods the result is much more mixed, the minimum being negative in six out of eighteen observations. Yet even for the subperiods the minimum percentage exceeds 50 for seven of the twelve positive observations.

Nonetheless, there is much absolute variation remaining to be accounted for after allowing for a constant velocity. The maximum coefficient of variation of the residual variability in velocity ranges from 3 to 34 percent for various periods and countries. The maximum standard deviation of the residual variability in rates of change varies from 0.4 to

---

9. Note that fitting a single straight-line trend to the logarithms of money and income would give results intermediate between those for the level figures for the period as a whole and the rate-of-change figures, since there are substantial differences between the single trends and trends fitted to subperiods.

10. Differentiate equation (a) of footnote 7 above with respect to time:

(h) $$\frac{1}{M}\frac{dM}{dt} = \frac{1}{Y}\frac{dY}{dt},$$

or, in simpler notation,

(j) $$g_M = g_Y.$$

Hence the rate of change of either variable is to be predicted from the rate of change of the other by assuming them equal. Again distinguish predicted from observed, and we have that the error in the predicted g_M is

$$g_M - \hat{g}_M = g_M - g_Y = g_k = -g_V.$$

Hence the root-mean-square of the rate of change of velocity is the root-mean-square error. Note that the root-mean-square is *not* equal to the standard deviation of g_V because g_V may not average zero. Rather,

$$(Eg^2_V)^{1/2} = [\sigma^2_{g_V} + (\bar{g}_V)^2]^{1/2}.$$

As for levels, the root-mean-square value is the same for g_M and g_Y, and both are maximum errors because of errors of measurement.

3.1 percentage points. These are appreciable magnitudes, and we shall have a highly imperfect understanding of monetary relations until we can account for them.[11] Yet they are generally much less than the total variation in levels or rates of change of money and income.

Table 6.1 makes it clear that a numerically constant velocity does not deserve the sneering condescension that has become the conventional stance of economists. It is an impressive first approximation that by almost any measure accounts for a good deal more than half of the phase-to-phase movements in money or income. Almost certainly, measurement errors aside, it accounts for a far larger part of such movements than the other extreme hypothesis—that velocity is a will-o'-the-wisp reflecting independent changes in money and income. Yet, for most of the period since the mid-1930s, the will-o'-the-wisp extreme has been nearly the orthodox view among economists!

Our ultimate objective is an explanation of the behavior of velocity, which is to say, of the quantity of money demanded, that takes account simultaneously of all the variables affecting velocity. Nonetheless, we believe that this ultimate objective is better approached indirectly, by examining variables one or two at a time, than by what has become the prevailing fashion in econometric work, the immediate computation of multiple regressions including all variables that can reasonably be regarded as relevant. We believe that the indirect approach yields insights that cannot be obtained from the more sweeping approach—that multiple correlations with many variables are almost impossible to interpret correctly unless they are backed by more intensive investigations of smaller sets of variables. Accordingly, we shall proceed in the following sections to consider variables one or two at a time, and reserve to section 6.7 estimating their simultaneous effect.[12]

---

11. In light of the contrast that we and others have drawn between Keynesian and quantity theories, it is fascinating that it was precisely with respect to this point that Keynes made his famous remark about the long run. Having noted "that the quantity theory is often stated" in a form in which velocity is a constant and output is determined independently of the quantity of money, he went on to say, "Now 'in the long run' this is probably true. If, after the American Civil War, the American dollar had been stabilised and defined by law at 10 per cent below its present value, it would be safe to assume that . . . [the price level] would now be just 10 per cent greater than [it actually is]. . . . But this *long run* is a misleading guide to current affairs. *In the long run* we are all dead. Economists set themselves too easy, too useless a task if in tempestuous seasons they can only tell us that when the storm is long past, the ocean is flat again."

Like much of Keynes's own subsequent research, our monetary studies and those of other scholars are an attempt to respond to the challenge stated so colorfully by Keynes. J. M. Keynes, *A Tract on Monetary Reform* [1923], Royal Economic Society edition (London: Macmillan, 1971), p. 65.

12. The indirect approach played a critical role in the formulation of the multiple regressions that we calculate in section 6.7. At the same time, the partial results in sections

6.3   Effect of Financial Sophistication

The character of the financial system clearly affects velocity—indeed, it affects what items we designate as money. The development of banks of issue led students of money to add bank notes to coins and specie; the development of government money issue, to add government fiduciary or fiat currency; and the development of commercial banking, to add deposits, though with much disagreement about the kinds of deposits.

The financial structures of the United States and the United Kingdom have had enough in common and have remained sufficiently constant for the past century that we have found it feasible to use the same basic definition of money for both countries and the whole period, with only one minor exception.[13] However, while the general character of the financial structures has remained the same, there have been substantial changes in detail.

We concluded in chapter 5 (sec. 5.1.2) that the more rapid spread of financial institutions in the United States than in the United Kingdom after 1880 was probably the main reason for the near elimination by 1903 of the wide difference in velocity that prevailed in 1876–77—a difference of 2.8 to 1. Clearly, we must somehow or other allow for this effect.

A full analysis would require identifying the features of financial organization that are most directly relevant to the demand for money and measuring the separate influence of each—such features as number of bank offices per capita, average minimum distance of a bank office from residents in a specified area, fraction of the population having deposit accounts, detailed costs of and returns from deposit accounts, variables connected with the "quality" of deposits as judged by depositors, and so on. More broadly, and particularly for countries other than the United States and the United Kingdom, a major feature is the use of giro rather than checking systems.[14]

Such a full analysis, though it would be extremely illuminating, is clearly beyond the scope of this study. In lieu thereof, we tried to see whether a few simple variables (such as the deposit-currency ratio as a proxy for the quality of deposits) could capture the major effects of the

---

6.4, 6.5, and 6.6 are similar to the results from the final regressions. Hence the reader who is interested primarily in the results and not their derivation may want to skip these sections. This comment does not apply to section 6.3.

13. That exception is the exclusion of large negotiable certificates of deposit from the United States money stock since 1961. See Friedman and Schwartz, *Monetary Statistics*, pp. 80–81.

14. A giro system was introduced in the United Kingdom in 1968. Although deposits grew from £10 to £145 million in March 1975, they were only 0.5 percent of United Kingdom commercial bank deposits at the later date. Bank of England, *Quarterly Bulletin* 15 (June 1975), table 11/1, p. 198.

spread of banking. These experiments were uniformly unsuccessful. We have therefore resorted to a simple statistical expedient to correct United States data for what, in chapter 5, we called the changing financial sophistication of the United States relative to the United Kingdom.

1. On the basis of chart 5.5, showing velocity (or number of weeks of income) in the United States and the United Kingdom, we conclude that the change was largely completed by the year 1903.

2. We assume that the change affected the amount of money held and therefore velocity by the same percentage each year from 1869 to 1903, increasing money holdings and decreasing velocity each year by that percentage, over and above any change that can be explained by other variables.

3. One way we estimate the magnitude of the change is by using a dummy variable. For statistical regressions in which the dependent variable is the *level* of money or income or number of weeks of income held as money, the dummy variable is taken equal to zero for the United States phase centered on 1904.0 and later phases, and to the number of years elapsing to 1903 for earlier phases. For regressions in which the dependent variable is the *rate of change* of one of the indicated magnitudes, the dummy variable is taken equal to zero for phases centered on 1906 and later phases and equal to one for earlier phases.

4. Different regressions yield different estimates, yet all are within a fairly narrow range. For one set of forty-eight regressions, for example, for different periods, for the United States separately, and for the United States and the United Kingdom, the estimates range from a low of .022 to a high of .032; that is, increasing financial sophistication added between 2.2 and 3.0 percent per year to United States cash balances from 1876 to 1903. Accordingly, a second, and main, way we allow for the change in financial sophistication is to construct an "adjusted" set of money estimates for the United States for years before 1903 by raising the logarithm of the actual money stock by a constant times the number of years elapsing to 1903. The constant we have used is .0250; that is, we treat increasing financial sophistication as adding 2.5 percent per year to desired United States money balances from 1876 to 1903. The adjusted rates of change of money, and of number of weeks of income held as money, are therefore 2.5 percentage points lower than the unadjusted, and the adjusted rates of change of velocity, 2.5 percentage points higher. The effect is to eliminate most of the sharp early decline in velocity that is so prominent a feature of the raw data.

The second way has the advantage that it keeps the allowance for financial sophistication the same while other variables are altered. The first way does not; in practice, other variables with definite trends, and particularly steeper trends before 1903 than after, tend to absorb the effect of financial sophistication in their coefficients.[15] Of course, this consideration is not decisive. It may be that our adjustment for financial sophistication is in fact absorbing part of the effect of these other variables. However, a variety of considerations lead us to conclude the opposite.

Allowing for the changing degree of financial sophistication by adjusting our money estimates has a substantial effect (table 6.2). As we have interpreted it, this factor operates for 30 percent of the total period and for three-quarters of the period before World War I. Yet for the United States the adjustment reduces the variance of the aggregate level of money by 16 percent, of real per capita money balances by 35 percent, and of velocity by over 70 percent. To put it differently, table 6.1 showed that constant velocity alone, with income treated as exogenous, accounts for at least 96.1 percent of the variance of money and leaves a maximum residual variation of 34.0 percent. For the adjusted money series, constant velocity alone, with income again treated as exogenous, leaves a residual variation of 18 percent (see table 6.3, line 1, col. 2). In consequence, constant velocity plus the adjustment for financial sophistication account for no less than 99 percent of the total variance of the initial money series.

Put the other way around, treating money as exogenous, the initial money series plus constant velocity account for at least 94.5 percent of the variance of nominal income; substituting the adjusted money series accounts for more than two-thirds of the residual variation, raising the percentage of the variance accounted for to at least 98.5.

The effect of adjusting the money series is much the same for the United States for the period excluding wars and is smaller, though still very substantial indeed, for the United States plus the United Kingdom, for either the total period or the period excluding wars. The effect is, of course, even larger for the pre–World War I period, where the whole of the adjustment is concentrated.

For rates of change, the adjustment has little effect on money—indeed, the adjusted variance is somewhat higher than the unadjusted. The unadjusted rates of change for the earlier period are not far from the average for the period as a whole, thanks to the high rates of change during World Wars I and II, so lowering them does not much affect the standard deviation of the rates of change of money. If the war phases are excluded, the adjustment does lower the variance. More important, the adjustment reduces very appreciably the variation of per capita real

15. A specially clear example is provided by population. In one set of level regressions, for example, the inclusion of population yields coefficients of the dummy variable ranging from .0011 to .0096 in absolute magnitude, far smaller than in other regressions.

Table 6.2   Effect of Changing Financial Sophistication on Variability in Money and Velocity

| | Variation (Percent or Percentage Points)[a] | | | | | | Fraction of Variance Accounted for by Increasing Financial Sophistication in U.S. | | |
| | Full Period | | Full Period Ex-Wars | | Pre–WW I | | Full Period | Full Period Ex-Wars | Pre–WW I |
	Original	Adjusted	Original	Adjusted	Original	Adjusted			
Level									
			United States						
Money	172.6	158.6	182.8	167.9	71.7	48.9	15.56	15.64	53.49
Per capita real money balances	77.8	62.5	80.8	64.3	47.6	23.9	35.46	36.67	74.80
Velocity	34.0	18.0	34.4	16.7	29.6	7.2	71.66	76.43	94.08
Level									
			United States and United Kingdom						
Money	148.6	142.2	156.9	149.9	56.6	47.2	8.43	8.72	30.46
Per capita real money balances	60.6	51.3	62.6	52.4	39.6	19.8	28.34	29.93	75.00
Velocity	29.2	18.2	29.2	16.6	33.0	13.3	61.15	67.68	83.76
Rate of Change									
			United States						
Money	4.45	4.53	3.61	3.26	1.99	2.12	−3.63	18.45	−13.49
Per capita real money balances	2.57	2.25	2.36	1.58	1.72	1.25	76.65	44.82	52.82
Velocity	2.59	2.31	2.23	1.85	1.74	1.54	20.45	31.18	21.67
Rate of Change									
			United States and United Kingdom						
Money	4.04	3.88	3.09	2.81	2.44	1.75	7.76	17.30	48.56
Per capita real money balances	2.30	2.04	1.98	1.49	1.98	1.15	76.66	56.63	33.73
Velocity	2.27	2.08	1.92	1.60	1.59	0.92	16.04	30.56	66.52

[a]For levels, figures given are standard deviations of natural logarithms multiplied by 100, which can be regarded as estimates of the coefficients of variation of the original observations, expressed as a percentage. For rates of change, figures are standard deviations of the rates of change expressed as percentages, hence are in percentage points.

Table 6.3 Standard Deviation of Logarithms of United States and United Kingdom Velocities: United States Velocity Based on Money Adjusted and Unadjusted for Changing Financial Sophistication

| | Phases | | Standard Deviation of Velocity (Percentage) | | | | |
| | | | United States | | United Kingdom | United States and United Kingdom | |
Period	United States	United Kingdom	Unadjusted (1)	Adjusted (2)	(3)	Unadjusted (4)	Adjusted (5)
1. Full	4–52	1–37	34.0	18.1	16.7	29.2	18.2
2. Full ex-wars	4–24	1–11	34.4	16.7	14.8	29.2	16.6
3. Pre–World War I		8–37	29.6	7.2	3.1	33.0	13.3
4. Equal financial sophistication	18–52		15.4		19.4	17.5	

balances for both the United States and the United States and the United Kingdom combined, for all periods considered.

Our adjustment for this factor treats it as no longer operative after 1903. That cannot be strictly valid. Many and sizable changes in financial organization have occurred since then in both the United States and the United Kingdom, particularly rapidly in recent decades. The apparent effect of such changes on United States money-holding propensities before 1903 raises the question whether they have not been an important factor in both countries since then. That possibility adds to the desirability of a full study of the effect of financial structure on the demand for money. However, comparison of the variability of velocity, adjusted and unadjusted, for different periods (table 6.3) suggests that the adjustment we have made for the United States before 1903 is of much greater magnitude than any further adjustment for this factor and renders the data for the different periods relatively homogeneous. The adjusted standard deviations for the periods including the pre-1903 period for the United States are much more like those for the United States for subsequent periods—the whole period after 1903 (line 4 of table 6.3), the interwar and post–World War II periods—than are the unadjusted standard deviations. In addition, the adjusted United States standard deviations are much closer to the standard deviations for the United Kingdom and for the two countries combined than the unadjusted—even though some of the adjusted standard deviations do differ significantly both between periods and countries.

Throughout the rest of the book, all references to United States money figures, unless otherwise noted, are to the figures adjusted for the changing degree of financial sophistication by the second of the two methods outlined above.[16]

6.4   Effect of Real per Capita Income

6.4.1 Levels

Equation (1), corresponding to a constant numerical velocity, is entirely in nominal terms. But it can be regarded as a special case of a more general function that separates out real per capita income and money from population and prices, for example, the function

$$(3) \qquad (\frac{M}{NP})(N)(P) = k\,(\frac{Y}{NP})^{\alpha} N^{\beta} P^{\gamma}$$

16. To make sure that this procedure did not introduce a bias, for almost all our calculations we made parallel estimates for the period after 1903, which we treated as corresponding to equal financial sophistication in the two countries. The results conformed so closely to those for the period as a whole based on adjusted observations that we have not thought it worthwhile to include the results for that period in the tables that follow.

where N is population and P is the price level so that M/NP, which we shall hereafter designate m, is real per capita cash balances and Y/NP, which we shall designate as y, is real per capita income. Equation (1) is a special case of equation (3) for $\alpha = \beta = \gamma = 1$.

In general, economists have tended to take $\beta = \gamma = 1$, on the grounds, for γ, that doubling all prices is equivalent simply to a change in units and will therefore double nominal money demanded for double the nominal income; for β, that the relevant function is for the individual economic unit—household or business—and that doubling the number of units would therefore double the nominal money demanded for double the nominal income.

This reasoning is unobjectionable for different levels of prices, all characterized by the same rate of change of prices (generally implicitly taken to be zero). However, it takes time for a change from one level to another to have its full effect. Hence the observed γ may not equal unity for a particular set of empirical observations. If it does not, it presumably would reflect incomplete adjustment to price changes and therefore be less than unity.

For population, the reasoning is unobjectionable if different sizes of population are obtained by changing the unit of observation—going from an individual state in the United States to a collection of states or to the country as a whole. However, the effect of a change of population is not at all clear for time-series observations for the same geographical area, such as those with which we are primarily concerned. Larger population means a higher density of population, which reduces the average distance between persons and enables different patterns of transactions to develop. It would be preferable to allow for such factors directly. However, if that is not done, and population is used as a proxy, it may well be that the observed value of β may not equal unity.

It is not clear a priori whether β will tend to exceed unity or be less than unity: the greater ease of transactions in a denser market would lead to a β less than unity; the greater division of labor and the more extensive chain of intermediaries between the provision of factor services and the ultimate consumer would lead to a β greater than unity.

For the rest of this section, we shall assume $\beta = \gamma = 1$, but in the next section we shall investigate this assumption to see whether it is indeed supported by our data.

For real per capita income, there is no a priori reason to expect α to equal unity or to have a constant value over time. Our earlier work has led us to the empirical conclusion that α is generally greater than unity; that is, that money is, in the terminology of consumption theory, a "luxury" rather than a "necessity."[17] As we noted in chapter 5, the

17. M. Friedman, *The Demand for Money: Some Theoretical and Empirical Results*, Occasional Paper 68 (New York: NBER, 1959), reprinted in M. Friedman, *The Optimum*

comparisons with the United Kingdom persuade us that our earlier estimates of the income elasticity of demand for real balances for the United States may be too high, biased upward by our failure to allow for changes in the degree of financial sophistication. Hence a reexamination of this issue is clearly called for.

With $\beta = \gamma = 1$, equation (3) can be rewritten

$$(4) \qquad m = ky^{\alpha} .$$

If both sides are divided by y, we have an equation for desired number of time units (e.g., weeks or years) of income held as money, or

$$(5) \qquad \frac{m}{y} = ky^{\alpha - 1}.$$

Taking the reciprocal of both sides gives

$$(6) \qquad V = \frac{1}{k} y^{1 - \alpha} ,$$

where V is velocity, turnovers per time unit.

If we take logarithms of equation (4), we have

$$(7) \qquad \log m = \log k + \alpha \log y.$$

This is the form in which we shall fit the equation statistically, both because it gives a linear equation to fit and because the error term that needs to be added to equation (7) to convert it into a stochastic function is more nearly homoskedastic in the logarithms than in the original values.

The use of per capita real balances and per capita real income is correct on economic grounds if $\beta = \gamma = 1$. However, it does introduce a purely statistical bias into equation (7) and similar equations. The basic data consist of separate estimates of Y, M, N, and P. We then calculate m and y from these estimates. The estimates of M, N, and P are statistically independent—the estimates of M coming from the books of financial institutions, of N from population censuses, and of P from price indexes or national income statistics. There is some dependence between the estimates of Y and P, since the price level we use is the price level implicit in the calculation of national income at constant prices. However, the national income calculations are mostly based on data for nominal income, and real income in individual sectors is derived by dividing by an independent price index. Hence, even for Y and P, the two magnitudes can be regarded as largely independent.

Quantity of Money and Other Essays (Chicago: Aldine, 1969); M. Friedman and A. J. Schwartz, "Money and Business Cycles," *Review of Economics and Statistics*, 45, no. 1, part 2, suppl. (February 1963): pp. 43–45, reprinted in M. Friedman, *Optimum Quantity of Money*; Friedman and Schwartz, *A Monetary History*, pp. 639, 679–82.

But if Y, M, N, and P are statistically independent magnitudes, m and y are not, since

$$\log m = \log M - \log N - \log P$$
$$\log y = \log Y - \log N - \log P.$$

On economic grounds, use of the same values of N and P to calculate both m and y is desirable, since in effect it enables us to impose the economic restriction that $\beta = \gamma = 1$. It would raise no statistical problem if N and P were measured without error. But obviously they are not. And errors of measurement in N and P introduce common errors into m and y, since the same numerical estimates are subtracted from $\log M$ and $\log Y$ in calculating $\log m$ and $\log y$. These common errors tend to bias the statistical estimate of α toward unity.[18] We know no simple way to estimate the size of this bias, so we shall have to allow for it only qualitatively.

---

18. Express the logarithm of each variable as the sum of a "true" value and an error of measurement, say

$$\log M = (\log M)^* + e_M$$
$$\log Y = (\log Y)^* + e_Y$$
$$\log NP = (\log NP)^* + e_{NP},$$

where an asterisk designates a true value and we have combined N and P because what matters for our purpose is only their product. We then have

$$\log m = (\log m)^* + e_M - e_{NP}$$
$$\log y = (\log y)^* + e_Y - e_{NP}.$$

Assume that e_M, e_Y, and e_{NP} are independent of the asterisked variables and of one another, and that all variables are expressed as deviations from their means. We have two "true" estimates of α, one from the regression of $(\log m)^*$ on $(\log y)^*$, the other from the regression of $(\log y)^*$ on $(\log m)^*$, say

$$\alpha_{my}^* = \frac{E[(\log m)^* \, (\log y)^*]}{\sigma^2_{(\log y)^*}},$$

$$\alpha_{ym}^* = \frac{\sigma^2_{(\log m)^*}}{E[(\log m)^* \, (\log y)^*]},$$

where E stands for expected value, and, if the coefficients are positive, $\alpha_{my}^* < \alpha_{ym}^*$.
We have two corresponding statistical estimates of α, say

$$\alpha_{my} = \frac{E[(\log m) \, (\log y)]}{\sigma^2_{\log y}} = \frac{E[(\log m)^* \, (\log y)^*] + \sigma^2_{e_{NP}}}{\sigma^2_{(\log y)^*} + \sigma^2_{e_Y} + \sigma^2_{e_{NP}}}$$

$$= \frac{\alpha_{my}^* + \dfrac{\sigma^2_{e_{NP}}}{\sigma^2_{(\log y)^*}}}{1 + \dfrac{\sigma^2_{e_Y} + \sigma^2_{e_{NP}}}{\sigma^2_{(\log y)^*}}},$$

The Separate Countries

Chart 6.1 gives scatter diagrams of log m and log y, panel A for the United States and panel B for the United Kingdom. In each panel three lines are drawn through the point corresponding to the mean values of log m and log y: a line with a slope of unity, which is the counterpart of

$$\alpha_{ym} = \frac{\sigma^2_{\log m}}{E[(\log m)(\log y)]} = \frac{\sigma^2_{(\log m)^*} + \sigma^2_{e_M} + \sigma^2_{e_{NP}}}{E[(\log m)^*(\log y)^*] + \sigma^2_{e_{NP}}}$$

$$= \frac{\alpha^*_{ym} + \dfrac{\sigma^2_{e_M} + \sigma^2_{e_{NP}}}{E[(\log m)^*(\log y)^*]}}{1 + \dfrac{\sigma^2_{e_{NP}}}{E[(\log m)^*(\log y)^*]}}.$$

The statistical estimates differ from the true values because of errors in measuring (a) Y and M and (b) NP.

With respect to (a), this is the standard regression effect, as can be seen by supposing NP to be measured without error, so that $\sigma_{e_{NP}} = 0$. We then have:

$$\alpha_{my} = \frac{\alpha^*_{my}}{1 + \dfrac{\sigma^2_{e_Y}}{\sigma^2_{(\log y)^*}}} < \alpha^*_{my} < \alpha^*_{ym} < \alpha^*_{ym} + \frac{\sigma^2_{e_M}}{E(\log m)^* \, (\log y)^*} = \alpha_{ym},$$

that is, the calculated regression coefficients will cover a wider range than the "true" ones.

To isolate the effect of (b), namely, errors in NP, suppose Y and M measured without error, so $\sigma_{e_Y} = \sigma_{e_M} = 0$. We then have:

$$\alpha_{my} = \frac{\alpha^*_{my} + \dfrac{\sigma^2_{e_{NP}}}{\sigma^2_{(\log y)^*}}}{1 + \dfrac{\sigma^2_{e_{NP}}}{\sigma^2_{(\log y)^*}}}$$

$$\alpha_{ym} = \frac{\alpha^*_{ym} + \dfrac{\sigma^2_{e_{NP}}}{E[(\log m)^*(\log y)^*]}}{1 + \dfrac{\sigma^2_{e_{NP}}}{E[(\log m)^*(\log y)^*]}}.$$

Both these expressions are of the form of weighted averages of the "true" coefficient and unity, the weights being 1 and $\sigma^2_{e_{NP}}/\sigma^2_{(\log y)^*}$ for α_{my} and 1 and $\sigma^2_{e_{NP}}/E[(\log m)^*(\log y)^*]$ for α_{ym}. Accordingly, the effect of errors in NP is to bias the computed coefficients toward unity by comparison with the true coefficients. This conclusion remains valid when the assumption that $\sigma_{e_M} = \sigma_{e_Y} = 0$ is dropped; that is, computed coefficients are biased toward unity compared with hypothetical coefficients computed under the assumption that $\sigma_{NP} = 0$ but σ_{e_M} and σ_{e_Y} are whatever they in fact are.

The possible magnitude of the regression effect can be judged by computing estimates of α from both regressions and regarding these as upper and lower limits of the correct values. There is no similar simple way that we know of to judge the size of the bias arising from the errors in N and P, since that depends on the size of the measurement errors in N and P compared with the variance of log Y and log M.

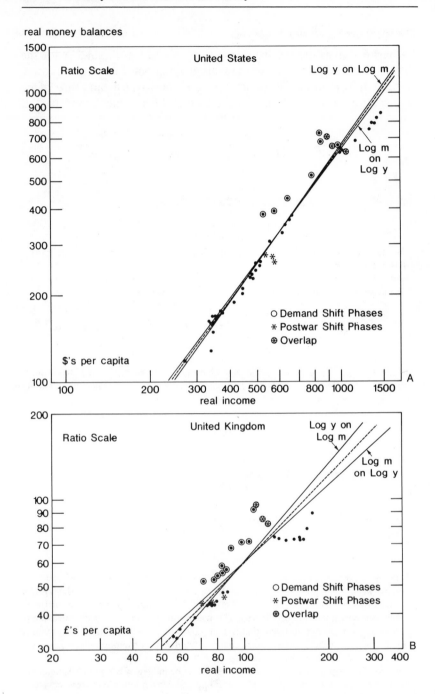

Chart 6.1   Scatter diagram of levels of real per capita income and real per capita money and regression lines.

Table 6.4   **Income Elasticities and Correlation Coefficients, Calculated from Levels of Real per Capita Money and Income**

Period and Country	Phase Numbers	Income Elasticities		Correlation Coefficient r (3)
		Lower Limit (1)	Upper Limit (2)	
United States				
Full period	4–52	1.26	1.31	.978
Full ex-wars		1.23	1.27	.983
Pre–World War I	4–24	1.20	1.28	.966
Interwar	28–36	0.37	4.32	.296
Postwar	40–52	0.59	0.75	.886
United Kingdom				
Full period	1–37	0.84	1.10	.874
Full ex-wars		0.78	0.93	.918
Pre–World War I	1–11	0.85	0.88	.984
Interwar	15–23	1.26	1.47	.926
Postwar	27–37	−0.02	−13.31	.080
United States and United Kingdom			·	
Full period	4–52, 1–37	1.13	1.27	.948
Full ex-wars		1.09	1.20	.957
Pre–World War I	4–24, 1–11	1.09	1.19	.961
Interwar	28–36, 15–23	0.85	2.04	.844
Postwar	40–52, 27–37	0.36	1.06	.976

Note: For United States plus United Kingdom, allowance is made for a difference in level between the two countries after converting the United Kingdom figures from pounds to dollars at the exchange rate of $4.862.

equation (1); and two regressions, one of log m on log y, the other of log y on log m, both computed from the phase average data for 1873 to 1975 for the United States, and from 1874 to 1975 for the United Kingdom. The slopes of these lines can be regarded as upper and lower estimates of α.[19] Table 6.4 gives, in columns 1 and 2, the numerical elasticities for these regressions, and also for regressions for the period before World War I, the interwar period, and the post–World War II period.

For the United States, for the period as a whole, the income elasticity is clearly greater than unity. The line with a slope of unity is above most observations for income and money below the mean and below most observations for income and money above the mean (indeed there are only three observations that do not conform to this pattern). Both regressions are steeper than the line with unit slope.

The points that are most out of line are for the 1930s, the World War II years, and the immediate post-World War II years. These indicate much

19. See the preceding note.

larger money holdings (i.e., lower velocity) than the others. We are inclined to attribute this result to the effects of the great contraction of 1929–33 and the war. Declining prices during the contraction meant that money balances had a substantial positive yield, and great uncertainty raised desired liquidity. These effects were partly offset by bank failures, which lowered the "quality" of deposits. The uncertainty lasted long after the contraction itself and was then reinforced by the war; in addition, during the war, the unavailability of goods reinforced uncertainty in raising desired money balances.

These discrepancies are reflected in the much less satisfactory results for the interwar and postwar periods than for the period as a whole or the pre–World War I period. The correlation for the interwar period is close to zero, and the elasticities for the postwar period are far lower than for the period as a whole.

The United Kingdom results differ in two respects. First, only one of the regression lines has a slope greater than unity. The scatter diagram as a whole does not suggest an elasticity greater than unity: about half the points for incomes below the mean are above the line with a slope of unity, and about the same fraction of points for incomes above the mean are below the line. Second, the scatter is much looser, with a correlation coefficient of .87, compared with .98 for the United States.

However, there are also some similarities, most strikingly the division of the points into two sets, one at a higher level than the other. The points at the higher level (circled in the charts) include the same period as those for the United States (1939–54) and in addition all the phases for the 1920s from 1921 on.[20] The additional phases are no less significant than the common ones. The United Kingdom's time of serious economic trouble started in the early 1920s and recovery began in 1932, before the Great Contraction ended in the United States. The forces we adduced to explain the discrepant points for the United States—namely, price deflation, uncertainty arising out of serious cyclical fluctuation reinforced by the outbreak of war, and the unavailability of goods during the war—all operated at least as strongly in the United Kingdom as in the United States but started nearly a decade earlier. It therefore supports this interpretation that higher-level-points for the United Kingdom span a period beginning earlier but ending at roughly the same date as the analogous United States points.

A second similarity between the two countries came to light when we studied the relations between rates of change (see sec. 6.4.2), namely, an immediate postwar adjustment that produced idiosyncratic rates of change after World War I and World War II in both the United States and the United Kingdom—in both countries, in opposite directions after the

20. In addition, because of the difference in reference dates, the final phase at the higher level ends in 1955 rather than 1954.

two wars but by roughly the same amount in the two countries. We had missed these perturbations when we first studied the level data because even a sizable deviation in a rate of change for a phase or two produces only a small effect on the levels.

However, once alerted to them, it is easy to see their effect. For the United States for World War I they are reflected in a substantial deviation of the phase centered on 1919 (designated by the lowest of the three uncircled *'s) below the lower of the two regression lines in chart 6.1, panel A. Indeed, it deviates more from the line than all but one other observation (for the phase centered on 1884). The level of the phase centered on 1920 is also below the line (the second lowest of the three uncircled *'s), the level of the phase centered on 1921 (the third of the uncircled *'s) is nearly on the line. The postwar adjustment reaction apparently carried too far, bringing the phase level centered on 1922.5 well above the line. The same pattern is repeated, but in the other direction, for World War II. The 1947.5 point is well above the upper line (the highest of the circled *'s marked on the chart), the largest deviation with one exception in the upper set. The 1949 point (the second highest circled *) is a trifle above the line, that for the 1952 phase (the third of the circled *'s) well below.

For the United Kingdom a similar, though initially less clear, pattern is present after World War I—the tendency to overshoot carrying the observations into the beginning of the period we isolated as reflecting an upward shift in liquidity. After World War II, the pattern of points for the United Kingdom around the upper regression line in chart 6.1, panel B is almost identical with that for the United States, except it comes later in time. The phase centered on 1949 (the highest circled * marked on the chart) is well above the line, with 1952, 1954, and 1957 moving toward and then below it, and the 1957 phase reflecting both the overshooting and the end of high liquidity preferences.

We shall refer to these postwar perturbations as the postwar shift and to the upward shift in liquidity preference as the demand shift.

When we analyze the effect of other variables influencing the quantity of money demanded later in this chapter, we shall see whether their fluctuations are such as to account for the two shifts: the demand shift and the postwar shift. In the meantime, in order to continue examining the effect of per capita real income by itself, we shall use the device of introducing two shift variables.

To allow for the apparent increase in liquidity preference in the interwar, war, and early postwar periods, we introduce a dummy variable that has the value of one for the phases in the upper cluster, of zero for the other phases. This procedure is equivalent to fitting separate regressions to the two clusters of points but imposing the requirement that they have the same slope, that is, income elasticity.

To allow for the postwar shift, we also introduce a dummy variable for the affected phases, but this one equal in absolute value to the time span beteen the midpont of the affected phase and the midpoint of the first normal postwar phase, and negative after World War I, positive after World War II. The reason, as explained below in section 6.4.2, is that we interpret the adjustment as reflecting a maximum change in the rate of change that holders of money are willing to undertake in these circumstances.[21]

Consistent with our visual impression, the postwar adjustment dummy produces an appreciable minor improvement in results for the level equations, if a less substantial improvement than for the rate of change equations or than the demand shift dummy does for the level equations.[22] Panels A and B of chart 6.2 repeat the scatters from chart 6.1 and add two pairs of parallel lines, one pair corresponding to the regression of log m on log y, the other to the regression of log y on log m, the difference between the lines in each pair reflecting the demand shift and also allowing for the postwar readjustment.

The improvement in fit is striking. Indeed, for the United States the correlation is so high that the log m on log y and log y on log m regressions are difficult to distinguish on a chart the size of chart 6.2, panel A.

The imposition of a common income elasticity on the two clusters seems to do no serious violence to the observed data. The larger number and wider scatter of observations in the lower cluster means that that cluster largely determines the numerical size of the slope. Yet even for the upper cluster the slope seems appropriate—though there is some indication for the United Kingdom that a slightly steeper slope would be preferable.

The remarkable feature of these charts is how closely a single pattern fits such widely separated observations as those before World War I and after World War II. Allowance for the demand and postwar shifts drastically reduces the differences between regressions for the period before World War I, when no shift variables are used, and similar regressions for the period thereafter, including shift variables. Once the shift variables are included, little is gained by distinguishing war phases from the other phases, or by any of the other subgroups we have used.[23]

21. See below, following equation (8), for a more detailed listing of the values of the dummy variables.

22. The t-value for the coefficient of the postwar adjustment dummy is 2.8 for the United States, 3.6 for the United Kingdom, and 2.1 for the two countries combined, compared with corresponding t-values for the demand shift dummy of 9.7, 10.8, and 9.9. The numerical size of the estimated coefficient of the postwar adjustment dummy is about 2 percent per year for both the United States and the United Kingdom, about 1.5 percent per year for the two countries combined, which is less than one-third of the estimate derived from the rate of change data.

23. We have consistently made calculations reported in the rest of this chapter for the

real money balances

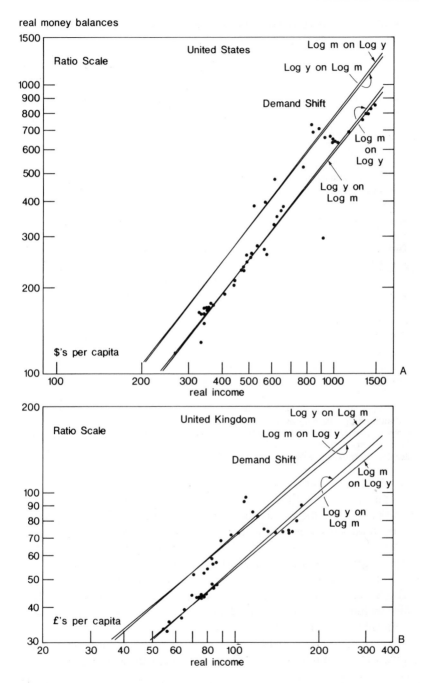

Chart 6.2 Scatter diagram of levels of real per capita income and real per capita money and regression lines isolating effect of demand shift.

Table 6.5   **Effect of Allowing for Postwar Adjustment and Shift Dummies on Difference between Variances and Regressions**

Source of Variation[a]	Simple Regressons, Dummies		Multiple Regressions, Dummies	
	Absent	Present	Absent	Present
Mean Sum of Squared Residuals				
United States				
Within first period (22)	.0038		.0028	
Within second period (27)(26)[b]	.0196	.0031	.0058	.0020
Two periods combined	.0127	.0034	.0045	.0024
Between two periods	.1254	.0222	.0443	.0048
United Kingdom				
Within first period (12)	.0005		.0004	
Within second period (25) (24)[b]	.0247	.0061	.0049	.0027
Two periods combined	.0153	.0038	.0032	.0018
Between two periods	.1968	.0060	.0507	.0114
F Values and Significance of Difference				
United States				
Between two periods in				
Residual variances	5.2**	0.8	2.1	0.7
Regressions	9.9**	6.5**	9.8**	2.0
United Kingdom				
Between two periods in				
Residual variances	49.4**	12.2**	12.2**	6.8**
Regressions	12.9**	1.6	15.8**	6.3**

[a]And number of observations, *not* degrees of freedom.
[b]Number of observations one greater for simple regressions than for multiple regressions.
*Significant at .05 level.
**Significant at .01 or more stringent level.

Table 6.5 summarizes the effect of allowing for the demand and postwar shift dummies on the difference between the period through 1918 (first period) and the period thereafter (second period) with respect to the residual variances within the two periods and also the regression equations for the two periods. We present these calculations for the simple regression equations that, aside from the dummies, include only per capita real money balances and per capita real income and also for the multiple regression equations that we finally settle on in section 6.7, which include in addition two independent variables measuring the yield on alternative assets.

The residual variance within the second period is reduced sharply by allowing for the dummies, by between 45 percent and 84 percent. For the

subperiods as well as for the period as a whole. However, we have found them for the most part to add so little to the single calculation including one or more shift variables that it has not seemed worth including them in the tables.

United States, the resulting residual variance for the second period does not differ significantly from that for the first: the set of data becomes homogeneous in that respect. For the United Kingdom there remains a significant difference, which reflects the abnormally low variance for the first period, in our opinion a statistical artifact arising from the extensive interpolation entering into the early United Kingdom data.

The variance of the difference between the two periods is reduced even more sharply, by between 78 and 97 percent. For the United States, the difference between the two periods remains statistically significant for the simple regression but not the multiple—apparently the time difference reflects primarily differences in average interest rates. For the United Kingdom the situation is reversed: there is no significant difference for the simple regression; there is for the multiple. However, in light of the major reduction in both the variance between periods and the F values, and our doubts about the statistical validity of the variance within the first period, we do not regard this one result as contradicting the validity of treating the whole period as homogeneous after allowing for the two shifts.

The main difference between the two countries is the steeper slope of the regression for the United States than for the United Kingdom—a higher than unit elasticity for the United States, a lower than unit elasticity for the United Kingdom.

Table 6.6 summarizes the numerical effect of allowing for the demand and postwar shifts. Remarkably, the size of both shifts is almost identical in the two countries. For the demand shift, desired money balances were apparently raised by about 30 percent at each level of per capita income by the factors associated with Depression and its aftermath and World War II. For the postwar shift, desired money balances were lowered after World War I and raised after World War II by the limited rate at which balances readjusted from their abnormal wartime levels to peacetime levels. The percentage discrepancy on this account narrowed at a rate equal to roughly two percentage points per year; that is, the percentage discrepancy was equal in absolute value to twice the time interval between each of the relevant phases and the first postwar phase we treated as normal (phases centered on 1922.5 and 1954.0 for the United States and on 1923.0 and 1957.0 for the United Kingdom).

The estimated income elasticity is 1.2 for the United States, about 0.8 for the United Kingdom. This difference raises a real puzzle. Does it reflect a fundamental difference between the two countries in the response of the quantity of money demanded to a change in real income? Or may it be a disguised reflection of a differential behavior in the two countries of other variables affecting the quantity of money demanded? We shall pursue that question in the later sections of this chapter. Here we may only note that the difference in computed elasticities is large

Table 6.6 Relation between Real per Capita Money and Real per Capita Income: Effect of Allowing for Upward Shifts in Money Demand during Interwar, World War II and Early Postwar Period, and for Postwar Shifts

	United States	United Kingdom	United States and United Kingdom
1a. Period of upward demand shift	1929–54	1921–55	
b. Period of postwar shift	1918–21, 1946–53	1918–21, 1946–55	
2a. Size of demand shift (percentage)[a]	27.7 (27.2)	29.6 (29.6)	30.9 (30.0)
b. Size of postwar shift (percentage)[a,b]	2.3 (2.3)	2.2 (2.0)	1.6 (1.4)
c. Difference in level between United States and United Kingdom (at market exchange rate, as percentage of United States level)[a]			10.7 (12.8)
3. Income elasticity, lower limit	1.19	0.79	1.07
4. Income elasticity, upper limit	1.21	0.83	1.12
5a. Simple correlation (money and income)	0.978	0.874	0.945
b. Partial correlation (allowing for shifts)	0.994	0.974	0.976
6. Multiple correlation, including shifts[a]	0.995 (0.994)	0.983 (0.975)	0.981 (0.980)

Standard Error of Estimate (%)

Real per capita money			
7. Total	62.5	32.6	51.3
Maximum residual after allowing for:			
8. Constant velocity	18.1	16.7	18.2
9. Constant elasticity	13.2	16.0	16.6
10. Constant velocity plus shifts	11.7	9.8	11.5
11. Constant elasticity plus shifts	6.5	6.3	10.1
Real per capita income			
12. Total	48.7	33.7	45.0
Maximum residual after allowing for:			
13. Constant velocity	18.1	16.7	18.2
14. Constant elasticity	10.3	16.6	13.9
15. Constant velocity plus shifts	11.7	9.8	11.5
16. Constant elasticity plus shifts	5.4	7.8	9.2

[a]Figures in parentheses from regressions of y on m and dummy (or dummies) solved for m; others from regression of m on y and dummy (or dummies).

[b]Note that the postwar shift is positive after World War I, negative after World War II.

enough, and the residual variation small enough, so that the elasticity difference is highly significant statistically, while the differences in shift effects are not.[24]

The constant velocity assumption of section 6.2 is equivalent to assuming an elasticity of unity between money and income. In view of the closeness of the estimated elasticities to unity, it is not surprising that

24. The relevant analysis of variance is as shown in table 6.N.1.

The difference in slope and in level are highly significant, the difference in shifts is not. Similarly, both the common demand shift and the postwar shift are highly significant, and of course the common slope is highly significant.

It should be noted that the partition of the sums of squares among the individual degrees of freedom is not invariant to the order in which the various effects are allowed for. We have generally followed the principle of allowing for the effects in the order of their significance, as indicated by t-values.

Table 6.N.1   **Analysis of Variance of Differences between Demand for Money Regressions for the United States and the United Kingdom Based on Levels**

Source of Variation	Degrees of Freedom	Sum of Squares	Mean Square	F
Within United States	45	.1900	.0042(.0039)[a]	
Within United Kingdom	33	.1310	.0040(.0044)[a]	
Within United States and United Kingdom	78	.3197	.0041	
Difference between United States and United Kingdom				
In slope	1	.4943	.4943	120.6
In shifts	2	.0170	.0085	2.1
In level, at market exchange rates	1	.4590	.4590	112.0
Subtotal	82	1.2900		
Attributable to				
Demand shift	1	1.4090	1.4090	343.7
Postwar shift	1	0.0450	0.0450	11.0
Slope	1	19.6680	19.6680	4797.1
Total	85	22.4120		

[a]The total sum of squares does not equal the sum of within country sums because of the need to allow for the effect of unequal weighting of observations. The mean squares within parentheses are estimates of the common mean square after adjustment for difference of weights. The common mean is the weighted average of the parenthetical figures, the weights being the number of degrees of freedom. The two parenthetical mean squares do not differ at a .05 level.

For 1 and 78 degrees of freedom, .05 F value is 4.0; .01 F value, 7.0; .001 F value, 11.8. For 2 and 78 degrees of freedom, the corresponding F values are 3.1, 4.9, and 7.6.

allowing for a constant elasticity instead of an elasticity of unity produces only a rather small reduction in the computed standard error of estimate for either real per capita money, with real per capita income taken as exogenous, or real per capita income, with real per capita money taken as exogenous (compare lines 8 and 9 and 13 and 14 in table 6.6). For reasons explained in chapter 5, these two standard errors cannot both be simultaneously valid measures of the variation in each of the variables independent of the variation in the other, because each assumes that the other variable is perfectly known. The entries in lines 9 and 14 of table 6.6, like the entries in lines 8 and 13, are therefore to be regarded as estimates of the *maximum* residual standard error. Simultaneously valid estimates of the independent variation in each variable would necessarily be lower.

Allowing for the demand and postwar shifts in liquidity preference in three out of four cases reduces the maximum residual standard error more drastically than allowing for the difference between constant elasticity and constant velocity; and allowing for both the shifts and the differences between constant elasticity and constant velocity does even better. Allowing for the shifts generally enhances the value of substituting constant elasticity for constant velocity. Together the two roughly cut the standard error in half and in addition, for real per capita money, though not income, bring the standard errors for the United States and the United Kingdom closer together. All these residual standard errors are below 10 percent—and these continue to be maximum estimates.

The constant velocity standard errors are constrained to be the same for money and income. For the United States, all of the rest are higher for money than for income, but for the United Kingdom they are higher for income than for money. The reason is linked to an elasticity higher than unity for the United States and lower than unity for the United Kingdom. The total variability of money is higher in the United States than the total variability of income—which helps to produce the higher than unit elasticity.[25] The reverse is the case in the United Kingdom, which helps to produce the lower than unit elasticity. But the usual convention regards the same fraction of the variance of each variable as "accounted for" by the regression, namely the square of the correlation coefficient given in line 5 of table 6.6. As a result, if the initial standard error is higher (or lower) for log m than for log y, so also must be the residual standard error. If, as we suspect, pure errors of measurement are higher for income than for money, then the "correct" fraction of variance accounted for may well be higher for money than for income, which

25. Because the lower limit is $r\,\frac{\sigma_m}{\sigma_y}$, and the upper limit, $\frac{1}{r}\frac{\sigma_m}{\sigma_y}$. Since r is necessarily less than unity, $\sigma m > \sigma y$ is a necessary but not sufficient condition for the lower limit to exceed unity, and a sufficient but not necessary condition for the upper limit to do so.

might well reverse the relation now shown in table 6.6 for the United States and increase the difference for the United Kingdom. We saw in the preceding chapter that the standard deviation of deviations about trend was higher for income than for money, and we shall see in the next section that the standard deviation of rates of change is also higher for income than for money, both of which suggest that the purely random component is higher for income than for money and that table 6.6 may show the opposite for the United States solely because of a statistical convention.

The figures in table 6.6 overstate the case for constant elasticity as compared with constant velocity. We are here dealing with per capita real magnitudes. These have lower variability than the nominal aggregates. A constant velocity (i.e., unit elasticity) demand function would enable us to predict total income from total money, if we assume money exogenous, or total money from total income, if we assume income exogenous. The constant elasticity per capita real demand function would not; we would need to know in addition what is happening to prices and population. Additional "explanation" is therefore bought at the expense of requiring more information.

The Two Countries Combined

Despite the statistically significant difference between the income elasticities for the United States and the United Kingdom derived from the regressions that allow for the demand and postwar shifts, the similarity of the regressions in other respects and the small magnitude of the elasticity difference suggest that it may be worth getting a single estimate by combining the data for the two countries, if only to explore some of the problems raised by such a combination.

We cannot combine the data directly, because the data for the United States are in dollars and those for the United Kingdom are in pounds sterling. One way to combine the data is to convert the United Kingdom figures to dollars at the exchange rate ($4.862) ruling in 1929 (the year that was the base for the price indexes used to estimate real money balances). That is the way we have combined them to get the standard deviations for the two countries in lines 7 and 12 of table 6.6. However, it is far from clear that the market rate of exchange is the relevant one for the purpose of calculating a single regression.

Both for this reason and also to allow for a possible difference in the level of money demand between the two countries, we include in all regressions for the two countries combined a dummy variable (Z) distinguishing the United Kingdom from the United States. With this addition plus dummy variables to allow for the demand (S) and postwar (W) shifts, equation (7) becomes:

(8) $$\log m = \log k + \alpha \log y + \lambda_1 W + \lambda_2 S + \lambda_3 Z \ ,$$

where $W = \ -T_i$ for the phases centered on 1919, 1920, and 1921 for the United States and the United Kingdom

$+T_i$ for the phases centered on 1947.5, 1949, and 1951.5 for the United States and 1949, 1952, and 1954 for the United Kingdom

0   for all other phases

$S = $ 1   for the phases from 1929 to 1954 in the United States and from 1921 to 1955 in the United Kingdom

0   for all other phases

$Z = $ 1   if the observation is for the United Kingdom

0   if the observation is for the United States

and where $T_i = $ time interval between the center of phase i and the center of the first postwar phase treated as normal (1922.5 and 1954.0 for the United States, and 1923.0 and 1957.0 for the United Kingdom.).

The parameter λ_3 encompasses two effects: a difference in level produced by the exchange rate required to convert pounds to dollars and any difference in the level of money demand for the two countries at that exchange rate. To demonstrate, distinguish by subscripts the observations for the United States and the United Kingdom. Let EX be the rate of exchange expressed in number of dollars per pound; let the original observations for the United States be in dollars and for the United Kingdom in pounds; and assume that α, λ_1, and λ_2 are the same for the two countries. We then have

(9) $$\log m_{us} = \log k_{us} + \alpha \log y_{us} + \lambda_1 W + \lambda_2 S$$

(10) $$\log EXm_{uk} = \log k_{uk} + \alpha \log EXy_{uk} + \lambda_1 W + \lambda_2 S$$

(11)   or $$\log m_{uk} = \log k_{uk} + (\alpha-1) \log EX + \alpha \log y_{uk} \\ + \lambda_1 W + \lambda_2 S$$

(12)   or $$\log m_{uk} = \log k_{us} + \alpha \log y_{uk} + \lambda_1 W + \lambda_2 S \\ + (\log k_{uk} - \log k_{us}) + (\alpha-1) \log EX.$$

If we now fit the combined data for the United States and the United Kingdom with equation (8), keeping the United States data in dollars and the United Kingdom data in pounds, it is clear that

(13) $$\lambda_3 = (\log k_{uk} - \log k_{us}) + (\alpha-1) \log EX.$$

The first term reflects any difference in the level of money demand between the two countries at the exchange rate of EX; the second reflects the difference in apparent level arising from the exchange rate.[26] If $\alpha = 1$, that is, income elasticity is unity, then no difference in apparent level arises from the exchange rate: velocity is then a constant and hence is independent of the level of income and equally of the monetary units in which income and money are expressed, provided the same rate of exchange is used for both money and income, which is why this problem did not arise in section 6.2, where we analyzed constant velocity.

If $\alpha \neq 1$, it is impossible to decompose the computed value of λ_3 into its two parts without a further assumption. (1) If we assume that the first term is zero, that is, that there is no difference in level, we can use equation (13) to estimate the implied value of EX, that is, the exchange rate that would produce identical relations for the United States and the United Kingdom (given that the slopes or elasticities and the size of the shifts are forced to be identical and that the same exchange rate is used for money and income). We shall consider later how to interpret such an implicit exchange rate. (2) Alternatively, if we assume a particular value for EX, say \$4.862, which was the market value in 1929, the base year for both the United States and United Kingdom real magnitudes, we can use equation (13) to estimate the difference in level between the United States and the United Kingdom relations. The result will of course be precisely the same as if we had calculated equation (8), using United Kingdom figures converted to dollars at that exchange rate.[27]

The entries in table 6.4 for the United States and United Kingdom combined were calculated using this dummy variable procedure but not allowing for the shifts (i.e., treating λ_1 and λ_2 as zero). The entries in table 6.6 for the two countries combined were calculated the same way except allowing for the shifts (i.e., from equation 8). They gave us estimates of the income elasticity and of the upward shifts that are free from any assumption about the exchange rate that is appropriate or about the size of the constant terms in equations (9) and (10).

---

26. If, instead of computing regression (8) from United States figures in dollars and United Kingdom figures in pounds, we were to use United Kingdom figures converted to dollars at the exchange rate EX', equation (13) would become:

(13') $\lambda_3 = (\log k_{uk} - \log k_{us}) + (\alpha - 1)(\log EX - \log EX')$

In effect, using pound figures is equivalent to using an $EX' = 1$, in which case equation (13') reduces to equation (13). Note that in equation (13') k_{uk} implicitly gives the level of the United Kingdom relation in dollars at the exchange rate of EX, not EX', just as it does in equation (13).

27. See preceding note.

For the 1929 market exchange rate of $4.862, the difference in level between the United States and the United Kingdom is 11 to 13 percent (line 2c of table 6.6). That is, at each level of real income per capita, real balances per capita tend, according to this combined estimate, to be 11 to 13 percent higher in the United Kingdom than in the United States.

Because the average elasticity (1.07–1.12) is so close to unity, it is clear that this estimate will not be highly sensitive to the precise exchange rate used to convert United Kingdom figures to dollars. For example, for reasons discussed in Appendix A to this chapter (sec. 6.8), the purchasing power parity exchange rate has a strong claim to be the relevant exchange rate to use in combining the data. An estimate of the purchasing power parity rate for various years can be constructed from the most recent independent estimate for 1970. That estimate sets it at $5.50 for 1929.[28] At this exchange rate, the difference in level, as computed from equation (13), would have been 10 to 12 percent instead of 11 to 13 percent. Clearly, no plausible adjustment of the market exchange rate can account for the difference in level.

A far more serious problem about the estimated difference in level arises from neglecting the effect of the significant difference in income elasticity between the two countries. This problem is illustrated by chart 6.3, which plots for the two countries the money on income regressions from equation (8)—these are the two parallel lines—and the regressions calculated for each country separately from the same equation, eliminating, of course, the term Z.[29] In all cases the regressions are for values of the shift dummy variables (W and S) set equal to zero (i.e., they correspond to the lower of the two parallel lines in chart 6.2).

The constraint to a common elasticity imposed by equation (8) fitted to pooled data for the two countries forces parallelism between the resulting lines for the separate countries and so gives a single estimate for the difference between the two countries for all levels of income—the 11 to 13 percent difference recorded in line 2c of table 6.6. But this parallelism clearly misrepresents the data—as the other two lines on the chart show. Because the United States line has a higher elasticity than the United Kingdom line, it starts below and ends above the United Kingdom line. At the roughly equal per capita income in the two countries at the beginning of our period (1876 or 1877), the United Kingdom regression gives a level of real per capita money 40 percent higher than does the United States regression. A century later, at the prevailing United Kingdom income, the United Kingdom level is 13 percent below the United States; at the prevailing United States income, now much higher than in

28. See appendix to this chapter, section 6.8.
29. For simplicity, we show only the money on income regressions. Because of the high correlations, the income on money regressions differ only trivially.

real per capita money (in $)

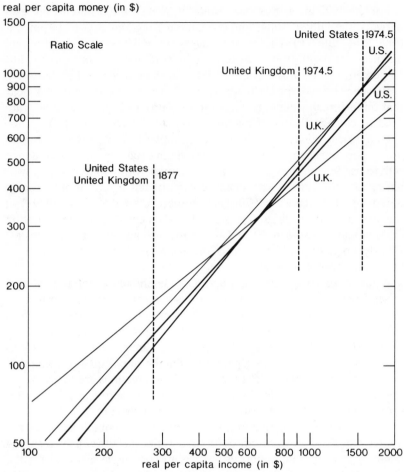

Chart 6.3   Regressions of real money per capita on real income per capita for United States and United Kingdom, elasticities different and constrained to be equal, eliminating common shift.

the United Kingdom, 30 percent. The single estimate of 11 percent is implicitly an average of these very different figures.

This chart puts a strong spotlight on the puzzle referred to above—Why the difference in elasticities? Why, at a comparable level of real income early in the century we cover, should United Kingdom real balances per capita have averaged close to 40 percent higher than United States balances, but at the end of the century, 13 to 30 percent lower? Does this difference reflect a basic discrepancy between the countries in the effect of higher real income, other major variables held constant? Or does it reflect the effect of a differential change between the two countries in those variables?

Any ambiguity about the exchange rate to use in pooling the data for the two countries has little to offer to the explanation of the differences we have found between the two countries. At most the use of a wrong exchange rate could help explain the difference in average level; it would contribute nothing to explaining the difference in slopes, which is derived from data for each country separately. As a result we have relegated a full examination of the problem of the exchange rate to use in pooling the data to Appendix A of this chapter (sec. 6.8).

Summary of Results for Levels of Money and Income

The results for the levels of real money per capita are fairly straightforward. For the whole century we cover, and for each country separately, the elasticity of real money per capita with respect to real income per capita appears to be a constant, numerically greater than unity (about 1.2) for the United States, less than unity (about 0.81) for the United Kingdom. There appears to have been a single upward shift in liquidity preference of about the same size (30 percent) in both countries, connected with economic depression and its aftermath and World War II and its aftermath. We estimate that the shift spanned the years 1929 to 1954 in the United States and 1921 to 1955 in the United Kingdom. There appears also to have been a postwar readjustment to bring demand back to its desired level—after the particularly low level of money demand during World War I and the high level during World War II—that was also of the same size in both countries. The postwar adjustment was less important in both size and duration than the demand shift. Together, constant elasticity plus the shifts account for at least 99 percent of the variation in real per capita money for the United States, if real per capita income is taken as exogenous, and 98 percent for the United Kingdom; and for 99 and 98 percent for the United States and the United Kingdom, respectively, of the variation in real per capita income, if real per capita money is taken as exogenous. The maximum residual standard error is less than 6.5 percent for money for the United States, 6.3 percent for the United Kingdom, less than 5.4 percent for income for the United States, and 7.8 percent for the United Kingdom.

We have constructed a single equation for the two countries, constraining the elasticities to be equal. The calculated common elasticity is about 1.1, and the estimated level of real per capita money for given real capita income is about 11 to 13 percent higher in the United Kingdom than in the United States. However, these estimates deserve little confidence because of the difference between the two countries in elasticity, which means that for real incomes as low as those in the early part of the period, United Kingdom real per capita money for given real per capita income is something like 40 percent higher than in the United States, and for levels of real income as high as those at the end of the period, some 13 to 30 percent lower.

This difference in elasticity is the chief puzzle. Moreover, since errors in population and prices bias these estimates toward unity, unbiased estimates would be higher for the United States and lower for the United Kingdom, giving a still larger difference to explain.

A major task for later sections of this chapter is to see whether changes over time in the other variables that we explore can account for the upward shift in both countries, and whether differential changes over time in these other variables for the two countries can account for the difference in elasticity.

6.4.2   Rates of Change

The situation is somewhat different for rates of change of real per capita money and real per capita income, as is clear from chart 6.4, panels A and B, which gives scatter diagrams for rates of change like those in chart 6.1, panels A and B, for levels.

If we differentiate equation (7) with respect to time, we have

$$(14) \qquad \frac{1}{m}\frac{dm}{dt} = \alpha\,\frac{1}{y}\frac{dy}{dt}$$

or

$$(15) \qquad g_m = \alpha\,g_y\,,$$

where g designates the rate of change of the variable designated by the subscript.

A value of $\alpha = 1$ corresponds to a constant velocity. Hence, if velocity is constant,

$$(16) \qquad g_m = g_y\,,$$

that is, money and income change at the same rate. The center line in each graph corresponds to equation (16). The other two lines are estimates of equation (15) obtained by regressing g_m on g_y and g_y on g_m, forcing the constant term to be zero. The computed values of α are given in table 6.7.

Clearly the scatters are very loose—more so for the United Kingdom than for the United States. The two limiting regressions are reasonably close together for the United States, a good deal farther apart for the United Kingdom.

This impression is confirmed by table 6.7. Columns 1, 2, and 3 are for equation (15). The correlations are clearly much lower than for the levels, but still most are appreciable. The limits on the income elasticity are much wider apart, but in general they include the narrower range in tables 6.4 and 6.6. However, much of the correlation, especially for the United Kingdom, comes from a common trend, as can be seen from columns 4, 5, and 6, which are for equation (15) modified by adding a constant term, that is,

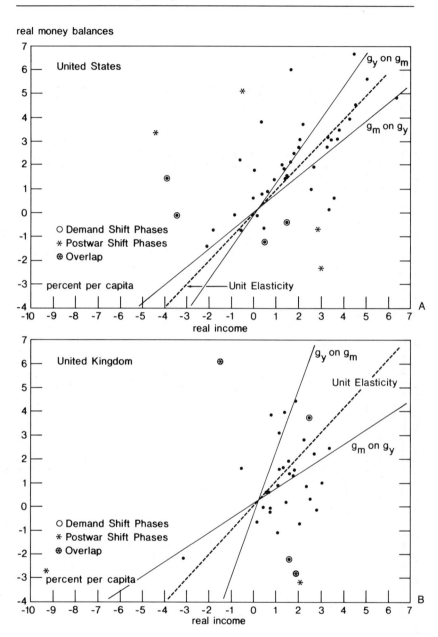

real money balances

United States

O Demand Shift Phases
* Postwar Shift Phases
⊛ Overlap

percent per capita

Unit Elasticity

g_y on g_m

g_m on g_y

real income

United Kingdom

O Demand Shift Phases
* Postwar Shift Phases
⊛ Overlap

percent per capita

Unit Elasticity

g_y on g_m

g_m on g_y

real income

Chart 6.4   Scatter diagram of rates of change of real per capita income and real per capita money and regression lines.

Table 6.7   Income Elasticities and Correlation Coefficients Calculated from Rates of Change of Real per Capita Money and Real per Capita Income, Various Periods, without and with Allowance for Trend by Inclusion of Nonzero Constant Term

	Zero Constant Term, No Allowance for Trend			Nonzero Constant Term, Allowance for Trend		
	Income Elasticity		Correlation Coefficient	Income Elasticity		Correlation Coefficient
	Lower Limit (1)	Upper Limit (2)	(3)	Lower Limit (4)	Upper Limit (5)	(6)
United States						
Full period	0.76	1.36	.751	0.48	1.60	.549
Full ex-wars	0.66	1.28	.721	0.41	1.18	.590
Pre–World War I	0.90	1.32	.826	0.37	1.44	.504
Interwar	0.30	1.49	.445	0.45	0.67	.822
Postwar	0.66	1.04	.798	1.02	2.10	.699
United Kingdom						
Full period	0.63	2.66	.487	0.14	23.42	.078
Full ex-wars	0.70	1.76	.633	0.50	7.51	.257
Pre–World War I	0.93	1.02	.955	1.19	1.51	.889
Interwar	1.15	1.59	.853	−0.09	−7.56	.110
Postwar	−0.05	−22.17	.049	−0.18	−78.74	.045
United States and United Kingdom[a]						
Full period	0.73	1.68	.657	0.47	2.80	.411
Full ex-wars	0.68	1.46	.682	0.42	2.38	.422
Pre–World War I	0.91	1.21	.868	0.70	1.61	.659
Interwar	0.57	1.55	.607	0.45	0.74	.782
Postwar	0.38	2.35	.400	0.87	6.07	.377

[a]Since basic observations are free of units, being rates of change, United States and United Kingdom observations were simply pooled for these regressions.

(17) $g_m = \kappa + \alpha g_y.$

Equation (17) is obtained by adding the term κT, with T for time, to equation (7) and then differentiating with respect to time, which is why we speak of it as allowing for a trend. The correlations for the United States in this part of the table are still respectable, but for the United Kingdom they are close to zero except for the pre–World War I period.

To some extent these rather unsatisfactory results simply reflect the statistical characteristics of our data. Our rates of change are comparable to first differences between equally spaced data, differing only in being based on observations that are unequally spaced and on three rather than two observations. Correlations between first differences typically tend to be much lower than between original values because the random component plays so much larger a role compared with the systematic component. Similarly, we would expect the correlations between the rates of change to be much lower than between the levels, especially given the strong secular trends in our variables. On this ground the lower but still respectable correlations for the United States are fully in accord with expectations. However, the sharp drop in the United Kingdom correlations, to a level that does not differ from zero by an amount that is statistically significant, is disturbing.

The contrast between the prewar period for the United Kingdom and the other periods gives a clue to the results for the latter. For both the United States and the United Kingdom, the results for periods other than the prewar period are distorted by two phenomena: (1) immediate postwar perturbations, which account for the most extreme observations for both the United States and the United Kingdom, and (2) the upward shift in liquidity preference discussed in the preceding section.

1. The points in chart 6.4, panels A and B marked * are the relevant postwar phases centered on 1920 and 1921 for both countries after World War I; on 1949 and 1951.5 for the United States; and 1952 and 1954 for the United Kingdom after World War II. In both countries the two sets of postwar points are extreme, though in opposite directions: the rate of growth of real per capita money is unusually high after World War I and unusually low after World War II. The opposite directions are the counterpart of the difference between the two wars that we discussed earlier (sec. 5.2): during World War I velocity rose, so after the war real money balances rose sharply to restore them to their usual relation to real income; during World War II velocity fell, so after the war real money balances had to fall sharply to restore the usual relation.

Two other features stand out. First, the deviations in the opposite directions from the central line are of roughly the same magnitude both for the two wars and for the two countries. At the risk of reading more into the data than may be there, this curious and, at least to us, unexpected result suggests that there may be a fairly constant maximum *rate* at which money holders are willing, under the kind of conditions prevailing at the end of the two wars, to readjust their money holdings from one desired *level* to another. Second, the postwar readjustment comes at the same time in the two countries after World War I but later in the United Kingdom after World War II. This again is a familiar phenomenon that we have referred to before.

2. Because our rates of change are calculated from three phase levels, the upward shift in liquidity preference isolated in our examination of levels affects two rates of change at the onset and two at its termination. These observations are circled in chart 6.4. For the United States, the circled observations do not overlap the ones marked *. For the United Kingdom, because the upward shift came earlier and the post-World War II readjustment later, there is an overlap, so that two observations are both *'s and circled.

The upward shift tends to make the rate of change of real per capita money unusually high when it began and unusually low when it ended. Seven out of eight circled points clearly conform to that expectation; the eighth, the United Kingdom one for 1923, is somewhat ambiguous, falling between the two regressions.

To estimate the quantitative effect of allowing for these two phenomena, we have added two dummy variables to equations (15) and (17), so that they become

(18) $$g_m = \alpha g_y + \lambda_1 W_g + \lambda_2 S_g$$

(19) $$g_m = \kappa + \alpha g_y + \lambda_1 W_g + \lambda_2 S_g \ ,$$

where W_g = $\begin{cases} +1 & \text{for the phases centered on 1920 and 1921 for the United States and the United Kingdom} \\ -1 & \text{for the phases centered on 1949 and 1951.5 for the United States and 1952 and 1954 for the United Kingdom} \\ 0 & \text{for all other phases} \end{cases}$

S_g = $\begin{cases} +T_{g_i} & \text{for the phases centered on 1928.5 and 1931 for the United States and 1921 and 1923 for the United Kingdom} \\ -T_{g_i} & \text{for the phases centered on 1954 and 1956 for the United States and 1954 and 1957 for the United Kingdom} \\ 0 & \text{for all other phases} \end{cases}$

where T_{g_i} is the time interval between the centered dates of phase $i + 1$ and phase $i - 1$. Note that W_g and S_g and T_{g_i} are equivalent to the time derivative of the corresponding variables, W, S, and T_i for levels.

The first dummy variable, W_g, allows for the postwar readjustment, the second, S_g, for the upward shift. This way of allowing for these phenomena constrains the postwar readjustment to have the same effect on the rate of change for each of the four phases involved, and the upward demand shift to have the same effect on the product of the rate of change and time duration for each of the four phases involved. For W_g, that constraint reflects the hypothesis that there is a maximum per-year desirable rate of readjustment of deficient or excessive money balances; for S_g it reflects our earlier conclusion that the level figures could be approximated by two parallel constant elasticity functions. For each of the four rate of change observations affected by the shift, the size of the step is the same, but since the period over which the adjustment occurs depends on the interval between the preceding and following phases, that implies a constant product of time interval and change in the rate of change.

The effect of introducing these dummy variables is summarized in table 6.8. These results are much more satisfactory than those in table 6.7. Though the correlations between rates of change after allowing for shifts are understandably still much lower than between levels, they are all positive and most differ significantly from zero. More important, the ranges of the income elasticities are not inconsistent with the ranges derived from the levels. The postwar shift plays a much larger role, and the demand shift a smaller role, for rates of change than for levels, but again the size of the shifts is about the same for the United States and the United Kingdom. The one important difference from the levels is that there is no clear difference between United Kingdom and United States income elasticities—but that may reflect simply the much lower correlation for rates of change and hence the wider limits on the estimated elasticity.

As for levels, the inclusion of the shift variables seems to make the data homogeneous for the different periods. There is no significant difference between the computed regressions for the pre-World War I period, for which dummies are irrelevant, and the rest of the period, if dummies are included.[30] Neither is there a significant difference between the United States and the United Kingdom regressions once dummies are included.[31]

It is hard to compare directly the variability of the rates of change and the levels because the standard deviations are in different units. For the level of United States real per capita money for the period as a whole, for example, the standard deviation is 62.5 percent. This means that roughly

---

30. The F values between the periods for regressions with a zero constant term of real per capita money on real per capita income and dummies are 1.3 for the United States (1 and 43 degrees of freedom); .01 for the United Kingdom (1 and 31 degrees of freedom); and .32 for the United States plus the United Kingdom (1 and 79 degrees of freedom). The results are similar for regressions including other variables, and for regressions with a constant term.

31. The relevant analysis of variance is as shown in table 6.N.2 on p. 252.

Table 6.8 Relation between Rates of Change of Real per Capita Money and Real per Capita Income: Effect of Allowing for Demand and Postwar Shifts, with Zero and Nonzero Constant Term

	Zero Constant Term			Nonzero Constant Term		
	U.S.	U.K.	U.S. and U.K.	U.S.	U.K.	U.S. and U.K.
1a. Period affected by demand shift	1927–32	1920–24		1927–32	1920–24	
	1953–57	1952–58		1953–57	1952–58	
b. Period affected by postwar shift	1919–21	1919–21		1919–21	1919–21	
	1948–53	1951–55		1948–53	1951–55	
2a. Size of demand shift (annual percentage)	0.51(0.68)	0.45(0.48)	0.48(0.65)	0.28(0.81)	0.48(0.31)	0.38(0.84)
b. Size of postwar shift (annual percentage)	4.59(5.59)	4.18(6.33)	4.32(5.39)	4.62(5.66)	3.76(10.72)	4.40(5.45)
3a. Income elasticity, lower limit	0.91	0.85	0.89	0.64	0.47	0.68
b. Income elasticity, upper limit	1.27	1.84	1.42	1.42	5.23	1.83
4a. Simple correlation, money and income	0.75	0.49	0.66	0.55	0.08	0.41
b. Partial correlation, allowing for shifts	0.85	0.68	0.79	0.67	0.30	0.61
5. Multiple correlation, including shifts	0.85(0.87)	0.74(0.72)	0.81(0.82)	0.73(0.78)	0.64(0.43)	0.70(0.68)

Standard Error of Estimate (%)

Real per capita money						
6. Total	3.31	2.08	2.61	2.25	1.75	2.04
Maximum residual after allowing for:						
7. Constant velocity	2.32	1.91	2.07	2.31	1.93	2.08
8. Constant elasticity	2.21	1.84	1.98	1.90	1.78	1.88
9. Constant velocity plus shifts	2.20	1.78	2.00	2.20	1.78	2.00
10. Constant elasticity plus shifts	1.80	1.46	1.57	1.59	1.42	1.49
Real per capita income						
11. Total	3.25	1.60	2.36	2.57	0.96	1.78
Maximum residual after allowing for:						
12. Constant velocity	2.32	1.91	2.07	2.31	1.93	2.08
13. Constant elasticity	2.17	1.42	1.79	2.17	0.97	1.63
14. Constant velocity plus shifts	2.20	1.78	2.00	2.20	1.78	2.00
15. Constant elasticity plus shifts	1.67	1.17	1.40	1.68	0.90	1.33

Note: Figures in parentheses from regressions of g_y on g_m and dummy or dummies solved for g_m; others from regressions of g_m on g_y and dummy and dummy (or dummies).

two-thirds of the observations are between 100/1.625, or 61.5 percent of the mean, and 162.5 percent of the mean. For rates of change there is little point in expressing the variation relative to the mean, since the mean may be zero or negative. The comparable rate of change standard deviation is 2.25 percentage points per year, which means that two-thirds of the annual rates of changes are within 2.25 percentage points of the mean annual rate of change. Perhaps one way to make the comparison is to note that the mean interval spanned by the three phases from which rates of change are calculated is four years for the United States, five and one-half years for the United Kingdom, so the standard deviation of the total percentage change in money over this interval is about 9 percent of the initial value for the United States, only a seventh of the 62.5 percent standard deviation of levels. For the United Kingdom, the corresponding figures are 32.6 and 1.75 percentage points per year, or about 10 percent for a five and one-half year span, less than a third of the standard deviation of levels. Clearly, eliminating the longer period movements by the use of rates of change has also eliminated most of the variability.

As a result, allowing for the effect of real per capita income on real per capita money (or of real per capita money on real per capita income) and of the shifts has a much less dramatic effect on the standard deviations, reducing them, if trend is allowed for by including a constant term, from 2.25 percentage points per year to 1.59 for the United States, and from

Table 6.N.2	Analysis of Variance of Differences between Demand for Money Regressions for the United States and the United Kingdom Based on Rates of Change			
Source of Variation	Degrees of Freedom	Sum of Squares	Mean Square	F
Within United States	44	.01428	.00032(.00030)*	
Within United Kingdom	32	.00684	.00021(.00023)*	
Within United States and United Kingdom	76	.01937	.00025	
Difference between United States and United Kingdom				
In slope	1	.00005	.00005	0.20
In shifts	2	.00001	.000005	0.02
Subtotal	79	.01943		
Attributable to				
Demand shift	1	.00546	.00546	21.84
Postwar shift	1	.00691	.00691	27.64
Slope	1	.02415	.02415	96.60
Total	82	.05595		

[a]See note 24, above.

1.75 to 1.42 for the United Kingdom (and for real per capita income from 2.57 to 1.68 for the United States, and .96 to .90 for the United Kingdom). Comparison of these reduced standard errors, multiplied by the average span on which they are based, with the residual standard errors of the levels, after allowing for real per capita income and the shifts, is much more illuminating than comparing the original standard deviations. For the United States the residual standard error of the level of real per capita money is 6.5 percent; four times the residual standard error of the rate of change is 6.4. For the United Kingdom, the residual standard error of the level is 6.3 percent; five and one-half times the residual standard error of the rate of change is 7.8 percent. The final results are therefore roughly the same: real per capita income and the shifts leave about the same residual error as the more sensitive adjustment for trend in the form of rates of change.

What these results mean is that the relatively small short-term movements of real money balances reflect primarily variables other than the contemporaneous changes in real per capita income or the shifts we have isolated. We have reached this conclusion before for movements within cycle phases. It is the basis for our suggestion that the demand for real money balances depends on permanent rather than measured income.[32] The present results indicate that a similar, but weaker, conclusion holds for the longer periods to which our rates of change refer—averaging four years for the United States, five and one-half for the United Kingdom. Over such periods, the variation in both real balances and real income is small, and each is heavily affected by variables that do not affect the other in the same way. Over longer periods, the changes in real money balances and real per capita income cumulate and become more and more important relative to the short-term perturbations.

6.5   Effect of Population and Prices

In the preceding section we assumed that $\beta = \gamma = 1$ in equation (3), that is, that any change in prices or population implied an equal percentage change in the quantity of money demanded (mathematically, the demand for money in nominal terms is homogeneous of the first degree in population and prices). This section tests that assumption. Take logarithms of both sides of equation (3), add terms to allow for the demand and postwar shifts, and rearrange to:

$$(20) \qquad \log m = \log k + \alpha \log y + (\beta - 1) \log N \\ + (\gamma - 1)\log P + \lambda_1 W + \lambda_2 S.$$

32. M. Friedman, *The Demand for Money: Some Theoretical and Empirical Results*, Occasional Paper 68 (New York: NBER, 1959); reprinted in Friedman, *Optimum Quantity of Money;* Friedman and Schwartz, "Money and Business Cycles," p. 44.

Alternately, solve equation (20) for log y, giving:

(21) $\log y = -(1/\alpha) \log k + (1/\alpha) \log m - [(\beta - 1)/\alpha] \log N - [(\gamma - 1)/\alpha] \log P - [\lambda_1/\alpha]W - [\lambda_2/\alpha]S.$

Clearly, if $\beta = \gamma = 1$, the coefficients of log N and log P are zero in both equations (20) and (21).

The values of k, α, β, and γ obtained by fitting equations (20) and (21) to the data for the United States and the United Kingdom are summarized in table 6.9.[33] For both countries, the calculated price elasticities as computed from the money on income and income on money regressions are consistent with the theoretical value of unity—one estimate exceeding, the other falling short of unity. For the United Kingdom, that is true also of the population elasticity, but it is not for the United States, for which both limits exceed unity. For the United States plus the United Kingdom, the range of both population and price elasticities excludes unity, but the limit for each is clearly not significantly different from unity. All in all, therefore, the only serious discrepancy from theoretical expectations is for the United States population elasticities.

Columns 5 and 6 provide an additional test by comparing errors of estimate of equations omitting population and prices (i.e., forcing $\beta = \gamma = 1$) and equations including them. For four of the six comparisons, the inclusion of population and prices explicitly has a sizable effect, reducing the standard error substantially. There is one exception for each country: the income on money regression for the United States, the money on income regression for the United Kingdom.

One possible explanation for these results is that population and prices are serving as proxies for other variables. For prices, the other variable may be interest rates, since there is the well-known Gibson paradox phenomenon of a positive correlation between prices and interest rates. For population, the obvious other variable is time trend, since we know that population moves very slowly over time.

The effect of including population and prices on the value of α is consistent with the interpretation of population as a proxy for trend. The lower and upper limits of α (from the regressions of money on income and income on money, respectively) are far wider apart in table 6.9 than in table 6.6, indicating that inclusion of population and prices has reduced the correlation between real money per capita and real income per capita, both of which display consistent upward trends. Some other variable, presumably population, is clearly serving as a trend term.

33. Note that because P and N enter explicitly in these equations, the statistical estimates of α are not subject to the bias arising from measurement errors in N and P discussed above.

Table 6.9 Relation between Levels of Real per Capita Money and Real per Capita Income: Estimates of the Effects of Population and Prices, Allowing for Demand and Postwar Shifts

Country and Regression	Constant (1)	Income Elasticity (α) (2)	Population Elasticity (β) (3)	Price Elasticity (γ) (4)	Standard Error of Estimate (Percentage) of per Capita Magnitude from Regressions among Real per Capita Money, Real per Capita Income, Shift Dummies, and			
					No Other Variables (5)	Population, Prices (6)	Interest Rate, Trend (7)	Interest Rate, Lagged per Capita Magnitude (8)
United States								
Money on income	−0.96	0.68	1.49	1.07	6.5	4.6	4.5	3.9
Income on money	−2.33	1.13	1.17	0.94	5.4	5.2	5.3	5.2
United Kingdom								
Money on income	−0.16	0.65	1.29	1.00	6.3	6.4	5.4	5.3
Income on money	0.70	1.62	−0.10	0.87	7.8	6.2	5.3	4.1
United States and United Kingdom[a]								
Money on income	−1.37	0.60	1.69	0.96	10.1	6.2	8.4	5.3
Income on money	3.66	1.45	1.01	0.75	9.2	6.6	5.6	6.1

[a]For United States and United Kingdom combined, country dummy (U.S. = 0, U.K. = 1) was also added to equation.

The final two columns in table 6.9 test this explanation by substituting a short-term interest rate for the price variable[34] and by allowing for trend instead of population—in column 7 by including time as a variable, in column 8 by including the lagged value of the dependent variable. These substitutions give lower standard errors of estimate in ten out of twelve comparisons, and in some comparisons decidedly lower standard errors.[35]

The equations including the interest rate term and trend (corresponding to column 7 of table 6.9) go even further than the equations including population and prices in the direction of absorbing some or most of the relation between money and income. For the United States and the United Kingdom, the effect is to widen the range between the lower and upper limits of the computed income elasticity—from .63 and 1.13 to .61 and 1.17 for the United States, from .65 and 1.62 to .42 and 2.54 for the United Kingdom. For the United States plus the United Kingdom, the effect, surprisingly, is the reverse, to narrow the range, from .60 and 1.45 to 1.23 and 1.86.

Parallel calculations for rates of change give very similar results. Differentiating equations (20) and (21) with respect to time gives:

(22) $$g_m = \alpha\, g_y + (\beta - 1)g_N + (\gamma - 1)g_P + \lambda_1 W_g + \lambda_2 S_g$$

(23) $$g_y = [1/\alpha]g_m - [(\beta - 1)/\alpha]g_N - [(\gamma - 1)/\alpha]g_P$$
$$- [\lambda_1/\alpha]W_g - [\lambda_2/\alpha]S_g.$$

Table 6.10, the counterpart for rates of change of table 6.9, gives almost identical results. The computed population and price elasticities are in general, though not uniformly, consistent with the hypothetical values of unity; the inclusion of population and prices explicitly has a trivial effect on the standard error of estimate for three comparisons, reduces it moderately for three; in the latter cases the same or an even greater reduction in the standard error is achieved by including an interest rate and a trend term instead of population and prices.[36]

As for levels, the inclusion of population and prices absorbs some of the effects of the correlation between money and income, widening the range of the estimated income elasticities (compare table 6.10 and table 6.8, zero-constant term). Replacing population and prices by interest rate

34. Tests summarized in section 6.6.1 indicate that a short-term rate generally gives better results than a long-term rate. However, the interest rate used here is not the differential interest rate we finally settled on in section 6.6.

35. We have also computed regressions including population and prices along with interest rates and a trend term. In general, these give standard errors of about the same size as those in columns 7 and 8. However, in a few cases the addition of population and prices does reduce the standard error appreciably, indicating that they are not simply proxies for interest rates and time.

36. Trend is allowed for simply by introducing a constant term into the regression. Equations (22) and (23) do not have a constant term.

Table 6.10   Relation between Rates of Change of Real per Capita Money and Real per Capita Income: Estimates of the Effects of Population and Prices, Allowing for Demand and Postwar Shifts

Country and Regression	Estimates of			Standard Error of Estimates (Percentage) of per Capita Real Magnitude from Regressions among Real per Capita Money, Real per Capita Income and			
	Income Elasticity (α) (1)	Population Elasticity (β) (2)	Price Elasticity (γ) (3)	No Other Variables (4)	Population, Prices (5)	Interest Rate, Trend (6)	Interest Rate, Lagged per Capita Magnitude (7)
United States							
Money on income	0.64	1.64	1.11	1.80	1.59	1.61	1.00
Income on money	1.37	0.95	0.90	1.67	1.69	1.69	1.52
United Kingdom							
Money on income	0.69	1.36	1.06	1.46	1.47	1.35	1.33
Income on money	3.49	−3.16	1.03	1.17	0.95	0.92	0.96
United States and United Kingdom[a]							
Money on income	0.67	1.57	1.08	1.57	1.48	1.47	1.23
Income on money	1.75	0.29	0.95	1.40	1.36	1.33	1.41

[a]For United States and United Kingdom combined, country dummy (U.S. = 0, U.K. = 1) was multiplied by demand shift and postwar shift dummies and added to equations.

and trend widens them further, modestly for the United States and United States plus the United Kingdom, substantially for the United Kingdom.[37]

The results for both levels and rates of change are reasonably consistent with the assumption $\beta = \gamma = 1$. Any apparent influence of population and prices can readily be interpreted as a disguised reflection of the influence of trend and interest rates.

The most interesting substantive result from our explorations is the effect on the computed elasticities of allowing explicitly for trend. For both the United States and the United Kingdom, introducing trend absorbs much of the effect of income and widens the range of the estimates of income elasticity. This result admits of two very different interpretations. One is that there is a secular trend in the quantity of money demanded produced by some secularly changing variables other than income itself—for example, urbanization, or increasing specialization in production—for which income is serving as a proxy and for which a trend term is a better proxy. This explanation is certainly plausible.

An alternative interpretation is that the quantity of money demanded is related to a longer term income magnitude than average income over a phase, and that the trend term itself is serving as a proxy for such a longer term magnitude. Numerous demand studies for money have shown that some concept of permanent real income or wealth is more closely connected with the real quantity of money demanded than is current income. However, these studies have mostly been for quarterly or annual data. We conjectured initially that our phase data would be closely enough linked to permanent income to make the distinction of little empirical significance. But perhaps that is wrong.

Column 8 of table 6.9 and column 7 of table 6.10 were included as a simple way to cast some light on this interpretation. Allowing for trend in a regression of money on income by including the lagged value of the quantity of money is equivalent to estimating permanent income as a weighted average of current and prior values of income with the weights given by an exponential whose value declines the earlier the income value weighted—this is the adaptive expectations approach—and hence to regarding the quantity of money demanded as a function of permanent income. Similarly, in a regression of income on money, including the lagged value of income is equivalent to regarding income as a function of "permanent money" estimated by the same kind of exponentially weighted average of present and past values of money.

The results are reasonably consistent with this interpretation. For the money on income regressions and for both levels and rates of change, the

37. For the United States, to 0.64 and 1.42; for the United Kingdom, to 0.40 and 5.40; for the United States and United Kingdom, to 0.68 and 1.79.

inclusion of lagged income consistently gives a lower standard error than the use of the trend term. For the income on money regression, this is true for only three out of six comparisons, and in general any effect is smaller in magnitude—which is certainly what would be expected if permanent income systematically affects desired money balances. It is difficult to give any persuasive interpretation to "permanent money" as determining real income, which is why the asymmetry of the results supports the alternative interpretation. Moreover, the regression coefficients are not unreasonable. They imply that the mean period of averaging in computing permanent income is roughly two or three phases, and that the elasticity of money demand with respect to permanent income is roughly the same as the lower limits computed more directly, allowing only for the shifts, as given in tables 6.6 and 6.8.[38]

6.6   Effect of Costs of Holding Money

The quantity of money that people wish to hold is affected by the costs and returns from holding money. The direct costs and returns—in the form of expected losses, storage charges, interest received—are generally neglected and treated as zero. However, Benjamin Klein has demonstrated that, at least for the United States, allowance for these direct costs and returns can appreciably improve the statistical estimates of demand

---

38. The estimated weight on the current phase value of income in computing permanent income (b), average period of weighting, in phase units ($1/b$), and estimated permanent income elasticity (dm/dy_p) are as follows for the United States and the United Kingdom, for levels and rates of change:

	Levels			Rates of Change		
	b	$1/b$	dm/dy_p	b	$1/b$	dm/dy_p
United States	.55	1.8	1.12	.40	2.5	1.55
United Kingdom	.62	1.6	0.79	.60	1.7	0.78

These estimates were derived from the coefficients of the following regressions:

$$m_t = \log k + \alpha y_t + \delta R_S + \Theta m_{t-1} + \lambda_1 W + \lambda_2 S,$$

$$g_{m_t} = \log k + \alpha g_{y_t} + \delta\, g_{R_S} + \Theta g_{m_{t-1}} + \lambda_1 W_g + \lambda_2 S_g.$$

We assumed that permanent income for the United States is estimated by adding a trend element of .02 per year, which for phases averaging two years in length means .04 per phase, to a weighted average of current and past measured incomes. On this assumption

$$b = 1 - \Theta + .04$$

$$\frac{dm}{dy_p} = \frac{\alpha}{b}.$$

For the United Kingdom, we assumed a trend element of .0125 per year, which multiplied by the 2.75 year phase average length of the United Kingdom phase, gives .034 as the trend allowance.

curves.[39] Klein obtains a statistical counterpart to these direct costs and returns by neglecting the direct costs and returns associated with currency and with losses from bank failures but including an allowance for interest paid on deposits, whether interest is paid directly, as was legal for all deposits in the United States before 1933 and for time deposits thereafter (and throughout in the United Kingdom),[40] or indirectly through rendering services without charge or granting loans at lower than market interest rates. He allows for both direct and indirect payments by assuming that banks pass on to their customers the net income they receive from their earning assets and estimating this net income on the basis of market interest rates. This procedure is equivalent to including the ratio of high-powered to total money as well as a market interest rate in the demand for money function.[41] We have experimented with this method of allowing for the direct costs and returns from holding money and report the results below.

The major return from holding money is indirect: the nonpecuniary services rendered by money. The adjustment we have made for increasing financial sophistication of the United States before 1903 already allows for one element of these services. For the rest, we treat this return

39. Benjamin Klein, "The Payment of Interest on Commercial Bank Deposits and the Price of Money: A Study of the Demand for Money" (Ph.D. diss., University of Chicago, 1970).

40. However, cartel agreements among the banks, dating from 1877 and effective from World War II on, prohibited direct interest payments on United Kingdom current accounts. In 1877 London joint stock banks agreed to abolish all interest payments on current accounts, although there is evidence that many banks evaded the agreement before World War I. Certain provincial banks did not end the practice of paying interest on current accounts until World War II, when all banks agreed not to compete for deposits by increasing interest payments. Cartel agreements among the banks dating to 1886 determined the rate of interest to be paid on deposit accounts by reference to the margin between bank rate and the deposit rate, but again there were many exceptions. See C. A. E. Goodhart, *The Business of Banking, 1891–1914* (London: Weidenfeld and Nicolson, 1972), pp. 178–88; B. Griffiths, "The Development of Restrictive Practices in the U.K. Monetary System," *Manchester School of Economics and Social Studies* 41 (March 1973): 6–7.

41. Let $H = C + B$ be high-powered money, with C = currency, and B = bank reserves defined as the banks' total holdings of high-powered money. Let R = a market interest rate on securities comparable to bank earning assets in period to maturity. Then Klein treats interest paid per dollar of deposits as equal to $R(1 - B/D)$, where D equals total bank deposits. This includes interest paid indirectly on demand deposits plus interest paid directly on time deposits. Income earned by a holder of money per dollar would then be a weighted average of the zero earned per dollar of currency and the above sum earned per dollar of deposits, or

$$\frac{C(0) + DR(1 - \frac{B}{D})}{C + D} = \frac{R(D - B)}{C + D} = \frac{R(M - H)}{M} = R(1 - \frac{H}{M}),$$

where $M = C + D$ = the money supply.

as embodied in the demand function, which means as primarily a function of the real quantity of money held. This procedure is incorrect insofar as technical changes have altered the productivity of money balances in yielding monetary services—as apparently they did to a marked extent in the United States before 1903 and must have to some extent in the United States since then and in the United Kingdom before and since.

The major indirect cost of holding money is the income foregone from the assets that could have been held instead of the money. The opportunity cost depends on the alternative considered and on the period of time for which the alternative is regarded as sacrificed. In addition, we must distinguish between the alternative cost ex post—the realized return on the alternative asset—and the alternative cost ex ante—the anticipated return. We can only measure the cost directly ex post, yet what is relevant to the demand function is the alternative cost ex ante.

As we noted in chapter 2, possible alternative assets are numerous for each holder of money and vary widely from holder to holder. For business enterprises, the key alternatives to holding money are larger holdings of financial and physical assets or reduced liabilities in the form of borrowing from banks, other short-term borrowing, long-term debt, and equity. For ultimate owners of wealth, and for our concept of money, the major alternatives include mutual savings deposits, savings and loan shares, government and private debt obligations, equities, and physical assets, or reduced liabilities in the form of mortgages on owned homes and debt on other consumer goods.

For each alternative, the ex post return in nominal terms that is sacrificed for any given period includes the explicit yield in nominal terms during that period plus the change in the nominal price of the asset during that period. For some alternatives, for example borrowing from banks (neglecting the possibility of default), mutual savings deposits, savings and loan shares, and series E United States government bonds, the change in price is zero because the obligation can be paid off or redeemed on demand at a fixed nominal price. For these alternatives also, the yield is generally known in advance so that there is no significant difference between the nominal return ex ante and ex post—though of course there may still be a difference between the real return ex ante and ex post. For marketable obligations, such as commercial paper, bonds, and particularly equities, a change in the nominal price of the asset may be an important component of the ex post return. For some obligations that have a stated maturity value such as commercial paper and bonds, the change in price will itself consist of two parts, one that results from the amortization of any premium over, or discount from, the value at maturity, the other, from the change in market yields. The first is embedded in calculated market yields and hence can be regarded as known ex ante.

The second cannot be known in advance and the ex ante equivalent to this part of the ex post return is an *anticipated* change in market yields.

For equities, which have no stated maturity value, and for physical assets such as fixed capital and inventories for business enterprises, or owned homes, automobiles and other consumer capital for ultimate wealth owners, the change in market price tends to be a still larger part of the nominal return and no part of the change is known ex ante. Almost the whole of the return on these assets must be based on anticipations.

The period of time for which the alternative is regarded as sacrificed and therefore for which the ex ante yield is relevant is an elusive concept. Money balances are held for a wide variety of possible contingencies, the timing of some of which, such as recurrent trips to market, is reasonably predictable, the timing of others, such as emergency needs for ready funds, is highly uncertain. In principle, the whole term structure of yields, for all possible holding periods, is relevant to the quantity of money demanded. For example, no one would hold money instead of an interest-bearing asset if he were *certain* that he would not have to draw on it for a very long time. Yet he may hold money even though there is a sizable possibility that he may not have to draw on it for a very long time. Whether he will do so depends on the return available from assets held for long periods.[42]

Given the multiplicity and complexity of the yields that are relevant, it is perhaps not surprising that statistical studies of the demand for money, which have had to use a small number of observable yields, have produced divergent and confusing results. Almost all such studies confirm the expected negative relation between yields on alternative assets and the quantity of money demanded. However, studies for different countries and periods, and even studies by different scholars for the same country and period, have yielded widely divergent conclusions about the particular yield that is most closely related to the quantity of money demanded. The studies have explored (1) short-term yields on nominal assets; (2) long-term yields on nominal assets; (3) yields on equities; (4) anticipated rates of price change, computed as weighted averages of past rates of price change and interpreted as the nominal yield on physical assets. And these four classes of yields have of necessity covered only a small part of the range of assets that are effective alternatives to the holding of money. For most such assets, there simply are no market yields to observe.

Item 4, anticipated price change, has generally been dominant whenever there has been substantial inflation, perhaps partly because governmental intervention has often made it impossible to observe the other

42. See Milton Friedman, "Time Perspective in the Demand for Money," *Scandinavian Journal of Economics* 79, no. 4 (1977): 397–416.

yields. For other countries and times, the effect of anticipated price change has been hard to detect, either because our measures are defective or because the bulk of its effect is allowed for by item 1, the yield on nominal assets, which tends to be raised by expectations of inflation. Item 3, yield on equities, is hard to measure and hence has been explored in only a few studies.

For countries and periods not characterized by substantial inflation, items 1 and 2, short- and long-term yields on nominal assets, have been the yields generally explored. These studies show no uniformity. Sometimes a short-term yield gives better results, sometimes a long-term yield, and when both are included the relative coefficients are unstable. This result is not inconsistent with theoretical reasoning, which suggests that the relative weight of yields for different holding periods should itself depend on the level and term structure of yields.

The consistent finding that the yield displays the expected negative relation with the quantity of money demanded presumably reflects the existence of a structure of yields that tends to move more or less together. If this is so, then the yield that is included in a demand study, or the small number of yields that are included, enter as a proxy or proxies for the whole structure of yields rather than in their own right. On this view, the particular yield that shows the closest relation depends on the yield that happens, in the particular circumstances, to be the best proxy for the yield structure as a whole.

We conclude that it would be desirable for the focus of research to change, that we should give up the attempt to find an asset or a small set of assets that can be regarded as the closest substitutes for money and instead recognize that money is so pervasive and the range of substitutes so broad that we should seek rather to find a compact way to describe the whole structure of yields—the "general" level; the "tilt" of the yield structure to maturity; and the "difference" between real and nominal yields—to suggest what seem offhand the key characteristics of that structure.[43]

---

43. H. Robert Heller and Mohsin S. Khan, "The Demand for Money and the Term Structure of Interest Rates," *Journal of Political Economy* 87 (February 1979): 109–29, have taken up this suggestion and applied it to United States quarterly data for 1960–1976. They approximate the term structure by a quadratic in maturity, then use the three parameters of the quadratic in a demand for money function, concluding that "this approximation performed favorably relative to standard specifications of the money-demand function that utilized only one interest rate as the opportunity-cost variable as well as the ones that introduce several interest rates. Furthermore, . . . the function using this particular approximation appeared to be stable during a period when standard functions using only one interest rate display significant shifts in parameters" (p. 127).

We have ourselves not been able to use this approach for the United States and the United Kingdom because of the large research expenditure that would have been required to get

6.6.1   Yield on Nominal Assets

Our own explorations of different nominal yields have simply confirmed the results of other studies.

In our calculations, we have generally used two interest rates for each country: one a rate on a security with a short maturity, the other a rate on a security with a long maturity.[44] For levels, we have fitted equations of the form:

(24) $\log m = \log k + \delta_S R_S + \delta_L R_L +$ terms in other variables,

where m, as earlier, is real per capita money balances (for the United States, adjusted for changing financial sophistication), all logarithms are natural logarithms, R_S is a short-term rate of interest, R_L a long-term rate, and k, δ_S, δ_L and similar coefficients of other terms are parameters to be estimated. Some equations include only R_S, others, only R_L; still others, both.

For rates of change, we have fitted equations of the form:

(25) $g_m = \kappa + \delta_S DR_S + \delta_L DR_L +$ terms in other variables,

where D is used as a symbol for a time derivative or absolute difference (as compared with the symbol g that we have used for a percentage rate of change or time derivative of a logarithm). Some equations include an intercept (κ)—which is equivalent to allowing for a constant time trend in

---

satisfactory term structure data for the United Kingdom. We report in an appendix to this chapter (see 6.9) some experiments we have made for the United States.

Perhaps the most interesting and exciting empirical implication of their and our calculations is the evidence they provide on a conclusion reached on purely theoretical grounds in Friedman, "Time Perspective in the Demand for Money" (see note 42), that a steepening in tilt of the term structure, that is, a rise in long-term rates accompanied by a decline in short-term rates sufficient to keep the average level of interest rates constant, will reduce the quantity of money demanded. Both bodies of data confirm that conclusion, though we note that the relevant evidence from the Heller-Khan data is not that which they themselves adduce.

44. In principle, holding period, not maturity, is the time-duration concept relevant to the demand for money. However, maturity is the only readily available proxy for holding period. The interest rates used are:

United States short rate: sixty-to-ninety-day commercial paper rate through 1923; thereafter four-to-six-month commercial paper rate.

United States long rate: high-grade corporate bond yield.

United Kingdom short rate: three month rate on bankers bills.

United Kingdom long rate: yield on consols.

Tables 5.7 and 5.8 give phase averages and rates of change for an alternative United States short rate, the call money rate ($R_{S'}$), and an alternative United States long rate, the basic yield on corporate bonds ($R_{L'}$). Our decision to use the ones listed above instead was based on a large number of trial regressions. In general the rates we use gave higher correlations than the alternatives, but the difference in results was often small and sometimes in the opposite direction.

the level variables, that is, to using the time differential of equation (24) when one of the other variables is time; other equations do not include an intercept, that is, force $\kappa = 0$, which makes equation (25) equivalent to the time differential of equation (24), when time is not included among the other variables. As for levels, some equations include only R_S; others, only R_L; still others, both.

The inclusion of interest rates rather than their logarithms in equations (24) and (25) implicitly assumes that the absolute rather than percentage change in interest rates is what matters for the demand for money—that a one-percentage point higher interest rate will produce the same percentage reduction in the quantity of money demanded whether it is added to a base rate of 5 percent or to a base rate of 10 percent. On this assumption, a semilogarithmic slope, like δ_S or δ_L, is the relevant measure of the interest rate effect, even though this parameter is not free from units of measure but has the dimension of time.

An alternative would be to include the logarithms of interest rates rather than the interest rates themselves. The corresponding regression coefficients would be interest elasticities, free from units of measure. This would assume that elasticities rather than slopes are the same at all levels of interest rates.

Theoretical considerations in favor of a constant slope rather than elasticity are: (1) per dollar of money held, the cost of a change in the interest rate depends on the absolute, not the relative change in the interest rate; to put this point differently, a doubling of an interest rate of 1 percent is much less of a stimulus to reduce cash balances than a doubling of an interest rate of 10 percent; (2) an interest rate of zero does not imply infinite desired cash balances, yet a constant elasticity other than zero produces infinite cash balances at an interest rate of zero; (3) an expected rate of price change is a measure of cost logically similar to a nominal interest rate, and it seems desirable to treat the two cost measures in the same way, yet the expected rate of price change can be negative, ruling out logarithms.

One consideration against a constant slope is that, at high interest rates, desired cash balances will be small and will be used for high-priority purposes so that a rise of one percentage point is likely to produce a smaller percentage reduction in money balances than a similar rise at lower levels of interest rates. However, that is not an argument for a constant elasticity but rather a warning that the linear approximation used in equations (24) and (25) cannot be expected to hold over more than a limited range of values of the interest rate or the expected rate of change in prices.

Empirically, the two approaches give similar results for interest rates in the general range of those observed in the past century in the United States and the United Kingdom. We have not compared the two approaches for the phase bases used in this book. However, in earlier work with annual data we concluded that the semilogarithmic form gave better results than the logarithmic.[45]

Before we discovered the critical importance of the postwar readjustment and the upward demand shift, our regression results were very mixed. We found it necessary to supplement regressions for the period as a whole by regressions for subperiods, and we also calculated a large number of alternative regressions to try out different interest rate series. All in all, we calculated literally hundreds of regressions for different periods and different sets of independent variables. The introduction of shift variables for the postwar readjustment and the upward demand shift brought order into our results, particularly by rendering the various subperiods homogeneous. As a result we have been able to simplify our exposition greatly by restricting attention to regressions for the whole period and, indeed, only a subset of those. We note here only that the conclusions we derive from the regressions we do present are entirely consistent with those we had earlier derived from a much more numerous set of regressions—which we now interpret as a cumbrous and inefficient way to allow for the postwar readjustment and the upward demand shift.

Table 6.11 summarizes regressions for both levels and rates of change, comparing short- and long-term interest rates as variables in money demand equations. Each successive line refers to a single regression. The lines come in triplets: the first is for a regression that includes only the short rate; the second, for one that includes only the long rate; the third, for one that includes both the short rate and the long rate. Columns 1 to 4 give limits on the semilogarithmic slope of real per capita balances with respect to the relevant interest rate. The remaining columns provide evidence on the goodness of fit. For pairs of equations containing the same variables except that one contains R_S and the other R_L, a higher t statistic implies a lower standard error of estimate, so that column 7 simply duplicates columns 5 and 6. For the third equation in the triplicate, containing both, this is also true, though less obviously: the standard error will be less or greater for the third than the first according as the t value for R_L is greater or less than unity. Similarly, it will be less or

45. See also a similar conclusion reached by C. A. E. Goodhart and A. D. Crockett, "The Importance of Money," *Quarterly Bulletin, Bank of England* 10 (June 1970): 192. M. J. Hamburger found that the semilogarithmic form gave better results than the logarithmic for quarterly German (1963–70) and United Kingdom (1963–71) demand functions ("The Demand for Money in an Open Economy: Germany and the United Kingdom," *Journal of Monetary Economics* 3 (January 1977): 29, 34). However, most authors of money demand functions have measured interest rates in logarithmic form. In particular, S. M. Goldfeld obtained good results from such a form for post–World War II United States data (see his "The Demand for Money Revisited," *Brookings Papers on Economic Activity*, no. 3 (1973) pp. 577–646).

greater for the third equation than for the second according as the t value for R_S is greater or less than unity.

The results are highly consistent: when only one interest rate is included in the regression, the interest rate slopes are negative, and, with one exception, the t values are higher for the short- than for the long-term rate; when both interest rates are included, the short rate dominates and, with one exception, the standard error is intermediate between those for the equations including only one interest rate. These are the results for level equations, for rate of change equations with a zero intercept, and for rate of change equations with a nonzero intercept. (The exception for t values is for the United States short-term rate, for rates of change, nonzero intercept; for standard errors, for the United Kingdom rates of change, zero intercept.) The conclusion is clear: the short-term interest rate is preferable to the long, and there is no justification for including both.

As to the magnitude of effect, the limits on the slopes are as usual farther apart for the rate of change equations than for the level equations, but generally the wider rate of change range includes the narrower level range, so the two sets of results from levels and rates of change confirm one another. There seems no appreciable difference in slope between the United States and the United Kingdom.

To judge from the results based on the greatest amount of evidence—for the United States and the United Kingdom combined and the level data—the slope for the short-term interest rate is between -2.8 and -11.8. Since the average value of the short-term interest rate was .037, this corresponds to an elasticity at that average value between $-.10$ and $-.44$.

6.6.2   Interest on Deposits

Nominal yields on assets other than money measure the return on substitutes for money—in terms of the usual demand function for a commodity, they are the counterpart of the price of a substitute, and the elasticities cited in section 6.6.1 are the counterpart of cross-elasticities.

The counterpart of own-price in the usual demand function is the yield on money itself in the form either of services rendered without charge or explicit interest paid on demand deposits or the time deposits we include in our concept of money. However, whereas the own-price is usually the first variable to be considered in demand studies for most commodities and services, we have left it next to last. It is ordinarily completely neglected in money-demand studies on the (implicit) ground that it can be treated as zero. As we noted earlier, Benjamin Klein's study is an exception, and he concluded that allowing for own-yield improves demand functions estimated for the United States from annual data.

Table 6.11   Comparison of Short-Term (R_S) versus Long-Term (R_L) Interest Rate as Variables in Money-Demand Equation

| Country | Interest Rate Slope[c] | | | | t Statistic[d] | | Standard Error of Estimate (%) (7) |
| | Short-Term Rate | | Long-Term Rate | | Short-Term Rate (5) | Long-Term Rate (6) | |
	Lower Limit (1)	Upper Limit (2)	Lower Limit (3)	Upper Limit (4)			
Levels							
United States	−2.85	−14.69			3.18		5.54
			−1.95	−25.60		1.86	5.93
	−3.70	−26.48	1.19	85.42	2.58	0.76	5.57
United Kingdom	−3.05	−9.45			3.78		5.37
			−3.06	−13.07		3.03	5.72
	−3.19	−27.28	0.18	584.64	1.96	0.10	5.47
United States and United Kingdom[a]	−2.75	−11.84			4.80		5.51
			−2.29	−18.53		3.28	5.88
	−3.55	26.59	1.10	98.45	3.40	0.92	5.51
Rates of Change (Zero Intercept)							
United States	−1.92	−27.32			1.78		1.57
			−2.22	−47.36		1.44	1.59
	−1.70	−67.51	−0.40	−554.60	1.03	0.17	1.59

United Kingdom	−1.73	−24.46		1.51		1.42
	−3.40	−31.94		1.86	0.45	1.46
					1.17	1.41
United States and United Kingdom[b]	−1.60	−27.95	−0.62	−93.15	2.15	1.45
	−2.52	−43.23	2.48	55.47	2.15	0.99
			−0.94	−74.68		1.01
			1.49	109.21		1.48 / 1.45

Rates of Change (Nonzero Intercept)

United States	−1.37	−33.86	−2.22	−40.00	1.32	1.55
			−1.87	−112.22		0.82
						1.49 / 1.47 / 1.49
United Kingdom	−0.33	−323.56	−1.13	−51.14	0.20	0.81
	−2.12	−19.63	1.98	64.43	1.88	0.94
					1.92	1.37 / 1.44 / 1.37
United States and United Kingdom[b]	−1.59	−25.78	−1.29	−51.06	2.21	1.39
	−2.02	−50.65	0.70	224.91	1.75	0.48
						1.40 / 1.42 / 1.40

Note: All regressions include real per capita income, postwar readjustment dummy, demand shift dummy, and rate of change of nominal income.
[a] Includes also dummy for country and product of country dummy and real per capita income to allow for different income elasticity in United States and United Kingdom.
[b] Includes also product of country dummy and real per capita income.
[c] "Upper" and "lower" limits refer to absolute value, not algebraic value.
[d] Absolute value.

Following Klein, we allow for own-yield by assuming that currency yields a zero nominal yield and that banks are forced to pass on to their depositors the bulk of the interest they receive on their assets. However, assets held in the form of reserves, that is, high-powered money, earn zero return; hence this approach is equivalent to assuming that the return on money is a weighted average of zero (the return on currency and the high-powered reserves that are the counterpart to some deposits) and the market interest rate (the return on the rest of deposits), the weights being H/M (the ratio of high-powered money to total money) and $1 - H/M$. This requires, in effect, including $R_S(1 - H/M)$, where R_S is the market interest rate, in regressions as an own-price, along with R_S as a price of a substitute.

Table 6.12 shows the effect of the inclusion of own-yield, namely $(1 - H/M)R_S$, in the demand for money regressions. The inclusion of own-yield, in addition to the short-term rate (R_S), consistently lowers the standard error of estimate (compare lines 1 and 2 in each triplet).

Theory suggests that the difference between the yield on close substitute assets and on money should be the relevant variable, since this difference measures the marginal cost of holding an extra dollar as money rather than as an alternative nominal asset. The closeness in absolute value of the coefficients of the short rate and the own rate (columns 1 and 2 for line 2 of each triplet) is consistent with this theoretical expectation. Accordingly, in line 3 of each triplet we include the difference in yield—that is, $R_S - (1 - H/M)R_S = R_SH/M$, which we designate R_N, the N referring to nominal. With two exceptions (levels for United Kingdom and for United States and United Kingdom) this equation yields a lower standard error than either of the others. Moreover, the resulting coefficients are very similar for the United States and the United Kingdom and are consistent for levels and rates of change.[46]

46. In an excellent article examining the statistical validity of Klein's results, John A. Carlson and James R. Frew ("Money Demand Regressions with the Rate of Return on Money: A Methodological Critique," *Journal of Political Economy* 88 [June 1980]: 598–607) correctly point out that the improvement in Klein's fit obtained by approximating R_M (yield on money) by $(1 - H/M) R_S$ and including R_M in a demand equation along with R_S may be spurious, reflecting errors of measurement common to m and H/M. If both numerator and denominator of H/M are divided by NP, the denominator becomes m. Errors of measurement in m that arise from errors in NP will not be common (they cancel out in H/M), but errors of measurement in M will be. They will tend to produce a spurious negative correlation between m and H/M, or a spurious positive correlation between m and $(1 - H/M)$. Carlson and Frew point out further that such common errors will also introduce spurious elements into the computed coefficients of R_S and R_M. (They note quite properly that the fact that R_S is common to R_S and R_M does not of itself introduce any bias in the estimates because both are independent variables. This may however affect the variances and covariances of the estimates.) The spurious element contributes to the coefficients

These results confirm Klein's and suggest including in the demand function the differential yield on nominal assets, rather than the short rate alone or the short rate plus own-yield. At the same time they also show that the effect of substituting the differential yield for the short rate alone, while statistically significant, is quantitatively small: for levels, the substitution reduces the standard error by 8 percent for the United States but raises it by 3 percent for the United Kingdom; for rates of change, the largest improvement is a reduction of the standard error by 2 percent. Hence, for some purposes in later chapters, where including the differential yield greatly complicates the analysis, we shall omit it and include instead the short rate.

---

having opposite signs and, if the coefficient of R_M is positive and that of R_S negative, as is the case in both Klein's and our calculations, to a higher absolute value of the coefficient of R_S.

Some sample calculations by Carlson and Frew for Klein's results suggest that the spurious element could explain his results, though they are careful to note that the case is not proved, since the economic forces Klein emphasizes would work in the same direction as the spurious correlation, and their sample calculations do not discriminate between the spurious and the real effects.

One implication of the Carlson-Frew analysis of spurious correlation, pointed out but not exploited by them, does differ from an implication of economic reasoning and hence provides a basis for discriminating between the spurious and the real effects. As noted in the text, economic forces suggest that the differential rate, $R_S - R_M$, is the relevant alternative cost of holding money. It follows that on economic grounds the semilog *slopes* of R_S and R_M should be numerically equal. On the other hand, Carlson and Frew point out that the spurious statistical effects would produce numerically equal *elasticities* (p. 601, especially footnote 1). For their replication of Klein's result, the slope of R_S is 12 percent less in numerical value than on the slope of R_M; the elasticity of R_S is 20 percent greater (our calculation for the elasticity at the mean values of R_S and R_M). So far as this calculation goes, it argues somewhat in favor of real forces rather than spurious correlation accounting for Klein's results.

The purely spurious statistical element that Carlson and Frew emphasize affects our results in the same direction as Klein's. However, the effect is very likely decidedly smaller quantitatively. Our basic data are phase averages, Klein's annual, which tends to reduce the variance of errors of measurement compared with "true" fluctuations. For rates of change, our estimating them from triplets of phases reduces still further the relative magnitude of pure errors of measurement. This conclusion is supported by a number of pieces of empirical evidence. (1) The correlation between M and H/M or their rates of change is uniformly small. For levels it is negative, as both the spurious element and the secular decline in H/M would imply, but only $-.135$ for the United States, $-.184$ for the United Kingdom. For rates of change it is positive, $.045$ for the United States, $.095$ for the United Kingdom. (2) Adding of R_M reduces the standard error of estimate far more in Klein's equation, as recomputed by Carlson and Frew, than in ours (in Klein's by 37 percent; in ours by a maximum of 12 percent in the three comparisons for levels; by much less, in the comparisons for rates of change). (3) Klein's equation yields statistically significant coefficients for both R_S and R_L in an equation including R_M, for R_L but not R_S in an equation excluding R_M. In our case R_S has a statistically significant coefficient in level equations (including and excluding R_L, including and excluding R_M) (see tables 6.11 and 6.12). (4) Including R_M raises the t-statistic (in absolute value) for R_S for Klein's equation from 1.4 to 11.9; for our calculations for United States levels, from 3.2 to 4.1; for United Kingdom

Table 6.12   Effect of Own Yield on Money in Money-Demand Function

Country	Slope			t Statistic[c]			Standard Error of Estimate (%)
	Short-Term Rate (1)	Own Rate (2)	Differential Rate (3)	Short-Term Rate (4)	Own Rate (5)	Differential Rate (6)	(7)
	Levels						
United States	−2.85			3.18			5.54
	−8.38	7.34		4.13	2.98		5.09
			−8.82			4.45	5.09
United Kingdom	−3.05			3.78			5.37
	−4.84	3.19		5.27	3.08		4.74
			−11.16			3.42	5.54
United States and United Kingdom[a]	−2.75			4.80			5.51
	−5.43	3.98		6.79	4.38		4.95
			−9.28			5.48	5.32
	Rates of Change (Zero Intercept)						
United States	−1.92			1.78			1.57
	−10.52	10.88		1.59	1.32		1.56
			−9.65			2.25	1.54

United Kingdom	−1.73	21.43		1.51	1.29		1.42
	−18.67			1.42		1.86	1.40
			−9.48				1.39
United States and United Kingdom[b]	−1.60	13.03		2.15	1.78		1.45
	−11.94			2.04			1.43
			−8.74			2.74	1.42

Rates of Change (Nonzero Intercept)

United States	−1.37	5.93		1.32	0.72		1.49
	−6.11			0.91		1.51	1.49
			−6.60				1.48
United Kingdom	−2.12	21.50		1.88	1.34		1.37
	−19.12			1.51		2.24	1.35
			−11.19				1.34
United States and United Kingdom[b]	−1.59	12.04		2.21	1.70		1.40
	−11.13			1.97		2.76	1.38
			−8.48				1.37

Note: All regressions include real per capita income, postwar readjustment dummy, demand shift dummy, and rate of change of nominal income.
[a]Includes also dummy for country and product of country dummy and real per capita income to allow for different income elasticity in United States and United Kingdom.
[b]Includes also product of country dummy and real per capita income.
[c]Absolute value.

6.6.3   Yield on Physical Assets

Alternatives to holding money include not only the nominal-value assets whose yields were considered in section 6.6.2 but also financial assets, such as equities, that have no stated nominal value and physical assets held directly, such as land, buildings, machinery, and consumer capital. The financial assets generally represent indirect titles to physical assets, so we shall refer to this class of assets as physical assets, in effect treating all nonhuman wealth as falling into one of three classes: money, other nominal-value assets, and physical assets.

The nominal yield on physical assets, like the yield on financial assets, consists of two parts: the direct yield—rent on literal physical assets, dividends on equities—and the change in the nominal price of the assets. And again, the relevant yields for determining the attractiveness of these assets relative to money are the *anticipated* yields.

Most money-demand studies that have included the yield on physical assets have allowed for only the second part of the yield and have approximated it by the rate of change of a price level, often consumer

---

levels, from 3.8 to 5.3; for the two countries together, the t-statistic is reduced a trifle, and that is also true for all but one of the rate-of-change comparisons.

Including R_M does raise the absolute value of the coefficient on R_S for all of our results as well as for the one result of Klein recomputed by Carlson and Frew. But that result is also the one predicted by economic theory, as also is the positive sign of the own rate and the numerically larger coefficient of R_N than of either R_S or R_M. Hence we do not regard these findings as having much bearing on the quantitative importance of the spurious correlation.

In "Competitive Interest Payments and the Demand for Money: Economic Forces or Spurious Correlation?" Michael Melvin recalculates Klein's demand for money function, 1919–70, substituting r_d, the return on deposits, for Klein's r_m variable, and tests the regression results for evidence of real rather than spurious effects. For the shorter period Melvin investigates, he finds that the slopes differ by more than the elasticities, suggestive of spurious effects.

With respect to slopes versus elasticities, our results for levels support real forces versus spurious effects much more strongly than Klein's. The slope of R_S is numerically greater than the slope of R_M for all three comparisons: by 14 percent for the United States, 52 percent for the United Kingdom, and 88 percent for the United States plus United Kingdom (the opposite direction from Klein's result). Since the elasticity is the product of the slope and the interest rate, and since R_S as calculated is necessarily greater than R_M, it follows that elasticities will differ in the same direction and by even more than the slopes. Evaluated at the mean values of R_S and R_M, the numerical elasticity is 58, 94, and 144 percent greater for R_S than R_M for the United States, United Kingdom, and United States plus United Kingdom, respectively.

For rates of change, the slope of R_S is numerically lower than of R_M for five out of six comparisons: by 3, 13, 9, 11, and 9 percent, and higher by 3 percent for the remaining comparison (United States nonzero intercept). The elasticity of R_S is numerically higher for all comparisons, the percentage excess corresponding to the above differentials for slopes, being 32, 11, 21, 12, 20, and, for the one in the same direction, 41 percent. In all but one case, the percentage difference is larger for the elasticity, and generally much larger.

All in all, we conclude that we can have considerable confidence that our results reflect primarily real effects rather than spurious statistical effects.

prices. This procedure has been dictated by paucity of data. There are no satisfactory measures of the direct yield, except for dividends on equities, or of the change in the nominal price of physical assets, except again for equity prices on organized markets. But such equities are only a small part of the total class of assets under consideration.

The use of the rate of change of prices—generally a weighted average of past rates of change—as a proxy for the anticipated nominal yield on physical assets raises the obvious problem that it may be a poor proxy. But it also raises a more subtle problem. Arbitrage on capital markets tends to equalize the attractiveness of the anticipated yields on different assets—which means not that the yields will be equal but that differences will reflect the value placed by investors on such features of assets as risk and liquidity. Anything that changes the yield on physical assets will be transmitted in whole or part also to nominal assets. As Irving Fisher taught many years ago, the anticipated nominal yield on any asset, expressed as a percentage of its value, can be regarded as the sum of an anticipated real yield—that is, a yield after allowance for the effect of inflation on both the income stream and the capital value—and an anticipated rate of change of prices.

Suppose we compute a multiple regression including as variables the nominal yield on nominal assets and the anticipated rate of inflation (rather than nominal yield) on physical assets. We are then measuring the effect of a changed anticipated rate of inflation for a *given* nominal yield on nominal assets. How can these coexist if there is arbitrage between the assets? Only if the implicit real yield changes in the opposite direction so that, for example, a higher inflation rate plus a lower real yield gives a nominal rate on physical assets roughly equivalent to the assumed unchanged rate on nominal assets. But in that case there are two opposite effects on desired balances; by itself, the rise in the rate of price change would lower desired balances; but, by itself, the decline in the real rate would raise desired balances. Hence, in principle, even the sign of the coefficient is ambiguous.[47] In practice there is not full adjustment; the nominal yield serves, as we have stressed, as a proxy for the structure of yields; the rate of price change is likely to enter as another proxy, and a rise in it with a particular nominal yield such as R_S held constant is probably to be interpreted as reflecting a rise in other yields at least as much as a fall in the real yield; hence there is some presumption that its coefficient will be negative. Nonetheless, the effect of the rate of price change is diluted by the failure to include the real rate explicitly.

One way to allow for the real rate is to use the rate of change of nominal income rather than of prices as a proxy for the nominal yield on physical

---

47. This point is developed fully by Norman Lefton, "The Demand for Real Cash Balances and the Expected Permanent and Contemporaneous Rates of Change of Prices" (Ph.D. diss., University of Chicago, 1972).

assets—a device employed by Maurice Allais on somewhat different grounds.[48] The use of the rate of change of nominal income has the purely statistical advantage that it is likely to be more accurately measured than the rate of change of prices, particularly during periods of price control (see secs. 4.1.3 and 4.2.3). But its main attraction is economic. The rate of change of nominal income is the sum of the rate of change of prices and the rate of change of output, and the rate of change of output is an estimate, though a downward biased estimate, of the real yield.[49] Hence the rate of change of nominal income can be regarded as a better proxy than the rate of change of prices alone for the *total nominal yield* on physical assets.

On these grounds we have experimented with both the percentage rate of change of prices (g_p) and the percentage rate of change of nominal income (g_Y) as proxies for the nominal return on physical assets in equations for levels of money holdings. In equations for rate-of-change of money holdings, we have used the time derivatives of these rates of change, designated $D_{g_P} D_{g_Y}$ respectively. One problem with both is that we need a measure of anticipated rather than actual rate of change. However, for our initial explorations we have assumed that for our phase data we can regard actual and anticipated rates of change as identical.

Table 6.13 summarizes our regressions for both levels and rates of change: g_Y clearly performs better than g_P; every t value for g_Y is higher than for g_P in absolute value. Hence we shall use it as our proxy for the nominal return on physical assets. The coefficients of g_Y uniformly have the expected negative sign. For the United States and the United States and United Kingdom combined, the coefficients deviate from zero by an amount that is statistically significant. That is not true for the United Kingdom alone. Even when statistically significant, however, the slope coefficients are not very accurately determined. The range between lower and upper limits is wide, so that while the ranges overlap for the United States and for the United Kingdom, and for levels and rates of change, that is no great comfort. The overlap may merely reflect the limited accuracy with which we can estimate the coefficients.

The slope for g_Y tends to be decidedly smaller than that for R_S. It is arithmetic that a one percentage point increase in the nominal yield, whether on physical assets or on nominal assets, raises the cost of holding money instead of the corresponding asset by the same amount. As a

---

48. See Maurice Allais, "Réformulation de la Théorie Quantitative de la Monnaie," *Bulletin Sedeis*, no. 928, suppl., 10 September 1965; "A Restatement of the Quantity Theory of Money," *American Economic Review* 56 (December 1966), 1123–57; "Growth and Inflation," *Journal of Money, Credit and Banking* 1 (August 1969), 355–426, in which the velocity function depends upon past rates of growth of nominal income.

49. See R. J. Gordon, ed. *Milton Friedman's Monetary Framework* (Chicago: University of Chicago Press, 1974), p. 37.

matter of economics, it does not follow that the two increases would have the same effect on cash balances. That depends on the composition of the asset portfolio that would be held instead of cash. If that portfolio consisted exclusively of nominal assets, a change in the yield on physical assets would have no effect on cash balances for a given yield on nominal assets, and conversely if the portfolio consisted exclusively of physical assets. We have no direct evidence on what the proportions are, though we do know that the bulk of all material wealth consists of physical assets, if all accounts are consolidated.[50] It does not follow that, at the margin, holders of money could not treat other nominal assets as the chief substitute for money, though it does render any such result rather implausible. If our computed slopes were accurate measures of the effect of a change in the corresponding yield, their relative values would provide a measure of the composition of the substitute portfolio.

The slope coefficients from table 6.11 for R_S are in general a substantial multiple of the corresponding slope coefficients from table 6.13 for g_Y.[51] The implication, if the observed multiples were accurate estimates of the

50. In such a consolidation the only nominal value assets are high-powered money plus government interest-bearing liabilities.
51. See table 6.N.3.

Table 6.N.3   **Comparison of Effect on Demand for Money of Yields on Nominal and Physical Assets**

	Slope Coefficient(R_S)		Slope Coefficient(g_Y)		Ratio of Coefficients(R_S/g_Y)	
	Lower Limit	Upper Limit	Lower Limit	Upper Limit	Lower Limit	Upper Limit
Levels						
United States	−2.85	−14.69	−0.71	−2.82	4.0	5.2
United Kingdom	−3.05	−9.45	−0.28	−8.83	10.9	1.1
United States and						
United Kingdom	−2.75	−11.84	−0.57	−3.97	4.8	3.0
Rates of Change (Zero Intercept)						
United States	−1.92	−27.32	−0.60	−2.20	3.2	12.4
United Kingdom	−1.73	−24.46	−0.28	−5.57	6.2	4.4
United States and						
United Kingdom	−1.60	−27.95	−0.45	−3.02	3.6	9.3
Rates of Change (Nonzero Intercept)						
United States	−1.37	−33.86	−0.45	−2.65	3.0	12.8
United Kingdom	−2.12	−19.63	−0.11	−14.95	19.3	1.3
United States and						
United Kingdom	−1.59	−25.78	−0.33	−4.03	4.8	6.4

Table 6.13 Comparison of Rate of Change of Nominal Income (g_Y) and of Prices (g_P) as Variables Representing Nominal Return on Physical Assets in Money-Demand Equation

| | Slope[c] | | | | t Statistic[d] | | Standard Error of Estimate (%) |
| | Rate of Change of Income | | Rate of Change of Prices | | | | |
Country	Lower Limit (1)	Upper Limit (2)	Lower Limit (3)	Upper Limit (4)	g_Y (5)	g_P (6)	(7)
			Levels				
United States	−0.71	−2.82	−0.64	−5.89	3.77	2.27	5.54
	−1.26	−5.86	0.86	13.53	3.35	1.67	6.05
							5.43
United Kingdom	−0.28	−8.83	0.04	45.18	1.00	0.16	5.37
	−1.84	−7.69	1.42	6.61	3.02	2.81	5.46
							4.84
United States and United Kingdom[a]	−0.57	−3.97	−0.26	−10.23	3.54	1.42	5.51
	−1.34	−6.04	0.98	8.58	4.26	3.12	5.87
							5.22
			Rates of Change (Zero Intercept)				
United States	−0.60	−2.20	−0.30	−9.51	3.96	1.17	1.57
	−0.91	−2.81	−0.65	6.42	4.44	2.15	1.81
							1.51

			Rates of Change (Nonzero Intercept)			
United Kingdom						
-0.28	-5.57	-0.12	-6.95	1.25		1.42
-0.61	-11.54	0.28	13.34	1.28	0.73	1.44
					0.79	1.43
United States and United Kingdom[b]						
-0.45	-3.02	-0.17	-7.61	3.66		1.45
-0.80	-4.19	0.43	6.26	4.20	1.30	1.56
					2.35	1.41
United States						
-0.45	-2.65	-0.17	-13.02	2.91		1.49
-0.73	-3.26	0.54	6.99	3.40	0.74	1.62
					1.83	1.44
United Kingdom						
-0.11	-14.95	-0.05	-15.48	0.46		1.37
-0.22	-36.79	0.09	44.43	0.41	0.31	1.37
					0.23	1.39
United States and United Kingdom[b]						
-0.33	-4.03	-0.09	-11.84	2.58		1.39
-0.63	-5.25	0.35	7.21	3.19	0.77	1.45
					1.96	1.37

Note: All regressions include real per capita income, postwar readjustment dummy, demand shift dummy, and short-term interest rate.

[a]Includes also dummy for country and product of country dummy and real per capita income to allow for different income elasticity in United States and United Kingdom.

[b]Includes also product of country dummy and real per capita income.

[c]"Upper" and "lower" limits refer to absolute value, not algebraic value.

[d]Absolute value.

"true" multiples, would be that, at the margin, the bulk of any change in money balances is as a substitute for nominal value assets. In light of the composition of total wealth, that implication seems extremely implausible.[52]

An alternative interpretation is that the market rate of interest is a better measure of the relevant nominal yield on nominal value assets than the rate of change of nominal income is of the relevant nominal yield on physical assets. The one is a direct measure of yield, the other an indirect measure; the one is quoted contemporaneously on a marketplace, the other must be computed from inexact measures of a hypothetical total after the event.

If nominal yields on nominal and physical assets tended to move together, either would serve as a proxy for the other. That is the case for short and long rates, which tend to move together. It is not, however, the situation for nominal and physical assets. The correlation between R_S and g_Y is $-.189$ for the United States, $-.153$ for the United Kingdom; between their rates of change, $-.102$ for the United States, $-.132$ for the United Kingdom, so that inclusion of g_Y introduces a variable largely independent of others. It follows that it is desirable to include yields on both nominal and physical assets in a demand equation for real balances.

6.7   Effect of All Variables Combined

The preceding sections suggest that the following variables should be included in functions for the United States and the United Kingdom to represent the demand for money, expressed in real terms and per capita (m):

1. Changing financial sophistication for the United States—for which we allow by replacing the raw monetary totals before 1903 by adjusted totals that allow for a 2.5 percent per year increase in the quantity of money demanded arising from this source alone.
2. Real per capita income (y).
3. The difference between the nominal yield on short-term securities and the hypothetical yield on money, as a proxy for the differential yield on nominal value assets sacrificed by holding money (R_N).
4. The rate of change of nominal income, as a proxy for the yield on physical assets (g_Y).

52. However, we should note that the standard Keynesian liquidity preference approach takes bonds as the only substitute for money and so assumes that the whole of any change in money balances is as a substitute for nominal value assets.

Even if physical assets are a decidedly poorer substitute for money per dollar than nominal assets, they are so much more plentiful that the fraction of an additional dollar added to or subtracted from money balances that is matched by an offsetting change in physical assets might be expected to be of at least the same order of magnitude as the fraction matched by an offsetting change in nominal assets.

5. A postwar readjustment, allowed for by including a dummy variable ($W = -T_i$ after World War I, and $+T_i$ after World War II)
6. An upward demand shift, produced by economic depression and war, allowed for by including a dummy variable ($S = 1$ for the phases affected, 0 for the remaining phases).

We found that these six variables enable a single demand function to describe fairly accurately the demand for money in each country for the whole of the century our data cover. In addition, variables 3, 4, 5, and 6 have had about the same quantitative effect in the two countries, provided allowance is made for the different time periods for which items 5 and 6 are relevant.

Item 1 refers only to the United States. The one significant difference of response to any of these variables that we have detected is with respect to item 2: real per capita income. The income elasticity of demand for money is apparently above unity for the United States, below unity for the United Kingdom.

Table 6.14 presents the final equations for the United States and the United Kingdom as derived in three ways: from the levels, from the rates of change with a zero constant term, and from rates of change allowing for a trend via a nonzero constant term. All the coefficients are of the correct sign, and most differ from zero by a statistically significant amount. Three features of these results are most encouraging:

1. The consistency of results from levels and rates of change for both the United States and the United Kingdom, though for reasons discussed earlier the postwar readjustment has a larger effect on rates of change than on levels and the upward demand shift has a larger effect on levels than on rates of change. As usual, the correlation is higher for levels than for rates of change.

Consistency does not mean that the coefficients are identical. The coefficients of the two shift variables aside, because these have a different meaning for levels and rates of change, all but one of the other coefficients is less in absolute value for the rate of change equations with a nonzero intercept than for the level equations. This is the relation to be expected. The coefficients are lower limits (in absolute value) because of the regression effect (the coefficient of income is also biased toward unity because of statistical errors in prices and population). The lower correlation for the rate of change equations means that the regression effect is larger for them.

The standard errors of estimate for level and rate-of-change regressions are not readily comparable. However, as earlier, we can make a rough comparison by multiplying the percentage per year standard errors from the rate of change equations by the average interval between the first and third of the triplet of phases from which each rate of change is calculated. The product should be comparable to the standard error of

Table 6.14   Demand Equations for Money: Final Estimates for Regressions of Real per Capita Money on Other Variables

								Standard Error of Estimate (%)
	Coefficients and t Statistic[a] (in Parentheses)							
Country	Constant	Real per Capita Income	Differential Yield on Money	Proxy Yield on Physical Assets	Postwar Readjustment	Demand Shift	R^2	
Levels								
United States	-1.53 (9.42)	1.15 (50.72)	-8.82 (4.45)	-0.59 (3.54)	0.025 (3.84)	0.17 (6.90)	.994	5.09
United Kingdom	0.16 (0.08)	0.88 (18.13)	-11.16 (3.42)	-0.22 (0.74)	0.014 (2.38)	0.21 (7.56)	.970	5.54
Rates of Change (Zero Constant)								
United States		1.09 (12.03)	-9.65 (2.25)	-0.54 (3.84)	0.033 (3.00)	0.0045 (3.45)	.807	1.54
United Kingdom		0.92 (5.41)	-9.48 (1.86)	-0.24 (1.08)	0.030 (2.26)	0.0030 (1.21)	.616	1.39
Rates of Change (Nonzero Constant)								
United States	0.008 (2.14)	0.88 (6.82)	-6.59 (1.51)	-0.42 (2.87)	0.036 (3.43)	0.0033 (2.40)	.618	1.48
United Kingdom	0.008 (1.81)	0.44 (1.44)	-11.19 (2.24)	-0.06 (0.26)	0.026 (2.03)	0.0027 (1.13)	.502	1.34

[a]Absolute value.

the level, which is a value at a point of time. For the United States, the result is modestly higher than the level standard error (6.16 and 5.92, for equations with a zero and a nonzero constant, vs. 5.09); for the United Kingdom, considerably higher (7.64 and 7.37 vs. 5.54).

These results are in line with the theoretical expectation that estimates from the level equations can be expected to be the most reliable of the three sets of estimates.

2. The closeness of the coefficients for the United States and the United Kingdom. Only the coefficients of the income term from the level equations differ significantly between the two countries. Even the standard errors of estimate are not far apart for the two countries.

For the income term from levels, the estimated elasticity for the United States is 1.15, for the United Kingdom, 0.88; the difference, 0.27, is roughly five times the standard error of the difference—highly significant. For the income term from rates of change, the difference is in the same direction as for levels, but is not statistically significant, being roughly equal to the standard error of the difference for both forms of rate-of-change equations.

The only other difference is in overall level of demand, on which we cannot use the results in table 6.14, since the United States data are in dollars and the United Kingdom data in pounds. We shall return to this point later.

Allowing for the yields has reduced the size of the difference between the United States and the United Kingdom in income elasticity, but unfortunately it has not eliminated the difference. The reason for this difference is the major mystery for which we have been unable to find an explanation.

The implication is that, income aside, the same basic forces affect money demand in the two countries, have the same quantitative impact, and leave the same residual to be explained by statistical error or omitted economic variables.

We shall exploit this implication by constructing a single equation for the two countries combined.

3. How far we have been able to go in accounting for fluctuations over a century in real money holdings on the basis of six variables only. The implication is that money demand is stable over time—in the sense of a demand function—as well as between countries.

This excellent overall result is misleading in one respect. Although the income elasticities can be regarded as having been estimated fairly precisely, the slopes of the two yield variables are much less precisely estimated. This is brought out by table 6.15, which gives upper and lower limits based on regressions run both ways for the coefficients of the three quantitative economic variables.

The generally far wider limits for the rate-of-change regressions than for the level regressions simply reinforce the earlier conclusion about the greater reliability of the level regressions.

But even for the level regressions the coefficients of the yield terms are not specified very precisely. Taking the results from the regressions for two countries, the range is from -9 to -40 for the slope of the differential yield on money and from -0.2 to -12 for the proxy yield on physical assets.

Note that these are slopes, not elasticities. To convert them into elasticities requires multiplying them by the value of the relevant yield. Doing so at the mean value of the yields gives an elasticity of -0.10 to -0.32 for the differential yield and -0.01 to -0.49 for the proxy yield.

As a final summary of our results, we present two single equations for the two countries combined, one computed from levels, one from rates of change. For the level equation, we add a country dummy ($Z = 1$ for the United Kingdom, 0 for the United States) to allow for the difference in level (and perhaps also for a deviation between the market and relevant exchange rate), and we add a term equal to the product of the country dummy and the logarithm of real per capita income (Z times log y) to allow for the difference in income elasticity between the United States and the United Kingdom. The result is

$$(26) \qquad \log m = -\ 1.47 + 1.14 \log y - 9.3\ R_N - 0.47\ g_Y$$
$$\qquad\qquad\quad (9.6)\ \ (52.1) \qquad\quad (5.5) \qquad (3.1)$$

$$+\ .019W +\ .193S + 1.64Z - 0.25\ Z \log y$$
$$(4.7) \qquad (10.8) \qquad (6.2) \qquad (6.0)$$

$$R^2 = .9899$$
$$SEE = 5.32 \text{ percent.}$$

For income elasticities, this gives 1.14 for the United States and 0.89 ($1.14 - 0.25$) for the United Kingdom as lower limits—or very much the same as for the separate country equations (table 6.15).

The -9.3 slope for the differential yield on money corresponds to an elasticity of -0.19, the -0.47 slope for the proxy yield, to an elasticity of $-.02$.

These results simply repeat the earlier ones.[53] The new result is the coefficient of Z, which indicates the difference in level for the United States and the United Kingdom. For this equation, the United Kingdom figures were converted to dollars at the 1929 exchange rate ($4.862 to the £). At that exchange rate table 6.16 gives the differences in level of money

---

53. We do not give upper limits because of difficulties in determining them produced by the $Z \log y$ term.

Table 6.15 Upper and Lower Limits[a] of Income Elasticity of Money Demand and Semilog Slopes of Differential Yield on Money, and Proxy Yield on Physical Assets

| | Income Elasticity | | Semilog Slope | | | |
| | | | Differential Yield on Money | | Proxy Yield on Physical Assets | |
Country	Lower Limit	Upper Limit	Lower Limit	Upper Limit	Lower Limit	Upper Limit
Levels						
United States	1.15	1.17	-8.82	-27.52	-0.59	-2.59
United Kingdom	0.88	0.96	-11.16	-39.76	-0.22	-11.92
Rates of Change (Zero Constant)						
United States	1.09	1.40	-9.65	-89.74	-0.54	-2.08
United Kingdom	0.92	1.86	-9.48	-91.49	-0.24	-6.29
Rates of Change (Nonzero Constant)						
United States	0.88	1.66	-6.59	-124.65	-0.42	-2.50
United Kingdom	0.44	6.62	-11.19	-75.94	-0.06	-26.71

[a]Upper and limits refer to absolute, not algebraic values.

Table 6.16   Differences in Level of Money Demand in the United States and the United Kingdom at Three Income Levels

Income Levels	Real per Capita Money Holdings (in Dollars)		Percentage Excess of United Kingdom Money Holdings over United States Money Holdings (%)
	United States	United Kingdom	
United States, 1877	109	136	+25
United Kingdom, 1975	454	423	−7
United States, 1975	832	679	−18

demand at the three income levels[54] isolated in chart 6.3, and at the values of the other variables for the United States at the corresponding dates.

Though the difference between the two countries is substantial, it is appreciably less than the difference when no allowance is made for differences between them in yields on alternative assets. The corresponding differences in chart 6.3 are +40 percent for 1877 income levels; −13 percent for the 1975 United Kingdom income level; −30 percent for the 1975 United States income level. Allowing for yields has cut these differentials almost in half. Nonetheless, the mystery of why there is a difference in income elasticity remains.

The rate-of-change equation for the two countries combined, calculated with a zero constant term, to correspond with the absence of a trend term in the level equation, is as follows:

$$(27) \qquad g_m = \underset{(10.9)}{1.03\ g_y} - \underset{(2.7)}{8.74\ DR_N} - \underset{(3.6)}{0.41\ Dg_Y} + \underset{(3.7)}{.030\ W_g}$$

$$+ \underset{(3.3)}{.0040 S_g} - \underset{(0.3)}{.04\ Zg_y}$$

$$R^2 = .72$$
$$SEE = 1.54 \text{ percent.}$$

The results are very similar to those for the level equation, except that the difference between the income elasticities for the United States and the United Kingdom is not statistically significant, as it was not for the separate country equations. As is to be expected, the regression bias is more serious, so that the coefficients of the income and rate-of-return

54. In 1877, United States and United Kingdom real per capita incomes (in 1929 dollars) were equal. In 1975, United States real per capita income was higher than that of the United Kingdom.

variables are lower in absolute value (except for the United Kingdom income elasticity).

6.8   Appendix A: Issues in Using the Exchange Rate to Pool United States and United Kingdom Data

This appendix explores the problem of the exchange rate to use in pooling the data for the United States and the United Kingdom.

The market exchange rate may not be the relevant exchange rate for our regressions for two different reasons. One has been discussed in chapter 5: the relation between the exchange rate and price levels in the two countries can be affected by the composition of the balance of payments, in particular the role of capital exports from or imports to each country and of income from abroad from sources other than the current sale of goods and services.[55] The second reason is more immediately pertinent. The domestic prices in the two countries of goods traded internationally for which there are no tariffs or export subsidies and for which transportation costs can be neglected are necessarily in the same ratio as the exchange rate. For example, if the exchange rate for the pound sterling is $4.86, then such a good which sells for £100 in the United Kingdom will sell for $486 in the United States. (This proposition is sometimes known in the literature of international economics as "the law of one price.") Of course, even for international goods, tariffs and transportation costs may be sufficiently important to introduce substantial deviations between the relative prices in different countries and the exchange rate. But for other goods and services that are not traded the deviation may be far greater. For each such good or service, an implicit exchange rate can be calculated from domestic prices that may differ widely from the market rate. For example, consider the price of an hour of roughly comparable domestic service in the United States and the United Kingdom. The exchange rate required to make these two prices— one in pounds and the other in dollars—equal when converted to a common currency might be, say, $10 to the pound rather than $4.86 if domestic service is cheaper relative to internationally traded goods in the United Kingdom than in the United States (as seems indeed to have been the case). There are as many implicit exchange rates as there are identifiable goods and services available in both countries. There is still a link between these implicit exchange rates and the market rate—via substitution of trade for production, substitution among factors of production, and migration of labor and capital—but these links may be very loose indeed.[56] The tighter they are, the closer relative prices for different

---

55. See notes 4 and 14 in chapter 5.

56. For an excellent summary discussion of many of these issues and references to the literature on them, see Irving B. Kravis, Alan W. Heston, and Robert Summers, "Real

goods in different countries will be to the market exchange rate; the looser they are, the wider will be the variation of relative prices for different goods from the market exchange rate.

Consider a money-holding unit (an individual, a business enterprise, or a government or other unit) deciding on the amount of money to hold. By holding an extra dollar (or pound) of money, it saves, say c cents (or pence) in pecuniary costs plus receiving, say, nonpecuniary returns it values at n cents (or pence). Neither c nor n, of course, is a constant; the size of both depends on the real amount of money held (m) and the level of real income (y) or wealth. By holding an extra dollar (or pound) of money, the unit incurs a cost of, say, R cents (or pence) that could have been earned by holding alternative assets (including, of course, borrowing less). And R too, of course, need not be a constant but may depend on m, y, and other variables. The unit will tend to hold an amount of money so that

$$c + n = R$$

for that amount of money and its level of income. In general, of course, the higher c and n, and the lower R, for given values of m and y, the higher will be desired m.

Each of the magnitudes introduced in the preceding paragraph (c, n, R, m, y) raises a problem in using the market exchange rate for international comparisons.

For c, the services in question are those that the use of money economizes, such as bookkeeping services. Casual observation suggests that the relevant services involve mostly personal labor-intensive white-collar services, and that such services have been cheaper relative to internationally traded goods in the United Kingdom than in the United States. If these casual impressions are correct, they establish a presumption that the relevant implicit exchange rate for such services (for 1929) is greater than $4.86.

For n it is difficult to be equally specific because the alternative ways of obtaining nonpecuniary services substituting for those rendered by money are harder to visualize specifically (presumably, alternatives include insurance, credit lines, credit cards, larger holdings of financial or physical assets, including such things as jewelry, and even different employment).

For R there is clearly an international capital market. Nonetheless, yields on domestic assets, for a country that has net foreign assets, are, as Ricardo pointed out long ago, likely to be lower than on actuarially

GDP *per Capita* for More Than One Hundred Countries," *Economic Journal* 88 (June 1978): 215–42.

equivalent foreign assets because of additional transactions costs associated with holding foreign assets, and because of the general preference for investing at home. In principle, both these factors are taken into account through c and n—the transactions costs through c, the preference for domestic assets through n—provided that the interest rate used is the higher yield on foreign assets. In practice, however, we use the domestic interest rate, so some effect may remain. However, a more important factor is probably the capital exporting or importing status of the country, which will affect not only the market exchange rate but also interest rates.

For M and Y, nominal money and income, the market exchange rate is clearly the relevant one—nominal dollars and pounds are internationally traded goods par excellence. But what of m and y, real money and real income per capita? For each country separately, we have followed the practice of deflating nominal money and nominal income by the same price index, the index implicit in estimates of real net national product. The same practice for intercountry as for intertemporal comparisons would mean using the same exchange rate for real money and real income. The common exchange rate comparable to the internal price index we use would be the purchasing power parity exchange rate, that is, the average obtained by weighting all implicit exchange rates for goods and services by the contribution of each good and service to national product. As noted earlier (sec. 6.4.1), an estimate of the purchasing-power-parity (PPP) exchange rate in 1929 can be made on the basis of a recent direct estimate for 1970. The estimated rate in $5.50.

Kravis, Heston, and Summers (1978) estimate that, for 1970, the purchasing-power-parity exchange rate of the United Kingdom pound in terms of the United States dollar was 117 percent of the market rate for traded goods, 173 percent of the market rate for nontraded goods, and 139 percent for both combined.[57] The large difference for traded goods may reflect primarily the definition of traded goods used in making this calculation rather than the effect of tariffs and transportation costs. Traded goods were defined as including all commodities as finally sold, so even the final prices for most commodities "contain large service elements attributable to trade and transport margins."[58]

The 1970 estimate of the ratio of the purchasing-power-parity exchange rate to the market rate can be extrapolated to a different year by multiplying it by the ratio of the change in internal prices between 1970 and that year in the United States to the corresponding change in the United Kingdom. If $PPP(t)$ is the estimate of the purchasing-power-parity exchange rate in year t, then

---

57. Ibid., p. 216.
58. Ibid., p. 224.

$$PPP(t_1) = \frac{P_{us}(t_1)/P_{us}(t_2)}{P_{uk}(t_1)/P_{uk}(t_2)} PPP_d(t_2),$$

where PPP_d is a direct estimate for time t_2 and P is the implicit price index for the country designated by the subscript and the indicated date. This is essentially the method used in footnote 5 of chapter 5 to get an estimate for 1873–78 based on 1929 data of the ratio of incomes in the United States and the United Kingdom. For 1929, this method gives a purchasing-power-parity exchange rate of $5.50 in 1929, or a ratio of 1.13, compared with the 1970 ratio of 1.39. Similar estimates for the ratio of the purchasing-power-parity to the United States–United Kingdom market exchange rate are plotted in chart 6.5, annually, 1868–1975.

Chart 6.5 shows that "the law of one price" came much closer to being satisfied before 1932 than from that year on. This is the first and most important conclusion. The first sharp isolated peak is for the year 1932. That point provides a dividing line for the periods before and after 1932. For the period before 1932, the average ratio was about 1.12; that is, on the average, the purchasing-power-parity exchange rate was 12 percent above the dollar exchange rate. The dollar exchange rate during the fixed exchange-rate period was $4.86, so the purchasing-power-parity change rate was 12 percent above that, or about $5.40, or very close to the estimated value of $5.50 for 1929, the year we use as the base for our real income and money series. What is even more interesting is the fluctuation about the mean. Before 1932, the highest ratio is only 10 percent above the average; the lowest ratio, only about 10 percent below. So the purchasing-power-parity exchange rate fluctuated within a narrow range of plus and minus 10 percent, which seems consistent with a reasonably unified market, given the statistical error in estimates extrapolated back by a period of 38 to 102 years (from 1970 to 1868 to 1932), plus the time it takes for adjustment. The main movements of the purchasing-power-parity rate seem to reflect inflation and deflation in the United States. The purchasing-power-parity exchange rate went down from the 1880s to the 1890s when prices were falling in the United States relative to prices in the United Kingdom and went up thereafter when prices were rising.

The situation after 1931 is very different. In September 1931 the United Kingdom went off the gold standard. Thereafter, the United Kingdom had an exchange rate that was sometimes floating but mostly pegged by the Bank of England, with occasional large devaluations— temporarily fixed but subject to change. The United States stayed on the gold standard for two more years and thereafter also had a mixture of floating and pegged rates. The source of the sharp spike in 1932 is that 1932 was the one year when the United Kingdom was off the gold standard and the United States stayed on it. The depreciation of sterling made United Kingdom goods cheap relative to United States goods;

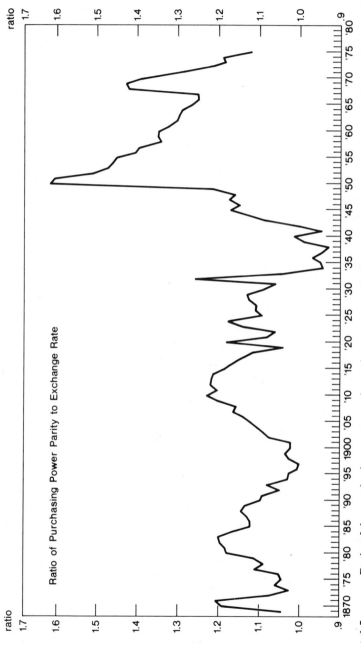

Chart 6.5   Ratio of the purchasing-power-parity exchange rate to the market exchange rate between the United States dollar and the United Kingdom pound, annually, 1868–1975.

equivalently, it meant that one pound could buy a larger quantity of goods than could the number of dollars corresponding to that pound according to the market exchange rate. In 1933 the United States went off the gold standard. The dollar depreciated even more than the pound had. As a result the ratio drops suddenly and drastically. From then on there were successive ups and downs. Each prominent peak in the series thereafter corresponds to a United Kingdom devaluation.

The picture is quite clear. Every now and then, for whatever reason, the United Kingdom government has stepped in and either devalued the currency deliberately or permitted it to depreciate. That has forced the purchasing-power-parity exchange rate out of line with the market exchange rate. Then market forces set in to correct it. The highest peak is for 1949–50, and that corresponds to the immediate post–World War II devaluation of the pound in 1949. The market then gradually starts to bring the ratio back down toward about 1.2. Before it gets there, another devaluation occurs and the ratio shoots up again. The market again brings it down, the United States devaluation in 1971 speeding up the process. Then, to go beyond the period covered by the chart, the depreciation of the pound in 1975 and 1976 pushed it up again. Once again, it has started coming down toward the range that market forces dictate.

The average for the period after 1931 is not much different from the average for the period before 1931—1.21 compared with 1.12. The real difference is in the fluctuations—plus and minus 10 percent before 1931, from minus one-quarter to plus one-third thereafter.

Since 1931 there have been tremendous improvements in communications and in transportation. The jet aircraft now spans the ocean in a few hours. Satellite transmission and television and radio communications link countries instantaneously and at relatively low cost. The cliché is it has become one world. In the economic world, the reality is clearly the reverse. The law of one price was far closer to being satisfied before 1931 than after. The technological improvements, which might have been expected to unify the world, have been more than offset by governmental intervention, which has fragmented the world into separate, isolated markets. Chart 6.5 demonstrates vividly how powerful and effective government intervention has been in rendering the law of one price far less applicable after 1931 than it was before.[59]

59. For an interesting approach to the same issue from a different perspective, see Sven Grassman, "Long-Term Trends in Openness of National Economies," *Oxford Economic Papers*, n.s., 32 (March 1980): 123–33. His broad conclusion is that "several European and North-American economies have roughly the same degrees of openness today as a century ago" (p. 123). His detailed tables for decades (tables A1 and A3) confirm our own finding about the difference between the periods before and after 1930. For decades before 1925, both foreign trade and foreign capital movements are more important for the United Kingdom relative to national income than for decades after 1944. That is on the average also true for the United States though less consistently.

It is worth repeating that the deviations of the purchasing-power-parity exchange rate from the market rate do not affect the slope of our money-income relations so long as the same adjustment is made for both money and income, but they do affect the United Kingdom income in pounds that is regarded as equivalent to the United States income in dollars. Hence they will affect our estimates of the difference in level of real money balances for a given real income—though even here, as we have seen, any effect is likely to be quantitatively minor.

The effects would be more far-reaching if a different adjustment were made for money than for income. But that issue is not basically one of how to make international comparisons; it arises for each country separately. For example, consider the use of time-series data to derive the relation between real food expenditure per capita and real income per capita. For such a study it might well be fruitful to deflate nominal food expenditure by a food price index and nominal income by a general price index. Using the latter index for both is equivalent to examining the effect of real per capita income not on real food expenditure but on the fraction of income spent on food—the counterpart to our relations that can be regarded as relating velocity to income. Put differently, our use of the same index for money and income means that we are in effect defining real money as the number of weeks' income to which it is equivalent.

The use of different index numbers for money and income could in principle contribute to explaining our puzzle of the different elasticities in the United States and the United Kingdom. For example, suppose that the ratio of the relevant price index for money to the relevant index for income fell in the United Kingdom over the century but remained constant in the United States. That would make the computed income elasticity of separately deflated money higher than the elasticity we computed. However, we know no student of the demand for money who has explored this route, we have not ourselves done so, and we have not thought of any feasible way to establish a presumption about the direction of effect. Hence we simply mention but do not further explore this possibility.

The same issue arises of course with respect to the unobserved variables c and n. If, for given real income, and other relevant variables, the ratio of the price index relevant to these variables to the general price index had fallen over time in the United Kingdom relative to the corresponding ratio for the United States, that would have reduced over time the ratio of desired m in the United Kingdom to desired m in the United States for the equivalent real incomes per capita—which would, in our calculations, have reduced computed United Kingdom elasticity relative to United States elasticity. Offhand, it seems more nearly feasible to pursue this possibility than the preceding one, by estimating purchasing-power-parity exchange rates for nontraded goods, on the assumption that

c, at least, and perhaps also n, depend disproportionately on the price of nontraded goods. However, that would be a far more laborious task than we have thought it justified to undertake for our purpose.

6.9   Appendix B: Incorporating the Term Structure of Interest Rates in the United States Demand for Money Equation

This appendix describes the experiment, referred to in footnote 43 above, to incorporate the term structure of interest rates in the United States demand for money equation. We first discuss the term structure data set, then the generation of the parameters to describe the term structure of yields, and finally the equation replacing the short-term interest rate with the term structure parameters.

6.9.1   United States Term Structure Data

Annual estimates of yield curves for the best grade corporate bonds are available since 1900.[60] For 1900–1941, the annual yield curves were derived from averages of high and low sale prices of the best-grade corporate bonds during each month of the first quarter of the year. Yields for 1941 were based on January and February prices, and yields for later years on February prices.

To match the period covered by our phase data, we needed term structure yields for 1873–99 for all five maturities available for 1900–1970 and for 1971–75 for the one-year-to-maturity yields.

Our basic source for the period before 1900 was Macaulay's tables of railroad bond yields.[61] He gives the yield of high-grade railroad bonds if held to maturity for each month of each year. Maturity date is given as part of the name for each bond. Following Durand, we used the February yields for each year, excluding any bond whose maturity exceeded fifty years—in some cases bonds with three hundred years to maturity were listed. For each year i we estimated a yield curve, using the quadratic function:

$$(A1) \qquad R_i(\tau) = a_{0i} + a_{1i}\,\tau + a_{2i}\,\tau^2 \,,$$

60. The estimating procedure is described in David Durand, *Basic Yields of Corporate Bonds, 1900–1942*, Technical Paper 3 (New York: NBER, 1942), p. 4. The data for five maturities (1, 5, 10, 20, and 30 years) are given in *Historical Statistics of the United States, Colonial Times to 1970*, Bicentennial Edition, part 2, (Washington, D.C.: Bureau of the Census, 1975), ser. X487-491, p. 1004. Data for 1979–75 for four maturities (5, 10, 20, and 30 years) are given in *Statistical Abstract of the United States, 1976* (Washington, D.C.: Bureau of the Census, 1976), p. 495. The Durand estimates were for the following years to maturity (0, 1, 2, 3, 4, 5, 6, 7, 8, 9, 10, 12, 14, 15, 20, 25, 30, 40, 50, 60).

61. F. R. Macaulay, *The Movements of Interest Rates, Bond Yields and Stock Prices in the United States since 1856* (New York: NBER, 1938), pp. A45–A78.

where R_i is the yield per bond in year i, τ is years to maturity, and a_{0i}, a_{1i}, and a_{2i} are parameters to be estimated for year i.[62] From this equation we calculated the estimated bond yield for each year from 1873 to 1902 for the five maturities (1, 5, 10, 20, and 30 years) that are available from 1943 to 1970. We linked these estimates to the corresponding Durand estimates by lowering the yield for each maturity by the average difference between each pair of series in the overlap period, 1900–1902.

To supplement the four longer maturities for 1971–75, we estimated the one-year yield to maturity, using the yields for the other four maturities (the only ones available for these years) for each year in the quadratic function.

Table 6.17 lists the anual yield to maturity estimates for 1873–1975. We then calculated the phase averages for each maturity to conform to the rest of our observations.

6.9.2 Estimating the Parameters of the Term Structure Yields

The estimation process described by Heller and Khan (see footnote 43 above) has two stages. In the first stage, estimates of a_0, a_1, and a_2 were obtained from the quadratic function $(A1)$ for individual phases rather than years. In the second stage, these parameters replace the phase single interest rate included in the standard version of the demand for money equation. As Heller and Khan note, a_0 "can be viewed as a shift parameter for the entire term structure of interest rates" (p. 114). The slope of the term structure equals $a_1 + 2a_2 \tau$, and the curvature $2a_2$. If the term structure slopes positively, at least initially, and is concave downward, generally taken to be normal, a_1 will be positive and a_2 negative. With a "U-shaped" yield curve, a_1 will be negative, and a_2 positive. Table 6.18 lists the parameters of the yield curve for each phase observation.

For pre–World War I phases, the yield curve alternated between a positive slope and negative curvature and negative slope and positive curvature. The latter shape dominated the interwar years until 1927–29. Thereafter, with only one exception through 1961–66, and again in the 1970s, the former shape predominated. Both parameters positive (1882–85, 1957–58) or negative (1914–18, 1967–69, 1969–70) was rare. Heller and Khan describe the case of negative slope and curvature as "fairly unrealistic and does not appear to have occurred during our sample period." The basic corporate yield data do, however, conform to such a yield curve in 1967–70.

---

62. Heller and Khan (see note 43 of this chapter) used the same quadratic function but fitted it to log R, instead of R, as we do.

Table 6.17   Estimated Yields of United States Corporate Bonds by Term to Maturity, 1873–1975 (Annual Percentage): Number of Years to Maturity

Date	1	5	10	20	30
1873	6.39	6.43	6.50	6.60	6.61
1874	6.15	6.24	6.35	6.51	6.53
1875	5.17	5.41	5.67	6.08	6.26
1876	4.42	4.79	5.19	5.72	5.84
1877	5.23	5.35	5.49	5.68	5.69
1878	4.41	4.79	5.18	5.66	5.67
1879	4.32	4.58	4.86	5.19	5.18
1880	4.41	4.55	4.72	4.98	5.08
1881	4.58	4.52	4.48	4.51	4.61
1882	4.36	4.35	4.38	4.51	4.69
1883	4.28	4.32	4.39	4.56	4.68
1884	4.40	4.38	4.38	4.44	4.51
1885	4.22	4.25	4.30	4.40	4.44
1886	3.79	3.82	3.87	3.97	4.03
1887	3.87	3.88	3.92	4.01	4.04
1888	4.12	4.07	4.05	4.05	4.07
1889	3.61	3.69	3.79	3.94	3.95
1890	4.10	4.05	4.01	3.97	3.93
1891	4.26	4.01	4.18	4.14	4.08
1892	4.30	4.01	4.14	4.06	3.99
1893	4.66	4.47	4.28	4.02	3.88
1894	4.88	4.61	4.33	3.98	3.84
1895	5.66	4.39	4.13	3.80	3.70
1896	4.59	4.32	4.05	3.73	3.62
1897	4.39	4.13	4.88	3.60	3.54
1898	4.02	3.79	3.59	3.38	3.38
1899	3.77	3.59	3.43	3.26	3.23
1900	3.97	3.36	3.30	3.30	3.30
1901	3.25	3.25	3.25	3.25	3.25
1902	3.30	3.30	3.30	3.30	3.30
1903	3.45	3.45	3.45	3.45	3.45
1904	3.60	3.60	3.60	3.60	3.60
1905	3.50	3.50	3.50	3.50	3.50
1906	4.75	3.67	3.55	3.55	3.55
1907	4.87	3.87	3.80	3.80	3.80
1908	5.10	4.30	4.02	3.95	3.95
1909	4.03	3.97	3.91	3.82	3.77
1910	4.25	4.10	3.99	3.87	3.80
1911	4.09	4.05	4.01	3.94	3.90
1912	4.04	4.00	3.96	3.91	3.90
1913	4.74	4.31	4.12	4.02	4.00
1914	4.64	4.45	4.32	4.16	4.10
1915	4.47	4.39	4.31	4.20	4.15
1916	3.48	4.03	4.05	4.05	4.05
1917	4.05	4.05	4.05	4.05	4.05
1918	5.48	5.25	5.05	4.82	4.75
1919	5.58	5.16	4.97	4.81	4.75

Table 6.17 (Continued)

Date	1	5	10	20	30
1920	6.11	5.72	5.43	5.17	5.10
1921	6.94	6.21	5.73	5.31	5.17
1922	5.31	5.19	5.06	4.85	4.71
1923	5.01	4.90	4.80	4.68	4.61
1924	5.02	4.90	4.80	4.69	4.66
1925	3.85	4.46	4.50	4.50	4.50
1926	4.40	4.40	4.40	4.40	4.40
1927	4.30	4.30	4.30	4.30	4.30
1928	4.05	4.05	4.05	4.05	4.05
1929	5.27	4.72	4.57	4.45	4.42
1930	4.40	4.40	4.40	4.40	4.40
1931	3.05	3.90	4.03	4.10	4.10
1932	3.99	4.58	4.70	4.70	4.70
1933	2.60	3.68	4.00	4.11	4.15
1934	2.62	3.48	3.70	3.91	3.99
1935	1.05	2.37	3.00	3.37	3.50
1936	0.61	1.86	2.64	3.04	3.20
1937	0.69	1.68	2.38	2.90	3.08
1938	0.85	1.97	2.60	2.91	3.00
1939	0.57	1.55	2.18	2.65	2.75
1940	0.41	1.28	1.95	2.55	2.70
1941	0.41	1.21	1.88	2.50	2.65
1942	0.81	1.50	2.16	2.61	2.65
1943	1.17	1.71	2.16	2.61	2.65
1944	1.08	1.58	2.20	2.60	2.60
1945	1.02	1.53	2.14	2.55	2.55
1946	0.86	1.32	1.88	2.35	2.43
1947	1.05	1.65	2.08	2.40	2.50
1948	1.60	2.03	2.53	2.73	2.80
1949	1.60	1.92	2.32	2.62	2.74
1950	1.42	1.90	2.30	2.48	2.58
1951	2.05	2.22	2.39	2.59	2.67
1952	2.73	2.73	2.73	2.88	3.00
1953	2.62	2.75	2.88	3.05	3.15
1954	2.40	2.52	2.66	2.88	3.00
1955	2.55	2.70	2.80	2.95	3.04
1956	2.70	2.78	2.86	2.99	3.09
1957	3.50	3.50	3.50	3.50	3.68
1958	3.21	3.25	3.33	3.47	3.61
1959	3.67	3.80	4.03	4.10	4.10
1960	4.95	4.73	4.60	4.55	4.55
1961	3.10	3.75	4.00	4.12	4.22
1962	3.50	3.97	4.28	4.40	4.42
1963	3.25	3.77	3.98	4.10	4.16
1964	4.00	4.15	4.25	4.33	4.33
1965	4.15	4.29	4.33	4.35	4.35
1966	5.00	4.97	4.91	4.80	4.75
1967	5.29	5.28	5.23	5.00	4.95
1968	6.24	6.24	6.20	6.00	5.93

Table 6.17 (Continued)

Date	1	5	10	20	30
1969	7.05	7.05	7.05	6.77	6.54
1970	8.15	8.10	8.00	7.60	7.60
1971	5.32	5.85	7.05	7.12	7.12
1972	6.26	6.50	7.05	7.05	7.01
1973	6.69	6.85	7.05	7.20	7.20
1974	7.32	7.47	7.67	7.80	7.80
1975	7.39	7.70	8.00	8.35	8.35

6.9.3   The Demand for Money, with the Term Structure of Interest Rates

We estimated the United States money demand equation, replacing R_S with the three parameters of the term structure shown in table 6.18. The results[63] for the alternate versions are as follows:

(A2)
$$\log m = -1.91 + 1.21 \log y - 2.85\, R_S$$
$$\quad (14.9) \quad (64.4) \qquad\quad (3.2)$$

$$\qquad\quad -0.71\, g_Y + 0.15 S + .019\, W$$
$$\qquad\quad\quad (3.8) \qquad\quad (4.3) \quad (2.6)$$

$$R^2 = .9919$$
$$SEE = 5.54 \text{ percent.}$$

(A3)
$$\log m = -1.93 + 1.21 \log y - 2.78\, a_0 - 298 a_1$$
$$\quad (15.1) \quad (60.2) \qquad\quad (2.6) \qquad (2.7)$$

$$\qquad\quad -13823\, a_2 - 0.71 g_Y + 0.185 S + 0.021\, W$$
$$\qquad\quad\quad (2.8) \quad\;\; (3.6) \qquad\; (4.8) \qquad (2.9)$$

$$R^2 = .9916$$
$$SEE = 5.64 \text{ percent.}$$

In terms of goodness of fit, equation (A3) with term structure parameters does about as well as equation (A2) using the short-term interest rate, and it yields statistically significant coefficients for all parameters. It provides more information than equation (A2) by indicating the effect on the demand for money of changes in the term structure of interest rates.

The intercept parameter has a clear meaning: an increase in a_0 by .01 implies a one percentage point rise in the whole term structure. Hence, the slope of the intercept parameter, a_0, indicates that a uniform upward

---

63. Note that in these equations, the values for R_S and for a_0, a_1, and a_2 are entered as decimals, not as percentage points, so that the values entered are 1/100 of values such as given in tables 6.17 and 6.18. That is true also, of course, of g_Y.

Table 6.18   **Parameters of the Yield Curve for Each Phase Observation (Interest Rates Expressed as Percentages)**

Phase Number	$100a_0$	$100a_1$	$100a_2$
4	5.2055	0.061700	− 0.001068
5	4.3764	0.040500	− 0.000638
6	4.3085	0.005876	0.000116
7	3.8986	0.010700	− 0.000090
8	3.9847	− 0.000119	0.000087
9	3.8424	0.008997	− 0.000148
10	4.1429	− 0.007933	0.000122
11	4.2070	− 0.011000	0.000195
12	4.6457	− 0.046800	0.000734
13	5.2581	− 0.127000	0.002630
14	5.1112	− 0.126400	0.002654
15	4.2360	− 0.038400	0.000363
16	3.8472	− 0.059800	0.001379
17	3.4065	− 0.012400	0.000313
18	3.5250	0.000000	0.000000
19	4.0921	− 0.064000	0.001619
20	4.8914	− 0.121300	0.003001
21	4.3506	− 0.046800	0.000996
22	4.1823	− 0.021100	0.000340
23	4.2330	− 0.026600	0.000553
24	4.6965	− 0.057400	0.001217
25	4.2981	− 0.001875	− 0.000092
26	5.5507	− 0.065100	0.001299
27	5.8662	− 0.080000	0.001647
28	6.5733	− 0.118600	0.002388
29	5.6752	− 0.060100	0.001042
30	5.0341	− 0.027600	0.000480
31	4.3279	0.028500	− 0.000772
32	4.3500	0.000000	0.000000
33	4.4089	− 0.020700	0.000473
34	4.0621	0.036700	− 0.000930
35	1.8658	0.180700	− 0.004025
36	0.7257	0.208500	− 0.004462
37	0.6257	0.179100	− 0.003708
38	0.8618	0.145700	− 0.003022
39	1.0643	0.126200	− 0.002581
40	1.5238	0.102300	− 0.002053
41	2.0426	0.053000	− 0.000937
42	2.4779	0.033600	− 0.000457
43	2.7208	0.020900	− 0.000217
44	3.3578	0.002016	0.000247
45	3.8492	0.015400	− 0.000247
46	4.0451	0.029800	− 0.000638
47	3.7954	0.055200	− 0.001254
48	5.1789	− 0.014400	0.000103
49	6.2397	− 0.009713	− 0.000141
50	7.6547	− 0.019200	− 0.000037
51	6.2427	0.102100	− 0.002409
52	7.1241	0.057300	− 0.001177

rise in the entire term structure by one percentage point will result in a decrease of the logarithm of money balances by .0278, or in money balances by 2.74 percent. This effect on money balances is almost identical, as of course it should be, with the effect obtained by using the short-term interest rate, namely, a reduction in the logarithm of money balances by .0285, or in money balances by 2.81 percent for each percentage point rise in R_S.

It is more difficult to interpret the coefficients of a_1 and a_2. If either a_1 or a_2 alone rises while a_0 and the other one are held constant, that will raise the value of the interest rate for every maturity given by equation (A1), and that in turn can be expected to reduce log m, as the negative coefficients in equation (A3) indicate. However, that simply repeats the finding for R_S from equation (A2) and for a_0 from equation (A3). The more interesting question is the effect of an increase in the slope of the term structure while at the same time an appropriate *average* rate is constant, namely, an average rate obtained by weighting different maturities (really holding periods) by their importance in determining desired money balances.[64] The calculated coefficients of the parameters a_0, a_1, a_2 have imbedded in them the appropriate weighting function, but we do not see any way to extract it.

This question has particular interest because a theoretical analysis of money demand implies that an increase in the slope in this sense, which decreases short rates while increasing long rates by enough to keep the appropriate average rate constant, will *decrease* the quantity of money demanded. This is counterintuitive. Short-term assets are a closer substitute for money than long-term assets, and hence our intuitive expectation is that a decline in short rates would tend to raise the quantity of money demanded by more than the associated rise in long-term rates would decrease it. The counterintuitive result reflects the countervailing influence of the weights. In general, closer substitutability of short-term than of long-term assets for money will mean that they get a higher weight in the appropriate substitute portfolio, which means that, to keep the average yield constant, long-term rates will have to rise by more than short-term rates fall, which offsets the closer substitutability of short-term assets. Moreover, the greater the difference in substitutability, the greater the difference in weights. Nonetheless, it is far from intuitively clear that the *net* result must be in the direction of decreasing the demand for money, which is why an empirical test is of great interest.[65]

---

64. For a fuller discussion, see M. Friedman, "Time Perspective in the Demand for Money," *Scandinavian Journal of Economics* 79, no. 4 (1977), equation (10) p. 408.
65. Ibid., pp. 410–11.

Aside from the unavailability of the appropriate weighting function, a further complication is that the slope is itself a function of maturity unless $a_2 = 0$.

Let $\bar{\tau}$ be a weighted average maturity, using the (unknown) appropriate weights. Then the average yield for the appropriately weighted portfolio is

$$(A4) \qquad \bar{R} = a_0 + a_1\bar{\tau} + a_2\bar{\tau}^2 = a_0 + a_1\bar{\tau} + a_2 (\bar{\tau}^2 + \sigma_\tau^2).$$

Suppose we concentrate on the slope of equation (A1) at $\bar{\tau}$, which is

$$(A5) \qquad DR\,(\bar{\tau}) = a_1 + 2a_2\bar{\tau}.$$

Consider a change of ΔS in the slope of equation (A1) at $\bar{\tau}$ produced by a change in a_1, from a_1 to $a_1 + \Delta a_1$, and in a_2 to $a_2 + \Delta a_2$, so that

$$(A6) \qquad \Delta a_1 + 2(\Delta a_2)\,\bar{\tau} = \Delta S.$$

The condition that $\bar{R}$ be unchanged requires that

$$(A7) \qquad (\Delta a_1)\,\bar{\tau} + (\Delta a_2)\,(\bar{\tau}^2 + \sigma_\tau^2) = 0.$$

Solving equations (A6) and (A7) simultaneously gives

$$(A8) \qquad \Delta a_1 = -\,\frac{\bar{\tau}^2 + \sigma_\tau^2}{\bar{\tau}^2 - \sigma_\tau^2}\,\Delta S,$$

$$(A9) \qquad \Delta a_2 = \frac{\bar{\tau}}{\bar{\tau}^2 - \sigma_\tau^2}\,\Delta S.$$

Let b_1 be the coefficient of a_1 in equation (A3); b_2, the coefficient of a_2. Then the change in $\log m$ produced by a change of Δa_1 and Δa_2 in a_1 and a_2 is

$$(A10) \qquad \Delta\log m = b_1\Delta a_1 + b_2\Delta a_2 \,.$$

To go further requires some assumption about the portfolio for which $\bar{\tau}$ and σ_τ^2 are to be calculated. We have considered two weighting patterns which are simple to handle mathematically because both are characterized by only a single parameter. One weighting pattern corresponds to a portfolio equally divided among all maturities from 0 to τ_o, or a weighting pattern of

$$(A11) \qquad w_1(\tau) = \frac{1}{\tau_o},$$

which has

$$(A12) \qquad \bar{\tau} = \frac{\tau_o}{2},$$

$$(A13) \qquad \sigma_\tau^2 = \frac{1}{12}\tau_o^2,$$

$$(A14) \qquad \Delta a_1 = -2\Delta S,$$

(A15) $\Delta a_2 = \dfrac{3}{\tau_o} \Delta S.$

The other weighting pattern involves triangular weights declining from 0 to τ_o, or a weighting pattern of

(A16) $w_2\,(\tau) = \dfrac{2}{\tau_o}(1 - \dfrac{\tau}{\tau_o}),$

which has

(A17) $\bar{\tau} = \dfrac{\tau_o}{3}$

(A18) $\sigma_\tau^2 = \dfrac{\tau_o^2}{18}$

and

(A19) $\Delta a_1 = -3\Delta S_1$

(A20) $\Delta a_2 = \dfrac{6}{\tau_o}\,\Delta S.$

The second pattern corresponds to the intuition that short-term securities should have a heavier weight than long-term securities.

It turns out that for both weighting patterns, and for the calculated values of b_1 and b_2, the effect on log m is the theoretically predicted negative effect for small τ_o. As τ_o rises, the negative effect becomes smaller in absolute value and ultimately turns positive. The value of τ_o at which it turns positive is 69.6 years, or a mean maturity of 34.8 years, for weighting pattern w_1; it is 92.8 years, or a mean maturity of 30.9 years, for weighting pattern w_2. These are far longer mean maturities than seem at all plausible for relevant actual portfolios—indeed, the mean maturity is longer than the longest maturities that we have used in calculating a_0, a_1, a_2. Hence, the theoretical implication about direction is amply confirmed.

What about magnitude of effect? Consider a rise in the slope at τ of .033 percentage points (.00033). That is equivalent to increasing the differential between maturities thirty years apart by one percentage point. And consider a value of $\bar{\tau}$ of 10 years, that is, a maximum maturity in the portfolio of twenty years for weighting pattern w_1 and of thirty years for weighting pattern w_2. That rise in slope, for fixed $\bar{R}$, would decrease desired m by

> 39 percent for weighting pattern w_1
> 46 percent for weighting pattern w_2.

These seem extremely large effects, hard to reconcile with the value of the coefficient of a_0 in equation (A3), or of R_S in equation (A2). However, the coefficients of a_1 and a_2 in equation (A3) are subject to large sampling errors, hence these estimates are subject to a large margin of error. To check this effect, we raised the absolute value of b_1 by one standard error and reduced the absolute value of b_2 by one standard error—both changes tending to raise $\Delta \log m$ algebraically. The result was still a reduction in desired m but by much smaller, and more plausible, amounts: by

16 percent for weighting pattern w_1
2 percent for weighting pattern w_2.

The inaccuracy of the estimate reflects the inaccuracy in the computed values of a_0, a_1, a_2 based as they are on only five observations, and these frequently not differing much. All in all, considering the element of chance error in our estimates, we regard these results as a strong confirmation of theoretical expectations.

A direct comparison of our results with those of Heller and Khan is not easy because of the different periods covered (1873 to 1975 versus 1960 to 1976); the different time unit (a cycle phase versus a quarter); the different form of the quadratic term structure equation (dependent variable R versus $\log R$); the different range of interest rates entering into the calculations (our one to thirty years versus their three months to twenty years); and the different demand equation (per capita real money and income versus aggregate real money and income, our inclusion and their exclusion of g_Y versus our exclusion and their inclusion of a lagged dependent variable).

In terms of direction, the coefficients of their counterparts of our a_0, a_1, a_2, are, like ours, all negative, though decidedly larger in absolute value when the difference between the use of R and the use of $\log R$ is allowed for, yet with roughly similar t values. In terms of the effect of an increase in slope holding $\bar{R}$ constant (in this case, $\overline{\log R}$, that is, the geometric mean), their results show a decrease in demand for τ_o less than 9.3 years for weighting pattern w_1, less than 12.35 years for weighting pattern w_2, or mean maturities of 4.6 or 4.1 years. It is perhaps not surprising that, given their short time unit and narrower range of maturities, these numbers are lower than those we found. In addition, the higher and more erratic inflation after 1960 than during most of our period could be expected to lead to considerably shorter-term portfolios, so, all in all, we regard their results as not inconsistent with ours.

Two recent studies by Bilson and Hale and by Allen and Hafer point out that Heller and Khan entered maturity incorrectly in computing the quadratic term structure. Bilson and Hale correct the error and also find that expressing the logarithm of the interest rate as a quadratic in the logarithm of maturity fits the term-structure data better than a quadratic in maturity. Allen and Hafer, using quarterly data for 1960–79, recompute both the Heller-Khan and the Bilson-Hale equations and also find that a cubic in the logarithm of maturity gives still better results.

The Bilson-Hale recomputation of the Heller-Khan equation strengthens its conformity with our results. The value of τ_o at which the effect on $\log m$ turns positive is 35.9 years for weighting pattern 1 and 48.1 years for weighting pattern 2, still less than the corresponding values for our equation but much closer to them.

The Bilson-Hale and Allen-Hafer use of the logarithms of interest rate and maturity rather than the interest rate and maturity complicates the comparison of their results with our own. However, it is straightforward to estimate the effect of a change in the slope of the term structure at the geometric mean maturity while keeping the geometric average yield constant. The results are that the effect of an increase in slope is in the theoretically predicted negative direction for weighting pattern 1 (weighting pattern 2) for τ_o less than 3.2 (5.1) months and between 7.4 (10.7) months and roughly 100 (300) years; it is in the opposite direction for τ_o between 3.2 (5.1) months and 7.4 (10.7) months, and greater than roughly 100 (300) years. These results, therefore, are in line with our own as well as with Heller and Khan's.

We have not attempted to analyze in the same way the Allen-Hafer equation using a cubic to approximate the term structure. However, the coefficients of the linear and quadratic terms (the counterparts of b_1 and b_2 in equation A11) are almost identical with those for the Bilson-Hale equation. Hence, the results cannot differ much.

7 Velocity and the Interrelations between the United States and the United Kingdom

The preceding chapter demonstrates that a single demand curve for money can be used for the United States and the United Kingdom, provided only that adjustment is made for a difference in the currencies used in the two countries and in the income elasticity. The largely common demand curve by itself does not, however, explain the striking finding in chapter 5 that velocity in the United States and velocity in the United Kingdom show parallel movements for most of the century our data cover, and that the rates of change of velocity are nearly identical in the two countries. If the variables affecting the demand for money and velocity had behaved very differently in the two countries, the same demand curve would have generated different realized time series of velocity. The similar behavior of velocity therefore requires in addition to a largely common demand curve the similar behavior of the variables affecting the demand for money. One possible explanation for the similar behavior of such variables is that the two countries were part of a single economic entity. National boundaries may have great political importance and economic significance in other respects, yet be consistent with a financial system that is unified over a much larger area. The international financial community presumably included (and includes) not only the United States and the United Kingdom but other countries as well. However, we perforce limit ourselves to the connections between the United States and the United Kingdom that are reflected in the similar behavior of velocity in these two countries. It would be highly desirable to extend the analysis to other countries as well, but we leave that to other scholars.

There is nothing novel or surprising about the existence of a unified financial community. What is novel and surprising is that the links should have been so close as to produce the degree of parallelism in velocity that is recorded in chart 5.5—given the extent to which the two countries failed to conform to the "law of one price," especially after 1931 (see chart 6.5, which plots the ratio of the purchasing-power-parity exchange rate to the market exchange rate).

From 1879 to 1914 and again from 1925 to 1931, the United States and the United Kingdom were both on a gold standard, and neither imposed appreciable controls on the movement of capital or engaged in exchange controls of the modern type (such exchange controls were invented only in 1934 by Hjalmar Schacht in Germany as part of the Nazi economic policy).

Before World War I, the United Kingdom had no tariffs. The United States did, but the tariffs were changed at infrequent intervals and were not used as an instrument of monetary or exchange policies. The United States and the United Kingdom almost literally had a single monetary system—a gold standard or, almost as descriptively, a sterling standard. As we demonstrated in *A Monetary History* (and as chart 6.5 confirms), there was a good deal of leeway for domestic monetary policy over short periods, but over periods of more than a few years, the quantity of money in each country was determined by the requirement that the price levels of the two countries move roughly in step in order to preserve equilibrium in the balance of payments. Similarly, the capital markets of the two countries were linked. There was little scope for interest arbitrage, since the exchange rates had to stay within the narrow gold points, so market interest rates could not differ much between the two countries. Hence rates of change in both prices and nominal interest rates were linked in the two countries.[1]

During World Wars I and II, the two countries were linked more fundamentally, the United States being either a major supplier of goods to the United Kingdom for wartime use or a partner of the United Kingdom. From 1925 to 1931, the gold standard was less rigid than in the pre–World War I period but even so, fixed exchange rates were maintained without effective capital or exchange controls,[2] so the links were still close. During the rest of the interwar period exchange rates were not rigidly fixed, yet the United States imposed neither exchange controls nor capital controls, and the United Kingdom imposed them only to a very minor extent. Interest arbitrage had more scope, but not much more,

1. A view that presents some empirical evidence for the United States and the United Kingdom for part of the period we cover is contained in Donald N. McCloskey and J. Richard Zecher, "How the Gold Standard Worked, 1880–1913," in *The Monetary Approach to the Balance of Payments*, ed. J. A. Frenkel and H. G. Johnson (London: George Allen and Unwin, 1976), pp. 357–85.

2. See D. E. Moggridge, "British Controls on Long-Term Capital Movements, 1924–1931," in *Essays on a Mature Economy: Britain after 1840*, ed. D. N. McCloskey (Princeton: Princeton University Press, 1971), pp. 113–38.

since exchange rate fluctuations were fairly small most of the time. Yet the years 1918 to 1925 and 1931 to 1939 were marked by a looser financial relation between the United States and the United Kingdom than the years 1879 to 1914 and 1925 to 1931.

The post–World War II period is more difficult to interpret. Until 1972, the sterling-dollar exchange rate was temporarily fixed but subject to change from time to time by official action. Sterling was devalued in 1949, again in 1967, and was permitted to float in 1972. Until October 1979, there was extensive exchange control in the United Kingdom, more sweeping in the early postwar period than later on, but significant throughout. Moreover, in the 1960s and until the early 1970s, the United States introduced restrictions on the movements of capital and exchange—the interest equalization tax, the tying of foreign aid and other foreign capital transfers, restrictions on bank loans and foreign investment by United States enterprises. Hence these postwar years are characterized by the loosest monetary linkage between the United States and the United Kingdom. They also display the most disparate movements of velocity (see chart 5.5) and of the ratio of the purchasing-power-parity exchange rate to the market exchange rate (chart 6.5).

7.1 The Reference Chronology

To judge from chronologies that we have used to define our basic phase observations, the financial linkages between the two countries were accompanied by—indeed, presumably were the source of—parallel movements in general economic activity.

As table 7.1 shows,[3] of thirty-nine United Kingdom turning points in the 109 years from 1867 to 1975, twenty come in the same year as a United States turning point of the same kind (i.e., a trough in the same year as a trough; a peak in the same year as a peak); eleven come one year later; four come one year earlier; and only four have no corresponding turning point within one year.[4] Of these four, three are in the post–World War II period, one in 1926. The 1926 trough, the only miss for the period of a gold standard, marked the end of the British general strike, which undoubtedly distorted cyclical behavior.

For the United States, recorded turning points total fifty-three rather than thirty-nine, so that fourteen additional turns do not match United Kingdom turns, making eighteen nonmatching turns in all for the United States. Twelve come before World War I, one in 1924, and the remaining

3. For comparison of datings, we have used the whole period after 1866 for which we have both chronologies and United States money data and not simply the period after 1870, when the United Kingdom money data begin.

4. A precise test of significance is not easy to make because of the condition that troughs and peaks alternate. But approximate tests of significance for troughs and peaks separately

five after World War II. The twelve before World War I all reflect extra movements (6 extra cycles) recognized in the United States chronology but not in the United Kingdom chronology, and so do two (one extra cycle) of the other six nonmatching turning points.

The extra United States turning points have generally been regarded as evidence of more marked cyclical movements in the United States than in the United Kingdom, leading to both briefer and larger cycles in the United States than in the United Kingdom. Our examination of the data leads us to enter a caveat. The extra United States turning points may simply reflect a greater plenitude of statistics for the United States than for the United Kingdom and a more searching examination of the United States data for cyclical movements.[5]

indicate that the agreement between the two chronologies is greater than could readily be expected from chance. Consider a contingency table for troughs (table 7.N.1).

Table 7.N.1   Comparison of Trough Reference Dates for the United States and the United Kingdom

Years from 1867 to 1975 That	Number of Years That Contain		
	United Kingdom Troughs	No United Kingdom Troughs	Total
Contain United States troughs	10	17	27
Precede United States troughs	2	25	27
Follow United States troughs	6	20	26[a]
Are none of above	2	27	29
Total	20	89	109

[a]Not 27, because the year following the 1975 trough is not included.

Chi-square for this table is 10.7, which is at the .02 level of significance for 3 degrees of freedom. The corresponding table, with years classified by United Kingdom troughs, yields a chi-square of 10.4. For peaks, the two corresponding tables yield chi-squares of 14.6 and 10.2. Adding the chi-squares for the corresponding trough and peak tables gives 25.3 and 20.6, which, for 6 degrees of freedom, would be exceeded by chance less than one time in a thousand.

5. The reference chronologies we use are based on the work done at the NBER, particularly by Arthur F. Burns and Wesley C. Mitchell. They did a far more exhaustive study of United States data than of United Kingdom data and had more United States data to study. In the course of our own reexamination of parts of the chronology that seemed questionable for one reason or another, we found that we were almost always inclined to recognize more turning points the broader the range of data we could examine. The concentration of extra turning points in the pre–1914 period strengthens the suspicion that we may be dealing with a statistical artifact: in the forty-eight years from 1866 to 1914, there are twenty-five United States turning points, 13 United Kingdom turning points; in the remaining sixty-one years, there are twenty-eight United States turning points, twenty-six United Kingdom turning points. There is a far greater difference between the statistical data available for the United States and the United Kingdom, and also between the effort that has been devoted to their analysis, for the pre–1914 than for the post–1914 period.

The major hesitation we have in accepting this interpretation is that the role of the British economy in the world was changed so drastically by World War I that the United Kingdom

Table 7.1   Relation between United Kingdom and United States Cyclical
Turning Points, 1867–1975

		Number of Turning Points		
		Trough	Peak	Both
1	Corresponding turning points (within one year of each other)	18	17	35
1a	United Kingdom one year earlier than United States	2	2	4
1b	United Kingdom same year as United States	10	10	20
1c	United Kingdom one year later than United States	6	5	11
2	No corresponding turning points (within one year of each other)			
2a	United Kingdom	2	2	4
2b	United States	9	9	18
	Total number of turning points			
1 + 2a	United Kingdom	20	19	39
1 + 2b	United States	27	26	53

One fascinating detail in table 7.1 is the tendency for nonsynchronous turning points in the United Kingdom to follow those for the United States. Of the fifteen matching turning points that do not come in the same year ín the United Kingdom and the United States, eleven come one year later in the United Kingdom and only four come one year earlier. Of the twenty that come in the same year, monthly reference dates indicate that twelve came later for the United Kingdom than for the United States, and six earlier (for two—1944 and 1946—we have no monthly United Kingdom chronology). One possible explanation is that cyclical fluctuations mostly originated in the United States and spread from the United States to the United Kingdom, rather than the other way—which would also be consistent with the greater amplitude and frequency of cyclical fluctuations in the United States. It is also the conclusion that we documented in *A Monetary History* for the worldwide contraction that began in 1929.[6]

cyclical pattern may also have changed. Britain's financial preeminence in the world before World War I may have enabled it to ride out fluctuations in the world that would have left echoes at home after World War I.

R. C. O. Matthews accepts fewer post–World War I turning points than we do, but even he reports phases of shorter average duration after 1914 than earlier, except for interwar upswings—resulting from his treatment of 1921–29 as one long expansion ("Postwar Business Cycles in the United Kingdom," in *Is the Business Cycle Obsolete?* ed. M. Bronfenbrenner (New York: Wiley, 1969), pp. 102–3).

6. Oskar Morgenstern reached the same conclusion for the pre-World War I period for three European countries (Great Britain, France, Germany): "In general in the prewar period the United States cycle led those of the three European countries at both peaks and troughs. . . . After the war the pattern was less definite although the United States cycles continued to lead British and French cycles at peaks" (*International Financial Transactions and Business Cycles*, Studies in Business Cycles, no. 8 [Princeton: Princeton University Press for NBER, 1959], p. 51).

This apparent lead of cyclical movements in the United States is not reflected in a simple correlation of annual velocity estimates for the United States and the United Kingdom. For the 105 years 1871 through 1975, the synchronous correlation coefficient is .492 and is slightly higher than the correlation for United States velocity leading (.486) or lagging United Kingdom velocity by one year (.46). Similarly, the synchronous correlation for year-to-year rates of change in velocity is .42, which is higher than the correlation for the rate of change in United States velocity leading (.19) or lagging (.29) the change in United Kingdom velocity by one year.

The close relation between the two chronologies suggests the desirability of using a single chronology for the two countries in order to provide matching observations that would permit a more detailed statistical investigation of the relations between them. The best way to get a single chronology would be literally to treat the United Kingdom and the United States as a single economic entity and construct a reference chronology for the combined entity comparable to the chronologies constructed for each country separately. However, that would be extremely laborious. Instead, we have substituted computer time for historical research. We have recalculated the United Kingdom phase bases on the United States chronology and the United States phase bases on the United Kingdom chronology. We then started out making two parallel analyses, one using the United States chronology for both countries, the other using the United Kingdom chronology for both countries. However, the results of the two parallel analyses were so close that we have simplified the exposition and analysis by generally using only the United States chronology.

One exception is in chart 7.1 which duplicates chart 5.5 except that velocity and its rate of change are calculated for the same chronological time units for the United States and the United Kingdom—in chart 7.1, panel A, the United States chronology, in chart 7.1, panel B, for the United Kingdom chronology.

Using the same chronology for both countries does not alter in any important way the story told by the earlier charts.

7.2 Correlation of United States and United Kingdom Velocities and Their Determinants

The visual impression given by chart 7.1, panels A and B, is confirmed by the numerical correlation coefficients in table 7.2 covering more than a century: .49 for velocity and .76 for its rate of change.

Of greater interest are the correlations for the variables we singled out in chapter 6 as most closely related to the demand for money and hence velocity: real per capita income; the differential interest rate on alternatives to money (the short rate times the ratio of high-powered money to money); the rate of change of nominal income (as a proxy for the nominal yield on physical assets); and the demand shift and postwar shift dummies.[7] Both the levels and the rates of change of these variables are highly correlated between the two countries, except only for the rate of change of real per capita income. Much of the common movement of velocity can therefore be attributed, as suggested above, to common movements of the determinants of velocity.

From this point of view, the exception is as significant as the high correlations. The low correlation between the *rates of change* of real per capita income means that the factors affecting the movements in real income over periods longer than a cycle but shorter than a sizable fraction of a century are largely independent in the two countries—apparently the high correlation for *levels* is primarily between trends. This result is entirely consistent with our interpretation of the common movements in velocity as reflecting a unified *financial* system. A unified financial system leaves much room for different physical development—as witness the differences among regions within the United States and the United Kingdom.

The contrast between *financial* unification and *physical* independence is brought out sharply by the correlations we have added at the bottom of table 7.2 for prices, nominal income, and money. The correlation for the level of prices is as high as for any other level variable; for the rate of change of prices it is decidedly higher than for any other rate-of-change variable. The correlation for the level of nominal income matches that for prices, but for the rate of change of nominal income is decidedly lower than for the rate of change of prices, reflecting the low correlation of the rate of change of per capita real income.

Although the quantity of money is as highly correlated between the countries as income and prices—reflecting the dominance of the trend—the rate of change of money displays the same correlation as the rate of change of income, and both are decidedly lower than the correlation for the rate of change of prices. At first glance this result may seem inconsistent with our interpretation of the United States and the United Kingdom as part of a larger monetary system, but it is not. The key linkage between the two countries is that prices, expressed in a common currency (i.e., adjusted for changes in exchange rates) must move in a way that will keep international payments in adjustment, which, broadly speaking, means that prices must move in harmony. If they do not, they will lead to exports or imports or capital movements that will produce balance-of-payments

---

7. For the United States, changing financial sophistication should also be listed. Allowance has implicitly been made for that variable by adjusting the quantity of money in the United States for phases before 1903.0.

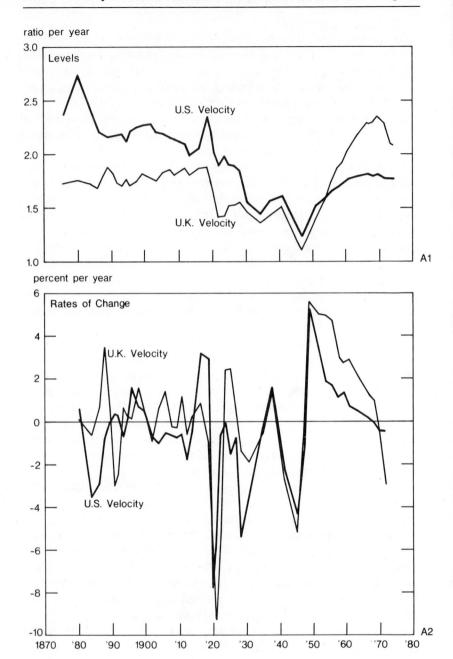

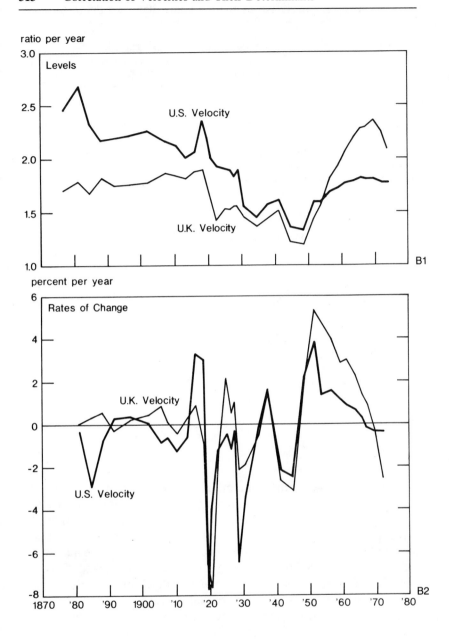

ratio per year

percent per year

Chart 7.1   Levels and rates of change of United States and United Kingdom velocity on United States and United Kingdom dates.

Table 7.2   Correlations of United States and United Kingdom Velocities and Their Determinants, and Also Prices, Nominal Income, and Money: Levels and Rates of Change, United States Dates

Variable	Correlation Coefficient
1. Velocity (log V)	.49
2. Real per capita income (log y)	.96
3. Differential yield on money (R_N)	.22
4. Rate of change of nominal income (g_Y)[a]	.71
5. Demand shift dummy	.84
6. Postwar shift dummy	.66
7. Rate of change of velocity (g_V)	.76
8. Rate of change of real per capita income (g_y)	.17
9. Rate of change of differential yield on money [$D(R_N)$]	.65
10. Rate of change of rate of change of nominal income (Dg_Y)	.66
11. Rate of change of demand shift dummy	.48
12. Rate of change of postwar shift dummy	.50
13. Prices (log P)	.99
14. Rate of change of prices (g_P)	.90
15. Nominal income (log Y)	.99
16. Rate of change of nominal income (g_Y)[a]	.73
17. Quantity of money (log M)	.99
18. Rate of change of money (g_M)	.73

[a]Level weights used to calculate line 4; rate of change weights used to calculate line 16.

deficits or surpluses, setting in motion the specie-flow mechanism. The requirement for money and nominal income (or exchange rates) is that they adjust in such a way as to keep prices in the appropriate relation. But this requirement is likely to imply a lower correlation for money and income than for prices, since, to keep prices in harmony, the quantity of money will have to adapt to differential changes in the demand for money (in the sense, of course, of "demand schedule" or "function"), and income will have to adapt to differential changes in output. Put differently, divergent movements in money and income will occur precisely in order to keep prices in line. Hence, the lower correlations for money and income than for prices are entirely consistent with, and indeed strengthen the evidence for, the two economies being part of a larger monetary system in which monetary adjustments serve as the key mechanism keeping the separate parts aligned with one another.

The linkage between prices in the two countries is reflected in chart 6.5.For the whole period before the Great Depression, the ratio of purchasing power parity to the exchange rate fluctuates within a rather narrow range—between a low of 1.00 (in 1896) and a high of 1.23 (in 1910)—and displays no clear trend. The loosening of the financial links between the two countries as a result of the depression, the 1931 departure of sterling from the gold standard, the wartime introduction and postwar continuation of exchange controls, and postwar devaluations, produced a major increase in the variability of the purchasing power ratio: from a low of .93 (in 1938) to a high of 1.62 (in 1950). The post–World War II period saw also the widest divergences in the movement of velocity in the two countries.

7.3   Role of Common Determinants of Velocity

Table 7.3 gives estimates of the role of various factors in accounting for the common and idiosyncratic movements of velocity in the two countries.[8] Consider first the columns for the level of velocity. If velocities

8. Five sources of variation in the velocity of each country can be distinguished:
1. The common movement in the two countries of the specified determinants
2. The common movement in the two countries of other common determinants
3. Differential movements in the specified determinants
4a. Differential movements in other common determinants
4b. All other determinants of measured velocity, including those specific to each country, chance, and measurement error.
We shall not be able to estimate the effects of 4a and 4b separately; so hereafter we refer to the two together as 4.

If items 1 and 2 were nonexistent, and yet velocity had varied in each country as it in fact did, the variance of the differences in the logarithms of velocities ($\log V_{uk} - \log V_{us}$) would be equal to the sum of the variances, or

A. $\qquad \sigma^2_{\log V_{uk} - \log V_{us}}$ (hypothetical) $= \sigma^2_{\log V_{uk}} + \sigma^2_{\log V_{us}}$.

The actual differences in velocity eliminate the effect of items 1 and 2. Hence

B. $\sigma^2_{\log V_{uk} - \log V_{us}}$ (measured) is an estimate of the combined effects of items 3 and 4.

Regressing the differences in velocity on the differences in the specified determinants eliminates the effect of item 3 as well as items 1 and 2. Hence

C. $(\text{SEE})^2_{\log V_{uk} - \log V_{us}}$, or the squared standard error of the residuals from such an equation, is an estimate of the effect of item 4.

Regressing velocity in each country on the specified determinants for that country eliminates the effects of items 1 and 3 for that country. Hence

D. $(\text{SEE})^2_{us} + (\text{SEE})^2_{uk}$, or the sum of the squared standard errors of the residuals from such regressions, is an estimate of the combined effects of items 2 and 4.

It follows that the entry in column 1 of table 7.3 in

Line 5   is A
Line 4   is C
Line 3   is B minus C
Line 2   is D minus C
Line 1   is line 5 minus the entries in lines 2, 3, and 4.

The same analysis applies for the rate of change of velocity by simply replacing velocity by the rate of change of velocity, so that the entries in column 3 of table 7.3 are derived in the same way.

Table 7.3   Role of Various Determinants in Producing Common Movements in Velocity in the United States and the United Kingdom

	Difference in Level of Velocity		Difference in Rates of Change of Velocity	
	Variance (1)	Percentage Distribution (2)	Variance (3)	Percentage Distribution (4)
Variances[a]				
Contribution to hypothetical variance of common movement in				
1. Specified determinants[b]	.0285	47.50	.000459	38.64
2. Other common determinants	.0019	3.17	.000441	37.12
All common determinants	(.0304)	(50.67)	(.000900)	(75.76)
3. Differential movements in specified determinants	.0236	39.33	.000116	9.76
4. Other factors	.0060	10.00	.000172	14.48
5. Hypothetical variance, if no common determinants	.0600	100.00	.001188	100.00
Standard Deviations[c]				
Factors considered				
6. Other factors only	.077		.013	
Factors other than common movements in:				
7. All determinants	.172		.017	
8. Specified determinants only	.178		.027	
9. Hypothetical, if no common determinants	.245		.034	

[a]For basis of computation, see footnote 8 of text.
[b]Log y, R_N, g_Y and demand and postwar shift dummies for levels; g_y, DR_N, Dg_Y, demand shift and postwar shift dummies for rates of change.
[c]Line 6: square root of line 4; line 7, of sum of lines 3 and 4; line 8, of sum of lines 2, 3, and 4; and line 9, of line 5.

in the two countries had been completely independent (i.e., the correlation between them had been zero) but velocity in each country had varied as much as it actually did, the variance of the difference between the logarithms of the two velocities ($\sigma^2_{\log V_{uk} - \log V_{us}}$) would have been the sum of the variances in each country separately or the .0600 in line 5 of column 1 of the table. The common movement of the determinants we have explicitly specified would have accounted for almost half of that hypothetical variance; together with other unspecified but common determinants, it would have accounted for slightly more than half. Differential movements in the specified determinants accounted for almost 40 percent, leaving 10 percent to be accounted for by all other factors—chance, measurement error, differential movements in unspecified but common determinants, and determinants of velocity specific to each country.

In terms of standard deviations, the standard deviation of that part of the difference between the two velocities that arises from all other factors is 7.7 percent; from these other factors plus the differential movement of the specified determinants, 17.2 percent. Common movements in unspecified determinants are of minor importance; including them raises the standard deviation only to 17.8 percent. Finally, the hypothetical standard deviation if the velocity series had been unrelated in the two countries would have been 24.5 percent.

The results are even more striking for rates of change. Common movements in determinants—those specified and others—account for over three-quarters of total variance. If there were no common determinants, the standard deviation of the difference between the rates of change of velocity in the two countries would be 3.4 percent. As it is, it is 1.7 percent.[9] For rates of change, the common movements in unspecified common determinants are more important than for levels: including them would raise the standard deviation to 2.7 percent.

7.4 Money and Income

Another way to explore the interrelations between the United States and the United Kingdom is to examine the effect of changes in the quantity of money in one country on income in the other.

---

9. We can use the residual difference in velocity between the two countries to get additional estimates of the effect of the several specified determinants by regressing these differences on the corresponding differences between the determinants in the two countries; and similarly for rates of change. We have done this with the phase data for both levels and rates of change and, for rates of change only, also with annual data. The results simply reinforce those of the previous chapter, without adding anything to them, so we simply summarize them in the appendix to this chapter.

A simple example will indicate the relevance of this approach. Suppose there were accurate estimates of nominal income and of the quantity of money in the state of Illinois. Suppose we then examined the relation between changes in income for the state of Illinois and changes in the quantity of money in Illinois or in the rest of the country. It would come as no surprise if income changes in Illinois were more closely related to monetary changes in the rest of the country than to monetary changes in Illinois itself. The reason is that Illinois is a small part of a broader economy using the same money. The quantity of money in Illinois is endogenous—determined by the amount that people in Illinois want to hold. They can always get the amount they want by bidding it away from other states. The forces running from income to money will dominate those running the other way. Moreover, in such a small unit there is much room for random perturbation in the demand for money.

For the country as a whole, on the other hand, the quantity of money comes closer to being exogenous. The forces running from money to income are likely to be more important relative to those running from income to money than for Illinois alone. And in such a large unit, random perturbations have more of an opportunity to cancel out.

At first glance, these considerations suggest only that the income-money relation for the United States as a whole will be closer than for Illinois alone. However, the free mobility of men, money, capital, and goods between Illinois and the rest of the country also makes it likely that Illinois income will be more closely related to the quantity of money in the United States as a whole than in Illinois alone. Income movements in Illinois must be highly correlated with income movements elsewhere. The random perturbations in that relation are likely to be less than the random perturbations in the Illinois demand for money. The Illinois relation alone may best be viewed in terms of Illinois income serving as a proxy for United States income; Illinois money, for United States money. Substituting actual United States money for its proxy removes one source of random disturbance.

Note that the question at issue is not simply whether economic developments in the rest of the country influence Illinois. Of course they do—very strongly. However, as in the classical specie-flow mechanism, or the more recently fashionable monetary theory of the balance of payments, that influence might operate primarily through balance-of-payments deficits or surpluses between Illinois and the rest of the country, or through arbitrage operations reflecting the "law of one price." Either adjustment mechanism forces the quantity of money in Illinois to change in line with prices and the quantity of money in the rest of the economy and so would be fully reflected in the Illinois quantity of money. The question is whether the monetary changes in the rest of the country exert an influence on Illinois beyond those influences reflected in the Illinois quantity of money.[10]

A similar example, closer to the United States–United Kingdom relation, is between Canada and the United States. This example is similar to the Illinois–United States example in the relative size of Canada and the United States and in the closeness of the economic links between them. It differs in the existence of two formally independent monies—Canadian dollars and United States dollars. This formal independence was largely irrelevant in those years when the two monies were connected by a fixed exchange rate and there was no extensive governmental exchange control. It was potentially much more relevant when exchange control was extensive and when the monies were linked by floating exchange rates. However, the periods of extensive exchange control were few, the controls were never thoroughly effective, and the floating rate has tended in practice to be relatively stable.

For this example, a number of empirical studies have indicated that the expectations expressed above for Illinois are indeed fulfilled for Canada: changes in nominal income in Canada are more closely related to changes in the quantity of money in the United States than to changes in the quantity of money in Canada, and still more closely related to a weighted average of the two.[11]

---

10. Note also that the question is not the one that has so preoccupied the proponents of the monetary theory of the balance of payments—whether movements in the balance of payments and in gold reflect (*a*) changes in the demand for money arising either from internal causes or from the direct effect on prices and income of the "law of one price" or (*b*) differential changes in prices in different countries reflecting perhaps autonomous changes in domestic quantities of money, which in turn set in motion the classical specie-flow mechanism.

In our opinion the much-exaggerated contrast between the classical specie-flow mechanism and the monetary theory of the balance of payments concerns the differential speed of adjustment of variables that all recognize as significant. The basic issue is empirical—the lag in reaction to different stimuli. However, some proponents of the monetary theory of the balance of payments mistakenly translate the question about the balance of payments into one of whether money determines income or, in an open economy with fixed exchange rates, income determines money.

In practice, both directions of influence are operative all the time. In any event, the lags in reaction would largely average out in our phase data. Whatever may cause the changes in the quantity of money within a country, those changes can in turn be expected to have predictable effects on nominal income, output, prices, and interest rates. We are dealing with a dynamic feedback system, not a one-way process. Hence, the controversy about the monetary theory of the balance of payments is largely irrelevant to the kind of relations between money and other variables that we explore in this book.

11. See Glenn P. Jenkins, "The Role of the United States Monetary Stock in a Model of the Canadian Economy," unpublished paper, Money and Banking Workshop, University of Chicago (April 1971); R. Argarwala, J. Drinkwater, S. D. Khosla, and J. McMenomy,

The United Kingdom economy is larger than the Canadian economy, geographical barriers to the movement of resources between the United Kingdom and the United States are greater than between Canada and the United States, and exchange controls have been more extensive and lasted longer in the United Kingdom. The empirical question is whether these differences are sufficiently important to seriously blur the effects of one country on the other beyond those that are incorporated in each country's money supply via the specie-flow mechanism or the "law of one price" or, for the period of floating exchange rates, via the adjustment of exchange rates, which alters relative money supplies expressed in a common currency.

7.4.1 Combined Money Stock

One simple test is to relate income (or prices) in each country separately to the total money stock in the two countries together rather than to the money stock in the country in question. Table 7.4 gives the results of such a test for both levels and rates of change of income and prices.

Before we can add the two money stocks, they must first be expressed in a common currency. We have done this by using the market exchange rate ruling in each year. This gives two series: one in dollars, one in pounds, depending on which country's money stock is converted into the currency of the other. When exchange rates are constant, as from 1879 to 1914, the two level series are of course, in a fixed ratio and the two rate-of-change series are identical. But, when exchange rates vary, neither property holds. To allow for the difference, we regressed the United States variables on the dollar combined money stock series and its rate of change and regressed the United Kingdom variables on the pound combined money stock series and its rate of change.

Columns 2 and 3 of table 7.4 give the regression coefficients for the two regressions (described as "simple," though in fact demand shift and postwar readjustment effects are allowed for); columns 9 and 10, the standard errors of estimate; and columns 13 and 14, the squared correlation coefficients.

"A Neoclassical Approach to the Determination of Prices and Wages," *Economica*, n.s., 39 (August 1972): 250–63.

Indirect evidence for closer relations between Canadian income and the United States quantity of money than between Canadian income and Canadian quantity of money is provided by a simulation of the effects of monetary restraint in the United States and Canada on the two countries. The United States restraint had a greater effect on Canada than Canadian restraint. This result, however, is critically dependent on the particular multiple-regression models for Canada and the United States employed in the simulation. See John Helliwell and Tom Maxwell, "Monetary Interdependence of Canada and the United States under Alternative Exchange Rate Systems," in *National Monetary Policies and the International Financial System*, ed. R. Z. Aliber (Chicago: University of Chicago Press, 1974), pp. 82–108.

The results are quite different for income and prices, and for prices, for the United States and the United Kingdom. For income, the combined money stock uniformly gives higher standard errors and lower correlations than own-country money; for prices, on the other hand, the combined money stock gives lower standard errors and higher correlations than own-country money for the United States, but higher standard errors and lower correlations for the United Kingdom. There is clearly something here requiring further exploration: Why should the United Kingdom money stock affect United States prices but not the other way around? And why should there be a greater effect on prices than on income?

7.4.2 Own-Country Money, Other-Country Money, and Other-Country Velocity

As a first step, instead of combining the two money stocks, we have included them as separate variables in multiple regressions. In the United States regressions, the United Kingdom money stock is converted to dollars; in the United Kingdom regressions, the United States money stock is converted to pounds. These results (columns 4 and 5, 11, and 15 in table 7.4) largely confirm those from combined money. For three out of the four income regressions, the standard error of the multiple regression is larger than for the simple regression with own-country money. The exception is for the United Kingdom level of income, for which United States money has a significant positive coefficient. For prices, the two United States equations again show a significant effect of United Kingdom money on United States prices. The two for Britain give a slightly mixed picture—the rate-of-change equation again showing no significant effect and the level equation showing an effect on the borderline of significance but in a negative direction; that is, a rise in United States money tends to lower United Kingdom prices for a given stock of United Kingdom money.

So far we have been considering only the effects operating through money stock. However, as we have seen earlier, a unified monetary system may require divergent movements in the stock of money in the several countries composing the system in order to offset autonomous changes in the quantity of money demanded. The linkage between prices and income is more fundamental than that between money stocks and may operate in other ways than through changes in the quantity of money of the other country (for example, through the "law of one price"). One way to allow for these more subtle effects is to include velocity in the other country as an additional variable.[12]

---

12. Statistically, the inclusion of velocity is equivalent to including income in the other country. For example, consider (Continued on p. 324)

Table 7.4 Regressions of Level and Rate of Change of Income and Prices in the United States and the United Kingdom on Level and Rate of Change of Own-Country, Other-Country and Combined-Country Money[a] and Other-Country Velocity: United States Dates, Full Period

Dependent Variable (1)	Regression Coefficient (and Absolute t Value) of Simple Regression		Regression Coefficient (and Absolute t Value) of Multiple Regression on				
	Own-Country Money (2)	Combined Money (3)	Own-Country Money (4)	Other-Country Money (5)	Own-Country Money (6)	Other-Country Money (7)	Other-Country Velocity (8)
$\text{Log } Y_{us}$	0.94 (171)	1.04 (147)	0.96 (21)	-0.03 (0.04)	0.91 (21)	0.03 (0.45)	0.27 (3.3)
$\text{Log } Y_{uk}$	1.05 (92)	0.74 (87)	0.76 (7.1)	0.19 (2.7)	0.82 (8.9)	0.18 (3.1)	0.57 (4.2)
$g_{Y_{us}}$	0.92 (14)	0.94 (12)	0.85 (8.6)	0.09 (0.92)	0.96 (12)	0.14 (1.8)	0.61 (5.1)
$g_{Y_{uk}}$	0.80 (11)	0.63 (8.3)	0.78 (7.2)	0.03 (0.31)	0.81 (12)	-0.004 (0.06)	0.73 (8.3)
$\text{Log } P_{us}$	0.36 (28)	0.40 (31)	0.10 (1.0)	0.44 (2.7)	0.08 (0.75)	0.47 (2.7)	0.14 (0.69)
$\text{Log } P_{uk}$	0.63 (42)	0.44 (36)	0.91 (6.2)	-0.18 (1.9)	1.01 (9.1)	-0.19 (2.6)	0.98 (6.1)
$g_{P_{us}}$	0.68 (11)	0.76 (15)	0.33 (5.4)	0.46 (7.5)	0.39 (7.1)	0.48 (9.2)	0.32 (4.0)
$g_{P_{uk}}$	0.88 (13)	0.70 (10)	0.84 (8.4)	0.05 (0.53)	0.87 (13)	0.02 (0.30)	0.63 (6.9)

Table 7.4 (Continued)

Dependent Variable	Standard Error of Estimate				R^2			
	Simple Regression		Multiple Regression		Simple Regression		Multiple Regression	
	On Own-Country Money (9)	On Combined Money (10)	Money in Two Countries (11)	Money in Two Countries and Velocity in Other Country (12)	On Own-Country Money (13)	On Combined Money (14)	Money in Two Countries (15)	Money in Two Countries and Velocity in Other Country (16)
Log Y_{us}	.0572	.0662	.0577	.0523	.9986	.9981	.9986	.9988
Log Y_{uk}	.0888	.0935	.0833	.0707	.9949	.9943	.9956	.9969
$g_{Y_{us}}$	.0176	.0198	.0176	.0139	.8886	.8589	.8908	.9336
$g_{Y_{uk}}$	.0206	.0248	.0209	.0129	.7523	.6412	.7529	.9074
Log P_{us}	.1322	.1207	.1241	.1248	.9474	.9561	.9547	.9552
Log P_{uk}	.1171	.1370	.1138	.0845	.9757	.9668	.9776	.9879
$g_{P_{us}}$	.0166	.0137	.0110	.0094	.7920	.8696	.9117	.9367
$g_{P_{uk}}$	.0190	.0236	.0192	.0132	.8030	.6981	.8043	.9096

[a]Also on dummies to allow for demand shift and postwar readjustment. Other-country money is converted to the currency of own-country money.

The multiple regression including the other-country velocity systematically gives a lower, and mostly substantially lower, standard error than the simple regression on own-country money, and with one minor exception (log P_{us}), also than the multiple regression on own- and other-country money. The inclusion of velocity does not appreciably alter the calculated coefficient of other-country money, though in several cases, notably the effect of United States money on United Kingdom income, it does substantially increase the corresponding t value. Clearly, the inclusion of velocity allows for a largely independent set of effects.

With two exceptions, velocity accounts for a much larger fraction of the variation not accounted for by own-country plus other-country money than other-country money does of the variation not accounted for by own-country money alone.[13] With these two exceptions, money in the

---

(a) $\log Y_{us} = a + b \log M_{us} + c \log M_{uk} + d \log V_{uk}.$

Now

(b) $\log V_{uk} = \log Y_{uk} - \log M_{uk},$

so (a) can be rewritten:

(c) $\log Y_{us} = a + b \log M_{us} + (c-d) \log M_{uk} + d \log Y_{uk}.$

The coefficient d and its associated partial correlation coefficient measure the relation between that part of $\log Y_{uk}$ which is not correlated with $\log M_{us}$ and $\log M_{uk}$ and that part of $\log Y_{us}$ which is not correlated with $\log M_{us}$ and $\log M_{uk}$. They thus measure the additional connection between the two countries over and above the effect operating through the money supply.

13. Consider table 7.N.2, derived from the entries in columns 13, 15, and 16 of table 7.4.

Table 7.N.2   Explanatory Value of Other-Country Money and Velocity

	Percentage of Variation Not Explained by	
	Own-Country Money	Own-Country and Other-Country Money
	Explained by	
	Other-Country Money[a]	Velocity[b]
Y_{us}	0	14.3
Y_{uk}	13.7	30.0
$g_{Y_{us}}$	2.0	39.2
$g_{Y_{uk}}$	0.2	62.5
P_{us}	13.9	1.1
P_{uk}	7.8	46.0
$g_{P_{us}}$	57.5	28.3
$g_{P_{uk}}$	0.7	53.8

[a]100 times (Column 15 minus column 13)/(1 minus column 13).
[b]100 times (Column 16 minus column 15)/(1 minus column 15).

other country is clearly a less potent vehicle for the transmission of influences from one country to another than are the forces that are reflected in velocity. Indeed, for the most part, other-country money has no significant effect at all.

The two exceptions are the level of and rate of change of prices in the United States—the same two that have been idiosyncratic throughout. They raise the most intriguing question of interpretation.

For a fuller analysis of these results, it is desirable to allow for the possibility that wartime observations are distorting the results; and to distinguish between different exchange-rate regimes.[14] Under a fixed-exchange-rate regime, changes in one country affect another through actual or potential discrepancies between the countries in the prices of identical goods and in relative prices of traded and nontraded goods, which in turn alter trade flows and produce specie flows and capital movements. Under variable exchange rates, exchange rate changes replace specie flows wholly or in part, depending on whether the exchange rate floats freely or is partly controlled by central bank intervention. If exchange rates float freely, the own-country money stocks are insulated from one another, and one channel of influence is closed off. There remain the other two—other-country money converted into own-country currency, which will reflect changes in exchange rates as well as in the nominal quantity of money, and velocity. But it would not be surprising if the closing off of one channel affected the operation of the others.

14. An example of the usefulness of separating out periods with different exchange-rate regimes is an article by Terry C. Mills and Geoffrey E. Wood, "Money-Income Relationships and the Exchange-Rate Regime," *Federal Reserve Bank of Saint Louis Review* 60 (August 1978): 22–27.

For the rest, their analysis is not directly relevant to the problem of this chapter, since the money-income relationship they examine is within each country separately whereas our main concern is with the effect of monetary and other changes in one country on income in the other country.

They correctly point out, as we have, that in a fixed exchange rate regime the quantity of money in one country is endogenous and cannot be determined, except for brief periods, by the monetary authorities. They use this insight to interpret statistical tests of "causality," arguing that the endogeneity of money means that "monetary policy cannot affect income, but rather income fluctuations produce accommodating monetary flows" (p. 24).

This statement, taken literally, is correct but, as written, highly misleading. Monetary policy cannot affect the quantity of money except temporarily; nonetheless, changes in the quantity of money, however produced, will affect income. Indeed, it is precisely because they do that a gold standard or other fixed exchange rate regime is self-adjusting. Similarly, while "income fluctuations [whether in the country in question or other countries to which it is linked] produce accommodating monetary flows," it is also true that monetary flows produce accommodating income fluctuations.

In short, the exchange rate regime does not affect the existence of a "causal" influence from money to income; it affects the forces determining the quantity of money and thereby whether the situation is one of a largely unidirectional influence from money to income or of simultaneous determination and interaction.

The fixed-exchange rate period includes 1879 to 1914 and 1925 to 1931. However, given the small number of phases in the period from 1925 to 1931, and the even smaller number of triplets of phases from which rates of change are calculated, there seems little loss, and a considerable gain in simplicity, in treating the whole period from 1914 on as corresponding to a variable-exchange-rate regime, and the pre-1914 period to a fixed-exchange-rate regime. Unfortunately, this confounds the effect of temporal change with the effect of exchange-rate regime, but history makes that inevitable, and the confounding would not be significantly reduced by including the six years from 1925 to 1931 with the thirty-six years before 1914.

Multiple regressions between the level and rate of change of income and prices, as dependent variables, and own-country money, other-country money, and velocity, as independent variables, are summarized in tables 7.5 and 7.6 for the whole period, peacetime phases, pre-1914 phases, post-1914 phases and post-1914 peacetime phases—in table 7.5 for income and in table 7.6 for prices.

Omitting the wartime phases does not have any major effect on the results. The division between the fixed-exchange-rate and variable-exchange-rate periods, on the other hand, has a major effect.

For the United States, neither other-country money nor other-country velocity has any significant influence on *income* for each period separately when own-country money is held constant. The only channel of influence appears to be own-country money.[15] The significant effect of other-country velocity for the period as a whole apparently is produced by the difference between the periods. That is true also for the *level of prices*—indeed for the pre-1914 period not even own-country money is significant. However, the situation is very different for *the rate of change of prices*: all three variables seem significant or close to significant for both the pre-1914 and the post-1914 periods, though decidedly more so for the later period.[16]

For the United Kingdom, the results for the gold standard period are the same as for the United States: only own-country money is significant

---

15. Note that this result is perfectly consistent, as we shall see, with prices in the United States being strongly affected by prices in the United Kingdom, provided that either the United States quantity of money reacts sufficiently rapidly to accommodate the price effect, or real output, rather than nominal income, absorbs the price effect, that is, moves in the opposite direction to prices, leaving nominal income unaffected.

16. Consider the *t* values for the pre–1914 and post–1914 periods:

	Own-Country Money	Other-Country Money	Other-Country Velocity
Pre–1914	5.9	2.6	1.9
Post–1914	4.7	7.3	3.0
Post–1914 peacetime	6.9	8.2	5.0

for income, none of the variables is significant for levels of prices; all are significant for rates of change of prices.

However, for the variable-exchange rate period, the results differ substantially. First, other-country money and other-country velocity have a significant influence on *income* for the whole post-1914 period and peacetime phases alike, with the exception only of rates of change of other country money.[17] Second, other-country money is not significant for *prices*, judged by either levels or rates of change; other-country velocity is significant for levels but not for rates of change for peacetime phases.[18]

Some of the puzzles raised for the period as a whole stand out in even sharper form for subperiods. (1) For the gold standard period, why should other-country money and velocity influence the rate of change of prices in both the United States and the United Kingdom but not the rate of change of nominal income? (2) For the variable-exchange-rate period, why the differences between the United States and the United Kingdom? (Both the level of and rate of change of nominal income in the United Kingdom but not in the United States are affected by other-country money and velocity. The rate of change of prices in the United States but not in the United Kingdom is affected by other-country money and velocity.)

Gold-Standard Period: Income versus Prices

The explanation for a significant effect of other-country variables on rates of change of prices but not of incomes seems straightforward. For each country separately, a relatively stable demand function for money with a close to unity real income elasticity means that the nominal quantity of money (or rate of change) and nominal income (or rate of change) must be consistent with one another, and each country is large enough so that its own money stock is a better proxy for the relevant monetary magnitude than any broader total including other countries—the interpretation we gave earlier for the corresponding income results for the period as a whole.

17. Consider these *t* values:

	Own-Country Money		Other-Country Money		Other-Country Velocity	
	Levels	Rates of Change	Levels	Rates of Change	Levels	Rates of Change
Post–1914	4.2	9.0	2.4	0.24	3.3	9.2
Post–1914 peacetime	6.5	6.8	3.1	1.5	1.5	2.4

18. Consider these *t* values:

	Own-Country Money		Other-Country Money		Other-Country Velocity	
	Levels	Rates of Change	Levels	Rates of Change	Levels	Rates of Change
Post–1914	6.3	8.9	0.24	0.61	6.5	6.2
Post–1914 peacetime	7.3	6.4	0.90	1.11	6.1	1.3

Table 7.5 Regressions of Level and Rate of Change of Income in the United States and the United Kingdom on Level and Rate of Change of Own-Country Money, Other-Country Money, and Other-Country Velocity:[a] United States Dates, Various Periods

Dependent Variable and Period	Constant	Regression Coefficient (and Absolute t Value)			Standard Error of Estimate	R^2
		Own-Country Money	Other-Country Money	Other-Country Velocity		
Log Y_{us} Whole Period	1.20	0.91	0.032	0.27	.0523	.9988
	(5.0)	(21)	(0.45)	(3.3)		
Peacetime	1.29	0.92	0.008	0.27	.0525	.9990
	(5.3)	(21)	(0.11)	(3.0)		
Pre–1914	2.13	0.93	−0.098	0.11	.0565	.9862
	(2.5)	(11)	(0.58)	(0.20)		
Post–1914	1.25	0.94	−0.012	0.23	.0500	.9979
	(3.7)	(16)	(0.13)	(2.1)		
Post–1914 peacetime	1.13	1.01	−0.063	0.04	.0460	.9984
	(2.9)	(16)	(0.69)	(0.22)		
Log Y_{uk} Whole period	0.00	0.82	0.182	0.57	.0707	.9969
	(0.00)	(8.9)	(3.1)	(4.2)		
Peacetime	0.01	0.88	0.138	0.44	.0658	.9977
	(0.04)	(10)	(2.4)	(3.1)		
Pre–1914	0.50	0.93	0.073	0.02	.0247	.9914
	(1.4)	(12)	(2.0)	(0.16)		
Post–1914	−0.22	0.73	0.267	0.66	.0840	.9934
	(0.44)	(4.2)	(2.4)	(3.3)		
Post–1914 peacetime	−0.65	0.82	0.252	0.26	.0572	.9974
	(1.7)	(6.5)	(3.1)	(1.5)		

$g_{Y_{us}}$	Whole period	−0.01 (2.0)	0.96 (12)	0.140 (1.8)	0.61 (5.1)	.0139	.9336
	Peacetime	−0.01 (1.6)	1.00 (11)	0.056 (0.70)	0.23 (1.6)	.0128	.9251
	Pre–1914	0.00 (0.19)	0.94 (5.1)	−0.13 (0.40)	0.27 (0.67)	.0165	.6466
	Post–1914	−0.01 (2.3)	0.95 (10)	0.205 (2.1)	0.68 (5.4)	.0128	.9619
	Post–1914 peacetime	−0.01 (1.6)	1.04 (11)	0.042 (0.48)	0.21 (1.4)	.0094	.9792
$g_{Y_{uk}}$	Whole period	0.01 (3.5)	0.81 (12)	−0.004 (0.06)	0.73 (8.3)	.0129	.9074
	Peacetime	0.00 (0.74)	0.86 (11)	0.136 (1.7)	0.40 (2.7)	.0130	.8703
	Pre–1914	0.00 (0.14)	1.05 (5.0)	0.051 (0.44)	0.11 (0.67)	.0104	.6262
	Post–1914	0.02 (4.0)	0.75 (9.0)	0.016 (0.24)	0.86 (9.2)	.0116	.9356
	Post–1914 peacetime	0.01 (2.0)	0.72 (6.8)	0.192 (1.5)	0.60 (2.4)	.0131	.9240

[a] Also demand shift and postwar readjustment dummies.

Table 7.6   Regressions of Level and Rate of Change of Prices in the United States and the United Kingdom on Level and Rate of Change of Own-Country Money, Other-Country Money, and Other-Country Velocity:[a] United States Dates, Various Periods

Dependent Variable and Period	Constant	Regression Coefficient (and Absolute t Value)			Standard Error of Estimate	R^2
		Own-Country Money	Other-Country Money	Other-Country Velocity		
Log P_{us} Whole period	-5.25 (9.2)	0.08 (0.75)	0.47 (2.7)	0.14 (0.69)	.1248	.9552
Peacetime	-5.27 (8.7)	0.07 (0.64)	0.47 (2.6)	0.21 (0.95)	.1299	.9583
Pre-1914	-0.43 (0.28)	0.10 (0.63)	-0.17 (0.54)	0.59 (0.57)	.1048	.1046
Post-1914	-4.43 (8.2)	0.33 (3.5)	0.10 (0.67)	-0.10 (0.58)	.0808	.9693
Post-1914 peacetime	-4.81 (8.2)	0.41 (4.4)	0.06 (0.46)	-0.34 (1.3)	.0704	.9795
Log P_{uk} Whole period	-6.77 (21)	1.01 (9.1)	-0.19 (2.7)	0.98 (6.1)	.0845	.9879
Peacetime	-6.80 (19)	1.04 (8.9)	-0.21 (2.8)	0.94 (5.0)	.0871	.9890
Pre-1914	-1.51 (2.0)	0.08 (0.49)	0.01 (0.17)	0.31 (1.4)	.0510	.1360
Post-1914	-6.15 (18)	0.74 (6.3)	-0.02 (0.24)	0.86 (6.5)	.0568	.9922
Post-1914 peacetime	-6.00 (19)	0.78 (7.3)	-0.06 (0.90)	0.90 (6.1)	.0487	.9950

$g_{P_{us}}$	Whole period	−0.03 (9.4)	0.39 (7.1)	0.48 (9.2)	0.32 (4.0)	.0094	.9367
	Peacetime	−0.03 (11)	0.45 (8.4)	0.41 (8.4)	0.46 (5.1)	.0077	.9207
	Pre–1914	−0.04 (6.6)	0.61 (5.9)	0.49 (2.6)	0.42 (1.9)	.0092	.7722
	Post–1914	−0.02 (6.2)	0.32 (4.7)	0.53 (7.3)	0.27 (3.0)	.0093	.9526
	Post–1914 peacetime	−0.02 (9.3)	0.38 (6.9)	0.41 (8.2)	0.42 (5.0)	.0054	.9791
$g_{P_{uk}}$	Whole period	−0.01 (3.7)	0.87 (13)	0.02 (0.29)	0.63 (6.9)	.0132	.9096
	Peacetime	−0.02 (5.8)	0.81 (13)	0.20 (3.1)	0.24 (2.0)	.0105	.9021
	Pre–1914	−0.02 (10)	0.67 (8.1)	0.30 (6.7)	0.18 (2.9)	.0040	.8905
	Post–1914	−0.01 (2.2)	0.93 (8.9)	−0.05 (0.61)	0.73 (6.2)	.0147	.9114
	Post–1914 peacetime	−0.01 (2.2)	0.79 (6.4)	0.16 (1.1)	0.36 (1.3)	.0149	.8982

[a] Also demand shift and postwar readjustment dummies.

Prices, however, are a different matter. For internationally traded goods, there is a single world price level and, as we saw in table 7.2, the correlation between the rate of change of prices in the two countries is higher than for any other rate-of-change magnitude. For a given rate of growth of nominal income in the United States, an increased rate of growth of nominal income in the United Kingdom would tend, at least in part, to take the form of a higher rate of growth of prices, which in turn would be reflected in United States prices—and conversely.

On this interpretation, the effect of both other-country money and other-country velocity is through income; that is, for fixed other-country money, a rise in other-country velocity means a rise in other-country income; for fixed other-country velocity, a rise in other-country money also means a rise in other-country income. But if both other-country money and other country velocity are affecting prices only via other-country income, their coefficients should be equal.[19] That condition is close to being satisfied for the rate-of-change equations. The coefficients are .49 and .42 for the United States and .30 and .18 for the United Kingdom, and the differences are not statistically significant.

The numerical value of these coefficients suggests roughly twice as great an effect of an increase in the rate of change of United Kingdom income on United States prices as the rate of change of United States income on United Kingdom prices. Three factors presumably combine to produce this result: first, international trade was more important for the United Kingdom than for the United States; second, during the gold standard period, the United Kingdom was the major trading country of the world. Both factors would make United Kingdom prices more representative of international prices than United States prices. Third, as chapter 9 demonstrates, other things the same, a larger fraction of a change in nominal income tends to be reflected in prices rather than output for the United Kingdom than for the United States.

The absolute sizes of the coefficients are not unreasonable on this interpretation. For the United States, a one percentage point increase in the rate of change of its own money stock (which implies roughly a one percentage point increase in the rate of change of its income), tends to produce a percentage point increase of about 0.6 in the rate of change of its prices; a one percentage point increase in United Kingdom velocity (i.e., income) tends to produce a percentage point increase of about 0.4—about two-thirds as much; perhaps somewhat high but not unreasonable considering the United Kingdom role in the world at the time. For the United Kingdom, a one percentage point increase in the rate of change of its own money stock tends to produce a slightly larger percentage point increase in the rate of change of its prices—nearly 0.7 percent-

19. See note 12 above.

age points, while a one percentage point increase in the rate of change of United States velocity (i.e., income) tends to produce an increase of only about 0.2 percentage point.

One final point: why should these effects show up on rates of change and not on levels? Presumably the answer is statistical: the level figures are dominated by trends, and so these effects show up only in the more sensitive rate-of-change figures.

Variable-Exchange-Rate Period

Different effects on nominal income, United States and United Kingdom. As we noted earlier, it would not be surprising if the partial or total blocking of one channel of influence—via specie flows—enhanced the importance of other channels of influence. That clearly happened for the United Kingdom, as judged not only by the significance of other-country money and velocity, but also by the decided decline in the coefficient of own-country money—from 0.93 and 1.05 for pre-1914 levels and rates of change of income to 0.73 and 0.75 for post-1914 phases, and 0.82 and 0.72 for post-1914 peacetime phases.

The puzzle is why the same phenomenon did not occur for the United States: with one exception, for rates of change for the post-1914 period as a whole, neither other-country money nor other-country velocity is more than marginally significant; and, with no exceptions, the coefficients of own-country money are higher after 1914 than before. The obvious explanation is the changed role of the United States and the United Kingdom. Not only did the size of the United States economy continue to rise relative to that of the United Kingdom economy, but the United States replaced the United Kingdom after 1914 as the financial center of the world. If before 1914 the world could have been said to be on a sterling standard, after 1914 it could be said to be on a dollar standard. In addition, after World War II, the United Kingdom had extensive foreign exchange and other controls. Given the continued importance of foreign trade and foreign capital to the United Kingdom, these controls could not insulate the United Kingdom from foreign influences, but they could, and presumably did, limit any reciprocal effect of United Kingdom developments on the United States.

This explanation is far from satisfactory, because, while the changes outlined could certainly be expected to produce a greater effect of United States variables on the United Kingdom than of United Kingdom variables on the United States, it seems implausible that they would eliminate any reverse effect, as they apparently did at least during post-1914 peacetime phases. However, we have been unable to find any other answer to the puzzle.

Another issue raised by our results for the United Kingdom is the channels through which the changes in the United States affected the

United Kingdom. For the gold standard period and the effect on prices, we found that our two other-country variables—money and velocity— could have been replaced by a single variable, other-country income. This is not true for the post-1914 period for United Kingdom income.[20] The coefficient of United States velocity is consistently higher —generally much higher—than the coefficient of United States money.[21] Apparently, changes in United States money and United States velocity that have the same effect on United States income have a different effect on United Kingdom income.

One reason this might be true for the post-1914 period is that other-country money reflects changes in exchange rates, whereas other-country velocity does not. For the United Kingdom income regression, United States money in dollars is converted into pounds by multiplying by the market price of the dollar in terms of pounds. As a result, a rise, for example, in United States money in terms of pounds for given velocity may reflect simply a change in the exchange rate without a rise in United States dollar income. Such a change in the exchange rate would not affect United States velocity, which is the ratio of the dollar aggregates.

However, United States money is not serving simply as a proxy for the exchange rate: if the exchange rate is substituted for other-country money in multiple regressions for United Kingdom income for the post-1914 period like those in table 7.5, three of the four coefficients are not statistically significant (t values of 0.8, .05, 1.4) though the corresponding coefficient of other-country money is.[22] The exchange rate, if anything, apparently dilutes the influence of other-country money—a result to be expected, since one of the effects of a floating exchange rate is to partly insulate countries from monetary changes in other countries.

---

20. In equation (c) of note 12, if $c = d$, as it apparently does for the pre–1914 period, the penultimate term has a coefficient of zero and drops out, whereas if $c \neq d$, as is true after 1914, both final terms are relevant.

21. The coefficients are as follows:

	Coefficients of	
	United States Money	United States Velocity
Post–1914 Period		
Levels	.27	.66
Rates of change	.02	.86
Post–1914 peacetime		
Levels	.25	.26
Rates of change	.19	.60

22. The fourth coefficient of the exchange rate, for rate of change, post–1914 peacetime, gives a t value of 2.9 compared with 1.5 for other-country money. This one case is suggestive but inconclusive.

For corresponding regressions for the United States, the t values for the exchange rate range from 0.13 to 1.3, simply duplicating the finding for other-country money.

What about United States velocity? A rise in velocity in the United States for a given United States (dollar) stock of money[23] will produce or accompany a rise in nominal income and be produced by or accompany also a rise in interest rates. The rise in nominal income will tend to raise United States imports, lower United States exports, and thus shift the current balance toward a deficit. The deficit (or reduced surplus) can be financed (1) by a money flow (the classical specie-flow movement), which would affect the own-country money term in our equations; or (2) by an offsetting capital movement stimulated by the higher interest rates; or it could be eliminated by a change in exchange rates, which would affect the other-country money term in our equations. The absence of any significant influence of other-country velocity before 1914 presumably reflects the dominance of item 1 under a gold standard; the significant influence of United States velocity on United Kingdom income after 1914, reflects the closing off of item 1, and the effect of item 2. Given a common capital market, higher interest rates in the United States would mean higher interest rates in the United Kingdom, which would in turn raise United Kingdom velocity and nominal income for a given United Kingdom stock of money.

We can test this explanation by replacing velocity in our multiple regression by a short-term interest rate. The results are favorable to the explanation: the coefficients of the United States interest rate in the United Kingdom income regressions are uniformly positive, the *t* values are 1.6, 1.7, 3.1, and 1.9, either approaching or exceeding a significant level, and in three of the four comparisons are less than the *t* values for velocity itself. This final result is favorable because the short-term interest rate is only one of the set of rates that might be expected to be associated with changed velocity, so velocity itself might be expected to have a greater influence than any single interest rate. Finally, the implied effect of the United States interest rate on United Kingdom velocity is consistent with the findings of chapter 6.[24]

Presumably the coefficient of the United States money-stock term reflects a diluted version of the same effect—diluted both because of exchange rate changes and also because a rise in United States income accompanied by a rise in United States money with constant velocity would tend to be associated with less of a rise in interest rates than a rise in

23. Note that other-country money is in pounds in our U.K. regressions.
24. The ratio of the coefficient of the interest rate term to the coefficient of the velocity term is an estimate of the interest slope (i.e., the derivative of the logarithm of velocity with respect to the interest rate). This ratio is 3.2 and 4.9 for levels of the post–1914 period as a whole and the peacetime phases, respectively, and 5.7 and 4.8 for the rates of change. These are well within the range of the corresponding lower- and upper-limit estimates (with changed sign) in note 51 of chapter 6.

United States income accompanied by a rise in velocity with constant United States money.

Different effects on the rate of change of prices, United States and United Kingdom. United Kingdom variables might be expected to influence United States prices in the post-1914 period for the same reason as in the pre-1914 period—because changes in United Kingdom income partly mirror changes in the world price level.[25] As for the pre-1914 period, the level equations show no effect of other-country variables on prices, the rate-of-change equations do; and the coefficients of money and velocity are nearly identical for post-1914 peacetime phases (.41 and .42), though not for the post-1914 period as a whole, just as they were before 1914. The one important difference between pre- and post-1914 results is the decline in the own-country money coefficient from 0.61 to 0.38. Perhaps this reflects the greater role of the United States in the world economy.

The remaining puzzle is why the United Kingdom does not show the same effect of other-country variables on the rate of change of prices after 1914 as before. The answer apparently is because a major part of the difference in United Kingdom price movements is reflected in, or produced by, changes in the exchange rate, and the relevant equations allow for this effect only indirectly through the conversion of United States money into its equivalent in pounds. If the rate of change of the exchange rate is substituted for the rate of change of other-country money in the multiple regressions for the rate of price change in the United Kingdom, it has a significant effect (*t* values 3.2 and 4.5 for the post-1914 period as a whole and peacetime phases, respectively). Even more important, for given rate of exchange rate change, the rate of change of other-country velocity has a significant effect (*t* values of 5.9 and 5.1), and its coefficient is much higher than in the prewar period (.61 and .69 compared with .18). For given exchange rates, a one percentage point increase in the United Kingdom rate of change of money tends to raise United Kingdom prices by roughly 0.8 percentage points; a one percentage point rise in United States velocity tends to raise United Kingdom prices by 0.6 to 0.7 percentage points—indicating the much greater role of the United States relative to the United Kingdom in the post-1914 period than in the pre-1914 period.[26]

25. Note that the two United Kingdom variables largely eliminate price changes specific to the United Kingdom, the money variable because it is converted to dollars, the velocity variable because it is a ratio of two magnitudes in pounds.

26. The equations in question (omitting dummies) are as follows for the post–1914 period as a whole and peacetime phases, respectively:

7.5 Conclusion

The common movements of velocity in the United States and the United Kingdom reflect a unified financial system in which monetary variables—prices, interest rates, nominal incomes, stocks of money—are constrained to keep largely in step except as changes in exchange rates alter the number of units of one country's currency equivalent to one unit of the other country's currency. Within the unified financial system, there is much room for divergence of physical magnitudes—movements in real per capita output are least closely linked between the two countries; movements in prices, expressed in a common currency, are most closely linked. Influence ran both ways across the Atlantic, though there is some evidence that real effects were stronger from west to east and price effects from east to west. Moreover, the changing role of the United States and the United Kingdom in the world economy leaves a clear impress on our data.

During the gold standard period before 1914, the influence of each country on the other country's nominal income was manifested entirely through its influence on the other country's money—the classical specie-flow process. Each country was sufficiently large so that using the money stock for a larger area does not appreciably improve the correlation with income. That remains true for the United States after 1914, when variable exchange rates were the rule, but not for the United Kingdom, the nominal income of which was affected by changes in United States money and velocity. These changes apparently affected United Kingdom income by altering interest rates in the United States, which, given a common capital market, affected United Kingdom interest rates and thereby also United Kingdom velocity. Apparently, blocking the gold-standard channel of influence via specie flows diverted the influence of United States monetary changes into other channels. The difference in results for the United States and the United Kingdom is something of a puzzle, only partly explained by the far greater role of the United States in the post-1914 world than earlier.

$$g_{P_{uk}} = -0.01 + 0.83 g_{M_{uk}} - 0.09 g_{EX} + 0.61 g_{V_{us}}$$
$$(3.1) \quad (14.4) \quad \quad (3.2) \quad \quad (5.9)$$

$$SEE = .0123$$

$$R^2 = .9379$$

$$g_{P_{uk}} = -0.01 + 0.75 g_{M_{uk}} - 0.17 g_{EX} + 0.69 g_{V_{us}}$$
$$(1.4) \quad (10.6) \quad \quad (4.5) \quad \quad (5.1)$$

$$SEE = .0096$$

$$R^2 = .9577$$

where g_{EX} is the rate of change of the exchange rate.

For both the gold standard period and the later variable-exchange rate period, price changes in each country are affected by monetary changes in the other, not only through effects on own-country money but also more directly—though to isolate this effect for the United Kingdom after 1914 requires allowing explicitly for changes in exchange rates. This is the counterpart of the closer linkage of prices throughout the world than of physical magnitudes—an expression of the "law of one price."

The one world we have been exploring clearly extends beyond the geographical boundaries of the United States and the United Kingdom, and our results show reflections of this wider world especially in the changing relation between the influences running west to east and east to west. A fuller analysis of this wider world, though it is beyond our scope, would much improve our understanding of the bilateral relations to which we have restricted our own work.

7.6   Appendix: Regressions of Velocity Differences in the United States and United Kingdom on Differences in Specified Determinants

Table 7.7 presents the coefficients calculated from regressions of velocity differences in the United States and United Kingdom on differences in the specified determinants. The first two lines are based on phase data, the third on annual data. In interpreting the coefficient of the real per capita income variable, note that unity must be subtracted from the elasticity of velocity and the sign changed in order to obtain an estimate of the elasticity of real per capita money. For the other variables, the sign but not numerical size of the coefficients must be changed to obtain estimates of the corresponding coefficients for a real per capita money equation.

Table 7.8 compares the estimates of the effects of specified determinants from our earlier regressions based on data for the separate countries and the regressions in table 7.7. It is clear that, allowing for sampling error, the estimates are similar. Note that, as always, the regression effect makes these estimates lower limits of the indicated effect.[27] The upper limits are straightforward to compute for the variables other than the income elasticity, and as for the level equations (see table 6.15) are very much above the lower limits.

---

27. For the regressions based on velocity differences, note that

$$\log V_{uk} - \log V_{us} = (\log y_{uk} - \log y_{us}) - (\log m_{uk} - \log m_{us}).$$

Since the difference between the logs of real per capita income is included as an independent variable, the results in table 7.8 are identical with those that would have been observed from a regression in which the dependent variable was based on the difference between real per capita money balances in the two countries.

Table 7.7   Regression of Differences between Logarithms of United States and United Kingdom Velocities and Their Rates of Change

Dependent Variable	Period and Data	Coefficient and (Absolute t Value)						Standard Error of Estimate
		Constant Log Term	y or g_y	R_N or DR_N	g_Y or Dg_Y	S or S_g	W or W_g	
$\log V_{uk} - \log V_{us}$	Whole period Phase data	-0.03 (0.14)	-0.0005 (0.005)	19.8 (7.4)	1.22 (3.7)	-0.24 (5.2)	0.004 (0.38)	.0774
$g_{v_{uk}} - g_{v_{us}}$	Whole period Phase data	—[a]	0.19 (2.1)	12.5 (3.8)	0.031 (2.1)	-0.0025 (1.9)	-0.004 (0.46)	.0131
$g_{v_{uk}} - g_{v_{us}}$	1872–1975 Annual data	—[a]	0.33 (4.2)	4.4 (3.7)	0.31 (6.1)	-0.0058 (0.50)	0.0062 (0.34)	.0401

[a]Intercept forced to zero.

Table 7.8   Estimates of Effects of Specified Determinants: Comparison between Results from Regressions Based on Separate Country Data and Those Based on Differences between United States and United Kingdom

| | Level Equations | | Rate of Change Equations — Dependent Variables | | | |
| | | | g_m | | $g_{V_{uk}} - g_{V_{us}}$ | |
	$\log m$	$\log V_{uk} - \log V_{us}$	Constant Term	Zero Constant	Phase Data	Annual Data
Income elasticity, m or g_m						
United States	1.15 ⎫	1.00	0.88	1.09 ⎫	0.81	0.67
United Kingdom	0.88 ⎭		0.44	0.92 ⎭		
Slope, R_N or DR_N						
United States and United Kingdom	−9.3	−19.8	−8.5	−8.7	−12.5	−4.4
Slope, g_Y or Dg_Y						
United States and United Kingdom	−0.47	−1.22	−0.29	−0.41	−0.31	−0.31
Demand shift						
United States and United Kingdom	0.19	0.24	0.0031	0.0040	0.0025	0.0058
Postwar readjustment						
United States and United Kingdom	0.019	−0.004	0.0308	0.0299	0.0040	−0.0062
Standard error of estimate	.0532	.0774	.0137	.0142	.0131	.0401
Estimated standard error of estimate for one country's level or rate of change	.0532	.0547	.0137	.0142	.0093	.0284

The final line of table 7.8 requires some explanation. The standard errors for the velocity equations in the penultimate line are for a difference between the two countries. If the errors of estimate are independent for the two countries but have the same variance for each—as we found in chapter 6, they do for the United States and the United Kingdom—then the standard error of the difference is $1/\sqrt{2}$ times the standard error for a single country. The entries for the velocity equations in the final line are therefore $1/\sqrt{2}$ times the entry in the penultimate line.

The differential velocity equations implicitly allow not only for the specified determinants allowed for by the money equation, but also for other unspecified determinants of velocity that tend to have common movements in the two countries. That might be expected to produce a smaller standard error. It does for the rate of change equations but not for the level equations—presumably because, as table 7.3 indicates, these common movements in unspecified determinants are far more important for short-term fluctuations than for longer-term ones (they account for only 3 percent of the hypothetical variance for levels, but for 37 percent for rates of change).

The higher standard error from the annual data than from the phase data reflects partly simply the longer interval to which the phase standard error refers—four years on the average for the United States, five and one-half for the United Kingdom. However, if this were the only effect, the standard error for the annual data would be between $\sqrt{4}$ and $\sqrt{5.5}$ times the standard error for the United Kingdom, or at most .0218 on the final line ($.0093 \sqrt{5.5}$). It is higher than that presumably because our phase data eliminate a systematic cyclical effect in addition to averaging out serially independent errors.

8   Monetary Influences on Nominal Income

Chapter 6 explores the hypothesis that the real quantity of money demanded can be regarded as a relatively stable function of a small number of variables. It isolated as the key variables entering into the demand function the degree of financial sophistication, real per capita income, the return on nominal-value assets, the return on physical assets, and two episodic sets of events handled by dummy variables—postwar readjustment and an upward shift in demand. A single function of these variables describes reasonably well the demand for real balances for the whole century our data cover and for both the United States and the United Kingdom, the one significant difference between the two countries being with respect to the income elasticity of demand for real balances. Chapter 7 explores the relations between the United States and the United Kingdom, documenting their roles as part of a unified monetary system. The major channel of influence during the gold standard system that prevailed before 1914 was through the stocks of money in each country. After 1914, when variable exchange rates came to prevail, this channel of influence was supplemented by others operating through exchange rates, interest rates, and perhaps other variables. These chapters give empirical content to "the generalization that changes in desired real balances (in the demand for money) tend to proceed slowly and gradually or to be the result of events set in train by prior changes in supply" (sec. 2.1).

Given a stable demand function and a variable nominal quantity of money, there remains for investigation the way in which changes in the nominal quantity of money work their way through the relatively stable demand function to alter nominal income, prices, interest rates, and output—how, in short, demand and supply interact, the theoretical issue with which much of chapter 2 deals.

For a hypothetical simple quantity theory world in which velocity is a numerical constant, prices are completely flexible, and reactions are instantaneous, the analysis of the interaction of supply and demand is trivial. Prices mirror instantly and perfectly the changes in the quantity of money. Output and the real yield on capital are unaffected, determined by other variables. Yet even in this hypothetical case, the effect of changes in the quantity of money on nominal interest rates depends on anticipated rates of price change and cannot be described without specifying how anticipations are formed.

Alter this hypothetical case in almost any respect and the analysis becomes far from trivial. For example, make velocity a function of nominal interest rates and let interest rates be connected with anticipated rates of price change, and the purely theoretical analysis becomes extremely complex—indeed, there is currently no satisfactory accepted theoretical analysis of this case, though with other specifications intact, output and real interest rates would still be unaffected by monetary changes.[1] Introduce lags in reaction, which is to say price or other rigidities, and output and real interest rates enter into the reaction process.

In principle, all the variables are simultaneously determined, and the effect of a monetary change on any one—say, nominal income—is linked to the way it affects the others—say, prices, output, and interest rates. However, to reduce the empirical problem to manageable scope, we propose to start with a simplified monetary theory of nominal income, which separates the effect of monetary change on nominal income from the effect on prices and output separately, and which treats interest rate changes as themselves traceable to earlier monetary change.[2] In chapter 9, we shall then investigate explicitly the division of changes in nominal income between prices and output, and, in chapter 10, the relation between monetary changes and interest rates.

We rely on the simplified model with some hesitancy, since it was designed to interpret short-term movements, and it is not clear therefore that it is appropriate for our phase-average data. However, that is one of the questions we shall explore.

1. See Fischer Black, "Active and Passive Monetary Policy in a Neo-classical Model," *Journal of Finance* 27 (September 1972): 801–4; Thomas Sargent and Neil Wallace, "The Stability of Models of Money and Growth with Perfect Foresight," *Econometrica* 41 (November 1973): 1043–48; idem, "Rational Expectations and the Dynamics of Hyperinflation," *International Economic Review* 14 (June 1973): 328–50; Thomas Sargent, "The Demand for Money during Hyperinflations under Rational Expectations: I," *International Economic Review* 18 (February 1977): 59–82; B. M. Friedman, "Stability and Rationality in Models of Hyperinflation," *International Economic Review* 19 (February 1978): 45–64; W. A. Brock, "Money and Growth: The Case of Long-Run Perfect Foresight," *International Economic Review* 14 (October 1974): 750–77.

2. See M. Friedman, "A Theoretical Framework," in *Milton Friedman's Monetary Framework*, ed. Gordon, pp. 34–43.

8.1   From the Demand for Balances to the Behavior of Nominal Income

To show how the demand function for real balances can be converted into a relation between nominal income and nominal money supply, let us start with the demand equations at the end of chapter 6 for the United States and the United Kingdom combined and for the full period.

(1) $$\log m = -1.47 + 1.64Z + (1.14 - 0.25Z)\log y \\ -9.3R_N - 0.47g_Y + 0.019W + 0.193S,$$

(2) $$g_m = (1.03 - 0.04Z)g_y - 8.7DR_N \\ -0.41Dg_Y + 0.030W_g + 0.004S_g.$$

Subtract $\log y$ from both sides of equation (1) and then reverse signs. Since $\log V = \log y - \log m$ (recall that y is per capita real income, m per capita real balances), we have

(3) $$\log V = 1.47 - 1.64Z - (0.14 - 0.25Z)\log y \\ + 9.3R_N + 0.47g_Y - 0.019W - 0.193S.$$

Replace $\log V$ by its equivalent expression, $\log Y - \log M$, and transfer $\log M$ to the right-hand side. This gives

(4) $$\log Y = 1.47 - 1.64Z + \log M - (0.14 - 0.25Z)\log y \\ + 9.3R_N + 0.47g_Y - 0.019W - 0.193S.$$

This expression now gives the level of nominal income consistent, for various values of other variables, with equality between actual and desired quantity of money if the desired level is determined by the demand equation defined by equation (1).

Similarly, subtract g_y from both sides of equation (2), reverse signs, replace g_V by $g_Y - g_M$, and we have

(5) $$g_Y = g_M - (0.03 - 0.04Z)g_y + 8.7DR_N + 0.41Dg_Y \\ - 0.030W_g - 0.004S_g.$$

This expression gives the rates of change of nominal income consistent, for various other variables, with equality between the actual and desired rate of change of money if the desired rate of change is determined by the demand equation defined by equation (2).

Of course, if we were dealing with exact relationships observed without error and properly specified, equation (5) would be the time derivative of equation (4), and the coefficients of corresponding variables would be equal. In fact, we concluded in chapter 6 that the differences were not statistically significant. In both equation (1) and equation (2), the coefficients are lower limits (in absolute value) because of the regression effect, which is more important in equation (2) dealing with rates of change than in equation (1) dealing with levels. This explains why all coefficients (other than that for W_g) are lower (in absolute value) in equation (2) than in equation (1). In addition, of course, the lower limits in both equations are themselves subject to statistical errors of measurement, and the coefficients of $\log y$ in equation (1) and of g_y in equation (2) are biased toward unity by errors of measurement of population and prices.

Equations (4) and (5) are still not in the form corresponding to the monetary theory of nominal income because they include real per capita income. The deviance is small, however, since the coefficients of the real per capita income variable are close to zero (-0.14 and -0.03 for the United States; $+0.11$ and $+0.01$ for the United Kingdom). It looks as if this variable can be omitted with little loss, though this conclusion must be qualified somewhat because of the statistical bias toward zero of these coefficients.

Rather than proceed further with these transformed demand equations, we can estimate directly general equations of the form of equations (4) and (5), say,

$$(6) \qquad \log Y = -\log k - \lambda_3 Z + \zeta \log M + (1 - \alpha - \lambda_4 Z) \log y \\ - \delta R_N - \epsilon g_Y - \lambda_1 W - \lambda_2 S \,,$$

$$(7) \qquad g_Y = \zeta g_M + (1 - \alpha - \lambda_4 Z) g_y - \delta DR_N - \epsilon Dg_Y \\ - \lambda_1' W_g - \lambda_2' S_g \,,$$

where $\log k$ is the constant term of demand equation (1) for the United States, λ_3 is the excess of the constant term for the United Kingdom over that for the United States, ζ is the elasticity of nominal income with respect to nominal money for given values of the other variables, α is the real per capita income elasticity of the demand for money in the United States, λ_4 is the excess of United Kingdom income elasticity over United States income elasticity, δ and ϵ are the semilogarithmic slopes of the demand for money with respect to the differential yield on nominal assets and the proxy yield on physical assets, respectively, λ_1 and λ_1' are the coefficients of the postwar adjustment dummy for levels and rates of change, respectively, and λ_2 and λ_2' of the upward demand shift dummy.

Equations (6) and (7) are special cases of equation (15) of chapter 2, equation (6) for $\phi = \infty$, which assures that M^S, or money supplied, always equals M^D, or money demanded; equation (7) for $\psi = \infty$, which assures that g_{M^D} always equals g_{M^S}.

If equations (1) and (2) were exact relations observed without error and properly specified, direct estimates of equations (6) and (7) would be identical with equations (4) and (5). In practice they will not be, for three reasons: (*a*) The coefficients of $\log M$ and g_M are free to take any value in equations (6) and (7), not restricted to unity, as they are in equations (4) and (5). (*b*) The changed dependent variable alters the bias resulting from errors of measurement. In equations (1) and (2), errors of measurement in population and prices bias the coefficients of log y and of g_y in equations (4) and (5) toward zero. In equations (6) and (7) , the errors in the measurement of Y and of population and prices introduce a very different bias. They bias $(1-\alpha)$ in these equations upward toward a positive number less than or equal to unity rather than toward zero.[3] In

3. Recall that

(a) $$\log Y = \log y + \log NP$$

or, as actually computed,

(b) $$\log y = \log Y - \log NP.$$

Using the notation of note 18 of chapter 6,

(c) $$\log Y = (\log Y)^* + e_Y = (\log y)^* + (\log NP)^* + e_Y$$

(d) $$\log NP = (\log NP)^* + e_{NP}$$

(e) $$\log y = (\log y)^* + e_y = (\log y)^* + e_Y - e_{NP}.$$

Assume as in that footnote that e_Y and e_{NP} are independent of the asterisked values and of one another and that all variables are expressed as deviations from their means.

Consider now estimates of $(1-\alpha)$ in equation (6), for a fixed value of M^*, and neglecting the other variables. The estimate of $(1-\alpha)$ from the regression of log Y on log y is

(f)
$$
\begin{aligned}
(1-\alpha)_{Yy} &= \frac{E \log Y \log y}{\sigma^2_{(\log y)}} \\[6pt]
&= \frac{E[(\log Y)^* + e_Y] [(\log y)^* + e_Y - e_{NP}]}{\sigma^2_{(\log y)^*} + \sigma^2_{e_Y} + \sigma^2_{e_{NP}}} \\[6pt]
&= \frac{E(\log Y)^*(\log y)^* + \sigma^2_{e_Y}}{\sigma^2_{(\log y)^*} + \sigma^2_{e_Y} + \sigma^2_{e_{NP}}}.
\end{aligned}
$$

From the basic demand equation we have that

(g) $$\log k + \alpha^* (\log y)^* + (\log NP)^* = (\log M)^*,$$

where α^* is the "true" value of α.

But the fixed value of $(\log M)^*$ is zero, given that we are dealing with deviations from means, so that

(h) $$(\log k) + (\alpha^* - 1) (\log y)^* + (\log Y)^* = 0$$

Multiply through by $(\log y)^*$ and take expected values. The result is

(i) $$E (\log Y)^*(\log y)^* = (1-\alpha^*) \sigma^2_{(\log y)^*}.$$

Substitute in (f) and we have

(j)
$$
\begin{aligned}
(1-\alpha)_{Yy} &= \frac{(1-\alpha^*) \sigma^2_{(\log y)^*} + \sigma^2_{e_Y}}{\sigma^2_{(\log y)^*} + \sigma^2_{e_Y} + \sigma^2_{e_{NP}}} \\[10pt]
&= \frac{(1-\alpha^*) \sigma^2_{(\log y)^*} + \left(\sigma^2_{e_Y} + \sigma^2_{e_{NP}}\right) \left(\dfrac{\sigma^2_{e_Y}}{\sigma^2_{e_Y} + \sigma^2_{e_{NP}}}\right)}{\sigma^2_{(\log y)^*} + \sigma^2_{e_Y} + \sigma^2_{e_{NP}}}
\end{aligned}
$$

or a weighted average of $(1-\alpha^*)$ and $\dfrac{\sigma^2_{e_Y}}{\sigma^2_{e_Y} + \sigma^2_{e_{NP}}}$.

For an income elasticity of unity or above, the average is necessarily greater than $(1-\alpha)^*$, so

terms of α, the income elasticity, the bias is downward, whereas in equations (4) and (5) it is toward unity. (c) In equation (6) for the United States and the United Kingdom combined, a single dummy variable will no longer suffice to allow fully for the difference between pounds and dollars. One dummy served in equation (1), despite the changes in the market exchange rate during the period the equation covers, because both real balances and real income are expressed in terms of 1929 prices, hence only the 1929 exchange rate is relevant. In equation (6), $\log Y$ and $\log M$ are in current prices. For $\zeta = 1$, this raises no problem because only the difference between $\log Y$ and $\log M$ (i.e., the logarithm of Y/M) is relevant, and this difference is not affected by the exchange rate. So this item is linked to item 1. For $\zeta \neq 1$, a real problem arises. We have dealt with it by converting the United Kingdom values of Y and M to dollars at the ruling exchange rate, and of y to dollars at the 1929 exchange rate. The coefficient of the dummy variable Z can then be regarded as reflecting any difference in the level of the demand function plus a constant percentage difference between the market exchange rate and the exchange rate that is relevant in comparing the services rendered by cash balances. In this way, for the United States and the United Kingdom combined, the form of the equation is given by equation (6) but the variables $\log Y$, $\log M$, and $\log y$ have a different meaning for the United Kingdom than they do in equation (4), or than they do in equation (6) estimated for the United Kingdom alone.[4]

---

the bias is definitely upward. For an income elasticity of less than unity, the same result is possible but not necessary unless $\sigma^2_{e_{NP}} = 0$. Since α^* according to our empirical results is higher than unity for the United States and not much below unity for the United Kingdom, there is a presumption that the bias is definitely upward.

For the regression of y on Y, the result is unambiguously an upward bias. That estimate is

(k)
$$(1-\alpha)_{yY} = \frac{\sigma^2 \log Y}{E \log_Y \log y} = \frac{\sigma^2 (\log Y)^* + \sigma^2_{e_Y}}{E(\log Y) * (\log y)^* + \sigma^2_{e_Y}}.$$

Multiplying equation (h) through by $(\log Y)^*$ and taking expectations, we have

(l)
$$\sigma^2_{(\log Y)^*} = (1-\alpha^*) E (\log Y) * (\log y)^*.$$

Substituting in equation (k) gives

(m)
$$(1-\alpha)_{yY} = \frac{(1-\alpha^*)E(\log Y) * (\log y)^* + \sigma^2_{e_Y}}{E (\log Y) * (\log y)^* + \sigma^2_{e_Y}},$$

or a weighted average of $(1-\alpha)^*$ and 1, which is necessarily greater than $(1-\alpha)^*$ for any positive income elasticity.

4. A simpler procedure would be to use the United Kingdom figures converted into dollars for both the United Kingdom alone and the United States and United Kingdom combined. We have not done so because that introduces a thoroughly extraneous element into the data for the United Kingdom alone. These data were generated in pounds not dollars; the holders of pounds received them as pounds, not as dollar equivalents. If the

The direct estimates are given in table 8.1 for equations (6) and (7).[5] Because of the bias in the coefficients of log y and g_y, and because of our interest in omitting these variables to correspond with the monetary theory of nominal income, we also estimated equations without these terms:

(6a)
$$\log Y = -\log k - \lambda_3 Z + \zeta \log M - \delta R_N \\ - \epsilon g_Y - \lambda_1 W - \lambda_2 S ,$$

(7a)
$$g_Y = \zeta g_M - \delta D(R_N) - \epsilon D g_Y - \lambda_1' W_g - \lambda_2' S_g .$$

For the two countries combined, the indirect and direct estimates compare as follows for levels:

(4)
$$\log Y = 1.47 - 1.64Z + \log M - (0.14 - 0.25Z)\log y \\ + 9.3R_N + 0.47g_Y - 0.019W - 0.193S,$$

(6)
$$\log Y = -0.39 - 0.92Z + 0.83 \log M \\ + (0.42 + 0.13Z) \log y + 11.4R_N + 0.16g_Y \\ - 0.020W - 0.11S,$$

(6a)
$$\log Y = 0.76 - 0.08Z + 0.97\log M + 15.1R_N \\ + 0.71g_Y - 0.014W - 0.15S,$$

and as follows for rates of change:

(5)
$$g_Y = g_M - (0.03 - 0.04Z)g_y + 8.7 DR_N + 0.41 Dg_Y \\ - 0.030 W_g - 0.004 S_g ,$$

(7)
$$g_Y = 0.77g_M + (0.46 + 0.02Z)g_y + 14.0 DR_N \\ + 0.28 Dg_Y - 0.020 W_g - 0.003 S_g ,$$

(7a)
$$g_Y = 0.87g_M + 10.5 DR_N + 0.53 Dg_Y \\ - 0.027 W_g - 0.004 S_g.$$

The most striking difference between the direct and indirect estimates is in the coefficient of the real income term, which, for the level equations, changes from -0.14 to $+0.42$ for the United States and from $+0.11$ to $+0.55$ for the United Kingdom and, for the rate-of-change equations, from -0.03 to $+0.46$ for the United States and from $+0.01$ to $+0.48$ for the United Kingdom. It is difficult to interpret these coef-

exchange rate had remained the same throughout, it would make no difference which procedure was used. However, with a variable exchange rate, it does make a difference.

One other parenthetical point. It may seem as if there should be a fourth effect, namely, a difference in the regression effect. However, this is not so. The direction of minimization of the sums of squares is the same since log y or g_y remains the independent variable.

5. We also made parallel calculations for equation (7) modified by adding a constant term. The constant term was statistically insignificant for each country separately, and at the margin of significance at a .05 level for the combined equation; it affected only slightly the standard error of estimate or the other coefficients. Hence, we do not present these calculations.

Table 8.1 Regressions of Nominal Income on Nominal Quantity of Money and Other Variables

Country	Equation[a]	Intercept	Log M or g_M	Log y or g_y	R_N or DR_N	g_Y or Dg_Y	S or S_g	W or W_g	Standard Error of Estimate	R^2
					Levels					
United States	(6)	−0.24	0.83	0.40	8.60	0.24	−0.14	−0.024	.0369	.9994
	(6a)	1.10	0.95		7.99	0.51	−0.17	−0.024	.0445	.9991
United Kingdom	(6)	−1.02	0.84	0.60	18.80	−0.08	−0.10	−0.009	.0394	.9990
	(6a)	0.38	1.01		14.17	0.53	−0.19	−0.011	.0599	.9977
United States and United Kingdom[b]	(6)	U.S. U.K. −0.39 −1.31	0.83	U.S. U.K. 0.42 0.55	11.45	0.16	−0.11	−0.020	.0389	.9992
	(6a)	0.76 0.68	0.97		15.11	0.71	−0.15	−0.014	.0602	.9981
					Rates of Change					
United States	(7)		0.74	0.49	12.51	0.29	−0.003	−0.025	.0108	.9804
	(7a)		0.88		10.29	0.58	−0.005	−0.031	.0131	.9704
United Kingdom	(7)		0.78	0.49	15.54	0.22	−0.002	−0.017	.0103	.9660
	(7a)		0.86		12.43	0.41	−0.003	−0.026	.0118	.9534
United States and United Kingdom[b]	(7)		0.77	U.S. U.K. 0.46 0.48	14.03	0.28	−0.003	−0.020	.0102	.9732
	(7a)		0.87		10.54	0.53	−0.004	−0.027	.0121	.9616

[a]For definition of equations, see text.

[b]The intercept for the United Kingdom is computed by adding the coefficient of Z to the regression intercept shown for the United States. Similarly, the entry for United Kingdom for the coefficient of log y or g_y is the regression coefficient shown for the United States plus the coefficient of Z log y.

ficients from equations (6) and (7) as reflecting an economic phenomenon. If they did, they would imply an income elasticity of demand for real balances of 0.58 or 0.54 for the United States and of 0.45 or 0.52 for the United Kingdom; yet our earlier evidence has led us to conclude that the income elasticity exceeds unity for the United States and is only a little less than unity for the United Kingdom.[6] A more likely explanation is the bias in these coefficients arising from the measurement errors common to Y and y. As noted, these errors bias the coefficients in equations (6) and (7) upward, whereas the errors in population and prices bias the corresponding coefficients of equations (4) and (5) toward zero.

The equations without the real income terms are consistent with this explanation. With only three exceptions out of sixteen comparisons (the coefficients of Z, R_N, and W), the coefficients of equations (6a) and (7a) for the two countries combined are closer to the coefficients of equations (4) and (5) than the corresponding coefficients of equations (6) and (7).[7] That is also the case for the equations for the separate countries, with only three exceptions out of twenty-six comparisons. In addition, the standard errors of estimate for equations (6) and (7) are uniformly lower than for equations (6a) and (7a). While this might be the effect of either common measurement errors or an economically meaningful influence of real per capita income on nominal income for given money stock and other variables, the economically implausible values of the coefficients argue in favor of common measurement errors.

On that interpretation, we can use the standard errors of estimate to construct estimates of the size of the common measurement errors. These turn out to range from 2.5 to 4.6 percent for the levels of nominal income; from 0.5 to 0.75 of a percentage point for the rate of change of nominal income.[8] These values are certainly not implausible as estimates of pure measurement error.

6. Note that the regression bias cannot explain the conflict with earlier evidence. The corresponding coefficients computed from regressions of log y (g_y) on log Y (g_Y) are higher, implying even lower estimates of elasticity than those cited in the text, and hence an even greater conflict with earlier evidence.

7. Note that this includes comparing the imposed values of zero for the coefficients of log y and g_y in equations (6a) and (7a) with the computed coefficients in equations (4) and (7), as well as the imposed value of unity for the coefficients of log M and g_M in equations (4) and (5) with the computed coefficients in the other equations.

8. Assume that measurement errors account for the difference between the standard errors of estimate of equations (6) and (6a), and of equations (7) and (7a), and that measurement errors can be treated as independent of the "true" values of the independent variables. It then follows that

$$\sigma_{e_Y} = \sqrt{[SEE\,(6a)]^2 - [SEE\,(6)]^2}$$

is an estimate of the standard deviation of the percentage measurement error in Y, where $SEE\,(\ )$ stands for the standard error of estimate of the equations in the parentheses, and

On the basis of this evidence, we shall proceed for most of this chapter to regard equations (6a) and (7a) as a valid representation of the relation between the nominal quantity of money and nominal income and shall treat the exclusion of real per capita income as a valid first approximation. We shall leave the division of the change in nominal income between prices and output for separate consideration in chapter 9.

How much better are equations (6a) and (7a) than simpler quantity theory relations that do not allow for the effect of asset yields as measured by R_N and g_Y? The final three columns of table 8.2 give one answer. Column 5 shows the standard deviation of log Y and the root mean square value of g_Y, which is to say, the coefficient of variation of nominal income itself and an estimate of the standard deviation of the rate of change of nominal income on the assumption that its mean value is zero. The next column shows the deviation that remains after allowing solely for log M or g_M (plus, for the United States, the changing degree of financial sophistication before 1903, and, for both countries, the postwar readjustment and upward demand shifts)—that is, standard errors of estimate from the equations

(8) $$\log Y = -\log k - \lambda_3 Z + \zeta \log M - \lambda_1 W - \lambda_2 S ,$$

(9) $$g_Y = \zeta g_M - \lambda' W_g - \lambda' S_g.$$

The final column shows the deviation that remains, after allowing also for the effect of asset yields, that is, the deviations from equations (6a) and (7a). Clearly, the simple quantity theory effect is far more important than the further refinement of allowing for changing yields, and this is true even for the rates of change, which largely eliminate the effects of common trends. But, equally clearly, the allowance for yields is important, always reducing the residual standard deviation appreciably—indeed, in some cases to not much above our estimate of pure measurement error.

One striking result in table 8.1 is that the coefficient of log M or g_M—the estimated elasticity of nominal income with respect to nominal money—is generally less than unity. Columns 1 to 4 of table 8.2 show that this result cannot be attributed to the regression effect. The upper limits are above unity only twice—for the United Kingdom level regressions for

---

$$\sigma_{e_{g_Y}} = \sqrt{[SEE\,(7a)]^2 - [SEE\,(7)]^2}$$

is an estimate of the standard deviation of the percentage point measurement error in g_Y. The values calculated this way are as follows:

	σ_{e_Y}	$\sigma_{e_{g_Y}}$
United States	.025	.0074
United Kingdom	.045	.0058
United States and United Kingdom	.046	.0065

Table 8.2   **Effect of Allowing for Asset Yields on Relation between Nominal Quantity of Money and Nominal Income**

Variable and Country	Elasticity of Nominal Income with Respect to Nominal Quantity of Money				Standard Deviation of Log Y[b] or Root Mean Square Value of g_Y[b] (5)	Standard Error of Estimate[b]	
	Equation (8) or (9)[a]		Equation (6a) or (7a)[a]			Equation (8) or (9) (6)	Equation (6a) or (7) (7)
	Lower Limit (1)	Upper Limit (2)	Lower Limit (3)	Upper Limit (4)			
Level of income (log Y)							
United States	0.935	0.937	0.950	0.951	141.37	5.72	4.45
United Kingdom	1.061	1.065	1.012	1.020	114.93	7.01	5.99
United States and United Kingdom	0.966	0.972	0.974	0.977	134.06	9.63	6.02
Rate of change of income (g_Y)							
United States	0.925	0.986	0.884	0.921	7.20	1.74	1.31
United Kingdom	0.908	0.985	0.858	0.918	5.08	1.40	1.18
United States and United Kingdom	0.918	0.987	0.873	0.922	5.97	1.51	1.21

Note: For definition of equations, see text.

[a]Lower limit is value of coefficient of log M or g_M in relevant regressions; upper limit is lower limit divided by square of corresponding partial correlation coefficient.

[b]Percentage (or percentage points).

which the lower limits are also above unity—and for the rest are below unity. A priori, one might expect allowance for yields to give an elasticity closer to unity than the simple regressions. That is the result for the level equations, but not for the rate-of-change equations. For them, allowance for yields appreciably improves the relation between nominal money and nominal income but generally lowers the elasticity.[9]

If all variables affecting nominal income other than the nominal quantity of money were allowed for, the elasticity of nominal income with respect to nominal money would be unity. The consistent tendency for the elasticity calculated from equations (6a) and (7a) to be less than unity means that some variables are omitted that are related in the opposite direction to nominal income for given quantities of money than they are to the quantity of money.

We have deliberately excluded one such variable, namely, real per capita income. If the income elasticity of demand for money is greater than unity, as we have concluded it is for the United States, then an increase in real income for a given money stock will tend to lower velocity, which is to say, to lower the level of nominal income corresponding to that quantity of money; and it will act conversely if the income elasticity is less than unity, as we have concluded it is for the United Kingdom. If, in addition, increases in nominal money tend to be associated with increases in real per capita income, as they have been in levels for both countries and in rates of change for the United States,[10]

9. The effect on the relation of allowing for yields can be shown by comparing the partial correlation coefficients between log Y or g_Y and log M or g_M, with and without allowance for yields.

Table 8.N.1   Effect of Allowing for Yields on Relation between Nominal Income and Nominal Money

| | Partial Correlation | | | |
| | Log Y and Log M | | g_Y and g_M | |
	Yields Not Allowed for	Yields Allowed for	Yields Not Allowed for	Yields Allowed for
United States	.9992	.9992	.9684	.9794
United Kingdom	.9982	.9960	.9602	.9663
United States and United Kingdom	.9967	.9985	.9646	.9731

Four out of six of the correlations are higher with allowance for yields than without, one is the same, the final one is lower.

10. The correlations, after allowing for dummy variables by the technique explained below in note 13, are as follows:

then the exclusion of real per capita income will mean that nominal money serves partly as a proxy for real per capita income. For the United States, that would tend to lower the elasticity of nominal income with respect to nominal money; for the United Kingdom it would tend to raise it. However, in view of the closeness of the income elasticity of demand for money to unity in both countries, it is hard to believe that this effect is of major importance.

Another set of variables that is excluded are yields other than those measured by R_N and g_Y. We know that R_N and g_Y are generally positively correlated with M, and DR_N and Dg_Y with g_M.[11] If other yields behave the same way, for fixed values of R_N and g_Y, their exclusion would tend to raise the computed elasticities, since higher yields tend to raise velocity and nominal income for a given quantity of money. The effect would be in the opposite direction from that required to explain elasticities less than unity and so would further raise the discrepancy to be explained. However, the correlations with M of the yields we use are generally very small, so they would not bias the results much, and we have no reason to suppose that other yields would show any higher correlation—or even be correlated in the same direction.

For quarterly or annual data, the observed elasticity of nominal income with respect to nominal money tends to be decidedly higher than unity, rather than lower as it is for our phase average data. We have interpreted the greater than unity cyclical elasticity as reflecting a difference between measured income—the observed variable used as the dependent variable—and permanent income—the unobserved variable that we regard as underlying the demand for money. Since measured income fluctuates cyclically more widely than permanent income, a unit elasticity with respect to permanent income would be, and a less than unit elasticity could be, converted into a greater than unit elasticity with respect to measured income.

This effect is presumably still present in our phase average data, though to a much smaller extent, since averaging over phases removes much of the difference between measured and permanent income.

	Levels (M and y)	Rates of Change (g_M and g_y)
United States	.990	.659
United Kingdom	.960	−.082

For a fuller discussion, see chapter 9.

11. The correlations, after allowing for dummies by the technique explained below in note 13 are:

	Levels		Rates of Change	
	United States	United Kingdom	United States	United Kingdom
M and R_N	−.68	.44	.50	.36
M and g_Y	.26	.48	.22	.24

However, to whatever extent it is present, it also is in the wrong direction to explain our results.

We have no fully satisfactory explanation of our finding that, for given yields on assets, a 1 percent increase in the nominal quantity of money tends to be associated with an increase of something less than one percent in nominal income—roughly, about 0.9 percent.

8.2 Replacing Yields by Prior Income and Money

Aside from the dummies, equations (6a) and (7a) relate nominal income to three contemporary variables: quantity of money, the differential yield on nominal assets, and the proxy for the nominal yield on real assets. The simplified monetary theory of nominal income sketched in an earlier publication contains only a single yield, "the" nominal interest rate, which is taken to be the sum of a real interest rate plus an anticipated rate of change of prices. It further assumes that the difference between the anticipated or trend real rate of interest and the anticipated or trend real rate of growth of real income can be regarded as a constant. If we take "the" interest rate to be the short rate, this gives

$$(10) \qquad R_S = k_o + (g_Y)^*.$$

It then interprets $(g_Y)^*$ as itself determined by current and prior movements of income, which in turn reflect current and prior movements of money, and so expresses current income as a functional of the prior course of money.

Equation (10) is in the same spirit as our use of g_Y as a measure of the yield on physical assets. However, our discussion of the observed coefficients of g_Y and R_S (or R_N) warns against regarding $(g_Y)^*$ and g_Y as equivalent. The observed interest rate in the market is a *direct* measure of *anticipated yield*, the observed rate of change of nominal income, an *indirect* measure of *actual yield*.

Nonetheless, as a first step in converting equations (6a) and (7a) into a relation between current income and current and prior money and income, it seems worth exploring the consequences of using equation (10) to eliminate R_S and assuming

$$(11) \qquad (g_Y)^* = g_Y,$$

that is, that actual and anticipated rates of change of nominal income are equal. We can greatly simplify this exploration by modifying equations (6a) and (7a) by replacing R_N by R_S, which, as we saw in chapter 6, gives only slightly less satisfactory results.[12]

---

12. The effect on the standard errors of equations (6a) and (7a) of replacing R_N by R_S is as follows:

Making these substitutions into modified equation (6a), which we shall refer to as (6a)′, and omitting for simplicity the dummy variables,[13] gives

$$(12) \qquad \log Y = -(\log k + \delta k_0) + \zeta \log M - (\delta + \epsilon) g_Y.$$

If we interpret Y and M as continuous series, g_Y is the time derivative of Y. Equation (12) is then a first-order differential equation in nominal income, whose solution would give nominal income as an exponentially weighted average of past quantities of money, the weights declining the farther back in time. Equation (12) is of the same form as the one connecting permanent and measured income in the Cagan-Koyck version of adaptive expectations.[14] Hence the solution is the same, with nominal income bearing the same relation to money as permanent income does to measured income.

In order for equation (12) to give a stable solution, $-(\delta + \epsilon)$ must be greater than unity, otherwise the slightest disturbance drives log Y to plus or minus infinity. If $-(\delta + \epsilon)$ is greater than unity, the equation implies that nominal income will be stabler than nominal money, because it will be a weighted average of nominal money. As just noted, this result is sharply contrary to experience for quarterly or annual data, since a striking cyclical phenomenon is the wider amplitude of fluctuations in nominal income than in nominal money.[15] This phenomenon, which is muted but no doubt still present in our phase average data, conceivably

	Standard Error of Estimate			
	Level Equation with		Rate of Change Equation with	
	R_N	R_S	DR_N	DR_S
United States	.0445	.0471	.0131	.0128
United Kingdom	.0599	.0578	.0118	.0121
United States and				
United Kingdom	.0602	.0627	.0121	.0120

13. For the later empirical calculations, we simplify the allowance for the postwar readjustment and upward demand shift by using the device employed to allow for increasing financial sophistication in the United States, namely, adjusting the money series in advance for their effect. We have used for this purpose the estimated coefficients of the dummy variables from the final demand equations in chapter 6.

14. For example, let x be any variable and x^* its "permanent" or "anticipated" value. The Cagan-Koyck version assumes that

$$(a) \qquad \frac{dx^*}{dt} = b\,(x - x^*),$$

if there is no secular trend,

$$(b) \quad \text{or} \qquad \frac{dx^*}{dt} = b\,(x - x^*) + c$$

if there is a linear trend.

Equation (b) is of the same form as equation (12), with (log Y) substituted for x^*, and $\zeta(\log M)$ for x, $b = 1/(\delta + \epsilon)$, and $c = -(\log k + \delta k_0) / (\delta + \epsilon)$.

15. See Friedman and Schwartz, "Money and Business Cycles," table 4.

could be consistent with equation (12) if it simply reflected a greater error of measurement in income than in money. However, in the absence of independent evidence on the relative size of the measurement errors, that seems an unsatisfactory way to reconcile the theoretical implications of equation (12) with the results of experience.

Our earlier results also indicate that equation (12) is unsatisfactory. Equation (12) is identical with equation (6a) with R_N omitted. In fitting that equation, and its companion (7a), the partial correlation of R_N with log Y (or of DR_N with g_Y) is almost invariably higher than the partial correlation of g_Y with log Y (or of Dg_Y with g_Y), indicating that if only one of the two variables R_N or g_Y is to be used, R_N is preferable. Moreover, the use of both rather than g_Y alone consistently produces a significant reduction in the standard error of estimate.[16]

Let us therefore drop assumption (11) while retaining assumption (10). This gives (see sec. 8.4):

$$(13) \qquad \log Y = - \ [\log k + \delta k_o + \lambda_3 Z] + \zeta \log M \\ - \delta g_Y^* - \epsilon g_Y.$$

If we now interpret $(g_Y)^*$ as determined by an adaptive expectations mechanism, that is, as determined by the past history of income, the effect will be to introduce higher derivatives of g_Y. The corresponding differential equation is of the second or higher order and no longer has the implication that led us to reject equation (12).

We could proceed to try to fit equation (13) by replacing $(g_Y)^*$ with a function of Dg_Y and perhaps still higher derivatives and then proceed to approximate g_Y and Dg_Y by the empirical counterpart of these variables we have used in earlier computations. However, for our present purpose of seeking to relate changes in nominal income to current and prior changes in money and income, this procedure has a serious defect. Our estimate of g_Y is based on a linear trend fitted to three successive phase average values of log Y. The slope is then taken as an estimate of g_Y corresponding to the central phase. Dg_Y is calculated from first differences of g_Y, divided by the interval between them. As a result, using our statistical counterparts for g_Y and Dg_Y would in effect relate log Y to future as well as past levels of money and income.

To avoid this problem, let us rewrite equation (13) as a difference equation. If we assume the Cagan-Koyck type of adaptive expectations for the determination of $(g_Y)^*$ and treat all phases as equal in length, this difference equation (as shown in sec. 8.4) will be of the form:

$$(14) \qquad \log Y(t) = a + b \log M(t) + c \log M(t-1) \\ + d \log Y(t-1) + e \log Y(t-2) + fZ.$$

---

16. Equivalent statements hold if R_S is substituted for R_N in the regressions.

The corresponding rate of change equation, based on modified equation (7a) [(7a)'], has the form:

(15) $$g_Y(t) = bg_M(t) + cg_M(t-1) + dg_Y(t-1) + eg_Y(t-2).$$

These equations correspond to equation (15) in chapter 2 for the special case of the monetary theory of nominal income.

The assumption that the phases are equal in length enters into the derivation of equations (14) and (15) in two rather different ways: (1) the weighting of past phases to estimate $(g_Y)^*$; (2) the calculation of g_Y from successive phase values. To use the equation as it stands with our phase data, we must (1) let the chronological time span over which expectations are assumed to be formed be a variable, depending on the length of the phases, and (2) compute rate of change per phase rather than per year.

Our initial view was that both item 1 and item 2 are defects. Further reflection, however, particularly in the light of some fundamental work by Maurice Allais, suggests that item 1 may be an advantage rather than a defect,[17] though we continue to regard item 2 as a defect and shall try to eliminate it. Allais argues that the rate at which people "forget" the past in judging the future—that is, the span of past time on which they base their anticipations—is variable and depends on the course of events themselves. If the relevant magnitude changes rapidly—for example, if prices change rapidly—then people also adapt their anticipations more rapidly, "forgetting" the past at a faster rate or using a smaller time span to form their anticipations, and conversely. Allais proposes a very specific and sophisticated hypothesis to connect "psychological" time, as he calls it, with chronological time. For our purpose, the general idea rather than its specific embodiment is relevant. A lengthy cycle phase means that economic events have been proceeding slowly; a brief cycle phase means they have been proceeding rapidly. Hence the chronological span over which anticipations are formed should, if Allais is correct, be longer when the phases are long than when they are short. The time period corresponding to the length of a phase, or to the interval between phases, might therefore come closer to representing a constant duration of psychological time than would a fixed chronological time interval.

And what is true of Allais's rate of forgetfulness is also plausible for the rate at which people eliminate discrepancies between desired and actual balances. If events move slowly, adjustments might well also move slowly.

17. Maurice Allais, "Réformulation de la théorie quantitative de la monnaie," *Bulletin Sedeis*, no. 928, suppl. (10 September 1965); "A Restatement of the Quantity Theory of Money," *American Economic Review* 56 (December 1966): 1123–57; "Forgetfulness and Interest," *Journal of Money, Credit and Banking* 4 (February 1972): 40–71.

But there is no corresponding justification for item 2, namely, using the rate of change of various variables per phase rather than per chronological time unit. The chronological rates of change are objective measurements. The change in the rate of forgetfulness in effect represents a changing evaluation of objective measurements; it affects the internal discount rate that is employed in choosing how much cash to hold, how much to save and spend, and so on.

Accepting item 1, but using chronological time in estimating g_Y from successive phase values, produces a more complex equation than equations (14) and (15), one that is a function of the same basic variables, but is not linear in its parameters.[18] It has the form

$$
\begin{aligned}
(16) \quad \log Y(t) = {} & \log Y(t-1) - (1/Q(t)) \{ w(\log k + \delta k_o + \lambda_3 Z) \\
& - \zeta[\log M(t) - \log M(t-1)] \\
& - w[\zeta \log M(t-1) - \log Y(t-1)] \\
& - [\epsilon(1-w)/\bar{n}(t-1)][\log Y(t-1) \\
& - \log Y(t-2)] \},
\end{aligned}
$$

where

$$
n(t) = \text{length of phase } t
$$

$$
\bar{n}(t) = \frac{n(t) + n(t-1)}{2}
$$

$$
Q(t) = 1 + \frac{\delta w + \epsilon}{\bar{n}(t)}.
$$

Although equation (16) seems at first glance linear in the parameters, it is not because $Q(t)$ is a function of δ, ϵ, and w. Accordingly, we have used an iterative nonlinear computer regression program to calculate equation (16), given initial values of the various parameters. The iterations converged in all cases, though in some it took a considerable number of iterations to arrive at a satisfactory result.

The corresponding rate of change equation has the form:

$$
\begin{aligned}
(17) \quad g_Y(t) = {} & g_Y(t-1) + (1/Q(t)) \{ \zeta[g_M(t) - g_M(t-1)] \\
& + w[\zeta g_M(t-1) - g_Y(t-1)] \\
& + [\epsilon(1-w)/\bar{n}(t-1)][g_Y(t-1) - g_Y(t-2)] \}.
\end{aligned}
$$

It was fitted by the same iterative program.

Table 8.3 compares the standard errors of the equations (14) to (17), which replace R_S and g_Y by earlier money and income, with the standard errors of the simple quantity theory equations (8) and (9) and equations (6a)′ and (7a)′ that incorporate R_S and g_Y directly. The table also in-

---

18. For derivation, see appendix to this chapter (sec. 8.4)

Table 8.3   Alternative Relations between Nominal Income and Other Variables: Standard Errors of Estimate

	Standard Error of Estimate: Income on Money				
	Only	and Yields	and Prior Phase's Money and Two Prior Phases' Income, with Phase Length		and Three Prior Phases' Money
			Assumed Constant	Allowed for	
	(8) and (9)[a]	(6a)' and (7a)'	(14) and (15)	(16) and (17)	(18) and (19)
Levels					
United States	.0599	.0463	.0520	.0513	.0601
United Kingdom	.0785	.0564	.0554	.0581	.0747
United States and United Kingdom	.0983	.0684	.0555	.0562	.0980
Rates of Change (Zero Intercept)					
United States	.0178	.0126	.0155	.0156	.0155
United Kingdom	.0146	.0118	.0146	.0140	.0153
United States and United Kingdom	.0158	.0119	.0149	.0145	.0153
Rates of Change (Nonzero Intercept)					
United States	.0179	.0123	.0156	.0158	.0143
United Kingdom	.0143	.0104	.0139	.0130	.0154
United States and United Kingdom	.0158	.0111	.0147	.0141	.0154

[a]Equations on which estimates are based.

cludes standard errors for rates of change for equations identical to equations (15) and (17) except that they include a constant term, and therefore allow for a trend, which may reflect the average effect of real income growth plus an $\alpha \neq 1$.

Equations (14) and (15), which implicitly neglect variability in phase length, give appreciably lower standard errors than the simple quantity equation, with only one exception (no change for United Kingdom rates of change with zero intercept). However, by comparison with equations (6a)' and (7a)', equation (14) for levels gives a lower standard error for only two out of three comparisons, and equation (15), for rates of change, gives a decidedly higher standard error for all six comparisons. The level equations presumably show an improvement because past values of income approximate the trend of income better than does the current value of money alone. The rate-of-change equations show a worsening because the trend factor is of negligible importance—though of enough importance to make the equations with an intercept generally slightly superior to those without. Either the failure to allow for differences in length of phases or the replacement of R_S and g_Y by earlier money and income introduces a significant source of error.

Equations (16) and (17) allow for differences in length of phase and so eliminate one of these sources of error. While allowing for differences in length of phases reduces the standard error in five out of nine comparisons, the reduction is trivial, as are the increases in the remaining four comparisons. The minor improvement is in line with theoretical expectations, but hardly worth the extra complication and, in any event, leaves the regressions that replace current yields by prior money and income decidedly less satisfactory than those that allow for yields directly.

Table 8.4 gives estimates of the structural parameters yielded by the various approaches: ζ, the elasticity of nominal income with respect to nominal money; δ, the slope of the logarithm of real per capita money with respect to the estimated yield (R_S) on nominal assets; ϵ, the slope of the logarithm of real per capita money with respect to the estimated yield (g_Y) on physical assets; and w, the weight given the current phase in estimating anticipated yields on real assets.

Like the comparisons of standard errors, these results are disappointing. The equations replacing current yields by earlier money and income give roughly the same estimates for ζ as the equations including current yields, but generally very different and more erratic estimates for δ and ϵ. For the United States, the estimates of δ and ϵ are at least mostly of the right sign (ten out of twelve); but for the United Kingdom alone most of the estimates are of the wrong sign—positive rather than negative.

The estimates of w are the only additional information provided by the table. The equations that do and do not allow for the length of phases give roughly the same results, though those for the equations that do not allow

Table 8.4   Estimates of Structural Parameters from Alternative Equations of Relations between Nominal Income and Other Variables

	Elasticity of Income with Respect to Money (ξ)			Slope of Log of Real per Capita Money with Respect to							
				Nominal Yield on Nominal Assets (δ)			Proxy Nominal Yield on Physical Assets (ε)			Weight of Current Phase in Forming Expectations (w)	
	(6a)' and (7a)'ᵃ	(14) and (15)	(16) and (17)	(6a)' and (7a)'	(14) and (15)	(16) and (17)	(6a)' and (7a)'	(14) and (15)	(16) and (17)	(14) and (15)	(16) and (17)
				Levels							
United States	0.93	0.93	0.92	−2.05	−0.46	−0.98	−0.53	0.14	0.40	0.45	0.50
United Kingdom	1.02	1.08	1.09	−3.28	2.44	1.97	−0.54	0.11	0.18	0.32	0.34
United States and United Kingdom	0.95	0.95	0.94	−3.62	0.81	0.24	−0.78	0.20	0.34	0.15	0.14
				Rates of Change (Zero Intercept)							
United States	0.86	0.84	0.88	−2.75	−0.26	−0.53	−0.64	−0.28	−0.10	0.48	0.58
United Kingdom	0.86	0.91	0.84	−2.96	0.48	−0.50	−0.45	−0.26	−0.10	0.45	0.39
United States and United Kingdom	0.86	0.86	0.87	−2.78	0.34	−0.50	−0.57	−0.27	−0.12	0.46	0.49
				Rates of Change (Nonzero Intercept)							
United States	0.79	0.90	0.88	−3.56	−0.20	−0.56	−0.67	−0.41	−0.09	0.47	0.58
United Kingdom	0.73	0.65	0.66	−3.35	1.68	−1.19	−0.48	0.16	0.09	0.42	0.43
United States and United Kingdom	0.77	0.74	0.77	−3.37	−1.13	−0.89	−0.59	−0.03	0.06	0.45	0.52

ᵃEquations on which estimates are based.

for length of phases are somewhat more homogeneous. In general, the value of w is lower for levels than for rates of change, particularly for the United Kingdom, a result to be expected from the greater importance of trends for levels. For rates of change and equation (15), all the estimates are close together, ranging from .42 to .48. The reciprocal of w is the *average* number of phases over which expectations are formed.[19] For rates of change and equation (15), that average varies only from 2.1 to 2.4 phases. In terms of years, the estimated average period over which expectations are formed is slightly over four years for the United States, about six years for the United Kingdom—periods that are eminently reasonable by comparison with similar estimates for different phenomena.

8.3   Replacing Prior Income by Prior Money

Equations (14) and (16) express current income as a function of the current and prior phases' money and the two preceding phases' income. Income for the two preceding phases can be replaced by the relevant similar expression, and so on, so that these equations can in principle be converted into equations expressing current income as a function solely of current and past levels of money. Similarly, equations (15) and (17) can be converted into equations expressing the current rate of change of income as a function solely of present and past rates of change of money.

This conversion is straightforward for equations (14) and (15), which treat the phases as equal in length, and, as we have seen, little if anything is gained by allowing for the variable length of phase. Repeated substitution converts these equations into equations of the form:

$$(18) \qquad \log Y(t) = a' + f'Z + b_0 M(t) + b_1 M(t-1)$$
$$+ b_2 M(t-2) + \ldots + b_i M(t-i) + \ldots$$

$$(19) \qquad g_Y(t) = b_0 g_M(t) + b_1 g_M(t-1) + b_2 g_M(t-2)$$
$$+ \ldots + b_i g_M(t-i) + \ldots ,$$

where the coefficients are functions of the coefficients of equations (14) and (15).[20]

19. The average is a weighted average of the time gap between prior phases and the current phase, the weights being the exponential weights assumed to be used in forming expectations.

20. The relation between the sets of coefficients is as follows:

$$a' = \frac{a}{1-d-e}$$

$$f' = \frac{f}{1-d-e}$$

$$b_0 = b$$

We have estimated equations (18) and (19) directly by cutting off the series at $M(t-3)$; that is, including the current and three prior phases for money. The final column of table 8.3 gives the standard errors of estimate of the resulting equations. The results are most unsatisfactory. Not only are the standard errors higher than those for the equations that allow for yields directly, and higher than or roughly the same as those for equations including prior phases' income, but also, for three of the nine comparisons, the standard errors are higher than those from the simple regression of income on current money alone—that is, adding the prior phases' money simply uses up degrees of freedom.

We have also estimated the coefficients in equations (18) and (19) indirectly for an indefinite number of phases from the computed coefficients of equations (14) and (15) by using the expressions in footnote 20 above.[21] The direct and indirect estimates are given in table 8.5 for both levels and rates of change, with a zero intercept. Three items are of interest in this table.

1. There is only a family resemblance between direct and indirect coefficients, somewhat closer for rates of change than for levels, but not really close for any pair. For the indirect estimates, coefficients are given separately for the current and six prior phases, but only the sum of the coefficients, always trivial, is given for the remaining phases. The greatest similarity is in the coefficient of current money, which is to be expected, since this term dominates most of the correlations.

2. Nine of the twelve reaction patterns—three for levels and all six for rates of change—conform to the patterns predicted in chapter 2 from

$$b_1 = db + c$$
$$b_2 = db_1 + eb_0$$
$$b_3 = db_2 + eb_1$$
$$\dots\dots\dots\dots\dots$$
$$b_i = db_{i-1} + eb_{i-2}$$

For derivation, see appendix to this chapter (sec. 8.4.).

A similar conversion is extremely complex for equations (16) and (17), which allow for differences in lengths of phases. We have not been able to express the result in a compact form suitable for presentation, much less for computation. Accordingly we have had to restrict ourselves to the simpler expressions (18) and (19). However, from the estimates of the structural parameters based on equations (16) and (17) it is possible to estimate coefficients of hypothetical equations (14) and (15) for equal length phases, and thence of hypothetical equations (18) and (19) for equal length phases. Equations (18) and (19) are specific versions of equation (36) in Gordon, *Milton Friedman's Monetary Framework*, p. 41.

21. We have also estimated them indirectly from the structural parameters derived from equations (16) and (17), which allow for the variable length of phases. However, we do not present those estimates because they add little or nothing to the results from equations (14) and (15).

Table 8.5   Relation between Nominal Income and Money in Current and Prior Phases

Country and Method of Estimation[a]	Coefficient of Money in Phase							Sum of Coefficients	
	t	t-1	t-2	t-3	t-4	t-5	t-6	Remaining Phases	All Phases
Levels									
United States									
Direct	1.024	−0.085	−0.011	0.000					0.928
Indirect	0.958	0.020	−0.024	−0.014	−0.007	−0.004	−0.002	−0.001	0.926
United Kingdom									
Direct	1.027	−0.201	0.096	0.144					1.066
Indirect	0.806	0.084	0.048	0.036	0.027	0.020	0.015	0.047	1.083
United States and United Kingdom									
Direct	0.994	−0.110	0.055	0.016					0.955
Indirect	0.836	0.070	0.010	0.005	0.004	0.003	0.003	0.023	0.954
Rates of Change (Zero Intercept)									
United States									
Direct	1.105	−0.214	−0.094	0.143					0.940
Indirect	1.144	−0.305	0.033	−0.021	−0.002	−0.003	−0.001	−0.001	0.844
United Kingdom									
Direct	1.070	−0.351	0.238	0.036					0.993
Indirect	0.926	−0.059	0.081	0.036	0.022	0.013	0.008	−0.116	0.911
United States and United Kingdom									
Direct	1.112	−0.282	0.026	0.105					0.961
Indirect	1.066	−0.201	0.015	−0.011	−0.003	−0.002	−0.001	−0.001	0.862

[a]Indirect estimates are based on coefficients of equations (14) and (15).

theoretical considerations. The six rate-of-change patterns plus two of the level patterns (direct estimates for the United States and for the United States plus the United Kingdom) correspond to the solid and dotted lines in chart 2.3. That is, there is an initial overshoot, in the sense of an initial percentage increase in nominal income in response to a 1 percent increase in the rate of monetary growth larger than the ultimate increase as measured by the sum of the coefficients, followed by a damped cyclical return. The pattern is highly damped, so that generally only the first two or three coefficients are appreciable in size. One additional level pattern (indirect for the United States) shows an initial overshoot followed by an asymptotic return. The remaining three level patterns do not overshoot. Two show a steady unidirectional approach to the final position. The assumptions we have used to convert the demand curve into a relation between current income and current and prior money permit a wide variety of patterns of adjustment, but the empirical results concentrate on only a few—especially an initial overshoot followed by cyclical return.

It is not surprising that the rate-of-change results correspond to theoretical expectations better than the level results. We are here exploring dynamic patterns, and these are likely to be registered more faithfully in the rate-of-change observations than in the trend-dominated level observations. The implication is that the rate-of-change results deserve greater weight for the present purpose than the level results.

3. The sum of coefficients is less than unity in ten out of twelve cases. The two exceptions are for the United Kingdom estimates from levels. The differences from unity are relatively small and may not be statistically significant. Nonetheless, the consistency of the tendency is intriguing.

The assumptions we have used to translate the demand curve for money balances into a relation between income and prior money imply that the sum of the coefficients should be unity. A real income elasticity of demand of unity implies a rate of growth of nominal income equal to the rate of growth of nominal money, even though real income changes over time. Suppose the rate of monetary growth rises from, say, 5 percent to 6 percent a year. The equilibrium rate of growth of nominal income would then, on our assumptions, also rise from 5 percent to 6 percent a year. True, at the higher rate of monetary growth prices would rise at a 1 percent higher rate, and hence nominal yields on nominal and physical assets would be 1 percent higher, which would affect the amount of money demanded for given income, but this would be a transient effect. Once nominal income adjusted to the new yields, income would again rise at the same rate as money.

The tendency for the sum of the coefficients to be less than one requires a closer examination of the effect of an income elasticity not equal to unity, and of transient effects. We shall discuss the effect of each separately, then present the results of our computations to test these effects for the two together.

8.3.1   Income Elasticity

If real per capita income grows, as it has in fact in the United States and the United Kingdom during the past century, an income elasticity different from unity would make nominal income grow at a different rate than nominal money—at a lower rate for the greater than unity elasticity that we have found to characterize the United States, and at a higher rate for the less than unity elasticity that we have found to characterize the United Kingdom.[22] However, so long as changes in the rate of monetary growth did not affect the *rate* of real growth, a one percentage point increase in the rate of monetary growth would still imply a one percentage point increase in the rate of income growth. In the example of the next to last paragraph, a 5 percent rate of monetary growth might imply a 4 percent rate of income growth—one percentage point of the monetary growth being absorbed, say, by a 1 percent per year rise in population, one percentage point directly by a 1 percent per year rise in per capita real income, one percentage point indirectly via higher real cash balances, and the remaining two percentage points by rising prices, so that the 4 percent rate of income growth would be half in prices, half in total output. A rise in the rate of monetary growth from 5 percent to 6 percent a year would, transitional effects aside, raise the rate of income growth from 4 to 5 percent, the extra one percentage point taking the form of a higher rate of price rise.

In our calculations, this effect would bias our estimated sum of coefficients. For the level equations, it means that the long-term trends of income and money would differ. Because of the strong trend component in money, its coefficients would reflect the trend effect. For rate-of-change equations, it means that a nonzero constant term equal to $(1 - \alpha)g_y$ is required, whereas we have used a zero constant term.[23] The differences in table 8.5 between the United States and the United Kingdom with respect to the sum of the coefficients are consistent with such a bias: The sum is uniformly higher for the United Kingdom than for the United States, precisely the result to be expected from a greater than unity elasticity for the United States and a less than unity elasticity for the United Kingdom. Similarly, the less than unity sums for the United States, and the greater than unity sums for levels for the United Kingdom

---

22. Nominal income growth (g_Y) would differ from nominal money growth (g_M) by $(1-\alpha)g_y$, where α is the income elasticity of demand for real balances per capita and y is per capita real income.

23. See appendix to this chapter (sec. 8.4).

are consistent with such a bias, but the below unity sums for the United Kingdom for rates of change are not. This exception presumably reflects the absence of a positive correlation for the United Kingdom between rates of monetary change and rates of real income change.

8.3.2   Transient Effects

We pointed out in chapter 2 that a movement from one rate of monetary growth to another rate of monetary growth would have transient effects—a once-for-all shift to bring real cash balances to the new level appropriate to the new rate of price change associated with the new rate of monetary growth. In the example of a rise in the rate of monetary growth depicted in chart 2.3, we described the transient effects by saying that the area between the adjustment path and the ultimate equilibrium rate of nominal income growth must be positive. In terms of the sum of the b's, this means that the observed sum would be greater than unity for a shift to a higher rate of monetary growth, less than unity for a shift to a lower rate of monetary growth. The equations we have so far used obviously do not embody this effect, since for a constant rate of monetary growth there is no way of knowing whether it came from a higher or a lower prior rate. Put differently, to allow for transient effects we must go to higher derivatives of monetary growth.

If the rate of monetary growth had fluctuated around the same level throughout the period, above-average rates of monetary growth would have offset below-average rates, so that no bias would have been introduced, though the transient effect would obviously introduce error into the statistical estimates. However, in practice, the rate of monetary growth on the average rose over the period as a whole. By itself, this should have tended to bias the sum of the b's upward.

We show in section 8.4 that one way to allow for the transient effects is to include terms in g_M in the level equations and terms in Dg_M in the rate-of-change equations. To keep down the number of parameters estimated, we have added only two terms—$g_M(t-1)$ and $g_M(t-2)$ to the level equations, $Dg_M(t)$ and $Dg_M(t-1)$ to the rate-of-change equations.[24]

8.3.3   The Effect of Nonunit Elasticity and
Transient Effects on the Sum of the b's

Table 8.6 summarizes the sum of the b coefficients for both direct estimates of equations (18) and (19) and indirect estimates, both allowing for and not allowing for trend and transient effects. Because of the difference in income elasticity between the United States and the United Kingdom, results are given only for the two countries separately. For the

24. We have used different lags for the level and rate of change equations because our method of calculating $g_M(t)$ uses $M(t+1)$, $M(t)$ and $M(t-1)$, while our method of calculating $Dg_M(t)$ uses only $g_M(t)$ and $g_M(t-1)$.

Table 8.6 Sum of b Coefficients: Effect of Allowing for Trend and Transient Effects; Significance of Difference from Unity

Country and Method of Estimation[a]	Sum of Coefficients, Allowing for			F Ratio for Significance of Difference between Unity and Sum of b Coefficients, Allowing for			
	Neither Trend nor Transient Effects (1)	Trend Only (2)	Both Trend and Transient Effects (3)	Neither Trend nor Transient Effects (4)	Trend Only (5)	Both Trend and Transient Effects (6)	.05 Value[b] (7)
Levels							
United States							
Direct	0.93	1.06	1.07	136.21	2.02	2.57	4.1
Indirect	0.93	1.03	1.09	9.27	0.17	1.60	
United Kingdom							
Direct	1.07	1.20	1.24	23.33	7.83	10.23	4.2
Indirect	1.08	1.14	1.27	2.64	0.33	2.48	
Rates of Change							
United States							
Direct	0.94	1.15	1.11	1.54	3.04	1.52	4.1
Indirect	0.84	0.91	0.88	5.48	0.66	1.06	
United Kingdom							
Direct	0.99	0.90	1.03	0.01	0.59	0.08	4.2
Indirect	0.91	0.65	0.78	0.48	3.84	1.51	

[a]Indirect method based on equations (14) and (15).
[b]Differences in degrees of freedom between columns 4, 5, and 6 do not affect F value to the one decimal given here.

United States, the results are in the direction to be expected from above unit income elasticity. The sum of the b's is raised by allowing for trend alone or trend and transient effects, in all eight comparisons. The effect is to make the sum higher than the theoretical unity rather than lower in six out of eight comparisons. For the United Kingdom the results are more mixed. The sum is raised, rather than lowered as would be expected from a below unit income elasticity, in all four level comparisons and in one of the four rate-of-change comparisons, though by a trivial amount. Three of the eight sums are below unity, five above.

With respect to the deviation from unity, allowing for trends or trend and transient effects increases the deviation from unity for eleven out of sixteen comparisons, a rather disappointing result. However, the F ratios indicate that this result is somewhat misleading. Even for some of the comparisons in which the deviation from unity is increased, the statistical significance of the deviation is sharply reduced. This effect is particularly marked for the level equations, and particularly for the direct estimates. The reason is that if trend is not allowed for explicitly, the deviation of the sum of b's from unity implicitly allows for trend: both income on the left-hand side of the equation and the values of M on the right-hand side have an upward trend. For the United States, the secular decline in velocity (after allowance for dummies) means that the trend in nominal money is steeper than the trend in nominal income; a sum of b's less than unity allows for this difference in trend. Similarly for the United Kingdom, a sum of b's greater than unity allows for a steeper trend in nominal income than in nominal money. If the sum of b's is forced to unity there is no way to allow for trend, which is why the difference from unity is so significant statistically. Once trend is explicitly allowed for, it takes up the variance previously accounted for by the difference between the sum of b's and unity, so the difference of the sum of the b's from unity is less important.

The same effect is present to a much lesser extent for the indirect estimates. The reason is that two of the variables on the right-hand side are prior incomes, which also have different trends from money, and thereby implicitly allow for the trend on the right-hand side.

Once trend is allowed for, only two F ratios are clearly significant (both for levels and for the United Kingdom), and one additional one is on the borderline, also for the United Kingdom but for rates of change. It is notable that a deviation of a given size yields a lower F ratio for the indirect than for the direct estimates. The reason is that the statistical error is compounded in computing the indirect estimates.[25] As earlier, the rate-of-change results are more satisfactory than the level results.

25. The condition for the sum of the coefficients to be greater than unity is that $b + c + d + e \lessgtr 1$; but the estimated sum of the coefficients is $\dfrac{b + c}{1 - d - e}$, which is less stable statistically than $b + c + d + e$. This sum alone is much less erratic but necessarily, of course, on the same side of unity as the numbers entered in the table.

Taken as a whole, and allowing crudely for the nonindependence of the various comparisons, restricting the sum of the b's to unity, which saves a degree of freedom and conforms to theoretical expectations, does not seem inconsistent with the data.

Another way of judging the effect of allowing for trend, and for transient effects, and also of restricting the sum of the b's to unity, is to compare the estimates of α obtained from the trend terms of the level equations and the constant terms of the rate-of-change equations. These estimates, summarized in table 8.7, suggest that restricting the sum of the b's to unity provides the more reasonable estimates of α. All such estimates are above unity for the United States, below unity and positive for the United Kingdom, whereas four of the estimates for the United Kingdom from the unrestricted equations are above unity and two are negative. All of the estimates from the restricted equations are either within or close to the limits on the elasticity in table 6.15, whereas many of the estimates for the unrestricted equations are not. These elasticity

Table 8.7   **Estimates of Income Elasticity Based on Trend Terms**

| Country and Method of Estimation | Estimated Value of Income Elasticity (α)[a] | | | |
| | Transient Effects Not Allowed for, Sum of b's | | Transient Effects Allowed for, Sum of b's | |
	Not Restricted	Restricted to Unity	Not Restricted	Restricted to Unity
	Levels			
United States				
Direct	1.20	1.11	1.45	1.24
Indirect	1.17	1.12	1.52	1.24
United Kingdom				
Direct	1.18	0.92	1.63	0.80
Indirect	1.08	0.89	1.66	0.71
	Rates of Change			
United States				
Direct	1.77	1.38	1.56	1.25
Indirect	1.29	1.62	1.10	1.52
United Kingdom				
Direct	0.60	0.89	0.66	0.58
Indirect	-0.40	0.65	-0.05	0.64

[a]For direct method, calculated from slope of trend term added to equation (18) or constant term added to equation (19), both truncated at t-3. These terms were set equal to $(1 - \alpha)\bar{g}_y$, where $\bar{g}_y$ is the slope of a straight-line trend fitted to per capita real income for the period 1873–1973.

For indirect method, calculated from coefficients of equation (14) with trend term added and equation (15) with constant term added by setting these terms equal to $(1 - \alpha)(1 - d - e)\bar{g}_y$.

See appendix equations (A71) and (A72).

estimates reinforce the desirability of restricting the sum of the b's to unity.

8.3.4　Estimates of the Transient Effect

The equations we have used to estimate the transient effect are as follows:

For levels,

(20)
$$\log Y = a + k\,T + b_0 M(t) + b_1 M(t-1) + b_2 M(t-2) \\ + b_3 M(t-3) + j_1 g_M(t-1) + j_2 g_M(t-2) + fZ,$$

(21)
$$\log Y = a' + k'T + b\,M(t) + c\,M(t-1) + d\,Y(t-1) \\ + e\,Y(t-2) + j_1 g_M(t-1) + j_2 g_M(t-2) + fZ,$$

where T is chronological time.

For rates of change,

(22)
$$g_Y = k + b_0 g_M(t) + b_1 g_M(t-1) + b_2\,g_M(t-2) \\ + b_3\,g_M(t-3) + j_0\,Dg_M(t) + j_1 Dg_M(t-1),$$

(23)
$$g_Y = k' + b\,g_M(t) + c\,g_M(t-1) + d\,g_Y(t-1) \\ + eg_Y(t-2) + j_0 Dg_M(t) + j_1 D\,g_M(t-1).$$

Equations (20) and (22) are the ones we have referred to as the direct estimates, (21) and (23) are the indirect estimates.

We show in section 8.4 that, if j_1 and j_2 or j_0 and j_1 fully captured all transient effects, their sum would theoretically equal $-(\delta + \epsilon)$, that is, the negative of the sum of the logarithmic slopes of the demand curve for real money balances with respect to nominal yields on nominal and physical assets. Accordingly, we give our direct estimates of $-(\delta + \epsilon)$ in the first column of table 8.8. The second column gives the sum of the j terms of equations (20) and (22) for the direct estimates and equations (21) and (23) for the indirect estimates, with the sum of the b's restricted to unity.[26] The next two columns give the individual coefficients.

Clearly the two terms we include have not captured anything like the whole of the theoretical transient effect. The largest sum is less than half of the theoretical estimate. For six of the eight sets of estimates, the initial calculated transient effect is positive and the second negative, indicating a cyclical reaction; for the other two, both are positive. Our failure to confirm a larger fraction of the theoretical effect may reflect our including only the first cycle in the reaction and not a later rebound, implying a rather long-lasting transient effect, given that our time unit is a phase. Some experimental calculations for annual data are not inconsistent with this interpretation.

26. For equations (21) and (23), this is equivalent to restricting $b + c + d + e$ to unity. We have also estimated similar equations without the restrictions with essentially similar results.

Table 8.8 **Estimates of Transient Effects and Tests of Their Statistical Significance (Sum of b's Restricted to Unity)**

Country and Method of Estimation	Sum of Transient Effects		Estimates of Separate Effects		F Ratio	
	Hypothetical (1)	Calculated (2)	Initial (3)	Second (4)	Calculated (5)	.05 Value (6)
Levels						
United States						
Direct	2.58	1.17	1.23	−0.06	2.6	3.2
Indirect		0.27	0.77	−0.51	1.4	
United Kingdom						
Direct	3.82	1.29	2.30	−1.01	1.9	3.4
Indirect		−0.17	0.62	−0.79	1.1	
Rates of Change						
United States						
Direct	4.23	0.72	0.20	0.51	2.2	3.2
Indirect		0.17	0.49	−0.32	1.0	
United Kingdom						
Direct	3.83	1.48	0.42	1.06	9.6	3.4
Indirect		0.52	1.12	−0.60	4.0	

All in all, these estimates are not statistically very firmly established, as the F ratios in column 5, as well as t values for individual coefficients, indicate. Only the United Kingdom estimates from rates of change are clearly statistically significant. Yet it is encouraging that, as theory suggests, seven out of the eight signs of the calculated effects in column 2 are positive, and that none of the sums exceed the theoretical total, indicating that we are capturing the transient effect, but only part of the whole.

For rates of change, the estimated United Kingdom transient effects are both larger in absolute value than those for the United States and statistically far more significant. Nonetheless, there does not appear to be a statistically significant difference between the rate-of-change equations for the United States and the United Kingdom.[27] However, there is no necessary contradiction. If Dg_M varied more relative to its mean value for the United Kingdom than for the United States, the transient effects would be more important for the United Kingdom than for the United States, they would be estimated more accurately, and they would appear statistically more significant; yet the coefficients estimated for the United Kingdom might give fairly good estimates of the effect of the narrower movements of Dg_M in the United States, and so the equations for the two countries might not differ significantly. And indeed that seems to be the case.

8.3.5   Summary

We summarize in table 8.9 and in chart 8.1 our final estimates of the reaction pattern of nominal income to nominal money. In all cases the sum of the b's is restricted to unity and the reaction patterns are based on the indirect equations including current money and past money and income, in order to have a full reaction pattern, and including terms to allow for transient effects. We have included not only patterns for the United States and the United Kingdom separately but also a pattern for the two combined that allows for a difference in income elasticity.[28]

The table gives (and the graph plots) the cumulated effect of a sustained increase in the rate of monetary growth by one percentage point—

27. The F ratio for the difference between the equations with the sum of the b's restricted to unity is 1.9 for the direct equations, 0.75 for the indirect, compared with a .05 F value of 2.3. The results are essentially the same for equations for which the sum of the b's is not restricted. Such tests are not readily available for the level equations because the data used in computing a United States plus United Kingdom level equation are not simply the combination of the data used in computing the United States and United Kingdom equations separately. As explained earlier (see footnote 4 above), for the combined equation, United Kingdom money and income figures were first converted to dollars, whereas for the separate United Kingdom equations they were kept in pounds.

28. The combined pattern for the two allows for the difference in income elasticity by including in the level equations not only a country dummy but also a dummy times the trend variable, and in the rate of change equations, a country dummy.

Table 8.9   Cumulative Effect on the Rate of Growth of Nominal Income of a Sustained One Percentage Point Increase in the Rate of Monetary Growth Initiated in Phase t, Eliminating and Including Transient Effects

Country	Trend (Annual Percentage)	Cumulative Effect at Phase							
		t	$t+1$	$t+2$	$t+3$	$t+4$	$t+5$	$t+6$	∞
Levels, Eliminating Transient Effects									
United States	−0.20	0.884	0.912	0.956	0.977	0.988	0.994	0.998	1.000
United Kingdom	0.09	0.650	0.829	0.900	0.937	0.959	0.973	0.982	1.000
United States and United Kingdom — U.S. U.K.	−0.12 0.07	0.811	0.942	0.972	0.984	0.991	0.995	0.997	1.000
Levels, Including Transient Effects									
United States	−0.20	0.884	1.284	0.712	0.977	0.988	0.994	0.998	1.000
United Kingdom	0.09	0.650	1.064	0.600	0.937	0.959	0.973	0.982	1.000
United States and United Kingdom — U.S. U.K.	−0.12 0.08	0.811	1.093	0.724	0.984	0.991	0.995	0.997	1.000
Rates of Change, Eliminating Transient Effects									
United States	−0.52	1.020	0.968	0.990	0.996	0.999	1.000	1.000	1.000
United Kingdom	0.18	0.321	0.701	0.925	1.012	1.028	1.020	1.010	1.000
United States and United Kingdom — U.S. U.K.	−0.38 0.03	0.702	0.941	0.999	1.006	1.004	1.002	1.001	1.000
Rates of Change, Including Transient Effects									
United States	−0.52	1.253	0.816	0.990	0.996	0.999	1.000	1.000	1.000
United Kingdom	0.18	0.746	0.474	0.925	1.012	1.028	1.020	1.010	1.000
United States and United Kingdom — U.S. U.K.	−0.25 0.05	1.047	0.733	0.999	1.006	1.004	1.002	1.001	1.000

Note: Computed indirectly from equations (21) and (23) with sum of b's restricted to unity. Patterns including transient effects calculated by using equations (A89) and (A90) of sec. 8.4. United States plus United Kingdom equations allow for difference in income elasticity by including in level equations not only a country dummy but a country dummy times T (chronological time) and in rate-of-change equations a country dummy.

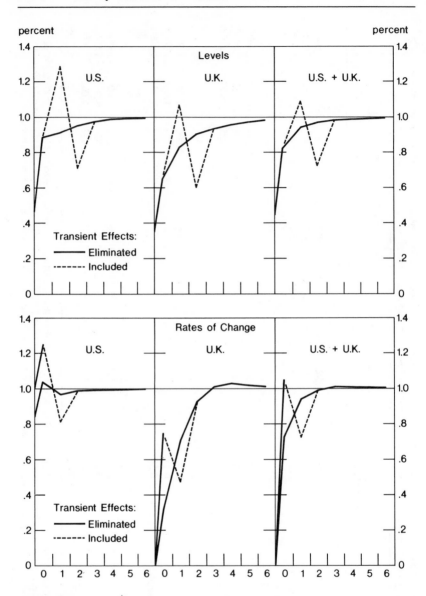

Chart 8.1   Reaction patterns of nominal income to monetary change.

that is, the values entered in the table and plotted on the chart are the cumulative sums of the b's. This makes the chart strictly comparable with chart 2.3, except that we have not shown explicitly the zero axis.[29] The solid lines beginning at t_o eliminate the transient effects, the dashed lines add them in.

29. The initial solid line segments in chart 8.1, if extended, would go through the zero horizontal axis at the midpoint of the prior phase.

For levels, the patterns for the United States and the United Kingdom are highly similar. Both show a gradual, roughly asymptotic movement to the new equilibrium position, somewhat slower for the United Kingdom than for the United States, but in neither case involving any overshooting. The failure to adjust immediately reflects a lag in adjustment, which is in a way a transient effect, but a very different one from that involved in the once-and-for-all shift to a higher level of velocity because of a higher rate of price rise and hence of nominal interest rates. That effect is embodied in the dashed line. The dashed lines, which incorporate the transient effect and thus show the predicted actual reaction pattern, involve an overshoot and then a cyclical reaction.

For rates of change there is more of a difference between the solid lines. For the United States there is almost immediate adjustment, for the United Kingdom, a long-delayed adjustment. But the dashed lines again show the same pattern for the two countries. Despite the apparent large difference in the solid lines, our earlier results indicate that the difference between them or between the dashed lines is not statistically significant.

For the United States plus the United Kingdom, the solid line for the levels, eliminating transient effects, repeats the gradual roughly asymptotic movement to the new equilibrium observed for the separate countries. The dashed line for the levels, including transient effects, shows an overshoot and then a cyclical reaction. For rates of change for the two countries combined, the solid line shows a delayed adjustment, less marked than in the case of the United Kingdom alone. The dashed line, as for the levels, shows an overshoot and a cyclical reaction thereafter.

We cannot claim to have pinned down the reaction pattern in any precise quantitative terms, yet the similarity among the patterns for the two countries and for levels and rates of change, and the concordance with theoretical expectations is encouraging, especially given the compounding of substantial errors of estimation by the indirect derivation of the patterns.

8.4   Appendix: Derivation of Relations between Nominal Income and Other Variables

8.4.1   Relation of Nominal Income to Real per Capita Income and Yields

Levels

We start with the demand equations of chapter 6, omitting for simplicity the postwar readjustment and demand shift dummies.[30]

30. In section 8.4.1, the omission is readily repaired by recognizing that it is only necessary to add terms for W and S or W_g and S_g duplicating those for Z. In section 8.4.2 the omission cannot be repaired, but in the computations based on the equations in that section we have taken account of these effects by adjusting the money series at the outset. See note 13.

(A1) $$\log m(t) = \log k + \lambda_3 Z + (\alpha + \lambda_4 Z) \log y(t) \\ + \delta R_N(t) + \epsilon g_{Y(t)} ,$$

where

$m(t)$ = per capita real money balances at time t

$y(t)$ = per capita real income at time t

$R_N(t)$ = differential interest yield at time t on nominal assets

$g_Y(t)$ = rate of change of nominal income at time t as proxy for nominal yield on physical assets

Z = dummy variable equal to 1 if the observations are for the United Kingdom, to 0 if they are for the United States. Note that Z is not a function of time, but only of country,

and

$\log k$ = constant term of demand function

α = elasticity of demand for real per capita money balances with respect to real per capita income

δ = percentage change in m for a one percentage point change in R_N, given y and g_Y, or semilogarithmic money demand slope with respect to differential yield on nominal assets

ϵ = percentage change in m for a one percentage point change in g_Y, given y and R_N, or semilogarithmic money demand slope with respect to nominal yield on physical assets

λ_3 = excess of level of $\log m$ in United Kingdom over that in United States for given y, R_N, and g_y. If y for United Kingdom is in pounds, for United States in dollars, includes adjustment for exchange rate

λ_4 = excess of income elasticity in United Kingdom over that in United States.

Given that the same price index and population are used to deflate aggregate nominal income and nominal money to per capita real income and per capita real money, we have

(A2) $$\log y - \log m = \log Y - \log M,$$

where

$$Y = \text{aggregate nominal income}$$
$$M = \text{aggregate nominal money.}$$

Solve equation (A2) for

(A3) $\log m = \log y - \log Y + \log M,$

substitute the right-hand side for $\log m$ in equation (A1), and solve for $\log Y$. This gives

(A4)
$$\begin{aligned}\log Y(t) = & - [\log k + \lambda_3 Z] + \log M(t) \\ & + (1 - \alpha - \lambda_4 Z) \log y(t) \\ & - \delta R_N(t) - \epsilon g_Y(t).\end{aligned}$$

Insert a free coefficient, ζ, before $\log M(t)$, and we have

(A5)
$$\begin{aligned}\log Y(t) = & - [\log k + \lambda_3 Z] + \zeta \log M(t) \\ & + (1 - \alpha - \lambda_4 Z) \log y(t) - \delta R_N(t) - \epsilon g_Y(t),\end{aligned}$$

which, except for dummies, is equation (6) of the text.

Let $\alpha = 1$, $\lambda_4 = 0$, and we have

(A6)
$$\begin{aligned}\log Y(t) = & - [\log k + \lambda_3 Z] + \zeta \log M(t) \\ & - \delta R_N(t) - \epsilon g_Y(t),\end{aligned}$$

which is equation (6a) of the text.

Rates of Change

The rate-of-change demand equation:

(A7) $g_m(t) = [\alpha + \lambda_4 Z]g_y(t) + \delta\, D[R_N(t)] + \epsilon D[g_Y(t)],$

by precisely similar steps can be expressed as

(A8)
$$\begin{aligned}g_Y(t) = & \zeta g_M(t) + (1 - \alpha - \lambda_4 Z)g_y(t) - \delta D[R_N(t)] \\ & - \epsilon D[g_Y(t)],\end{aligned}$$

and

(A9) $g_Y(t) = \zeta g_M(t) - \delta D[R_N(t)\,] - \epsilon D[g_Y(t)\,],$

which are the counterparts of equations (7) and (7a) of the text.

8.4.2   Relation of Nominal Income to Current
          and Prior Money and Income

Levels

Assume that

(A10) $R_S(t) = k_o + g_Y^*(t)\,,$

(A11) $g_Y^*(t) = w\, g_Y(t) + (1 - w)\, g_Y^*(t - 1)\,,$

the appropriate adaptive expectations equation if g_Y has no anticipated trend,[31]
and that

(A12) $$g_Y(t) = \frac{\log Y(t) - \log Y(t-1)}{\bar{n}(t)},$$

where

(A13) $\quad n(t) = $ length of phase t, with t interpreted as number of phase, not chronological date,

(A14) $\quad \bar{n}(t) = \dfrac{n(t) + n(t)}{2} = $ average length of phase t and $t-1$, or period between central points of two successive phases.

In the rest of this book we have estimated $g_Y(t)$ by the slope of a straight line trend fitted to three successive phase values of log Y, but we shift to this form at this point for reasons outlined in the text.

Substitute from equation (A10) into equation (A5), modified to substitute R_S for R_N, in order to simplify the subsequent analysis,

(A15) $$\begin{aligned} \log Y(t) = &- [\log k + \delta k_o + \lambda_3 Z] \\ &+ \zeta \log M(t) + (1 - \alpha - \lambda_4 Z) \log y(t) \\ &- \delta g_Y^*(t) - \epsilon g_Y(t), \end{aligned}$$

which for $\alpha = 1$, $\lambda_4 = 0$, is the counterpart of equation (13) of the text.

Write equation (A15) for $(t-1)$, and subtract $(1-w)$ times that rewritten equation from (A15), modified by replacing $g_Y^*(t)$ by the right-hand side of equation (A11). The result is

(A16) $$\begin{aligned} \log Y(t) = &(1-w) \log Y(t-1) - w [\log k + \delta k_o + \lambda_3 Z] \\ &+ \zeta[\log M(t) - (1-w) \log M(t-1)] + (1 \\ &- \alpha - \lambda_4 Z) [\log y(t) - (1-w) \log y(t-1)] \\ &- \delta w g_Y(t) - \epsilon[g_Y(t) - (1-w) g_Y(t-1)]. \end{aligned}$$

Replacing the g_Y terms by the relevant expressions from equation (A12) and rearranging terms yields

---

31. If g_Y has an anticipated exponential trend, the relevant adaptive expectations equation is

(11)′ $\qquad g_Y^*(t) = w\, g_Y(t) + (1-w)\,(1+k)\, g_Y^*(t-1).$

If it has an anticipated linear trend, the relevant equation is

(11)″ $\qquad g_Y^*(t) = w g_Y(t) + (1-w)\, [g_Y^*(t-1) + k].$

We have assumed k to be zero because, in fact, g_Y has had no unambiguous trend.

(A17) $$\log Y(t)\left[1+\frac{\delta w+\epsilon}{\bar{n}(t)}\right]$$

$$
\begin{aligned}
= &\left[1+\frac{\delta w+\epsilon}{\bar{n}(t)}\right]\log Y(t-1)\\
&-w(\log k+\delta k_o-\lambda_3 Z)+\zeta[\log M(t)\\
&-\log M(t-1)]+(1-\alpha-\lambda_4 Z)[\log y(t)\\
&-(1-w)\log y(t-1)]+w[\zeta\log M(t-1)\\
&-\log Y(t-1)]\\
&+\epsilon(1-w)\frac{[\log Y(t-1)-\log Y(t-2)]}{\bar{n}(t-1)}.
\end{aligned}
$$

Let

(A18) $$Q(t)=1+\frac{\delta w+\epsilon}{\bar{n}(t)},$$

and divide both sides of equation (A17) by $Q(t)$. The result is

(A19) $$\log Y(t)=\log Y(t-1)-w\frac{[\log k+\delta k_o+\lambda_3 Z]}{Q(t)}$$

$$+\zeta\frac{[\log M(t)-\log M(t-1)]}{Q(t)}$$

$$+(1-\alpha-\lambda_4 Z)\frac{[\log y(t)-(1-w)\log y(t-1)]}{Q(t)}$$

$$+w\frac{[\zeta\log M(t-1)-\log Y(t-1)]}{Q(t)}$$

$$+\epsilon(1-w)\frac{[\log Y(t-1)-\log Y(t-2)]}{\bar{n}(t-1)Q(t)}.$$

For $\alpha=1$, $\lambda_4=0$, this is equation (16) of the text.

As explained in the text, we used an iterative nonlinear computer regression program to calculate this equation, given initial values of the various parameters. The iterations converged in all cases.

To get the equivalent of equation (14) of the text, assume

(A20) $$n(t)=n=\text{constant independent of } t$$

so that

(A21) $$Q(t)=1+\frac{\delta w+\epsilon}{\bar{n}(t)}$$

$$=Q \text{ a constant independent of } t.$$

Rearrange the terms in equation (A19) to get:

(A22)
$$\log Y(t) = -w\frac{[\log k + \delta k_o]}{Q} - \left[\frac{w\lambda_3}{Q}\right]Z$$

$$+ \frac{1-\alpha-\lambda_4 Z}{Q}[\log y(t) - (1-w)\log y(t-1)]$$

$$+ \frac{\zeta}{Q}\log M(t) - \frac{(1-w)\zeta}{Q}\log M(t-1)$$

$$+ \left[1 - \frac{w}{Q} + \frac{\epsilon(1-w)}{nQ}\right]\log Y(t-1)$$

$$- \frac{\epsilon(1-w)}{nQ}\log Y(t-2).$$

For $\alpha = 1$, $\lambda_4 = 0$, this is now precisely in the form of equation (14) of the text:

(A23)
$$\log Y(t) = a + b\log M(t) + c\log M(t-1) \\ + d\log Y(t-1) + e\log Y(t-2) + fZ,$$

where

(A24)
$$a = \frac{-w(\log k + \delta k_o)}{Q},$$

(A25)
$$b = \frac{\zeta}{Q},$$

(A26)
$$c = \frac{-\zeta(1-w)}{Q},$$

(A27)
$$d = 1 - \frac{w}{Q} + \frac{\epsilon(1-w)}{nQ},$$

(A28)
$$e = \frac{-\epsilon(1-w)}{nQ},$$

(A29)
$$f = \frac{-\lambda_3 w}{Q},$$

(A30)
$$Q = 1 + \frac{\delta w + \epsilon}{n},$$

and n is a number that we may set equal to the average length of a phase.

We can solve these equations for the structural parameters, except that we can estimate only $\log k + \delta k_o$, not $\log k$ and k_o separately. Divide equation (A26) by equation (A25) and solve for w:

(A31) $$w = 1 + \frac{c}{b}.$$

Replace the final term of the right-hand side of equation (A27) by its equivalent, $-e$, from equation (A28), then replace w by its equivalent from equation (A31) and solve for Q:

(A32) $$Q = \frac{1 + \frac{c}{b}}{1 - d - e}.$$

Substitute from equations (A31) and (A32) into equations (A24), (A25), (A28), and (A29):

(A33) $$\log k + \delta k_o = - \frac{a}{1 - d - e}$$

(A34) $$\zeta = \frac{b + c}{1 - d - e}$$

(A35) $$\epsilon = \frac{e\, n(b + c)}{c(1 - d - e)}$$

(A36) $$\lambda_3 = - \frac{f}{1 - d - e}$$

From equation (A30),

(A37) $$\delta = \frac{(Q - 1)n - \epsilon}{w}.$$

Substitute into equation (A37) from equations (A31), (A32), and (A35) and simplify:

(A38) $$\delta = -n\,b \left[\frac{1}{b + c} + \frac{\frac{e}{c} - \frac{1}{b}}{1 - d - e} \right].$$

Equations (A31), (A34), (A35), (A36), and (A38) were used to calculate the estimates of structural parameters in table 8.4.

Though the equations in this and the next section for rates of change are expressed in a general form in which they apply to the United States plus the United Kingdom as well as to each country separately, it should be noted that such an application requires assuming not only that all phases are the same length in each country separately but also that they are of the same length in the United States and the United Kingdom; yet we know that, as we have defined the phases, they are longer on the average in the United Kingdom than in the United States. This difference could in principle be allowed for in equation (A22), but only at the cost of adding inordinate complexity to an already unduly complex equation. Accordingly, we have not tried to do so. As a result, any computations in the text based on this and related equations for the two countries combined deserve less confidence than the computations for the separate countries.

Rates of Change

The rate-of-change equation corresponding to equation (A19) is derived starting from equation (A8) in the same way as equation (A19) is derived from equation (A5). In doing so, we have not used equation (A12), as the basis for computing g_Y and g_M but have continued, as in the rest of the work, to use as g_Y and g_M the slopes of straight lines fitted to successive triplets of values of log Y and log M, because this raises no problem at this level about different time references on the two sides of the final equation. Since we have throughout calculated $D(g_Y)$ and $D(g_M)$ from first differences of successive values of g_Y and g_M, no problem arises for them similar to the problem that arose for g_Y and g_M themselves, so $D(g_Y)$ and $D(g_M)$ are calculated by the equivalent of equation (A12). The counterparts to equations (A10) and (A11) are simply the derivatives of those equations, or

(A39a) $$D[R_S(t)\,] = D[g^*{}_Y(t)\,]$$

(A39b) $$D[g^*{}_Y(t)\,] = wD[g_Y(t)\,] + (1-w)\,D\,[g^*{}_Y(t-1)\,].$$

The final equation is then

(A40) $$g_Y(t) = g_Y(t-1)$$

$$+ (1-\alpha-\lambda_4 Z)[\frac{g_y(t) - (1-w)g_y(t-1)}{Q(t)}]$$

$$+ \zeta\,[\frac{g_M(t) - g_M(t-1)}{Q(t)}]$$

$$+ w[\frac{\zeta g_M(t-1) - g_Y(t-1)}{Q(t)}]$$

$$+ \epsilon(1-w)[\frac{g_Y(t-1) - g_Y(t-2)}{\bar{n}(t-1)Q(t)}].$$

If we assume that all phases are of equal length, the counterpart to equation (A22) is

(A41) $$g_Y(t) = \frac{1-\alpha-\lambda_4 Z}{Q}[g_y(t)-(1-w)g_y(t-1)]+\frac{\zeta}{Q}g_M(t)$$

$$-\frac{(1-w)\zeta}{Q}g_M(t-1) + [(1-\frac{w}{Q}\epsilon+\frac{(1-w)}{nQ}]g_Y(t-1)$$

$$-\epsilon\frac{(1-w)}{nQ}g_Y(t-2),$$

and, for $\alpha = 1$, $\lambda_4 = 0$, the counterpart to equation (A23) is

(A42) $$g_Y(t) = bg_M(t) + cg_M(t-1) + dg_Y(t-1) + eg_Y(t-2).$$

Equations (A31), (A34), (A35), and (A38), as they stand, express the structural coefficients w, ζ, ϵ, and δ in terms of these coefficients b, c, d, and e, which is why we have used these letters interchangeably as coefficients of both the level equations and the rate of change equations.

8.4.3 Relation of Nominal Income to Current and Prior Money Only

Levels

On the most general level, we can replace log $Y(t-1)$ and log $Y(t-2)$ in equation (A19) by their equivalents obtained by writing equation (A19) for $t-1$ and $t-2$; replace log $Y(t-2)$ and log $Y(t-3)$ in the result by their equivalents obtained by writing equation (A19) for $t-2$ and $t-3$; and so on; and in this way, for $\alpha = 1$ and $\lambda_4 = 0$, end up with an equation expressing log $Y(t)$ as a function solely of earlier monetary history. However, the resulting expressions quickly become unmanageably complicated because of the presence of terms in $Q(t)$ and $\bar{n}(t)$, and so we finally gave this transformation up as a bad job.

Instead we have restricted ourselves to the case in which we can treat phases as equal in length, that is, to equation (A23).

Using the lag operator L, where $L\ X(t) = X(t-1)$, we can write equation (A23) as

(A43) $$\log Y(t) = a + (b+cL)\log M(t)$$
$$+ (dL+eL^2)\log Y(t)+fZ.$$

Solve for log $Y(t)$:

(A44) $$\log Y(t) = \frac{a}{1-dL-eL^2} + \frac{b+cL}{1-dL-eL^2}\log M(t)$$
$$+ \frac{f}{1-dL-eL^2}Z.$$

Since a and fZ are the same for all time units, the constant term and the coefficient of Z can be obtained by setting $L = 1$, giving

(A45) $$\log Y(t) = \frac{a}{1-d-e} + \frac{b+cL}{1-dL-eL^2}\log M(t) + \frac{f}{1-d-e}Z.$$

Write the middle term on the right hand side as

(A46)
$$
\begin{aligned}
f(L)\log M(t) &= \frac{b+cL}{1-dL-eL^2}\log M(t) \\
&= (b_0 + b_1 L + b_2 L^2 + \ldots + b_i L^i \\
&\quad + \ldots)\log M(t) = b_0 \log M(t) \\
&\quad + b_1 \log M(t-1) + b_2 \log M(t-2) \\
&\quad + \ldots + b_i \log M(t-1) + \ldots .
\end{aligned}
$$

The sum of the b's is obtained very simply, since that is the value of $f(L)$ if $\log M(t) = \log M(t-i)$ for all i, which is again equivalent to setting $L = 1$. This gives

(A47) $$\sum_{i=0}^{\infty} b_i = \frac{b+c}{1-d-e}.$$

The values of the individual b's are given by:

(A48)
$$
\begin{aligned}
b_0 &= b \\
b_1 &= c + d\,b \\
b_i &= d\,b_{i-1} + e\,b_{i-2} \text{ for } i > 1.
\end{aligned}
$$

To prove that these are the correct values of b, write

(A49)
$$
\begin{aligned}
f(L) &= \sum_{i=0}^{\infty} b_i L^i = b_0 + b_1 L + \sum_{i=2}^{\infty}(d\,b_{i-1} + e\,b_{i-2})L^i \\
&= b_0 + b_1 L + dL \sum_{i=2}^{\infty} b_{i-1}L^{i-1} + eL^2 \sum_{i=2}^{\infty} b_{i-2}L^{i-2} \\
&= b_0 + b_1 L + dL\left[\sum_{i=0}^{\infty} b_i L^i - b_o\right] + eL^2\left[\sum_{i=0}^{\infty} b_i L^i\right] \\
&= b_0 + b_1 L - b_0 dL + dLf(L) + eL^2 f(L).
\end{aligned}
$$

Solve for $f(L)$:

(A50) $$f(L) = \frac{b_0 + (b_1 - b_0 d)\,L}{1-dL-eL^2}.$$

Replace b_0 and b_1 by their values from equation (A48):

(A51) $$f(L) = \frac{b+cL}{1-dL-eL^2}. \quad \text{Q.E.D.}$$

We have used equation (A48) to estimate in the text the coefficients of equation (A45) from the coefficients of equation (A23).

Rates of Change

Equation (A42) is identical in form to equation (A23) except for $a = f = 0$. Hence, it yields equations identical to (A45), (A46), and (A48), except for setting $a = f = 0$, or

(A52)
$$g_Y(t) = b_0 g_M(t) + b_1 g_M(t-1) + b_2 g_M(t-2) \ldots$$
$$+ b_i g_M(t-i) + \ldots$$

with

(A53)
(Identical
to A48)
$$b_0 = b$$
$$b_1 = c + d\,b$$
$$b_i = d\,b_{i-1} + e\,b_{i-2} \text{ for } i > 1.$$

We have used equations (A53) to estimate in the text the coefficients of equation (A52) from the coefficients of equation (A42).

Effect of Nonunit Income Elasticity

Equation (A52) is homogeneous of zero degree in g_Y and g_M because of our assumption that the income elasticity of demand for real balances per capita (α) is unity. As noted in the text, this assumption introduces a bias into the computed b's that seems greater than any comparable bias in earlier equations, so it is desirable to generalize equations (A45) and (A52) to include an $\alpha \neq 1$.

At this point we shall drop any attempt to keep our analysis sufficiently general to apply to the United States plus the United Kingdom as well as to each country separately. Our earlier conclusion that the real income elasticity is different in the two countries would require us to allow not only for the difference in level measured by the parameter λ_3, but also for the difference in elasticities measured by the parameter λ_4. That alone would render what follows extremely complex. But in addition either we would have to neglect the difference in the average length of phases in the two countries as well as in the average rate of real income growth, or else we would have to introduce additional parameters to allow for such a difference. The added complexity would be so great that we have decided that the better part of wisdom is to proceed from here on to develop our equations only for each country separately—which is equivalent to setting $Z = 0$ in the earlier equations and interpreting the parameters as applying only to the country in question.

For $\alpha \neq 1$ and $Z = 0$, the counterpart to equation (A23) can be written as

(A54) $\log Y(t) = a + b \log M(t) + h \log y(t)$

$$+ c \log M(t-1) + h(\tfrac{c}{b}) \log y(t-1)$$
$$+ d \log Y(t-1) + e \log Y(t-2),$$

where we have written $h(c/b)$ as the coefficient of $\log y(t-1)$ instead of a free coefficient, to incorporate the restriction that the coefficients of $\log y(t)$ and $\log y(t-1)$ must be in the same ratio as the coefficients of $\log M(t)$ and $\log M(t-1)$, and where

(A55) $h = \dfrac{1-\alpha}{Q}$, so that

(A56) $\alpha = 1 - hQ = 1 - \dfrac{h}{b}\dfrac{b+c}{1-d-e}.$

In the same way, for rates of change, the counterpart to equation (A42) is

(A57) $g_Y(t) = b\, g_M(t) + h\, g_y(t) + c\, g_M(t-1) + h(\tfrac{c}{b})g_y(t-1)$

$$+ d\, g_Y(t-1) + e\, g_Y(t-2).$$

If we proceeded, as before, to eliminate from equations (A54) and (A57) the earlier nominal income terms, we could end up with equations like equations (A45) and (A52) except that each would also include a series of current and past values of $y(t)$, for equation (A54), and $g_y(t)$ for equation (A57), with coefficients of the same form as in equations (A48) and (A53).[32]

We do not propose to explore this in detail, partly because it introduces the serious problem of spurious correlation arising from the fact that $\log y(t)$ is a component of $\log Y(t)$, and partly because of the number of degrees of freedom that would have to be used up. However, to free the b's from bias, we can allow for the *average* rate of growth of real income per capita by assuming that

(A58) $\log y\,(t) = A + \bar{g}_y\, T(t),$

where $\bar{g}_y$ is the average per year rate of growth, and $T(t)$ is the chronological date corresponding to phase t.

This would convert equation (A54) into the expression:

(A59) $\log Y(t) = [a + h\,A\,(1+\tfrac{c}{b}) - h\,\tfrac{c}{b}\,\bar{g}_y n]$

$$+ b \log M(t) + c \log M(t-1) + d \log Y(t-1)$$
$$+ e \log Y(t-2) + h\bar{g}_y(1+\tfrac{c}{b})\,T\,(t),$$

32. The only difference is that b in equations (A48) and (A53) would be replaced by h and c would be replaced by $h\,(\tfrac{c}{b})$.

and equation (A57) into

(A60) $$g_Y(t) = h\bar{g}_y(1 + \frac{c}{b}) + b\, g_M(t) + c\, g_M(t-1)$$
$$+ d\, g_Y(t-1) + e\, g_Y(t-2),$$

that is, a constant term, say $k' = h\bar{g}_y(1 + \frac{c}{b})$, would be added to equation (A42).[33]

If we now proceed to eliminate from equation (A59) the earlier values of log Y, the result will be to modify equation (A44) by adding an additional constant term and a term in T, that is, a trend term. In order to have only the phase number t as a variable and not also chronological time T, we can replace T by nt, on the assumption that the phases are all equal in length. The final result is

(A61) $$\log Y(t) = \frac{a'}{1 - dL - eL^2} + \frac{k'n}{1 - dL - eL^2}t$$
$$+ \frac{b + cL}{1 - dL - eL^2}\, M(t),$$

where

(A62) $$a' = a + hA(1 + \frac{c}{b}) - h\frac{c}{b}\bar{g}_y n$$

and

(A63) $$k' = h\bar{g}_y(1 + \frac{c}{b}).$$

As before, we can get the constant term by setting $L = 1$, and the successive coefficients of $M(t-1)$, namely b_i, will be given by equation (A48). To get the coefficient of the t term, write

(A64) $$\frac{k'n}{1 - dL - eL^2}t = k'\left[\sum_{i=0}^{\infty} b_i' L^i\right]nt$$
$$= n\, k'\sum_{i=0}^{\infty} b_i'(t-i)$$
$$= n\, k'\left[t\sum_{i=0}^{\infty} b_i' - \sum_{i=0}^{\infty} ib_i'\right].$$

33. It may offhand seem as if the constant term should be
$$k' = h\bar{g}_y(1 + \frac{c}{b})\, n$$
instead of
$$k' = h\bar{g}_y(1 + \frac{c}{b}).$$

That would be correct if g_Y represented the rate of change per phase. But we have used it to designate the rate of change per year, so the differentiation involved in passing from level to rate of change equations is with respect to T or (nt), not (t). We use k' to distinguish it from the k which enters into the constant term of the demand function for money.

By setting $L = 1$, we know that

(A65) $$\Sigma b_i' = \frac{1}{1-d-e}.$$

To estimate $\Sigma_{i=0}^{\infty} i\, b_i'$, we can show, by a proof comparable to that used to demonstrate that equation (A48) is correct, that

(A66) $$\begin{cases} b_0' = 1 \\ b_1' = d \\ b_i' = d\, b_{i-1}' + e\, b_{i-2}' \text{ for } i > 1. \end{cases}$$

(A67) $$\sum_{i=0}^{\infty} i\, b_i' = \sum_{i=1}^{\infty} i\, b_i' = d + \sum_{i=2}^{\infty} [d\, b_{i-1}' + e\, b_{i-2}']i$$
$$= d + d \sum_{i=2}^{\infty} [b_{i-1}'(i-1) + b_{i-1}']$$
$$+ e \sum_{i=2}^{\infty} [b_{i-2}'(i-2) + 2b_{i-2}']$$
$$= d + d \sum_{i=1}^{\infty} b_i' + 2e \sum_{i=0}^{\infty} b_i'$$
$$+ d \sum_{i=1}^{\infty} b_i' i + e \sum_{i=0}^{\infty} b_i' i.$$

From which

(A68) $$\sum_{i=0}^{\infty} i\, b_i' [1 - d - e] = d + d[\frac{1}{1-d-e} - 1] + 2e[\frac{1}{1-d-e}]$$
$$= \frac{d - d^2 - ed + d - d + d^2 + de + 2e}{1-d-e}$$
$$= \frac{d + 2e}{1-d-e},$$

so that

(A69) $$\sum_{i=0}^{\infty} i\, b_i' = \frac{d+2e}{(1-d-e)^2}.$$

We then have

(A70) $$\log Y(t) = \frac{a'}{1-d-e} - k'n \frac{d+2e}{(1-d-e)^2} + \frac{k'n}{1-d-e} t$$
$$+ \sum_{i=0}^{\infty} b_i M(t-i),$$

where the values of b_i are given by equation (A48).

If we proceed to eliminate from equation (A60) the earlier values of g_Y, we get, as the counterpart of equation (A52),

(A71) $$g_Y(t) = (1 - \alpha)\bar{g}_y + b_0 g_M(t) + b_1 g_M(t-1)$$
$$+ b_2 g_M(t-2) + \ldots + b_i g_M(t-i) + \ldots$$

with the values of the b's again given by equations (A53).

The constant term of equation (A71) is intuitively obvious. If the income elasticity is unity, then real income growth does not affect the equality of g_Y and g_M for steady g_M. But if the income elasticity is higher than unity, then g_y will tend to be less than g_M by the percentage rate of rise of real balances expressed as weeks of income (i.e., percentage rate of decline of velocity), which is precisely $(\alpha - 1)g$.

If we wish to derive the constant term of equation (A71) not by direct estimate but from equation (A60), we must divide the constant term of equation (A60) by 1-d-e, giving

(A72) $$(1 - \alpha)\bar{g}_y = \frac{k'}{1-d-e} = k''.$$

There is no way of deriving $\bar{g}_y$ from the computed coefficients, but it can be estimated by the actual trend of real per capita income, which gives an estimate of α.

This is the expression we have used in table 8.7 to estimate the constant term of equation (A71).

8.4.4 Allowing for Transient Effects

Consider demand equation (A1) for $Z = 0$ and R_N replaced by R_S but for the moment assume $\epsilon = 0$, so that we have

(A73) $$\log m = \log k + \alpha \log y + \delta R_S.$$

Convert this equation into one in nominal income:

(A74) $$\log Y = -\log k + \log M + (1 - \alpha) \log y - \delta R_S.$$

Assume that the real interest rate, the rate of growth of real per capita income, and the rate of growth of population are all constant equal to ρ_o, $\bar{g}_y$, and $\bar{g}_N$ respectively, and that the actual and expected rates of change are equal. We will then have:

(A75) $$R_S = \rho_o + g_P$$

and

(A76) $$g_P = g_M - \alpha \bar{g}_y - \bar{g}_N.$$

Substitute equation (A76) in equation (A75) and the result in equation (A4), with Z and $\epsilon = 0$ and R_N replaced by R_S, to get

(A77) $$\begin{aligned} \log Y = {} & -\log k + \log M + (1-\alpha) \log y - \delta[\rho_o \\ & + g_M - \alpha\bar{g}_y - \bar{g}_N] \\ = {} & [\log k - \delta\rho_o + \delta\,\alpha\bar{g}_y \\ & + \delta\bar{g}_N] + (1-\alpha) \log y + \log M - \delta g_M. \end{aligned}$$

If g_M were a constant over time, this reduces to our earlier results simply adding another term to the constant term. If either $\log y$ is constant, or $\alpha = 1$, $\log Y$ equals $\log M$ aside from a constant and $g_Y = g_M$. If g_M is not constant, we have the result described in chapter 2, that, with $\delta < 0$, a rise in the rate of monetary growth will raise income relative to money, that is, raise velocity; a fall in the rate of monetary growth will lower velocity.

If $\epsilon \neq 0$, the effect in equation (A77) is to replace δ by $\delta + \epsilon$.

Along the lines of equation (A58), assume that we can replace $\log y$ by a time trend:

(A78) $\log y = A + \bar{g}_y T.$

Substitute equation (A78) for $\log y$ in equation (A77) and denote the constant term by a. We then have

(A79) $\log Y(t) = a + (1 - \alpha)\bar{g}_y T + \log M(t) - \delta g_M(t).$

This equation is for full equilibrium. To get a corresponding equation that allows for a distributed lag in adjustment, we can replace equation (A79) by:

(A80)
$$\log Y(t) = a + (1-\alpha)\bar{g}_y T + \sum_{i=0}^{\infty} b_i \log M(t-i)$$
$$+ \sum_{i=0}^{\infty} j_i g_M(t-i),$$

where the theory suggests that

(A81) $\Sigma\, b_i = 1,$

(A82) $\Sigma\, j_i = -(\delta + \epsilon).$

To use this in practice, we have estimated it directly, by setting $b_i = 0$ for $i > 3$, and $j_0 = j_i = 0$ for $i > 2$. The reason for setting $j_0 = 0$ is that our method of calculating $g_M(t)$ uses $M(t + 1)$, and we have wanted to use only current or past data.

We have also used the results of the earlier sections of this appendix to estimate equation (A80) indirectly from

(A83) $\log Y(t) = a + k\,T + b\,\log M(t) + c\,\log M(t - 1)$
$\qquad\qquad\qquad + d\,\log Y(t - 1) + e\,\log Y(t - 2)$
$\qquad\qquad\qquad + j_1 g_M(t - 1) + j_2 g_M(t - 2).$

Take the time derivative of equation (A79):

(A84) $g_Y(t) = (1 - \alpha)\bar{g}_y + g_M(t) - \delta D g_M(t).$

Again in distributed lag form, we have estimated it by

(A85) $g_Y(t) = (1-\alpha)\bar{g}_y + \sum_{i=0}^{\infty} b_i g_M(t-i) + \sum_{i=0}^{\infty} j_i D g_M(t-i),$

this time setting $b_i = 0$ for $i > 3$ and $j_i = 0$ for $i > 2$, since our method of calculation does not raise the same problem for Dg_M as for g_M.

For an indirect estimate, we have computed

$$(A86) \qquad \begin{aligned} g_Y(t) = {} & k' + b\, g_M(t) + c g_M(t-1) + d g_Y(t-1) \\ & + e g_Y(t-2) + j_0\, Dg_M(t) + j_1\, D\, g_M(t-1). \end{aligned}$$

If all phases were in fact equal in length, the j terms in equations (A80) and (A85) would be redundant because $g_M(t)$ and $Dg_M(t)$ would be expressed as linear combinations of $\log M(t - i)$, which would render the determinant of the least-squares equations zero. However, the phases are not equal in length, and differences in length are taken into account in computing $g_M(t)$ and $Dg_M(t)$. For equation (A86), the j_o terms would be redundant if phases were equal in length. However, the j terms in equation (A83) would not be redundant, and neither would the j_1 term in equation (A86), because they are based on values of $M(t - i)$ or $g_M(t - i)$ that do not otherwise enter the equations explicitly.

Given estimates for the j_i, an average reaction pattern excluding transient effects is given by the b_i coefficients estimated directly from equations (A80) and (A85), or the b_i coefficients estimated indirectly from equations (A83) and (A86). An average reaction pattern including transient effects can be obtained from equations (A80) and (A83) by setting

$$(A87) \qquad g_M(t-i) = \frac{\log M(t-1) - \log M(t-i-1)}{\bar{n}},$$

and in equations (A85) and (A86) by setting

$$(A88) \qquad Dg_M(t-i) = \frac{g_M(t-i) - g_M(t-i-1)}{\bar{n}},$$

and then collecting like terms, in equations (A83) and (A86) after replacing the mixed money and income terms by the equivalent terms in M alone.

For equations (A83) and (A86), as we have estimated them, the coefficients including the transient effects (designated by a prime) are:

$$(A89) \qquad b_1' = b_1 + \frac{j_1}{\bar{n}},$$

$$b_2' = b_2 - \frac{j_1}{\bar{n}} + \frac{j_2}{\bar{n}}$$

$$b_3' = b_3 - \frac{j_2}{\bar{n}},$$

and all other b's are the same primed and unprimed.

For rates of change,

(A90)
$$b'_o = b_o + \frac{j_o}{\bar{n}} \,,$$

$$b'_1 = b_1 - \frac{j_o}{\bar{n}} + \frac{j_1}{\bar{n}},$$

$$b'_2 = b_2 - \frac{j_1}{\bar{n}},$$

and all other b's are the same primed and unprimed.

9 Division of Change in Income between Prices and Output

On the average of the 102 years from 1873 to 1975, nominal income in the United States rose 4.9 percent per year, divided between a rise of 3.1 percent per year in output and 1.8 percent per year in prices. The corresponding figures for the United Kingdom are 4.0 percent per year in nominal income, 1.7 percent per year in output and 2.3 percent per year in prices. On the average, rising prices accounted for over one-third of the rise in nominal income in the United States, for over one-half in the United Kingdom.

These proportions varied greatly over time. For example, in both the United States and the United Kingdom, prices fell from 1880 to the mid-1890s while nominal income rose, so prices accounted for a negative fraction of the rise in nominal income. In the United Kingdom, output fell during World War I while nominal income rose sharply, so prices accounted for more than the whole of the rise in nominal income.

The theory sketched in chapter 2 to interpret the division of a change in nominal income between prices and output distinguishes between long-run forces that determine what are there called the anticipated or permanent levels of nominal income, prices, and output, and the shorter-run forces that determine the discrepancy between the actual and anticipated levels. It regards the long-run behavior of output as determined primarily by real factors and of prices primarily by monetary factors. The shorter-run discrepancies between actual and anticipated levels cannot be so sharply dichotomized. The shorter-run movements in both prices and output were treated in chapter 2 as depending on both monetary and real factors, and as reflecting an adjustment process involving a feedback from past observed values.

That chapter was silent about the chronological counterpart of "short run" and "long run"—as is economic theory in general, since the distinction is analytical and its chronological counterpart may vary from problem to problem or country to country or time to time. In applying the theory of chapter 2 to our phase-average data on prices and output, we implicitly treat the short run as corresponding to changes over periods longer than a phase (which averages two years in duration for the United States, 2.8 years for the United Kingdom). We are encouraged to proceed in this way by the results of earlier chapters, which show that the adjustment to monetary disturbances is fairly slow, even in terms of phases. That confidence is reinforced by the results of this chapter. Nonetheless, there is no assurance that the conclusions we derive for phases will apply, either in general or in detail, to the intracycle movements lasting a few months or a few quarters. Though this caveat is equally applicable to earlier chapters, it seems especially relevant to this one, since the interplay between movements in output and prices has been at the heart of much business-cycle analysis.

As we explained in chapter 2, the simple Keynesian and quantity theory hypotheses can be regarded as special cases of the more general theory. So also can a third simple theory: namely, that the division of a change in nominal income between prices and output depends only on the size of the change in nominal income (or what comes to the same thing, depends on the same variables as determine the change in nominal income, and no others).[1] This third simple theory can be regarded as a particular extension to prices and output of the monetary theory of nominal income.

Section 9.1 examines these three special cases in their most rigid form and shows that all can be rejected, though the simple quantity theory hypothesis conflicts with the evidence less than either of the others.

In the course of section 9.1, we uncover a tendency for observed price and output changes to be correlated negatively instead of positively, as is typically assumed in theories of general economic fluctuations. We explore this tendency in section 9.2, with special reference to purely statistical reasons for the observed phenomenon.

Section 9.3, like section 9.1, is a preliminary empirical exploration of one feature of the theoretical analysis, namely, the division between "long run" and "short run." It explores that feature by examining how the division of a change in nominal income between prices and output is affected by lengthening the period averaged in computing rates of change. The results are suggestive but inconclusive.

Section 9.4 constructs a framework for the further analysis of the more general theory embedded in equations (12) and (13) of chapter 2, which allows both anticipations about prices and deviations of actual output

---

1. In the linearized version in chapter 2, this special case is obtained by setting $\xi = 0$ in equations (12) and (13).

from potential output to affect the division of changes in nominal income between prices and output.

That framework links the analysis of the present chapter with that of chapter 8. Sections 9.5 and 9.6 apply to prices and output separately two special cases analyzed for nominal income, one that allows for the effect of the current variables affecting nominal income—money and yields (sec. 9.5); the other that expresses these variables in terms of current and prior money and prior income (sec. 9.6). These sections use the same variables for prices and output separately as were used in chapter 8 for nominal income.

Sections 9.7 and 9.8 bring into the analysis variables special to the division of nominal income between prices and output—in particular, anticipations about inflation and the degree of utilization of capacity. The results suggest that inflation anticipations are far more important in determining the rate of price change than the level of utilization of capacity.

9.1   Alternative Simple Explanations

The scatter diagram in chart 9.1 depicts the variable contribution of prices and output to changes in income. The chart plots phase rates of change of prices and output for both the United States (squares) and the United Kingdom (triangles), and the mean rates of change for the United Kingdom and the United States. War phases are circled.

The scatter diagram enables us to reject a number of possible simple explanations of the division of the change in nominal income between prices and output.

One possible explanation is that the same variables that determine the change in nominal income determine changes in prices and output and that they do so in such a way as to establish a one-to-one correspondence between the change in nominal income and in prices and output separately. In that case the changes in prices and output separately could be predicted from the change in nominal income and the points in chart 9.1 for each country would fall on a single curve—in the simplest case, that of strict proportionality between changes in prices and output, on a straight line through the origin and the point designating the mean rates of change. Clearly, the points do not conform to that explanation.

A second possible explanation is the simple Keynesian view that a change in nominal income is wholly absorbed by output until the "point of full employment" is reached, and by prices thereafter. In that case rapid rates of growth of output (in the limit, infinite) would be associated with low rates of growth of prices (in the limit, zero), and slow rates of growth of output (in the limit, zero) with high rates of growth of prices (in the limit, infinite). In terms of chart 9.1, the points would tend to cluster

Rate of Change in Prices (percent per year)

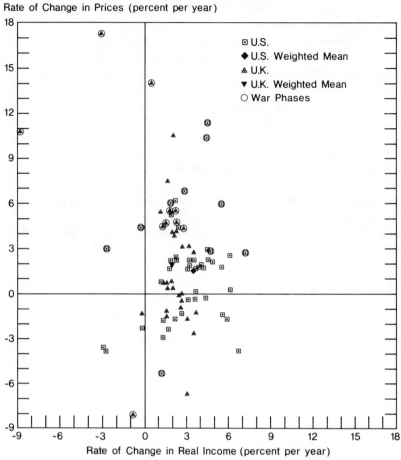

Rate of Change in Real Income (percent per year)

Chart 9.1   Scatter diagram of rates of change of real income and implicit prices, United States and United Kingdom, 1873–1975.

either in the lower right-hand corner (high output growth, low price growth), or in the upper left-hand corner (low output growth or decline, high price growth), with few or no points between the two clusters. Clearly, the points do not conform to that explanation either.

A third possible explanation is the simple quantity theory view that changes in output and prices are independent of one another; that changes in output respond to changes in resources and technology that alter the feasible output of the economy, while changes in prices respond to changes in the quantity of money per unit of output. In that case, changes in output would tend to be independent not only of changes in the price level but also in the quantity of money. The points in chart 9.1 conform more closely to this explanation than to either of the others, since the correlation between price change and output change is clearly small. Yet they do not conform fully to this explanation either, though for rather different reasons for the United States and the United Kingdom.

For the United States, the correlation between prices and output is positive for the period as a whole, including or excluding wartime phases, and for two out of three nonwar subperiods; though for the pre–World War I subperiod, the correlation is close to zero (.06) (table 9.1). The other three positive correlations differ significantly from zero at a .05 or .01 level. The one jarring note is for the period after World War II, when the correlation not only is negative, but differs significantly from zero. The correlation between money and output is consistently positive, though close to zero (.03) for the post–World War II period, and is consistently higher than that between prices and output. All in all, the hypothesis that output changes are independent of changes in prices and money must be rejected.

For the United Kingdom, the correlation between prices and output is consistently negative, though only the correlation for the period as a whole differs significantly from zero at a .05 level. The correlation between money and output is negative for the period as a whole and for the

Table 9.1   Correlations between Phase Rates of Change in Money,[a] Nominal Income, Prices, and Output

Period and Country	Rates of Change in Money and			Rates of Change in Prices and Output	Number of Observations
	Nominal Income	Prices	Output		
Full period					
United States	0.94**	0.88**	0.64**	0.36*	47
United Kingdom	0.91**	0.92**	−0.24	−0.33*	35
Full ex-wars					
United States	0.96**	0.83**	0.79**	0.43**	37
United Kingdom	0.92**	0.92**	0.03	−0.08	25
Pre–World War I					
United States	0.80**	0.78**	0.37	0.06	19
United Kingdom	0.90**	0.57	0.49	−0.33	9
Interwar					
United States	0.97**	0.88**	0.95**	0.78*	7
United Kingdom	0.80*	0.95**	−0.32	−0.28	7
Post–World War II					
United States	0.95**	0.76**	0.03	−0.60*	11
United Kingdom	0.98**	0.98**	−0.41	−0.53	9

[a]Money series adjusted for effect of postwar readjustment and upward demand shift.
*Significant at .05 level.
**Significant at .01 level.

interwar and postwar periods, essentially zero for the nonwar phases, and positive for the pre–World War I period. However, none of these correlations differs significantly from zero at the .05 level. All in all, the United Kingdom comes closer to conforming to the simple quantity theory than the United States, but the consistent negative relation between prices and output and occasionally even between money and output gives pause before that interpretation can be accepted.

Chart 9.2, which replots the points in chart 9.1 as time series rather than as a scatter diagram, reflects these correlations. For the United States there is a positive correlation between rates of change in prices and output up to Word War II, when it becomes equally clearly negative. For the United Kingdom there is a negative correlation throughout, though it is much more marked for the post–World War II period.

One other feature brought out by chart 9.2 is the greater stability of output growth in the United Kingdom than in the United States—certainly if World War I is excluded. As table 9.2 shows, the standard deviation of the rate of change of output is consistently higher for the United States than for the United Kingdom. The difference is least for the post–World War II period. For prices the situation is more complicated. Prices were decidedly more stable in the United Kingdom before World War I, somewhat less stable during the interwar period, and much less stable in the post–World War II period. The roughly equal standard deviations for the United States and the United Kingdom for the period as a whole simply average out these substantial differences between the subperiods.

For the United Kingdom, prices are consistently more variable than output; for the United States that is also true for the post–World War II period, trivially so for the pre–World War I period, and the reverse for the interwar period. The greater importance of price change relative to output change for the United Kingdom than for the United States is a phenomenon that we shall document repeatedly in later sections of this chapter.

The much stabler output for the United Kingdom reinforces the impression from chart 9.1 that the United Kingdom comes closer to conforming to the simple quantity theory than does the United States. The changing pattern of price stability presumably reflects the changed role of the United Kingdom in the world monetary system discussed in chapter 7. Before World War I, the United Kingdom was the center of the international monetary system; changes in internal prices generated a rapid response in its international payments, so it had little leeway for departing from the pattern of world prices in gold: the "law of one price" operated with full force. The United States was more isolated; it could have a more idiosyncratic pattern of price movement; hence prices were less stable in the United States than in the United Kingdom. The interwar

percent per year

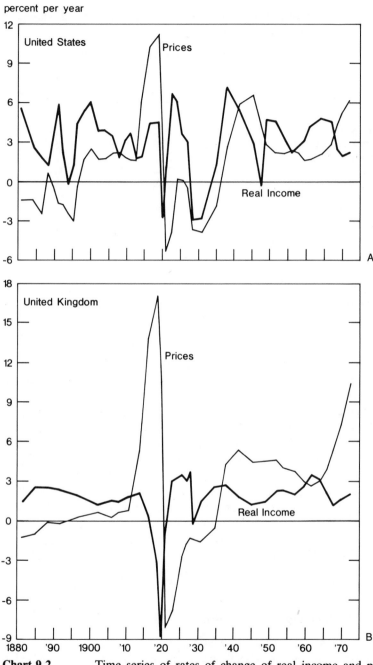

Chart 9.2   Time series of rates of change of real income and prices, United States and United Kingdom, 1880–1975. Points are plotted at the midpoint of central phase of the triplet from which rate of change is computed.

Table 9.2   **Variability of Phase Rates of Change in Money,[a] Nominal Income, Prices, and Output**

Period and Country	Standard Deviation of Rates of Change				Number of Observations
	Money	Nominal Income	Prices	Output	
Full period					
United States	4.95	5.10	3.53	2.61	47
United Kingdom	3.55	3.33	3.52	0.95	35
Full ex-wars					
United States	4.00	4.33	2.54	2.58	37
United Kingdom	2.55	2.52	2.49	0.63	25
Pre–WW I					
United States	2.12	2.53	1.75	1.73	19
United Kingdom	0.81	0.73	0.71	0.52	9
Interwar					
United States	4.40	4.56	1.51	3.28	7
United Kingdom	2.32	2.00	2.03	1.03	7
Post–WW II					
United States	1.51	1.18	1.44	1.10	11
United Kingdom	4.02	2.29	2.58	0.70	9

[a]Money series adjusted for effect of postwar readjustment and upward demand shift.

period was a period of transition, though the United States was definitely assuming a larger role. Equally important, while the United States stayed on the prewar gold standard until 1933, the United Kingdom was on the prewar gold standard only between 1925 and 1931. So price variability in the United Kingdom was moderately greater than in the United States. After World War II the United Kingdom's role in the international financial system continued to decline, while that of the United States grew, as the world—at least until 1971—essentially adopted a dollar standard. The United States was now more strongly affected by the "law of one price"; the United Kingdom had greater autonomy, reflected in occasional changes in official exchange rates before 1971, and subsequent floating thereafter, and in the control of foreign exchange transactions (until 1979). One result was that price variability increased in the United Kingdom and decreased in the United States.

9.2   Price and Output Correlations

Most students of cyclical fluctuations doubtless share our own initial expectation that on the whole price and output changes are positively correlated; yet the evidence for the two countries combined is that the phase rates of change more frequently show a negative than a positive correlation. What explains this result?

On analysis, the phenomenon that turns out to need explanation is less the empirical result than the initial expectation. There are strong statistical and economic reasons to expect a negative relation.

Consider first the statistical reason. The three magnitudes—nominal income, real income, and prices—are not statistically independent. In general, nominal income and one of the remaining two magnitudes are independently calculated, and the third is obtained by division. As a result, errors of estimate of real income and prices are negatively correlated.

The economic reasons are twofold. The first is essentially the same as the statistical reason. Any economic force that impinges autonomously on prices or output will tend to produce a negative relation between them. A good or bad harvest, for example, that raises or lowers real output without affecting, at least for the time being, the quantity of money or any other determinant of nominal income will tend to affect prices in the opposite direction. Only those autonomous influences that affect nominal income spill over to both prices and output and introduce a positive correlation.

But even the influences that affect nominal income have some effects that may reduce or reverse the positive correlation. This second economic reason, which is much more complex, arises from the difference in the temporal reaction pattern of output and prices to autonomous changes in nominal income produced by monetary, or indeed, other forces. In general, output is affected sooner than prices: an initial acceleration in nominal income, for example, leads to an acceleration in output after a brief lag (about six to nine months for the United States and the United Kingdom) and has little effect initially on prices. Later the impact shifts to prices (after about another fifteen to twenty months for the United States and the United Kingdom). As prices take over, output decelerates in response. The positive correlation between prices and output imparted by a change in nominal income thus tends to be offset by the temporal differences in response.

It follows from these considerations that a positive correlation is to be expected only when the autonomous forces affecting nominal income are sufficiently dominant to overcome both the statistical and the economic forces making for a negative relation. And that is precisely what our results show.

The only significant positive correlation between rates of change of prices and output for a subperiod is for the United States for the interwar period (0.78), and that is also the subperiod for which the standard deviation of the rate of change of nominal income (and also of money) is the highest: 4.56 percentage points, almost twice as high as the next highest, 2.53, which is for the United States pre–World War I, the only other subperiod for which the price-output correlation is positive (.06) (tables 9.1 and 9.2). At the other extreme, the negative price-output correlation that is largest in absolute value is for the United States for the post–World War II period (− .60), and that is the subperiod for which the standard deviation of nominal income (and also of money) is next to the lowest(1.18). The lowest for both money and income is for the United Kingdom pre–World War I.

A glance at chart 9.2 for the United States reinforces and amplifies this explanation. For the period before World War I, the positive correlation reflects the deep depression of the 1890s—an episode when there were exceptionally wide fluctuations in nominal income as a result of auton-omous forces—in our opinion, predominantly monetary—affecting nominal income. For the rest of the period the correlation appears negative. The essentially zero correlation for the whole pre–World War I period reflects an averaging out of the positive correlation from the end of the nineteenth century through the beginning of the twentieth, and the negative correlation before and after that episode.

For the interwar period, two similar episodes—the sharp contractions of 1920–21 and of 1929–33 and their aftermath—are the source of the positive correlation. Again, these are episodes that were characterized by exceptionally wide fluctuations in nominal income as a result of auton-omous forces—in our opinion, again predominantly monetary—affecting nominal income.

We suspect that these episodes—so dramatic and so important—ex-plain our initial expectation that the correlation would be positive.

The one puzzle that remains from tables 9.1 and 9.2 is the relation between the variability of money and of income. As the preceding paragraphs indicate, we interpret fluctuations in the rate of change of nominal income as associated with fluctuations in the rate of change of money. As table 9.2 indicates, there is in general a close relation between the standard deviations of money and of income. However, the relation for the post–World War II period differs from that for the earlier periods. For the United States, income is more variable than money for the pre–World War I and interwar periods; money is more variable than income for the post–World World War II period. For the United King-dom, money is uniformly more variable than income, but the difference is small for the first two periods—11 percent for the pre–World War I period, 16 percent for the interwar period—much larger for the post–World War II period—76 percent. For both countries, therefore, the post–World War II period displays enhanced variability of money rela-tive to income.

Chart 9.3 suggests that the explanation for this phenomenon is the length of time that it took for both countries to readjust to the major wartime disturbance of the monetary relations. In both countries that disturbance took the form of a sharp decline in the velocity of circulation

percent per year

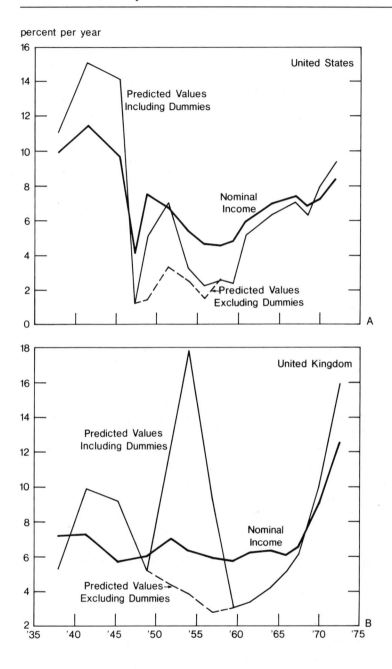

United States

Predicted Values
Including Dummies

Nominal
Income

Predicted Values
Excluding Dummies

A

United Kingdom

Predicted Values
Including Dummies

Nominal
Income

Predicted Values
Excluding Dummies

B

'35   '40   '45   '50   '55   '60   '65   '70   '75

Chart 9.3   Actual and predicted rates of change of nominal income,
post-1937 phases (predicted from regression of pre-1937
phases of rates of change of nominal income on rates of change
of money in current and three prior phases).

of money—that is, a larger rise in money than in income. The two panels of the chart plot the actual rates of change of income and the rates of change predicted from a regression relating the rate of change of income to the rate of change of money in the current and three prior phases and based solely on data for the period before Word War II.[2]

Two sets of predicted values are plotted for the postwar phases affected by postwar readjustment and upward demand shift. The points connected by a solid line allow for these shifts on the basis of the effects of the corresponding shifts after World War I. Since those estimated effects are very unreliable, because based on very few observations, we also plot the points connected by a dashed line, which make no allowance for the shifts. Allowance for the shifts improves the predictions for the United States. For the United Kingdom the allowance is in the right direction but excessive in magnitude. For our present limited purpose, the predictions that neglect the shifts are the more illuminating.

For both countries the predicted pattern is similar to the actual pattern but differs in amplitude. The predicted is above the actual during wartime—the counterpart to the decline in velocity—and then below the actual after the war—the counterpart to the recovery in velocity. Income did not rise as much as might have been expected on the basis of monetary growth during the war, but it rose more after the war. The reaction took a long time in the United States and even longer in the United Kingdom. In the United States, the reaction was largely completed by the early 1960s, in the United Kingdom, not until the end of the 1960s.

Once the reaction was completed, the actual is remarkably close to the predicted, especially for an extrapolation of more than twenty-five years for the United States and more than thirty years for the United Kingdom. A particularly remarkable feature is that in both countries the agreement is closer at the end of the period of extrapolation than at the beginning—a rather impressive testimonial to the stability of the link between money and income. The wider fluctuation of the predicted rates of change of income than of the actual means that the variability of money relative to predicted income would have been decidedly less than its variability relative to actual income. It follows that the wider relative variability of

---

2. Whereas in most of chapter 8 and the rest of this chapter we have used rates of change of money adjusted for the postwar readjustment and upward demand shift, for the present purpose we did not, but rather included dummy variables for these shifts in the regression equation fitted to the pre–World War II data. The reason is that the parameters used in calculating the adjusted money figures are based on regressions for the period as a whole and hence the use of the adjusted money figures would mean that the predicted values were not based on completely independent observations.

The earliest rate of change observations we have for money are for phases centered on 1870 for the United States and 1881.5 for the United Kingdom. Accordingly, the period covered by the dependent variable in these regressions is 1878 to 1937 for the United States, 1890 to 1937 for the United Kingdom.

money after World War II reflects the war and its aftermath rather than a fundamental structural change.

9.3   The Effect of Lengthening the Period

In *A Monetary History* we concluded that, over long periods, differential rates of monetary growth are reflected primarily in differential rates of inflation and have little effect on output whereas, over brief periods, differential rates of monetary growth affect both prices and real income.[3] That is also the result implied by the theory of chapter 2. The question is, How brief is "brief"?

As a first step to answering that question, we have computed rates of change from groups of four, five, six, seven, eight, and nine successive phases, so moving from the average span of about four years for the United States or six years for the United Kingdom for our standard rates of change computed from triplets of phases to an average span of about seventeen (United States) or twenty-three (United Kingdom) years for rates of change computed from nonets of phases.[4] The rates of change for triplets and for the longest periods, nonets of phases, are plotted in chart 9.4—for money in A panels, for nominal income, real income, and prices in B, C, and D panels. Some numerical results are given in table 9.3 for all phases.

Lengthening the period smooths out the minor perturbations in the money and nominal income series and significantly raises the simple correlation between them: from .94 for triplets to .99 for nonets for the United States, from .91 to .94 for the United Kingdom. Of more interest for the present purpose, lengthening the period sharply reduces the amplitude of the movements in real income relative to those in both prices and money for the United States but not for the United Kingdom. For the United States, the standard deviation of output is 74 percent that of price for triplets, 39 percent for nonets; for the United Kingdom, the corresponding percentages are 27 and 29.[5] In this sense our generalization in *A Monetary History* is confirmed by the charts and the table for the United States but not for the United Kingdom—another manifestation of the difference we have been finding between the United States and the

---

3. *A Monetary History*, pp. 694–95.

4. The interval between the first and last phase in a rate of change computed from i phases is $(i-1)\bar{n}$, where $\bar{n}$ is the average length of a phase, which is 2.1 years for the United States, 2.8 for the United Kingdom.

5. An interesting detail is that, to the three decimal places given in the table, the standard deviation of prices is identical for the United States and the United Kingdom for each of the seven period lengths—differences appear only in the (unreported) fourth decimal place. This coincidence is a minor but impressive testimonial to the international character of price movements.

percent per year

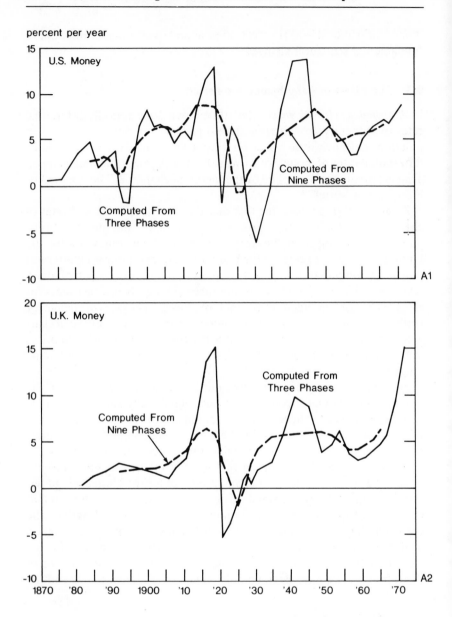

percent per year

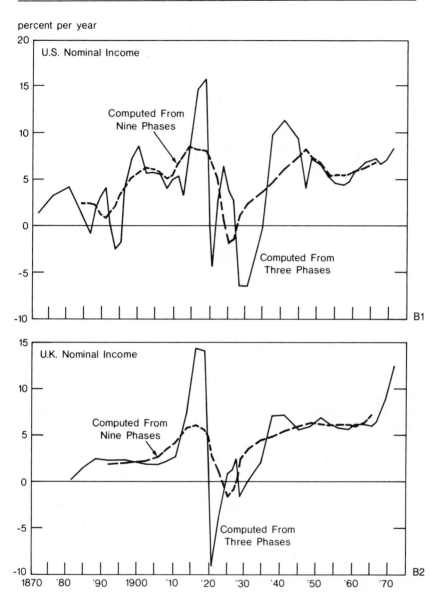

Chart 9.4   Rates of change computed from three- and nine-phase average values, for money, nominal income, real income, and prices, United States 1870–1975, United Kingdom 1881–1975.

percent per year

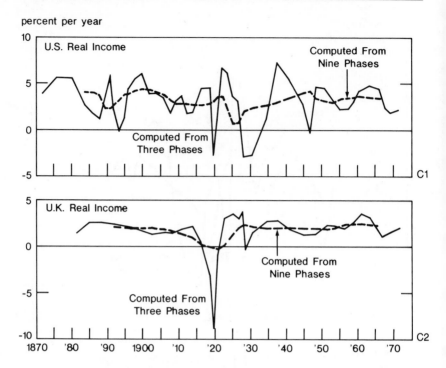

United Kingdom in respect of the relative price and output reactions to monetary change. For the United States, the residual mild fluctuations in the rate of growth of real income remain positively correlated with those in money. The simple correlation for nonets is .70, the partial correlation is .80, holding prices constant. For the United Kingdom the simple correlation for nonets is negligible and negative (− .10), though the partial correlation, holding prices constant, is positive (.47), as in the United States.

These results seem to contradict our earlier generalization that over long periods rates of monetary growth have little effect on output. A reconciliation is suggested by the dating of the residual fluctuations in the rate of change of real income (see chart 9.4, C panels). For the United States, the residual fluctuations reflect primarily the impact of the deep depressions in the 1890s, 1920s, and 1930s; for the United Kingdom, the one major residual fluctuation reflects the effect of the First World War. In each case the smoothing process has spread the influence of the deep depressions and wars over a considerable period, has shifted the dating of the turning points, and, by averaging out the smaller fluctuations, has given a larger role to these major episodes.

For the United States, the positive correlation between monetary and real income changes for nonets of phases can therefore be regarded as a reflection of another of our major generalizations in *A Monetary His-*

percent per year

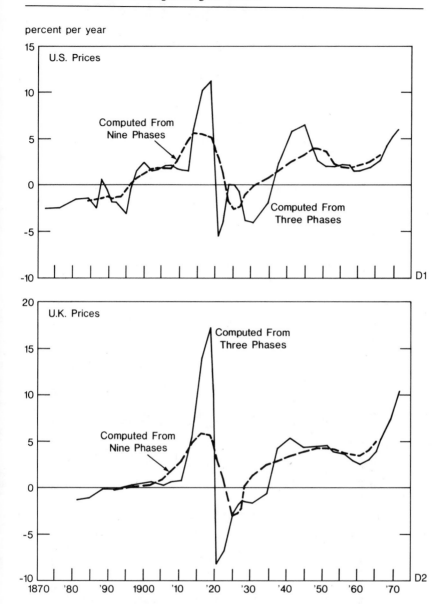

tory—the one-to-one relation between severe economic contractions and severe monetary contractions, a cyclical relation of such importance that it takes more than a seventeen-year period to average it out.

The generalization that sustained monetary changes are reflected primarily in prices rather than in real income is strongly supported by the final columns of table 9.3, which give regression coefficients and hence measure quantitative effects. For the United States, a one percentage point change in the rate of monetary growth for a three-phase span is

Table 9.3 Rates of Change Computed from Varying Number of Phases: Selected Statistical Characteristics of Money,[a] Nominal Income, Prices, and Real Income

Number of Phases	Standard Deviations				Correlation Coefficients				Partial Correlation Coefficients			Regression Coefficients			
	σ_M	σ_P	$\sigma_{y'}$	σ_Y	r_{MY}	r_{MP}	$r_{My'}$	$r_{Py'}$	$r_{MP \cdot y'}$	$r_{My' \cdot P}$	$r_{Py' \cdot M}$	b_{PM}	$b_{y'M}$	$b_{PM \cdot y'}$	$b_{y'M \cdot P}$
							United States								
3	.050	.035	.026	.051	.937	.882	.638	.363	.906	.723	−.548	.627	.337	.780	.752
4	.043	.032	.021	.045	.944	.887	.650	.385	.907	.723	−.544	.658	.314	.817	.697
5	.038	.029	.016	.039	.966	.902	.695	.421	.934	.805	−.664	.688	.305	.900	.742
6	.033	.026	.013	.034	.978	.918	.722	.460	.954	.852	−.741	.725	.290	.967	.768
7	.029	.024	.011	.030	.982	.934	.724	.490	.963	.853	−.752	.758	.268	.987	.771
8	.026	.022	.009	.028	.984	.948	.716	.515	.968	.834	−7.36	.786	.248	.986	.779
9	.024	.021	.008	.026	.985	.960	.700	.530	.972	.803	−.706	.810	.233	.974	.806
							United Kingdom								
3	.036	.035	.010	.033	.906	.921	−.240	−.334	.919	.184	−.298	.914	−.064	.885	.120
4	.032	.032	.008	.030	.926	.930	−.269	−.396	.931	.296	−.413	.937	−.072	.894	.199
5	.028	.029	.008	.026	.944	.939	−.253	−.412	.947	.427	−.524	.977	−.071	.928	.319
6	.025	.026	.007	.024	.950	.942	−.238	−.406	.952	.466	−.554	1.003	−.068	.955	.360
7	.022	.024	.006	.022	.948	.942	−.211	−.374	.952	.450	−.531	1.019	−.061	.977	.359
8	.020	.022	.006	.021	.946	.940	−.168	−.331	.951	.447	−.517	1.032	−.050	.999	.374
9	.019	.021	.006	.020	.944	.937	−.102	−.278	.950	.470	−.523	1.040	−.033	1.019	.412

[a]Money series adjusted for effect of postwar readjustment and upward demand shift.

accompanied on the average by a 0.63 percentage point change in prices and a 0.34 percentage point change in real income (the simple regression coefficients), so that even for a span of four years prices account on the average for nearly two-thirds of the total effect. The sum of the two effects gradually rises from 0.96 for triplets to 1.04 for nonets, and the relative importance of the price effect rises, so that for nonets prices account for nearly four-fifths of the total effect. For the United Kingdom the results are even more clearly in line with the generalization. The output effect is throughout negative and small, while the price effect rises from 0.91 percentage points to over 1 percent, and, as in the United States, the sum rises from 0.85 for triplets to 1.01 for nonets. These results reflect the consistent finding that the United Kingdom tends to come closer to conforming to a simple quantity theory than does the United States.

The changes recorded in the table proceed continuously so that they do not permit a sharp demarcation between "brief" and "long"—the question we started with. We shall explore this question further, and in a more sophisticated way, in later sections.

9.4 Framework for Further Analysis

The theory outlined in chapter 2 implies that a permanent one percentage point increase in the rate of monetary growth will ultimately be reflected in a one percentage point increase in the rates of growth of both nominal income and prices, leaving the rate of growth of output unchanged.[6]

The proposition is a special case of the more general view that economic actors are concerned with real variables and do not consistently err in their estimates of real variables because of purely monetary changes. Money illusion, to use the earlier terminology, is a transitory phenomenon, if it occurs at all. Expectations, to use more recent terminology, are rational.

On this view, the average growth of output over long periods is determined by real factors such as natural resource endowment, social institutions, human capacities, technology, invention, enterprise, and thrift. It is independent of *anticipated* changes in nominal magnitudes except as they affect real magnitudes—for example, the real interest rate or the real quantity of money.

Over shorter periods as well, output growth will be affected by real factors. However, over such periods output will also be affected by

---

6. As to level of output, the effect would be to reduce the level of output properly measured because the higher cost of holding money will lead to smaller real balances (higher velocity) and hence to a lower stream of productive and nonpecuniary services of money balances (see M. Friedman, *Optimum Quantity of Money*).

unanticipated changes in nominal magnitudes. Deviations of nominal income from its anticipated growth path, produced by deviations of monetary growth from its anticipated path, will produce deviations in output from the path that would be mandated by real factors alone.

The real factors that determine the potential output of an economy at any point in time generally change slowly and gradually. For both the United States and the United Kingdom, the absence of any secular trend in the rate of growth of output indicates that the effect of these trend factors on the growth of potential output has been roughly constant over the century we study.[7]

Occasionally real factors do affect output and output potential appreciably over shorter periods. For the period we study, the most important have been wars and, at the very end of the period, the emergence of the Organization of Petroleum Exporting Countries (OPEC) and the accompanying drastic alteration in the conditions of supply of crude oil. War affects output during active hostilities and, in addition, the destruction of physical and human capital reduces potential output for at least a time after the initial period of reconversion. The impact of OPEC is similarly capable of being long lasting. However, that episode came too late to affect our results appreciably.

Other real factors that affect output over short periods, such as weather conditions affecting agricultural output and construction, labor disputes and similar temporary disruptions of supply, or the bunching of new innovations, can almost surely be neglected for our purpose. Our data are for the United States and the United Kingdom as a whole, which averages out many local real elements, and for cycle phases as a whole, which further averages out transitory and cyclical phenomena. Of course the averaging out is far from complete. The Great Depression leaves an unmistakable impress on our data. But we are inclined to interpret that depression as an example of a major economic movement produced primarily by monetary rather than real phenomena.

Hence, in analyzing in more detail the division of a change in nominal income between price and output change, we shall neglect all real factors other than wars plus those that operate slowly or gradually. We shall allow for wars by presenting results only for nonwar phases. That restriction recommends itself also for a different reason—the questionable reliability of the price series during wars even after we adjust them for price controls.[8] We shall allow for the real factors that operate slowly by including a trend term in equations based on observations for levels and a constant term in equations based on rates of change.

---

7. The correlation coefficient between the phase rates of change of output and time is $-.084$ for the United States, .022 for the United Kingdom, values that would be exceeded by chance well over half the time if the true correlation were zero.

8. That problem also arises with respect to our post–World War II observations, but we regard it as less serious.

Although we neglect other real factors that affect the division of a change in nominal income between prices and output, we do not assume away changes in output. On the contrary, we neglect these real factors in order to concentrate attention on the effect of *unanticipated* changes in money and nominal income on fluctuations in output.

Unanticipated changes in nominal income alter the demand for particular products. They affect output because sellers and producers of these products have no way at the outset of knowing whether the change in demand for their products is a change relative to the demand for other products, to which it is in their interest to react by expanding or contracting output, or a change in general nominal demand, to which the appropriate response is an adjustment of prices.[9]

In chapter 2 this effect was embodied in equations (9) and (10), or in linearized form, in equation (12) and (13). These equations are:

$$(1) \qquad g_p = g_P^* + \eta \, (g_Y - g_Y^*) + \xi \, (\log y' - \log y'^*)$$

$$(2) \qquad g_{y'} = g_{y'}^* + (1 - \eta) \, (g_Y - g_Y^*) - \xi \, (\log y' - \log y'^*),$$

where the values with asterisks are anticipated or permanent values. The first term on the right-hand side of these equations relates price and

---

9. An important source of misunderstanding about the distinction between "anticipated" and "unanticipated" changes is the failure to specify the time unit involved. Many of the criticisms of "rational expectations models," and of their implications for policy, are really criticisms of the implicit assumption in some of these models that the same time unit, relatively brief, is relevant to anticipations for all variables. Longer or shorter time units may be relevant for different variables. Anticipations in active financial markets may be for very short periods, since commitments are for short periods, whereas anticipations are likely to be for much longer periods for construction or labor contracts. Once this point is recognized, much of the appeal of some simple rational expectations models disappears, but so also do many of the criticisms of a more sophisticated use of the concept of rational expectations.

A recent example is the criticism by George A. Akerlof of rational expectations models on the grounds that they are inconsistent with relatively long spells of unemployment, because they assume continuous market clearing. That is a valid criticism of models that assume that anticipations are for brief periods, and that errors are serially independent. It is not a valid criticism of models that allow for long contract periods. See Akerlof, "The Case against Conservative Macroeconomics: An Inagural Lecture," *Economica* 46 (August 1979): 219–37. On the effect of contract length, see J. A. Gray, "On Indexation and Contract Length," *Journal of Political Economy* 86 (February 1978): 1–18. See also note 33 below and sections 10.1.1 and 10.7.3.

Karl Brunner, Alex Cukierman, and Allan H. Meltzer have combined the distinction between anticipated and unanticipated with the distinction between permanent and transitory shocks to construct formal models in the spirit of the analysis of chapter 2 and this section but much more detailed. See "Stagflation, Persistent Unemployment, and the Permanence of Economic Shocks," *Journal of Monetary Economics* 6 (October 1980): 467–92; and "Money and Economic Activity, Inventories and Business Cycles" (March 980, unpublished).

output change to *anticipated* changes in the corresponding magnitudes; the second term relates them to *unanticipated* changes in nominal income; and the third term relates them to the deviation of actual output from permanent and potential output, itself the cumulated residue of earlier unanticipated changes in nominal income.[10]

Equation (15) of chapter 2 relates the unanticipated change in nominal income to monetary change, in linearized form, as

$$(3) \qquad g_Y - g_Y^* = \Psi \, (g_{M^S} - g_{M^D}) + \Phi \, (\log M^S - \log M^D).$$

where the superscripts S and D refer to "supplied" and "demanded." In chapter 8 we explored two special cases of equation (3), one that assumed an instantaneous adjustment of M^S to M^D or of g_{M^S} to g_{M^D} and another that corresponded to the monetary theory of nominal income. The results were encouraging though by no means fully satisfactory. They gave equations for nominal income and the rate of change of nominal income in terms of current money and current yields for the first special case, and in terms of current money and past money and past income, or current and past money alone, for the second special case.

As a first step in investigating empirically equations (1) and (2), we shall in sections (9.5) and (9.6), resort to the same special cases for prices and output separately. This requires modifying equations (1) and (2) (and their counterparts for levels) by setting $\xi = 0$, replacing g_Y (or Y) by an equation relating g_Y (or Y) to current money and yields, or to current money and earlier money and income, or to current and earlier money, and replacing η by a vector of parameters multiplying the individual coefficients of the several independent variables used in the price and output regressions.

As a second step, we replace equation (3) by the simpler version:

$$(4) \qquad g_Y - g_Y^* = \Psi \, (g_M - g_M^*).$$

Equation (4) simplifies equation (3) in three ways. It neglects the stock adjustment term on the ground that it is likely to be less important for output than the stock adjustment term in equations (1) and (2) and, in any event, is likely to be highly correlated with that term.[11] It replaces g_{M^S} by g_M on the ground that M can be regarded as predominantly exogenous.

10. These equations suffer from the defect discussed in the preceding footnote that they do not explicitly allow for the time period that anticipations cover, or for the possibility that different time periods are relevant for different sectors of the economy. That defect is less serious for our empirical work, which uses as a time unit a phase, than for studies using, say, quarterly data, because a phase is long enough to allow for the bulk of the relevant contract periods, though as chapter 10 suggests, the defect is not completely eliminated.

11. Because, if past deviations of g_M from g_M^* have, for example, left M^S above M^D, they can also be expected to have left y' above y'^*.

It replaces g_{MD} by g_M^* on the ground that, wartime apart, the real factors affecting the demand for money can be regarded as changing slowly.

In section 9.7 we use the Phillips curve as a convenient device for examining the effect of the degree of utilization of capacity and of inflationary anticipations as approximated by a linear function of the rate of inflation in the prior phase. The results are intriguing, enough so that we are led in section 9.8 to introduce more sophisticated hypotheses about the formation of inflationary anticipations. None of those hypotheses proves nearly as satisfactory as the simpler formulation of section 9.7. However, the approach does yield some interesting results about the role of capacity utilization.

9.5 Effect of Money and Yields

By definition, the sum of the logarithms of price and output equals the logarithm of nominal income. It follows that, since current money and yields have a consistent relation to nominal income, they must also be related to prices or to output or to both.

For most of the previous chapter, we could separate the behavior of nominal income from its division into prices and output by treating the real income elasticity of demand for money as if it were unity. This assumption enabled us to write nominal income as a function of nominal money and yields alone, without also introducing real income, and it meant that the rate-of-change equations connecting nominal income with nominal money and yields would, in principle, have zero intercepts.

When we break nominal income down into its price and output components separately, even the assumption that the real income elasticity of demand is unity will not enable us to omit real income or to eliminate the constant term from the rate-of-change equations. Consider equation (6) of chapter 8, simplified by omitting the dummy variables.

$$(5) \qquad \log Y = -\log k + \zeta \log M + (1 - \alpha) \log y - \delta R_N - \epsilon g_Y$$

plus the identity

$$(6) \qquad \log P = \log Y - \log y - \log N,$$

where y is per capita real income and N is population.

Substitute equation (5) into equation (6):

$$(7) \qquad \log P = -\log k - \log N + \zeta \log M - \alpha \log y - \delta R_N - \epsilon g_Y.$$

Similarly, the rate of change equation becomes:

$$(8) \qquad g_P = -g_N + \zeta g_M - \alpha g_y - \delta DR_N - \epsilon Dg_Y.$$

Setting $\alpha = 1$ eliminates the term in $\log y$ from equation (5) and reduces it to the simplified form of equation (6a) of chapter 8, but it does not eliminate the term in y from equations (7) and (8). The one simplification it introduces is to permit per capita real income and population to be combined in a single term corresponding to total output, and to fix the coefficient of that term at unity.

Unfortunately, it seems undesirable statistically to include either per capita output or total output in equations for prices (and conversely, prices in equations for output). The reason is that the two variables are generally not statistically independent. The estimates of nominal income are generally derived independently, and then a separate estimate is made either of output at constant prices or of prices, and the remaining variable derived by dividing the nominal income estimate by the output estimate or the price estimate. As a result, errors of measurement of the estimates of prices and output are negatively correlated. We decided in chapter 8 that this problem was significant empirically and seriously distorted the direct estimates of equation (6) of that chapter. We resolved it there by assuming a real income elasticity of unity.

We resolve it here by approximating population and real income by expressions in terms of other variables. We show in the appendix to this chapter (sec. 9.10) that if we replace population by an exponential trend and assume that deviations of real per capita income from an exponential trend (which can be regarded as an estimate of anticipated or permanent or potential per capita output) are related to M, R_N, and g_Y, we can express equations (7) and (8) as

$$(9) \qquad \log P(t) = -\log k_P - \lambda_{3P}Z - [\bar{g}_P + \lambda_{5P}Z]T(t) \\ + \zeta_P \log M(t) - \delta_P R_N(t) - \epsilon_P g_Y(t),$$

$$(10) \qquad g_P(t) = -\bar{g}_P - \lambda_{5P}Z + \zeta_P g_M(t) - \delta_P D[R_N(t)] \\ - \epsilon_P D[g_Y(t)],$$

where

$$\begin{aligned}
\log k_P &= \log k &+ A_N &+ (\alpha + \lambda_4 Z)A_y, \\
\lambda_{3P} &= \lambda_3 &+ \lambda_{3N} &+ (\alpha + \lambda_4 Z)\lambda_{3y}, \\
\bar{g}_P &= \bar{g}_N &+ &(\alpha + \lambda_4 Z)\bar{g}_y, \\
\lambda_{5P} &= \lambda_{5N} &+ &(\alpha + \lambda_4 Z)\lambda_{5y}, \\
\zeta_P &= \zeta &- &(\alpha + \lambda_4 Z)\zeta_y, \\
\delta_P &= \delta &- &(\alpha + \lambda_4 Z)\delta_y, \\
\epsilon_P &= \epsilon &- &(\alpha + \lambda_4 Z)\epsilon_y,
\end{aligned}$$

$T(t)$ is the chronological date corresponding to phase t, and A_N, A_y, $\bar{g}_N$, and $\bar{g}_y$ are the constant and exponential trend terms for the United States in the equations used to approximate population and real income respectively; λ_{3N}, λ_{3y}, λ_{5N}, and λ_{5y} are the excess of the corresponding terms for the United Kingdom over those for the United States, and ζ_y, δ_y, and ϵ_y are the coefficients of log M, $R_N(t)$, and $g_Y(t)$ in an equation like equation (9) for log y. Similar equations hold for output (see appendix equations A14 and A17). In using these equations, and throughout the rest of this chapter, we replace R_N by R_S for reasons explained in chapter 8.

Table 9.4 gives multiple regressions for nonwar phases between nominal income, prices, and output as dependent variable, and (1) money and trend alone or (2) money, trend, and yields as independent variables. Only two out of each set of three regressions are independent, since the price and output regressions must add to the income regression, but we give all three because t values and standard errors of estimate are of interest for prices and output separately. We have computed similar regressions for all phases; also for three subperiods: before World War I, the interwar years, and after World War II; and also for the United States plus the United Kingdom, using dummy variables to allow for country effects. As already indicated, we present the results for nonwar phases to allow for possible wartime real effects. However, it is worth noting that the level equations for all phases differ only inconsequentially from those for nonwar phases. The rate-of-change equations differ more appreciably, yet none of our major results would be affected by using all phases instead of all nonwar phases.[12] We use in later tables some of the results of the regressions for separate periods. However, they are individually rather unreliable because of the small number of observations on which some of them are based.[13] Similarly, in some of the later tables we use results for the United States and United Kingdom combined.

12. The biggest difference is that for the United States, the coefficient of g_M is greater for prices, and smaller for output, for all phases than for all nonwar phases, a difference that turns out to be traceable to the heavier weight in the nonwar than in all phases of the interwar observations, with their two major contractions.

13. The maximum number of observations is as shown in table 9.N.1 (fewer when lagged variables are included).

Table 9.N.1   **Number of Level- and Rate-of-Change Observations, by Nonwar Subperiods, Available for Regressions for Separate Periods**

	Levels		Rates of Change	
Period	United States	United Kingdom	United States	United Kingdom
Pre–World War I	21	11	19	9
Interwar period	9	9	7	7
Post–World War II	13[a]	11[a]	11	9
All nonwar phases	43[a]	31[a]	37	25

[a]One fewer when rate of change of nominal income is an independent variable.

Table 9.4   **Relation of Nominal Income, Prices, and Output to Money and Yields, Nonwar Phases**

Country	Dependent Variable (1)	Intercept (Level Equation) (2)	t Value	Trend (Time or Intercept of Rate of Change) (3)	t Value	M or g_M (4)	t Value	R_s or DR_s (5)	t Value	g_Y or Dg_Y (6)	t Value	Standard Error of Estimate (7)
United States	Y	0.94	6.1	−0.007	3.2	1.06	26.9					.054
	Y	1.05	7.6	−0.004	1.9	1.01	24.3	1.07	1.7	0.77	4.1	.044
	P	−5.51	23.7	−0.027	8.6	0.85	14.2					.082
	P	−5.64	21.9	−0.031	7.3	0.92	11.8	−1.54	1.3	0.19	0.5	.083
	y'	6.44	26.5	0.021	6.2	0.20	3.3					.086
	y'	6.69	27.0	0.026	6.5	0.10	1.3	2.61	2.2	0.58	1.7	.080
United Kingdom	Y	0.02	0.1	−0.002	0.9	1.10	23.0					.062
	Y	0.51	3.9	0.002	1.2	0.97	24.1	3.28	4.8	1.10	4.1	.041
	P	−5.94	35.1	−0.016	7.7	1.03	19.5					.068
	P	−5.99	31.1	−0.015	7.4	1.02	17.4	0.94	0.9	−1.10	2.8	.060
	y'	5.96	27.0	0.014	5.3	0.08	1.1					.088
	y'	6.50	34.2	0.017	8.3	−0.05	0.9	2.34	2.4	2.20	5.7	.059

United States	g_Y	-0.0052	1.9	1.04	19.8	1.74	1.8	0.50	4.1	.0126
	g_Y	-0.0003	0.1	0.91	12.6					.0105
	g_P	-0.0172	5.4	0.53	8.9	2.75	2.2	0.10	0.6	.0143
	g_P	-0.0104	2.4	0.37	3.9					.0138
	$g_{y'}$	0.0120	3.4	0.51	7.6	-1.01	0.7	0.40	2.3	.0161
	$g_{y'}$	0.0100	2.1	0.54	5.3					.0149
United Kingdom	g_Y	0.0044	1.5	0.90	11.0	2.80	3.5	0.05	0.2	.0103
	g_Y	0.0072	2.8	0.76	9.4					.0085
	g_P	-0.0164	5.7	0.90	11.2	2.73	4.0	-0.41	1.7	.0100
	g_P	-0.0133	5.9	0.77	11.0					.0074
	$g_{y'}$	0.0208	11.3	0.0075	0.1	0.06	0.1	0.47	2.3	.0065
	$g_{y'}$	0.0205	11.3	-0.01	0.2					.0060

Note: Number of observations is 42 for United States levels, 30 for United States rates of change, 37 for United Kingdom levels, 25 for United Kingdom rates of change.

Nominal income regressions in this table differ from those in chapter 8. Chapter 8 regressions do not exclude wartime phases and do not include time as a variable in the level equations and an intercept in the rate-of-change equation.

Table 9.4 confirms the quantity theory expectation that monetary change affects prices more than output. In seven out of eight comparisons, the t value for the coefficient of money is greater for prices than for output (the exception is for United States rates of change for the equation including yields) and, indeed, for five of the eight equations, including all four for the United Kingdom, the coefficient for output does not differ significantly from zero at a .05 level. These results are in accord with a more extreme form of the quantity theory for cycle phases than we outlined in chapter 2—what we called in section 9.1 the "simple" quantity theory—and tend to confirm our finding in section 9.1 that the "United Kingdom comes closer to conforming to the simple quantity theory than the United States."

Examination of similar equations for the subperiods shows that the statistically significant coefficients of money for three of the four United States output equations are produced by the interwar period. We have four parallel equations for each of three subperiods, or twelve in all. None of the eight coefficients for the pre–World War I and post–World War II periods differs significantly from zero; all four for the interwar period do. Similarly, the coefficient for a similar equation for the pre–World War I period and the post–World War II period combined does not differ significantly from zero. The different result for the interwar period reflects the two major contractions (1920–21 and 1929–33) during that period. The changes in output during those contractions were so large that, as noted in section 9.3, even averaging over as many as nine phases does not eliminate them.

The significant coefficients for the output equations for the interwar years represent a conflict with the simple quantity theory; but of course they do not conflict with the more sophisticated quantity theory outlined in chapter 2. As we have repeatedly emphasized, we regard these major contractions as a response to monetary disturbances that produced unanticipated changes in the quantity of money of sufficient size and duration to produce important effects on output.

Despite the lack of statistical significance of most of the separate coefficients on money in the output equations, the results as a whole give some evidence of a systematic influence both in the few significant coefficients and in the generally positive signs of the coefficients. Six out of the eight coefficients in table 9.4 are positive, and so are fifteen out of twenty-four of the coefficients for the subperiods.

Including yields in the equations reduces the standard error for three out of four price equations and for all four of the output equations. However, some of the reductions are trivial. Similarly, only about half of the coefficients of yields for the price and output equations are statistically significant at a .05 level. Nonetheless, it is interesting that some coefficients are significant not only for prices but also for output. Indeed, a few more of the coefficients are significant for output than for prices, and for six out of the eight comparisons the t values of the yield terms are greater for output than for prices. One other suggestive detail is that, whereas the coefficient of R_S has a higher t value than the coefficient of g_Y for three out of four price equations, the opposite is true for three out of four output equations. While obviously not very firmly based statistically, this result has considerable theoretical appeal. R_S is the nominal yield on nominal assets; g_Y is our proxy for the nominal yield on physical assets; it is therefore plausible that g_Y would have the greater effect on output, as a better indicator of the incentive to expand or contract output. All four of the coefficients of g_Y for output are positive, as this interpretation suggests, while two of the coefficients of g_Y for price are negative, which also fits this interpretation, suggesting that the output effect of a higher or lower yield on physical assets more than offsets the effect on prices via its impact on the demand for money. Note that the coefficient for income, which reflects only the impact through the demand function for money, is uniformly positive (though for one equation trivial in size), which is the sign to be expected.

The tendency for prices and output to be negatively correlated, discussed in section 9.2, is reflected in table 9.4 in the standard errors of estimate in column 7. If prices and output were statistically independent, the standard error for income would be larger than the standard errors for price and output separately.[14] Yet that is true for only two out of the eight comparisons in table 9.4 (both for United Kingdom rates of change). For the other six comparisons, the standard error of estimate is uniformly less for income than for prices, and also than for output.[15] This result must reflect a negative correlation between prices and output when the independent variables are held constant.

These correlations between prices and output are given directly in table 9.5 both for all nonwar phases and for the subperiods. All but two are negative, the two being for the United Kingdom interwar period for levels and rates of change when money and trend are allowed for, and even these are converted to negative coefficients when yields are allowed for. This result is of course to be expected for the reasons outlined in section 9.2. If these equations accounted for all systematic influences on income, prices, and output, the only thing left would be measurement error; and, given the calculation of either price or output as a residual, any measurement error in one would be perfectly correlated negatively

---

14. Since $\sigma^2_{\log Y} = \sigma^2_{\log P} + \sigma^2_{\log y'} + 2r_{\log P,\ \log y'}\ \sigma_{\log P}\ \sigma_{\log y'}$.

15. For subperiods, the standard error is greater for income than for both prices and output for four out of twenty-four comparisons (two for the United States, two for the United Kingdom), less for income than for both prices and output for ten out of twenty-four comparisons, and less for income than one of the others for ten out of twenty-four comparisons.

Table 9.5   Correlation between Price and Output, after Allowing for Money and Trend and for Money, Trend, and Yields

Period and Country	Correlation Coefficient between Price and Output after Allowing for	
	Money and Trend	Money, Trend, and Yields
Levels		
All nonwar phases		
United States	−0.80	−0.85
United Kingdom	−0.72	−0.76
Pre–World War I		
United States	−0.40	−0.50
United Kingdom	−0.85	−0.72
Interwar		
United States	−0.61	−0.71
United Kingdom	0.38	−0.46
Post–World War II		
United States	−0.29	−0.52
United Kingdom	−0.61	−0.58
Rates of Change		
All nonwar phases		
United States	−0.66	−0.74
United Kingdom	−0.28	−0.21
Pre–World War I		
United States	−0.41	−0.50
United Kingdom	−0.84	−0.80
Interwar		
United States	−0.33	−0.92
United Kingdom	0.09	−0.54
Post–World War II		
United States	−0.95	−0.98
United Kingdom	−0.72	−0.90

Note: See note to table 9.4.

with the measurement error in the other. Of course, the equations do not account for all systematic influences, but comparing the standard errors with our estimates in the preceding chapter of the order of magnitude of measurement errors indicates that measurement errors may account for an appreciable fraction of residual variability.

Table 9.6 summarizes the evidence from the regressions in Table 9.4 and similar regressions for the subperiods on the division between prices and output of the change in nominal income accompanying a change in money. One striking feature is the difference between the United States and the United Kingdom. The percentage absorbed by prices in the United Kingdom exceeds that in the United States in fourteen out of sixteen comparisons. The two exceptions are for rates of change pre–World War I, when yields are not allowed for, and post–World War II,

Table 9.6   **Percentage of Nominal Income Change Associated with Monetary Change That Is Absorbed by Prices When Allowance Is Also Made for Trend, or for Trend and Yields**

	Percentage of Nominal Income Change Absorbed by Price Change in Regressions with	
Period and Country	Money and Trend	Money, Trend, and Yields
Levels		
All nonwar phases		
United States	81	90
United Kingdom	93	106
Pre–World War I		
United States	84	81
United Kingdom	90	82
Interwar		
United States	30	20
United Kingdom	111	93
Post–World War II		
United States	102	104
United Kingdom	146	133
Rates of Change		
All nonwar phases		
United States	51	40
United Kingdom	99	101
Pre–World War I		
United States	68	62
United Kingdom	61	73
Interwar		
United States	30	21
United Kingdom	120	86
Post–World War II		
United States	97	110
United Kingdom	113	95

Note: See note to table 9.4.

when yields are allowed for. This is further evidence of the difference between the United States and the United Kingdom remarked on in section 9.1.

The only significant difference we have hitherto found between the United States and the United Kingdom is in the elasticity of the demand for money with respect to real per capita income. At first it seems that we may have found another one here in the division of income change between prices and output. However, the situation is more complex and the evidence weaker than appears at first glance. As before, the major difference between the United States and the United Kingdom is for the interwar period, for which, according to the estimates in table 9.6, prices

Table 9.7   Tests of the Significance of the Difference between the United States and the United Kingdom for Relations between Nominal Income, Prices, and Output, and Nominal Money and Yields

Period	F Value			.05 Value
	Income	Prices	Output	
Nonwar phases	1.17	4.61	6.73	2.38
Nonwar phases other than United States interwar	0.70	0.49	0.32	2.42
Pre–World War I	0.34	0.52	0.12	2.71
Interwar	2.63	5.79	3.94	4.39
Post–World War II	2.52	0.13	0.16	3.11

Note: All variables are rates of change.

In making these comparisons, a country dummy was included in the United States plus United Kingdom equations to allow for the difference over the period as a whole in average rates of growth in output arising from the differences between the two countries in population and per capita income trends.

account for 20 to 30 percent of the change in income for the United States, but for 86 to 120 percent in the United Kingdom. There is no doubt that the price-output response was very different for the United States in this period than for the United Kingdom.

For the remaining periods there is nothing like so clear a difference. True, for six out of eight comparisons in table 9.6 for the other subperiods, the percentage accounted for by price is greater for the United Kingdom than for the United States, but some of the differences are trivial and none anything like so large as for the interwar period. Table 9.7, which tests the significance of the difference between the rate-of-change equations for the United States and the United Kingdom, confirms this judgment.[16] Only the equations for price and output for all nonwar phases, and for prices for interwar phases, differ significantly at the .05 level. For the rest, the United States and the United Kingdom appear homogeneous.

The United States interwar period is clearly unique. Its dramatic character gave it far-reaching influence. It played an important role in leading Keynes himself, and his American followers even more, to regard prices as rigid and output as flexible, to interpret income change as corresponding primarily to output change and not at all, or hardly at all, to a change in prices. The percentages in table 9.6 for the United States for the interwar period are certainly consistent with that view—but they are the only ones that are. The rest of the data contradict the hypothesis Keynes was led to formulate. But that fact has not even yet been fully recognized.

16. These comparisons are restricted to rate of change equations for the reason given in note 27 of chapter 8.

9.6   Effect of Current and Prior Money and Prior Income

It is shown in the appendix (sec. 9.10) that, if we treat all phases as n years in length, equations (9) and (10) of the preceding sections can be expressed as:

$$(11) \qquad \log P(t) = a_P + f_P Z + (a'_P + f'_P Z)T(t) \\ + b_P \log M(t) + c_P \log M(t-1) \\ + d_P \log Y(t-1) \\ + e_P \log Y(t-2)$$

$$(12) \qquad g_P(t) = a'_P + b_P g_M(t) \\ + c_P g_M(t-1) + d_P g_Y(t-1) + e_P g_Y(t-2),$$

with similar equations for output. The relations connecting these coefficients with the structural parameters are much more complicated than the corresponding relations for the nominal income equation, because the structural parameters for both the nominal income equation and the price equation enter in.

Similarly, equations (11) and (12) can be converted into relations with prior money alone, but again the coefficients of the money relations are a function of both the coefficients of equations (11) and (12) and the nominal income equations that are the counterparts of equations (11) and (12). Equations (11) and (12) can be written as:

$$(13) \qquad \log P(t) = a''_P + k''_P T(t) + \sum_{i=0}^{\infty} b_{P_i} \log M(t-i)$$

and

$$(14) \qquad g_P(t) = k''_P + \sum_{i=0}^{\infty} b_{P_i} g_M(t-i),$$

where

$$(15) \qquad \begin{cases} b_{P_0} = b_P \\ b_{P_1} = c_P + d_P b_0 \\ b_{P_i} = d_P b_{i-1} + e_P b_{i-2} \text{ for } i > 1, \end{cases}$$

and

$$(16) \qquad \sum_{i=0}^{\infty} b_{P_i} = b_P + c_P + (d_P + e_P) \left[\frac{b+c}{1-d-e} \right],$$

where b_i in equation (15) are the coefficients of the nominal income counterpart of equations (13) and (14) and the other terms are defined in section 9.10. Similar equations are valid for output.

It will be recalled that

$$(17) \qquad \sum_{i=0}^{\infty} b_i = \left[\frac{b+c}{1-d-e} \right].$$

We concluded in the preceding chapter that we can regard the sum of the b's for the nominal income equation as equal to unity. It follows from equation (16) that the sum of the b's for the price equation is then an estimate of the fraction of the change in income that is absorbed by prices. Similarly, the sum of the b's for the corresponding output equation is, under the same assumption, an estimate of the fraction of the change in income that is absorbed by output. However, unless the cross-equation restriction that the sum of the b's for prices plus those for output add to unity is imposed on the price and output equations in computing them, there is no assurance that the two sums will add to unity. Rather, they will add to the sum of the b coefficients from the income equation calculated without imposing the restriction that those coefficients add to unity. In that case the estimated fraction of the change in income absorbed by prices is given by the ratio of the right-hand sides of equations (16) and (17), and that result will be consistent with the corresponding fraction for the output equations.

Table 9.8 summarizes both the sum of the b's for the price equation and the percentage of the income change absorbed by price change calculated from the ratio of the right-hand sides of equations (16) and (17). The results are remarkably consistent for different methods of estimation.

The estimated cumulative percentage change in prices, like the percentages in table 9.6, are uniformly higher for the United Kingdom than for the United States for the period as a whole. However, that result is reversed for five of the eight comparisons for which the interwar period is excluded for the United States. For the estimated percentage of nominal income change absorbed by price change, the relation is reversed for levels, even for the period as a whole: the percentage change in income is so much higher in the United Kingdom than in the United States that the higher price effect constitutes a smaller percentage of the income effect.

We are puzzled by this result. The rate of change results seem much more reasonable. When the interwar period is excluded for the United States, the percentage absorbed by prices is consistently raised for the United States but still remains below the percentage for the United Kingdom. We found in table 9.6 that, for all nonwar phases, the various estimates of the percentage of the income change absorbed by prices varied from 40 percent to 90 percent for the United States, from 93 to 106 percent for the United Kingdom. The estimates in table 9.8 vary from 68 to 96 percent for the United States, from 84 to 114 percent for the United Kingdom. When interwar phases are excluded for the United States, the estimated percentage absorbed varies for the United States from 92 to 114, very closely matching the range for the United Kingdom.

The rate-of-change estimates for the United Kingdom in table 9.8, like those in table 9.6, conform almost precisely to the quantity theory implication that prices should ultimately absorb the whole of the change in

Table 9.8 Cumulative Effect on Prices of a One Percent Increase in the Quantity of Money, and Percentage of Income Change Ultimately Absorbed by Price Change, Estimated from Equations Relating Price Change to Current and Prior Money (Direct) or Current and Prior Money and Prior Income (Indirect); Nonwar Phases, United States, and United Kingdom, and for United States also Excluding Interwar Phases

	Cumulative Percentage Change in Prices						Percentage of Nominal Income Absorbed by Prices					
	Levels			Rates of Change			Levels			Rates of Change		
	U.S.		U.K.	U.S.		U.K.	U.S.		U.K.	U.S.		U.K.
Basis of Estimates	All	Excluding Interwar		All	Excluding Interwar		All	Excluding Interwar		All	Excluding Interwar	
Transient effects not allowed for												
Direct	98	120	108	88	104	124	96	114	92	79	94	100
Indirect	95	117	111	70	93	89	95	112	84	68	92	114
Transient effects allowed for												
Direct	96	119	104	79	95	124	93	108	85	73	94	100
Indirect	93	111	109	71	94	107	92	106	84	80	94	99

income associated with a monetary change. The estimated percentages clearly do not differ from 100. For the United States, the rate of change percentages are below 100 even when the interwar period is excluded. However, they do not differ significantly from 100.

All in all, we conclude that if the interwar period for the United States is treated as exceptional, the remaining evidence for both countries is remarkably consistent with the quantity theory implication that a monetary change should ultimately affect only prices.[17]

The evidence is also consistent with the absence of any significant difference between the United States and the United Kingdom in the relation between prices and earlier money and income, provided the United States relation is based on data excluding the interwar period.[18]

Our judgment that the interwar period in the United States is excep-

17. This conclusion is in general supported by F tests of the difference between Σb_{P_i} and unity. Table 9.N.2 shows the results of those tests for the sums based on the indirect approach. The only significant values are for the United States rate of change for all nonwar values—which we attribute to the interwar period—and for levels for the United States for all nonwar excluding interwar phases if transient effects are not allowed for—which reflects a sum of b's greater than unity.

Table 9.N.2 F **Values for Differences between** Σb_{P_i} **and Unity**

| Period and Country | Transient Effects | | .05 Value Col. 1 | .05 Value Col. 2 |
	Not Allowed for (1)	Allowed for (2)	(3)	(4)
Levels				
United States				
All nonwar	0.47	0.98	4.11	4.13
All nonwar excluding interwar	7.19	4.04	4.21	4.24
United Kingdom,				
all nonwar	0.63	1.41	4.32	4.38
Rates of change				
United States				
All nonwar	12.48	8.25	4.15	4.17
All nonwar excluding interwar	0.37	0.22	4.24	4.28
United Kingdom				
All nonwar	0.00	0.19	4.45	4.54
United States and United Kingdom				
United States				
nonwar excluding interwar				
period plus all United				
Kingdom nonwar	0.01	0.18	4.05	4.06

18. The tests of significance are as shown in table 9.N.3. All but one of the F's for all nonwar phases are significant; none of the F's is when the interwar phases for the United States are excluded.

Table 9.N.3   **F Values for Differences between Countries**

	Transient Effects					
	Not Allowed for			Allowed for		
Period and Treatment of Σb_P's	Direct	Indirect	.05 Value	Direct	Indirect	.05 Value
Σ of b_P's not restricted						
All nonwar phases	5.17	5.60	2.30	3.87	4.02	2.15
United States interwar phases excluded	1.88	0.89	2.32	1.33	0.90	2.19
Σb_P's restricted to unity						
All nonwar phases	4.38	5.94	2.41	1.84	5.22	2.22
United States interwar phases excluded	1.48	0.98	2.43	0.76	1.01	2.25

tional and our exclusion of that period from some of the statistical calculations do not mean that we regard the period as unimportant or uninstructive. On the contrary, its very exceptional character reveals dramatically the power of monetary policy and monetary disturbances to influence the economy—which was why we were led to devote nearly half of the text of *A Monetary History* to these twenty years out of the ninety-three years our *History* covers. However, just as wartime periods are instructive yet may introduce undesirable heterogeneity and bias into statistical analysis, so the United States interwar period requires separate treatment rather than being lumped with the remaining episodes—and, we may add, we suspect that it is better treated by the episodic approach of *A Monetary History* than by the statistical approach of this book.

In chapter 8, we concluded that the cumulative effect of a 1 percent change in money can be taken to be a 1 percent change in nominal income (i.e., that $\Sigma b_i = 1$), and imposed that restriction in calculating the reaction pattern of nominal income in response to monetary change. It now seems that, the interwar period for the United States aside, the cumulative effect of a 1 percent change in money can be taken to be a 1 percent change in prices (i.e., that $\Sigma b_P = 1$). Accordingly, we shall impose that restriction as well in most of the rest of this section.

Table 9.9 compares the transient effect for prices with that for income. For levels, the sum of the transient effects for prices for the United States is in the wrong direction, negative instead of positive, yet statistically significant for two out of the four comparisons. For the United Kingdom the results are more nearly consistent with expectations. For rates of change, which might be expected to give more reliable estimates of transient effects, seven out of the eight sums of transient effects are positive, and the one negative sum is not statistically significant, whereas five of the seven positive sums are. The transient effect for prices is sometimes higher than for income, sometimes lower, as is consistent with our finding that output effects are small or nonexistent.

Table 9.10 summarizes the effect of allowing for alternative sets of variables on the residual variability of prices and output. For prices, money and trend are obviously far and away the most important variables, as has been true throughout earlier chapters as well. Allowing for yields generally makes an appreciable improvement. Substituting prior money for yields generally reduces the variability further, and allowing in addition for transient effects uniformly leaves a lower variability than adding yields to money and trend. This result is consistent with the theoretical model that we used to justify replacing yields by prior money. However, it cannot be regarded as strong confirmatory evidence for that theoretical model, since it could readily be that earlier money is replacing not yields but some other variable omitted in the money, trend, and yield regressions such as variables producing serial correlation in prices. Unfortunately our data, even though they stretch over a century, did not seem rich enough to enable us to explore such possibilities. The final pair of columns, which include income in the first and second prior phases instead of money in the second and third prior phases, give slightly poorer results for levels and for United States rates of change, mixed results for United Kingdom rates of change.

For output, the results for the United States are roughly the same as for prices. For the United Kingdom the most interesting result is for rates of change, for which all the measures are roughly the same. The rate of growth of output in Britain from cycle phase to cycle phase—at least as recorded in the imperfect figures we have available—has been highly stable and not affected significantly by any of the variables, including earlier income, implying essentially a series corresponding to a random walk or white noise. It is noteworthy that the total variability of output rates of change for all nonwar phases for the United Kingdom is not much more than half the lowest *residual* variability for United States nonwar phases. The situation is different for the rate of change of prices. Total variability is about the same in the two countries—reflecting the "law of one price." However, the variables we have considered had a greater influence on United Kingdom than on United States prices, so that *residual* variability is decidedly less for the United Kingdom than for the United States.

All in all, we regard as the most reliable and instructive relations those for rates of change for all nonwar phases for the United Kingdom and all nonwar phases excluding interwar phases for the United States, as well as the combination of these two.

Table 9.11 gives a different kind of summary of our results, namely, the estimated reaction of prices and output to a sustained 1 percent increase in the quantity of money. These estimates are based on the relations summarized in the final two columns of table 9.10, except that the restriction is imposed that the ultimate cumulative effect on prices be unity and on output zero, in accordance with our earlier finding that these theoretical expectations are not contradicted by our data. This table is the counterpart of table 8.9 for income except that it is restricted to all nonwar phases excluding interwar phases for the United States, and to all nonwar phases for the United Kingdom.

Chart 9.5 plots the reaction patterns based on rates of change. We regard these as most reliable not only for the reasons already cited but because technical considerations prevented us from estimating a transient effect from levels for the initial phase in which the monetary change is introduced. The price reaction obviously dominates. For both the United States and the United Kingdom it overshoots, but not until the second phase after the initial phase for the United States and the fourth phase for the United Kingdom, and then only modestly. The milder, yet

Table 9.9   Estimates of Transient Effect on Income and Prices and Tests of Significance of Transient Effects on Prices (Σb's Restricted to Unity for both Income and Prices): Nonwar Phases, United States, and United Kingdom, and for United States also Excluding Interwar Phases

Country, Method of Estimation, and Period	Sum of Transient Effects			Estimates of Separate Effects		F Ratio for Prices	
	Income		Prices				
	Hypothetical	Calculated	Calculated	Initial	Second	Calculated	.05 Value
Levels							
United States							
All nonwar phases							
Direct	1.84		-2.15	-1.57	-0.58	2.56	3.27
Indirect		-0.28	-2.38	-2.06	-0.32	5.41	
Pre–World War I, post–World War II							
Direct	1.62		-1.40	-1.51	0.11	1.81	3.37
Indirect		-0.27	-2.23	-1.78	-0.45	7.25	
United Kingdom							
All nonwar phases							
Direct	4.39		2.52	1.93	0.59	4.78	3.49
Indirect		0.46	0.93	1.40	-0.47	0.57	

Rates of Change

United States							
All nonwar phases							
Direct	2.24	0.59	1.56	0.26	1.30	6.10	3.31
Indirect			-0.86	-0.64	-0.22	1.44	
Pre–World War I, post–World War II							
Direct	1.82	0.64	1.39	0.68	0.71	4.06	3.40
Indirect			0.39	1.04	-0.65	3.22	
United Kingdom							
All nonwar phases							
Direct	2.84	1.91	3.65	2.49	1.16	7.24	3.63
Indirect			2.54	2.70	-0.16	2.47	
United States and United Kingdom							
Pre–World War I plus post–World War II, United States; all nonwar, United Kingdom[a]							
Direct	2.91	0.78	1.81	1.03	0.78	14.88	3.20
Indirect			1.09	1.25	-0.16	4.82	

[a]A country dummy was included in the United States plus United Kingdom equations.

Note: Transient effects from direct income calculations are not shown because there was no occasion to estimate them in chapter 8.

Table 9.10   Variability of Prices and Output, before and after Allowing for Effects of Money; Money and Yields; Current and Prior Money; Current and Prior Money and Prior Income; and Trend

Period and Country				Measure of Variability[a]			
					After Allowing for Trend and Money		
				and Prior Money		and Prior Money and Prior Income	
	Total[b,c] (1)	Only[c] (2)	and Yields[c] (3)	Only (4)	Plus Transient Effects (5)	Only (6)	Plus Transient Effects (7)
Levels							
United States							
All nonwar	57.16	8.24	8.26	7.52	7.20	7.98	7.13
All nonwar, excluding interwar	64.26	5.98	5.69	4.66	4.81	5.72	4.98
United Kingdom							
All nonwar	74.82	6.77	5.97	3.68	3.33	4.13	4.14
Rates of Change							
United States							
All nonwar	2.54	1.43	1.38	1.21	1.01	1.31	1.35
All nonwar, excluding interwar	2.21	1.35	1.33	1.04	0.93	1.24	1.15
United Kingdom							
All nonwar	2.49	1.00	0.74	0.82	0.57	0.71	0.66
United States and United Kingdom							
All nonwar, excluding interwar, United States	2.39	1.11	0.96	0.97	0.76	0.95	0.88

Prices

Levels							
United States							
All nonwar	95.75	8.61	7.95	6.58	5.91	6.70	5.86
All nonwar, excluding interwar	107.62	6.18	5.76	4.66	4.39	4.66	4.01
United Kingdom							
All nonwar	52.44	8.85	5.90	7.59	5.96	6.25	6.27
Rates of Change							
United States							
All nonwar	2.58	1.61	1.49	1.33	1.35	1.19	1.15
All nonwar, excluding interwar	1.52	1.51	1.46	1.10	1.04	0.95	0.97
United Kingdom							
All nonwar	0.63	0.65	0.60	0.64	0.65	0.68	0.67
United States and United Kingdom							
All nonwar excluding interwar, United States	1.29	1.00	0.95	0.91	0.93	0.85	0.86

[a]For levels, measure of variability is standard deviation of logarithm times 100, which is equivalent to coefficient of variation of original observations in percent. For example, a measure of 10 means the standard deviation is 10 percent of the mean. For rates of change, measure is standard deviation of percentage rate of change. For example, a measure of 2 means that, if the residuals are normally distributed, two-thirds will be between +2 percent and −2 percent per year.

[b]Number of observations is as follows:

	Cols. 1–3	Cols. 4–7		Cols. 1–3	Cols. 4–7
Levels			**Rates of Change**		
United States			United States		
All nonwar	42	42	All nonwar	37	37
Nonwar excluding interwar	33	33	Nonwar excluding interwar	30	30
United Kingdom			United Kingdom		
All nonwar	28	26	All nonwar	25	22

[c]Note that the variability estimates for United Kingdom nonwar phases in cols. 1, 2, and 3 are not strictly comparable to those in columns 4 to 7 because they are based (as footnote b indicates) on more observations. However, the differences are small and would not affect our conclusions; hence we have given only one set of measurements.

Table 9.11 Cumulative Effect on the Rate of Growth of Prices and Output of a Sustained One Percentage Point Increase in the Rate of Monetary Growth Initiated in Phase t; Eliminating and Including Transient Effects: United States, All Nonwar Phases Excluding Interwar; United Kingdom, All Nonwar Phases; United States Plus United Kingdom, All Nonwar Phases Excluding United States Interwar

Country				Cumulative Effect at Phase				
	t	$t+1$	$t+2$	$t+3$	$t+4$	$t+5$	$t+6$	∞
				PRICES				
			Levels, Eliminating Transient Effects					
United States	1.501	1.015	0.971	0.991	0.999	1.000	1.000	1.000
United Kingdom	0.304	0.784	0.880	0.944	0.978	0.995	1.007	1.000
			Levels, Including Transient Effects					
United States	1.501	0.161	0.753	0.991	0.999	1.000	1.000	1.000
United Kingdom	0.304	1.314	0.703	0.944	0.978	0.995	1.007	1.000
			Rates of Change, Eliminating Transient Effects					
United States	0.118	0.992	1.005	1.005	1.003	1.001	1.000	1.000
United Kingdom	−0.540	0.348	0.668	0.925	1.037	1.052	1.031	1.000
United States and United Kingdom	−0.053	0.664	0.819	0.930	0.986	1.005	1.008	1.000
			Rates of Change, Including Transient Effects					
United States	0.617	0.678	1.005	1.005	1.003	1.001	1.000	1.000
United Kingdom	0.484	0.289	0.668	0.925	1.037	1.052	1.031	1.000
United States and United Kingdom	−0.490	0.590	0.819	0.930	0.986	1.005	1.008	1.000

OUTPUT

Levels, Eliminating Transient Effects							
United States	−0.443	0.060	0.045	0.009	0.000	0.000	0.000	0.000
United Kingdom	0.167	−0.019	0.038	0.041	0.030	0.016	0.002	0.000
Levels, Including Transient Effects								
United States	−0.443	1.018	0.030	0.009	0.000	0.000	0.000	0.000
United Kingdom	0.167	−0.003	−0.155	0.041	0.030	0.016	0.002	0.000
Rates of Change, Eliminating Transient Effects								
United States	0.360	−0.226	−0.100	−0.041	−0.015	−0.005	−0.001	0.000
United Kingdom	0.176	−0.152	0.086	0.113	0.066	0.020	−0.003	0.000
United States and United Kingdom	0.235	−0.102	0.014	0.036	0.026	0.013	0.004	0.000
Rates of Change, Including Transient Effects								
United States	0.295	−0.036	−0.100	−0.041	−0.015	−0.005	−0.001	0.000
United Kingdom	0.061	−0.278	0.086	0.113	0.066	0.020	−0.003	0.000
United States and United Kingdom	0.222	−0.226	0.014	0.036	0.026	0.013	0.004	0.000

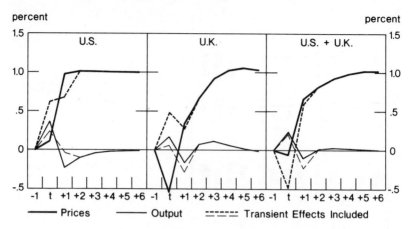

Chart 9.5   Reaction patterns of price and output to monetary change: United States, United Kingdom, and United States and United Kingdom (based on rates of change for all nonwar phases excluding United States interwar)

appreciable, output reaction is cyclical—first positive, reflecting the delay in the reaction of prices, then negative, as prices take over, then again positive.

These reaction patterns are suggestive, but we do not regard them as at all firmly established. They are a highly manufactured product and hence sensitive to small errors in the coefficients of the equations from which they are derived. For example, the patterns for the United States and the United Kingdom differ substantially, yet there is no statistically significant difference between the equations from which they are derived.

For the two countries together, the price pattern is very smooth, almost approximating an exponential approach to equilibrium. The output pattern remains cyclical as for each country separately and is quite sharply damped. The transient component is small, as it is for each country separately.

Though none of these patterns is statistically very reliable, they do correspond to the kind of pattern of reaction that is suggested by the theoretical analysis of chapter 2 and therefore give no reason to modify that analysis. Accordingly, we proceed to a more sophisticated application of it.

9.7   Effect of Output Capacity and Anticipations: The Phillips Curve Approach

By assuming up to now that $\xi = 0$ in equations (1) and (2), we have so far ruled out the effect that A. W. Phillips[19] incorporated in his famous

19. "The Relation between Unemployment and the Rate of Change of Money Wage Rates in the United Kingdom, 1861–1957," *Economica* 25 (November 1958): 283–99.

curve and that has played such an important part in the post–World War II economic literature bearing on the relation between inflation and unemployment. This literature has almost all been concerned with cyclical fluctuations rather than the longer-term movements with which we deal, yet it offers a convenient and familiar framework for investigating the factors affecting the division from phase to phase of changes in nominal income between prices and output. Moreover, as we have seen, in these matters the "short run" may not be very brief chronologically.

In his original article, Phillips related the level of utilization of capacity, which he measured inversely by the unemployment rate, to the rate of change of nominal wages. He argued that a high level of unemployment (a low level of utilization of capacity) was a sign that the quantity of labor offered at the going rate exceeded the quantity of labor demanded and hence exerted downward pressure on wage rates and conversely. Later writers extended the relationship from wages to prices, on the ground that prices move with costs and that labor costs dominate total costs. The theoretical argument is unexceptionable if "wages" are interpreted as "real wages."[20] However, Phillips himself, and for a long time most of his followers, interpreted "wages" as nominal wages.

It is interesting to note that in 1926 Irving Fisher studied precisely the same statistical relationship but justified it theoretically in a very different way, as an effect running from the rate of change of prices to employment rather than the other way.[21]

In terms of our framework, the Phillips curve explanation, if expressed in linear form, can be regarded as a special case of equations (1) and (2) of this chapter. If we replace $g_Y - g_Y^*$ in equations (1) and (2) by its equivalent from equation (4), they become

(18) $$g_P = g_P^* + \eta \Psi(g_M - g_M^*) + \xi(\log y' - \log y'^*)$$

(19) $$g_{y'} = g_{y'}^* + (1 - \eta) \Psi(g_M - g_M^*) - \xi(\log y' - \log y'^*),$$

where η is the fraction of an unanticipated change in nominal income that is absorbed by unanticipated price change and Ψ is the multiplier relating unanticipated change in nominal income to unanticipated change in money.

In the initial version of the Phillips curve, it was implicitly assumed that $g_P^* = 0$, though nothing essential is altered if g_P^* is assumed equal to a constant other than zero. In addition, its strictest form, which regards the level of unemployment as the only factor affecting the rate of change of

20. See Milton Friedman, "The Role of Monetary Policy," *American Economic Review* 58 (March 1968): 1–17, reprinted in *The Optimum Quantity of Money*, pp. 95–110, especially p. 102.

21. "A Statistical Relation between Unemployment and Price Changes," *International Labour Review* 6 (June 1926): 785–92, reprinted in the *Journal of Political Economy* 81 (March/April 1973): 496–502.

prices, is equivalent to assuming $\eta = 0$. On these assumptions, equations (18) and (19) become:

(20) $$g_P = g_P^* + \xi \log (y'/y'^*), \text{ and}$$

(21) $$g_{y'} = g_{y'}^* + \Psi(g_M - g_M^*) - \xi \log (y'/y'^*),$$

or, since $\Psi g_M^* = g_Y^*$ and $g_Y^* = g_P^* + g_{y'}^*$,

(22) $$g_{y'} = -g_P^* + \Psi g_M - \xi \log (y'/y'^*).$$

This version is the obvious counterpart of the simple Keynesian hypothesis. Monetary change impinges in the first instance entirely on output, and affects prices only through the ratio of actual to potential output.

"Unfortunately for this hypothesis, . . . evidence failed to confirm it. Empirical estimates of the Phillips curve relation were unsatisfactory. More important, the inflation rate that appeared to be consistent with a specified level of unemployment did not remain fixed: in the circumstances of the post–World War II period, when governments everywhere were seeking to promote 'full employment,' it tended in any one country to rise over time and to vary sharply among countries. Looked at the other way, rates of inflation that had earlier been associated with low levels of unemployment were experienced along with high levels of unemployment. The phenomenon of simultaneous high inflation and high unemployment increasingly forced itself on public and professional notice, receiving the unlovely label of 'stagflation.' "[22]

Our data for cycle phases confirm this generally negative verdict.[23] To fit equations (20) and (22), we need an empirical counterpart to y'/y'^* in addition to our rates of change of money, prices, and output. One approach would be to treat y'^* as an unobservable anticipated magnitude, as we have treated Y^*. We have not followed that approach but rather have interpreted y'^* as corresponding to long-run potential output, and hence $\log y'/y'^*$ as the logarithm of the ratio of actual to potential output, capable of being directly apprehended by the economic actors. We have simply tried to find an empirical proxy for this concept. After much experimentation, we settled on the logarithm of the ratio of real income per capita for each phase to an exponential trend fitted to the phase averages of real income per capita. The trend allows for slow changes in productive capacity, the ratio to trend for shorter period

22. See Milton Friedman, "Inflation and Unemployment" (Nobel Lecture, 1976), reprinted in *Journal of Political Economy* 85 (June 1977): 451–72; quotation from p. 455.

23. For the rest of this chapter, we restrict the empirical analysis to rates of change instead, as hitherto, of making dual calculations for levels and rates of change. This economy is justified by the earlier sections of this chapter. When the results differed for levels and rates of change, we have generally decided in favor of the rate of change results.

changes in the rate of utilization of capacity. We term this measure the output ratio and denote it by $R_{y'}(t)$.[24]

Table 9.12 summarizes the estimates of equations (20) and (22), with g_P^* treated as a constant. For all nonwar phases in the equation for g_P, the coefficient of $R_{y'}$ is positive for both the United States and the United Kingdom. However, it does not differ significantly from zero for the United States at the .05 level, and barely does so for the United Kingdom. Moreover, for the United States, the sign of the coefficient is reversed if the idiosyncratic interwar period is excluded. For all three

24. The chief alternative we considered was the average fraction of the labor force employed during each phase. For the United States, we use the complement of the unemployment rate for 1890–1939 constructed by Stanley Lebergott (*Manpower in Economic Growth* [New York: McGraw-Hill, 1964], pp. 43–512) that he linked to the Census Bureau's Current Population Survey P-50 reports for 1940–46; thereafter we work with the figures given in *Economic Report of the President Transmitted to the Congress January 1979*, table B-27, p. 21. For the United Kingdom, we use the complement of the unemployment rate for 1870–1965 in C. H. Feinstein (*National Income, Expenditure and Output of the United Kingdom, 1855–1965* [Cambridge: Cambridge University Press, 1972], table 57, pp. T125–27), extended by us for 1966–75 by adding figures for Great Britain (*Annual Abstract of Statistics* 113 [1976]: 150) and for Northern Ireland (*Digest of Statistics* 47 [March 1977]: 8, 13) for civilian working population and unemployment to derive the United Kingdom unemployment rate. We interpret a high fraction of the complement as meaning a high ratio of utilization of capacity and conversely. We shall refer to this measure as the employment ratio.

Neither measure is satisfactory—the output ratio, because a single exponential trend is an unduly crude representation of the long-run change in productive potential, the employment ratio, because it refers to only one category of productive resources and, in addition, is not very reliable statistically.

For the United States there seems a clear case for preferring the output ratio: first, the output ratio is available for the whole of our period, the employment ratio, only since 1890: second, the two ratios are highly correlated (for phase averages, .72 from 1890–91 to 1973–75; for annual observations, .90 from 1890 to 1975); third, a considerable number of test correlations using the two measures as alternatives generally yielded more reasonable and statistically more reliable results when the output ratio served as the measure of capacity utilization.

For the United Kingdom, the choice is less clear. First, both measures are available for the whole of our period. Second, the correlation between them, while positive, is much lower than for the United States (for phase averages, .59 from 1874–79 to 1973–75; for annual observations, .61 from 1874 to 1975). Third, in test correlations, sometimes one measure yields more reasonable and statistically more reliable results, sometimes the other. On the whole, the output ratio perhaps has a slight margin in its favor, but that margin could be readily reversed by a different implicit weighting of the test correlations.

In the absence of a clear case for the United Kingdom, we have used the output ratio for both countries in order to maintain comparability. We have checked to make sure that our major conclusions would not be reversed for the United Kingdom by the substitution of the employment ratio.

The output ratio has recently been used in related contexts in two articles in a single issue of the *American Economic Review* 70 (March 1980): Vito Tanzi, "Inflationary Expectations, Economic Activity, Taxes, and Interest Rates," pp. 12–21; and Jeffrey Sachs, "The Changing Cyclical Behavior of Wages and Prices," pp. 78–90.

Table 9.12 **Estimates of Simple Phillips Curve, Nonwar Phases**

Equations Fitted $g_P = a + c\,R_{y'}$
$g_{y'} = a' + b'\,g_M + c'\,R_{y'}$

Country and Period	Dependent Variable	Coefficient (and Absolute t Value)			Number of Observations	Variability[a]	
		Constant Term	Monetary Growth (g_M)	Output Ratio ($R_{y'}$)		Total	Residual
United States							
All nonwar	g_P	0.001 (0.3)		0.053 (1.9)	37	2.54	2.45
	$g_{y'}$	0.014 (3.5)	0.464 (5.8)	0.022 (1.0)		2.58	1.61
All nonwar excluding interwar	g_P	0.016 (3.2)		-0.117 (2.0)	30	2.21	2.10
	$g_{y'}$	0.026 (3.4)	0.160 (1.2)	0.084 (2.1)		1.52	1.43
United Kingdom							
All nonwar	g_P	0.003 (0.6)		0.118 (2.2)	24	2.54	2.35
	$g_{y'}$	0.022 (11.1)	0.002 (0.04)	-0.015 (1.0)		0.64	0.65

[a]Standard deviation of percentage rates of change.

equations, the reduction in variability by taking $R_{y'}$ into account is trivial in size. In addition, while equations (20) and (22) have constant terms and coefficients of $R_{y'}$ that are equal in size and opposite in sign for the g_P and $g_{y'}$ equations, all constant terms in table 9.12 are positive, and the coefficients of $R_{y'}$ for the United States for all nonwar phases are of the same sign for g_P and $g_{y'}$. For the other pair of United States equations, the two coefficients are opposite in sign and do not differ significantly in size. For the United Kingdom pair, the coefficients are opposite in sign but differ significantly in size. As always for United Kingdom output, the series looks like white noise. At most, the calculations show only a trace of a simple Phillips curve effect.[25]

One reaction to the failure of the simple Phillips curve was an attempt by many economists to retain the basic idea, by keeping $\eta = 0$, but to eliminate the conflict with observation by treating the anticipated rate of inflation g_P^*, in equation (20) as a variable adapting to experience rather than a constant. Such an expectations-adjusted Phillips curve is indirectly a way to move from nominal wages to real wages.[26]

This modification leaves a "short-run" trade off between the level of unemployment and the rate of inflation because g_P^* is taken to be relatively sluggish, adapting only gradually to experience. However, taken as it stands, equation (20) would deny any "long-run" trade off, since once expectations adapt to experience, $(g_P - g_P^*) = 0$ and hence, with $\eta = 0$, $\log y' = \log y'^*$, which means that there is no relation between the absolute rate of inflation and the observed level of utilization of capacity. (This has come to be known as the "accelerationist hypothesis.")

To retain the possibility of a long-run trade off, investigators have rewritten equation (20) by attaching a coefficient to g_P^* that can differ from unity, but still assuming $\eta = 0$.

In addition, they have kept the idea of a constant element in inflationary expectations by adding a constant term. This gives[27]

(23) $$g_P = a_0 + a_1 g_P^* + \xi R_{y'},$$

(24) $$g_{y'} = -a_1 g_P^* + \psi g_M - \xi R_{y'}.$$

25. The results for subperiods are consistent with this general conclusion.

26. For a fuller discussion, see Milton Friedman, *Price Theory* (Chicago: Aldine, 1976), pp. 221–29.

27. Stephen J. Turnovsky, "On the Role of Inflationary Expectations in a Short-Run Macro-economic Model," *Economic Journal* 84 (June 1974): 317–37, gives an excellent analysis of this approach and summarizes some of the statistical studies using it. His equation (11) is, except for notation and a linear approximation to the final term, identical with equation (23).

Investigators have then explored whether $a_1 = 1$ in the long run. Most have concluded that a_1 is less than unity, implying that there remains a long-run trade off. However, this conclusion has been questioned as reflecting both statistical bias and mistaken specification of the appropriate test.[28] The essential criticisms are twofold: (1) That the statistical studies have stressed exclusively the influence running from employment to prices, neglecting entirely the reverse influence that is given primary pride of place by Irving Fisher in his 1926 article. Essentially this criticism is that it is inappropriate to treat η as equal to zero in deriving equation (20).[29] (2) That the studies have used models for the formation of

28. For the criticisms, see Thomas J. Sargent, "A Note on the 'Accelerationist' Controversy," *Journal of Money, Credit and Banking* 3 (August 1971): 721–25, and his "Rational Expectations, the Real Rate of Interest, and the 'Natural' Rate of Unemployment," *Brookings Economic Papers*, no. 2 (1973), pp. 429–72. Robert E. Lucas, Jr., "Econometric Testing of the Natural Rate Hypothesis," in *The Econometrics of Price Determination Conference*, ed. Otto Eckstein (Washington: Board of Governors of the Federal Reserve System and Social Science Research Council, 1972); Robert E. Lucas, Jr., "Some International Evidence on Output-Inflation Trade-offs," *American Economic Review* 63 (June 1973): 326–34; and R. Auerbach and R. Moses, "A Comment on Rothschild's 'The Phillips Curve and All That,'" *Scottish Journal of Political Economy* 21 (November 1974): 299–301.

For attempts to estimate a_1 in equation (23) concluding that it is less than unity, see R. M. Solow, "Recent Controversy in the Theory of Inflation: An Eclectic View," in *Inflation: Its Causes, Consequences and Control*, ed. S. W. Rousseas (Wilton, Conn.: Kazanjian Economics Foundation, 1968), and idem, *Price Expectations and the Behavior of the Price Level* (Manchester: Manchester University Press, 1969); R. J. Gordon, "Inflation in Recession and Recovery," *Brookings Papers on Economic Activity*, no. 1 (1971), pp. 105–58; S. J. Turnovsky, "The Expectations Hypothesis and the Aggregate Wage Equation: Some Empirical Evidence for Canada," *Economica* 39 (February 1972): 1–17; S. J. Turnovsky and M. L. Wachter, "A Test of the 'Expectations Hypothesis' Using Directly Observed Wage and Price Change Expectations," *Review of Economics and Statistics* 54 (January 1972): 47–54.

Three recent review articles contain additional references: R. J. Barro and S. Fischer, "Recent Developments in Monetary Theory," and R. J. Gordon, "Recent Developments in the Theory of Inflation and Unemployment," both in *Journal of Monetary Economics* 2 (April 1976): 133–67, 185–219; and A. M. Santomero and J. J. Seater, "The Inflation-Unemployment Trade-off: A Critique of the Literature," *Journal of Economic Literature* 16 (June 1978): 499–544.

See also the papers and references in Bennett T. McCallum, ed., "Rational Expectations: A Seminar Sponsored by the American Enterprise Institute," *Journal of Money, Credit and Banking* 12 (November 1980, part 2): 691–836.

29. Some of the studies are subject to still other criticism. For example, Solow, in *Price Expectations and the Behavior of the Price Level*, fits an equation like equation (23) except that, to allow for costs as well as demand, he includes on the right-hand side the rate of change of wages. There is no reason to expect a_1 to be unity in such an equation, which is concerned with the margin between prices and wages rather than the behavior of either separately. Let the anticipated rate of inflation go up by one percentage point but the rate of change of wages be unchanged. Any resulting rise in prices would stimulate output by increasing selling prices relative to costs, which implies that, even if a_1 in equation (23) were unity, Solow's counterpart would be less than unity.

expectations(g_P^*) that may not be "rational," in the sense that they do not involve the full utilization of the data available to participants in forming their expectations.[30] This criticism applies equally to the adaptive expectations models that we have used in previous chapters and that we use in the next section.

In a series of very interesting and important papers, Lucas and Sargent have explored the implication of the rational expectations hypothesis and have tried to derive empirical tests of the slope of the long-run Phillips curve without the possibly misleading assumption of adaptive expectations.[31]

Their empirical tests use a different kind of information. For example, one implication of a rational expectations hypothesis is that, in a country in which prices have fluctuated a great deal, expectations will respond to changes in the current rate of inflation much more rapidly than in a country in which prices have been relatively stable. It follows that the observed short-run Phillips curve will be steeper in the first country than in the second. (We explore this effect with our data below.) Comparisons among countries in this way, as well as other tests, seem so far entirely consistent with what any reasonable person must surely expect: that, *since you can't fool all the people all the time, the true long-run Phillips curve is vertical.* However, the evidence is by no means all in, so we cannot regard the matter as settled.

On the more limited issue of whether it is appropriate to regard $\eta = 0$, and the output ratio as the major determinant of the deviation of the rate of inflation from its anticipated value, we can alter equation (20) by including a term in g_M. For this purpose, a crude and yet simple way of allowing for both inflationary anticipations (g_P^*) and anticipations about monetary growth (g_M^*) seems adequate. Accordingly, we do so in equation (18) by approximating ($g_P^* - \eta\psi g_M^*$) by $g_P(t-1)$ times a coefficient.[32]

---

30. Note the words "may not be." The adaptive expectations models that we and other investigators have used may or may not be "rational," depending on the assumed stochastic structure of disturbances. Brunner, Cukierman, and Meltzer, in their formal models constructed in the papers referred to in footnote 9 above, assume a stochastic structure under which adaptive expectations are "rational."

31. This and the following paragraph are from Milton Friedman, *Price Theory*, p. 231. The papers alluded to are: Robert E. Lucas, Jr., "Econometric Testing of the Natural Rate Hypothesis," in *The Econometrics of Price Determination Conference*, ed. Otto Eckstein, and "Econometric Policy Evaluation: A Critique," in *The Phillips Curve and Labor Markets*, ed. K. Brunner and A. H. Meltzer (Carnegie-Rochester Conference Series on Public Policy, vol. 1, 1976), pp. 19–46; Thomas J. Sargent, "Rational Expectations, the Real Rate of Interest, and the 'Natural' Rate of Unemployment," *Brookings Papers on Economic Activity*, no. 2, pp. 429–72.

32. One way of rationalizing this approach is by supposing that $g_P(t)$ is a random walk, so that the best estimate of $g_P^*(t)$ is $g_P(t-1)$, and that $g_M^*(t)$ can be regarded as a roughly constant fraction of $g_P^*(t)$, so that a proxy for $g_P^*(t)$ is also a proxy for $g_P^*(t) - \eta\psi g_M^*(t)$. Of course, there are many other possible rationalizations.

The resulting equations are:

(25) $g_P(t) = a_o + a_1 g_P(t-1) + \eta\psi g_M(t) + \xi R_{y'}(t)$

(26) $g_{y'}(t) = a_o' - a_1 g_P(t-1) + (1-\eta)\psi g_M(t) - \xi R_{y'}(t)$.

Table 9.13 reports estimates of these equations computed without the cross-equation restrictions on their coefficients embedded in equations (25) and (26).

These results make it clear that monetary growth is far more important than the output ratio—in our terms, if either η or ξ is to be set equal to zero, far better to set $\xi = 0$, certainly for the price equations. The only statistically significant coefficient of $R_{y'}$ in any of the price equations is for all United States nonwar phases, and for that equation the effect is in the wrong direction, the estimated ξ being negative rather than positive—a point to which we shall return.

For both price and output equations, the t value for the coefficient of g_M is consistently higher than for the coefficient of $R_{y'}$, and all but one of the coefficients of g_M is statistically significant. Not surprisingly, that one is for United Kingdom output—a series we have consistently been unable to explain. It appears, so far as we can tell, to be a purely random series.

The prior rate of price change has a statistically significant effect in all equations other than the United Kingdom output equation. For all three price equations, it is the single most important variable; for the two United States output equations, monetary growth is.

For the United States, the coefficients of $g_P(t-1)$ and g_M are not inconsistent with the restrictions embedded in equations (25) and (26): the coefficients of prior price change for the price and output equations are opposite in sign and not significantly different in size; the coefficients of monetary growth add up to 1.07 and 0.94, respectively, which are consistent with a theoretically anticipated value of ψ of about unity. For the United Kingdom, neither restriction is well satisfied—another example of our inability to interpret real income movements in the United Kingdom.

The residual variability is consistently lower, except again for the United Kingdom output equation, than the lowest variability obtained in table 9.10. This result may simply reflect the high serial correlation of g_P. However, it may also be evidence in favor of the validity of the approach incorporated in equations (18) and (19), except for the condition that ξ is either zero or not well identified. To illustrate, consider the price equations for the United States, excluding the interwar period, and for the United Kingdom for all nonwar phases, omitting, for both countries, the statistically not significant term in $R_{y'}$:

(27)   United States $g_P(t) = -0.009 + 0.686 g_P(t-1)$
                                        $+ 0.296\, g_M(t)$

Table 9.13   Estimates of Relations between Rates of Change of Prices and Output, and Prior Price Change and Output Ratio, Nonwar Phases

Equations Fitted: $g_P = a + b\,g_P(t-1) + c g_M(t) + d\,R_{y'}(t)$

$g_{y'} = a' + b'\,g_P(t-1) + c'\,g_M(t) + d'\,R_{y'}(t)$

Country and Period	Dependent Variable	Coefficient (and Absolute t Value) of				Number of Observations	Variability	
		Constant Term	Prior Price Change $g_P(t-1)$	Monetary Growth g_M	Output Ratio $R_{y'}$		Total	Residual
United States								
All nonwar	$g_P(t)$	−0.008 (3.6)	0.614 (9.1)	0.314 (6.4)	−0.036 (3.6)	37	2.54	0.75
	$g_{y'}(t)$	0.001 (0.4)	−0.627 (6.3)	0.760 (10.5)	0.022 (1.5)		2.58	1.10
All nonwar excluding interwar	$g_P(t)$	−0.009 (1.8)	0.686 (6.5)	0.296 (2.8)	−0.014 (0.5)	30	2.21	0.74
	$g_{y'}(t)$	0.009 (1.2)	−0.615 (3.6)	0.645 (3.7)	−0.001 (0.0)		1.52	1.20
United Kingdom								
All nonwar	$g_P(t)$	−0.006 (2.5)	0.582 (6.1)	0.422 (4.9)	0.014 (0.9)	24	2.54	0.58
	$g_{y'}(t)$	0.020 (7.0)	−0.113 (1.1)	0.086 (0.9)	−0.008 (0.5)		0.64	0.65

(28)   United
              Kingdom $g_P(t) = -0.006 + 0.582g_P(t-1)$
                           $+ 0.422g_M(t).$

The first observation suggested by these results is that the two equations are very similar. They clearly do not differ significantly.

A second observation is that both equations imply that in the long run (when $g_P(t) = g_P(t-1)$), the difference between g_M and g_P is roughly a constant, the relevant equations being:

(29)   United States $g_P(t) = -0.029 + 0.94g_M$

(30)   United Kingdom $g_P(t) = -0.014 + 1.01g_M.$

The constant term in principle is equal in numerical value but opposite in sign to the long-term rate of output growth times the income elasticity of demand for real balances, which is close to unity for both countries. The computed constant term does approximate the long-term rate of output growth, which was 3.1 percent per year for the United States, 1.7 percent per year for the United Kingdom. The coefficient of g_M is not significantly different from unity for either equation—the strict quantity theory conclusion.

A third observation is that, if we can take Ψ to be close to unity, the coefficient of g_M in equations (27) and (28) is an estimate of η—the fraction of unanticipated change in nominal income (i.e., the difference between actual and anticipated nominal income growth) absorbed by unanticipated price change (i.e., the difference between actual and anticipated inflation). The estimate is in the neighborhood of one-third for both countries. Other studies have shown a strong and systematic effect of unanticipated monetary growth on output but most such studies have been for quarterly or annual data.[33] Our results suggest that the averaging

33. Robert J. Barro, "Unanticipated Money Growth and Unemployment in the United States," *American Economic Review* 67 (March 1977): 101–15: "Unanticipated Money, Output, and the Price Level in the United States," *Journal of Political Economy* 86 (August 1978): 549–80; Robert J. Barro and Mark Rush, "Unanticipated Money and Economic Activity," in *Rational Expectations and Economic Policy*, ed. Stanley Fischer (Chicago: University of Chicago Press, 1980), pp. 23–48.

Robert J. Gordon, in his comment on the Barro-Rush paper (ibid. pp. 55–63) points out that the evidence in these papers does not reject the hypothesis that anticipated as well as unanticipated monetary changes affect real output, and he presents statistical evidence to support his skepticism. Gordon's analysis and evidence are persuasive. We suspect, however, that the key issue is not "anticipated" versus "unanticipated" but the time period discussed in footnote 9 above. Two time points are relevant: the date at which anticipations are formed; the date to which they refer. A change at time t anticipated at time $t-1$ may have been unanticipated at time $t-2$. It will presumably not affect real output decisions made at time $t-1$; it will affect those made at time $t-2$.

Barro's approach defines "unanticipated" entirely in terms of a one-year time span. Given the existence of longer term contracts, what Gordon designates as "anticipated" may

involved in calculating cycle phases does not eliminate such an effect. As we also noted in section 9.3, the period of adjustment to unanticipated changes is surprisingly long.

One implication of the theory of rational expectations that was pointed out by Lucas and mentioned above is that the response to monetary change might well depend on anticipations not only about the level of inflation but also about the variability of inflation. In an economy in which the rate of change in the general level of prices has been highly stable, anticipations about that rate of change might be expected to be held with considerable confidence. Much new evidence will be required before participants in the economy come to interpret changes in the nominal demand for their products and services as reflecting changes in the rate of inflation rather than in relative demand. Conversely, in an economy that has experienced frequent and substantial changes in the rate of inflation, participants will readily alter their inflationary anticipations. We would expect a changed rate of monetary growth to be reflected initially more in output and less in prices in the first economy than in the second (that is, we would expect η to be smaller), and a longer period to elapse before the change was fully reflected in prices.

Lucas explored this implication in terms of differences among countries. In an interesting paper, Benjamin Klein has done so for time-series data for the United States.[34] As a measure of what he calls "short-term price unpredictability," Klein initially used a moving variance of rates of inflation. In his calculations for the United States with annual data, he related this variable to "long-term price unpredictability" to show an upward shift in the amount of long-term relative to short-term price uncertainty dating from the mid-1950s.

---

well have been unanticipated at the time the contracts were entered into. An attempt by Stanley Fischer to test the effect of including forecast errors for a two-year as well as a one-year time span yielded a lower residual variability. However, the effect was small (ibid., pp. 234–35).

Our own results suffer from the same difficulty as Barro's but to a lesser extent because of the longer and variable time unit.

In a recent article, Gordon provides independent confirmation, based on annual data for the United States, of our estimate that about one-third of the unanticipated change in nominal income is absorbed by unanticipated prices change. He writes: "nominal GNP changes have been divided consistently, with two-thirds taking the form of output change and the remaining one-third the form of price change. ("A Consistent Characterization of a Near-Century of Price Behavior," *American Economic Review Papers and Proceedings* 70 [May 1980]: 243–49; quotation from p. 243).

34. "Our New Monetary Standard: The Measurement and Effects of Price Uncertainty, 1880–1973," *Economic Inquiry* 13 (April 1975): 461–84. Klein included his "short-term price unpredictability" variable in demand for money regressions. The variable produced an increase in voluntarily held money balances ("The Demand for Quality-Adjusted Cash Balances: Price Uncertainty in the U. S. Demand for Money Function," *Journal of Political Economy* 85 (August 1977): 691–715).

Subsequently, in response to criticisms from Ibrahim and Williams, Klein developed what he regarded as superior measures of expected price variability.[35] We have calculated phase averages for both Klein's initial variable and his subsequent revised version of short-term price unpredictability (which we designate EVP), for both our United States and our United Kingdom data, and have added EVP to the regressions for $g_{y'}$ summarized in table 9.13 to test its usefulness.[36] Unfortunately the results were not encouraging. The coefficient of EVP does not differ significantly from zero for any of the three regressions corresponding to those in table 9.13.

These results do not invalidate the theoretical expectation that a high expected variability of prices will make for a fuller and more prompt adjustment of prices and a smaller adjustment of output in response to changes in monetary growth. We suspect that our results reflect much more the defects of the particular measure of expected variability of price plus the small number of degrees of freedom available to test its role.

One bit of evidence that our negative results may reflect the defect of our measure of uncertainty comes from a study by Donald Mullineaux of the effect of inflation uncertainty on employment and output in the United States during the post–World War II period. He uses two measures: "a moving-standard deviation of the observed inflation rate"—similar in kind though not in detail to the Klein measure—and "a time-series of standard deviations calculated from cross-section surveys of inflation anticipations." He found that the second measure "significantly affected unemployment and production" for both a longer (1950–75) and a shorter (1958–75) period he examined but that the first affected them only for the shorter period. Unfortunately, the cross-section measure of uncertainty that he used is available only for the post–World War II period, so we could not test it with our data.[37]

A more promising body of evidence for a test of the role of uncertainty over a longer period might be obtained from cross-country comparisons, such as those suggested by Lucas.

35. See B. Ibrahim and R. Williams, "Price Unpredictability and Monetary Standards: A Comment on Klein's Measure of Price Uncertainty," *Economic Inquiry* 16 (July 1978): 413–37; Benjamin Klein, "The Measurement of Long- and Short-Term Price Uncertainty: A Moving Regression Time Series Analysis," *Economic Inquiry* 16 (July 1978): 438–52.

36. We are grateful to Klein and to Michael Melvin for constructing the relevant United Kingdom series for us.

37. Donald J. Mullineaux, "Unemployment, Industrial Production, and Inflation Uncertainty in the United States," *Review of Economics and Statistics* 62 (May 1980): 163–69.

9.8   Effect of Output Capacity and Anticipations: The Approach through Alternative Models of the Formation of Anticipations

The results of the previous section seemed sufficiently encouraging to justify trying to adopt a more sophisticated approach to the formation of anticipations about g_P^*, $g_{y'}^*$, and g_M^* than the assumption that $g_P(t-1)$ is a satisfactory proxy for $g_P^* - \eta\psi g_M^*$. Accordingly, we have considered a number of alternative hypotheses in an attempt to approximate these unobservable magnitudes. Though our experiment unfortunately turned out to be unsuccessful, we did have one rather interesting by-product, not about anticipations but about the role of capacity utilization.

9.8.1   Alternative Hypotheses

Since

$$g_P^* + g_{y'}^* = g_Y^* \, ,$$

only two of three anticipated magnitudes are independent. We have earlier assumed that g_Y^* can be regarded as given by the Cagan-Koyck adaptive expectations mechanism (see equation A11 in sec. 8.4). That assumption yielded reasonably satisfactory results. We have therefore retained it and concentrated here on $g_{y'}^*$, treating g_P^* as given by $g_Y^* - g_{y'}^*$.

We list in the text below the alternative hypotheses we have considered, relegating the details about the equations that embody them to section 9.10.5.

Unchanging Anticipations

The simplest approach is to suppose that economic actors treat both $g_{y'}^*$ and g_M^* as constants.

In view of the absence of any long-period trends in $g_{y'}$ and the dependence of its secular movements primarily on basic institutional elements, it would not have been unreasonable for participants to have regarded $g_{y'}^*$ as a constant, except perhaps during the wars. The situation with respect to g_M^* is very different. In the first place, g_M has been much more variable than $g_{y'}$ (see table 9.2), so there is more incentive to take its fluctuations into account. In the second place, g_M is much more subject to direct government control than is $g_{y'}$ and is known to be so subject. This consideration is important for both the United States and the United Kingdom after World War II, when both countries were explicitly committed to using monetary and fiscal policy to promote full employment. It is least important for both the United States and the United Kingdom before World War I. The United States had no central bank—though the

Treasury Department acted in many ways like one—and was firmly committed to an international gold standard, so that the quantity of money was not a policy variable. The United Kingdom had a central bank, but it too was firmly committed to an international gold standard.

For both countries, the interwar period is intermediate. In the United States a central bank (the Federal Reserve) had been established in 1914, but it was new and untried; it proclaimed its dedication to the international gold standard until 1933; and it adopted a passive role thereafter. Nonetheless, the existence of the Federal Reserve as an intermediary in the transmission of monetary influences from abroad with the capacity to sterilize or reinforce gold movements did significantly alter the determination of the quantity of money.

In the United Kingdom, despite the post–World War I determination to return to gold at the prewar parity, the delay of the return to gold until 1925 and the subsequent departure in 1931 meant that throughout most of the period after the outbreak of World War I, the United Kingdom was on a fiduciary standard operated primarily to promote domestic objectives.

We conclude that the assumption that $g_{y'}^*$ and g_M^* were treated by economic actors as constants is plausible for both countries in the pre–World War I period; more plausible for the United States than for the United Kingdom in the interwar period; highly implausible for both in the post–World War II period; and highly implausible for both during the two wars.

Unchanging Anticipations for Output: Adaptive Anticipations for Money

A more complex approach is to assume that the economic actors regarded $g_{y'}^*$ as a constant but estimated g_M^* on the basis of earlier values of g_M, the kind of adaptive expectations we used for g_Y^* in chapter 8. One justification of this approach is that serial correlations of g_M tend to be higher than of $g_{y'}$; that is, earlier values of g_M contain more information about current values of g_M than earlier values of $g_{y'}$ contain about current values of $g_{y'}$ (the only exception is for the aberrant United States interwar period).[38]

38. The serial correlations are as follows:

	g_M	$g_{y'}$
Pre–World War I		
United States	.62	.34
United Kingdom	.49	.34
Interwar		
United States	.47	.50
United Kingdom	.90	.46

This approach leads to equations that are not linear in the parameters. Hence we have had to resort to an iterative procedure to estimate them.

Adaptive Anticipations for both Output and Money:
Rate of Adaptation Equal (w = w')

Though $g_{y'}$ has no long-term trend, it does have considerable fluctuations, and there is positive serial correlation between its successive values (see footnote 38 above). Hence, a further complication is to assume that the economic actors also estimate $g_{y'}^*$ on the basis of earlier values of $g_{y'}$. We again do so by Cagan-Koyck adaptive anticipations.

The simplest case arises if the weight (w') attached to the current value of $g_{y'}$ in deriving $g_{y'}^*$ is equal to the weight (w) attached to the current value of g_M in deriving g_M^*.

Adaptive Anticipations for both Output and Money:
Rates of Adaptation Not Equal (w ≠ w')

If $w \neq w'$, the final equations are much more complex. Like those for the second hypothesis above, they are not linear in the parameters.

9.8.2 Comparison of Alternative Hypotheses

Although we have derived in the Appendix (sec. 9.10) pairs of equations—one for price, one for output—we need estimate only one to test the various hypotheses. Both contain the same unknown parameters, and both will give the same numerical estimates because of the identities connecting price, output, and income. We have chosen to concentrate on the output equation both because it is generally the simpler of the two and because the simple quantity theory implies that none of the variables included in these equations should have any significant influence on output (that is, on the simple quantity theory hypothesis, $\eta = \xi = 0$). And we have found repeatedly that the simple quantity theory hypothesis comes closer to being satisfied than the other simple hypotheses we have considered.

Table 9.14 indicates that for the United Kingdom none of the hypotheses contributes anything to the explanation of the rate of change of output for all nonwar phases. The simple quantity theory is confirmed again—as we have repeatedly found with respect to output for the United Kingdom. The total variability of the rate of change of output is 0.64

Post–World War II		
United States	.74	.54
United Kingdom	.88	.57
All nonwar phases		
United States	.61	.35
United Kingdom	.81	.47

percentage points; the lowest residual variability in table 9.10, which summarizes the effects of allowing for money and yields, prior money, prior income, and trend, is 0.60; the residual variability in table 9.13, which allows for prior price change and the output ratio, is 0.65; and in table 9.14 it is 0.62. Five out of six measures of residual variability in table 9.10, the residual variability in table 9.13, and six out of the eight measures in Table 9.14 are higher than the total variability. The situation is the same for interwar and post–World War II periods. For the pre–World War I period, all the measures of residual variability in table 9.14 are less than the total variability and a number are less than half the total variability. But these measures are based on only four to six degrees of freedom and hence are at best suggestive. All in all, it appears for the United Kingdom that neither the deviation of monetary growth from its anticipated value nor the ratio of actual output to anticipated output has any significant influence on the deviation of the rate of growth of output from its anticipated value—or alternatively, that none of our hypotheses about the formation of anticipated values provides a satisfactory approximation. The only hint of a different conclusion is for the pre–World War I period.

For the United States the situation is different—as is indicated at the outset by the much greater variability of output growth (more precisely, estimated output growth) for the United States than for the United Kingdom. All but two of the thirty-five estimates of residual variability in table 9.14 are less than the corresponding total variability, and many are much less. However, it is noteworthy that only two of the measures of residual variability for all nonwar phases and two for the period excluding interwar phases are as low as the residual variability for the simple Phillips-curve type of hypothesis in table 9.13. On the whole, the hypothesis of adaptive anticipations for money (cols. 5 through 10) gives appreciably lower variability than the hypothesis of constant anticipations (cols. 3 and 4) regardless of the hypothesis about output or the effect of capacity utilization with which it is combined.

To go beyond that statement, it is necessary to separate the results for an assumed zero and nonzero effects of the output ratio. For a zero effect ($\xi = 0$), adaptive anticipations for money, constant for output (column 5), is clearly the most satisfactory hypothesis: it gives the lowest residual variability of any of the $\xi = 0$ results except only for the idiosyncratic interwar period. Moreover, the residual variability for both all nonwar phases and for nonwar phases excluding interwar phases is lower than the lowest measure in table 9.10 (0.98 vs. 1.15 for all phases; 0.91 vs. 0.95, excluding interwar), and both are lower than the residual variability in table 9.13 (0.98 vs. 1.10 and 0.91 vs. 1.20).

For an assumed nonzero effect of the output ratio ($\xi \neq 0$), the hypothesis of adaptive anticipations for money, constant for output, requires

Table 9.14   Comparison of Alternative Hypotheses about Anticipations: Residual Variability of Output after Allowing for Anticipations

			Standard Error of Estimate (in Percentage Points) of Rate of Change of Output Hypothesis about Anticipated Rates of Money and Output Growth and Effect of Output Ratio							
			Constant		Adaptive for Money, Constant for Output		Adaptive for Both, Rates of Adaptation Equal		Adaptive for Both, Rates of Adaptation Unequal	
Period and Country	Number of Phases (1)	Total (2)	$\xi=0$ (3)	$\xi\neq0$ (4)	$\xi=0$ (5)	$\xi\neq0$ (6)	$\xi=0$ (7)	$\xi\neq0$ (8)	$\xi=0$ (9)	$\xi\neq0$ (10)
Number of parameters estimated		1	2	3	3	4	1	3	3	4
Nonwar phases										
United States										
All	37	2.58	1.61	1.61	0.98	1.01	1.53	1.12	1.30	Δ
Excluding interwar	30	1.52	1.51	1.43	0.91	Δ	1.35	0.81	1.28	Δ
United Kingdom										
All	24	0.64	0.67	0.67	0.62	0.63	0.89	0.73	0.74	0.68
Pre–World War I										
United States	19	1.73	1.65	1.49	1.08	Δ	1.62	0.92	1.57	1.09
United Kingdom	8	0.53	0.32	0.36	0.36	0.31	0.43	0.40	0.49	0.36
Interwar										
United States	7	3.28	1.17	1.23	1.29	0.65	1.86	0.86	1.12	0.35
United Kingdom	7	1.03	1.07	1.15	0.98	Δ	1.55	1.50	1.37	1.53
Post–World War II										
United States	11	1.10	1.16	1.16	0.57	Δ	0.73	0.45	0.68	0.69
United Kingdom	9	0.70	0.68	0.74	0.65	Δ	0.60	0.58	0.58	0.57

Note: Δ Nonlinear estimates did not converge.

nonlinear estimation (column 6), which failed to converge for three out of five sets of United States observations. Needless to say, we do not know whether this result reflects a defect of the nonlinear program or of our initial approximate parameter estimates, or whether it is a valid judgment on the economic validity of the hypothesis.

It does mean that, if the output ratio is allowed for ($\xi \neq 0$), our best results are for the hypothesis of adaptive anticipations for both money and output, with equal rates of adaptation (column 8). The residual variability for this hypothesis for the United States is slightly lower for all nonwar phases combined than the lowest measure in table 9.10 (1.12 vs. 1.15) and appreciably lower for nonwar phases excluding the interwar phases (0.81 vs. 0.95), and both are lower than the residual variability in table 9.13.

As between the hypothesis that is best when the output ratio is omitted ($\xi = 0$) and the one that is best when the output ratio is allowed for ($\xi \neq 0$), the evidence is conflicting. For the separate periods, the residual variability is consistently less for the United States when the output ratio is allowed for (column 8) than when it is not (column 5). That is also true for nonwar phases excluding interwar phases. However, for all nonwar phases combined the situation is reversed, implying that not allowing for the output ratio gives more homogeneous results for different periods than allowing for it. For the United Kingdom, the residual variability is higher when the output ratio is allowed for (col. 8) than when it is not (col. 5) for all nonwar phases and for interwar phases, lower for pre–World War I and post–World War II. One further minor bit of evidence for the hypothesis of column 5 is from the United Kingdom: it is the only hypothesis, excluding those for which some estimates are missing, for which the residual variability is consistently less than the total variability.

As further evidence, table 9.15 gives the parameter estimates for these two alternative hypotheses. The estimate of ψ (the response of nominal income to nominal money) is the same for both hypotheses. For combined phases, the values of ψ do not differ significantly from unity—the result we have repeatedly observed. For separate periods, with small numbers of observations, the estimates vary widely.[39]

---

39. The estimates differ significantly from unity for both countries for the post–World War II period and for the United Kingdom for the pre–World War I period. The low postwar values are somewhat paradoxical and reflect the particular pattern of the postwar reaction to the wartime decline in velocity.

The postwar rise in velocity at first suggests that the estimated ψ should be greater rather than less than unity. However, equation (A44) of the appendix is based on second derivatives, the acceleration of income and money, rather than the first derivatives, the rates of change. The postwar pattern was that the rate of monetary growth fell sharply in the early postwar period, then rose sharply, whereas the rate of income growth fell less, was fairly flat

Table 9.15   Estimates of Parameters on Two Alternative Hypotheses

	Number of Phases	Estimates of Parameters for Hypotheses about Anticipated Rates of Money and Output Growth and Effect of Output Ratio							
		Adaptive for Money, Constant for Output, $\xi = 0$				Adaptive for Both Money and Output, Rates of Adaptation Equal, $\xi \neq 0$			
Period and Country		ψ (1)	$g_{y'}^*$ (2)	η (3)	w (4)	ψ (5)	η (6)	w (7)	ξ (8)
Nonwar phases									
United States									
All	37	1.05	.0182	0.19	0.38	1.05	0.74	2.71	−0.08
Excluding interwar	30	0.97	.0281	−0.28	0.58	0.97	0.65	2.11	−0.10
United Kingdom									
All	24	0.81	.0208	0.14	0.77	0.81	0.68	1.36	−0.01
Pre–World War I									
United States	19	1.03	.0279	−0.44	0.63	1.03	0.73	2.37	−0.12
United Kingdom	8	0.49	.0174	−1.05	0.49	0.49	0.13	3.17	−0.02
Interwar									
United States	7	1.10	.0098	0.20	0.39	1.10	−0.16	−3.36	0.54
United Kingdom	7	1.87	.0147	−1.62	0.84	1.87	0.60	0.10	0.15
Post–World War II									
United States	11	0.63	.0229	−0.33	0.29	0.63	−0.07	0.89	0.01
United Kingdom	9	0.51	.0241	0.95	0.36	0.51	0.62	−0.70	−0.16

Note: Calculated from output regressions.

With respect to the remaining parameters, which differ between the two hypotheses, neither set of estimates is very appealing, though the estimates for the hypothesis of column 5 of table 9.14 seem preferable. For that hypothesis, the estimated permanent rate of real output growth is of the right order of magnitude—though perhaps a little low for the United States, a little high for the United Kingdom. Similarly, w, the estimated weight attached to current monetary growth in computing anticipated growth, is reasonable, being consistently between zero and unity and implying that the current phase receives from one-third to four-fifths of the weight in forming anticipations about monetary growth. However, the estimated values of η, the fraction of an unanticipated change in nominal income absorbed by an unanticipated change in prices, seem much too low, only 19 percent for all nonwar phases for the United States, and actually negative for pre–World War I and post–World War II phases. That negative result implies that a monetary growth higher than was anticipated would mean an inflation rate *lower* than was anticipated. Though not necessarily inconsistent with the observed positive relation between measured monetary growth and measured inflation, the result is certainly implausible.[40]

For the hypothesis of column 8 of table 9.14, the estimated values of η are more in line with expectations, but those of w and ξ are wholly out of line. Only two out of the nine estimates of w are within the anticipated zero to unity range; and only three of the estimates of ξ have the anticipated positive sign. The relatively good fit of the underlying equation for the United States clearly cannot be regarded as evidence in favor of the hypothesis from which it was derived.

All in all, the results from the much simpler relations of section 9.7 seem much more in line with expectations. They too yield a $\psi = 1$, but a value of η of roughly a third.

We have here a special case of a general proposition: the same empirical relation can be generated by more than one alternative hypothesis. As

---

for a time, and then rose, though less sharply than money. This meant that acceleration of both money and income was first negative, then positive, but the swing in money had a greater amplitude than in income, thereby producing an estimated ψ less than unity.

40. The reason a negative η is not necessarily inconsistent with a positive correlation between g_M and g_P is the assumed positive relation (indeed, equality) between g_M^* and g_P^* and the heavy weight of $g_M(t)$ in estimating $g_M^*(t)$. For example, for the parameters $\eta = -0.28$, $\psi = 0.97$, and $w = 0.58$, a one percentage point jump in g_M would increase $g_M^*(t)$ by 0.58 percentage points and mean a deviation of 0.42 percentage points between g_M and g_M^*. That would mean introducing a deviation of $0.97 \cdot 0.42 \cdot (-0.28)$ equal to -0.11 percentage points between g_P and g_P^*. If, before the disturbance, $g_P^* = g_Y^* - g_{y'}^* = g_M^* - 0.0281 = 0$, say, then subsequent to the disturbance, g_M^* would become $.0281 + .0058 = .0339$, and g_P^* would become $.0058$. Since $g_P - g_P^* = -0.0011$, the final result would be that g_P would be 0.0048, i.e., a one percentage point jump in g_M would be accompanied by a 0.48 percentage point immediate jump in inflation, compared with the 0.62 percentage point change in table 9.11 in the initial period.

it happens, the hypotheses underlying columns 5 and 8 of table 9.14 yield equations in observable variables very similar to some of those considered in section 9.6, namely, relating current output growth to earlier growth in money and income. The key difference for column 5 is the inclusion of an earlier value of output growth rather than of nominal income growth. The minor improvement in results presumably reflects the serial correlation of output growth from phase to phase. The key difference for column 8 is the inclusion of the current and lagged output ratio in addition to earlier monetary growth. In both cases, the variables that make a difference are only very loosely related to our alternative assumptions about the formation of anticipations.

We conclude that, while our results may give some evidence on the role of the output ratio, they do not provide any reliable evidence on the process of the formation of anticipations. From that point of view we must simply record an unsuccessful experiment.

The evidence on the role of the output ratio is provided by the estimated values of ξ—which measure the response of output and prices to the output ratio. A positive ξ, the sign to be expected on Phillips-curve lines, means that a high ratio of output stimulates inflation relative to output growth; a low ratio means the reverse. The fascinating feature of the values given in table 9.15 is that they are generally negative rather than positive. Instead of a high ratio of output to capacity tending to increase the price response and reduce the output response to a change in monetary growth, it appears to have precisely the opposite effect. For the United States, the negative values for combined periods (the first two lines of table 9.15) differ significantly from zero; for the United Kingdom the negative value does not.[41] The one appreciable exception is for the United States interwar period, for which the estimated value of ξ is positive and significantly different from zero at a .05 level.[42]

These are fascinating results. First, they reinforce the conclusion of section 9.5 that the United States interwar period is both idiosyncratic and the only period that is consistent with the Keynesian analysis—in this case, the post-Keynesian analysis embodied in the so-called Phillips curve. In the second place, they suggest that, for the other periods, the Phillips curve, insofar as it applies, is positively rather than negatively sloped.[43]

41. The absolute value of t for these three estimates of ξ are 2.4, 3.7, and 0.6; the first is significant at a .05 level, the second at a .01 level.

42. The t value is 3.8 and there are 4 degrees of freedom.

43. This conclusion, based on the equation underlying column 8 of table 9.14, is also consistent with the estimates of ξ based on the equations corresponding to columns 4, 6, and 10. Out of twenty such estimates, 13 are negative, seven positive; and of the four that are statistically significantly different from zero at a .05 level, all are negative. For the United Kingdom separately, the evidence is weaker, as is to be expected from the lack of statistical significance of most of the regressions. Of the ten estimates for the United Kingdom for

This result, though wholly out of tune with professional views in the 1950s and 1960s, seems far less so from the perspective of the late 1970s. As the postwar period unfolded, higher inflation tended to be accompanied by higher, not lower, unemployment, leading to the hypothesis of a positively sloped Phillips curve.[44] Our results suggest that that hypothesis may apply over a much longer time span than the post–World War II period alone. However, we hasten to repeat that our evidence on this particular point is weak and is suggestive rather than conclusive.

9.9   Conclusion

The results of this chapter are at the same time disappointing and most informative.

They are disappointing because we have not succeeded, as we had hoped we would, in giving satisfactory empirical content to the sophisticated theoretical analysis in chapter 2 bearing on the division over short periods of a change in nominal income between prices and output. The empirical analysis in section 9.8 comes closest in sophistication to the theoretical analysis—yet that section, while it yields some fascinating results, also records an unsuccessful experiment.

One possible interpretation of our failure to give satisfactory empirical content to the theoretical analysis is a point noted at the outset of this chapter—that we have used too lengthy a unit of observation, and that a similar empirical analysis using monthly or quarterly data might uncover empirical intracycle relations corresponding to our theoretical hypothesis. The results of section 9.3, on the effect of lengthening the period, as well as the many regressions in this and previous chapters using observations for earlier phases, rather argue against that interpretation. We have repeatedly found that the adjustment time is long, to be measured in cycle phases, not in months. Nonetheless, it may be that, for the particu-

---

equations corresponding to columns 4, 6, and 10, five are positive, five negative. However, the only one significantly different from zero at the .05 level is negative.

The only bit of contradictory evidence comes from equations for the United Kingdom corresponding to columns 4 and 8 of table 9.14, but using the employment ratio rather than the output ratio. While for the output ratio four of the eight estimates are positive, four are negative, and none is statistically significantly different from zero, for the employment ratio, five of the eight estimates are positive, three are negative, and one differs significantly from zero; that one is positive, and is for all nonwar phases and the equation corresponding to column 8. (The estimated value of ξ is 0.31, and the t value is 2.3, with 19 degrees of freedom.) However, the equation involved has a residual standard error higher than the initial standard deviation, so this result does not deserve much confidence; presumably, it reflects intercorrelations among the independent variables rather than a relation to the dependent variable.

44. For a fuller discussion of these issues, see Milton Friedman, "Inflation and Unemployment," referred to in note 22 above.

lar problem of the relative roles of prices and output, timing differences measured in months are vital, and that these are obliterated by our phase bases.

The results are informative in three rather different ways: (1) they narrow sharply the phenomena requiring explanation; (2) they suggest that much "conventional wisdom" reflects overgeneralization of a special case; and (3) they suggest that what "conventional wisdom" currently regards as a special case may be the norm.

1. For the United Kingdom there seems little if any relation between monetary change and output: a simple quantity theory that regards price change as determined primarily by monetary change and output by independent other factors fits the evidence for the period as a whole (excluding wars, which we have largely omitted from our analysis). The whole of a change in the quantity of money is absorbed sooner or later by prices and, in the early stages, more by changes in velocity than by changes in output. The output series bears little or no relation to any monetary factors, either the quantity of money, in the current or prior phases, or yields. From that point of view, the rate of change of output appears to be a random series (though not one displaying complete serial independence). Finally, the rate of change of output is much less variable over time than the rate of change of prices. Its variability is of the same order of magnitude as that which would be produced simply by measurement error.

For the United States, for the period as a whole, there is a positive relation between monetary change and output change, and price change absorbs a smaller percentage than in the United Kingdom of the change in the quantity of money, and of the related change in nominal income. In sharp contrast to the United Kingdom, the rate of change of output is more variable than the rate of change of prices.

On further examination, and this leads on to point 2, it turns out that much of the difference between the United States and the United Kingdom reflects the United States interwar period—a twenty-year span containing three major contractions. That period seems idiosyncratic. If it is omitted, and the pre–World War I and post–World War II periods combined, the two periods together conform to a simple quantity theory about as well as the United Kingdom data for the period as a whole. Indeed, we cannot find any statistically significant difference between the United States and the United Kingdom relations—though it does remain true that the rate of change of output varies more than the rate of change of prices in the United States and less in the United Kingdom.

We must confess to being surprised at our failure—if the United States interwar period is excluded—to find a positive relation between price change and output change. Misled by the "conventional wisdom," we expected a positive relation between price and output change and between both and monetary change, and we searched long and diligently—and we believe, not simple-mindedly—to uncover such a relation. On the contrary, a negative relation between price and output change is more typical, for both statistical and economic reasons (section 9.2). We are reminded of Keynes's dictum expressed in another connection:

> I find myself moved, not for the first time, to remind contemporary economists that the classical teaching embodied some permanent truths of great significance, which we are liable today to overlook because we associate them with other doctrines which we cannot now accept without much qualification. There are in these matters deep undercurrents at work, natural forces, or even the invisible hand, which are operating towards equilibrium.[45]

2. We have concluded that the widely held belief in a positive relation between price and output change and in the inadequacy of the quantity theory stems largely from a tendency to regard the United States interwar period as the norm rather than, as we found it, idiosyncratic. That period generated Keynes's *General Theory* and sparked the Keynesian revolution. It appears that Keynes's theory, far from being general, is highly special, a view that has often been expressed but seldom documented as fully as we believe we have been able to.

3. One of the most important of the by-products of the Keynesian revolution was the "Phillips curve"—the notion that there is a stable tradeoff between inflation and unemployment and conversely; or, equivalently, that a high level of output relative to capacity (the output ratio) will be reflected in a high level of inflation, a low output ratio in a low level of inflation.

This relation has clearly broken down in the postwar period as country after country has experienced stagflation—higher inflation accompanied by higher unemployment, not lower. However, this empirical positively sloped Phillips curve has been regarded as an exception, and the postwar period as idiosyncratic.

Sections 9.7 and 9.8 indicate that this conclusion is not justified. Section 9.7 demonstrates rather decisively that past price change is far more important than the output ratio as a determinant of inflation. Section 9.8 demonstrates that, insofar as there is any relation between the output ratio and inflation, it is in the direction called for by a positively sloped Phillips curve. This is true not solely for the post–World War II period but throughout—the idiosyncratic interwar period for the United States alone excepted.

---

45. J. M. Keynes, "The Balance of Payments of the United States," *Economic Journal* 56 (June 1946): 172–87. Quotation is from p. 185.

9.10   Appendix: Derivation of Price and Output Relations

9.10.1   Relation of Prices and Output to Real per Capita
            Income and Yields

To convert the equations in the appendix to chapter 8 into equations for prices and output separately, we make use of the identities:

(A1) $\log Y(t) = \log P(t) + \log y(t) + \log N(t)$,

where N is population,
and

(A2) $g_Y(t) = g_P(t) + g_y(t) + g_N(t)$.

Start with equation (A5) of chapter 8, which is

(A3) $\log Y(t) = -[\log k + \lambda_3 Z] + \zeta \log M(t)$
                 $+ (1 - \alpha - \lambda_4 Z) \log y(t)$
                 $- \delta R_N(t) - \epsilon g_Y(t)$,

and subtract $\log y(t) + \log N(t)$ from both sides. This gives

(A4) $\log P(t) = -[\log k + \lambda_3 Z] - \log N(t) + \zeta \log M(t)$
                 $- (\alpha + \lambda_4 Z) \log y(t)$
                 $- \delta R_N(t) - \epsilon g_Y(t)$.

Subtract $\log P(t)$ from both sides of equation (A1). This gives

(A5) $\log y'(t) = \log y(t) + \log N(t)$.

Similarly for rate of change equations, we start with equation $(A8)$ of the appendix to chapter 8, or

(A6) $g_Y(t) = \zeta g_M(t) + (1 - \alpha - \lambda_4 Z)g_y(t) - \delta D[R_N(t)]$
                 $- \epsilon D[g_Y(t)]$,

and subtract $g_y(t) + g_N(t)$ to get

(A7) $g_P(t) = \zeta g_M(t) - (\alpha + \lambda_4 Z)g_y(t) - g_N(t) - \delta D[R_N(t)]$
                 $- \epsilon D[g_Y(t)]$.

Subtract $g_P(t)$ from both sides of equation (A2). This gives

(A8) $g_{y'}(t) = g_y(t) + g_N(t)$.

These equations make one point explicit: even if $\alpha = 1$, the behavior of real output per capita and of population cannot be neglected in discussing the breakdown of nominal income between prices and output.

To determine the influence of the variables so far discussed on the breakdown between prices and output, we must express $\log y$ and $\log N$ as functions of these variables.

With respect to population, we found in chapter 5 that population contributed a trivial fraction of the variation of money and income about their trend. Accordingly, we shall assume that we can represent population by

(A9) $$\log N(t) = A_N + \lambda_{3N}Z + [\bar{g}_N + \lambda_{5N}Z]T(t),$$

where $T(t)$ is the chronological date corresponding to the midpoint of phase t. The parameter λ_{3N} is the excess of the constant term of the trend equation for the United Kingdom over that for the United States, λ_{5N} is the excess of the slope term, and similarly with subsequent coefficients of Z.

By differentiating equation (A9) with respect to T, we can represent the rate of change of population by

(A10) $$g_N(t) = \bar{g}_N + \lambda_{5N}Z.$$

With respect to real income per capita, we cannot neglect the deviations from trend, but we can assume that they are related to variables affecting nominal income, namely, $M(t)$, $R_N(t)$, and $g_Y(t)$, and that the relation is the same in the United States and the United Kingdom. On that assumption, we can represent per capita income by

(A11) $$\log y(t) = A_y + \lambda_{3y}Z + (\bar{g}_y + \lambda_{5y}Z)\ T(t) + \zeta_y \log M(t) - \delta_y R_N(t) - \epsilon_y g_Y(t),$$

and the rate of change of real income per capita by

(A12) $$g_y(t) = (\bar{g}_y + \lambda_{5y}Z) + \zeta_y g_M(t) - \delta_y D[R_N(t)] - \epsilon_y D[g_Y(t)].$$

Substitute equations (A9) and (A11) in equations (A4) and (A5) to get:

(A13) $$\log P(t) = -\log k_P - \lambda_{3P}Z - [\bar{g}_P + \lambda_{5P}Z]T(t) + \zeta_P \log M(t) - \delta_p R_N(t) - \epsilon_P g_Y(t),$$

and

(A14) $$\log y'(t) = A_{y'} + \lambda_{3y'}Z + [\bar{g}_{y'} + \lambda_{5y'}Z]T(t) + \zeta_y \log M(t) - \delta_y R_N(t) - \epsilon_y g_Y(t)$$

where

(A15a)
$$
\begin{cases}
\log k_p &= \log k &+ A_N &+ (\alpha + \lambda_4 Z)A_y \\
\lambda_{3P} &= \lambda_3 &+ \lambda_{3N} &+ (\alpha + \lambda_4 Z)\lambda_{3y} \\
\bar{g}_P &= \bar{g}_N &+ &(\alpha + \lambda_4 Z)\bar{g}_y \\
\lambda_{5p} &= \lambda_{5N} &+ &(\alpha + \lambda_4 Z)\lambda_{5y} \\
\zeta_p &= \zeta &- &(\alpha + \lambda_4 Z)\zeta_y \\
\delta_P &= \delta &- &(\alpha + \lambda_4 Z)\delta_y \\
\epsilon_P &= \epsilon &- &(\alpha + \lambda_4 Z)\epsilon_y
\end{cases}
$$

and

(A15b)
$$\left\{ \begin{array}{rcl} A_{y'} &=& A_N + A_y \\ \lambda_{3y'} &=& \lambda_{3N} + \lambda_{3y} \\ \bar{g}_{y'} &=& \bar{g}_N + \bar{g}_y \\ \lambda_{5y'} &=& \lambda_{5N} + \lambda_{5y}. \end{array} \right.$$

Similarly, for rate of change equations, substitute equations (A10) and (A12) into equations (A7) and (A8) to get:

(A16)
$$g_P(t) = -\bar{g}_P - \lambda_{5P}Z + \zeta_P g_M(t) - \delta_P D[R_N(t)] \\ - \epsilon_P D[g_Y(t)],$$

and

(A17)
$$g_{y'}(t) = \bar{g}_{y'} + \lambda_{5y'}Z + \zeta_y g_M(t) - \delta_y D[R_N(t)] \\ - \epsilon_y D[g_Y(t)].$$

So far, we have made no assumptions about income elasticity. Real income per capita (y) does not enter on the right-hand side of the equations, but α does in equation (A13) though not equation (A14) (see equations A15a and A15b). One consequence is that fitting equation (A13) for the United States and the United Kingdom combined in its most general form (i.e., $\alpha \neq 1$ and $\lambda_4 \neq 0$) would require using three country parameters ($\lambda_{3P}, \lambda_4, \lambda_{5P}$). This is feasible, since values of α and λ_4 could be taken from the estimated demand equation for the two countries, but it would be complex and, in view of our reliance on the assumption of $\alpha = 1$ and $\lambda_4 = 0$ in chapter 8, hardly worthwhile. We have introduced the approximations of equations (A11) and (A12) not to avoid that assumption but because, even with that assumption, real income per capita enters the price and output equations. Accordingly, in what follows we shall, in combining the two countries, proceed as if $\alpha = 1, \lambda_4 = 0$. The assumption of $\alpha = 1$ is not implicit in the equations for each country separately.

A second and more subtle consequence of an $\alpha \neq 1$, affecting the equations for the separate countries as well as for the two combined, has to do with the comparability of the equation for nominal income with the equations for price and output separately. If $\alpha = 1$ and $\lambda_4 = 0$, then the sum of equations (A13) and (A14) will, as a mathematical matter, give equation (A3), for $\alpha = 1$ and $\lambda_4 = 0$. However, suppose we estimate equations (A13) and (A14) by straightforward multiple regression. Their sum will equal the corresponding regression estimate of equation (A3) with the term in log $y(t)$ omitted only if we impose the cross-equation conditions that

$$\log k_P - A_{y'} = \log k$$

(A18)
$$\lambda_{3P} - \lambda_{3y'} = \lambda_3$$

$$\bar{g}_P = \bar{g}_{y'}$$

$$\lambda_{5P} = \lambda_{5y'},$$

that is, conditions on the estimated constant terms and the coefficients of Z, T, and ZT in equations (A13) and (A14).

If we do not impose any cross-equation conditions, then the sum of the regressions corresponding to equations (A13) and (A14) will equal

$$
\begin{aligned}
\text{(A19)} \qquad \log Y(t) = {} & - \log k - \lambda_3 Z + \bar{g}_Y T(t) + \lambda_5 T(t) \\
& + \zeta \log M(t) - \delta R_N(t) - \epsilon g_Y(t).
\end{aligned}
$$

If, empirically, α is close to unity and λ_4 to zero, then the estimated $\bar{g}_Y$ and λ_5 will be close to zero. However, there is nothing that requires that result. Accordingly, to avoid the complexity of introducing cross-equation conditions, we have introduced terms in T in the equations for Y in tables 9.4, 9.5, and 9.6, and in T and ZT for corresponding equations for the combined United States and United Kingdom (not reported). As a result, they do not correspond precisely to those presented in chapter 8. In effect, this involves indirectly allowing for an $\alpha \neq 1$.

The same problems arise for the rate of change equations (A16) and (A17) and mean that in computing these equations for the two countries combined, we implicitly assume $\alpha = 1$, $\lambda_4 = 0$; and that in computing the corresponding equations for the rate of change of nominal income, we include a constant term plus, for the two countries combined, a term in Z.

9.10.2 Relation of Prices and Output to Current and Prior Money and Income

If we replace R_N by R_S, we can express R_S and $D(R_S)$ and g_Y and $D(g_Y)$ in terms of earlier money and income by the same procedure as was used in the appendix to chapter 8. The final result, however, is much more complicated because, in replacing $R_S(t)$ by $k_0 + g_Y{}^*(t)$ and $g_Y{}^*(t)$ in turn by its value in terms of earlier money and income, it is necessary to use the equations for $\log Y(t)$, not for $\log P(t)$, or $\log y'(t)$. Hence the final equations cannot be obtained, as might at first appear, by simply replacing ζ by ζ_P or $\zeta_{y'}$, δ by δ_P or $\delta_{y'}$, and so on. Both sets of structural parameters enter in. However, the final results, on the assumption that all phases are equal in length, can still be expressed in the same form as equations (A23) and (A42) of the appendix to chapter 8.[46] The results are

---

46. The steps in the derivation of the equation for $\log P$ are as follows:

(i)   In equation (A13) of this appendix, with R_S substituted for R_N, replace $R_S(t)$ by $k_0 + w g_Y(t) + (1 - w) g_Y^*(t-1)$.
    [Denote the resulting equation by (i), and similarly for later steps.]

(ii) Do the same in equation (A6) of the appendix to chapter 8, modified by substituting R_S for R_N.

(iii) Write modified equation (A6) of the appendix to chapter 8 for $(t-1)$, and replace $R_S(t-1)$ by $k_0 + g_Y^*(t-1)$.

(iv) Multiply both sides of equation (iii) by $(1-w)\delta_P/\delta$

(v)   Subtract equation (iv) from equation (i).

(A20) $\log P(t) = a_P + a'_P T(t) + f_P Z + f'_P ZT(t) + b_P \log M(t)$
$+ c_P \log M(t-1) + d_P \log Y(t-1)$
$+ e_P \log Y(t-2),$

(A21) $\log y'(t) = a_{y'} + a'_{y'} T(t) + f_{y'} Z + f'_{y'} ZT(t) + b_{y'} \log M(t)$
$+ c_{y'} \log M(t-1) + d_{y'} \log Y(t-1)$
$+ e_{y'} \log Y(t-2),$

where

$$a_P = -\log k_P - w\delta_P k_0 + (1-w)\log k \, \delta_P/\delta$$
$$+ \frac{w(w\delta_P + \epsilon_P)(\log k + \delta k_0)}{nQ}$$

(A22a)

$$a'_P = -\bar{g}_P$$

$$f_P = -\lambda_{3P} + \lambda_3(1-w)\delta_P/\delta + \frac{w(w\delta_P + \epsilon_P)}{nQ}\lambda_3$$

$$f'_P = -\lambda_{5P}$$

$$b_P = \zeta\left(\frac{\zeta_P}{\zeta} - \frac{w\delta_P + \epsilon_P}{nQ}\right)$$

$$c_P = -(1-w)\zeta\left(\frac{\zeta_P}{\zeta} - \frac{w\delta_P + \epsilon_P}{nQ}\right)$$

$$d_P = \frac{\delta_P}{\delta}(1-w)\left(1+\frac{\epsilon}{n}\right)$$

$$+ \frac{w\delta_P + \epsilon_P}{nQ}\left(w - \frac{(1-w)\epsilon}{n}\right)$$

$$e_P = -(1-w)\frac{\epsilon}{n}\left(\frac{\delta_P}{\delta} - \frac{w\delta_P + \epsilon_P}{nQ}\right)$$

and the corresponding coefficients for equation (A21) are

(vi) In equation (v), replace $g_Y(t)$ by $[\log Y(t) - \log Y(t-1)]/n$, and $g_Y(t-1)$ by the corresponding expression.

(vii) In equation (vi), replace $\log Y(t)$ by its equivalent from equation (A23) of the appendix to chapter 8.

The procedure for deriving the equation for $\log y'$ is the same except starting with equation (A14) of this appendix instead of equation (A13).

$$a_{y'} = A_{y'} - w\delta_y k_0 + (1-w) \log k \, \delta_y/\delta$$
$$+ \frac{w(w\delta_y + \epsilon_y)(\log k + \delta k_0)}{nQ}$$

$$a'_{y'} = \bar{g}_{y'}$$

$$f_{y'} = \lambda_{3y'} + \lambda_3(1-w)\delta_y/\delta + \frac{w(w\delta_y + \epsilon_y)}{nQ}\lambda_3$$

$$f'_{y'} = \lambda_{5y'}$$

(A22b)
$$b_{y'} = \zeta\left(\frac{\zeta_y}{\zeta} - \frac{w\delta_y + \epsilon_y}{nQ}\right)$$

$$c_{y'} = -(1-w)\,\zeta\left[\frac{\delta_y}{\delta} - \frac{w\delta_y + \epsilon_y}{nQ}\right]$$

$$d_{y'} = (1-w)\frac{\delta_y}{\delta}\left(1+\frac{\epsilon}{n}\right)$$
$$+ \frac{w\delta_y + \epsilon_y}{nQ}\left(w - \frac{(1-w)\epsilon}{n}\right)$$

$$e_{y'} = -(1-w)\frac{\epsilon}{n}\left(\frac{\delta_y}{\delta} - \frac{w\delta_y + \epsilon_y}{nQ}\right).$$

The corresponding rate of change equations are

(A23)
$$g_P(t) = a'_P + f'_P Z + b_P g_M(t) + c_P g_M(t-1)$$
$$+ d_P g_Y(t-1) + e_P g_Y(t-2),$$

(A24)
$$g_{y'}(t) = a'_{y'} + f'_{y'} Z + b_{y'} g_M(t)$$
$$+ c_{y'} g_M(t-1) + d_{y'} g_Y(t-1) + e_{y'} g_Y(t-2).$$

As with equations (A13) and (A14) and (A16) and (A17), so with equations (A20) and (A21) and (A23) and (A24), the equations for the countries combined implicitly assume $\alpha = 1$, $\lambda_4 = 0$. For the rate of change of nominal income for each country separately, the equations obtained by summing $(A23)$ and $(A24)$ are the same as those computed in chapter 8 with a constant term (to allow for trend). For the two countries combined, a term in Z is also required.

9.10.3   Relation of Prices and Output to Current and Prior Money Only

To express equations (A20) and (A21), and (A23) and (A24) in terms of earlier money alone, we make use of equations (A70) and (A71) of the appendix to chapter 8. These are for each country separately; that is, $Z = 0$, to which we restrict our analysis in this section, as we did in the corresponding section of the appendix to chapter 8.

They can be written as

(A25) $$\log Y(t) = a'' + \frac{k'}{1-d-e} nt + \sum_{i=0}^{\infty} b_i M(t-i),$$

(A26) $$g_Y(t) = \frac{k'}{1-d-e} + \sum_{i=0}^{\infty} b_i g_M(t-i),$$

where

(A27) $$\begin{cases} b_0 &= b \\ b_1 &= c + bd \\ b_i &= db_{i-1} + eb_{i-2} \text{ for } i > 1. \end{cases}$$

Replacing t by $t-1$ and $t-2$ successively, we may substitute the results for $\log Y(t-1)$ and $\log Y(t-2)$ in equations (A20) and (A21), and for $g_Y(t-1)$ and $g_Y(t-2)$ in equations (A23) and (A24). The results for prices are:

(A28) $$\log P(t) = \left[a_P + (d_P + e_P)a'' - (d_P + 2e_P)\frac{k'n}{1-d-e} \right]$$

$$+ \left[a_P' + (d_P + e_P)\frac{k'}{1-d-e} \right] nt$$

$$+ \sum_{i=0}^{\infty} b_{P_i} \log M(t-i),$$

and

(A29) $$g_P(t) = a_P' + (d_P + e_P)\frac{k'}{1-d-e} + \sum_{i=0}^{\infty} b_{P_i} g_M(t-i),$$

where

(A30) $$\begin{cases} b_{P_0} &= b_P \\ b_{P_1} &= c_P + d_P b_0 \\ b_{P_i} &= d_P b_{i-1} + e_P b_{i-2} \text{ for } i > 1. \end{cases}$$

From equation (A30) it follows that

(A31) $$\sum_{i=0}^{\infty} b_{P_i} = b_P + c_P + (d_P + e_P)\sum_{i=0}^{\infty} b_i$$

$$= b_P + c_P + (d_P + e_P)\frac{b+c}{1-d-e}.$$

If $\Sigma b_i = 1$, which has been imposed on the final equations in chapter 8, then

(A32) $$\sum_{i=0}^{\infty} b_{P_i} = b_P + c_P + d_P + e_P \text{ for } \Sigma b_i = 1,$$

so that the sum of the coefficients of the money and income terms is an estimate of the fraction of the change in nominal income that ultimately takes the form of price change. More generally, that fraction is given by

(A33)
$$\frac{\Sigma b_{P_i}}{\Sigma b_i} = \frac{(b_P + c_P)(1 - d - e)}{b + c} + d_P + e_P.$$

The condition that this fraction equal unity, that is, that the whole of a change in monetary growth ultimately be reflected in prices, is then

(A34)
$$\frac{1 - d_P - e_P}{b_P + c_P} = \frac{1 - d - e}{b + c}.$$

The equations for output are identical with those for prices, except that y' replaces P wherever P appears as a subscript.

The sum of the price and output equations estimated separately from the regressions on current and prior money and prior income will equal the corresponding equation for income if the latter is estimated without imposing the restriction that $\Sigma b_i = 1$. If that restriction is imposed, then the separate equations will sum to the income equation only if cross-equation restrictions are imposed assuring that outcome.

However, the condition that $\Sigma b_{P_i} = 1$ can be imposed along with the condition that $\Sigma b_i = 1$, by imposing the condition on the price equation that $b_P + c_P + d_P + e_P = 1$.

9.10.4   Transient Effects

The treatment of transient effects in the appendix to chapter 8 carries over directly to prices and output separately, except only that the theoretical value given by equation (A82) of that section applies to the sum of price and output transient effects.

9.10.5   Alternative Hypotheses about Anticipations

Unchanging Anticipations

If $g_{y'}^*$ and g_M^* are treated as constants, equations (18) and (19) of the text reduce to

(A35)
$$g_P(t) = -(g_{y'}^* + \eta\psi g_M^*) + g_Y^*(t) + \eta\psi g_M(t) \\ + \xi\log R_{y'}(t),$$

(A36)
$$g_{y'}(t) = [g_{y'}^* - (1 - \eta)\psi g_M^*] + (1 - \eta)\psi g_M(t) \\ - \xi\log R_{y'}(t).$$

As written, equation (A36) makes $g_{y'}$ a function of current g_M only. In chapter 8 we introduced prior monetary change by making the demand for money a function of nominal interest rates and nominal interest rates in turn a function of expected rate of change of nominal income. However, a constant g_M^* would also imply, in the thoretical model of chapter 2, a constant g_Y^*, and, together with a constant $g_{y'}^*$, a constant g_P^*. Hence that analysis gives no reason here to introduce directly prior values of g_M in either equation (A35) or equation (A36). The only justification for doing so on these assumptions would be to allow for discrepancies between actual and desired cash balances. Such discrepancies may well be extremely important for monthly, quarterly, or even annual time units, but we have so far neglected them for periods as long as our phases, and we shall continue to do so.

Unchanging Anticipations for Output:
Adaptive Anticipations for Money

On this approach, we supplement equations (18) and (19) of the text with

(A37) $$\frac{dg_M^*}{dt} = D(g_M^*) = w(g_M - g_M^*),$$

the solution of which, as usual, can be approximated, for discrete data, by

(A38) $$g_M^*(t) = wg_M(t) + (1 - w)g_M^*(t - 1),$$

where, for reasons explained in chapter 8, we treat the phase as a time unit, even though phases differ in chronological duration, and where we regard w, the rate of adaptation, as being the same for g_M^* as for g_Y^*.

Substitute equation (A38) and its counterpart for g_Y^*, in equations (18) and (19) of the text, which gives

(A39) $$\begin{aligned} g_P(t) = g_Y(t) - g_{y'}^* - (1 - w)\,[g_Y(t) - g_Y^*(t - 1)] \\ + \eta\psi(1 - w)[g_M(t) - g_M^*(t - 1)] + \xi\log R_{y'}, \end{aligned}$$

(A40) $$\begin{aligned} g_{y'}(t) = g_{y'}^* + (1 - \eta)\psi(1 - w)[g_M(t) - g_M^*(t - 1)] \\ - \xi\log R_{y'}\,. \end{aligned}$$

Write equations (18) and (19) of the text for $(t - 1)$, multiply by $(1 - w)$, subtract the results from equations (A39) and (A40), and simplify to get

(A41) $$\begin{aligned} g_P(t) = -wg_{y'}^* + (1 - w)g_P(t - 1) + wg_Y(t) \\ + \eta\psi(1 - w)[g_M(t) - g_M(t - 1)] \\ + \xi[\log R_{y'}(t) - (1 - w)\log R_{y'}(t - 1)\,], \end{aligned}$$

(A42) $$\begin{aligned} g_{y'}(t) = wg_{y'}^* + (1 - w)g_{y'}(t - 1) \\ + (1 - \eta)\psi(1 - w)\,[g_M(t) - g_M(t - 1)\,] \\ - \xi\,[\log R_{y'}(t) - (1 - w)\log R_{y'}(t - 1)\,]. \end{aligned}$$

These equations now contain only observable variables but are nonlinear in the parameters.[47,48]

The sum of equations (A41) and (A42) does not contain the output ratio. If we divide the sum by $(1 - w)$, the result is

(A43) $$g_Y(t) - g_Y(t - 1) = \psi[g_M(t) - g_M(t - 1)],$$

or, dividing by $\bar{n}(t)$, the interval between the midpoints of phases t and $t - 1$,

(A44) $$D[g_Y(t)] = \psi D[g_M(t)].$$

We can use this equation to estimate ψ.

Adaptive Anticipations for both Output and Money:
Rates of Adaptation Equal

The counterpart for output of equation (A38) is:

(A45) $$g_{y'}^* = w'g_{y'}(t) + (1 - w')g_{y'}^*(t - 1),$$

where w' is the weight attached to current output growth.

The case considered here is one in which the rates of adaptation are equal for money and output ($w = w'$).

Substitute equations (A38) and (A45), and their counterpart for g_Y^*, into equations (18) and (19) of the text to get:

(A46) $$\begin{aligned} g_P(t) = {} &wg_Y(t) + (1 - w)g_Y^*(t - 1) - w'g_{y'}(t) \\ &- (1 - w')g_{y'}^*(t - 1) \\ &+ \eta\psi(1 - w)[g_M(t) - g_M^*(t - 1)] + \xi \log R_{y'}(t). \end{aligned}$$

(A47) $$\begin{aligned} (1 - w')g_{y'}(t) = {} &(1 - w')g_{y'}^*(t - 1) \\ &+ (1 - \eta)\psi(1 - w)[g_M(t) - g_M^*(t - 1)] \\ &- \xi \log R_{y'}(t). \end{aligned}$$

For $w = w'$, write equations (18) and (19) of the text for $t - 1$, multiply by $(1 - w)$, and subtract from equations (A46) and (A47). After simplification, the result is

(A48) $$g_P(t) - g_P(t - 1) = \eta\psi[g_M(t) - g_M(t - 1)] \\ + \xi\left[\frac{\log R_{y'}(t)}{1 - w} - \log R_{y'}(t - 1)\right],$$

47. If equation (A41) is expressed in a series of terms, there will appear to be six regression coefficients, but there are only five independent parameters: w, $g_{y'}^*$, η, ψ, and ξ, and η and ψ only appear as a product, so there are really only four independent parameters. Similarly, equation (A42) yields five linear regression coefficients, but there are only four independent parameters, w, g^*d2y', $(1 - \eta)\psi$, and ξ.

48. A less rigid approach would be to regard g_M^* as a weighted average of current and earlier values of g_M but without restricting the weights to the exponential form implied by equation (A38). However, without imposing additional restrictions on the weights, it becomes difficult or arbitrary to identify ψ separately from the weights.

(A49)
$$g_{y'}(t) - g_{y'}(t-1) = (1-\eta)\psi[g_M(t) - g_M(t-1)]$$
$$-\xi\left[\frac{\log R_{y'}(t)}{1-w} - \log R_{y'}(t-1)\right].$$

Unlike equations (A41) and (A42), these equations are linear in the parameters and can be estimated directly.

If ξ is set equal to zero, and the equations are divided through by $\bar{n}(t)$, equations (A48) and (A49) reduce to

(A50)
$$D[g_P(t)] = \eta\psi D[g_M(t)],$$

(A51)
$$D[g_{y'}(t)] = (1-\eta)\psi D[g_M(t)],$$

and their sum to equation (A44), the same as the sum of equations (A41) and (A42), implying the same estimate of ψ.

Adaptive Anticipations for both Output and Money:
Rates of Adaptation Not Equal ($w \neq w'$)

Write equations (18) and (19) of the text for $(t-1)$, multiply by $(1-w')$ and subtract from equations (A46) and (A47) of the preceding section to get, after some rearrangement,

(A52)
$$(1-w')[g_P(t) - g_P(t-1)] = (w-w')[g_Y(t) - g_Y^*(t+1)]$$
$$+ \eta\psi(1-w)[g_M(t) - g_M(t-1)]$$
$$- \eta\psi(w-w')[g_M(t-1) - g_M^*(t-1)]$$
$$+ \xi[\log R_{y'}(t) - (1-w')\log R_{y'}(t-1)],$$

(A53)
$$(1-w')[g_{y'}(t) - g_{y'}(t-1)]$$
$$= (1-\eta)\psi(1-w)[g_M(t) - g_M(t-1)]$$
$$- (1-\eta)\psi(w-w')[g_M(t-1)$$
$$- g_M^*(t-1)]$$
$$- \xi[\log R_{y'}(t) - (1-w')\log R_{y'}(t-1)].$$

Replace $g_M^*(t-1)$ and $g_Y^*(t-1)$ by their equivalents for $(t-1)$ from equation (A38) and the corresponding equation for $g_Y^*(t)$. Subtract equations (A52) and (A53) rewritten for $(t-2)$ and multiplied by $(1-w)$ from the resulting equations, The final results are:

(A54)
$$g_P(t) = g_P(t-1) + (1-w)[g_P(t-1) - g_P(t-2)]$$
$$+ \frac{(1-w)(w-w')}{(1-w')}[g_Y(t) - g_Y(t-1)]$$
$$+ \eta\psi\frac{(1-w)}{(1-w')}[g_M(t) - g_M(t-1)]$$
$$- \eta\psi(1-w)[g_M(t-1) - g_M(t-2)]$$
$$+ \frac{\xi}{(1-w')}[\log R_{y'}(t) - (1-w)\log R_{y'}(t-1)]$$
$$- \xi[\log R_{y'}(t-1) - (1-w)\log R_{y'}(t-2)],$$

(A55)
$$g_{y'}(t) = g_{y'}(t-1) + (1-w)[g_{y'}(t-1) - g_{y'}(t-2)]$$
$$+ (1-\eta)\psi \frac{(1-w)}{(1-w')} [g_M(t) - g_M(t-1)]$$
$$- (1-\eta)\psi(1-w)[g_M(t-1) - g_M(t-2)]$$
$$- \frac{\xi}{(1-w')} [\log R_{y'}(t) - (1-w) \log R_{y'}(t-1)]$$
$$+ \xi [\log R_{y'}(t-1) - (1-w) \log R_{y'}(t-2)].$$

Like equations (A41) and (A42), these equations are nonlinear in the parameters. The sum of equations (A54) and (A55) is

(A56)
$$g_Y(t) - g_Y(t-1) = \frac{(1-w)(1-w')}{(1-w)^2 + w(1-w')} [g_Y(t-1)$$
$$- g_Y(t-2)]$$
$$+ \frac{\psi(1-w)}{(1-w)^2 + w(1-w')} [g_M(t) - g_M(t-1)]$$
$$- \frac{\psi(1-w)(1-w')}{(1-w)^2 + w(1-w')} [g_M(t-1) - g_M(t-2)].$$

Divide both sides by $\bar{n}(t)$ to get

(A57)
$$D[g_Y(t)] = \frac{(1-w)(1-w')}{(1-w)^2 + w(1-w')} D[g_Y(t-1)] \frac{\bar{n}(t-1)}{\bar{n}(t)}$$
$$+ \frac{\psi(1-w)}{(1-w)^2 + w(1-w')} D[g_M(t)]$$
$$- \frac{\psi(1-w)(1-w')}{(1-w)^2 + w(1-w')} D[g_M(t-1)] \frac{\bar{n}(t-1)}{\bar{n}(t)},$$

from which, in principle, it is possible to estimate ψ, w, and w'. In practice, the estimates are wholly unacceptable.

10   Money and Interest Rates

No part of this book has been so subject to obsolescence between first draft and final version as this chapter. When the first draft was completed (1966), the Keynesian liquidity preference approach held full sway. It was widely taken for granted that more money meant lower interest rates and a faster rate of monetary growth meant declining interest rates, and conversely. Hume's warning of two centuries earlier—"Lowness of interest is generally ascribed to plenty of money. But money, however plentiful, has no other effect, *if fixed*, than to raise the price of labour"— was mostly neglected. Irving Fisher's pathbreaking work, dating from 1896, distinguishing between nominal and real interest rates and examining the empirical role of inflationary expectations was hardly known and was certainly not part of the received wisdom. Accordingly, our first draft, which presented a full theoretical analysis incorporating Fisher's work, was devoted mostly to testing his conclusions with our United States data.

In the interim there has been a veritable explosion of work in this area, some stimulated by our first draft, the theoretical part of which was published in 1968,[1] but most in reaction to the emergence in the advanced countries of accelerating monetary growth and rising interest rates that made it impossible to continue to regard a stable Keynesian liquidity preference function relating the nominal quantity of money inversely to nominal interest rates as an adequate tool for analyzing the effect of monetary changes on interest rates.

The first round of the explosion, like our first draft, consisted largely of studies along the lines pioneered by Irving Fisher, both redoing his work

1. Milton Friedman, "Factors Affecting the Level of Interest Rates," in *Proceedings of the 1968 Conference on Savings and Residential Financing* (Chicago: United States Savings and Loan League, 1968), pp. 10–27.

and extending it by introducing more sophisticated devices for estimating inflationary expectations. These studies largely confirmed Fisher's results—in particular, his conclusion that inflationary expectations were formed on the basis of a long past period and only slowly adjusted to experience. This conclusion was the centerpiece of his work and the basis for his interpretation of the Gibson paradox—the long-observed positive correlation between interest rates and the *level* of prices.[2] But then some disturbing notes crept in. Results for recent years seemed drastically different from those for the earlier periods, suggesting that the period of experience on which expectations were based shortened drastically after the mid-1960s.[3] In addition, examination of the statistical properties of the estimates constructed by Fisher and by more recent investigators raised doubts about their interpretation.[4]

A second round of the explosion carried the analysis on to a different plane by linking it to the theory of "rational expectations" pioneered by John Muth and the theory of efficient markets developed by Eugene Fama and others.[5] This approach fully accepts Fisher's theoretical framework but rejects his hypothesis about the formation of expectations on the ground that it assumes that profitable market opportunities are neglected. The "efficient market" approach appears to work well in the United States for the period since World War II,[6] but unfortunately not

2. Irving Fisher, *Appreciation and Interest* (Cambridge, Mass.: American Economic Association, 1896); idem, *The Rate of Interest* (New York: Macmillan, 1907); idem, *The Theory of Interest* (New York: Macmillan, 1930); William E. Gibson and George G. Kaufman, "The Sensitivity of Interest Rates to Changes in Money and Income," *Journal of Political Economy* 76 (June 1968): 472–78; William E. Gibson, "Price-Expectations Effects on Interest Rates," *Journal of Finance* 25 (March 1970): 19–34; Thomas Sargent, "Anticipated Inflation and the Nominal Rate of Interest," *Quarterly Journal of Economics* 86 (May 1972): 212–25. Richard Roll, "Interest Rates on Monetary Assets and Commodity Price Changes," *Journal of Finance* 27 (May 1972): 251–78, is a useful survey of these studies.

3. William P. Yohe and Denis S. Karnosky, "Interest Rates and Price Level Changes," *Federal Reserve Bank of Saint Louis Review* 51 (December 1969): 19–36; William E. Gibson, "Interest Rates and Inflationary Expectations," *American Economic Review* 62 (December 1972): 854–65; Karen Johnson, "Inflation and Interest Rates: Recent Evidence," Discussion Paper no. 10, Stanford Workshop on the Microeconomics of Inflation (May 1977).

4. Thomas Sargent, "Interest Rates and Prices in the Long Run: A Study of the Gibson Paradox," *Journal of Money, Credit and Banking* 5, part 2 (February 1973): 385–449.

5. J. F. Muth, "Rational Expectations and the Theory of Price Movements," *Econometrica* 29 (July 1961): 313–35. For summaries of studies along these lines, and bibliographical references, see Maurice D. Levi and John H. Makin, "Fisher, Phillips, Friedman, and the Measured Impact of Inflation on Interest," *Journal of Finance* 34 (March 1979): 35–52; Kajal Lahiri and Jungsoo Lee, "Tests of Rational Expectations and the Fisher Effect," *Southern Economic Journal* 46 (October 1979): 413–24; J. J. Sijben, *Rational Expectations and Monetary Policy* (Germantown, Md.: Sijthoof and Noordhoff, 1980).

6. Robert J. Shiller, "Rational Expectations and the Structure of Interest Rates," Ph.D. diss., Massachusetts Institute of Technology, 1972; Eugene Fama, "Short-Term Interest

for the United States or the United Kingdom before World War II.[7] Yet the Gibson paradox seems to prevail for much of the period after as well as before World War II—though it has apparently disappeared in the decade of the 1970s. We are left with no single satisfactory interpretation of that supposedly well-documented empirical phenomenon. We start this chapter by restating the theoretical analysis that links changes in the quantity of money with interest rates (sec. 10.1). This part of the chapter is largely unchanged from our first draft. We then proceed to exploit our data for the United States and United Kingdom first, to estimate the average value over a century of the nominal interest rate and the real interest rate (sec. 10.2), and then, after a digression on the measurement of yields (sec. 10.3), to estimate the average values in subperiods (sec. 10.4). This leads into the relation between the yields on nominal and physical assets (sec. 10.5) and between nominal yields, price levels, and the rate of change of prices (sec. 10.6). We use these results as a background to evaluate alternative explanations of the Gibson paradox (sec. 10.7), and to interpret an apparent structural change since the end of World War II (sec. 10.8). Finally we return to the initial theme of the relation between monetary changes and interest rates, to find that the statistical results are far less clear-cut than the initial theoretical analysis (sec. 10.9).

10.1 The Theoretical Analysis

The complexity of the relation between money, interest rates, prices, and output derives from two main sources: the interaction between monetary and real disturbances, and the different time patterns of various reactions to either a monetary or a real disturbance. By a monetary disturbance we mean an autonomous change in the nominal quantity of

---

Rates as Predictors of Inflation," *American Economic Review* 65 (June 1975): 269–82. However, see Patrick J. Hess and James J. Bicksler, "Capital Asset Prices versus Time Series Models as Predictors of Inflation," *Journal of Financial Economics* 2 (December 1975): 341–60; also Charles R. Nelson and G. William Schwert, "Short-Term Interest Rates as Predictors of Inflation: On Testing the Hypothesis That the Real Rate of Interest Is Constant," *American Economic Review* 67 (June 1977): 478–86; Robert J. Shiller and Jeremy J. Siegel, "The Gibson Paradox and Historical Movements in Real Interest Rates," *Journal of Political Economy* 85 (October 1977): 891–907; Kenneth Garbade and Paul Wachtel, "Time Variation in the Relationship between Inflation and Interest Rates," *Journal of Monetary Economics* 4 (November 1978): 755–65; and John A. Carlson, "Short-Term Interest Rates as Predictors of Inflation: Comment," *American Economic Review* 67 (June 1977): 469–75. These papers criticize Fama's results, primarily on grounds that his assumption of a constant real rate is incorrect rather than that markets were not efficient. Fama contends in his reply to his critics ("Interest Rates and Inflation: The Message in the Entrails," *American Economic Review* 67 [June 1977]: 487–96), that the "model remains a useful approximation to the world" (p. 487).

7. See Sargent reference in note 4 above.

money or in the conditions determining the nominal quantity of money; by a real disturbance we mean an autonomous change in the conditions of production (the production function), or in the supply of productive resources, or in the conditions of demand for goods and services (including the demand for capital goods and for real balances).

To isolate the effect of a monetary disturbance, we shall first trace the effect of a systematic change in the rate of change of the quantity of money, on the assumptions (1) that the system starts from a position of equilibrium, and (2) that any real disturbances are transitory, not systematic.[8] We shall then consider more briefly the effect of a systematic real disturbance in a stable monetary framework.

10.1.1   Monetary Disturbances

For the monetary analysis we shall, for definiteness, take the initial position at time t_o to be one in which output and the quantity of money have both been increasing at 3 percent per year, velocity and prices have both been stable, and the nominal interest rate is 4 percent. Initial systematic changes in velocity and prices would complicate the exposition but not alter the analysis. We shall take the systematic monetary change to be a shift at time t_o from a steady 3 percent rate of monetary growth to a steady 8 percent rate. We postpone briefly the question of where the additional money comes from.

The effect of such a shift from one rate of monetary growth to another can be usefully classified under three headings: (1) the impact effect, which includes the Keynesian liquidity effect and a first-round loanable funds effect; (2) an intermediate-run effect on real income and the price level; and (3) a long-run price anticipation effect, associated with the name of Irving Fisher, though he analyzed all three sets of effects.[9] These effects depend on whether the change in the quantity of money is anticipated—in which case the first two sets of effects largely disappear—or is unanticipated. We shall assume throughout that initially the change is unanticipated.

Impact Effect

Liquidity effect. Keynes introduced, and the textbooks of the past few decades have popularized, the liquidity preference function as drawn in chart 10.1, showing the quantity of money (M) that the public desires to hold as a function of the interest rate (R). As drawn, the diagram

---

8. Disturbances range along a continuum from strictly momentary to the longest-lasting; however, it will simplify the analysis to replace the continuum by a dichotomy.

9. Similarly, Henry Thornton, a century earlier, was aware of all three effects. See *An Enquiry into the Nature and Effects of the Paper Credit of Great Britain* [hereafter, *Paper Credit of Great Britain*] [1802], ed. F. A. von Hayek (London: George Allen and Unwin, 1939), appendix 1, pp. 256–57, 296–97; appendix 3, p. 336.

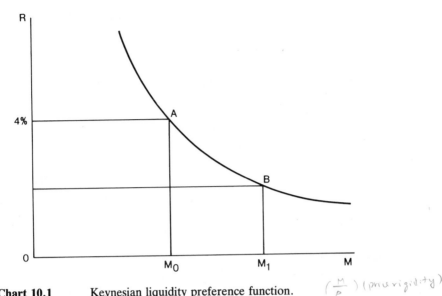

Chart 10.1   Keynesian liquidity preference function. $\left(\frac{M}{P}\right)$ (price rigidity)

embodies three crucial simplifications. First, measuring "the" nominal rate of interest on the vertical axis implicitly assumes that the concept of money for which it is drawn pays no interest; otherwise the vertical axis should record the difference between "the" rate of interest and the rate of interest paid on cash balances (either explicitly or implicitly in the form of services rendered without charge). This simplification reflects Keynes's assumption that the financial assets available to be held could be regarded as consisting either of money bearing no interest or long-term bonds.[10] Second, and more important for our purposes, the horizontal axis should be in terms of the real stock of money (M/P or M/Y), not the nominal stock of money. The failure to distinguish the nominal from the real quantity of money reflects Keynes's assumption that prices could be taken as rigid and that any effects on income would be on real income.[11] We shall relax this assumption in considering the intermediate output and price effect, as well as the long-run price anticipation effect. Third, the diagram neglects, as Keynes did not, the role of the level of income in determining the demand for money. The curve drawn is to be interpreted as holding for a particular level of income (both nominal and real, given the fixed price assumption, or real, if the horizontal axis is interpreted as real money stock). A higher level of income would be associated with a higher curve, a lower level with a lower curve.

10. See section 2.5.3.
11. See section 2.5.2.

The curve as drawn is for a particular time t_o. For our initial assumptions, with M growing at 3 percent a year, the curve is moving over time to the right at 3 percent per year along with output, and the quantity measured on the horizontal axis is doing the same. More simply, we may interpret M as corrected for a 3 percent secular trend.

A shift at time t_o to an 8 percent rate of monetary growth means that cash balances will start to rise at a 5 percent a year rate relative to their previous trend. So far as our present restricted framework is concerned, nothing will happen initially except that the public will hold the excess cash—after all, the rise is unanticipated and cash is held as a shock absorber. But presumably this interval will be brief. As excess cash accumulates, holders of cash, finding the composition of their portfolios disturbed, will try to adjust the portfolios by replacing cash with other assets (including both securities and physical assets). In the process they will bid up the price of other assets and force down the rate of interest. This is the pure liquidity effect.

Note that chart 10.1 gives the demand for a *stock* at a point of time, and the assumed change is a change in a *flow*. Hence this effect would involve not a once-for-all shift from one to another on the demand curve, but a sliding down the curve from point A toward, say, point B, which we may take to correspond to the (trend-adjusted) quantity of money available at the end of a year. Expressed in terms of a time scale, the behavior of the rate of interest that would be produced by this effect is as described in chart 10.2, namely, an indefinite decline.

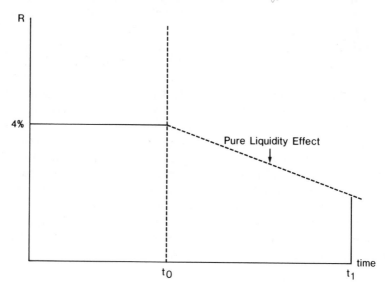

Chart 10.2   Pure liquidity effect on the interest rate of an increase in the rate of monetary growth.

Note also the crucial role of the rigid price assumption. Suppose that we interpret the horizontal axis as referring to M/P, that the shift to an 8 percent rate of monetary growth is announced in advance and fully taken into account and is simultaneously accompanied by a 5 percent rate of price rise. Then, if we neglect the price-anticipation effect on the interest rate considered later, the public would stay at point A in chart 10.1, since real (trend-adjusted) balances would be constant.

The liquidity effect as just described underlay the academic opinion in the Keynesian era that "easy" money could be regarded as equivalent to both lower interest rates and more rapid monetary growth. A rather different effect underlay the corresponding opinion held by bankers, commercial and central, for a far longer period.

The first-round loanable funds effect. Where does the extra money come from? How is it put in circulation? In the present financial system, it is natural to view the increased rate of monetary growth as coming through the banking system, via larger open market purchases by the central bank, which add to reserves of commercial banks, inducing them to expand more rapidly their loans and investments. In the first instance, therefore, the higher rate of monetary growth appears to take the form of an increase in the flow supply of loanable funds. Taken by itself, without allowing for any subsequent effects on ouput or prices of the expenditures financed with the additional funds, or for any liquidity effect, the increase in the supply of loanable funds would produce a once-for-all drop in the interest rate to a new level as in chart 10.3.

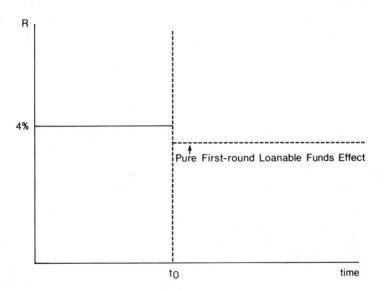

Chart 10.3   Pure first-round lonable funds effect on the interest rate of an increase in the rate of monetary growth.

Note that there are two slips 'twixt the cup and the lip with respect to the first-round effect. The first is that the increase in the quantity of money need not come through an increase in loanable funds. Historically, it has sometimes come through gold discoveries; currently, it is likely to come through government spending. In each case, the first-round effect, as John Stuart Mill stated more than a century ago, will depend on the initial use made of the new money.[12] If, for example, the monetary increase came through gold production, the first-round effect would be not on the flow of loanable funds and interest rates, but on the wages of gold miners and the prices of commodities they bought.[13]

The second slip is that the rise in the supply of loanable funds via money issue may not be a net rise. Whether it is depends on the behavior of the issuers of new money. The new money represents a source of revenue to the issuers, and there is no reason why the issuers would use the whole of the increase in revenue to add to their assets. It seems much more reasonable that they will use revenue from this source in the same way as other revenue. Even if legal or institutional arrangements require the issuers to put the money in circulation by purchasing assets, the issuers can offset the increase in holding of these assets by disposing of other assets, including the equity in the right to issue money. In that case there is no first-round effect on loanable funds at all.

The use of new money to finance government spending can be regarded as a special case of this slip instead of the first. However, this slip has much wider relevance, since it is the key issue in the extensive discussions of forced saving.[14]

On the empirical level, the two components of the impact effect imply different relations. The liquidity effect would produce a relation between the interest rate and the level of the nominal quantity of money or equivalently between the rate of change in the interest rate and the rate of monetary growth; the first-round loanable funds effect, between the

12. "It is perfectly true that . . . an addition to the currency almost always *seems* to have the effect of lowering the rate of interest: because it is almost always accompanied by something which really has that tendency. The currency . . . is all issued in the way of loans, except such part as happens to be employed in the purchase of gold and silver. The same operation, therefore, which adds to the currency, also adds to the loans. . . . Now, though, as currency, these issues have not an effect on interest, as loans, they have." John Stuart Mill, *Principles of Political Economy*, 5th ed. (London: Parker, Son and Bourn, 1862), book 3, chap. 23, par. 4.

13. See J. H. Cairnes, "Essays toward a Solution of the Gold Question," in *Essays in Political Economy* (London: Macmillan, 1873), pp. 1–165.

14. See the discussion by Phillip Cagan, *The Channels of Monetary Effects on Interest Rates* (New York: NBER, 1972), pp. 29–39.

John L. Scadding has examined this issue in greater detail, both theoretically and empirically, and has concluded that the second slip may well eliminate the bulk of any forced saving or first-round loanable funds effect. "Monetary Growth and Aggregate Savings," Ph.D. diss., University of Chicago, 1974, pp. 27–28, 56–58, 61–68.

interest rate and the rate of change of the nominal quantity of money or, equivalently, the rate of change of the interest rate and the acceleration of the quantity of money.[15]

Combined liquidity and loanable funds effects. Of course, the liquidity effect and the loanable funds effect operate together so that charts 10.2 and 10.3 cannot be simultaneously correct—in this simplified analysis there is only one interest rate. The reconciliation is the same as in other problems of capital theory in which demand and supply depend on both levels and rate of change.[16] The liquidity preference curve depicted in chart 10.1 must be treated as a function of the rate of change of the quantity of money—for our present purpose, of the excess of the actual over the anticipated monetary growth rate.

Chart 10.4 shows the demand situation incorporating this effect—the right-hand panel for stocks, the left for flows. The stock demand curve is depicted as a function not only of the level of balances but also of the rate of change (g_M in both panels is to be interpreted as only the unanticipated component of the rate of change). The flow demand is in its turn a function of the level of the stock. A shift of the rate of change of the quantity of money from zero to 5 percent per year produces an immediate decline in the level of interest rates via a downward shift in the stock demand curve to intersect with the vertical monetary supply curve at A'. As the quantity of money grows, the interest rate declines along the new stock demand curve from A' to B', which as before represents the temporary position at the end of a year. In the left-hand panel for flows, the flow demand curve declines as the quantity of money increases, the market interest rate at B' corresponding to a rate of monetary growth of 5 percent. The result is a time pattern of interest rates which reflects simply the super-position of chart 10.2 on chart 10.3, as in chart 10.5.

Intermediate Income Effect

As time passes, the initial impact effects will be superseded by more basic effects. Even though unanticipated, the rising money balances and

---

15. Cagan in his study of intracycle movements found evidence of the impact effect, in the form of both a negative synchronous correlation between the level of interest rates and short-term monetary growth, and a tendency for the rate of interest to decline for some six months after an acceleration in monetary growth. Cagan interprets his findings as reflecting primarily a portfolio or liquidity effect, with a first-round loanable funds effect playing a definite but secondary role (see Cagan, *op. cit.*, *Channels of Monetary Effects*, chaps. 3, 4, and 7). However, it is not clear that this interpretation is fully satisfactory. See William Poole, *Journal of Political Economy* 82 (May/June 1974): 665–68. Cagan recognizes that the liquidity and loanable-funds effects cannot be distinguished by relating the interest rate to monetary growth, but argues that his analysis distinguishes between them by introducing bank credit as an additional variable.

16. For a full analysis, see Milton Friedman, *Price Theory* (Chicago: Aldine, 1976), chap. 17, pp. 283–322.

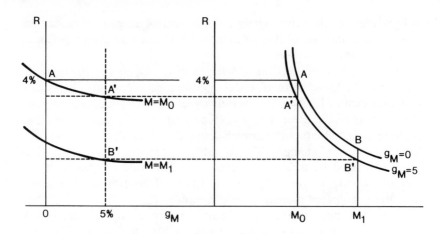

Chart 10.4   Liquidity preference curve as a function of rate of change of quantity of money.

initially lower interest rates will stimulate spending, the spending will affect both prices and output, and these effects will feed back on the demand for money. And sooner or later the increase in the rate of monetary growth will cease to be unanticipated. These effects begin to operate along with the impact effects as soon as the rate of monetary growth changes. However, initially they are negligible and build up only gradually, which is why it is convenient to separate them for purposes of analysis.

The existence and character of the intermediate income effect does not depend on any doctrinal position about the way monetary forces affect the economy. Along strict Keynesian income-expenditure lines, the initial liquidity and loanable funds effects produce lower interest rates, and the lower interest rates stimulate business investment, which in turn has a multiplier effect on spending. Along the broader monetary lines we prefer, the attempt to correct portfolio imbalance raises the prices of sources of service flows relative to the prices of service flows themselves, which leads to an increase in spending on both the service flows and the production of new sources of service flows. Put differently, reported interest rates are only a few of a large set of rates of interest, many implicit and unobservable, that are affected by the changed rate of monetary growth. As a result, higher monetary growth affects a much broader area than on the Keynesian view. In either case, a higher rate of monetary growth will tend, after some lag, to raise the rate of growth of nominal spending and hence nominal income.

For a moment, retain the Keynesian assumption that the whole of the acceleration in nominal income takes the form of an acceleration in output, while prices remain constant. The acceleration in real income will

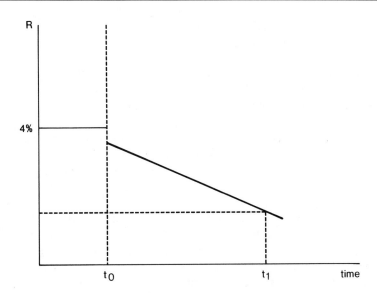

Chart 10.5   Combined impact effect: liquidity plus loanable funds effects on the rate of interest.

shift the liquidity preference curve of chart 10.1 to the right and also raise the demand for loanable funds—that is, it will shift the whole set of curves in the right hand panel of chart 10.4 to the right. These shifts will tend to raise interest rates, counteracting the downward pressure from the liquidity and first-round effects.

Sooner or later the acceleration in nominal income will have to take the form of rising prices, since the initial position was assumed to be one of equilibrium and we have introduced nothing to change the long-run trend of real income. Indeed, the initial acceleration in real income will presumably be followed at some point by a deceleration that brings it below the long-run trend so that the cumulative effect on real income cancels out. However, the qualitative effect on interest rates is the same whether the acceleration in nominal income takes the form of an acceleration in output or in prices. In either case the liquidity preference function, if the horizontal axis is in nominal terms, shifts to the right. If the horizontal axis is in real terms, the rising prices will instead be translated into a slowing or reversal of the right-hand movement of real balances, which also tends to raise interest rates.

The impact and intermediate effects together would, by themselves, ultimately produce a return to the initial rate of interest.[17] The 8 percent

17. As Henry Thornton put it in 1802, "It seems clear . . . that when the augmented quantity of paper shall have been for some time stationary, and shall have produced its full effect in raising the price of goods, the temptation to borrow at five per cent will be exactly the same as before" (*Paper Credit of Great Britain*, pp. 256–57).

rate of rise in money would be matched by an 8 percent rate of rise in nominal income, divided into a 5 percent rate of price inflation and a 3 percent rate of real income growth. Real balances and the real supply of and demand for loanable funds would be at their initial level.

As we know from chapter 2, this is not really a stable long-run equilibrium position because of the price anticipation effect. Even if we continue to abstract from this effect, the time path of interest rates produced by the combination of the impact and income effects would be not the smooth path described by curve *A* in chart 10.6 but the cyclical path involving overshooting described by curve *B*. In the first place, both the initial acceptance of excess balances and the delay between portfolio effects on interest rates and the effect of changes in interest rates on spending will produce an initial lag in the reaction of income. In chart 10.7, similar to chart 2.3 the lag means that, for some time after t_o, nominal income will tend to follow line *C* rather than line *B*. (Note that these lines are not in proper scale; their slopes are exaggerated to make the difference between them more obvious.) This will require a catch-up phase during which nominal income will have to rise more rapidly than 5 percent a year to get to line *B*. The rate of change of nominal income will certainly overshoot, and this may, though it need not, lead to an overshooting of the interest rate as well. Second, the initial unanticipated acceleration in output is likely to be regarded by the public as transitory, as in fact it will prove to be. It will therefore not raise their permanent income proportionately. If, as we have argued, demand for money is related to permanent income,

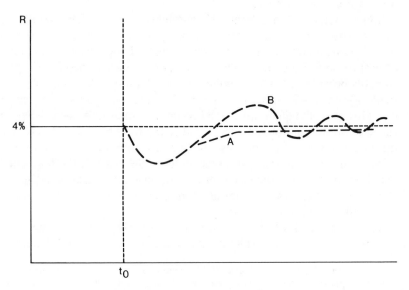

Chart 10.6   Combination of impact and income effects on the rate of interest.

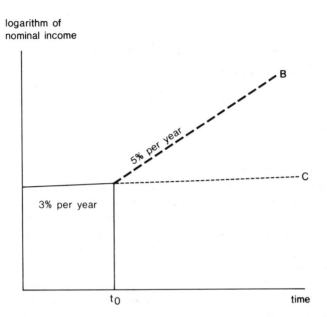

logarithm of
nominal income

B

5% per year

C

3% per year

t_0

time

Chart 10.7   Combination of impact and income effects on nominal income.

the liquidity preference curve in charts 10.1 and 10.4 (with the horizontal axis interpreted as the nominal quantity of money adjusted for trend) will initially shift to the right in lesser proportion than the rise in (similarly trend-adjusted) nominal income, though ultimately it will have to shift in full proportion. This will make for a more rapid rise in nominal income and a slower upward effect on interest rates in the initial stages when most of the increase in nominal income is in output.[18] This will contribute to an overshooting in the upward direction of the rate of change of nominal income and subsequently an overshooting in the downward direction. For interest rates, it means a slower recovery from the initial decline and may, though it need not, mean subsequently a rise above the final level.

If, for simplicity, we assume that the reaction pattern of interest rates to a monetary change is independent of the level of interest rates and of past and subsequent monetary change, we can express the composite effect of the impact and intermediate effects in the equation

(1) $$R(T) = R_o + \int_{-\infty}^{T} b(T - T') \, g_M(T') dT',$$

where $R(T)$ is the interest rate at time T and $g_M(T')$, the rate of monetary growth at time T' and where

(2) $$\int_{-\infty}^{T} b(T - T') dT' = 0,$$

18. We are indebted to Michael Darby for this refinement with respect to income.

and

(3)
$$b(T-T') \begin{matrix} < 0 \text{ for } (T-T') < \tau_1 \\ > 0 \text{ for } (T-T') > \tau_1 \end{matrix} \Big\}$$

if there is no overshooting (curve A in chart 10.6) and

(4)
$$b(T-T') \begin{matrix} < 0 \text{ for } (T-T') < \tau_1 \\ > 0 \text{ for } \tau_1 < (T-T') < \tau_2 \\ < 0 \text{ for } \tau_2 < (T-T') < \tau_3 \\ \dots\dots\dots\dots\dots\dots \end{matrix} \Bigg\}$$

when there is overshooting (curve B in chart 10.6).

Condition (2) assures that the impact and intermediate effects cumulate to bring the interest rate back to its initial position, which so far as we have gone is independent of the rate of monetary growth and is symbolized by R_o. R_o is of course to be regarded not as a numerical constant but as a function of whatever variables other than monetary growth affect the interest rate.

Condition (3) expresses the initial negative influence of the liquidity and first-round effects and the subsequent positive income effect, and condition (4) expresses these plus the subsequent cyclical adaptation mechanisms. τ_1 is the time delay between the acceleration of monetary growth and the subsequent initial trough of the interest rate (or the deceleration and subsequent initial peak).[19]

Price Anticipation Effect

When, in our example, prices are rising at 5 percent a year, the public will sooner or later come to anticipate the price rise. As a result, the 4 percent initial interest rate can no longer be the equilibrium rate. We can no longer neglect the distinction to which Irving Fisher called attention between the nominal rate of interest and the real rate of interest. Initially both equaled 4 percent. If the nominal yield were to stay 4 percent, the real yield would be -1 percent. Nothing has happened in the real sector, in the tentative equilibrium resulting from the impact and income effects alone, to reduce the equilibrium real yield. As the inflation come to be anticipated, lenders will come to demand higher interest rates and borrowers will be willing to pay higher interest rates. The nominal interest rate must rise above its initial level.[20]

---

19. Cagan in his study has tried to estimate an equation like equation (1) and has concluded that τ_1 is of the order of magnitude of six months and that the sum of the weights first totals zero, that is, the interest rate returns to its initial level, after about fifteen months. Cagan, *Channels of Monetary Effects*, p. 102.

20. As Henry Thornton put it in 1811, "Accordingly, in countries in which the currency was in a rapid course of depreciation, supposing that there were no usury laws, the current rate of interest was often . . . proportionably augmented" (speech, 7 May 1811, in the debate in the House of Commons on the Report of the Bullion Committee, in Thornton, *Paper Credit of Great Britain*, appendix 3, p. 336).

More formally, designate the nominal interest rate on nominal assets by R, the real interest rate on nominal assets by ρ, the rate of change of prices by g_P. Then the real yield actually realized after the event, the ex-post real yield,[21] will be

$$(5) \qquad \rho = R - g_P.$$

R is observed directly in the market. It corresponds to the yield to maturity of a security with specified maturity and interest payments if it is purchased at the market price. ρ is not observable in the market at the time the security is purchased. It can be calculated only after the event, when the security has matured and the rate of price rise over its life is known. Hence ρ cannot be a variable that directly influences behavior. What influences behavior is the *anticipated* real yield, or

$$(6) \qquad \rho^* = R - g_P^*,$$

where g_P^* is the rate of price change anticipated over the period to the maturity of the security to which R refers.

Note that a whole spectrum of equations like equations (5) and (6) exists at any point in time, one for each possible maturity. For convenience, we can treat these equations as referring to some standard maturity or, alternatively, to a maturity approaching zero as a limit, so they refer to a continuous rate of yield at a moment of time. The important consideration in any calculation of nominal and real yields is that the price change refer to the same period as the holding period for the security. As the term "holding period" suggests, the yield can be calculated for a period less than the stated maturity of a security. However, in that case the price of the security at the end of the holding period will also affect the yield and will, like the price change, generally not be a known quantity at the initial date. It too, like the rate of price change, will have to be determined ex post or treated as an anticipated magnitude.

In our example, initially

$$R = \rho = \rho^* = 4 \text{ percent.}$$

When the public comes to anticipate the 5 percent price rise, R will have to be higher than initially, and R will have to differ from ρ and ρ^* by 5 percentage points. The precise terminal value of R—whether it is 9 percent or higher or lower —depends on what happens to ρ^*. Will it remain 4 percent?

To answer this question we must examine the effect of the higher value of R on cash balance holdings. The higher value of R makes interest-bearing nominal assets more attractive relative to non-interest-bearing money and so will tend to reduce the real value of cash balances held: at the terminal position, velocity will be higher than at the initial position.

---

21. Equation (5) is exact only for continuous compounding.

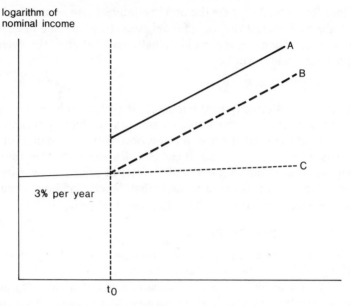

logarithm of
nominal income

A

B

3% per year

C

t_0

Chart 10.8   Effect of an increase in rate of monetary growth on the equilibrium path of nominal income.

The higher velocity has a number of important effects. In the first place, as we pointed out in chapter 2, the equilibrium path of nominal income will not be line *B* in chart 10.7 but line *A* in chart 10.8, parallel to *B* but higher (like chart 10.7, chart 10.8 is not drawn to scale). This in turn means that income will at some time or other have to overshoot its ultimate equilibrium rate of growth for a more basic reason than those cited earlier.

In the second place, and more important for our purpose, if terminal real nonhuman wealth held in nonmonetary form were the same as initially, total real nonhuman wealth would be less. The purely monetary disturbance we have assumed which produces a steady anticipated inflation has the *real* effect of lowering the equilibrium real wealth held in the form of money.[22] The reduction in real balances would in turn lead to an increase in other forms of real nonhuman wealth, either as a substitute for some of the cash balances that served as a productive resource or as a replacement for some of the cash balances held by ultimate wealth holders. Robert Mundell has argued that the result would tend to be a lower real yield on capital. However, that is by no means clear on a purely theoretical level. Everything depends critically on the determinants of the wealth/income ratio desired by ultimate wealth holders. For example,

22. See M. Friedman, *Optimum Quantity of Money*, and Robert Mundell, "Inflation and Real Interest," *Journal of Political Economy* 71 (June 1963): 280–83.

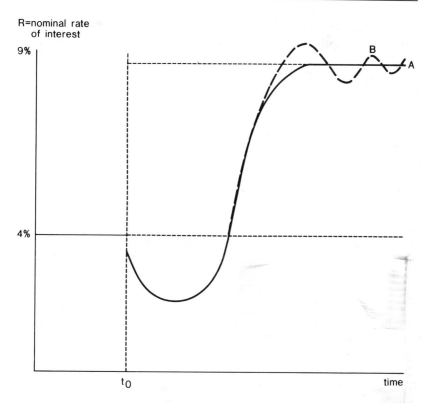

R=nominal rate
of interest

Chart 10.9   Full effect of an increase in monetary growth on the nominal
interest rate.

if they have a constant internal rate of discount when in wealth equilibrium, the ultimate result would be a higher real level of nonmoney nonhuman wealth, but a sufficiently lower real level of total nonhuman-wealth that the yield of the smaller amount of now less productive capital would be the same as before.[23]

If the real rate were unaffected by inflation, the final pattern of interest rate behavior for our example would be as depicted in chart 10.9, with curve A showing a monotonic ultimate approach to the final equilibrium, curve B, a cyclical approach.

Equation (1) could still be used to describe the composite effect of the anticipation effect as well as the impact and intermediate effects, but equation (2) would change, since the integral would equal unity instead of zero, so that a permanent increase in $g_M(T)$ by unity in equation (1) would ultimately raise the interest rate by unity. For some purposes, it

23. An even more bizarre possibility is that nonhuman nonmoney capital is sufficiently complementary with money balances that nonhuman nonmoney capital must decline along with real money balances to keep the yield constant.

might be useful to keep separate the impact and intermediate effects from the price anticipation effects by writing the equation for the interest rate as

(7)
$$R(T) = R_o + \int_{-\infty}^{T} b(T - T')\, g_M(T')dT'$$
$$+ \int_{-\infty}^{T} c(T - T')g_M(T')dT',$$

where

(8)
$$\int_{-\infty}^{T} b(T - T')dT' = 0$$

and

(9)
$$\int_{-\infty}^{T} c(T - T')dT' = 1 .$$

Conditions (3) or (4) would apply to the b function, but it is not easy to write corresponding conditions for the c function, since that depends on how monetary change is incorporated into price anticipations, a subject yet to be considered. In this form, R_o equals the real interest rate plus the hypothetical rate of inflation when the monetary growth rate is zero.

The terminal value of ρ^* might be less than the initial value, in which case the terminal value of R would be above the initial value by less than the rate of inflation. In that case the final pattern of interest rate behavior for our example would be as depicted in chart 10.9 except that curves A and B would both be lowered somewhat. It is more difficult to alter the equations in any simple way because there is no reason why the shortfall from unity in equation (9) should be the same for all rates of monetary growth.

The effect of moderate rates of anticipated inflation on the real rate is likely in practice to be negligible. Non-interest-bearing money is a small fraction of total wealth.[24] Even a substantial reduction in real balances would amount to a small reduction in total nonhuman wealth. In addition, the real yield on capital is almost surely highly insensitive to the size of the stock of capital, that is, the demand on the part of producing enterprises for the real stock of capital is highly elastic. That is the implication of the rather stable real rate of interest realized on the average over long periods of time. We conclude that the theoretically possible effect of anticipated inflation on the equilibrium real rate of interest can be neglected and the real rate regarded as unaffected by *anticipated inflation.*[25]

---

24. For the United States, M_2 in 1979 was roughly about six months' national income, M_1 was less than three months' national income, and high-powered money was about two-thirds of one month's national income. Total nonhuman wealth is typically something like three to five years' national income, so at most M_2 would be about one-sixth of total wealth, M_1 about one-twelfth, and high-powered money about one-fortieth.

25. A formal theoretical analysis that presents an explicit model leading to results such as those in chart 10.9 and equations (8) and (9) is developed in Dean G. Taylor, "The Effects of Monetary Growth on the Interest Rate," Ph.D. diss., University of Chicago, 1972.

A more important practical complication is taxation. Currently in the United States, nominal interest payments are taxed to the recipient and deductible in computing taxable income to the borrower. For the real after-tax yield to the lender to be unaffected by anticipated inflation, the differential between the nominal and real yield must exceed anticipated inflation by an amount that depends on the relevant marginal tax rate. If the marginal tax rate is t, the differential must be $1/(1-t)$ times anticipated inflation. If the borrower is subject to the same marginal tax rate as the lender and is permitted to deduct interest payments in computing taxable income, the same differential keeps the net real rate paid unchanged.[26] With the present high marginal rates of tax, the effect is potentially of considerable quantitative significance. For example, at a 50 percent rate, the differential between the real and nominal rate would have to be twice the anticipated rate of inflation to keep the real rate unchanged.[27]

Unanticipated inflation or, even more important, highly variable inflation is a different matter and almost surely is capable of having a major effect on real yields. Unanticipated inflation makes the ex-post real yield differ from the ex-ante real yield and hence makes the real yield obtained from physical capital differ from the real yield to holders of financial securities, particularly fixed interest securities. "The" real yield no longer has any meaning, even if we continue to neglect problems raised by

26. There has been much recent discussion of this issue. See Michael Darby, "The Financial and Tax Effects of Monetary Policy on Interest Rates," *Economic Inquiry* 13 (June 1975): 266–76; Jack Carr, James E. Pesando, and Lawrence B. Smith, "Tax Effects, Price Expectations and the Nominal Rate of Interest," *Economic Inquiry* 14 (June 1976): 259–69; Martin Feldstein, "Inflation, Income Taxes and the Rate of Interest: A Theoretical Analysis," *American Economic Review* 66 (December 1976): 809–20; Vito Tanzi, "Inflation, Indexation and Interest Income Taxation," *Banca Nazionale del Lavoro Quarterly Review*, no. 4 (1975), pp. 319–28; Arthur E. Gandolfi, "Taxation and the 'Fisher Effect,' " *Journal of Finance* 31 (December 1976): 1375–86. John A. Carlson, "Expected Inflation and Interest Rates," *Economic Inquiry* 17 (October 1979): 597–608, examines empirical evidence on the tax effect, finding some evidence of its existence during the 1960s, much less evidence for the 1950s and 1970s. In general the existence of the theoretically expected tax effect has evaded the several efforts to isolate it and, as yet, no satisfactory explanation for the failure has been forthcoming.

In an unpublished paper, Arthur E. Gandolfi has examined the effect of different income, capital gains, and depreciation tax arrangements and has concluded that the existence or nonexistence of the tax effect may depend on the specific tax arrangements. This is a matter on which much further work can be expected.

27. Vito Tanzi, "Inflation and the Incidence of Income Taxes on Interest Income: Some Results for the United States, 1972–74," *IMF Staff Papers* 24 (July 1977): 500–513, calculates the interest rates persons in various income brackets would have had to receive in 1972, 1973, and 1974 to have realized a zero net real return after allowing for inflation and taxes, and the net gain or loss because of the tax treatment—gain to debtors, loss to creditors. He concludes that, while actual interest rates in 1972 yielded positive net real returns to creditors in most income brackets, they did not do so for high income groups in 1973 and did so for almost no groups in 1974. He finds that middle-income groups are net debtors and therefore gained from the tax treatment; lower- and upper-income groups are net creditors and therefore lost.

different maturities, different degrees of default risk, and so on. These effects are reinforced if inflation is both high on the average and highly variable, even if the *average* rate is largely anticipated. Highly variable inflation tends to destroy financial intermediation, rendering the capital market both limited and inefficient—a tendency that is in practice strongly reinforced by government controls and restrictions on financial transactions. As a result, not only may the yield to the holder of securities deviate widely from the yield on the physical capital to which the securities are linked, but also the real yield on physical capital may differ widely from one enterprise or industry to another.

Unanticipated inflation has been important for the United States and the United Kingdom for the period we cover, but not highly variable inflation. Highly variable inflation has been much more important for less developed countries, particularly in South America. However, highly variable inflation has more recently plagued the United Kingdom and the United States as well.

The general effect of anticipated inflation on nominal interest rates is apparent from comparisons across countries: nominal interest rates are invariably higher in countries that have experienced substantial inflation for some time than in countries that have not. But the precise relation is much more difficult to pin down. The major problem is the difference between actual and anticipated inflation, so that any analysis requires combining a hypothesis about the formation of anticipations with a hypothesis about the behavior of real rates and the relation between real and nominal interest rates.

If price change were perfectly and instantaneously anticipated, rapid rates of price rise would be associated with high nominal interest rates and low rates of price rise with low nominal interest rates, but there would be no correlation between high prices and high interest rates or between rising prices and rising interest rates; yet the Gibson paradox is the allegation that such a correlation does exist.

Chart 10.10 illustrates this point. Suppose that the historical record of prices were the one plotted, where the ordinate is the logarithm of price so that straight lines correspond to constant rates of price change. If this price pattern were fully anticipated and were the only factor altering the nominal interest rate, the nominal interest rate would be high for periods a and c and low for periods b and d, as shown by the dashed steps. The difference in height between the two steps would be the rate of inflation in steps a and c plus the rate of deflation in steps b and d. There would be no correlation between the level of prices and the level of interest rates: half the time, a high interest rate would be associated with an above-average price level; half the time, with a below-average price level; and similarly for low interest rates. There would be perfect correlation between the level of interest rates and the rate of change of the price level.

log i, P

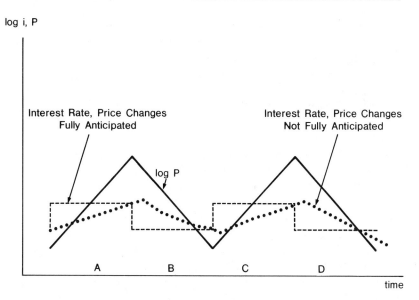

Chart 10.10   The effect of perfectly and imperfectly anticipated price changes on the interest rate.

This description applies rigorously only to the continuous interest rate at a moment of time. For a finite maturity, the interest rate at any point in time would reflect the rate of price change expected over the period from then to maturity. If price changes were correctly anticipated, the interest rate would equal a moving average of the step function in chart 10.10, the length of the average would be equal to the maturity, and the average would be plotted at the *initial* date of the moving average. The result would be to smooth the step function and to shift its turning dates earlier.

The actual relation, as we shall see below, is more like the wavy dotted line in chart 10.10 than like the step function. The turning dates are in practice shifted later, not earlier. To explain this pattern requires introducing discrepancies between actual and anticipated inflation, or movements in real interest rates, or some combination of the two. The particular explanation of this phenomenon, termed the Gibson paradox by J. M. Keynes, that has received most attention is the one offered by Irving Fisher. It combines an assumed rough constancy in the real rate with a lagged adjustment of price anticipations to the actual price movement. We shall discuss his and other explanations in greater detail in section 10.7, after we have first established in sections 10.2 through 10.6, as best we can, the phenomena to be explained.

10.1.2   Real Disturbances

The monetary disturbances analyzed in the preceding section have systematic effects on real interest rates. An unanticipated acceleration in monetary growth to a new steady rate produces at first a decline in the ex-post real instantaneous rate realized by lenders, then a rise, and ultimately a return roughly to its initial level. In the interim the ex-post real rate is likely to fluctuate above and below that level. The ex-ante real rate follows a similar qualitative course, but the timing may be quite different. The ex-post and ex-ante real rates on loans of different durations will tend to be appropriately weighted averages of the instantaneous rates.

It would be gratifying to be able to present a parallel systematic analysis for real disturbances. However, there is no way to do so because the pattern of effects on nominal and real interest rates depends on the character of the real disturbance. For that reason this section will be briefer and vaguer than the preceding and purely illustrative.

Compare for example, two hypothetical real disturbances: first, a Wicksellian or Schumpeterian surge of innovations that raises the real yield on a wide range of physical capital; second, innovations in the use of cash balances of the kind Irving Fisher expected to produce an upward trend in the transactions velocity of circulation of money. Initially, for both, assume given monetary conditions in the sense of a given rate of monetary growth.

A Surge of Innovations Raising the Yield on Physical Capital

An upward shift in the stock demand for capital in response to a surge of innovations will be accompanied by a similar shift in the flow demand curve for investment funds that will tend to raise nominal interest rates, which, in turn, will tend to raise the velocity of circulation of money. As in response to a monetary disturbance, this effect will be spread over time. The higher velocity will mean for a time a more rapid rise in nominal income which, given that it is unanticipated, will initially be reflected primarily in greater output rather than in prices. At this stage the rise in the nominal interest rate will be accompanied by a rise in both the ex-post and the ex-ante real rates. As time passes, the higher nominal income will be translated into higher prices, output will decline to its earlier level and, for a time, below it. Ex-post real rates will decline as the price adjustment occurs and may fall below the initial level. However, the rise in velocity is a once-for-all effect. There is nothing in the process so far considered to produce a continuing rise in velocity. Hence, when velocity has adjusted, prices will resume their prior rate of change, and the differential between nominal and real interest rates will return to its prior level. Both nominal and real interest rates will continue at higher than initial levels until the increased stock demand for physical capital is gradually satisfied by the higher savings called forth by the higher interest rate, possibly reinforced by saving out of the higher income generated by the assumed surge of innovations.[28] Depending on the wealth-holding preferences of the community, interest rates may ultimately return to their initial level or may settle at a higher or, possibly, even a lower level.

For our purpose, the important phenomenon is that the real disturbance produces an initial rise, then a later decline in nominal and real interest rates, with all sorts of possible detours in between.

A different monetary system, of the kind assumed by Wicksell, for example, would alter the results in detail but not in broad outline. In Wicksell's model, the initial rise in the "natural" rate would be resisted by banks, which would lead to a rise in the initially assumed rate of monetary growth, thereby partly reinforcing, partly offsetting the rise in velocity. But this effect too would tend to be a once-for-all phenomenon rather than a continuing process.

A Surge of Innovations in the Use of Cash Balances

The initial effect on interest rates of a surge of innovations in the use of cash balances (e.g., faster computer clearing, reducing average balances required) would be precisely the opposite of the Wicksellian surge of innovations. The innovations would have the same effect as more rapid monetary growth, tending to lower nominal interest rates through the attempt of holders of now-redundant cash to acquire interest yielding assets. Velocity would tend to rise as in the preceding case, but the rising velocity would itself be an autonomous force, not a response to a higher interest rate, and so would tend simultaneously to make for higher prices, as in the preceding case, but lower interest rates. If we assume, with Fisher, an upward *trend* in velocity rather than a once-for-all shift, the effects on interest rates would be precisely the same as that attributed in the preceding section to an increase in the rate of monetary growth, which means that ultimately nominal interest rates would settle at a permanently higher level, though real interest rates would return to their initial level.

The response of interest rates to this surge of innovations is very nearly the reverse of the pattern in response to the Wicksellian surge.

Perhaps this comparison will explain why we do not embark on a detailed analysis of real disturbances comparable to our earlier discussion of the effect of a more precisely specifiable monetary disturbance. We shall consider real disturbances further in section 10.7, which examines alternative explanations of the Gibson paradox.

10.1.3   Conclusion

The preceding general theoretical analysis of this chapter will perhaps prepare readers for a major feature of the empirical findings that follow:

28. The exact process is highly complicated. See M. Friedman, *Price Theory*.

the complexity of the behavior of interest rates and the difficulty of identifying any simple and consistent pattern connecting interest rates with price levels, rates of price change, or rates of monetary growth. Because interest rates connect the future with the present, they are necessarily sensitive to judgments about the future, about the formation of which we have little confirmed knowledge. Because interest rates connect large stocks to relatively small flows, they can display wide variations as a result of apparently trivial changes. Because they connect holders of financial assets to holders of physical assets, they are sensitive to the process whereby nominal and real magnitudes are linked. Finally, the same disturbance can have effects in opposite directions over different periods of time, so the observed behavior of interest rate is sensitive to variations in the reaction time of different groups in the population.

Like prices and money, interest rates are a pervasive and crucial phenomenon entering into every aspect of economic activity. But the special features just mentioned make their empirical behavior an even more challenging subject of scientific study.

10.2   Average Yields

Table 10.1 summarizes the average yields for over a century on various categories of assets. For this purpose we have used three measures of yield: (1) a short-term rate—the rate on commercial paper (sixty to ninety days through 1923, four to six months since) for the United States and the rate on three-month bank bills for the United Kingdom; (2) a long-term rate—the yield to maturity on high-grade corporate bonds for the United States and the consol yield (coupon divided by price) for the United Kingdom; (3) the proxy for the nominal yield on physical assets that we used in chapter 6 (g_Y)—namely, the rate of change of nominal income.[29] We shall, for simplicity, refer to this proxy as "the yield on physical assets."

For the more than a century that our data cover, the several average yields display a relation consistent with expectations from earlier studies.

1. For both the United States and the United Kingdom, the short-term nominal yield is less than the long-term nominal yield—by 0.68 percent-

29. For the United States we have experimented also with the two other interest rates on nominal assets: the call money rate and the basic yield on long-term bonds. The results largely duplicated those for the two in table 10.1: hence we have omitted them.

For the proxy yield, and also the rates of change of prices and money, we have departed from our usual procedure of calculating them from exponential trends fitted to triplets of phases. Instead they are calculated as the average of the annual rates of change within phases. The reason for this departure is to make them as closely comparable as possible to the matching interest rates. Interest rates are initially observed as rates, hence their phase averages are derived solely from rates within the several phases. Our notation for these rates of change is $g_Y.A$, $g_P.A$, and $g_M.A$.

age points for the United States, 0.77 for the United Kingdom. This difference presumably reflects a liquidity premium that various more detailed studies of the term structure of interest rates have shown to exist.[30]

2. For both the United States and the United Kingdom, the nominal yield on physical assets is between the nominal yields on short- and long-term securities—about halfway between for the United States, close to the long yield for the United Kingdom. In that mythical stationary state in which arbitrage between physical and nominal assets is effective, all assets of the same maturity and risk would provide the same return. These results therefore add to our confidence that g_Y can be treated as an approximation to the nominal yield on physical assets, and also that the physical assets for the yield on which it proxies are intermediate in maturity and risk between short- and long-term securities. As we shall see later, this equality does not hold for short periods. Indeed, the difference between the nominal yield on nominal assets and the nominal yield on physical assets is a sensitive index of economic conditions.

3. The nominal yields average about 0.5 percentage points higher for the United States than for the United Kingdom—0.68 points for the short rate, 0.59 points for the long rate, 0.33 points for the yield on physical assets. However, United States and United Kingdom yields are not directly comparable because of changes in the exchange rate. The price of the pound in dollars at the end of the period was lower than at the beginning, the rate of decline averaging 0.94 percent per year. Hence, a hypothetical long-lived Englishman who had purchased United States assets at the beginning of the period, held them throughout the period, and converted them back to pounds at the end of the period would have earned in pounds 0.94 percentage points more than the nominal United States yield given in table 10.1. Alternatively, an American who did the same with United Kingdom assets would have earned in dollars 0.94 percentage points less than the nominal United Kingdom yield. The

---

30. The literature on the term structure is immense. The most careful examinations of the existence of a liquidity premium are perhaps Reuben Kessel, *The Cyclical Behavior of the Term Structure of Interest Rates*, Occasional Paper 91 (New York: NBER, 1965); Phillip Cagan, "A Study of Liquidity Premiums on Federal and Municipal Government Securities," in *Essays on Interest Rates*, vol. 1, ed. P. Cagan and J. Guttentag (New York: NBER, 1969), pp. 107–42. These authors view the liquidity premium as reflecting the value of the services of short-term securities as substitutes for money balances. An alternative view is that long-term securities carry a yield premium, given an aversion to the risk of capital losses, resulting from a general belief that interest rates return to their "normal" level over the long run, with higher yields on long- relative to short-term securities when interest rates are relatively low because long securities are then especially subject to capital losses, and the converse when rates are high. For this view see J. Van Horne, "Interest-Rate Risk and the Term Structure of Interest Rates," *Journal of Political Economy* 73 (August 1965): 344–51; Franco Modigliani and Richard Sutch, "Innovations in Interest Rate Policy," *American Economic Review* (May 1966): 195–96.

Table 10.1   Nominal and Real Ex-Post Yields: Averages, Standard Deviations, Correlations for All Phases and All Nonwar Phases

	All Phases				All Nonwar Phases			
	United States		United Kingdom		United States		United Kingdom	
	Nominal	Real	Nominal	Real	Nominal	Real	Nominal	Real
Number of Phases	49		37		43		31	
	Means (Percentage Points)							
Nominal assets								
Short-term rate	4.15	2.62	3.47	0.88	4.41	3.83	3.77	2.54
Long-term rate	4.83	3.29	4.24	1.66	5.02	4.43	4.38	3.15
Physical assets								
Yield[a]	4.53	3.00	4.20	1.62	3.48	2.90	3.17	1.94
Rate of price change[a]	1.54		2.58		0.58		1.23	
Rate of monetary growth[a]	4.97		4.10		3.81		2.83	
Rate of change of exchange rate[a]			-0.94				-0.21	
	Standard Deviations (Percentage Points)							
Short-term rate	1.80	4.26	2.15	4.87	1.58	3.20	2.12	3.26
Long-term rate	1.31	4.14	2.14	4.68	1.20	3.23	2.33	3.08
Yield on physical assets	5.82	3.61	5.04	2.63	5.24	3.53	4.61	2.12
Rate of price change	3.72		5.26		2.98		4.16	
Rate of monetary growth	4.79		5.22		3.98		4.50	
	Correlation Coefficients							
Short-term and long-term rates	.908**	.981**	.893**	.979**	.873**	.970**	.926**	.963**
Short-term rate and yield on physical assets	-.136	-.285	.318	.294	-.022	-.336*	.505**	-.052
Long-term rate and yield on physical assets	-.164	-.265	.457**	.355*	-.071	-.301	.604**	.023

[a]See footnote 29 of text for method of calculation of phase rates of change of nominal income (i.e., nominal yield on physical assets), prices, money, and the exchange rate of the pound for dollars.
*Significantly different from zero at .05 level.
**Significantly different from zero at .01 level.

difference between the yields in the two countries measured in comparable terms is therefore roughly 1.27 to 1.62 percentage points rather than 0.33 to 0.68 percentage points. This difference is consistent with the net outflow of capital from the United Kingdom to the United States for much of the period, offset not by private return flow induced by interest rate differentials but by government repatriation of capital during World Wars I and II.

4. The ex-post real yield has been calculated from the nominal yield for all three categories of assets simply by subtracting the rate of change of prices (the implicit price index); hence the relation among the three ex-post real yields is the same as the relation among the nominal yields. However, as between the two countries, the real yields are directly comparable. No further adjustment for exchange rate changes is required because all yields are, as it were, expressed in the prices, and hence exchange rate, of a given base date. The difference between the two countries is 1.74 percentage points for the short rate, 1.63 for the long rate, and 1.38 for the yield on physical assets, somewhat higher than the differentials estimated in the preceding paragraph. The differentials are somewhat higher because the excess rate of rise of prices in the United Kingdom of 1.04 percentage points per year is slightly higher than the 0.94 percentage point per year decline in the exchange rate. The near-identity of these two numbers is to be expected from the theory of purchasing power parity. The United Kingdom's shift from a capital-exporting to a capital-importing country might have been expected to make the excess rate of rise of prices greater than the rate of decline in the exchange rate, and, according to our estimates, this is what happened (see sec. 6.8).

5. The average real yield varies from 2.6 to 3.3 percent for the different categories of assets for the United States, from 0.9 to 1.7 percent for the United Kingdom.

6–9. Excluding the wartime phases, which reduces the period covered from 103 years to 88 for the United States and from 102 to 87 for the United Kingdom, has a minor though systematic effect on the results.

6. The excess of long rates over short rates is reduced slightly, from 0.7 percentage points for the United States and 0.8 for the United Kingdom to 0.6 for both countries.

7. The differential between the two countries remains about 0.5 percentage points for nominal yields unadjusted for the change in the exchange rate and about 1.25 percentage points for real yields. Since exchange rate changes were greatest in wartime phases, the decline in the price of the pound in dollars in nonwar phases was 0.21 percent per year, only about a fifth of the decline over the full period.

8. The major change is that the yield on physical assets is decidedly

lower for the nonwar phases alone than the yield on both short- and long-term nominal assets—roughly one percentage point lower than the short rate. The major reason is that the war phases are inflationary phases. More than half the average rate of inflation for the period as a whole is accounted for by the wartime phases. Prices in the United States rose on the average by 0.58 percent per year during the nonwar phases alone, compared with 1.54 for the period as a whole, and in the United Kingdom by 1.23 percent per year compared with 2.58. As we shall see below, yields on physical assets have tended to be higher than yields on nominal assets during inflationary periods and lower during deflationary periods. A secondary reason is the deliberate government policy of holding down interest rates during World War II, so that the average nominal yields on nominal assets are higher during nonwar phases than during all phases, while our measure of the nominal yield on physical assets is lower.

9. The changed difference between the return on nominal and physical assets reflects primarily a different behavior in war and nonwar phases of the returns on nominal, not on physical assets. The nominal return on physical assets is higher for all phases than for all nonwar phases by roughly the differential rate of inflation, so that the real return on physical assets is about the same for all phases as for nonwar phases only. By contrast, the nominal return on nominal assets is about the same for all phases as for all nonwar phases, so that the real return is appreciably less for all phases. The wartime periods simply highlight a point that we shall examine below for other periods: yields on nominal assets for the most part behave as if price changes up or down were unanticipated.

We have included in the table the average rate of change of the quantity of money, both as something of an alternative proxy for the nominal yield on physical assets and because our major interest is the relation of monetary growth to interest rates. We know from earlier chapters that the rate of monetary growth is closely related to the rate of growth of nominal income, and that is about all these averages show.

Table 10.1 also gives measures of the variability of the yields from phase to phase. The most interesting feature of these standard deviations is that, whereas for nominal assets nominal yields are less variable than real yields, the reverse is true for physical assets. The reason is straightforward. The nominal yields on nominal assets, at least as measured here (see further discussion of holding period yields below), are contracted in advance; they are both ex post and ex ante. They are affected by anticipated price changes but not by unanticipated price changes. The ex-post real yield reflects in full the unanticipated price changes, and the high variability of the ex-post real yield indicates that the actual price changes have been largely unanticipated. For physical assets, on the other hand, neither the nominal nor the real yield, as measured here, is contracted in advance. Both are subject to random variation. However, price changes affect both cost and return on physical assets; there is a measure of automatic indexing, as it were. Hence, the real yield tends to be less variable than the nominal yield.

The bottom section of table 10.1 shows the correlation between the various yields. Short- and long-term yields on nominal assets both real and nominal are highly correlated for both countries. The correlations between yields on nominal and physical assets, both real and nominal, show an interesting difference for the two countries. For the United States they are consistently negative, though generally not significantly different from zero; for the United Kingdom, seven out of eight are positive, and four are sufficiently large to differ significantly from zero. However, all correlations for both the United States and the United Kingdom are lower in size than between short and long nominal rates.[31] However adequate the arbitrage between physical and nominal assets may be over a century, it appears to be weak for periods as short as a phase—which highlights one of the key problems requiring attention.

10.3   A Digression on the Measurement of Yields

The precise time reference of the yields for individual phases and, connected with that, their ex-post or ex-ante character, is not important for averages for long periods but is important for correlations, standard deviations, and the analysis in the rest of this chapter of relations over briefer periods.

Consider, first, *nominal yields on nominal assets*. The basic observations averaged to obtain the rates we have used are the yield to maturity calculated from the market price of a security at a point in time. That is both the ex-ante and the ex-post yield for a purchaser of the security who holds it to maturity. It is neither for a purchaser who intends to hold it or does hold it for a shorter period. For such a purchaser, the yield depends also on the price of the security when it is sold. For our purposes, this difference between holding period yield and yield to maturity can safely be neglected for commercial paper or bank bills, since our basic observations are averages for a year, and we further average these into phase averages, so the timing problem is trivial.[32] For long-term bonds the

31. All correlations between real yields have an upward statistical bias, because the same value of g_P is subtracted from the two yields correlated. Insofar as g_P is incorrectly measured, this introduces a common statistical error into both variables.

32. As a check on this presumption, we calculated for the United States the correlation from 1926 to 1974 for annual data between the annual holding-period yield on Treasury bills, as calculated by Ibbotson and Sinquefield, and the commercial paper rate. Despite the difference between the two securities, the correlation is .988. We do not use the Treasury bill series in our analysis because it is available for only part of the period we study. See Roger C. Ibbotson and Rex A. Sinquefield, "Stocks, Bonds, Bills, and Inflation: Year-by-Year Historical Returns (1926–1974)," *Journal of Business of the University of Chicago* 49, no. 1 (January 1976): 11–47.

In addition, we have experimented for the United States with the use of call money rates, which are one-day rates. The correlation with the commercial paper rate is high.

yield (percent per year)

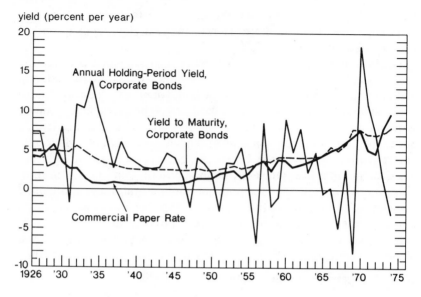

Chart 10.11   Nominal yields on nominal assets for annual holding periods and to maturity, annually, United States, 1926–74.

difference is far from trivial, since the period to maturity is substantial relative to the time units we use in our analysis. Chart 10.11 indicates the difference for annual data for the United States from 1926 to 1974. The yield to maturity of long-term bonds behaves like the commercial paper rate—as the high correlations in table 10.1 foreshadow. But the annual holding-period yield fluctuates widely. The yield to maturity cuts through the annual holding period like a trend series, though the two series are not correctly dated relative to one another.[33]

The annual holding-period yield is strictly an ex-post yield. It cannot be observed or known in advance. Its wide variability reflects this feature plus the large unanticipated element in the market price of the securities.

We have no corresponding direct evidence for the United Kingdom, but none is necessary. The consol yield is never strictly a realized holding-period yield, though obviously it approaches one as the holding period lengthens indefinitely. The annual, or other short-term holding period, yield of the consols fluctuates widely as the price of the consol varies.

For *real yields on nominal assets* there is the additional problem of matching the period for which the price change is calculated with either the period to maturity or the holding period. Again, no significant problem arises for the short-term rate. Our procedure of subtracting the

---

33. The yield to maturity series is plotted at the initial date whereas, to correspond in timing to the holding period series, it should be plotted later by an interval corresponding to some concept of average effective maturity.

average price change from one calendar year to the next from the average rate during the second of those years is not accurate; the price change should be for a year beginning seven and a half to eight and a half months later than the calendar year, but that error is negligible for our purpose. However, for long-term bonds, our procedure introduces serious error, since the nominal yield is calculated to maturity, but the rate of price change is not.

The real yields on nominal assets are ex-post yields. To get ex-ante yields requires some advance independent estimate of the anticipated rate of price change.

Given the very high correlation between short- and long-term nominal yields to maturity, the computational problems involved in correctly computing real yields to maturity, and the large erratic element in holding-period yields on long-term securities, we have bypassed these problems in the rest of this chapter by using only the short-period rates for our detailed analysis. Our interest is not in the term structure of rates but in the relation of monetary change to interest rates. For that purpose it seems adequate to use the short rate as a proxy for the whole structure of rates. In effect, that is equivalent to taking the average remaining maturity of the short-term instrument whose yield we use as the ex-ante holding period the return for which is being studied. Arbitrage across maturities assures that ex-ante yields for other maturities will differ only by liquidity or risk premiums, and these are not our primary concern.

For nominal yields, we can identify the ex-post with the ex-ante return, neglecting, for the series we use, the default risk. For real yields, even for short-term securities, we cannot do so. True, prices tend to move rather sluggishly; so for short periods it might be supposed that anticipated price movements will not differ much from actual price movements. However, the shorter the period, the smaller the yield, not as an annualized percentage, but as a percentage of the capital value. There is no reason to suppose a priori that the error in estimating price change declines any more rapidly than the yield. The pure measurement error in price change must rise as a fraction of the price change as the period shortens, but this component would tend to average out in our annual and even more phase averages and hence would not by itself be a reason for rejecting the identity of ex-post and ex-ante real yields.

For *nominal and real yields on physical assets*, the timing problem does not arise. Our proxies can be regarded as corresponding to holding-period yields. However, since they are based on differences between the logarithms of calendar year nominal and real income series, they are dated as of the end of the year; that is, they correspond to fiscal years ending 30 June rather than to calendar years. There is therefore a six-month difference in dating between the proxy series and the series on yields on nominal assets. Given that our time unit is generally a phase, this timing difference will generally be of minor significance.[34] Our proxies are necessarily ex post not ex ante, and there seems no way of getting a corresponding ex-ante measure.

The major measurement problem that arises for our proxies is whether they are valid proxies for the nominal and real yield on physical assets. The successful use of the nominal proxy in the demand functions of chapter 6, and the closeness of the averages for a century to the corresponding averages for the yields on nominal assets, is substantial evidence in their favor but can hardly be regarded as conclusive. We have therefore made a number of additional tests by comparing our proxies with two alternative estimates of returns on real assets for the United States for the period 1929 to 1969: (1) the Ibbotson and Sinquefield series of annual holding-period return on common stocks; and (2) the rate of return on capital for the United States private national economy, as estimated by Christensen and Jorgenson.[35] Chart 10.12 plots our proxies against these series, in panel A for nominal yields, in panel B for real yields, and table 10.2 gives means, standard deviations, and correlations for the several series.[36]

Our proxies compare very well with the Christensen and Jorgenson (CJ) rate of return on capital, having roughly similar mean values, a high positive correlation of nominal yields, and a low though statistically significant positive correlation for real yields. The main difference is that the CJ rate of return is much less variable, particularly the CJ real rate of return. Perhaps that means that it is closer to an ex-ante than to an ex-post return, perhaps it simply reflects the large measure of smoothing and interpolation that has gone into the construction of the CJ rate of return measures.

The common stock holding-period yields are much more variable than either of the others—hardly surprising given the volatility of the stock market prices from which they are derived. The high mean yield, double or more than double that shown by the other two measures, may be a return for risk or an artifact of the selective nature of the stock market or period. The correlation between the stock market returns and either of the others is trivial, though it is positive for three out of four comparisons.

So far as this evidence goes, it strengthens our confidence in the proxies as valid measures of returns on physical assets. The disagreement with common stock yields seems more reasonably interpreted as an indication

34. We have tested this proposition by computing phase averages from fiscal year interest-rate observations. The results were sufficiently similar to those derived from calendar year observations that we decided for simplicity to retain the latter.

35. Laurits R. Christensen and Dale W. Jorgenson, "U.S. Income, Saving, and Wealth, 1929–1969," *Review of Income and Wealth*, December 1973, pp. 344–45.

36. Though these charts cover 1926–74 for the proxies and holding-period returns, the Christensen-Jorgenson estimates are available only for 1929 to 1969, which is why table 10.2 is restricted to that period.

yield (percent per year)

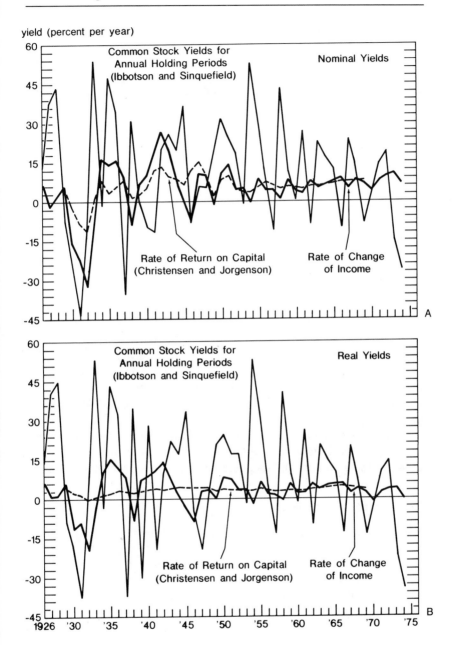

Chart 10.12   Three measures of yields on United States physical assets, 1926–74.

Table 10.2   Three Measures of Yields on Physical Assets, United States Annual
Data, 1929-69

	Nominal Yields	Real Yields
	Mean (Percentage Points)	
Physical assets (proxy)	5.2	3.1
Common stocks, annual holding period	10.8	8.9
CJ rate of return on capital	5.9	3.5
	Standard Deviation (Percentage Points)	
Physical assets (proxy)	10.8	7.1
Common stocks	22.6	23.1
CJ rate of return	5.0	1.1
	Correlation Coefficient	
Physical assets (proxy) and common stocks	.23	.06
Physical assets (proxy) and CJ rate of return	.82	.44
Common stocks and CJ rate of return	.15	−.06

of the highly special character of the subset of physical assets reflected in stock market securities than as evidence against our proxies for what they purport to be: yields on the broad spectrum of assets, both human and nonhuman, whatever the financial claims, if any, that are their counterpart.

One further minor bit of evidence is that the correlation between the commercial paper rate and the CJ nominal rate of return on capital, as between the commercial paper rate and our proxy, is essentially zero.

10.4   Yields in Subperiods

Table 10.3 repeats table 10.1 for a series of subperiods, except that we have omitted the long rates. We have subdivided the pre–World War I period into the period before 1896, when prices were generally falling, and the subsequent period, when prices were generally rising, have separated out the war periods, and have treated the interwar period as one unit, because of the paucity of observations, even though the behavior of prices varied greatly during these nearly two decades. As the mean rate of change of prices shows, the interwar period was certainly on the average a period of falling prices. The postwar period requires no subdivision. It clearly is a period of generally rising prices.

We therefore have two periods of generally falling prices (pre-1896, interwar), two wartime periods of rising prices, and two peacetime periods of rising prices (1896–1914, post–World War II).

Table 10.3 Nominal and Real Ex-Post Yields for Subperiods, 1873–1975

	Yields											
	Pre–World War I								World War I Phases			
	Falling Prices (Pre-1896)				Rising Prices				United States		United Kingdom	
	United States		United Kingdom		United States		United Kingdom		Nominal	Real	Nominal	Real
	Nominal	Real	Nominal	Real	Nominal	Real	Nominal	Real		3		3
Number of Phases	11		6		10		5		3		3	
Means (Percentage Points)												
Nominal assets												
Short-term rate	5.12	6.77	2.60	3.25	4.70	2.84	3.26	2.58	5.07	−4.33	4.33	−10.80
Physical assets												
Yield[a]	1.60	3.30	1.57	2.22	5.09	3.23	1.95	1.27	12.95	3.55	12.55	−2.58
Rate of price change[a]	−1.65		−0.65		1.86		0.68		9.40		15.12	
Rate of monetary growth[a]	1.80		1.63		5.97		2.22		12.53		14.10	
Rate of change of exchange rate[a]			−0.45[b]				0.07				−4.30	
Standard Deviations (Percentage Points)												
Short-term rate	0.60	1.71	0.36	1.69	0.42	0.94	0.21	0.43	1.14	3.26	0.61	2.02
Yield on physical assets	3.60	2.86	2.96	1.91	4.18	3.74	1.92	1.73	4.19	3.09	4.00	6.24
Rate of price change	1.69		1.51		0.83		0.36		2.14		2.25	
Rate of monetary growth	3.87		1.27		1.87		1.76		0.83		2.13	
Correlation Coefficients												
Short-term rate and yield on physical assets	.066	−.183	−.358	−.498	−.499	−.633*	.099	−.321	−.829	−.322	−.616	.938

Table 10.3 (Continued)

	Interwar Phases				World War II Phases				Postwar Phases			
	United States		United Kingdom		United States		United Kingdom		United States		United Kingdom	
	Nominal	Real	Nominal	Real	Nominal	Real	Nominal	Real	Nominal	Real	Nominal	Real
Number of Phases	9		9		3		3		13		11	
Means (Percentage Points)												
Nominal assets												
Short-term rate	3.54	5.31	3.06	4.76	0.82	−4.70	0.85	−4.02	4.20	1.03	5.70	0.08
Physical assets												
Yield[a]	0.09	1.86	0.03	1.73	9.13	3.61	6.65	1.78	6.23	3.07	7.85	2.22
Rate of price change[a]	−1.76		−1.70		5.52		4.87		3.17		5.62	
Rate of monetary growth[a]	1.11		−0.24		11.30		7.32		5.82		6.73	
Rate of change of exchange rate[a]			0.67				−4.21				−0.84	
Standard Deviations (Percentage Points)												
Short-term rate	1.92	4.28	1.76	4.77	0.17	0.91	0.22	2.01	2.15	1.12	2.66	2.32
Yield on physical assets	8.37	5.82	4.85	3.48	6.71	5.89	3.49	1.44	1.88	1.73	3.22	1.12
Rate of price change	3.34		4.30		0.90		2.12		1.77		3.40	
Rate of monetary growth	4.87		3.97		4.52		3.69		2.62		5.37	
Correlation Coefficients												
Short-term rate and yield on physical assets	−.247	−.591	−.411	.037	−.358	−.955	.394	−.950	.443	−.073	.719*	.288

[a]See footnote 29 of text for method of calculation of phase rates of change of income (i.e., yield on physical assets), prices, money, and the exchange rate of the pound for dollars.

[b]Reflects appreciation of the dollar and so shift in the exchange rate of the pound from a premium before United States resumption in 1879 to par thereafter.

*Significant at .05 level.

The division into periods adds to the conclusions derived from the averages for the period as a whole in respect to, first, the differences between the United States and the United Kingdom; and second, the effect of price experience on the differential between the yields on nominal and on physical assets.

10.4.1   United States versus United Kingdom

For the period as a whole, the short rate averaged 0.7 percentage points higher for the United States than for the United Kingdom, or 1.6 percentage points higher if allowance is made for changes in the exchange rate, which is equivalent to allowing for the differential behavior of prices in the two countries.

Table 10.4, which records the United States–United Kingdom differential for the various subperiods and yields, shows that the excess of the United States nominal short rate over the United Kingdom rate declined steadily from period to period, particularly sharply from the first to the second. This sharp and regular decline can in principle be attributed to any of three factors: (1) a decline in the differential real yield available on physical assets in the two countries; (2) a change in the relative behavior of prices, as reflected in the exchange rate; (3) a change in the effectiveness of financial intermediation leading to a relative decline in the United States in the differential between nominal yields on nominal assets and on physical assets.

All three factors apparently played a role, though each at a different time; the first, for the decline from the second prewar period to the

Table 10.4   **United States–United Kingdom Yield Differences, Subperiods, 1873–1975**

| | United States Yield Minus United Kingdom Yield (Percentage Points) | | | |
| | Nominal Yields | | Real Yields | |
Subperiod	Nominal Assets[a]	Physical Assets[b]	Nominal Assets[a]	Physical Assets[b]
Pre–World War I:				
Falling prices (before 1896)	2.52	0.03	3.52	1.10
Rising prices	1.44	3.14	0.26	1.96
World War I	0.74	0.40	6.47	6.13
Interwar	0.48	0.06	0.55	0.13
World War II	−0.03	2.48	−0.68	1.83
Postwar	−1.50	−1.62	0.95	0.85

[a]Commercial paper rate for United States, rate on three-month bank bills for United Kingdom.
[b]Rate of change of income.

interwar period; the second, for the decline from the interwar to the postwar period; and the third, for the decline from the first to the second prewar period.

1. The final column of table 10.4 indicates that, excluding war periods, the excess of the real yield in the United States over that in the United Kingdom was about one percentage point higher before World War I than after.[37] This clearly matches the 0.96 percentage point decline in the United States–United Kingdom nominal short-rate differential from the 1896–World War I period to the interwar period.

2. The sharp further decline of 1.98 percentage points in the nominal short-rate differential from the interwar to the postwar period corresponds fairly closely to the 2.39 percentage point decline in the rate of price rise in the United States relative to that in the United Kingdom.[38] This differential rate of price decline was reflected in the depreciation of the British pound relative to the United States dollar by 1.51 percent per year.

3. Finally, the sharp fall in the nominal short-rate differential from the first period to the second period cannot be attributed to item 1, since there is no corresponding decline in nominal differential yields on physical assets—rather, there is a rise. It cannot be attributed to item 2, because the pound appreciated by 0.52 percent per year between the two periods, reflecting differential behavior of average rates of price change, which would work against the change in the interest differential that actually occurred.[39] Our first impression was that item 3 must have been triggered by the substantial increase in the degree of financial sophistication in the United States relative to that in the United Kingdom that we identified in chapter 6, and to which we attributed much of the differential behavior of velocity in the United States and the United Kingdom up to about 1903. It seemed reasonable that increased financial sophistication would also produce a decline in the market rate of interest on securities like commercial paper traded in active financial markets.

37. As a rough estimate, a simple average of the excess for the two pre–World War I periods is 1.53, for the interwar and post–World War II periods, 0.49, or a difference of 1.04 percentage points. Alternatively, the difference between the prewar and interwar periods of falling prices is 0.97, between the prewar and postwar periods of rising prices, 1.11.

38. As table 10.3 shows, during the interwar period prices fell in the United States by 1.76 percentage points, in the United Kingdom, by 1.70 percentage points, or by .06 percentage points more in the United States. Prices rose in the United States during the postwar period by 3.17 percent; in the United Kingdom, by 5.62 percent, or by 2.45 percentage points less in the United States. Consequently, United States prices fell relative to those in the United Kingdom in both periods, but by 2.39 percentage points more after World War II than in the interwar period.

39. Before 1896 prices fell more rapidly in the United States than in the United Kingdom; after 1896 they rose more rapidly in the United States than in the United Kingdom. The differential changed by 2.18 percentage points. This factor alone should have made for a rise in the United States interest rate relative to the United Kingdom, not a fall.

percentage points

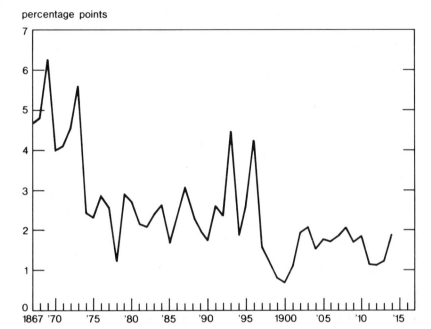

Chart 10.13   Excess of United States commercial paper rate over United Kingdom rate on bank bills, annually, 1867–1914.

However, chart 10.13, which plots the United States–United Kingdom differential year by year, contradicts this interpretation. That chart does not show a gradual reduction in the differential such as might be expected from a gradual growth in financial sophistication. On the contrary, it shows an abrupt drop from one level, 1874 through 1896, to another level, 1897 to 1914, with sizable year-to-year fluctuations about those levels. The peaks in 1893 and 1896 suggest an explanation for the drop in level. The peak in 1893 is connected with the banking panic of that year. The initial banking difficulties reinforced fears, endemic before 1896 because of silver politics, that the United States would go off gold and the dollar would depreciate. The restriction of cash payments by banks after July produced a premium in the market on currency (i.e., it took more than $100 of deposits to buy $100 of currency), which was equivalent to a depreciation of the United States dollar vis-a-vis the British pound, for a time converting the fear into a reality. The peak in 1896 is connected with the capital flight of that year accelerated by Bryan's nomination, which greatly strengthened fears that the United States would leave gold.[40] In both cases, fear of devaluation meant that owners of United Kingdom capital were reluctant to participate in the United States short-term

40. *A Monetary History*, pp. 107–13.

market except at a substantial premium. The election of McKinley changed the situation drastically. It made United States retention of the gold standard secure for the time being, and the subsequent flood of gold from South Africa, Alaska, and Colorado removed all doubts.

The sudden reversal of confidence in the sterling value of the dollar had the effect of an equally sudden improvement in the effectiveness of the financial market. The United States short-term market became linked, as it were, to the United Kingdom market as an equal participant rather than as a poor relative. The gradual improvement in the United States market by itself, which doubtless was proceeding, was overshadowed by the drastic one-time shift to a new level. Hereafter, financial intermediation was available at lower cost and could be expected to reduce the differences in rates charged in different markets.

The United States–United Kingdom nominal short-rate differential for the pre-1896 period in table 10.4 averages 1.08 percentage points higher than for the 1896–World War I period. We shall take this as measuring the magnitude of the shift.

One point about this shift deserves special mention. The fear that the United States would leave gold was equivalent to a fear that the United States would inflate at a faster rate than the United Kingdom (or deflate at a slower rate). The fear of inflation also animated the domestic opponents of free silver. As we pointed out in *A Monetary History*,[41] the paradoxical effect was to produce deflation—or more rapid deflation than would otherwise have occurred. The paradox shows up to the full in interest rates. Before 1896, prices were falling one percentage point per year faster in the United States than in the United Kingdom. That alone should have produced a 1 percent per year appreciation of the United States dollar and a one percentage point *lower* interest rate. However, the fear of inflation more than countered the fact of deflation; it kept the currency in danger of being devalued; and made interest rates in the United States one percentage point higher relative to those in the United Kingdom than they were after the fear was resolved.

The contrast between *fact* and *belief* continued after 1896. In the subsequent eighteen years, prices rose in the United States by roughly one percentage point more per year than in the United Kingdom. The *fact* of inflation by itself should have produced a 1 percent per year depreciation of the United States dollar and a one percentage point higher interest rate in the United States. However, the altered attitudes and the almost complete elimination of the silver issue meant that the exchange value of the dollar was never threatened and that United States interest rates, while higher than those in the United Kingdom, were one percentage point less so than before 1896. Put most simply, the *facts* of

41. Ibid., p. 132.

inflation would have justified a two percentage point rise in the differential from before to after 1896. The *beliefs* about inflation produced a one percentage point decline! We shall revert to this issue later in our discussion of the Gibson paradox.

The two war periods are obviously special. Yet, so far as nominal rates are concerned, the United States–United Kingdom differentials for the war periods are intermediate between the preceding and following periods.

To summarize: We conclude that the decline in the United States–United Kingdom differential for the nominal short rate from before to after 1896 reflects the resolution of fears that the United States would experience inflation and the United States dollar would be devalued; the further decline from pre–World War I to the interwar period reflects a decline in the real yield on physical capital in the United States relative to that in the United Kingdom, and the further decline from the interwar period to the post–World War II period reflects greater inflation in the United Kingdom than in the United States and an accompanying depreciation of the pound sterling.

10.4.2 Yields on Nominal and Physical Assets

If arbitrage had worked as well for each subperiod as it did for the period as a whole, yields on nominal and physical assets would either have been equal or would have differed by a constant reflecting the average preference for nominal versus physical assets (or the reverse). As noted in our earlier comparison between averages for all phases and averages for all nonwar phases, arbitrage did not work as well for the subperiods as for the period as a whole. For the two periods of falling prices, the yield on nominal assets was decidedly higher in both countries than the yield on physical assets. Deflation was not anticipated. Lenders did well. Borrowers did poorly. Since entrepreneurs generally borrow in nominal terms to acquire physical assets, it follows that rentiers did well, entrepreneurs badly—which is of course conventional (which does not always mean correct) wisdom, merely another way of expressing the widely believed generalization that a period of unanticipated deflation is adverse to enterprise and growth.

With one exception (the United Kingdom after 1896), the relation is reversed during periods of inflation, including the war periods: the yield on physical assets was higher than the yield on nominal assets. Apparently inflation too was not anticipated. Entrepreneurs did well, rentiers did poorly; capital was transferred from savers to borrowers—which is of course another way of expressing the widely believed generalization that unanticipated inflation is favorable to enterprise and growth.

As Irving Fisher put this point in 1907: "While *imperfection* of foresight transfers wealth from creditor to debtor or the reverse, *inequality* of foresight produces overinvestment during rising prices and relative stagnation during falling prices."[42]

Yet, like many widely believed generalizations, the generalization that unanticipated inflation is favorable to growth and unanticipated deflation unfavorable may be an illusion—a money illusion that is part and parcel of the same phenomenon as the failure to anticipate inflations and deflations. According to table 10.3, in both the United States and the United Kingdom, real growth (our proxy for the real yield on physical assets) was greater during the pre-1896 period of falling prices than during the post-1896 period of rising prices.[43] But the public perception at the time was clearly the reverse. Alfred Marshall referred to the possible contradiction between perception and reality in 1886 when he wrote, "I think there is much less difference than is generally supposed between the net benefits of periods of rising and falling prices."[44]

The situation is different for the interwar and postwar periods: real growth was greater in both countries during the postwar period of rising prices than during the interwar period of falling prices. However, the emergence of stagflation in both countries at the end of and following the period we cover, plus the special role of the Great Depression, suggests that this is a fragile piece of evidence for the generalization in question.

Table 10.5 brings out more clearly the effect of the rate of change of prices on the difference between the yields on nominal and physical assets. It lists the subperiods by the rate of price change, disregarding both chronology and country—even though, as the preceding section demonstrates, there are systematic differences between the United States and the United Kingdom. If the price change had been fully anticipated and the real yields had been independent of the rate of price change, the nominal yields on nominal assets in column 2 would rise as we go down the table, the real yields on nominal assets in column 4 would stay constant. In fact, the nominal yields in column 2 fluctuate about a roughly constant level, so that the effect of inflation is reflected primarily in a sharp decline in the real yield on nominal assets in column 4.[45] The hypothetical pattern of yields for a fully anticipated inflation comes closer to being realized for physical assets. Their nominal yield rises with inflation and their real yield fluctuates about a more or less constant level. However, this pattern does not reflect anticipations so much as the

42. *The Rate of Interest*, p. 286.

43. We are indebted to Arthur Gandolfi for calling our attention to the contradiction between our table 10.3 and the common belief.

44. Alfred Marshall, *Official Papers* (London: Macmillan, 1926), p. 9.

45. Note that the pre-1896 nominal yield is the most out of line, and that this is the yield that we decided in the preceding section was held up by fears of inflation despite the fact of deflation. Lowering this yield by one to three percentage points would produce a tendency for the nominal yield for peacetime periods to rise slightly along with the rate of inflation.

Table 10.5   Difference between Yields on Physical and Nominal Assets, Related to Rate of Change of Prices (Percentage Points)

Period and Country	Rate of Price Change (1)	Nominal Yield		Real Yield		Excess of Yield on Physical Assets over Yield on Nominal Assets Col. 3 Minus Col. 2 or Col. 5 Minus Col. 4 (6)
		Nominal Assets (2)	Physical Assets (3)	Nominal Assets (4)	Physical Assets (5)	
Interwar, United States	−1.76	3.54	0.09	5.31	1.86	−3.45
Interwar, United Kingdom	−1.70	3.06	0.03	4.76	1.73	−3.03
Pre-1896, United States	−1.65	5.12	1.60	6.77	3.30	−3.47
Pre-1896, United Kingdom	−0.65	2.60	1.57	3.25	2.22	−1.03
1896–World War I, United Kingdom	0.68	3.26	1.95	2.58	1.27	−1.31
1896–World War I, United States	1.86	4.70	5.09	2.84	3.23	0.39
Postwar, United States	3.17	4.20	6.23	1.03	3.07	2.03
World War II, United Kingdom	4.87	0.85	6.65	−4.02	1.78	5.80
World War II, United States	5.52	0.82	9.13	−4.70	3.61	8.31
Postwar, United Kingdom	5.62	5.70	7.85	0.08	2.22	2.15
World War I, United States	9.40	5.07	12.95	−4.33	3.55	7.88
World War I, United Kingdom	15.12	4.33	12.55	−10.80	−2.58	8.22

physical character of the assets and the real character of the yields. For nominal assets, investors fix rates in nominal terms and contract for a period ahead: prescience is therefore required if these rates are to reflect future price behavior. For physical assets, investors may fix no rates—certainly not in nominal terms—and generally make no contracts about either real or nominal yields for a period ahead. The yield is generated out of the economic activity in which the asset is employed. It requires no prescience for the nominal yield on physical assets to reflect current price behavior, only that the physical assets participate along with other assets in the nominal income and spending flows.

Column 6 gives the excess of the yield on physical assets over that on nominal assets. It is negative for deflation, positive for inflation. This pattern comes out clearly in chart 10-14, which plots the excess yield on physical assets against the rate of price change. If inflations were fully anticipated, the difference between yields on physical and nominal assets might be expected to be roughly a constant, reflecting any preference among asset holders for one category or the other of assets. Clearly the points are very far from clustering around such a horizontal line. If inflations were wholly unanticipated and there were no preference for

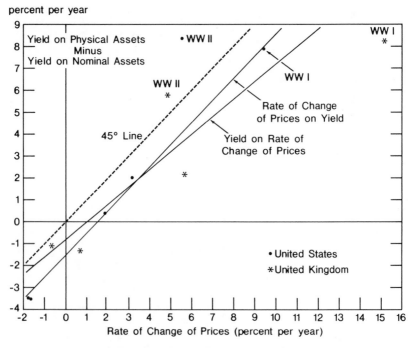

Chart 10.14   Excess of yield on physical over yield on nominal assets versus rate of change of prices.

one or the other category of assets, the points would fall along the dashed forty-five-degree line, since, ex post, the nominal yield on physical assets would reflect the actual rate of inflation, whereas the ex-ante nominal yield on nominal assets would not. In fact the points come rather close to approximating a line with a forty-five-degree slope but displaced downward by about one percentage point, as is indicated by the two regression lines, implying a preference of that amount for physical over nominal assets, that is, a willingness to accept that much less in yield in order to hold a physical rather than a nominal asset.[46]

Chart 10-14 diverges appreciably from the pattern that would be produced by wholly unanticipated inflations only with respect to the points for the final three wartime episodes in table 10.5: both United States wartime episodes and, especially, World War I for the United Kingdom. These lie roughly on a horizontal line, as if they corresponded to anticipated inflations. But interpreting them this way implies a very great preference (about eight percentage points) for nominal assets during wartime periods over physical assets—which seems most implausible. We are inclined therefore to treat the United Kingdom World War I point as an aberration—perhaps statistical, perhaps economic—rather than as an indication of correct anticipation of wartime inflation.[47]

The generalization that these results suggest is that, for the period our data cover, there was a preference of about 1.25 percentage points for physical over nominal assets and both inflation and deflation were wholly unanticipated—which, combined with risk aversion, would justify the preference for physical assets as reflecting a desire to hedge real returns against both unanticipated inflation and unanticipated deflation.

These results are inconsistent with the hypothesis that the ex-ante nominal yields on nominal assets incorporate correctly anticipated rates of inflation—which merely confirms what has long been known, that the public has not in fact been able to form correct anticipations of inflation—at least, until possibly very recently (see section 10.8). They give little evidence on a more interesting proposition: Is there within the periods a gradual recognition of and adjustment to inflation or deflation of the kind that was postulated by Irving Fisher? To answer that question, we need to

---

46. The simple correlation for the points in chart 10.14 is .89, and the regression equations calculated both ways are

$$\text{Differential yield} = -.84 + .80\, g_P.A$$
$$= -1.54 + 1.01\, g_P.A .$$

Note that the second equation is obtained simply by solving the regression of $g_P.A$ on the differential yield for the differential yield.

47. Excluding this point, the correlation is .93 and the two regressions are:

$$\text{Differential yield} = -1.22 + 1.09\, g_P.A$$
$$= -1.62 + 1.27\, g_P.A .$$

go beyond the subperiod averages and look at the observations within the periods.

10.5   Relation between Yields on
Nominal and Physical Assets

Our proxy for the real return on physical assets was far from being the same in the various periods, ranging for the six periods for the United States from 1.9 to 3.6 and for the United Kingdom from − 2.6 to 2.2. Yet these yields varied far less than the ex-post real yield on nominal assets, which ranged from − 4.7 to 6.8 for the United States and from − 10.8 to 4.8 for the United Kingdom. Moreover, one extreme item accounts for most of the range for the United Kingdom for the real return on physical assets. Omitting World War I which, as we have seen, appears to be an aberration, leaves five observations ranging from 1.3 to 2.2. No remotely comparable reduction in the range can be achieved for the real yield on nominal assets for either the United States or the United Kingdom by omitting the most discrepant observation.

These results suggest that it may not be a bad first approximation—for the purpose of studying monetary influences on interest rates—to follow Irving Fisher and assume that the ex-post real return on *physical assets* can be taken to be roughly constant on the average over time—though at a higher level in the United States than in the United Kingdom—and to accept our proxy as a reasonably accurate measure of that real return.

On these lines, the wide variation among subperiods in the difference between returns on nominal and physical assets reflects primarily the failure of nominal yields on nominal assets to adjust to the actual rate of inflation. As a result, ex-post real returns on *nominal assets* vary widely. The implication of rough constancy of real returns on physical assets is that the variation in ex-post real returns on nominal assets reflects primarily unanticipated changes in inflation.[48]

48. As Fisher says in his chapter "Inductive Verification (Monetary)" in *The Rate of Interest*, "In general the latter factor—unforseen monetary change—is the more important [compared with factors affecting the real rate on physical assets]. . . . It is, of course, not to be assumed that commodity-interest [the real yield] ought to be absolutely invariable; but it is practically certain that its variations would not be three and a half times the variations in money-interest, unless the price movements were inadequately predicted" (pp. 279–80).

In the chapter in his later book, *The Theory of Interest*, in which he presents his statistical calculations relating interest rates to past price change, Fisher does not explicitly discuss the constancy or variability of the real return on physical assets until the final two sentences of the chapter. He writes, "while the main object of this book is to show how the rate of interest would behave if the purchasing power of money were stable, there has never been any long period of time during which this condition has been even approximately fulfilled. When it is not fulfilled, the money rate of interest, and even more the real rate of interest [i.e., the *ex-post* real return on nominal assets] is more affected by the instability of money than by

Suppose now that the nominal yields do not adjust to the actual rate of inflation, but along Fisher's lines do adjust to the anticipated rate of inflation, which in turn adjusts to actual inflation after a considerable lag. We would then expect to find that shortly after a change from, say, falling to rising prices, the yield on physical assets would exceed considerably the yield on nominal assets, reflecting the incorporation in the yield on nominal assets of the lagged anticipations of falling prices. As prices continued to rise, the differential would decline and approach the equilibrium difference reflecting (inversely) any general preference for physical over nominal assets (or the converse).

On this interpretation, real yields on nominal assets would be highly variable within the subperiods, but real yields on physical assets would be relatively stable. The standard deviations of ex-post real returns in table 10.1 for the period as a whole show such a difference. However, those for nonwar phases alone do not for the United States and table 10.3 demonstrates that, for both the United States and the United Kingdom, the higher variability of ex-post real returns on nominal assets reflects largely differences between periods, not within periods. For five out of six within-period comparisons for the United States and three out of six for the United Kingdom, the ex-post real yield on physical assets is more variable than the ex-post real yield on nominal assets. Clearly, there is no systematic tendency the other way.

Chart 10.15 permits a more detailed examination of the intraperiod relation. It plots for each phase the excess of the return on physical assets over the return on nominal assets—which we shall refer to for brevity as the "differential"—against the rate of change of prices. The vertical lines separate the subperiods distinguished in table 10.3.

For both countries, the positive correlation between the differential and the rate of price change that we found to hold between periods clearly is present also within periods, though somewhat less consistently. Again, the correlation reflects the failure of yields on nominal assets to be adjusted promptly or at all to the actual course of prices.

For the United States, for the two prewar periods, there is a very clear and distinct shift in the rate of price change from a rate of decline of about 2 percent per year to a rate of rise of about 2 percent (see table 10.5, col. 1), so this pair of periods seems almost ideal for examining the effect of a shift from reasonably steadily falling prices to reasonably steadily rising

those more fundamental and more normal causes connected with income impatience, and opportunity, to which this book is chiefly devoted" (p. 451).

In the earlier part of the chapter, the assumption of a fixed real return on physical assets is imbedded in all of his calculations since they include no variables to adjust for changes in the real return.

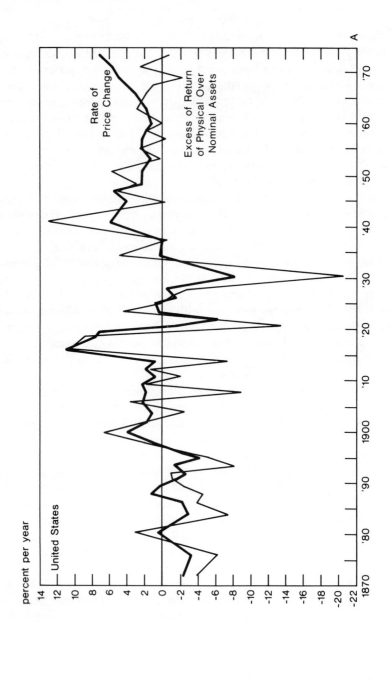

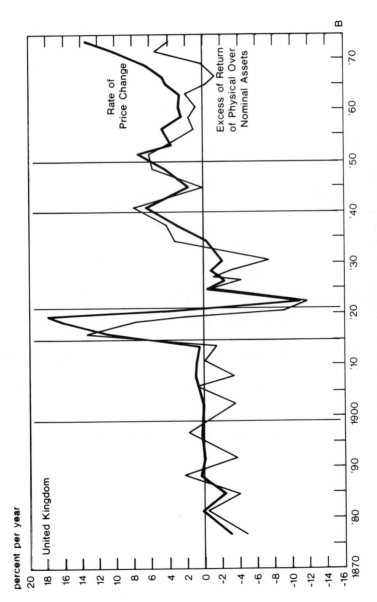

percent per year

United Kingdom

Rate of
Price Change

Excess of Return
of Physical Over
Nominal Assets

Chart 10.15   Excess of return on physical over nominal assets and the rate of price change, phase averages.

prices. However, we have already seen that this appearance is deceiving: the first period was one in which inflation was anticipated, even though deflation was experienced. Hence, the lower differential in the first period than in the second is consistent with the adjustment of the differential to the anticipated movement in prices, though the magnitude of the difference between the two periods (3.86 percentage points; see table 10.5, col. 6) is larger than can readily be accounted for in this way. With respect to movements within the periods, the differential shows no tendency to rise in the first period as would be expected from a gradual adjustment of anticipations. However, as chart 10.16 shows, the nominal rate on nominal assets does decline during the period. The failure of the differential to decline reflects the decline also in the nominal yield on physical assets. In the second period, the differential starts out sizably positive and then does decline, fluctuating around zero. This second period, therefore, conforms in part to the pattern for the differential sketched earlier. However, a closer examination indicates that this conformity, like the nonconformity for the first period, is partly spurious. As chart 10.16 shows, the decline in the differential in the second period is produced mostly by a decline in the yield on physical assets (both nominal and real), rather than by a rise in the yield on nominal assets, though the latter does rise mildly. These intraperiod patterns are therefore only very loosely consistent with a gradual adjustment of nominal rates to incorporate inflationary expectations.

The United Kingdom data for the pre–World War I period plotted in panel B of chart 10.15 do not show any clearer evidence of the Fisherian pattern than the United States data. The differential in the main fluctuates about a roughly constant level. That level shows at the most a very mild rise during the first period of falling prices but no decline during the later period of rising prices. However, the nominal short-term yield does fall mildly during the first period as if it were adjusting to expectations of deflation and rise mildly during the second as if it were adjusting to expectations of inflation. The United Kingdom was, of course, at the time a much more sophisticated financial market than the United States, so it might have been expected to conform to the Fisherian pattern more closely than the United States. In fact, any difference in this respect is trivial.

For World War I, for both the United States and the United Kingdom, the differential primarily mirrors price changes: nominal yields rose only slightly along with inflation, while our proxy for nominal yields on physical assets reflected the inflation—fully for the United States, largely for the United Kingdom. Clearly, no Fisherian pattern is evident here—nor should it be, given the widespread recognition that war is after all special and not to be extrapolated, plus the extensive government intervention into the financial system.

For the interwar period, for both the United States and the United Kingdom, there is some minor evidence of the Fisherian pattern. Nominal yields fall sharply toward the end of the period, the lowest level being reached after the rate of price change has shifted from negative to positive. The adjustment is sizable in terms of the usual variation in short-term rates but mild compared to the drastic changes in the rate of price change. On the other hand, yields on physical assets fully reflect the change in the rate of price change. As a result, the differential largely mirrors, as during the two wars, price changes. The low level of short-term yields in the succeeding period that we have designated as in World War II, though it begins in 1937, may partly reflect the Fisherian process. However, that lower level owes as much to government controls as to the incorporation of deflationary expectations in the low short-term yields during the highly inflationary war.

The post–World War II period shows the clearest evidence of the Fisherian pattern. For both the United States and the United Kingdom, the differential falls during most of the postwar period of rising prices, though not continuously so. More important, the differential is mostly inversely rather than positively related to the rate of price change, the nominal short-term yield is as variable as our proxy for the nominal yield on physical assets, the nominal short-term yield rises steadily throughout the period, the ex-post real yield on nominal assets rises sharply in the early part of the period and then fluctuates about a more or less constant level, and our proxy for the real yield on physical assets shows no steady trend.

All in all, this detailed examination of the intraperiod movements of yields supports the Fisherian interpretation at most for the post–World War II period.

10.6   Nominal Yields, Price Levels, and Rates of Change of Prices

The inconclusive results of the preceding section suggest examining more closely the relation between nominal yields and both the level of prices and the rate of change of prices.

On theoretical grounds, there is no reason to expect any direct relation between the nominal rate of interest and the level of prices. The rate of interest is a pure number except for its temporal dimension: dollars per dollars per year. The level of prices is not a pure number; it has the dimensions of dollars. There is a strictly arbitrary element in the price level related to the monetary unit. Clearly, if prices double because of a change in the unit—as happened, for example, in Rhodesia when it shifted in 1965 from the British pound as its currency to the Rhodesian

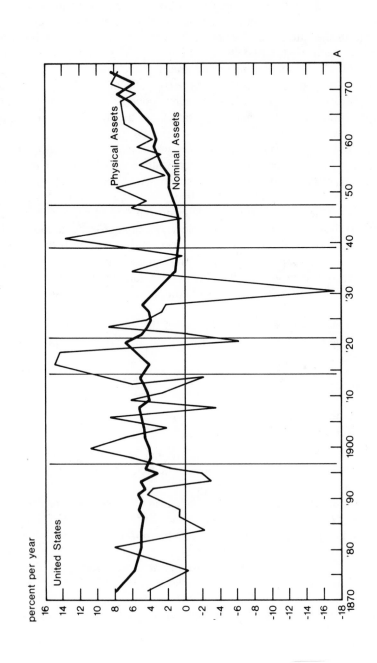

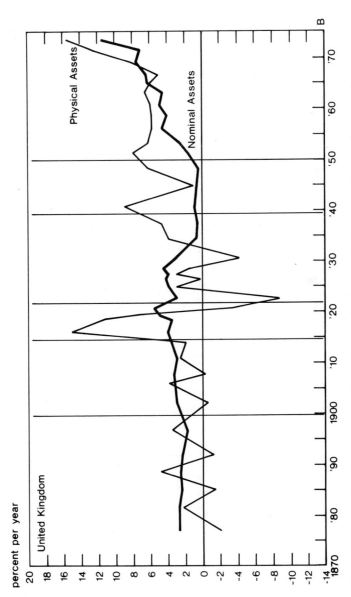

percent per year

Chart 10.16 Nominal return on physical assets versus nominal return on nominal assets, phase averages.

dollar at an initial exchange rate of $2 to the pound—there is no reason for any interest rate to be affected. If prices double, not because of a change in units, but because of a doubling of the amount of money per unit of output as a result, say, of war finance, there is again no reason to expect the rate of interest to change on this score once the country has adjusted to the new situation.

Dimensionally, the rate of change of prices, not the level of prices, is comparable to the interest rate. It too is dollars per dollar per unit of time and has the dimension of the reciprocal of time. And, as Fisher pointed out, theoretical considerations suggest that the nominal interest rate should be related to the rate of change of prices—either actual or anticipated.

Yet, empirically, the "tendency of prices and interest rates to rise together . . . and to fall together" was described by J. M. Keynes in 1930 as "one of the most completely established empirical facts within the whole field of quantitative economics." He termed it the "Gibson paradox," after a British financial journalist, A. H. Gibson, and this name has stuck despite the fact that the phenomenon had been described and analyzed three decades earlier by Knut Wicksell.[49]

Keynes's unqualified and colorful assertion helped to render the Gibson paradox a largely unchallenged generalization despite Macaulay's subsequent conclusion, in the course of one of the most perceptive examinations of the paradox that has yet been published, that while "it is true that, in various countries and often for long periods of time, the movements of interest rates (or rather bond yields) and commodity prices have been such as to suggest that they might be rationally related to one another in some direct and simple manner . . . the exceptions to this appearance of relationship are so numerous and so glaring that they cannot be overlooked."[50]

We now have data for nearly five decades more than were available to Keynes and nearly four decades more than were available to Macaulay, so it will be well to reexamine how well and with what exceptions Keynes's empirical assertion holds.

49. J. M. Keynes, *A Treatise on Money*, vol. 2 (1930), ed. Royal Economic Society (London: Macmillan, 1971), pp. 177–86. Keynes's failure to refer to Wicksell in connection with the Gibson paradox is curious, since in volume 1 of the *Treatise* he discusses Wicksell's work and refers to Wicksell's analysis as largely coinciding with his own and as deserving "more fame and much more attention than it has received from English-speaking economists" (*Treatise*, 1: 167). Wicksell discussed in English what Keynes called the Gibson paradox in his article "The Influence of the Rate of Interest on Prices," *Economic Journal* 17 (June 1907): 213–20.

50. Frederick R. Macaulay, *The Movements of Interest Rates, Bond Yields and Stock Prices in the United States Since 1856* (New York: NBER, 1938), p. 185. See also his implicit criticism of Keynes's "adjustments" to the data, pp. 163–64.

Chart 10.17 plots phase averages of the short-term nominal rate and of the rate of price change. For the United States, these more detailed data, like the earlier analysis simply in terms of periods of rising and falling prices, show only the loosest relation. Before 1950 there are occasional coincidences, such as the 1896 dip in both commercial paper rates and price change, or lagged relations, such as the World War I price explosion and the subsequent peak in commercial paper rates. But these are more plausibly interpreted in terms of specific historical circumstances than as a Fisherian allowance for anticipated inflation. The first coincidence is very likely the common result of the measures taken to end the threat to the gold standard. The 1921 peak in interest rates is related to the price inflation, not through allowance for anticipated inflation but through monetary policy. The sharp contractionary monetary measures taken by the Federal Reserve to end the postwar inflationary boom had an initial liquidity effect that drove up short-term rates.

The interesting feature of the United States chart is the striking contrast between the period before and after 1950. For the post–World War II phases there is a close correlation between the rate of interest and the rate of price change.

Fot the United Kingdom, panel B of chart 10.17 again confirms the earlier judgments. Before the early 1950's there is little relation. After World War II, except only for the first two phases, there is a close correlation.

One feature common to both countries is the much wider variability in the rate of price change than in the rate of interest, except for the one post–World War II period. The wider variability in the rate of price change may be simply a statistical artifact, reflecting greater measurement error in the series on price change than in the series on interest rates. A more plausible explanation is economic: before World War II, the wider variability of prices reflects the existence of monetary and other disturbances that were stochastic and could not readily be anticipated. After World War II, variability was large but was attributable to policy, not chance. We shall return to this line of reasoning later.

First, however, let us examine the relation between the short-term rate and the price level. These series are plotted in chart 10.18. The difference in dimensionality makes the association of scales for the two series arbitrary. We have resolved this arbitrariness for the basic price scale by locating it so as to put the mean price level for the pre–World War I period on the same point on the ordinate as the mean interest rate for that period. The interval on the logarithmic price scale was chosen so as to yield about the same amplitude for prices in that period as the arithmetic scale for interest rates yields for interest rates.

The continuous series plotted for a century resolve a major part of the so-called Gibson paradox and support Macaulay's doubts: interest rates

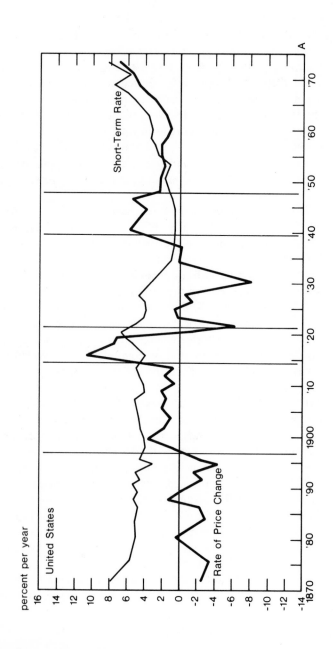

percent per year

United States

Short-Term Rate

Rate of Price Change

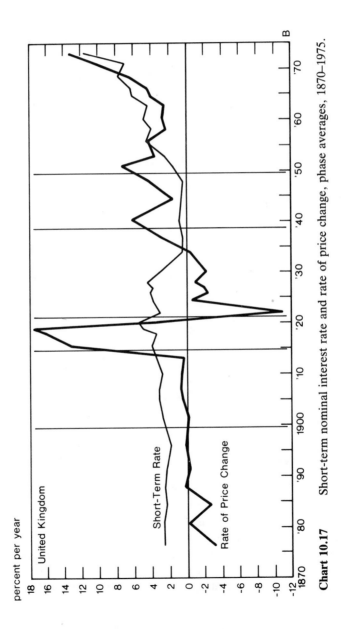

percent per year

United Kingdom

Short-Term Rate

Rate of Price Change

Chart 10.17 Short-term nominal interest rate and rate of price change, phase averages, 1870–1975.

price level (ratio scale)   short-term rate (percent per year)

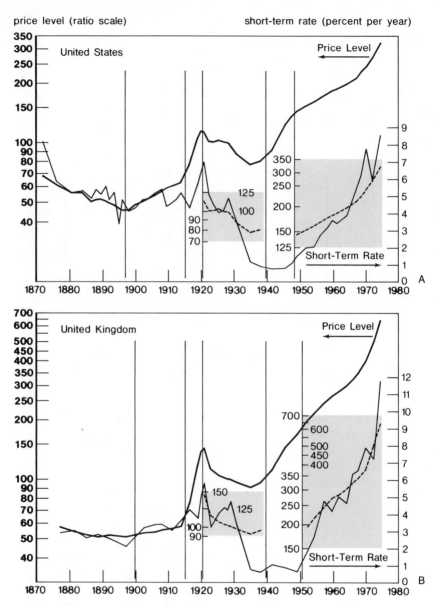

Chart 10.18   Short-term nominal interest rate and price level, 1870–1975.

do *not* follow major changes in price level. The theoretical expectation that jumps in the level of prices should leave no imprint on the rate of interest is fully confirmed. For both countries, the jumps in prices during World Wars I and II are not matched by any corresponding jump in interest rates. That much, at least, is eminently clear.

On the other hand, the close relation between interest rates and the level of prices during the pre–World War I period is striking, the only significant deviations being for the United States in the early years, when interest rates are out of line on the high side, and the final few years, when they are out of line on the low side.

To bring out any similar relation for the interwar and postwar periods, we have replotted the segment of the price series for those periods, shifting the origin of the vertical scale so as to make the average price level for each period coincide with the average rate of interest. For both the United States and the United Kingdom there is a definite correlation for both periods but a less close correlation than for the pre–World War I period, and for the post–World War II period it is not clear that the relation reflects more than common trends. Furthermore, for both countries, but more clearly for the United States, there seems to be a distinct break for the period after 1960 corresponding to the break we found earlier in the relation between the interest rate and the rate of price change. When interest rates start to parallel price *changes*, they start departing from parallelism with the price *level*.

The contrast between the relation of the interest rate to the rate of price change and the price level, as well as between the intraperiod and long-period relations, is brought out clearly in table 10.6. The only significant correlations for individual periods between interest rates and the rate of price change are for the post–World War II period. On the other hand, all the correlations for the three nonwar individual periods between the interest rate and the level of prices are positive and statistically significant.

For the period as a whole, none of the United States correlations with the rate of price change or the price level is statistically significant, either including or excluding wars. Three of the four United Kingdom correlations are significantly positive, both of those for the price level, and the correlation for nonwar phases for the rate of change of prices.

A more detailed description of the Gibson relation for nonwar periods is given in table 10.7. For both the United States and the United Kingdom, the intercepts clearly differ significantly between the periods—as was abundantly clear from chart 10.18. As is obvious from that chart, the slopes differ significantly for the United States, not for the United Kingdom.[51] One remarkable point brought out by the table and not by the charts is the close similarity between the countries. The average slopes for the three periods are almost identical, once allowance is made for differences in intercepts (compare lines 9 and 10); when a single slope is used for the three periods, the intercepts for the United States exceed

51. Herewith a summary analysis of variance (table 10.N.1, following page). Note that the F value for the United States corresponding to the 2 degrees of freedom for the three slopes is 17.2, highly significant.

Table 10.N.1   Significance of Differences among Periods in Regression of Interest Rate on Price Level

Source of Variation	Degrees of Freedom		Mean Square		F	
	United States	United Kingdom	United States	United Kingdom	United States	United Kingdom
Slope	1	1	.000001	.007497	0.0	110.2
Differences in intercept	2	2	.004151	.002111	133.9	31.0
Differences in slope	2	2	.000533	.000028	17.2	0.4
Residual	37	25	.000031	.000068		

Critical Values of F

n_1	n_2	.05 Value	.01 Value
1	37	4.10	7.37
1	25	4.24	7.77
2	37	3.26	5.23
2	25	3.38	5.57

Table 10.6   Relation between Nominal Interest Rate and Rate of Change and Level of Prices

	Number of Observations		Correlation between Interest Rate and	
			Rate of Change of Prices	Logarithm of Price Level
Period and Country	Col. 3 (1)	Col. 4 (2)	(3)	(4)
Pre–World War I				
United States	20	21	−.339	.538*
United Kingdom	10	11	.120	.719*
World War I				
United States	5	3	−.830	.991
United Kingdom	5	3	−.689	.449
Interwar				
United States	7	9	−.133	.961**
United Kingdom	7	9	−.297	.706*
World War II				
United States	5	3	−.769	.774
United Kingdom	5	3	.335	−.995
Post–World War II				
United States	11	13	.800**	.956**
United Kingdom	9	11	.711*	.955**
All, excluding wars				
United States	38	43	.114	.009
United Kingdom	26	31	.664**	.746**
All				
United States	48	49	−.192	−.032
United Kingdom	36	37	.205	.594**

*Significantly different from zero at .05 level.
**Significantly different from zero at .01 level.

those for the United Kingdom by 2.68, 1.38, and 1.44 percentage points for the three successive periods. More surprising perhaps is the closeness of the residual standard error of estimate, both when a single slope is used (0.0075 versus 0.0081), and when separate slopes are (0.0056 versus 0.0083). This similarity, like the corresponding examples in earlier chapters, is further evidence of how integrated the United States and United Kingdom economies have been. It cannot be taken as further evidence for the reality of the Gibson phenomenon. It is simply a reflection of the tendency for price levels and interest rates in the two countries to move together, though not identically.

The Gibson paradox remains, but cut down to much more manageable size and stripped of its greatest element of mystery.[52]

52. Gerald P. Dwyer, Jr., "An Explanation of the Gibson Paradox," Ph.D. diss., University of Chicago, 1979, explores the relation between interest rates and prices for

Table 10.7   Equations Relating Nominal Interest Rate to Logarithm of Level of Prices

Period and Country	Number of Observations	Intercept (Percentage	Slope of Log P Points)	Standard Error of Estimate
Pre–World War I				
1. United States	21	6.78	2.94	.0048
2. United Kingdom	11	7.22	7.04	.0033
Interwar				
3. United States	9	4.67	14.08	.0057
4. United Kingdom	9	2.77	9.65	.0133
Post–World War II				
5. United States	13	−1.85	8.86	.0066
6. United Kingdom	11	−2.70	7.29	.0084
All nonwar				
Single equation				
7. United States	43	4.42	0.02	.0160
8. United Kingdom	31	3.61	1.99	.0144
Separate period intercepts		10.20 ⎫		
9. United States	43	4.22 ⎬	8.36	.0075
		−1.51 ⎭		
10 United Kingdom	31	7.52 ⎫	7.51	.0081
		2.84 ⎬		
		−2.95 ⎭		
Separate intercepts and slopes				
11. United States	43	(same as in		.0056
12. United Kingdom	31	lines 1–6)		.0083

Note: Interest rates expressed as decimal (e.g., 5 percent is .05). Price level expressed as ratio to 1929 level (e.g., 1929 = 1.0).

The indication that there may have been a structural change in the relation between interest rates and prices in the post–World War II period is so intriguing that it seems worth exploring this point in more detail by exploiting data for time units shorter than phases. As it happens, monthly data are available from 1913 for the United States and 1915 for the United Kingdom on both consumer prices and interest rates. As background, chart 10.19 duplicates chart 10.17 except that it uses the consumer price index, rather than the price index implicit in the national income estimates, and monthly data, with the rate of price change averaged over six-month intervals to avoid extreme variability, rather than phase average data.[53]

France, Belgium, and Germany, as well as the United States and the United Kingdom. His conclusion parallels ours: "There is no stable relationship between interest rates and prices" (p. 79). He finds periods of positive correlation for the United Kingdom and the United States, especially before 1914 and after World War II, but not for the other countries.

53. It is unclear how best to date the price series matched with the interest rate series. The interest rate recorded for the month of January, for example, refers to a contract that will

The monthly series plotted in chart 10.19 bring out more clearly than our phase averages two respects in which the post–World War II period— or much of it—differs from the earlier period: the first starting in the early or mid-1950s, the second, somewhat later.

The first respect is the drastic decline in the variability of the recorded price series after the mid-1950s in both countries. Before that period the rate of price change is many times more variable than the interest rate; after that date it is still more variable, particularly in the United Kingdom, but the difference is much less. The change in the variability of the price series may be simply a statistical artifact. In both countries the reduction in variability coincides with a comprehensive statistical revision in the price index—in 1953 in the United States, in 1956 in the United Kingdom.[54] It may be that the recorded fluctuations in prices before these dates reflected largely measurement error.[55]

---

terminate some months later (for the United States, sixty to ninety days later through 1923, four to six months later thereafter; for the United Kingdom, three months later). The realized real return will depend on what happens to prices in the subsequent period. For that purpose, the January interest rate should be matched with a rate of price change corresponding to the period from January to the termination month. On the other hand, at the time the contract is entered into, data are available only on prices up to that point. To relate the January interest rate only to information available at the time requires using a rate of price change for a period terminating in January. Given that we are using a rate of price change based on a six-month interval, that means matching the January interest rate with the rate of price change from prices in the prior July to January, or a rate centered on October. That is what we have done in chart 10.19.

Note that in relating the January interest rate "only to information available at the time" we distinguish between two concepts of information: personal observation over time based on efficient knowledge of the market versus the official statistics of prices released in February for the month of January. Neither concept is right, but we judge the historical one to be better than the official release.

Correlation experiments relating interest rates to price changes subsequently to the date of the interest rate produced no persuasive evidence to justify a different dating.

54. See United States Department of Labor, Bureau of Labor Statistics, *Handbook of Methods of Surveys and Studies*, Bulletin no. 1458, October 1966, chap. 10, on consumer prices, pp. 69–90, for a description of the comprehensive revision of the index in January 1953.

The United Kingdom retail price index was introduced in 1956 as the successor to the cost of living index, the first officially published index of this sort, which started in 1915. The cost of living index was designed to show the effect of price changes on the basic goods consumed by working-class families before August 1914. The retail price index measures changes in prices of a much more comprehensive basket of goods and services reflecting the average spending pattern of the great majority of households, including those of practically all wage earners and most salary earners. See Great Britain, Central Statistical Office, *Method of Construction and Calculation of the Index of Retail Prices*, Studies in Official Statistics, no. 6 (London: HMSO, 1964).

55. In a private communication before his death, Julius Shiskin noted that, for a period of six months after the 1953 revision, the United States Bureau of Labor Statistics continued the old series, using the same samples, weights, and procedures in existence before the revision. There was greater variability in the old series for the overlap period. Phillip Cagan,

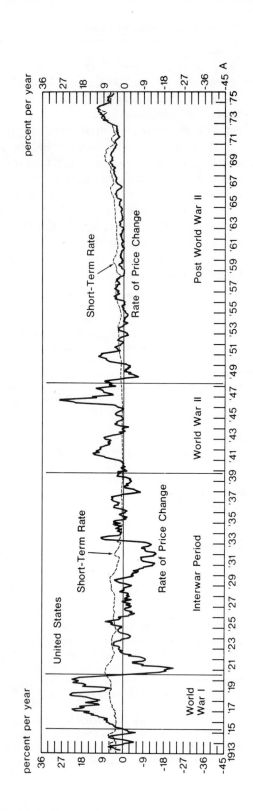

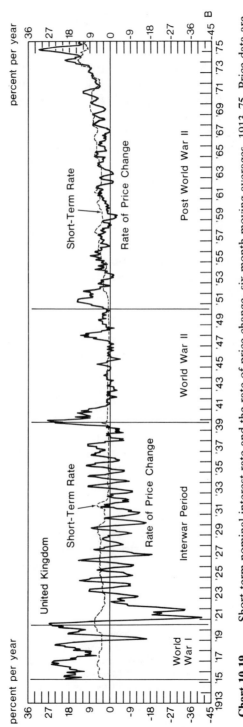

Chart 10.19   Short-term nominal interest rate and the rate of price change, six-month moving averages, 1913–75. Price data are six-month changes centered on the fourth month.

The second respect is the changed relation between the interest rate and the rate of price change. Up to the 1950s at least, there is only the vaguest of hints of any systematic short-term relation in either country between the interest rate and the recorded rate of price change—every once in a while there is a movement in the interest rate that can be connected to a movement in the same direction in the price-change series, but most of the time the two series seem to move independently of one another. This lack of relationship may be a consequence of the large measurement error in the rate of price change—the statistical noise in the recorded price series may have drowned out a systematic relation between interest rates and the "true" rate of price change.

However, the subsequent behavior of the series, particularly in the United States, suggests that statistical noise is at best a partial explanation. For some five to ten years in the United States after the 1953 statistical revision, there is no closer relation between the interest rate and the price series than there was earlier. Then the relation becomes closer and closer, at first in the general movement, then even in the minor ups and downs. The change is gradual so that there is no sharp dividing line, yet after, say, 1965 the relation is clearly very close.

The United Kingdom picture is less clear-cut, partly because the rate of price change retains more variability after the statistical revision, partly because the relation never gets as close as in the United States, partly because of the final spike in the rate of price change unmatched by any movement in the interest rate—a spike that may be connected with changes in price control. Statutory price controls were in effect from November 1972 to February 1974, followed by voluntary controls for the next six months and then by the reimposition of compulsory controls a year later, in August 1975. Nonetheless, with the benefit of the hindsight provided by the United States experience, a very similar pattern can be seen in the United Kingdom data, with 1965 again a convenient dividing line.

The looser relation between the two series for the United Kingdom than for the United States may well reflect statistical defects in both series: for the rate of price change, the more important and frequent use of price controls than in the United States; for the interest rate, its administered character. It is clear from the charts that the rate on bank bills in the United Kingdom is a managed rate, remaining constant for

---

however, informs us that he doubts that the decline in variability after 1953 is due to improvement in the United States consumer price index. He bases his judgment on a study of wholesale prices, in which he examined some components of the wholesale price index in the 1920s and post–World War II years and found a considerable decline in the dispersion of price changes for cycles of roughly the same severity. He attributes the decline to changed market behavior or a changed composition of markets and products ("Changes in the Recession Behavior of Wholesale Prices in the 1920s and Post-World War II," *Explorations in Economic Research* 2 [winter, 1975]: 54–104).

months at a time, while the United States commercial paper rate is an effective market rate.[56]

Chart 10.20 provides a closer look at the relation between the interest rate and the rate of price change for the period after 1965 ending in 1979, rather than 1975, the final cyclical turning point of our trend period. It differs from Chart 10.19 both in an enlarged time scale and in a different time reference of the rate of price change. Chart 10.19 plotted the price change retrospectively; that is, the price change associated with, say, a January interest rate is the change during the prior six months, or the information that could have been available to the lenders and borrowers when they entered into their contract. Chart 10.20 plots the price change prospectively; that is, the price change associated with, say, a January interest rate, is the change that is estimated to occur during the period of the loan contract. Hence the vertical difference is the realized real rate of return, and the price change is the one that the transactors would, if they had perfect foresight, take into account.[57]

For the United States the relation is very close indeed throughout the period. The shifting of dates does not improve the relation as judged by simple correlations, though visually it appears to do so at a number of points.[58] These results leave very much open the question whether partici-

56. John Foster, "Interest Rates and Inflation Expectations: The British Experience," *Oxford Bulletin of Economics and Statistics* 41 (May 1979): 145–64, comments (p. 152, n. 24): "It is worth emphasizing that short-term securities in the United Kingdom differ from those in the United States in that the latter are generally viewed as market determined whereas the former have been administered through Bank Rate policy and, more recently, through alterations in the Minimum Lending Rate [introduced in 1972]."

57. The actual matching is approximate. For the United States, we treated the four-to-six month commercial paper rate as if it always referred to six-month paper, which makes the six-month price change the relevant change, and gives the simple dating of matching the January interest rate (which for six-month paper refers to a contract terminating in July) with the January to July rate of price change.

For the United Kingdom, the interest rate is for a three-month bill, and the correct matching would be with a three-month price change. However, both for consistency with the United States and to reduce variability, we decided to retain a six-month price change and simply match as closely as possible the central dates of the interest rate contract and the price change. A January interest rate refers to a contract terminating in April; its central date is midway between February and March. The price change from November to May is centered in February, the price change from December to June, in March, so either one differs in dating by one-half month. We arbitrarily chose to match the December to June price change with the January interest rate.

58. Herewith the simple correlation coefficients for 1965–79:

Interest Rate Matched with Price Span Terminating	Correlation Coefficient
Same month	0.835
One month later	0.833
Two months later	0.823
Three months later	0.804
Four months later	0.782

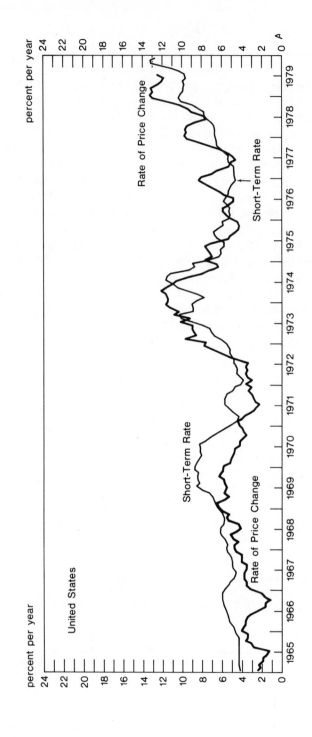

United States

percent per year

Rate of Price Change

Short-Term Rate

Short-Term Rate

Rate of Price Change

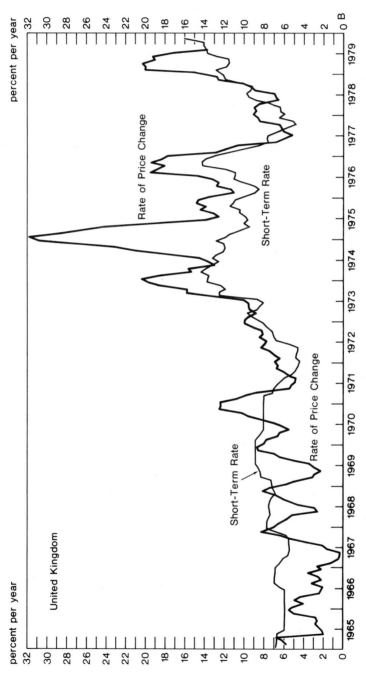

Chart 10.20 Relation between interest rates and price change, United States and United Kingdom, monthly, 1965–79.

pants in the market can successfully predict the movement of prices for a few months ahead.

For the United Kingdom the relation is far looser. As we noted earlier, this difference may reflect the statistical defects of the United Kingdom series rather than a basic economic difference between the two countries.

10.7   Alternative Explanations of the Gibson Paradox

The preceding sections narrow more than has hitherto been done the Gibson phenomenon to be explained: first, the alleged relation does not hold over periods witnessing a substantial shift in the price level, but only within briefer periods; second, the markets may have learned their Fisher and so have made Gibson obsolete. But this narrowing of the paradox does not eliminate it; it still represents a striking empirical regularity in search of an explanation.

The most famous and most fully explored explanations that have been proposed are the monetary explanation suggested by Irving Fisher and the real explanation suggested first by Knut Wicksell and later by J. M. Keynes.

10.7.1   The Fisher Explanation

As already noted, Fisher's proposed explanation hinges on a lag between a change in the direction of price movements and the public's perception of that change. In his 1907 *Rate of Interest*, which largely overlaps his 1896 *Appreciation and Interest*, he expresses this explanation in very general terms:

> Three general facts have now been established: (1) Rising and falling prices and wages are directly correlated with high and low rates of interest; (2) The adjustment of interest to price-movements is inadequate; (3) This adjustment is more nearly adequate for long than for short periods.
>
> These facts are capable of a common explanation expressing the manner in which the adjustment referred to takes place. Suppose an upward movement of prices begins. Business profits (measured in *money*) will rise. . . . Borrowers can now afford to pay higher "money-interest." If, however, only a few persons at first see this, the interest will not be fully adjusted, and borrowers will realize an extra margin of profit after deducting interest charges. This raises an expectation of a similar profit in the future and this expectation, acting on the demand for loans, will raise the rate of interest. If the rise is still inadequate, the process is repeated, and thus by continual trial and error the rate approaches the true adjustment. . . .
>
> Since at the beginning of an upward price-movement the rate of interest is too low, and at the beginning of a downward movement it is too high, we can understand not only that the averages for the whole

periods are imperfectly adjusted, but that the delay in the adjustment leaves a relatively low interest at the beginning of an ascent of prices, and a relatively high interest at the beginning of a descent. And this is what we found to be true. That the adjustment is more perfect for long periods than for short periods seems to be because, in short periods, the years of non-adjustment at the beginning occupy a larger relative part of the whole period.[59]

When Fisher returned to the problem some two decades later, he converted this general hypothesis into a much more rigid and formal one—and one, incidentally, with less economics. In the interim he had developed distributed lags, and he applied them to this problem. He expressed the nominal interest rate as the sum of a real interest rate, implicitly assumed constant, and an anticipated rate of price change, and then approximated the anticipated rate of price change by a weighted average of prior price change, with the weights declining linearly and summing to unity—that is, a triangular weighting pattern.[60] Whereas in 1907 he had explained the changes in interest rates as produced by shifts in the demand for loans arising from the result of unanticipated inflation on profits, a process that requires no explicit formation of inflationary anticipations, here the anticipations take center stage.

For the delayed formation of anticipations to explain Gibson's paradox empirically, the time it takes people to form their anticipations must have a particular relation to the duration of the long swing in prices. If people formed their anticipations very rapidly—much more rapidly than the duration of a price rise or a price fall—interest rates would rise only briefly when prices started to rise and soon would be high but constant; and similarly when prices started to fall. Interest rates would look more like the steps in chart 10.10 than like the wavy dotted line. A close correlation between rising prices and rising rates requires that the time it takes for people to adjust their anticipations must be roughly comparable to the duration of the long swings in prices. It is not surprising, therefore, that when Fisher estimated the lag in forming anticipations by using observed interest rates and prices he found that the average period of the distributed lag of anticipations behind prices was 7.3 years (i.e., triangular weights covering twenty years) for United States long rates computed from annual data from 1900 to 1927; 10.7 years (i.e., triangular weights covering thirty years) for United States short rates computed from quarterly data from 1915 to 1927; 10.0 years (triangular weights covering twenty-eight years) for United Kingdom long rates computed from annual data from 1898 to 1924.[61]

59. *The Rate of Interest*, pp. 284–85.
60. Irving Fisher, *The Theory of Interest* (New York: Macmillan, 1930), pp. 407–44.
61. Ibid., pp. 421, 422, 427. The mean period of continuous triangular weights is one-third the total period of the weights. For discontinuous weights, for which the initial

Frederick Macaulay, in his 1938 book, was highly critical of Fisher's analysis, partly on purely statistical grounds. He pointed out serious errors in Fisher's appendix tables, correction of which substantially reduced the already low correlation between levels of interest rates and the rate of change of prices. He noted that "rates and yields were usually more highly correlated with 'the weighted average of sundry successive' price changes than they were with the individual price changes; *but not so highly correlated as they were with the raw prices.*"[62] He then pointed out, as did others many years later when there was a resumption of interest in the subject, that "as the number of [past rates of change of prices] included in the [triangularly weighted average of price change] is increased, the configuration of [the weighted average] usually approximates more and more closely the configuration of [the price level]."[63] In consequence, he argued that Fisher's correlations were only a disguised reflection of the Gibson phenomenon, not an explanation thereof. He stressed also the difference in results for different periods, a point to which we shall recur. Macaulay admitted the existence of a real puzzle but believed that Fisher had not provided a satisfactory resolution.

In recent years a number of scholars have repeated and extended Fisher's calculations, with only slight modifications. The results have been highly consistent. For periods including World War I or World War II and some ways beyond, the results reproduce Fisher's finding that long lags yield the highest correlations.[64] However, for recent years that is not the case. Yohe and Karnosky and Robert Gordon find that, for the later years of the postwar period, a shorter weighted average of past price changes yields price anticipations that best explain interest rate movements.[65]

This finding, plus the understandable skepticism about the plausibility of such long lags that has all along hindered the acceptance of Fisher's conclusions, stimulated efforts to find other tests of Fisher's hypothesis. For the period since 1947, an independent series of price forecasts for the

---

weight is taken as dated minus one time unit, the mean period is one-third the total period plus either two-thirds or one-third of a time unit, depending on whether a total period of T units is interpreted as corresponding to discontinuous weights 1, 2, . . . , T, or to discontinuous weights 0, 1, 2, . . . , $T-1$. Fisher is inconsistent in converting total periods into mean periods. He sometimes converts by dividing by three, sometimes by dividing by three and adding two-thirds. We have used means obtained by dividing by three and adding two-thirds, since this corresponds to a change that Fisher made in listing errata for page 423.

62. Macaulay, *Movements of Interest Rates*, p. 171 (italics in original).

63. Ibid., p. 174.

64. See Suraj Gupta, "Expected Rates of Change in Prices and Rates of Interest," Ph.D. diss., University of Chicago, 1964.

65. W. P. Yohe and D. S. Karnosky, "Interest Rates and Price Level Changes" (note 3, above); Robert J. Gordon, "Inflation in Recession and Recovery," *Brookings Papers on Economic Activity*, no. 1, (1971), pp. 145–48.

United States has been compiled by Joseph Livingston from responses by a panel of business economists. Several studies have correlated this series with interest rates and used it to test hypotheses about the formation of expectations. The major findings relevant to our present purpose are that expectations are highly correlated with interest rates but that a short rather than a long weighted average of past price behavior gives the best fit to inflation forecasts.[66]

66. John A. Carlson, "A Study of Price Forecasts," *Annals of Economic and Social Measurement* 6, no. 1 (1977): 27–56, contains the most thorough description and presentation of these data that we have seen.

For analyses of these data see William E. Gibson, "Interest Rates and Inflationary Expectations"; Kajal Lahiri, "Inflationary Expectations: Their Formation and Interest Rate Effects," *American Economic Review* 66 (March 1976): 124–31; James E. Pesando, "A Note on the Rationality of the Livingston Price Expectations," *Journal of Political Economy* 83 (August 1975): 849–58; David H. Pyle, "Observed Price Expectations and Interest Rates," *Review of Economics and Statistics* 54 (August 1972): 275–81; Stephen J. Turnovsky, "Some Empirical Evidence on the Formation of Price Expectations," *Journal of the American Statistical Association* 65 (December 1970): 1441–54; Stephen J. Turnovsky and Michael L. Wachter, "A Test of the 'Expectations Hypothesis' Using Directly Observed Wage and Price Expectations," *Review of Economics and Statistics* 54 (February 1972): 47–54; Lahiri and Lee, "Tests of Rational Expectations."

Gibson does not test the relation between the Livingston expectations and prior price behavior but solely between them and interest rates, finding a good correlation, but suggesting that there is evidence of a break in the relation around 1965. Turnovsky is more directly concerned with expectations formation. He too finds a break in the data during the early 1960s and finds a good relation between the expectations and prior price behavior only after the early 1960s. A similar finding is reported in A. B. Holmes and M. L. Kwast, "Interest Rates and Inflationary Expectations: Tests for Structural Changes, 1952–1976," *Journal of Finance* 34 (June 1979): 733–41.

Quarterly interpolations of the Livingston expectations series and also of a series based on Survey Research Center surveys have been published by F. Juster and P. Wachtel, "Inflation and the Consumer," *Brookings Papers on Economic Activity*, no. 1 (1972), pp. 71–114. These series were updated in P. Wachtel, "Survey Measures of Expected Inflation and Their Potential Usefulness," *Analysis of Inflation, 1965–1974*, ed. Joel Popkin, Studies in Income and Wealth, vol. 42 (Cambridge, Mass.: Ballinger, 1977), pp. 361–94. G. de Menil and S. S. Bhalla, "Direct Measurement of Popular Price Expectations," *American Economic Review* 65 (March 1975): 169–80, used the Survey Research Center series to explain wage changes. S. J. Feldman has used both expectations series to examine their relation to interest rates from 1955 to 1971 and to various weighted averages of past price changes. He concludes, as did Gibson, that there is a close relation between price expectations and interest rates but finds no evidence of any change in the relation. Like Turnovsky, he does find a break in the 1960s in the relation between directly observed price expectations and the weighted averages of past price changes. He concludes that "distributed lag hypotheses are poor proxies for anticipated inflation" and that "how the market forecasted inflation has altered." "The Formation of Price Expectations and the Nominal Rate of Interest: Is Fisher Right?" unpublished Federal Reserve Bank of New York Research Paper no. 7416, July 1974.

Cukierman and Wachtel relate the variance of the two expectations series to the variance of nominal income change and of the inflation rate. They find that periods with large variances of nominal income change and of the inflation rate are also periods of close

Unfortunately, no similar independent estimates of price expectations are available for the earlier period, so there is no way of knowing whether this finding simply is another reflection of a major break in recent decades or is evidence against the long lags for the earlier period as well.[67]

---

association between the level of interest rates and the variability of expectations, and they suggest "the need to reformulate Fisher's theory of interest for the case of heterogeneous expectations" (p. 607). A. Cukierman and P. Wachtel, "Differential Inflationary Expectations and the Variability of the Rate of Inflation: Theory and Evidence," *American Economic Review* 69 (September 1979): 595–609.

For the United Kingdom, see J. A. Carlson and M. Parkin, "Inflation Expectations," *Economica* 42 (May 1975): 123–38; and D. Demery and N. Duck, "The Behavior of Nominal Interest Rates in the United Kingdom, 1961–73," *Economica* 45 (February 1978): 23–27. Demery's and Duck's finding that there is a great deal of evidence that inflation expectations have some role in determining nominal interest rates is disputed by John Foster, "Interest Rates and Inflation Expectations: The British Experience," *Oxford Bulletin of Economics and Statistics* 41 (May 1979): 145–64, who reports only limited evidence, "certainly from 1961–66 and probably from 1966–77" (p. 162). See also K. Holden and D. A. Peel, "An Empirical Investigation of Inflationary Expectations," *Oxford Bulletin of Economics and Statistics* 39 (November 1977): 291–99.

Australian data on price expectations of consumers reported quarterly for a five-year period are analyzed by L. V. Defris and R. A. Williams, "Quantitative versus Qualitative Measures of Price Expectations," *Economic Letters* 2, no. 2, (1979): 169–73. They conclude that the quantitative level of expected price change was "about right" and that "prediction of quarter-to-quarter fluctuations was moderately successful" (p. 173), but that qualitative forecasts were of little value. The paper was concerned solely with the price expectations.

67. One approach that has been attempted to obtain an independent series of anticipations is to derive them from futures prices of commodities as recorded on futures markets. Unfortunately this approach has foundered on the highly special composition of the commodities traded on active futures markets so that anticipations about changes in the relative price of these commodities appear to have swamped anticipations about changes in the general price level.

A more successful experiment is contained in an interesting paper by Jacob A. Frenkel, in which he used the forward exchange rate to estimate price anticipations during the German hyperinflation ("The Forward Exchange Rate, Expectations, and the Demand for Money: The German Hyperinflation," *American Economic Review* 57 [September 1977]: 653–70). However, this approach is available only during periods of floating exchange rates and even then gives expectations of changes in relative prices in two countries—limitations of no importance for the German hyperinflation, but of great importance for these periods.

Another approach is used by Cukierman with Israeli data, where the coexistence of indexed and nonindexed bonds provides a reasonably direct measure of the anticipated rate of inflation (not exact because of differences in the time duration and risk elements of the two categories of securities). In an interesting and important paper, he uses such a measure to test various assumed expectational processes, concluding that what he calls a "generalized linear process" gives the best approximation. The process, a modified version of a process presented by J. A. Frenkel ("Inflation and the Formation of Expectations," *Journal of Monetary Economics* 1 [October 1975]: 403–21), is one in which the anticipated rate of inflation is a weighted average of past rates, the set of weights being decomposable into two components, one, extending over a few months only, which is extrapolative, the other, extending over thirty months, which is regressive. The process is dominated by the regressive component, the weights for which first rise and then decline. Cukierman concludes that "the generalized linear expectational process is not inconsistent with the concept of rational

A more indirect approach that has been increasingly adopted in recent studies of the Gibson paradox and Fisher's hypothesis has been to ask whether it would have been rational for people to form their anticipations by such a long weighted average of past price experience. The answer is by no means clear or simple. The question, stated differently, is dual: first, insofar as past prices give information on future rates of inflation, does the long weighting pattern required to explain interest rate behavior extract that information efficiently? Second, was there information readily available to participants in the relevant markets, other than past prices, which would have enabled them to improve their prediction of future rates of inflation? If the answer to the first question were no, or the answer to the second yes then participants would have overlooked profit-making opportunities if they had neglected such information and had insisted on using the long weighted averages Fisher attributed to them: markets would have been inefficient. If the answer to the first question were yes, but the answer to the second no, Fisher's procedure would encapsulate the entire anticipatory process. Finally, if the answer to both questions were yes, Fisher's procedure would be incomplete, but not necessarily invalid, since it would correspond to the extraction from the price data of the information that it contains.

If Fisher's explanation of the Gibson paradox is not valid, that does not of course mean that markets are inefficient. It may rather reflect a lack of constancy in the ex-ante real rate or a different process of forming anticipations.

This indirect approach, like the calculations along Fisher's lines, has yielded very different results for recent and earlier decades. For the post–World War II period for the United States, Shiller and Fama conclude that short and long interest rates are consistent with both a constant real rate and rational expectations.[68] Two more recent papers question Fama's finding of a constant real rate, but not of an efficient market.[69] Rutledge finds that, for recent decades, information other than

---

expectations" (p. 749). Alex Cukierman, "A Test of Expectational Processes Using Information from the Capital Market—the Israeli Case," *International Economic Review* 18 (October 1977): 737–53.

68. Shiller, "Rational Expectations and the Structure of Interest Rates" Fama, "Short-Term Interest Rates as Predictors of Inflation." See note 6 above.

69. Hess and Bicksler, "Capital Asset Prices versus Time Series Models"; Nelson and Schwert, "Short-Term Interest Rates as Predictors of Inflation." See note 6 above. Both pairs of authors find Fama's procedure defective in allowing only for a single monthly autocorrelation of interest rates rather than a longer series. In a later article that makes no reference to either of these papers, Fama finds evidence of variation in the real rate but concludes that "only a trivial fraction of the sample variance" of the ex-post real return on one-month Treasury bills "can be attributed to the measured variation" in the ex-ante expected real rate. Eugene F. Fama, "Inflation Uncertainty and Expected Returns on Treasury Bills," *Journal of Political Economy* 84 (June 1976): 427–48; quotation from p. 444.

past price movements, namely, past monetary growth rates, can be used to improve predictions of future inflation. However, Feige and Pearce reach the opposite conclusion for roughly the same period and price data but by a different set of statistical procedures.[70] Dwyer concludes, along with Rutledge, that "Fisher's hypothesis is able to explain the upward movement of interest rates and price levels since the early 1950's."[71]

While the results for recent decades confirm the broad outlines of Fisher's approach, they reject his particular empirical hypothesis about the formation of expectations. Indeed, they come close to denying the existence of the Gibson paradox, which was the occasion for his hypothesis.

The situation is very different for earlier decades. For the United States for 1870–1940, Sargent finds that the weighted average of past price changes that gives the best predictions of future inflation has a much shorter average lag than the weighted average that Fisher used—an average much more like that which Yohe and Karnosky found for the 1960s. Sargent concludes that "it is difficult *both* to accept Fisher's explanation of the Gibson paradox *and* to maintain that the extraordinarily long lags in expectations are 'rational.'" However, this conclusion is based on calculations that include World War I, when, as we have seen, there was no Gibson paradox to explain. Siegel and Shiller conclude for both the United States and the United Kingdom for a much longer pre–World War II period that the data are not consistent with a constant real rate plus rational anticipations of inflation.[72] In a highly perceptive comment on Sargent's paper, Gordon points out that, through World War II, the major instances of significant inflation and deflation were concentrated in time and connected with episodes that were widely

70. John Rutledge, *A Monetarist Model of Inflationary Expectations* (Cambridge, Mass.: Lexington, 1974); Edgar L. Feige and Douglas K. Pearce, "Economically Rational Expectations: Are Innovations in the Rate of Inflation Independent of Innovations in Measures of Monetary and Fiscal Policy?" *Journal of Political Economy* 84 (June 1976): 499–522. Rutledge uses multiple correlation and relates an interest rate to other series; Feige and Pearce use Box-Jenkins techniques and do not use interest rates, instead investigating whether the residuals from ARIMA models fitted to time series of prices are correlated with residuals from ARIMA models fitted to time series of various monetary aggregates and the full employment surplus. They find no correlation. This procedure is eminently sensible for investigating the best way to forecast short-term movements in prices. However, it provides only limited evidence on the very different question of the effect of monetary or fiscal forces on the course of prices, since for the most part the important question about those effects has to do with the longer-term systematic movements that are expressly abstracted from in the ARIMA models.

71. Dwyer, "Explanation of the Gibson Paradox," p. 112.

72. Sargent, "Interest Rates and Prices in the Long Run," quotation from p. 402; Shiller and Siegel, "Gibson Paradox." See also Thomas J. Sargent, "Interest Rates and Expected Inflation: A Selective Summary of Recent Research," *Explorations in Economic Research* 3 no. 3 (summer 1976): 303–25.

recognized as special (World Wars I and II, post–World War I contraction, and the Great Depression). Hence, he argues, it would have been irrational to extrapolate them mechanically to the future. He interprets post–World War II experience as more favorable to a mechanical extrapolation, though with a short lag, because inflation has become a part of a standard political-economic response mechanism.[73]

Any shortcoming of Fisher's explanation of the Gibson paradox does not, of course, in any way diminish the importance of his distinction between real and nominal interest rates, or his distinction between ex-post and ex-ante real rates, or his emphasis on the anticipated rate of inflation as affecting both the demand for and supply of loanable funds. But it does put in serious doubt his highly special composite hypothesis that for the purpose of studying monetary influences on interest rates the ex-ante real rate can be treated as constant, and that interest rates follow the level of prices because borrowers and lenders estimate future inflation by a long weighted average of past rates of inflation.

Gordon's comment brings out a key limitation of all the empirical work covering long periods, including not only that of Sargent and of Siegel and Shiller, but also that of Fisher himself. With one minor exception for Sargent, to which we shall return, and more extensive exceptions for Fisher, all the calculations on which they base their conclusions span the World War I period. But we have seen that there was no Gibson phenomenon from before to after World War I. Their results may simply reflect the attempt to explain a nonexistent phenomenon and may be entirely consistent with a very different verdict on the Fisher hypothesis for the pre–World War I period alone, or for the interwar period alone.

It is noteworthy that while in the text Fisher stressed the periods including World War I, he systematically got lower correlations and shorter mean lags for periods excluding World War I: for United States short rates, only 10.2 quarters or two and one-half years for 1890–1914, compared with over ten years for 1915–1927; for United Kingdom long rates, 7.1 years for 1820–64, and 8.2 years for 1865–97, compared with ten years for 1898–1924.

The one exception in Sargent's paper is a calculation for 1880–1914 of the optimum prediction of the change in the annual wholesale price index on the basis of an exponentially weighted average of past price changes. He estimates that the optimum mean lag is very short (one quarter).[74]

73. Robert J. Gordon, "Interest Rates and Prices in the Long Run: A Comment," *Journal of Money, Credit and Banking* 5, no. 1, part 2 (February 1973): 460–65.

74. Sargent, "Interest Rates and Prices in the Long Run," table 2.1, p. 398. Let g_P refer to the continuous rate of price change (first difference of the natural log of price), and let

$$g_P^*(t+1) = b \sum_{i=0}^{\infty} (1-b)^i g_P(t-i),$$

where b is the weight given $g_P(t)$.

However, that optimum gives essentially no information on future price changes, since the weighted average computed from weights adding to unity is to be multiplied by 0.06. In effect, his formula reduces to a weighted average of a zero price change and an exponentially weighted average of prior price changes, with the zero price change receiving 94 percent of the weight. Moreover, the correlation between his exponentially weighted average and the actual subsequent price change is close to zero (for thirty-five observations, it is .062),[75] which is, of course, why it receives so little weight. Taken at its face value, Sargent's conclusion is that a zero price change was the optimum prediction for each year 1880–1914 based solely on past price data.

Sargent's result cannot, however, be accepted at face value. In the first place, it is disproportionately influenced by the one year 1880, in which wholesale prices averaged more than 11 percent higher than in 1879 as a result of the reaction to resumption—again, one of those special events that participants were surely aware of at the time and would not have regarded as simply another year to be extrapolated. Omit 1880, and Sargent would have come out with a much longer optimum lag (probably averaging about six to nine years) and would have given it greater weight in averaging it with a zero price change prediction.[76]

In the second place, the correlation between the interest rate and the actual annual price change, though low, is higher than between the interest rate and Sargent's predicted price change both including 1880 and excluding 1880.[77] The implication is that market participants had information in addition to price changes ending a year earlier. And of course they did. They not only knew about such events as resumption, the silver agitation, the defeat of free silver in 1896, and the like, but also had more current price information. Except at the very outset of a calendar year, the participants had price information for the earlier part of that calendar year itself.

Then the average period of the weights is $b \sum i(1 - b)^i = \frac{1-b}{b}$.

Given that the result is to be used for the next calendar year, the average period of the lag can be described as $1 + \frac{1-b}{b}$.

Sargent's estimate of b is .79, or a mean period of weights of roughly one quarter, or prediction lag of one and one-quarter years.

In this formula the weights are for discrete time units. The version for continuous time is given in note 83.

75. We have calculated this and all later correlations for annual data using the implicit price index as well as wholesale prices. The results differ only in detail.

76. Omitting 1880 raises the correlation between price change a year later and the weighted average from .06 to .24 for $b = .79$ but from .14 to .35 for $b = .14$, that is, a mean weight lag of about six years; and from .16 to .32 for $b = .10$, that is, a mean weight lag of about nine years.

77. The correlations are .24 and .02 including 1880; and .29 and .04 excluding 1880.

In the third place, our comparison of United States and United Kingdom interest rates led us to conclude that anticipated inflation in the United States was systematically above the actual before 1896 and perhaps the reverse after because of abatement of the fears of devaluation engendered by the free silver movement. We assessed the United Kingdom–United States difference on this account as one percentage point, which may well be a decided underestimate of the effect of the resolution of the free silver issue on anticipations.[78] If the interest rate before 1896 is adjusted for this effect by subtracting one percentage point, the correlation of the adjusted interest rate with the actual rate of price change (excluding 1880) is raised from .29 to .46, the correlation of the adjusted interest rate with Sargent's predicted price change, from .04 to .31; and with a predicted price change using a longer lag averaging six or nine years, from .03 or .06 to .45.[79] It also raises the Gibson paradox correlation of the interest rate with the price level from .23 to .57.

Using the annual data solely for 1880–1914, instead of, as Sargent does in most of his calculations, for 1880–1940 and allowing for the effect of other information than prior price change, thus gives a rather different impression. Fisher's explanation of the Gibson phenomenon is by no means confirmed, but, at the very least, it cannot be ruled out.

Similar calculations for the United Kingdom for annual data for 1880–1914 show a higher Gibson correlation of the interest rate with the price level for the United Kingdom than for the United States (.60 versus .30 for the United States unadjusted interest rate and .45 for the United States adjusted interest rate), and also a higher correlation with the rate of price change than for the United States unadjusted interest rate (.44 versus .24), but a slightly lower correlation with the rate of price change than for the United States adjusted interest rate (.44 versus .49). However, for the United Kingdom, an estimate of anticipated inflation using Sargent's weights gives a higher correlation with interest rates than estimates using the weights extending over a longer period.[80] This result reflects the higher contemporaneous correlation with the rate of price change and presumably also a higher serial correlation of the rate of price change in the United Kingdom than in the United States. In any event, all the correlations with anticipated inflation are higher than for the United States, so that United Kingdom data in no way contradict the tentative conclusion for the United States stated in the preceding paragraph.

78. The 1 percent estimate relies on the same exchange rate throughout, but we have seen that purchasing power party would have called for 1 percent per year appreciation of the United States dollar before 1896 and 1 percent per year depreciation of the United States dollar thereafter. Adding these effects would give an estimate of three percentage points as the effect of the resolution of the free silver issue on anticipations.

79. A larger adjusment equal to the three percentage points of the preceding footnote would make all these effects considerably greater.

80. Correlations of .42 for Sargent's weight for $b = .79$, .37 for $b = .14$, .40 for $b = .10$.

Dwyer reaches essentially the same conclusion for the pre-1914 period for the United States and the United Kingdom on the basis of a more complex test of the consistency of the price and interest rate series with rational expectations plus a random real rate with a constant expected value.[81]

Similarly, Harley, in a recent careful study of British pre–World War I experience concludes "that during periods of sustained price movement, the money market adjusted to price expectations and there was little effect on real interest rates." He thus supports Fisher's interpretation and our own finding. He estimates that the mean lag in formulating expectations of future price changes from past price changes was about seven years for short-term rates, about ten to thirteen years for long-term rates. These are even longer lags than Fisher got for the pre–World War I data for both the United States and the United Kingdom. Hence, though Harley's results seem strongly to support Fisher's interpretation of the United Kingdom Gibson phenomenon, they must share the doubt that attaches to such long estimated lags.[82]

One incidental by-product of our analysis is to illustrate a limitation of much recent work on rational expectations. One way that concept has been made operational is by regarding rationality of expectations as requiring that on the average the expectations are correct and hence by testing rationality of expectations by direct or indirect comparison of expectations with the actual subsequent values of the variables about which expectations were formed. But consider the period from 1880 to 1896. It was surely not irrational according to a commonsense interpretation of that term for participants in the financial markets to fear that growing political support for free silver would lead the United States to depart from the gold standard and to experience subsequent inflation— and this despite actual deflation during the period. Indeed, the longer the deflation proceeded, the more pressure built up for free silver, and the higher an intelligent observer might well have set his personal probability of inflation within, say, three years.

As it happened, the departure from gold was avoided. That does not prove that the persons who bet the other way were wrong—any more than losing a two to one wager that a fair coin will turn up heads proves that it was wrong to take the short end of that wager. Given a sufficiently long sequence of observations, of course, it could be maintained that all such events will ultimately average out, that in the century of experience our data cover, for example, there are enough independent episodes so that it is appropriate to test rationality of expectations by their average

81. Dwyer, "Explanation of the Gibson Paradox," pp. 106, 112.
82. C. Knick Harley, "The Interest Rate and Prices in Britain, 1873–1913: A Study of the Gibson Paradox," *Explorations in Economic History* 14 (February 1977): 69–89, quotation from p. 73.

accuracy. But that is cold comfort, since few studies cover so long a period, and our aim is surely to derive propositions that can be applied to shorter periods. Moreover, even one hundred years contain only six periods as long as that from 1880 to 1896, hardly a sufficiently large sample to assure "averaging out." Beyond these practical considerations there is a tantalizing intellectual question—What meaning, if any, can be given to the assertion: "Mr X's personal probability about a specified event was correct [or wrong]"?

To return to our main theme, our analysis of the annual data for 1880 to 1914 confirms the tentative indications of our earlier examination of charts 10.15, 10.16, and 10.17. There is some muted evidence of the Fisher effect, but it is clearly not the only, or even the most important effect at work—which still leaves the possibility that it may well be the feature that explains the Gibson phenomenon, since that too turns out, in a longer context, to be a much more limited relation than it is often represented as being.

We can use our phase average data to explore further the Fisher explanation for the subperiods excluding wars, in order to estimate the mean periods over which expectations would have had to be formed to explain the observed relation between the price level and interest rates, and to compare these mean periods for the two countries and the three nonwar subperiods.

We start with equation (6) rearranged and renumbered for convenience:

$$(10) \qquad R = \rho^* + g_P^*.$$

This is simply a definitional equation, defining the ex-ante anticipated real yield, ρ^*, as a function of the observed interest rate R and the anticipated price change. To give equation (10) content, assume that ρ^* can be treated as a constant except for random disturbances, and that g_P^*, aside from any special adjustments such as we have made above for the period 1880–96, can be regarded as determined by a simple adaptive expectational model:

$$(11) \qquad D(g_P^*) = \beta(g_P - g_P^*),$$

where $D(g_P^*)$ is the time derivative of g_P^*. This, of course, gives the usual exponentially weighted average of past price changes as an estimate of g_P^*, that is

$$(12) \qquad g_P^*(T) = \beta \int_{-\infty}^{T} e^{-\beta(T - T')} g_P^*(T') dT' ,$$

with a mean lag $= \dfrac{1}{\beta}$.[83]

---

83. This is the continuous version of the discontinuous form of footnote 74 above. The b of that footnote is equal to $1 - e^{-\beta}$, which, for small β, is approximately equal to β.

Differentiating equation (10) with these assumptions and adding a random disturbance term, we have

(13) $$D(R) = D(g_P^*) + \epsilon = \beta(g_P - g_P^*) + \epsilon.$$

Now let β be small, so anticipations are formed only gradually; that is, in the long moving average of imperfectly correlated terms that defines g_P^*, a long period of prior price change receives an appreciable weight. Such a moving average will tend to vary less than its elements, and the longer the moving average, the less variable it will be. As β approaches zero, g_P^* approaches the price level, which is nearly a constant by comparison with the rates of price change. Hence, the smaller β, the more will equation (13) be dominated by the term in g_P.[84]

---

84. The relative importance of the two terms in equation (13) depends on the relative variance of g_P and g_P^*. Assume that g_P^* has been expressed as a deviation from its expected value, so we can take it as having a mean of zero (this is equivalent to adding a constant to equation 11), then from equation 12,

(a) $$\sigma_{g_P^*}^2 = E[\beta \int_{-\infty}^T e^{-\beta(T-T')} g_P(T')dT'] [\beta \int_{-\infty}^T e^{-\beta(T-T'')} g_P(T'') dT'']$$
$$= \beta^2 \int_{-\infty}^T \int_{-\infty}^T e^{-\beta(T-T')-\beta(T-T'')} E[g_P(T')g_P(T'')] dT'dT'',$$

where E stands for expected value.

$E[g_P(T') g_P(T'')]$ is the covariance function. If $g_P(T')$ is a stationary time series, we can for $T' > T''$ write the covariance function as

(b) $$E[g_P(T') g_P(T'')] = \sigma_{g_P}^2 r(T' - T''),$$

where $r(T' - T'')$ is the correlogram giving the correlation coefficient between $g_P(T')$ and $g_P(T'')$ as a function of the interval between T' and T''. Note further that the double integral in equation (a), with limits running from $-\infty$ to T for both T' and T'' equals twice the integral over the half phase from $T' = -\infty$ to T, $T'' = -\infty$ to T,' thanks to the symmetry of the integral around $T' = T''$. Converting the double integral to twice the integral over the half phase, replacing $(T-T'')$ in the exponent of e by $(T-T' + T' - T'')$ and substituting equation (b) into equation (a) gives:

(c) $$\sigma_{g_P^*}^2 = 2\sigma_{g_P}^2\beta^2 \int_{-\infty}^T \int_{-\infty}^{T'} e^{-2\beta(T-T') - \beta(T'-T'')} r(T' - T'') dT''dT'.$$

Make the transformation:

$$T' = T'$$
$$\hat{T} = T' - T''$$
$$dT' dT'' = -dT' d\hat{T},$$

noting that $\hat{T}$ goes from $+\infty$ to 0 as T'' goes from $-\infty$ to T'. This gives

(d) $$\sigma_{g_P^*}^2 = 2\sigma_{g_P}^2 \beta^2 \int_{-\infty}^T \int_0^\infty e^{-2\beta(T-T') - \beta\hat{T}} r(\hat{T}) d\hat{T} dT',$$

or

(e) $$\sigma_{g_P^*}^2 = \sigma_{g_P}^2 [\beta \int_0^\infty e^{-\beta\hat{T}} r(\hat{T}) d\hat{T}][2\beta \int_{-\infty}^T e^{-2\beta(T-T')}dT'].$$

The second bracket is equal to unity. The first is a weighted average of the correlogram with exponentially declining weights summing to unity. Call this $\bar{r}(\beta)$. We then have

(f) $$\sigma_{g_P^*}^2 = \bar{r}(\beta)\sigma_{g_P}^2,$$

Since $r(\hat{T})$ is less than unity, so is $\bar{r}(\beta)$, hence $\sigma_{g_P^*}^2$ is less than $\sigma_{g_P}^2$ for all β. Moreover, so

At the extreme, if we suppose g_P^* to be roughly a constant, equation (13) is a linear relation between the rate of change of interest rates and the rate of change of prices. This is the mathematical translation, for a special case, of Fisher's explanation of the Gibson paradox.

Without going to this extreme, we can use equation (13) to construct an estimate of β. If the disturbance term ϵ is uncorrelated with g_P and g_P^*, the least-squares regressions of $D(R)$ on g_P and of g_P on $D(R)$ give upper and lower limits for β.[85]

These limits have some rather interesting properties. As β approaches zero, the percentage difference between β and the lower limit approaches zero, while both the percentage and the absolute difference between β

---

long as $r(\hat{T})$ declines on the average with $\hat{T}$ and approaches zero as $\hat{T}$ approaches infinity, $\bar{r}(\beta)$ will decline as β declines and approach zero as β approaches zero.

85. The expected value of the slope of the least-squares regression of $D(R)$ on g_P is given, to a first approximation, by

(g)
$$E\, b_{D(R)g_P} = \frac{E[D(R)\,g_P]}{E(g_P)^2} = \frac{\beta\, E[g_P - g_P^*]\, g_P + E\epsilon g_P}{\sigma^2_{g_P}},$$

where $D(R)$, g_P, and g_P^* are expressed as deviations from their mean values. If we assume that ϵ is uncorrelated with g_P, equation (g) reduces to

(h)
$$E\, b_{D(R)g_P} = \beta\, (1 - \frac{E g_P\, g_P^*}{\sigma^2_{g_P}}).$$

If we multiply g_p^* as given by equation (12) by g_P, take expected values, and replace $E\, g_P\, g_P^*$ by $r(T' - T'')\sigma^2_{g_P}$ from equation (b) of footnote 83, we have

(i)
$$E g_P\, g_P^* = \bar{r}(\beta)\, \sigma^2_{g_P} = \sigma^2_{g_P^*}$$

by equation (f). Substituting in equation (h)

(j)
$$E\, b_{D(R)g_P} = \beta[1 - \bar{r}(\beta)].$$

Since $\bar{r}(\beta)$ is necessarily less than unity,

(k)
$$E\, b_{D(R)g_P} < \beta.$$

Similarly, the expected value of the reciprocal of the slope of the least-squares regression of g_P on $D(R)$ is given to a first approximation by

(l)
$$E(\frac{1}{b_{g_P D(R)}}) = \frac{E[D\,(R)]^2}{E[\,D(R)\,g_P]} = \frac{\beta^2\, E[g_P - g_P^*]^2 + \sigma^2_\epsilon}{\beta\, \sigma^2_{g_P}\, [1 - \bar{r}(\beta)]},$$

where σ^2_ϵ is the variance of the random disturbance. Also

(m)
$$\begin{aligned} E[g_P - g_P^*]^2 &= \sigma^2_{g_P} + \boxed{\sigma^2_{g_P^*}} - 2E(g_P g_P^*) \\ &= \sigma^2_{g_P} + \bar{r}(\beta)\sigma^2_{g_P} - 2\bar{r}(\beta)\sigma^2_{g_P} \\ &= \sigma^2_{g_P}\, [1 - \bar{r}(\beta)], \end{aligned}$$

from equations (f) and (l). It follows that

(n)
$$E\, \frac{1}{b_{g_P D(R)}} = \beta[1 + \frac{\sigma^2_\epsilon}{\beta^2\sigma^2_{g_P}[1 - \bar{r}(\beta)\,]}\,] > \beta,$$

since both numerator and denominator of the fraction in the brackets are positive.

and the upper limit increase without limit. Hence, the lower β, the better the lower limit and the worse the upper limit as approximations. Another interesting property is that the lower limit is not affected by the size of the random disturbances in $D(R)$, while the upper limit is. The upper limit is a better approximation the smaller such random variation in R relative to the random variation in g_P, and it approaches β as the variance of R approaches zero relative to the variance of g_P.[86] From the earlier calculations in this chapter, it seems clear that recorded values of g_P have a much higher variance than recorded values of $D(R)$, which strongly suggests that the upper limit may prove a pretty good approximation to β.[87] Note that the upper limit for β gives the lower limit for the mean lag.

Table 10.8 gives the limits on β computed from the regressions of g_P on $D(R)$ and $D(R)$ on g_P. The results are reasonably satisfactory for the pre–World War I period, for which the Gibson phenomenon is most marked.[88] The limits are both farther apart and lower for the United States than for the United Kingdom. However, given the small number of degrees of freedom for the United Kingdom, the United States and United Kingdom limits do not differ significantly. Moreover, adding additional values of price change in the multiple correlation has almost no effect on the standard error of estimate for the United States—which is as it should be, since their only role is as proxies for g_P^* which, on the interpretation under discussion, is contributing little to the relation. The sharp reduction for the United Kingdom is meaningless, since including all the additional variables leaves only one degree of freedom.

The implied mean period of averaging of past price behavior is between five and twenty-five years for the United States, three and five

86. These statements follow directly from equations (j) and (n) of the preceding footnote, plus the fact that $\bar{r}(\beta)$ approaches zero as β approaches zero.

One other factor affecting the closeness of the limits to β is the serial correlation of g_P. The lower that correlation for each time interval between the items correlated, the lower is $\bar{r}(\beta)$ for each β and hence the closer the limits to one another and to β.

87. The standard deviations of $D(R)$ and g_P (in percentage points) are as follows for the three nonwar periods:

	United States		United Kingdom	
	$D(R)$	g_P	$D(R)$	g_P
Pre–World War I	0.18	1.87	0.10	0.37
Interwar	0.24	1.51	0.32	2.02
Post–World War II	0.21	1.44	0.26	2.58

Of course these standard deviations include systematic as well as random variation, and measurement error as well as random variation in the magnitude being measured, so they are only suggestive rather than conclusive. But the differences are so large and so consistent as to establish a strong presumption that the random variation in g_P as measured is very large compared with that in $D(R)$ as measured.

88. For the United States, the pre–World War I limits without adjustment for the free silver effect are .04 to .019. so that the adjustment has little effect.

Table 10.8 Estimates of β: Upper and Lower Estimates Based on Regressions between Rate of Change in Interest Rates and in Prices; Standard Errors of Estimate from Simple and Multiple Correlations (Percentage Points)

Period and Country	Number of Observations (1)	Limits on β — Lower (2)	Limits on β — Upper (3)	Standard Deviation of $D(R)$ (4)	Simple Regression $D(R)$ on g_P (5)	Standard Error of Estimate of $D(R)$ from $D(R)$ on $g_P(t), g_P(t-1), g_P(t-2), g_P(t-3)$ (6)
Pre–World War I						
United States [a]	18	0.04	0.22	.181	.167	.162
United Kingdom	6	0.21	0.37	.103	.076	.016
Interwar						
United States	7	0.10	0.25	.242	.201	.114
United Kingdom	7	(negative)		.319	.336	.123
Postwar						
United States	11	0.01	2.78	.206	.217	.188
United Kingdom	9	0.06	0.18	.255	.227	.289

[a] All calculations based on interest rate series adjusted for effect of free silver campaign on expectations by subtracting one percentage point from recorded interest rate, 1867 through 1896.

years for the United Kingdom. These intervals differ from Fisher's own estimates, which are shorter for the pre-1914 period for the United States (2.5 years), longer for the United Kingdom long rates for the pre-1914 period (7.3 for 1820–64, and 8.7 for 1865–97).

As we noted earlier, the lower relative variation in $D(R)$ than in g_P suggests that the upper estimate of β—which corresponds to the lower mean period—is the closer approximation to the true β. If so, that would suggest a mean period of about three years for the United Kingdom, five years for the United States, which is somewhat shorter than the mean period obtained earlier in our reanalysis of the annual data for the United States, 1881 to 1914. Certainly, periods of this length seem more plausible than the periods running two or three times as long that Fisher and others estimate for data spanning World War I.

For the interwar period, the United States results are very similar, again consistent with a mean period of four to ten years. However, for the United Kingdom, the slope of the regression is negative, which gives unacceptable results. For the postwar period, we again see the break we have repeatedly encountered in this chapter: for the United States, zero correlation between $D(R)$ and g_P; for the United Kingdom, a mild correlation, but one which gives a mean period of five to sixteen years.

For the pre–World War I period we have also used the phase averages to duplicate the calculations made earlier for the annual data from 1880 to 1914 for different weighting patterns. In these calculations, we have used the phase as the time unit and have converted the values of b equal to 0.10, 0.14, and 0.79 to corresponding values for phases by allowing for the average length of a phase.[89] The results are again that the longer average weighting patterns, corresponding to annual b's equal to 0.10 and 0.14, give higher correlations for the United States than the shorter weighting pattern derived by Sargent. For the United States it is striking also that for annual b's equal to 0.10 and 0.14 the correlation of the adjusted commercial paper rate with the expected rate of price change is higher than with the price level, thereby meeting one of Macaulay's objections. That is not true for the United Kingdom.[90]

89. Our procedure was first to calculate the value of β equivalent to each value of b, multiply the resultant values of β by the average length of a phase, and then convert back to b's. The resulting values of b are .186, .255, and .952 for the United States, .318, .422, and .997 for the United Kingdom.

In making these calculations, we used $g_P.A$ instead of g_P.

90. The correlations are as follows:

Correlation	Annual b		
	0.10	0.14	0.79
R and g_P^*			
United States (unadjusted)	.14	.11	− .32
United States (adjusted)	.72	.73	.43
United Kingdom	.42	.44	.47

All in all, the net result of these additional calculations is to reinforce our earlier suggestion that Fisher's hypothesis is plausible for the pre–World War I period, somewhat plausible for the interwar period, but not at all plausible for the post–World War II period.

10.7.2 The Wicksell-Keynes Explanation

Writing at the turn of the century, Knut Wicksell suggested that the parallel movement of prices and interest rates reflected long swings in the real yield on capital mediated through the commercial banking system. A rise, for example, in the productivity of capital would produce a rise in the demand for credit and in the "natural" rate of interest—the rate that would equate desired saving with desired investment in a situation of "monetary neutrality" or "monetary equilibrium," that is, without monetary creation. Faced with an increase in the demand for loanable funds, Wicksell argued, banks would expand their loans by creating money, letting the ratio of their liabilities to their reserves rise, and would only belatedly and sluggishly raise the rate of interest they charge. The "market" rate would respond to the increased demand, but too little and too late. The monetary expansion would raise prices; the reaction of banks would slow the rise in market interest rates but not prevent a rise from occurring, so that prices and interest rates would rise together. Some three decades later, Keynes suggested essentially the same explanation.[91]

Cagan has examined this hypothesis in detail for the United States. He found that changes in monetary growth primarily reflected changes in high-powered money rather than in bank-created money, as required by the Wicksell hypothesis. Lars Jonung has since carried out a similar analysis for Sweden. His conclusion is the same as Cagan's: the sources of changes in monetary growth are inconsistent with the Wicksell hypothesis.[92]

A different test of the Wicksell hypothesis can be made using our proxy for the real yield on capital. On the Wicksell hypothesis, the moving force in the whole process is the real yield on capital. Its fluctuations produce

---

R and P	
United States (unadjusted)	.54
United States (adjusted)	.64
United Kingdom	.72

91. For an excellent summary statement of this hypothesis, see Wicksell, "The Influence of the Rate of Interest on Prices." For Keynes's later presentation, see *A Treatise on Money*, 2: 182–84.

92. Phillip Cagan, *Determinants and Effects of Changes in the Stock of Money, 1875–1960* (New York: NBER, 1965), pp. 252–55; Lars Jonung, "Money and Prices in Sweden, 1732–1972," in *Inflation in the World Economy*, ed. J. M. Parkin and George Zis (Manchester: Manchester University Press, 1976), pp. 295–325.

parallel fluctuations in the price level and the nominal market rate. Accordingly, the Wicksell hypothesis implies a Gibson phenomenon for real and not merely nominal yields. Chart 10.21 and table 10.9 demonstrate that no such phenomenon exists either for our proxy for the real yield or for the ex-post real yield on short-term securities: with minor exceptions, there is a negligible correlation between the level of prices and the real yields, not only for the long periods for which, as we have seen, no nominal Gibson phenomenon exists, but also for the shorter subperiods. This test too therefore rejects the Wicksell hypothesis.

10.7.3   Other Real Explanations

The Wicksell hypothesis is a special case of a broader class of hypotheses that postulate common real disturbances that affect the price level and nominal interest rates in the same direction. Among others, Sargent has suggested an explanation of this class in the form of a specific hypothetical model of the economy.[93]

To illustrate such an explanation, consider the brief business cycles during which there is clearly a tendency for prices and interest rates to rise and fall together—indeed, in his discussion of the Gibson paradox Keynes referred to his initial belief, subsequently rejected, "that Mr. Gibson's surprising results were to be attributed to nothing more than the well-established and easily explained tendency of prices and interest to rise together on the upward phase of the credit cycle, and to fall together on the downward phase *plus* a gracious allowance of mere coincidence."[94]

Any theory of business cycles, be it a "real" theory relying on waves of optimism and pessimism à la Pigou, or bunchings of innovation à la Schumpeter, or an unstable investment function à la Keynes, or even Jevonian sunspots, or be it a monetary theory relying on fluctuations in monetary growth, could produce (1) a cyclical rise and fall in the demand for loanable funds relative to the supply of loanable funds and so a cyclical rise and fall in real and nominal interest rates; (2) a cyclical rise and fall in nominal income relative to permanent income and so a procyclical movement in measured velocity; (3) reinforcement of the movement in measured velocity by a reaction of the quantity of money demanded to the cyclical movement in interest rates; (4) a procyclical movement in monetary growth in reaction to the cyclical movement in the demand for loanable funds and in interest rates, which would reinforce the cyclical movement in nominal income, while damping somewhat the movement in interest rates and in velocity; and (5) a cyclical rise and fall in prices (or in prices relative to trend) as a result of the changes in

93. "Interest Rates and Prices in the Long Run." Sargent's model could indeed almost be regarded as a formal translation of Wicksell.
94. *Treatise*, 2: 177.

Table 10.9   **Tests of a Gibson Phenomenon for Real Yields**

Period and Country	Number of Observations		Correlation between Price Level and Real Yields	
	Col. 3 (1)	Col. 4 (2)	Proxy Real Yield on Physical Assets[a] (3)	Ex-Post Real Yield on Nominal Assets (4)
Pre–World War I				
United States	21	21	−0.20	0.13
United Kingdom	11	11	−0.36	0.47
Interwar				
United States	9	9	−0.08	0.52
United Kingdom	9	9	−0.68	0.33
Postwar				
United States	13	13	−0.36	0.45
United Kingdom	11	11	−0.04	−0.03
All excluding wars				
United States	43	43	−0.06	−0.42
United Kingdom	31	31	0.02	−0.37
All				
United States	49	49	−0.09	−0.32
United Kingdom	37	37	−0.02	−0.25

[a]$g_{y'}.A.$

nominal income. Items 1 and 5 together would produce the Gibson phenomenon of a positive correlation of interest rates and price levels, and it would produce it for both nominal and real rates—in sharp contrast to the Fisher interpretation, which posits such a correlation solely for nominal rates.

Actual experience during business cycles differs in important respects from this hypothetical sequence—notably in the empirical timing patterns of interest rates, monetary growth, and measured velocity, as well as in the apparent independence of monetary growth from interest rates—but it also has many similarities. In any event, the hypothetical sequence illustrates the kind of alternative hypothesis that Sargent and others suggest.

For the longer-period swings that are our concern, as for the cyclical fluctuations, there is no need for there to be a single source of real disturbances. All that is required is that real disturbances that tend to raise nominal interest rates should also tend to raise prices; and real disturbances that tend to raise prices should also tend to raise interest rates; or at least that one of these be correct and the other not reversed. The real forces could operate on prices and interest rates through any of a number of possible channels: on prices, through velocity or high-powered money or bank-created money or volume of output; on interest rates,

price level (ratio scale)   real rate of return (percent per year)

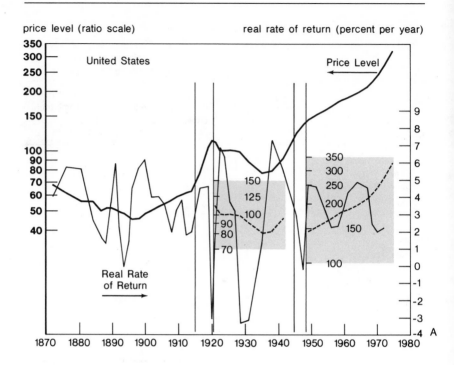

through the equilibrium real interest rate or preferences for nominal versus physical assets or preferences for nonhuman assets or the relative quantities of various kinds of assets.

However, the finding that there is apparently no real Gibson phenomenon for the longer swings (our correlations of phase bases give no evidence on the intracycle movement) rules out any such explanation that involves higher real returns along with prices. The real disturbances would have to operate by affecting the relation between nominal and real returns or in some other way be consistent with nominal but not real returns moving in the same direction as prices.

The only explicitly spelled-out hypothesis of this kind that we are aware of is one that was suggested by Macaulay some three decades ago and that has recently been formally developed by Siegel as reflecting distributional effects.[95] Siegel suggests that, if price rises are unanticipated they will tend to produce a transfer of wealth from lenders on fixed interest terms to borrowers on such terms—a phenomenon that we have certainly documented. He goes on to argue that this is a wealth transfer from risk-averse persons to risk-takers, which would tend to raise the

95. Macaulay, *Movements of Interest Rates*, pp. 206–8; Jeremy J. Siegel, "The Correlation between Interest and Prices: Explanations of the Gibson Paradox" (unpublished manuscript, University of Pennsylvania, 1975).

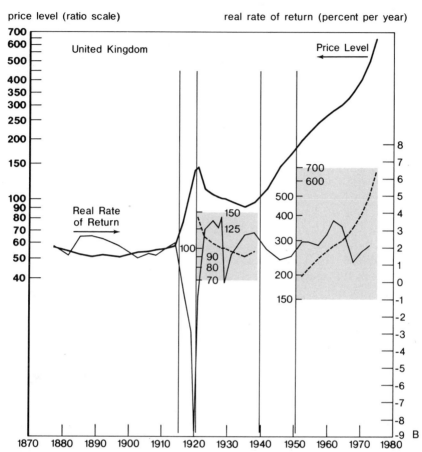

Chart 10.21   Price level and real rate of return on physical assets, United States and United Kingdom, 1870–1975.

differential between yields on securities attractive to the risk-averse and those attractive to risk-takers. If recorded nominal rates are rates on securities attractive to the risk-averse, the transfer could account for rising nominal interest rates along with rising prices.

This ingenious explanation is, however, not satisfactory without additional highly special assumptions. Why would this effect not simply produce an initial rise in the interest rate as the holders of nominal securities lose wealth and then a fall as they seek to restore their wealth and succeed in doing so? After all, the initial distribution of wealth is itself the result of an equilibrating process, not an accidental position. As in the Fisher explanation, there must be a coordination of various adjustments to produce the result to be explained. Throughout most of a price rise, it must continue to be unexpected, it must continue to transfer wealth cumulatively (in order that rates of interest keep on rising), and this cumulative transfer must not be offset by the saving adjustments of the risk-averse or the risk-takers or by the adjustment of interest rates to actual inflation.

A good deal more elaboration of this hypothesis and testing of its implications is required before it can be treated as more than an ingenious speculation.

10.7.4   Other Nominal Explanations

A more promising approach is to proceed along Fisher's lines of stressing the role of inflationary expectations but to alter his particular hypothesis about the formation of expectations and possibly to include an allowance for changing real returns on physical assets as well.[96] In effect, this is what we have done in our examination of the pre–World War I period for the United States by taking into account the effect of the free silver movement on expectations and in our treating World War I and World War II as special cases to be analyzed separately. It may be, however, that such a largely episodic interpretation can be replaced, or at least more fully supplemented, by a more formal model of the formation of expectations. The extensive studies along these lines of the post–World War II period may yet yield results that can be applied to the much longer pre–World War II period, though as yet they have not done so.

One feature of the strict Fisher expectations hypothesis that seems particularly objectionable in light of our empirical results—especially the failure of the Gibson phenomenon to hold over major wars—is the use of a single chronological time scale in converting past price experience to an estimate for the future. We have already had occasion to refer to Maurice Allais's perceptive distinction between chronological and psychological time to explain why it might be more appropriate to use the cycle phase rather than the year as our basic unit of time.[97] This is what we have done in using our phase average data to analyze the pre–World War I relations.

In the present context, however, a wider-ranging interpretation is called for. In judging the future, participants look back for past evidence

96. John Rutledge, "Irving Fisher and Autoregressive Expectations" (*American Economic Review Proceedings* 67 [February 1977]: 200–205) argues that Fisher included changes in real rates as part of his analysis, and Sargent makes a similar point (*Quarterly Journal of Economics* 86 [May 1972]: 224–25). Both are correct but the role is played primarily by changes in the ex-post real yield on nominal assets rather than by changes in either the ex-ante real yield on nominal assets or the ex-ante or ex-post real yield on physical assets. The latter do play a minor role in Fisher's analysis, but primarily in his analysis of cyclical fluctuations rather than of Gibson swings, which are the real puzzle. Of course he makes qualitative remarks that indicate his recognition of the existence of variability in real returns of all kinds, and he stresses over and over the variability of ex-post real returns on nominal assets, since they play, explicitly or implicitly, a crucial role in his analysis both of the cycle and of the Gibson swings. See note 48 above.

97. See chap. 8, n. 17.

that they regard most relevant to the current situation. That may involve a very different retrospective time span at different times. Much of the time it may involve looking back at a comparable stage of the business cycle—that is the rationalization for using the cycle phase as a basic time unit. But on some occasions that will not be relevant. For example, consider the situation in the United States after World War II. According to the first available Livingston forecasts, dated June 1947, the average forecast for the succeeding eighteen months was for declining prices at the rate of 5.8 percent per year for the consumer price index and of 8.7 percent per year for the wholesale price index, and the eighteen-month forecasts stayed negative, though smaller in magnitude, until the Korean War broke out in 1950.[98] Actual prices dipped briefly in 1949 and early 1950, but at nothing like the forecast rate. This expectation of deflation, which was surely widespread, was obviously not based on any simple weighted average of immediately prior rates of inflation—any such average would have led to a forecast of inflation. And it would have been most unreasonable to use any such average. Wars are highly unusual events known to be episodic. It was natural for participants to look back at what had occurred after past wars: the war of 1812, the Civil War, and the First World War. In each case the wartime inflation had been followed by a postwar deflation that ultimately brought the level of prices back to roughly its prewar level. It was not unreasonable to extrapolate that experience, even though that involved averaging experience covering roughly 150 years.

This example involves a process of formation of anticipations that is in the spirit of Fisher's model but cannot be confined within its fixed mechanical structure. Similarly, in allowing for the Great Depression it would have been reasonable for participants to revert back to other major cyclical contractions rather than to use an unchanging past time scale.

10.8   The Structural Change in the 1960s

Whether or not a more adequate explanation is developed for the Gibson paradox than Fisher's supplemented by episodic events, there remains the problem of accounting for the apparent difference between pre–World War II relations and postwar relations, particularly after the mid-1960s, when the Gibson relation largely disappears and is replaced by a close relation between interest rates and the rate of change of prices.

An extremely appealing explanation of the difference has been offered in an important paper by Benjamin Klein.[99]

98. Carlson, "A Study of Price Forecasts," table 1, p. 33, table 2, p. 35.
99. "Our New Monetary Standard: The Measurement and Effects of Price Uncertainty, 1880–1973," *Economic Inquiry* 13 (December 1975): 461–83. Klein has recalculated his measures of short- and long-term price unpredictability in "The Measurement of Long- and

Klein argues that there has been a fundamental change in the character of the monetary system since World War II, that before World War II, and to a lesser extent to the end of World War II, the United States and the United Kingdom were regarded as being on specie standards which limited the price *level*. Prices might rise or fall over short periods, but the price level was widely expected to revert to a roughly constant level, and it did. The price level in the United Kingdom in 1912 was roughly the same as in 1729—so far as it can be measured over such long periods. After the World War I rise, it again reverted to its prewar level by 1931 or 1932 and was lower than it had been during most of the nineteenth century.[100] In the United States wholesale prices were at roughly the same level in 1914 and in 1790 and, again after more than doubling during World War I, had reverted to their 1790 level by 1932.[101] Under this system, Klein argues, there was considerable short-term unpredictability of prices but much less long-term unpredictability. Current rates of price change contained little information about future rates of price change. On the other hand, the level of prices did contain such information. A price level that was high relative to "normal" implied a subsequent decline in prices and conversely.

In the post–World War II period, short-term unpredictability of price change, Klein points out, has been less than earlier. However, there is no longer a specie anchor to the price system. The monetary system is strictly fiduciary. There is no widespread anticipation that the price level will revert to any "normal" level; it (or perhaps its derivative) is now nearly of the nature of a random walk, perhaps with drift. Current rates of price change contain information about future rates of price change. It is rational to take this information into account, and interest rates now respond to recent rates of price change as they did not do before.

This analysis is highly plausible as an explanation for the change after World War II. Before World War I, and to a lesser extent in most of the interwar period, the government's role in the economy in both the United States and the United Kingdom was relatively minor and certainly did not include, and was not perceived to include, the kind of attempt at fine-tuning the economy that we have become so familiar with in recent decades. At most, government's role was to step in at time of crisis or panic and to administer a specie system. The sources of inflation or deflation were largely international and were mostly acts of God rather

Short-Term Price Uncertainty: A Moving Regression Analysis," *Economic Inquiry* 16 (July 1978): 438–52; see also I. B. Ibrahim and R. M. Williams, "The Fisher Relationship under Different Monetary Standards," *Journal of Money, Credit and Banking* 10 (August 1978): 363–70.

100. For a long-term United Kingdom price series, see Shiller and Siegel, "The Gibson Paradox," fig. 1.

101. Based on Warren and Pearson and BLS index numbers.

than deliberate acts of men. The basic institutions were highly stable, so it made sense to take a long view, and there was no easy way to predict the short-run or intermediate-run fluctuations of the price level. Given the physical or at least nondeliberate character of most of the forces producing such fluctuations, it made sense for participants to extrapolate the past along Fisher's lines. And, given the large degree of random fluctuation and the meagerness and inaccuracy of the available data, it made sense to base extrapolations on a fairly long past period.[102] The Fisher hypothesis, or some variation of it, plus allowance for special events—such as the free silver campaign in the United States or the Boer War in the United Kingdom—plus a good deal of random perturbation plus confidence in the long-run stability of the monetary system and the price level could explain reasonably well the greater short-run stability in the nominal yield than in the ex-post real yield, as well as the systematic covariation of the nominal yield with the longer swings in the price level.

Beginning with the Great Depression, the situation changed drastically. Government began to accept responsibility for the short-term movements in the economy. World War II interrupted the process and doubtless postponed the incorporation of the new role of government into the performance of financial markets. After the war there was a transitional period of adjustment to wartime distortions. In addition, there was widespread anticipation of a repetition of prior postwar experience, namely, a sharp decline in the price level and a severe recession or depression. These anticipations dominated the market for more than a decade after the war, producing the expectation of price decline despite the experience of gradual inflation. The result was low nominal interest rates and negative ex-post real yields—the mirror image of the situation in the decade preceding 1896, when expectations of inflation coincided with the actuality of deflation and produced high nominal rates and ex-post real yields.

By the mid- or late 1950s, the participants in the market were adjusting to the new circumstances, along the lines outlined by Klein. They came to regard the price level and the level of economic activity as largely affected by government authorities, and they saw the specie standard as a histori-

102. We should note that we are here departing from Klein's specific formulation because it is not consistent with the Gibson phenomenon. If the public based its anticipation of price movements on the relation between the current level of prices and some independently estimated "normal" level, as Klein implies, then it should have interpreted high prices as implying a subsequent decline. But this would mean low nominal interest rates when prices were high and high nominal rates when prices were low—precisely the reverse of the observed positive Gibson correlation. Alternatively, if the public took the current price level as its best estimate of the "normal" level, that would imply that it took the anticipated rate of price change as equal to zero at all times. Such anticipations would produce a zero correlation between prices and interest rates, not the observed positive Gibson correlation.

cal relic. The final explicit step in this transformation did not occur until the formal severing of the United States link with gold in 1971 and the explicit adoption of a floating exchange rate system in 1973 and thereafter. But the postwar devaluations and revaluations of many currencies, together with the obvious primacy of domestic considerations in the formulation of government economic policy in essentially all countries, affected attitudes long before this final step.

These changes in institutional arrangements made it easier to predict short-term movements at the same time that, as Klein emphasizes, they increased long-term uncertainty. They were also accompanied by improvements in statistics and in methods of analyzing data—as evidenced particularly by the explosive growth of the short-term economic forecasting industry—and in the sophistication and breadth of financial markets. All this appreciably shortened the horizon of market participants and increased their ability to make short-term projections. Simultaneously, the incentive to make such projections and to embody them in financial decisions was increased by the rise in the rate of inflation to levels seldom experienced before in the peacetime experience of the United States and the United Kingdom and by the considerable variation in the rate of inflation over periods of several years. The net result has apparently been to replace the long-term Gibson phenomenon with the short-term direct Fisher relation between nominal rates and price change. Whether this is a permanent or a temporary change is hard to judge. Presumably that depends in part on whether high rates of inflation, and substantial variation in rates of inflation, persist.

One further element has encouraged the switch to the short-term Fisher relation and perhaps has made it seem more complete than it really is. That element is the high marginal tax rates levied on nominal yields. As we saw in section 10.1.1 under "Price Anticipation Effect," the effect of such taxation is to widen substantially the margin between the nominal rate and the real rate required to keep unchanged the net real after-tax yield to the lender. Some studies of the relation between nominal and real rates that have concluded that nominal rates have fully adjusted to inflation have neglected this tax effect.[103] What they take to be a full adjustment is therefore less than full. For the United States, most long-term bonds are apparently held by institutions not subject to tax on the interest return (e.g., pension funds, insurance companies, tax-exempt institutions). However, an appreciable fraction appears to be held by taxable individuals. To judge from the differential return on taxable and tax-exempt securities, the relevant marginal tax rate is over one-third.[104] If such a tax rate had applied in the United States during all nonwar

103. E.g., Fama, "Short-term Interest Rates as Predictors of Inflation."

104. In December 1979 the yield on corporate triple Aaa bonds was 10.74, on long-term Treasury securities, 10.07, both taxable; on state and local Aaa bonds, exempt from federal taxes, 6.50, equivalent to a marginal tax rate of 35 percent compared with Treasury

Table 10.10   **Nominal Rates of Interest Required, at Inflations of 6 or 10 Percent, to Yield Average Ex-Post after-Tax Real Yields Recorded in Table 10.1**

	Rate of Inflation			
	6 Percent		10 Percent	
	All Phases	All Nonwar Phases	All Phases	All Nonwar Phases
United States				
Commercial paper	12.9	14.7	18.9	20.7
Corporate bonds	13.9	15.6	19.9	21.6
United Kingdom				
Banker bills	10.3	12.8	16.3	18.8
Consols	11.5	13.7	17.5	19.7

phases averaged in table 10.1, the ex-post after-tax real short-term yield would have been 2.3 percent instead of the 3.8 percent recorded there without allowing for the effect of taxation, and the ex-post real long-term yield would have been 2.7 instead of 4.4. To obtain the ex-post after-tax real yields in table 10.1 with a 6 percent inflation and with a 10 percent inflation for a hypothetical marginal tax rate of one-third would require the nominal rates shown in table 10.10.

Actual commercial paper rates in the United States exceeded 11 percent only briefly in 1974 when the contemporaneous recorded inflation rate was running over 10 percent for consumer prices. At about the same time corporate bond rates hit a peak of only a bit over 9 percent. In the United Kingdom the short-term rate hit a peak of a bit over 14 percent in early 1974, a year in which the average rate of inflation was over 20 percent for consumer prices and the long-term rate a peak of 17.4 percent. Clearly, interest rates did not adjust anything like fully to recent rates of inflation, once the tax effect is taken into account. As in earlier periods, much of the inflation must be regarded as unanticipated, so that lenders have received real returns lower than the real yield on capital. The difference from earlier periods is twofold. There has apparently been a greater relative adjustment to inflation than in earlier periods. And governments in their capacities as borrowers have benefited to a larger extent than in earlier episodes from the transfer of wealth from lenders to borrowers.

We are still clearly in a transition that has not yet been completed and may never be.[105]

securities, of 39 percent compared with corporate securities. These differentials are not atypical for recent years.

105. Even in 1980, after the end of our period, interest rates did not adjust anything like fully to inflation, if taxes at a marginal rate of one-third are allowed for. In the United States, the commercial paper rate hit a peak of over 16 percent, when inflation, as measured by the Consumer Price Index, averaged 13 percent; in the United Kingdom, the short-term rate hit

10.9   Correlations with Money

This long detour through price effects may seem a digression from the explicit subject of this chapter—money and interest rates. It is not. The impact effects via liquidity and loanable funds, and the intermediate effects via income, described in the initial theoretical analysis, can be expected to be most important within cycles and largely to average out for our cycle phases. That leaves the price effect as the major one for our purpose. The long-term effect of money on interest rates can therefore be analyzed best by considering the effect of money on prices—as we did in chapter 9—and then of prices on interest rates, as we have done in this chapter.

10.9.1   Impact and Intermediate Effects

Something of a check on these statements is provided by tables 10.11 and 10.12, which give correlations between money and interest rates relevant to the impact and intermediate effects, and table 10.13, which gives correlations relevant to the price effect.

The liquidity impact effect would tend to produce a negative correlation between R (the interest rate) and M (the stock of money) or between $D(R)$ (the rate of change of the interest rate) and g_M (the rate of change of the stock of money). The simple correlations in column 3 between R and M (table 10.11) and $D(R)$ and g_M (table 10.12) give little evidence of any liquidity effect. Only two of the ten correlations between R and M, and also between $D(R)$ and g_M, are negative, and the largest absolute correlations are all positive. Clearly the Gibson effect—which would produce positive correlations—has overwhelmed any liquidity effect for periods as long as our phases.[106]

The loanable funds impact effect would produce negative correlations between R and g_M, and between $D(R)$ and $D(g_M)$ (the acceleration of the stock of money). The simple correlations in column 4 show only a little stronger evidence of the loanable funds effect than those in column 3 do of the liquidity effect: three of the ten correlations between R and g_M, and also between $D(R)$ and $D(g_M)$ are negative, but this time one of the negative correlations is numerically the largest.[107]

---

a peak of a trifle over 18 percent when retail prices were rising at a rate in excess of 20 percent.

106. For the United States, for the pre–World War I period, we have computed all the correlations in tables 10.11 and 10.12 also for interest rates not adjusted for the effect of free silver. The results differ only trivially from those in the tables.

107. In an interesting paper that analyzes the relation between monetary policy and long-term interest rates using United States quarterly data for 1954–76, Frederic S. Mishkin finds little or no evidence of the impact effect, which suggests that, for that period, our failure to uncover it may not simply reflect our use of phase averages but may correspond to the impact effect's small or negligible size even for periods as short as a quarter. That

Table 10.11   Measures of Impact and Intermediate Income Effects: Correlations of Levels of Interest Rates with Money and Trend

| Period and Country | Number of Observations | | Simple Correlation | | Multiple Correlation with M and g_M | | | | | Multiple Correlation with M, g_M, and Trend | | | | | | | |
	Col.3 (1)	Other Cols. (2)	M (3)	g_M (4)	M Coefficient (5)	M t Value (6)	g_M Coefficient (7)	g_M t Value (8)	Corrected R^2 (9)	M Corrected Coefficient (10)	M t Value (11)	g_M Coefficient (12)	g_M t Value (13)	Trend Coefficient (14)	Trend t Value (15)	Corrected R^2 (16)
Pre–World War I[a]																
United States	21	21	.40	.48	0.002	0.7	0.078	1.5	.17	0.030	3.4	0.089	2.0	−0.001	−3.3	.46
United Kingdom	11	10	.39	.20	0.011	1.2	−0.042	−0.3	−.01	−0.051	−0.7	−0.012	−0.1	0.001	0.9	−.05
Interwar																
United States	9	9	.44	−.13	0.065	1.3	−0.079	−0.5	−.03	0.028	2.0	−0.099	−2.6	−0.003	−9.2	.93
United Kingdom	9	9	−.24	−.69	−0.035	−0.8	−0.374	−2.4	.36	0.034	1.0	0.831	2.3	−0.008	−3.4	.77
Postwar																
United States	13	12	.95	.59	0.036	6.5	0.056	0.4	.86	0.021	0.5	0.048	0.3	0.001	0.3	.84
United Kingdom	11	10	.96	.56	0.056	5.9	−0.090	−1.0	.85	0.026	0.6	−0.066	−0.6	0.002	0.8	.84
All, excluding wars																
United States	43	42	.09	.18	−0.001	−0.6	0.082	1.3	−.01	0.035	4.2	0.077	1.4	−0.002	−4.3	.30
United Kingdom	31	29	.70	.39	0.009	3.6	0.014	0.2	.39	0.038	3.5	0.006	0.8	−0.001	−2.7	.51
All																
United States	49	48	−.02	−.15	−0.001	−0.6	−0.043	−0.8	−.01	0.042	4.8	−0.026	−0.6	−0.002	−4.9	.33
United Kingdom	37	35	.52	.14	0.008	2.6	−0.019	−0.3	.13	0.042	3.4	−0.019	−0.3	−0.001	−2.8	.29

[a]For the pre–World War I period, the United States rate of interest was adjusted for the effect of free silver by subtracting one percentage point from the recorded rates, 1879–96.

Table 10.12   Measures of Impact and Intermediate Income Effects: Correlations of Rates of Change of Interest Rates with Rate of Change of Money and Trend

| Period and Country | Number of Observations | | Simple Correlation | | Multiple Correlation with g_M and $D(g_M)$, Nonzero Intercept | | | | |
	Col. 3 (1)	Other Cols. (2)	g_M (3)	$D(g_M)$ (4)	g_M Coefficient (5)	g_M t Value (6)	$D(g_M)$ Coefficient (7)	$D(g_M)$ t Value (8)	Corrected R^2 (9)
Pre–World War I									
United States[a]	19	19	.56	.42	0.037	2.5	0.046	1.6	.33
United Kingdom	9	8	−.13	−.79	−0.045	−1.1	−0.302	2.6	.56
Interwar									
United States	7	7	.51	−.26	0.051	2.7	−0.088	−2.3	.51
United Kingdom	7	7	−.51	.32	−0.063	−1.0	0.109	0.4	−.06
Postwar									
United States	11	11	.23	−.26	0.052	1.1	−0.148	−1.2	−.01
United Kingdom	9	9	.62	.49	0.068	1.4	−0.128	−0.6	.23
All, excluding wars									
United States	37	37	.77	.13	0.066	7.5	−0.053	−1.9	.61
United Kingdom	25	24	.51	.13	0.069	2.9	−0.130	−1.1	.23
All									
United States	47	47	.57	.04	0.038	5.2	−0.041	−1.8	.35
United Kingdom	35	34	.35	.20	0.022	1.7	0.015	0.4	.06

[a]For the pre–World War I period, the United States rate of interest was adjusted for the effect of free silver by subtracting one percentage point from the recorded rates, 1879–96.

The intermediate-term income effect would produce positive correlations between R and g_M, and $D(R)$ and $D(g_M)$, thus offsetting the negative impact of the loanable funds impact effect. Clearly, the intermediate income effect too is not strongly reflected in the contemporaneous correlations of tables 10.11 and 10.12. Neither is it strongly reflected in other correlations (not shown in the table) that allow for a lag in effect. The most one can say is that perhaps the intermediate income effect and the loanable funds impact effect are largely offsetting one another in our phase average data, with sometimes one and sometimes the other dominating, thereby producing mixed signs and small correlations. But there is no direct support for that interpretation.

The multiple correlations are an attempt to allow simultaneously for the various effects, instead of considering them one at a time. The coefficient of M in the correlation with R reflects the liquidity effect, and the coefficient of g_M reflects the loanable funds effect, as perhaps offset by the intermediate income effect. Similarly in the correlation with $D(R)$, the coefficient of g_M reflects the liquidity effect, the coefficient of $D(g_M)$, the mixed loanable funds and income effects. These multiple correlations, like the simple correlations, show only muted reflections of the impact and intermediate effects, though there are more negative coefficients—three out of ten for M and six out of ten for g_M in the correlations with R; two out of ten for g_M and seven out of ten for $D(g_M)$ in the correlations with $D(R)$—and several of the negative coefficients differ significantly from zero.

As a further bit of evidence, in the correlations with R for the subperiods, we have also included a time term to correct for trend. These correlations give little evidence of an appreciable liquidity or loanable funds effect—only one of the ten coefficients of M is negative, and only five of the ten coefficients of g_M, and only one of these six negative coefficients differs significantly from zero. The generally positive coefficients presumably reflect the long-term price effect. Only the correlations with $D(R)$ give any appreciable evidence of any other effect, and those support only a loanable funds effect.

All in all, these results suggest that our phases are long enough so that averages for them show at most strongly damped impact and intermediate effects and are dominated by the price effects.

---

conclusion fits in well with the emergence of the Fisher effect as dominating the Gibson effect in the later post–World War II period, that is, with the importance of the effect of monetary changes on anticipations. However, for that very reason, Mishkin's result cannot confidently be generalized to earlier periods when the Gibson effect was more important than the Fisher effect ("Monetary Policy and Long-Term Interest Rates: An Efficient Markets Approach," *Journal of Monetary Economics* 7 [January 1981]: 29–55).

Table 10.13　　**Relation of Interest Rates to Current and Prior Monetary and Price Change**

Period and Country	Number of Observations (1)	Standard Deviation of Interest Rate (Percentage Points)		
			Residual Multiple Correlation	
		Total (2)	g_M (3)	g_P (4)
Pre–World War I				
United States (unadjusted)	19	0.494	0.538	0.540
United States (adjusted)	19	0.592	0.377	0.449
United Kingdom	6	0.561	0.458	0.615
Interwar				
United States	7	1.575	0.592	1.340
United Kingdom	7	1.533	1.060	0.994
Postwar				
United States	11	1.765	1.080	0.831
United Kingdom	9	1.733	0.983	0.950
All, excluding wars, Dummies for subperiods				
United States (unadjusted)	37	1.332	1.160	1.270
United States (adjusted)	37	1.273	1.050	1.170
United Kingdom	22	1.786	1.180	1.280
All, excluding wars				
United States (unadjusted)	37	1.332	1.220	1.350
United States (adjusted)	37	1.273	1.070	1.230
United Kingdom	22	1.786	1.540	1.340
All Dummies for subperiods				
United States (unadjusted)	47	1.707	1.110	1.180
United States (adjusted)	47	1.638	1.070	1.140
United Kingdom	32	1.916	1.250	1.280
All				
United States (unadjusted)	47	1.707	1.670	1.700
United States (adjusted)	47	1.638	1.580	1.600
United Kingdom	32	1.916	2.010	1.910

10.9.2　Price Effects

To supplement our earlier analysis of price effects we have calculated the correlation between the level of interest rates and current and prior rates of change of both money and prices (table 10.13). It is not at all clear a priori which of these correlations should give a better relation. If the secular movement of interest rates is dominated by the price effect of

	Money					Prices			
Constant Term (Percentage Points) (5)	Coefficient				Constant Term (Percentage Points) (10)	Coefficient			
	$g_{M(t)}$ (6)	$g_{M(t-1)}$ (7)	$g_{M(t-2)}$ (8)	$g_{M(t-3)}$ (9)		$g_{P(t)}$ (11)	$g_{P(t-1)}$ (12)	$g_{P(t-2)}$ (13)	$g_{P(t-3)}$ (14)
4.726	−0.001	−0.030	0.064	−0.000	4.854	−0.049	−0.038	0.021	0.059
3.431	0.117	−0.017	0.110	0.017	4.301	0.108	0.044	0.046	0.073
1.836	0.608	−0.987	0.594	0.368	3.133	−0.779	0.682	−0.057	0.592
2.361	−0.046	0.298	0.011	0.244	5.655	0.054	0.860	0.023	0.383
4.546	−0.934	−0.047	0.054	−0.334	1.104	−2.585	1.287	−0.509	0.042
−0.819	1.190	−1.155	1.169	−0.345	2.981	0.831	0.513	−0.974	−0.065
7.240	0.435	−0.401	0.136	−0.639	7.851	1.275	−2.173	1.420	−1.299
4.028	0.090	−0.029	0.245	0.093	4.815	0.206	−0.107	0.194	−0.086
3.087	0.152	−0.040	0.297	−0.090	4.283	0.298	−0.048	0.222	−0.056
3.629	0.535	−0.950	0.294	−0.301	2.640	0.867	−0.994	0.111	−0.149
3.887	0.065	−0.019	0.235	−0.145	4.326	0.157	−0.135	0.203	−0.174
3.244	0.113	−0.052	0.287	−0.121	3.986	0.211	−0.125	0.213	−0.129
2.744	0.504	−0.393	0.253	−0.065	2.982	0.796	−0.503	0.074	0.019
4.388	0.038	−0.031	0.201	−0.088	4.865	0.024	−0.051	0.227	−0.088
3.547	0.085	−0.036	0.232	−0.082	4.339	0.096	−0.050	0.272	−0.074
2.781	0.114	−0.242	0.285	−0.146	2.790	−0.004	0.112	−0.056	0.066
3.915	−0.122	0.078	0.041	0.041	4.042	−0.171	0.126	0.029	0.052
3.353	−0.075	0.061	0.067	0.060	3.717	−0.115	0.108	0.053	0.081
2.852	0.018	−0.110	0.071	0.046	2.866	0.028	0.118	−0.066	0.148

monetary changes and if some version of Fisher's interpretation of how price anticipations are formed is accepted, then one might expect the price correlations to be closer, on the argument that factors other than money affect price movements and that such price movements should have the same effect on interest rates as price movements reflecting monetary change. On the other hand, the price series very likely are subject to greater measurement errors than the monetary series, and monetary changes can be expected to affect interest rates through the impact and intermediate effects, not only the price effects. On these grounds one might expect the monetary correlations to be higher.

The empirical comparison of the two multiple correlations in table 10.13 is hindered by the small number of degrees of freedom available for many of the computations for subperiods. Given that five constants are fitted, only one degree of freedom remains for the United Kingdom for the prewar period, only two for the interwar period for both countries and four for the post–World War II period for the United Kingdom, and only six for the United States for the post–World War II period. The period as a whole, both excluding and including war phases, provides more degrees of freedom but is unsatisfactory because of the significant differences among the periods. Accordingly, we have computed additional correlations for the period as a whole including dummies to allow for differences in the level of the interest rate in different periods.

For the three key nonwar periods separately, four of the money correlations (including all three for the pre–World War I period) are superior to the price correlations and three are inferior, as shown by the residual standard errors in columns 3 and 4.

All the results for the combined periods for both the United States and the United Kingdom, when dummies are included, yield a lower residual standard error for the money than for the price correlations, though some of the differences are small. When dummies are not included, that is also the result for the United States; but for the United Kingdom the residual standard error is lower for the price correlations.

For the prewar period we have given correlations for the United States for the original interest rate and also for the interest rate adjusted for the free silver effect by subtracting one percentage point from values for years before 1897. The adjusted results are markedly superior, and we may concentrate our attention on them.

Given the small number of degrees of freedom and the paucity of individual regression coefficients that differ significantly from zero, little confidence can be attached to the time pattern of coefficients. Somewhat, though not much, more can be attached to their sum. Moreover, theory indicates that in principle their sum, if enough terms are included, should approximate unity: that is, an indefinitely continued increase of one percentage point per year in the rate of monetary growth will tend ultimately to add one percentage point to the rate of price increase; and a one percentage point higher rate of price increase will tend to widen the difference between the nominal and real interest rates by one percentage point and, if the real interest rate is unaffected (the qualification that accounts for the "approximate" before unity), to raise the nominal interest rate by unity.

Table 10.14   **Combined Effect of Current and Past Price and Monetary Changes and Estimate of Real Interest Rate**

Period and Country	Estimate of Real Interest Rate from Correlation with		Sum of Coefficients of Current and Past	
	Money (1)	Prices (2)	Money (3)	Prices (4)
Pre–World War I				
United States (unadjusted)	4.73	4.85	0.03	−0.01
United States (adjusted)	3.44	4.30	0.23	0.27
United Kingdom	1.85	3.13	0.58	0.44
Interwar				
United States	2.37	5.66	0.51	1.32
United Kingdom	4.51	1.10	−1.26	−1.76
Postwar				
United States	−0.79	2.98	0.86	0.31
United Kingdom	7.23	7.85	−0.47	−0.78
All, excluding wars, dummies				
United States (unadjusted)	4.03	4.82	0.21	0.21
United States (adjusted)	3.10	4.28	0.32	0.42
United Kingdom	3.62	2.64	−0.42	−0.16
All, excluding wars				
United States (unadjusted)	3.89	4.33	0.14	0.05
United States (adjusted)	3.25	3.99	0.23	0.17
United Kingdom	2.75	2.98	0.30	0.39
All, dummies				
United States (unadjusted)	4.39	4.86	0.12	0.11
United States (adjusted)	3.55	4.34	0.20	0.24
United Kingdom	2.78	2.79	0.01	0.12
All				
United States (unadjusted)	3.92	4.04	0.04	0.04
United States (adjusted)	3.36	3.72	0.11	0.13
United Kingdom	2.85	2.87	0.13	0.23

As table 10.14 shows, the sum of the coefficients for money is between zero and unity for the United States throughout, but for the United Kingdom this is true only before World War I. However, these sums are decidedly short of unity.[108] For the three nonwar periods combined, and for the adjusted United States interest rate, the sum is less than one-third; for the United Kingdom for the pre–World War I period alone it is less than .6. The shortfall from unity may reflect the inability to include more terms. More likely, it reflects our inability to allow for many other factors affecting interest rates, which produce a downward bias in the regression coefficients arising from error in the estimates of both monetary change

108. This contrasts sharply with Harley's results. He finds the effect to be unity for the United Kingdom before World War I ("Interest Rate and Prices in Britain," p. 77).

and interest rates and from correlated disturbances. For prices the results are even less satisfactory.

We can also use the equations to estimate the interest rate that would result if price change were zero: the ex-ante "real" interest rate implied by these equations. For the price equations, this estimate is given directly by the constant term, because that is the value corresponding to all rates of price change being zero. For the money equations, the estimate requires inserting in the equations the rate of monetary change that could be expected to produce a zero price rise. We have estimated this for each period and country by assuming a real per capita income elasticity of 1.1 for the United States and 0.9 for the United Kingdom, which are roughly the values suggested by the results of chapter 6.[109] Inserting the resultant value of monetary change in the multiple regression provides the estimates in column 1 of table 10.14.

The estimates for the subperiods are highly erratic, a reflection of the small number of observations. In particular, the drastic rise from period to period in the real return for the United Kingdom, as estimated from the money equations, seems implausible. For all nonwar periods, as a whole, the results seem much more reasonable and much more in line with the ex-post real returns as recorded in table 10.1, as the summary in table 10.15 indicates.

For the three periods combined, the estimated ex-ante real returns are generally a bit higher than the average realized real rates, implying that on the average the realized rates were affected more by unanticipated inflation than by unanticipated deflation.

10.10   Conclusion

A well-developed theory reveals the complexity of the relation between monetary change and nominal interest rates. In the first place, the impact effect of unanticipated accelerations or decelerations of monetary growth is in the opposite direction from the intermediate and long-range effects. Second, part of the impact effect produces an abrupt shift in the interest rate (the loanable funds effect) while another produces a continuing movement (the liquidity effect). Third, the magnitude and time span of both impact effects depend critically on how rapidly anticipations adjust, and on the extent to which changes in nominal income take the form of changes in output and in prices—about which, as we saw in

109. That is, we have multiplied the rate of change of per capita real income by 1.1 or 0.9, then added the rate of population growth to get the rate of monetary change consistent with zero price rise. For the United States, the monetary figures used in computing the multiple correlations were already adjusted for the period before 1903 for increasing financial sophistication. For both the United States and the United Kingdom the money figures have been adjusted for dummy variables, as explained in chapter 8.

Table 10.15   **Estimated Real Return on Nominal and Physical Assets, Ex-Post and Ex-Ante, All Nonwar Periods**

Period and Country	Estimated Real Return			
	Ex-Post (Table 10.1)		Ex-Ante (Table 10.14)	
	Nominal Assets	Physical Assets	Money Equation	Price Equation
All nonwar				
United States (unadjusted)	3.83	2.90	3.89	4.33
United States (adjusted)			3.25	3.99
United Kingdom	2.54	1.94	2.75	2.98

chapters 2 and 9, we have neither a well-developed, agreed-on theory nor any soundly based and simple empirical generalizations. Such changes in output and prices are the prime source of the intermediate and long-range effects. Fourth, although the intermediate effects tend to offset and ultimately completely cancel the impact effects, in the process there are good grounds for expecting overshooting that produces a cyclical reaction pattern of interest rates to monetary disturbances. Finally, the long-range effect operates through price expectations, and these in turn are affected by monetary disturbances that raise or lower the rate of monetary growth for long periods at a time and so leave their impress on price movements, or monetary disturbances that it is widely believed will have this effect even if they do not in fact—a case that is well exemplified by United States experience during the free silver movement of the nineteenth century. Anticipations of inflation will, perhaps later rather than sooner, make for high nominal interest rates, and anticipations of deflation, for lower ones.

Unfortunately, there is no equally well developed theory of the effect of real disturbances on nominal interest rates. We know of course that changes that raise the real yield on capital will tend to raise nominal rates and conversely. But beyond this we have no satisfactory analysis of the time pattern or magnitude of their likely impact on the relation between nominal and real rates.

In view of the complexity of the effect of monetary disturbances, and the absence of a well-developed theory of the impact of real disturbances, it is not surprising that the empirical part of this chapter has produced no simple generalizations, independent of time and place, that would enable an observer to predict the effects on nominal interest rates of monetary change. Our theoretical framework provides important insight into the empirical behavior of interest rates, but that insight is far richer in understanding particular episodes than in producing a simple empirical generalization covering a wide range of such episodes.

Our empirical analysis has been devoted largely to two related themes: the relation between yields on nominal and on physical assets, and the effect of the level and rate of change of prices on interest rates. Money enters as a factor producing short-term effects, a large part of which averages out within the cycle phases that are our unit of analysis, and as a source of price changes. In principle, price changes arising from other sources should have the same effects on interest rates as those arising from monetary change. Yet it turns out that though nominal interest rates are not very closely connected with current and prior monetary change, they are more closely connected with such monetary changes than with current and prior price changes. We conjecture that this result reflects partly the greater statistical accuracy of our monetary series and partly the impact and intermediate effects that remain in our phase bases.

10.10.1   Yields on Nominal and Physical Assets

The capital markets that determine the interest rates we study serve the economic function of mediating between the suppliers of capital, who prefer to hold assets denominated in nominal terms, and the demanders of capital, who in the main use the capital to acquire physical assets. Financial intermediaries, such as banks, insurance companies, and the like, which have both assets and liabilities denominated in nominal terms, complicate and hide but do not invalidate this fundamental function of the markets in nominal assets. In order to study the relation between the yields on nominal assets and on physical assets, we have employed the rate of change of income as a proxy for the yield on physical assets: that of nominal income as a proxy for the nominal yield on physical assets, and that of real income as a proxy for the real yield on physical assets. Such evidence as we could assemble indicates that our proxy, which we initially used in the analysis of the demand for money, serves its purpose reasonably well, certainly far better than any available alternative.

For the century that our data cover, the average yield on nominal assets was roughly equal to the average yield on physical assets in both the United States and the United Kingdom—itself one of the bits of evidence on the validity of our proxy. The nominal yield on short-term assets averaged 4.2 percent for the United States, 3.5 percent for the United Kingdom; on long-term assets it averaged 4.8 percent for the United States, 4.2 percent for the United Kingdom. The real yield, after subtracting the rate of inflation from the nominal yield, averaged roughly 2.6 percent and 3.3 percent for the United States for short- and long-term assets, 0.9 and 1.7 percent for the United Kingdom. The difference in real yields is wider than in nominal yields because British prices rose on the average more rapidly than United States prices, a difference that was reflected almost precisely in the average behavior of the exchange rate.

The excess of the United States over the United Kingdom yield varies greatly over the century. Before 1914, the United Kingdom was a capital exporter, the United States mainly a capital importer. This situation implies that the yield on capital would be expected to be higher in the United States than in the United Kingdom, and that the difference would be greater than it was after World War I, and this is the case—the excess of United States over United Kingdom real yields being about one percentage point higher before 1914 than in subsequent peacetime periods. Before 1896, the differential between the nominal yields in the two countries was widened, and from 1896 to 1914 it was narrowed by the shift from expectations of devaluation and inflation before 1896 arising out of the free silver campaign, despite the fact of exchange rate stability and deflation, to confidence in the stability of the dollar-pound exchange rate and the avoidance of inflation, despite the fact of inflation. This shift was of course produced by the election of McKinley in 1896 and confirmed by a flood of gold, mostly from South Africa. While the United States–United Kingdom differential in real yields was roughly the same in the interwar and post–World War II periods, the differential in nominal rates shifted from higher United States nominal rates to higher United Kingdom nominal rates as a result of the depreciation of the pound relative to the dollar.

Like the United Kingdom–United States differential, the relation between yields on nominal and physical assets varies greatly from period to period. Equality of yields on nominal and physical assets holds only for the century as a whole. From phase to phase there was essentially no relation between the movements in yields on nominal and physical assets. Over longer periods, the relation depended critically on price movements—in periods of rising prices, the yield on physical assets tended to exceed the yield on nominal assets; in periods of falling prices, the yield on physical assets tended to be less than the yield on nominal assets. Clearly, a large part of the price movement was not anticipated, so that lenders did not succeed in advance in protecting the yield on their nominal assets from being eroded by rising prices, and borrowers did not succeed in advance in protecting their payments from being raised, in real terms, by declining prices. These failures to adjust for price movements had their effect through nominal yields. Between periods displaying different price movements, the real yields on physical assets were far more alike than the real yields on nominal assets, but a similar phenomenon does not hold within periods.

10.10.2   Interest Rates and Prices

Perhaps the most important single conclusion from our examination of the relation between interest rates and prices is to confirm the doubts expressed by Frederick Macaulay in the late 1930s about the validity of Keynes's unqualified assertion that the "tendency of prices and interest rates to rise together . . . and to fall together" is "one of the most completely established empirical facts within the whole field of quantitative economics." This alleged fact, which Keynes properly regarded as inconsistent with theoretical expectations and so dubbed the "Gibson paradox," simply is not a fact, at least since 1914. As Macaulay said, "the exceptions . . . are so numerous and so glaring that they cannot be overlooked" (p. 185). The relation holds over neither World War I nor World War II. It is dubious whether it holds for the post–World War II period, particularly since the middle 1960s. For the period our data cover, it holds clearly and unambiguously for the United States and the United Kingdom only for the period from 1880 to 1914, and less clearly for the interwar period. Dwyer has examined the relation for France, Germany, and Belgium, as well as for the United States and the United Kingdom, and finds no clear-cut Gibson phenomenon for the other countries.

The failure of the relation to hold over wartime price changes—which means over the major price changes—eliminates the major element of paradox but nonetheless leaves a striking empirical phenomenon demanding an explanation. One of two principal explanations that have been offered is Fisher's, that the relation between interest rates and *price level* reflects a relation between interest rates and the anticipated *rate of price change* plus the delayed formation of anticipations by extrapolating past price changes. The other is Wicksell's, also later in a variant suggested by Keynes, that the relation reflects fluctuations in the real yield on capital that are transmitted to both prices and nominal interest rates through commercial banks, which delay the impact of changes in real yields on nominal rates by altering the quantity of money.

Investigators of the Gibson paradox have increasingly come to reject both explanations. Our analysis supports the rejection of the Wicksell-Keynes explanation, partly on the basis of earlier studies by others, partly because we cannot detect in our data the Gibson phenomenon for *real* yields, as well as nominal yields, that is implied by the Wicksell-Keynes explanation. Our analysis does not, however, support the rejection of the Fisher explanation. We found that earlier investigators have been misled because they tested the explanation largely for periods over which the Gibson phenomenon is nonexistent. The Fisher explanation, plus allowance for such episodic phenomena as the free silver movement in the United States, seems to us to remain a highly plausible explanation for the observed relations. However, we are led by this reexamination to regard the period of past price change entering into the formation of price anticipations as being distinctly shorter than the period estimated by Fisher and some others—weights on past price change extending over a period covering something like six to nine years, instead of Fisher's longer periods.

Our data confirm a sharp break in the relation between interest rates and prices in both the United States and the United Kingdom in the mid- or late 1960s that has been reported by other investigators. From then on there is a much closer relation between interest rates and contemporaneous rates of inflation than existed earlier. Gibson disappears and the original Fisher emerges. Apparently lenders and borrowers have been better able than earlier to protect themselves against price changes.

We are inclined to accept an explanation offered by Benjamin Klein for this shift: a drastic change in the character of the monetary system from a largely specie standard to a fiduciary standard and a belated and gradual recognition of this shift by market participants. At an earlier date changes in the quantity of money and in price levels in the connected economies of the United States and the United Kingdom were perceived to be largely the result of such autonomous events as gold discoveries, banking developments, including occasional crises, and the like. They were not, and were not perceived to be, the deliberate consequence of government policy—though obviously measures by government were among the autonomous events that affected the quantity of money. The government was regarded, and regarded itself, as constrained by the requirement to maintain convertibility of the national money into specie, directly or indirectly. In recent decades the situation has changed drastically. Deliberate government management of the quantity of money as part of a policy of steering or tuning or controlling the economy has taken the place of the specie standard.

The change in the monetary standard altered the information relevant to predicting the future course of prices. In addition, it has been accompanied by less short-term but more long-term variability in rates of inflation and by much higher levels of inflation than had been experienced in peacetime in the United States and the United Kingdom during the period we cover. The result was to provide a greater incentive for participants in the market to seek to allow for future price movements, along with a greater possibility of doing so.

The extent of the change may have been exaggerated by the failure of many investigators to allow for the effect of taxes on the difference between nominal and real yields on nominal assets. Even a modest allowance on this score means that borrowers have not succeeded in protecting themselves at all fully from the effect of inflation on real yields. Moreover, the apparent shift may prove temporary. Whether it does, or whether it is carried even further, may very well depend on whether future rates of inflation remain as high and as variable as in the past decade (or even higher and more variable) or whether rates of inflation resume their peacetime behavior.

11   Long Swings in
         Growth Rates

We noted earlier that lengthening the period used to compute rates of change eliminates short, erratic movements but reduces only moderately the amplitude of the fluctuations in money and nominal income, leaving long, relatively smooth swings (sec. 9.3, especially chart 9.4). Chart 11.1 highlights this phenomenon. It gives rates of change computed from three, five, seven, and nine successive phase averages for money in panel A, nominal income in panel B, real income in panel C, and price level in panel D.

11.1 Past Work on Long Swings

For the United States, these long swings are members of the same species as those that have been studied by Kuznets, Burns, Abramovitz, and other investigators. That is clear from table 11.1, which compares three earlier chronologies for the United States with the turning points in our rate of change series for money, nominal income, and real income.[1]

1. See Simon Kuznets, "Long-Term Changes in the National Income of the United States of America since 1870," *Income and Wealth in the United States, Trends, and Structure*, Income and Wealth Series, vol. 2 (Cambridge: Bowes and Bowes, 1952), pp. 29–241; "Quantitative Aspects of the Economic Growth of Nations. I. Levels and Variability of Rates of Growth," *Economic Development and Cultural Change* 5 (October 1956): 1–94; "Long Swings in the Growth of Population and Related Economic Variables," *Proceedings of the American Philosophical Society* 102 (February 1958): 25–52; *Capital in the American Economy: Its Formation and Financing* (Princeton: Princeton University Press for the NBER, 1961), pp. 54, 316–88. The dates in table 11.1 are from the latter source, p. 352, referring to GNP, based on decadal levels in 1929 prices.

Arthur F. Burns, *Production Trends in the United States since 1870* (New York: NBER, 1934), pp. 174–252, esp. p. 196. Burns gives two sets of dates, one that regards his decade rates of growth as the slopes of secular trends at the midpoint of the decade, the second, in terms of decades of rapid and slow growth. The dates given in table 11.1 are the former,

For our series, we have entered every turning point, regardless of the size of the movement. As the average durations at the foot of the table show, the three-phase rates yield cycles roughly comparable in length to those dated by Abramovitz, though somewhat shorter; the nine-phase rates, longer cycles intermediate in length between those dated by Kuznets and by Burns. The exact dating differs somewhat for our three series, and, for each series for matching three-phase and nine-phase turns. However, there are comparably large differences among the dates assigned by the other investigators, and there is clearly more than a family resemblance among all the dates.

For the United Kingdom we have no satisfactory independent chronologies, despite a number of studies of long swings in the United Kingdom patterned after the Kuznets study for the United States. These studies examine the same phenomena but for the most part have not attempted to settle on a specific chronology.[2] Table 11.2 therefore gives only the

since the method used seems more nearly comparable with that implicit in the dating of the money series.

Moses Abramovitz, *Resource and Output Trends in the United States since 1870*, NBER Occasional Paper 52 (1956; reprinted from *American Economic Review* 46 [May 1956]: 5–23), pp. 19–23. See *Hearings on Employment, Growth and Price Levels*, Joint Economic Committee, 86th Cong., 1st Sess., part 2: "Historical and Comparative Rates of Production, Productivity, and Prices" (Washington, D.C.: Government Printing Office, 1959), 411–66, for an excellent summary and analysis of the evidence on long swings in the rate of growth. The dates in table 11.1 are from his "The Nature and Significance of Kuznets Cycles," *Economic Development and Cultural Change* 9 (April 1961): 225–48. They are designated as referring to swings in "economic activity or GNP."

See also Abramovitz, *Evidences of Long Swings in Aggregate Construction since the Civil War*, NBER Occasional Paper 90 (1964); R. A. Easterlin, *The American Baby Boom in Historical Perspective*, NBER Occasional Paper 79 (1962), and his *Population, Labor Force and Long Swings in Economic Growth* (New York: Columbia University Press for NBER, 1968); Manuel Gottlieb, *Estimates of Residential Building, United States, 1840–1939*, NBER Technical Paper 17 (1964), and his *Long Swings in Urban Development* (New York: Columbia University Press for NBER, 1976).

2. See in particular Brinley Thomas, *Migration and Economic Growth* (Cambridge: Cambridge University Press, 1954), and P. J. O'Leary and W. Arthur Lewis, "Secular Swings in Production and Trade, 1870–1913," *Manchester School* 23 (May 1955), reprinted in [American Economic Association] *Readings in Business Cycles*, ed. R. A. Gordon and L. R. Klein (Homewood, Ill.: Irwin, 1965), pp. 546–72.

The one long swing that has been identified by some United Kingdom investigators is a slowdown in United Kingdom growth rates in the 1880s and early 1890s. Others dispute this finding, in particular, S. B. Saul, *The Myth of the Great Depression* (London: Macmillan, 1969), whose main focus is fifty-year swings (so-called Kondratiev cycles) rather than the twenty-year swings that are the subject of this chapter.

Thomas does provide a more extensive chronology, by giving dates of the British building cycle in his table 52, p. 175. For our period, these show a trough in 1871, peak in 1899, trough in 1912, and peak in 1920. Thomas notes that these give cycles inverse to those in the United States but of the same average duration.

Kuznets, in *Economic Growth of Nations* (Cambridge: Harvard University Press, 1971), pp. 43–50, summarizes data on long swings in the United Kingdom, Germany, Sweden,

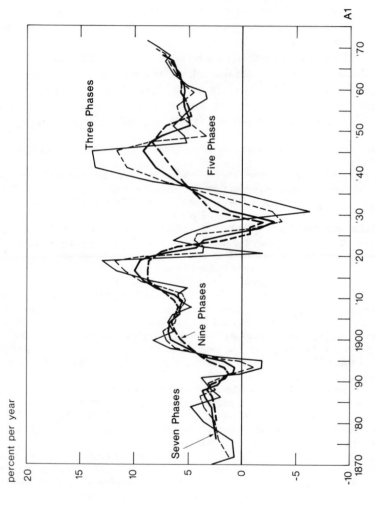

Chart 11.1 Rates of change computed from three, five, seven, and nine overlapping phase averages: money stock, nominal income, real income, United States, United Kingdom. **A1**, United States money.

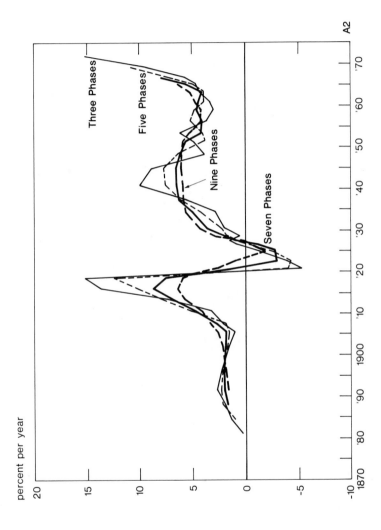

A2, United Kingdom money.

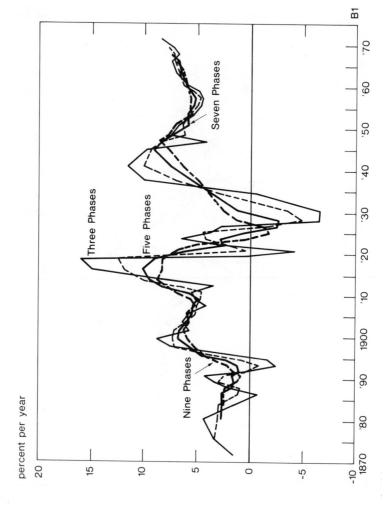

percent per year

B1, United States nominal income.

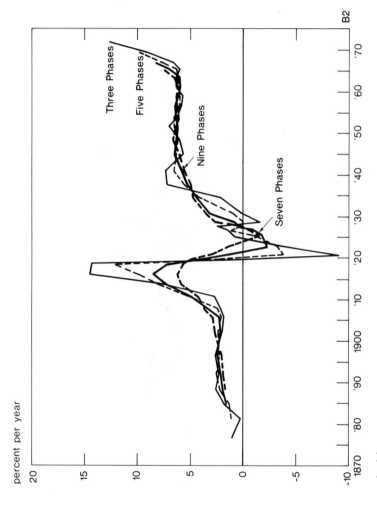

B2, United Kingdom nominal income.

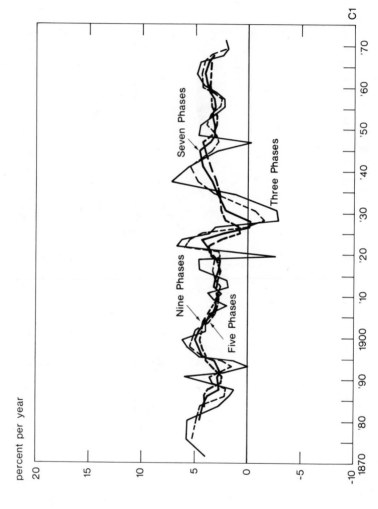

C1, United States real income.

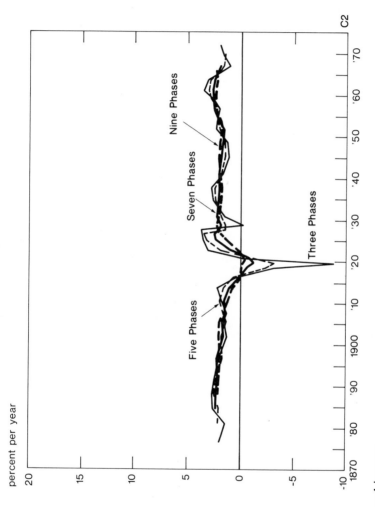

C2, United Kingdom real income.

percent per year

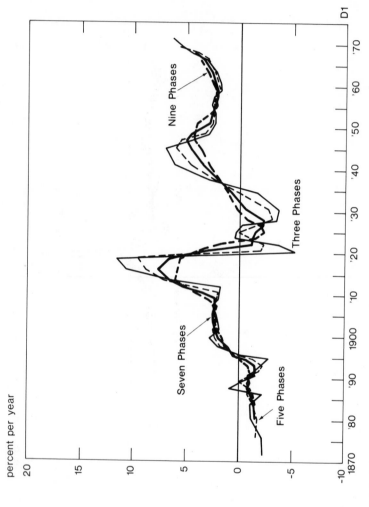

D1, United States price level.

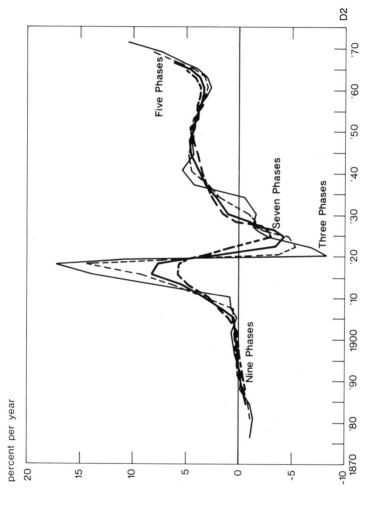

D2, Unitd Kingdom price level.

Table 11.1   Long Swings: Alternative Chronologies for the United States

Turning Point (1)	Kuznets (2)	Burns (3)	Abramovitz (4)	Money		Nominal Income		Real Income	
				Three-Phase Rates (5)	Nine-Phase Rates (6)	Three-Phase Rates (7)	Nine-Phase Rates (8)	Three-Phase Rates (9)	Nine-Phase Rates (10)
T	1873.5		1874.75	1872		1872			
P	1882.5	1880	1881.5	1884	1880.5	1880.5	1884	1876	1884
T			1887	1886.5	1888	1886.5		1888	
P		1890	1890.25	1891		1891	1891	1891	1891
T	1893.5		1892.75	1895	1892	1893.5		1893.5	
P		1900	1899.5	1900		1900		1900	1900
T				1902		1902	1902	1902	
P				1904	1904	1904		1904	
T	1908.5			1908	1908	1908	1908	1908	1909.5
P		1910		1911		1911		1911	1911
T			1911.5	1912.5		1912.5		1912.5	
P		1915	1915	1919	1914	1919	1914	1919	1916.5
T	1916.5	1920	1920.75	1921		1921		1920	
P	1926.5		1923.5	1924		1924		1922.5	1922.5
T	1934.5		1930.75	1931	1927	1931	1925.5	1928.5	1925.5
P			1939	1945.5	1947.5	1941.5	1947.5	1938	1947.5

	2	3	4	5	6	7	8	9	10
T				1947.5		1947.5		1947.5	
P	1950.5			1951.5		1949	1954	1949	1954
T				1958	1954	1958	1956	1956	1961
P				1967	1964	1967	1959.5	1964	1967
T				1968.5	1968	1968.5	1967	1970	
P				1972		1972		1972	
Mean duration of swing[a]	22.0	16.0	11.7	9.5	17.5	9.5	16.6	9.6	15.1

Source, by column: 2. Kuznets, *Capital in the American Economy*, p. 352, table 66, line 1,

3. Burns, *Production Trends*, p. 196 (midpoints of decades).

4. Abramovitz, "Nature and Significance of Kuznets Cycles," p. 231, col. headed, "Economic activity or gross national product" (redated in accordance with convention used here, as described in note, below).

5, 7, 9. See table 5.9, above, cols for g_Y, g_M, and g_Y, except for period of dummy adjustment of money figures described in chapter 8.

6, 8, 10. Based on rates of change computed from moving nine-phase averages shown in chart 9.4 above, panels A, B, and C.

Note: 1900.0 = 1 January 1900
1900.25 = 31 March 1900
1900.5 = 30 June 1900
1900.75 = 30 September 1900

[a]Calculated by dividing differences between terminal and initial date in each column by number of swings, counting a final rise or final fall not matched by a subsequent fall or rise as 0.5 swing.

Table 11.2   Long Swings: Alternative Chronologies for the United Kingdom

Turning Point (1)	Money		Nominal Income		Real Income	
	Three-Phase Rates (2)	Nine-Phase Rates (3)	Three-Phase Rates (4)	Nine-Phase Rates (5)	Three-Phase Rates (6)	Nine-Phase Rates (7)
T	1881.5		1881.5		1881.5	
P			1888.5	1888.5	1888.5	1888.5
T	1892	1892	1892		1902.5	
P			1897		1906	
T	1906		1906		1908	
P					1914	
T	1919	1916.5	1916.5	1916.5	1920	
P	1921	1925.5	1921	1925.5	1925.5	1921
T					1927	
P	1928		1928		1928	1929
T	1929		1929		1931	
P					1938	1938
T	1941.5		1941.5		1945.5	1945.5
P			1945.5		1952	
T	1949	1949		1949	1954	1952
P	1954		1952	1954		
T	1959.5	1957	1959.5	1959.5	1961.5	1959.5
P			1964	1961.5	1967.5	
T		1966	1966	1966		1966
P	1972.5		1972.5		1972.5	
Mean duration of swing[a]	16.5	29.6	12.1	22.1	10.6	22.1

Source by column: 2, 4, 6. Table 5.10 above, cols. for g_Y, g_M, and $g_{y'}$.
3, 5, 7. Based on rates of change computed from moving nine-phase averages shown in chart 9.4 above, panels A, B, and C.
[a]See notes to table 11.1.

turning points in the three-phase and nine-phase rates of change computed from our United Kingdom money, nominal income, and real income series.

The three-phase rates yield longer swings for the United Kingdom than for the United States. For nominal and real income this difference reflects primarily the pre–World War I period. For the period after World War I, the swings in real income are on the average slightly shorter for the United Kingdom than for the United States; in nominal income, slightly longer. For the period before World War I, we are uncertain whether the longer recorded swings in the United Kingdom than in the United States reflect a real phenomenon or simply the unsatisfactory and highly interpolated measurements for the United Kingdom. For money the situation is different. The longer United Kingdom swings reflect not only pre–World War I experience, but also the post–World War II period when it took so much longer in the United Kingdom than in the United States for velocity to recover from the war.

It is clear from chart 11.1 that the nine-phase rates for the United Kingdom retain only two major swings, one for each of the two wartime and postwar periods, plus a final upsurge in money and nominal income but not real income. (Note that, although table 11.2 identifies 1888.5—the first observation for the nine-phase rates—as a peak for real income, one can see on the chart only essential flatness in the observations before World War I; there is no cycle in real income until after World War I.) To judge from our data alone, it is doubtful that, with the exception of wartime and postwar periods, the United Kingdom experienced long swings comparable to those of the United States economy. This ambiguity is consistent with the absence of anything like a consensus on a pre–World War I chronology of United Kingdom long swings and the difficulty that investigators have had in establishing the existence of long swings in the United Kingdom. The absence of long swings in real income is also consistent with our finding in chapter 9 that, excluding wars, the rate of change of real income in the United Kingdom seems to be a random series.

Australia, and the United States for the pre–World War I period. He reports deviations from straight-line trends in the rate of growth of per capita output, population, and total output between successive decades, each pair of decades separated by five years. He gives no chronology, but the peaks and troughs for the United Kingdom in the reported deviations for per capita and total output show only one full swing with perhaps an initial half swing. The dates are: initial peak, 1867; trough 1874–75; peak, 1889–90; trough, 1904–5, implying a swing averaging twenty-five years in duration, or only slightly longer than those Kuznets identified for the United States. His final peak corresponds to the initial peak in column 7 of table 11.2.

Kuznets gets swings for Germany and Sweden roughly comparable to those for the United Kingdom but swings for Australia that are inverse to those for the European countries.

The long swings etched by the undulations in chart 11.1 for the United States clearly correspond to widely diffused movements common to an extraordinary variety of economic and quasi-economic phenomena— from gross capital expenditures by railroads to immigration, from non-farm residential construction to fertility of different population groups, from nonagricultural prices and shares traded on the New York Stock Exchange to number of patents issued.[3] The swings are present not only in real income but also in money and nominal income: indeed, the most striking feature of the chart is the decidedly larger amplitude of the swings in money and nominal income than in real income.

The less clearly marked and milder swings in real income in the United Kingdom than in the United States correspond to less clearly marked and milder swings in money. Where this is not the case, as during the wartime years when the United Kingdom monetary swings are as wide as those in the United States, the swings in real output are also as wide as those in the United States.

Yet in all the extensive literature on long swings, there is hardly a mention of money! The only studies we know of that explore the role of money in long swings are the second edition (1973) of Brinley Thomas's book (the original study is cited in footnote 2 above) and an unpublished study by Moses Abramovitz that was stimulated by an earlier draft of this book.[4] Two survey articles on long swings deal only with series in real terms: one uses fifteen such series for Sweden and the United Kingdom, as well as four for the United States; the other uses thirty British series.[5]

3. Kuznets, *Capital in the American Economy*, pp. 321, 352; Abramovitz, *Long Swings in Aggregate Construction*, p. 35; Easterlin, *American Baby Boom*, p. 25; Burns, *Production Trends*, pp. 223–41.

4. Thomas notes that in the first edition of his book, "Monetary influences were not ignored, but they did not form an important part of the mechanism of interaction" (p. 246), which stressed real factors. In the second edition he assumes that "A monetary cobweb is superimposed on the real instability inherent in the interplay of the real magnitudes" (p. 250) in the period 1870–1913. Moses Abramovitz ("The Monetary Side of Long Swings in U.S. Economic Growth," Memorandum no. 146, Stanford University Center for Research in Economic Growth, April 1973) proposes a model of United States long swings in which nominal income growth and its handmaiden, money stock growth, are governed by the growth rate of the sum of current merchandise and net capital imports.

Saul's study of the United Kingdom, 1873–96, is another exception to the general omission of a role for money. He concedes that money is "the oldest [explanation] and is one which could have the all-pervading effects mentioned" (p. 16) and "that we may have to put money back where it used to be as a major force in the price movement" (p. 19).

5. Benjamin P. Klotz, "Oscillatory Growth in Three Nations," *Journal of the American Statistical Association* 60 (September 1973): 562–67; John C. Soper, "Myth and Reality in Economic Time Series: The Long Swing Revisited," *Southern Economic Journal* 41 (April 1975): 570–79.

Kazushi Okhawa and Henry Rosovsky in *Japanese Economic Growth: Trend Acceleration in the Twentieth Century*, Studies of Economic Growth in Industrialized Countries (Stanford, Calif.: Stanford University Press, 1973) stress long swings in Japanese economic

Kuznets in a conclusion to a 1958 article says, "long swings would probably be found in a much wider range of phenomena . . . than was indicated above. For example, they would presumably be evident in the financial aspects of economic performance and structure," to which he adds three sentences elaborating on this possibility.[6] Aside from this one reference, we have found no mention of money or monetary phenomena in any of Kuznets's writings on long swings.[7] Similarly, the leading British article on long swings, by O'Leary and Lewis, does not mention money.[8]

The omission of money from the studies of long swings doubtless reflects the prevailing Keynesian temper at the time the basic studies were undertaken—characterized as it was by the view that "money does not matter."[9] The omission of money from later studies reflects the tendency of later investigators to stay in well-worn ruts rather than to strike out for themselves. In light of our own findings about the relation between changes in the quantity of money and in nominal and real income, as well as the wider amplitude of the long swings in money than of the associated long swings in real output, it may well be that Hamlet has been left out of the long-swing drama.

This chapter does not explore in detail the relation between long swings in monetary and real magnitudes—we leave that to investigators concerned more centrally with long swings. Our aim is much more modest: (1) to call attention, as we have already done, to the existence of long swings in money and to their apparent temporal association with the long swings that have been studied so extensively in real phenomena; (2) to indicate the relevance of our data to the question whether the swings are episodic or cyclical; and (3) to make some tentative suggestions about the way monetary changes are diffused through the economy and spread out in time.

---

development related to the absorption of advanced foreign technology by the Japanese modern sector.

6. Kuznets, "Long Swings in Population Growth and Related Economic Variables." This paper is reprinted in Kuznets, *Economic Growth and Structure* (New York: Norton, 1965), pp. 328–78; quotation from p. 352.

7. For example, his book *Economic Growth of Nations* contains no entry in the index under money, or monetary.

8. O'Leary and Lewis, "Secular Swings in Production and Trade."

9. A monetary role in long swings is logically entirely consistent with Keynes's pure theory, through the effect of monetary change on interest rates and thereby on investment. However, the view that "money does not matter" led to a complete neglect of this possibility.

Somewhat paradoxically, a rigid simple quantity theory—which regards long-run output as determined independently of monetary changes—would rule out any role for money in long swings. However, no scholar immersed in the quantity theory approach of the pre- or post-Keynesian era would neglect to consider the possible role of money—as we have been led to do.

11.2   Are the Swings Episodic or Cyclical?

The widespread diffusion of the swings through the economy and their apparent smoothness over time are consistent with their being either episodic or cyclical. Let the economy, or some sector of it, be affected by a large "disturbance"—that is, an unsystematic movement, whether favorable or unfavorable—and the disturbance will affect sectors other than those in which it arose, some immediately, some after a lag. These secondary disturbances will in turn produce further effects, including a feedback to the sector in which the disturbance arose. The question is whether the appearance of smooth swings in rates of change is produced by such reactions to occasional episodic disturbances, plus the effect of the statistical devices used to smooth the series,[10] or whether they reflect an internal cyclical mechanism that converts a reasonably steady stream of disturbances into a roughly periodic and recurring pulsation.

Earlier investigators have tended to favor the cyclical interpretation, though recognizing that it is far from established, and have offered tentative hypotheses about the cycle-generating mechanism. The neglect of monetary phenomena has meant that the suggested mechanisms all rely on real phenomena. In light of our own results, these hypotheses are either wrong or, at the very least, seriously incomplete. They are wrong if the monetary phenomena play a significant role in generating the observed swings. They are incomplete even if the monetary phenomena are simply reflections of independent real swings because they do not account for the systematic monetary changes that accompany the real swings.

One technique that has been used extensively in the attempt to determine whether the swings are episodic or cyclical is spectral analysis.[11] Since spectral analysis is a purely descriptive technique, it is not contaminated by defects in the theoretical explanations that have been offered for the real swings. However, because the spectral analysis has relied solely on real series, it has failed to use all of the information available. This failure is particularly unfortunate because the results of spectral analysis have so far been inconclusive, interpreted by some investigators as rejecting the existence of long swings, except as episodic disturbances, by others as mildly favoring that hypothesis.[12]

---

10. This possibility has been suggested and explored by Bird, Desai, Enzler, and Taubman, "'Kuznets Cycles' in Growth Rates: Their Meaning," *International Economic Review* 6 (May 1965): 229–39.

11. See, for example, J. P. Harkness, "A Spectral-Analytic Test of the Long-Swing Hypothesis in Canada," *Review of Economics and Statistics* 50 (November 1968): 429–36; M. Hatanaka and E. P. Howrey, "Low Frequency Variation in Economic Time Series," *Kyklos* 22, no. 3 (1969): 752–63; E. P. Howrey, "A Spectrum Analysis of the Long-Swing Hypothesis," *International Economic Review* 9 (June 1968): 228–52.

12. See Soper, "Myth and Reality in Economic Time Series," for a convenient summary.

The rough temporal coincidence between the swings that earlier investigators found in real magnitudes, the swings in our real income series, and the swings in the stock of money suggests that the real and monetary swings are part of the same process and require a common explanation. In *A Monetary History* we examined in detail the sources of the large changes in the United States in rates of monetary growth. We concluded that each had a fairly straightforward specific explanation. We attributed the four successive substantial rises recorded in chart 11.1 to the reaction to successful resumption of specie payments in 1879, the development of a commercially feasible cyanide process for the extraction of gold, the financing of World War I, the reaction to the Great Contraction plus the financing of World War II. We attributed the four successive substantial declines to the worldwide price decline in the 1880s exacerbated by silver agitation and terminating in the deep depression of the early 1890s, the tapering off of the gold expansion plus the 1907 panic, the post–World War I monetary contraction, which, in the severe smoothing imposed by the nine-phase rates of change merges into the even more drastic monetary contraction from 1929 to 1932, and, finally, the cessation of the rapid monetary expansion of World War II.

We have not made a similarly exhaustive study of United Kingdom monetary history. However, the two wars and postwar periods were characterized by essentially the same pattern of monetary growth in the United Kingdom as in the United States. In the interwar period there is a substantial difference: based on midpoint dates of our three-phase rates of change, United States monetary growth declines sharply from 1924 to 1931 and only then starts to rise to a World War II peak; United Kingdom monetary growth rises sharply, though irregularly, from 1923 to 1941 with only a minor dip marking the Great Contraction. This difference can plausibly be attributed to the different foreign exchange policies: the United States retention of gold until 1933, the United Kingdom departure from gold in 1931. In the pre–World War I period, British monetary growth, as recorded, is much stabler than United States growth, rising moderately in response to the rise in the international supply of gold and then settling back along with United States monetary growth as that impact was absorbed.

These events seem mostly episodic rather than cyclical in character. They are, of course, linked. The worldwide decline in prices expressed in terms of gold before 1890 must have stimulated the search for gold and for better processes of extracting gold from low-grade ore. World War I certainly set in motion political forces that played a part in the strains leading to World War II. In the United States, the monetary panic of 1907 played a large role in producing the agitation for monetary reform that led to the enactment of the Federal Reserve Act and so to the establishment of the monetary institutions that served as the channel of wartime inflation and that were responsible for the severe monetary contractions of 1919–21 and 1929–33. The severe post–World War I contraction in the United Kingdom plus the effects of the return to gold in 1925 certainly laid the groundwork for the early departure from gold in 1931 and the accompanying and subsequent rapid monetary growth. However, these links are of the general kind that connect all major historical events. It is hard to see in them the kind of economic self-generating long cycle mechanism that is embodied in the tentative hypotheses offered by earlier investigators.

While this evidence favors an episodic interpretation of the long swings, it is not decisive. It can be rendered consistent with the self-generating long cycle mechanism in two different ways.

1. It can be maintained that the reaction mechanism of the economy to a major episodic disturbance is cyclical in character, but damped, so that the cycle would die away unless another major disturbance occurred to keep it going. If the damping is assumed to be substantial, the explanation is indistinguishable from a simple episodic explanation, hence it must assume relatively slow damping, so that many observed swings are not episodic.

2. It can be maintained that the particular dramatic events we associate with the monetary changes took the form they did and had the monetary effects they had only because the underlying self-generating cycle mechanism produced a climate favorable to them. Had the same "disturbances" occurred at a different stage of the cycle, they might have passed off without important consequences. Plausible examples are the deep depression of the 1890s and the panic of 1907. In both cases it can be maintained that, unless there had been underlying real forces working for retardation in rates of growth of output, the silver agitation in the earlier case or the failure of a number of banks in the later would not have triggered appreciable monetary contraction. It is much more difficult, on the qualitative evidence available to us, to accept a similar interpretation for the other episodes.

The principal events that are candidates for "random disturbances," the smoothing of which might be regarded as generating the long swings are clearly, for the United States, the deep contractions that have punctuated American economic history since at least as far back as 1808, and for both the United Kingdom and the United States, the major wars. One way, therefore, to get some evidence bearing on the episodic or cyclical character of long swings is to determine the extent to which the long swings reflect these two categories of events.

In order to use phase averages for this purpose, we divided the phases into two sets: "special" phases, which correspond to the wars and deep contractions for the United States and to wars alone for the United Kingdom, and "other" phases, which correspond to the "usual" or "normal" expansions and contractions. In doing so, we treated as deep contraction phases not only the contraction phases themselves, but also the following expansion phases, because of the finding in our other work that there is a close relation between the amplitude of contractions and of succeeding expansions (though not of preceding expansions).[13] The succeeding expansion, as it were, reflects a reaction to, or a rebound from, the deep contraction. Put differently, we treat the period from a peak to a subsequent peak as a deep contraction, containing a contraction and an expansion phase. For the same reason we include as a war phase the expansion phase following the contractions that started at the end of the wars (1918–19 and 1944–46). In all, for the period from 1873 to 1975 for the United States and 1874 to 1975 for the United Kingdom, we classified six phases as war phases and, for the United States, an additional eleven phases as deep contraction phases.[14] Since our rates of change are based on triplets of phases, the rate of change associated with a phase just preceding, or just following, a special phase is affected by the special phases. Accordingly, in the analysis of rates of change which follows, we treat ten observations as corresponding to war phases—for the six war phases proper plus the two that precede and follow each triplet of war phases—and, for the United States, twenty-five observations as corre-

---

13. *A Monetary History*, pp. 97, 139, 173, 241, 493; "The Monetary Studies of the National Bureau," in *The National Bureau Enters Its 45th Year*, 44th Annual Report (June 1964), pp. 14–18. Reprinted in M. Friedman, *The Optimum Quantity of Money* (Chicago: Aldine, 1969), pp. 271–75.

14. The phases classified as war phases are:

Contraction		*Expansion*	
United States	United Kingdom	United States	United Kingdom
1918–19	1918–19	1914–18	1914–18
1944–46	1944–46	1919–20	1919–20
		1938–44	1938–44
		1946–48	1946–51

The phases classified as deep contraction phases for the United States are as follows:

Deep Contraction	*Following Expansion*
1892–94	1894–95
1895–96	1896–99
1907–8	1908–10
1920–21	1921–23
1929–32	1932–37
1937–38	1938–44

We classify both 1892–94 and 1895–96 as deep contractions because the troubled situation of the period straddled two contraction phases. The 1938–44 expansion is also classified as a war phase, and hence reduces the number of deep contraction phases to eleven.

sponding to all special phases.[15] For the United Kingdom, there remain twenty-five observations corresponding to other phases, for the United States, twenty-two. In terms of years covered, the special observations for the United Kingdom cover twenty-three of the 101 years in the period as a whole; for the United States they cover about half of the 102 years in the period as a whole.

The importance of the special observations in determining the amplitude of fluctuations in our series is brought out dramatically by chart 11.2. In each panel, the first pair of curves (part 1) shows the actual rates of change—for money and nominal income in panel A for the United States, panel B for the United Kingdom; for prices and real income in panel C for the United States, panel D for the United Kingdom. The second panel (part 2) shows hypothetical rates of change in which the special observations are replaced by the average value of the other observations. Eliminating the special observations eliminates the bulk of the variability in the series. Moreover, even some of the variability that remains seems fairly clearly to be a reaction to the special observations—particularly for nominal income for the United Kingdom. It would be hard to justify a long-swing hypothesis as more than random perturbations on the basis of the nonspecial observations alone. If there is any kind of a nonepisodic long swing, wars and deep depressions must be of its essence.

Tables 11.3 and 11.4 supplement the graphs, table 11.3 for means, table 11.4 for variance. For both countries the war phases, as we have noted repeatedly, are characterized by high average rates of growth in money, nominal income, and prices. Real income grew at a higher rate during wars in the United States than during all other phases,[16] but at a somewhat lower rate in the United Kingdom. The United States nonwar deep depression observations are, as expected, at the opposite extreme from the war observations: lower rate of growth in all variables than during nonspecial phases.

Table 11.4 is more significant for the present purpose. It allocates the total variability of rates of change to various sources depending on the type of observation. Taking all special together,[17] for the United States, they account for 54 percent of the degrees of freedom, but for 81 to 95 percent of the variability, so that the variation per degree of freedom of the special observations is between three and a half and fifteen times as

15. Adding phases that precede and follow each set of deep contraction phases, listed in note 14 above, gives a total of twenty phases. Five of these are included in the ten observations corresponding to war phases. Hence, other special phases number fifteen, for a total of twenty-five.

16. The average value for the thirty-seven nonwar observations is 3.0.

17. The inclusion of the one degree of freedom "between special and other" with special rather than with other is called for by the hypothesis being tested, namely, that the "other" phases are the "norm," so that the difference in means between the special and other phases is to be attributed to the special ones.

large as per degree of freedom of the other observations.[18] The only interesting feature of the more detailed sources of variation is that for the nominal magnitudes (money, nominal income, and prices), the one degree of freedom corresponding to the difference between the war and nonwar deep depression observations accounts for 44 to 48 percent of the variance, reflecting the wide difference between the corresponding means in table 11.3. For real income, on the other hand, this degree of freedom contributes 16.5 percent.

For the United Kingdom, the war observations account for twenty-nine percent of the degrees of freedom, but for from 60 to 69 percent of the variability, so that the variation per degree of freedom of the war observations is between three and five times as large as per degree of freedom of the other observations.[19] Once again, the one degree of freedom between war and other observations is extremely important for the nominal magnitudes, much less so for real income.

These results simply confirm the tale of charts 11.1 and 11.2: wars and deep depressions are the major source of wide variability in money, nominal income, prices, and real income. Unless these events can be regarded as integral parts of a self-generating long swing, the empirically observed swings must be regarded as reflecting episodic phenomena smoothed both by the economic reaction to them and by the statistical treatment of the economic data.

The importance of deep depressions for the United States, and their apparent unimportance for the United Kingdom, seems to us further evidence against the cyclical interpretation. In *A Monetary History* we concluded the United States deep depressions reflected predominantly monetary collapse. On that interpretation, the difference between the two countries for the periods concerned is readily explained by the difference in monetary institutions and history. The United Kingdom during this period had some serious monetary disturbances—as in 1890 connected with the Baring crisis—but it had no major financial panics of the kind that were experienced in the United States.[20] On the other hand,

18. These *F* values would be exceeded by chance distinctly less than one-tenth of 1 percent of the time.

19. For money, nominal income, and prices, the *F* ratios would be exceeded by chance less than 1 percent of the time; for real income, less than one-tenth of 1 percent of the time.

20. Baring Brothers was threatened with insolvency in November 1890 as a result of imprudent investments in issues of the governments of Argentina and Uruguay. The Bank of England thereupon mobilized a guarantee fund of £17m., subscribed to by the bank and a syndicate of private and joint stock banks, to enable the Barings to discharge their obligations in an orderly way over a period of years. There was no panic on the Stock Exchange, no run on banks, no internal drain of funds, no external run on sterling. See Sir John Clapham, *The Bank of England, 1694–1914* (Cambridge: Cambridge University Press, 1945), 2:326–39; L. S. Presnell, "Gold Reserves, Banking Reserves, and the Banking Crisis of 1890," in *Essays in Money and Banking in Honour of R. S. Sayers*, ed. C. R. Whittlesey and J. S. G. Wilson (Oxford: Clarendon Press, 1968), pp. 167–68, 192–207.

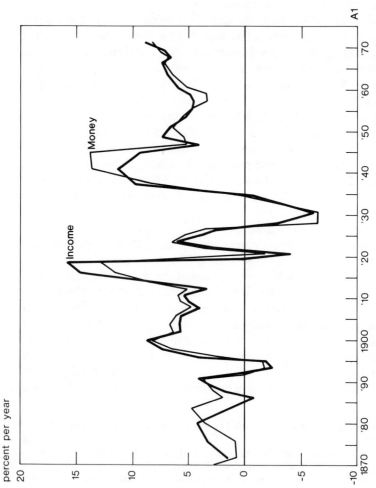

percent per year

Chart 11.2 Actual and hypothetical rates of change of money and nominal income, and of prices and real income, United States, United Kingdom. (Hypothetical rates that replace actual values for special phases are average actual values for nonspecial phases.) **A1**, United States money and nominal income, actual.

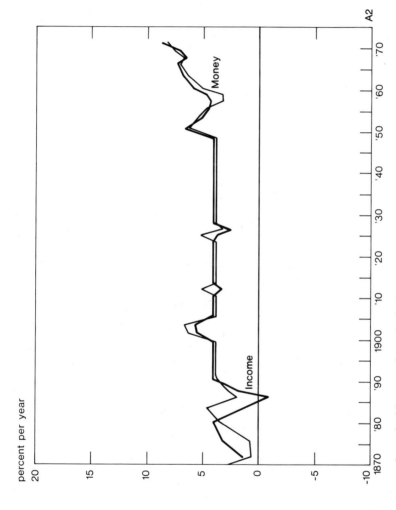

A2, United States money and nominal income, hypothetical.

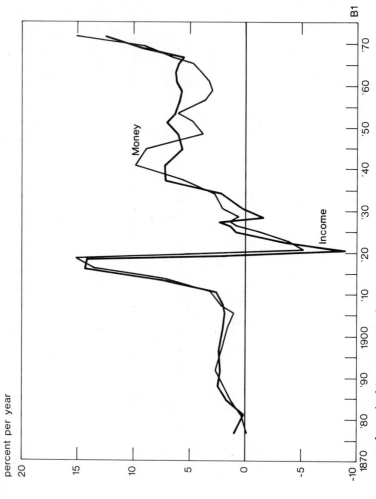

B1, United Kingdom money and nominal income, actual.

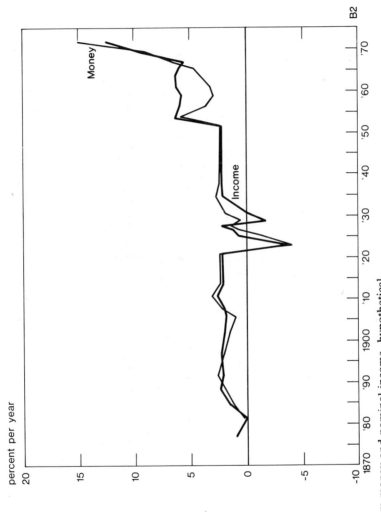

B2, United Kingdom money and nominal income, hypothetical.

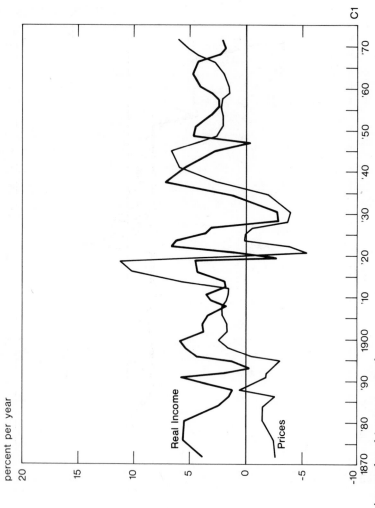

C1, United States prices and real income, actual.

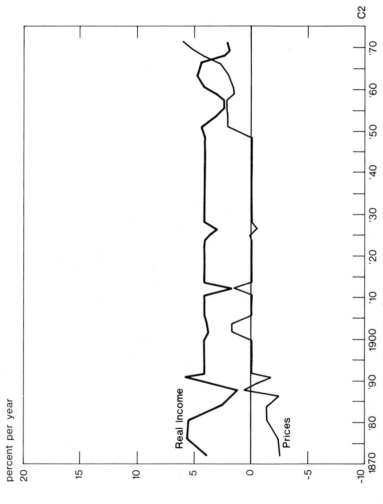

C2, United States prices and real income, hypothetical.

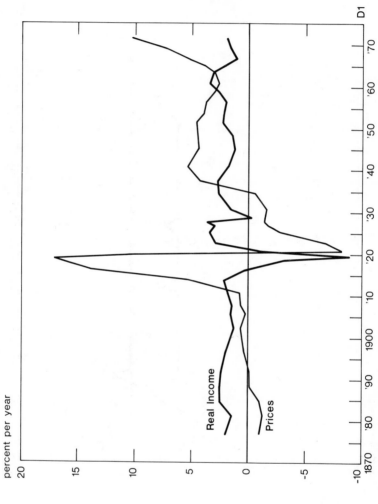

D1, United Kingdom prices and real income, actual.

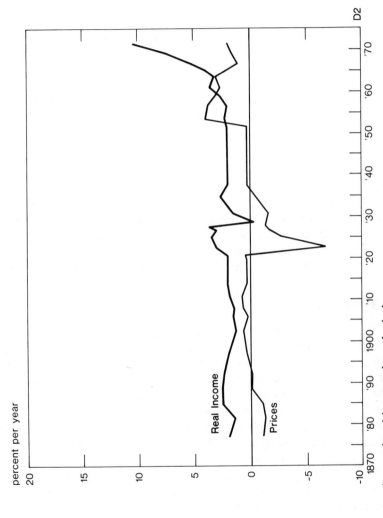

D2, United Kingdom prices and real income, hypothetical.

Table 11.3   Mean Rate of Change of War, Additional Special, and
               Other Phase Observations

Type of Phase	Number of Observations	Number of Years	Rate of Change			
			Money	Nominal Income	Prices	Real Income
United States, 1873–1975						
War	10	20	10.3	9.9	5.1	4.8
Other special	15	29	0.6	0.2	−1.2	1.4
All special	25	49	5.9	5.5	2.2	3.2
Other	22	53	5.2	4.8	0.9	3.9
All	47	102	5.5	5.2	1.6	3.5
United Kingdom, 1874–1975						
War	10	23	7.5	7.0	5.3	1.6
Other	25	78	2.5	2.7	0.6	2.1
All	35	101	3.9	3.9	1.9	2.0

the hypothesis that observed experience reflects primarily a self-generating long swing in real output produced by real forces cannot be accepted without a persuasive explanation of why these forces should have produced such different results in the two countries—an explanation that is at the moment notable by its complete absence.

11.3   The Role of Money in Long Swings

The episodic character of the long swings is consistent with a small set of economic variables playing a crucial role in their occurrence and diffusion, and the same set playing that role in all long swings. The variables could be peculiarly subject to disturbance and closely linked to other activities, and hence a likely bridge for the diffusion of disturbances; or, alternatively, they could be an essential element in the transmission mechanism, so that disturbances, wherever they originate, have diffused effects if and only if they trigger changes in such variables.

Our results strongly suggest that the quantity of money is such a key variable: for both the United States and the United Kingdom, the amplitude of changes in the quantity of money and the associated nominal magnitudes (nominal income and prices) is much wider than in real output; monetary institutions can be the source of serious disturbances, and the greater susceptibility of the United States institutions to such disturbances than of the United Kingdom institutions seems a likely source of the different incidence of deep depressions in the two countries; money is a pervasive element throughout the economy, so changes in the quantity of money will have widely diffused effects and will be a channel

Table 11.4 Analysis of Variance of Rates of Change during War, Additional Special, and Other Phase Observations

Source of Variation	Number of Degrees of Freedom	Percentage Distribution — Sum of Squares					Mean Square per Degree of Freedom			
		Degrees of Freedom	Money	Nominal Income	Prices	Real Income	Money	Nominal Income	Prices	Real Income
				United States, 1873–1975						
Within war	9	20	10.6	8.6	15.1	15.8	13.3	11.3	9.6	5.5
Within other special	14	30	33.8	37.1	15.8	51.2	27.3	31.6	6.4	11.5
Between war and other special	1	2	47.7	43.5	45.0	16.5	538.1	519.8	257.4	52.0
Within special	24	52	92.1	89.2	75.9	83.5	43.3	44.4	18.1	10.9
Between special and other	1	2	2.6	2.4	5.1	3.4	29.4	28.5	29.2	10.7
Total special	25	54	94.7	91.6	81.0	86.9	42.8	43.7	18.5	10.9
Within other	21	46	5.3	8.4	19.0	13.1	2.8	4.8	5.2	2.0
Total	46	100	100.0	100.0	100.0	100.0	24.5	26.0	12.4	6.8
				United Kingdom, 1874–1975						
Within war	9	26	24.6	27.1	29.2	66.6	11.7	11.3	13.7	2.3
Between war and other	1	3	38.9	32.4	35.4	2.1	166.7	121.7	149.1	0.6
Total war	10	29	63.5	59.5	64.6	68.7	27.2	22.4	27.2	2.1
Within other	24	71	36.5	40.5	35.4	31.3	6.5	6.4	6.2	0.4
Total	34	100	100.0	100.0	100.0	100.0	12.6	11.1	12.4	0.9

through which other disturbances are transmitted. Wide variability in the quantity of money is associated with wide variability in nominal income and real income both within the United States and the United Kingdom, between the two countries, and among a much wider range of countries.[21] We conclude that substantial changes in monetary growth are very likely both a necessary and sufficient condition for the emergence of substantial long swings in economic activity.

11.4 The Transmission Mechanism

Chapter 2 gives a theoretical analysis of the way changes in the quantity of money are transmitted to other variables and why a change in monetary growth is likely to give rise to a cyclical reaction pattern in nominal income, prices, real income, and interest rates. Chapters 5 through 10 document this process empirically. They demonstrate the close empirical relation between monetary changes and contemporaneous and subsequent changes in other magnitudes. Most important, for the present purpose, they demonstrate the gradual nature of the adjustment process and the long time it takes for a monetary change to be fully reflected in other phenomena, in particular, in public anticipations about the future behavior of prices.

A swing produced by monetary disturbances can, on the basis of this evidence, be expected to take a considerable time, as the observed swings do, and to display a consistent pattern of reaction of both nominal and real magnitudes, as the observed swings do. Our purpose has led us to concentrate on aggregates, but the same reasoning leads one to expect that monetary disturbances will produce systematic patterns in the reaction of such components of output as construction, other investment, consumption, and so on.

It follows that there is no inconsistency between our tentative judgment that changes in monetary growth are a crucial element in the generation of long swings and the finding of other investigators that there are systematic long-swing patterns in the behavior of real output.

11.5 Summary

Our chief conclusions can be stated briefly. First, Hanlet has been left out of most work to date on long swings. Second, those swings appear to represent smoothing of episodic disturbances rather than an internal cyclical mechanism that produces a roughly periodic and recurrent pulsation.

21. See J. R. Lothian, "The Demand for High-Powered Money," *American Economic Review* 66 (March 1976): 56–68; A. A. Walters, *Money in Boom and Slump*, 3d ed., Hobart Paper 44 (London: Institute of Economic Analysis, 1971); M. Friedman and A. J. Schwartz, "Money and Business Cycles," *Review of Economics and Statistics* 45, suppl. (February 1963): 32–64.

12　　The Role of Money

One conclusion keeps rising to the surface throughout our lengthy examination of the role of money in the economic trends of the past century: John Maynard Keynes "shunted the car of Economic science on to a wrong line"—to use the words that William Stanley Jevons applied to an earlier brilliant economist, David Ricardo.[1] Keynes's *General Theory* was a reaction to the circumstances of the troubled interwar years. It offered an hypothesis to explain what seemed a conflict between experience and the implications of "orthodox" monetary theory. The hypothesis was

> the right kind of theory in its simplicity, its concentration on a few key magnitudes, its potential fruitfulness. [We] have been led to reject it, not on these grounds, but because [we] believe that it has been contradicted by evidence: its predictions have not been confirmed by experience. This failure suggests that it has not isolated what are "really" the key factors in short-run economic change.
>
> *The General Theory* is profound in the wide range of problems to which Keynes applies his hypothesis, in the interpretations of the operation of modern economies and, particularly, of capital markets that are strewn throughout the book, and in the shrewd and incisive comments on the theories of his predecessors. These clothe the bare bones of his theory with an economic understanding that is the true mark of his greatness.[2]

The conclusion in this book that Keynes's hypothesis was unsuccessful is based on money and income data that were not available to Keynes himself. That is true for the pre–World War I period and for the interwar

1. *The Theory of Political Economy*, preface to the 2d ed. (London: Macmillan, 1879), p. lvii.

2. Milton Friedman, "Comments on the Critics," in *Milton Friedman's Monetary Framework* ed. Robert J. Gordon (Chicago: University of Chicago Press, 1974), p. 134.

period itself. In addition, of course, we now have evidence for more than four decades that have elapsed since the *General Theory* was published.

Our examination of this body of evidence reveals that Keynes was generalizing from an idiosyncratic episode—the interwar period in the United States. The pre–World War I period in the United States and the United Kingdom, even the interwar period in the United Kingdom, and the post–World War II period in both countries do not reveal the phenomena that Keynes regarded as contradicting "orthodox" monetary theory. On the contrary, experience during these periods and in these countries conforms to that theory very well. Indeed, one of the ironies of our examination of the evidence is that experience in Keynes's native United Kingdom conforms to the simplest version of the "orthodox" theory he attacked better than does experience in the United States.

The view that Keynes's theory, far from being general, as he labeled it, is highly special, has often been expressed but never documented as fully as we believe we have been able to do.

12.1 The Phillips Curve

The clearest conflict betweeen our evidence and the expectations engendered by a Keynesian vision is with respect to the relation between prices and output. Keynes's emphasis on aggregate demand as the prime mover in economic fluctuations—whether short-term movements within business cycles or the longer-term movements between cycle phases that we take as our basic unit in order to abstract from cyclical fluctuations—led to the expectation that output and prices would move together, both rising and falling together relative to longer-term trends. That view is embodied most directly in the negatively sloped Phillips curve, the idea that if output is high relative to capacity, so that unemployment is low, prices will tend to rise relative to trend (or inflation to accelerate), and if output is low relative to capacity, so that unemployment is high, prices will tend to fall relative to trend (or inflation to decelerate).

We were surprised to find that the typical relation is the reverse, that prices and output tend to be related negatively for our phase averages, not positively; that, so far as it exists at all, the Phillips curve—at least for units of time as long as our cycle phases (averaging two years for the United States, 2.8 years for the United Kingdom)—is positively, not negatively, sloping, except only for the idiosyncratic United States interwar period (chap. 9).

12.2 Two Extreme Theories

It has been common to contrast two supposedly extreme theories: the simple quantity theory of money and the simple Keynesian income-expenditure theory (chap. 2). The first theory implies that the velocity of circulation of money—the ratio of nominal income to the quantity of money—is a constant aside from errors of measurement of its numerator and denominator, so that changes in income (i.e., income in dollars or pounds by contrast with "real" income) mirror changes in the nominal quantity of money—in Irving Fisher's evocative phrase, income fluctuations are a "dance of the dollar." A somewhat more sophisticated version that dates back at least two hundred years treats velocity as a stable function of a small number of variables, including the earlier behavior of the quantity of money.[3] The second theory implies that the velocity of circulation of money is a "will-o'-the-wisp" consisting of the ratio of two essentially independent magnitudes. Fluctuations in nominal income are linked to fluctuations in investment through the "consumption multiplier," so that income is a dance of investment rather than of the dollar. A somewhat more sophisticated version gives money, and velocity, some independent status via the possible effect of changes in the quantity of money on interest rates and thence on investment—both "interest rates" and "investment" being defined rather narrowly.

Neither theory, in its simple or more sophisticated version, has anything systematic to say about how a change in nominal income is divided between a change in prices and in output. The quantity theory supposes output to be determined predominantly by nonmonetary forces and supposes changes in nominal income that are produced by changes in money to be reflected ultimately entirely in prices. The Keynesian theory supposes prices to be determined by nonmonetary forces and supposes changes in nominal income that are produced by changes in investment to be reflected entirely in output (so long as employment is less than "full"). Of course, users of both theories have recognized that neither extreme is correct and have made many illuminating side comments on this issue. But neither group has succeeded in developing a satisfactory formal theory to fill this major gap.

We have offered some suggestions about how to do so in our theoretical framework (secs. 2.6–8), but these are highly tentative. Further, the chapter in which we attempt to give empirical content to these suggestions (chap. 9) largely records an unsuccessful experiment—though it does yield some highly important results to which we have already referred.

The broad survey of our basic time series with which we begin our empirical analysis (chap. 5) is sufficient to demonstrate that the simple

3. For example, see David Hume, "Of Money" (discourse 3) and "Of Interest" (discourse 4) in David Hume, *Political Discourses* (Edinburgh: Fleming, 1752), pp. 41–59, 61–78; and M. Friedman, "Discussion," at American Economic Association session "The Rediscovery of Money," *American Economic Review Papers and Proceedings* 65 (May 1975): 176–78.

Keynesian view can be rejected; the movements in the level of income and its rate of change parallel extraordinarily closely for more than a century the contemporaneous movements in the quantity of money and its rate of change, and this is equally true for the United States and the United Kingdom. Whichever is the "cause" and whichever the "effect," the two magnitudes are clearly not independently determined. Velocity varies far less than either nominal money or nominal income. Even more striking, the movements of velocity in the United States parallel those in the United Kingdom, and so do movements in the rate of change of velocity.

The one important difference between the two countries that emerges in this broad survey is that price change accounts for a larger fraction of the fluctuations in nominal income, and output change for a smaller fraction, for the United Kingdom than for the United States—a phenomenon that we encounter repeatedly in later chapters.

12.3 The Demand for Money

Velocity is a "real," not a "nominal" magnitude, the monetary units in numerator and denominator canceling out. Its reciprocal has the dimension of time, measuring the amount of money held in terms of the number of time units of income to which that amount of money is equal—so many weeks or months or other time units of income. In consequence, an analysis of velocity is equivalent to an analysis of the demand for money in "real" terms.

We begin our study of the demand for money (chap. 6) by examining in more detail the agreement between our data and the alternative simple theories. The conclusion is clear: both can be rejected, but the simple quantity theory comes far closer to explaining experience than does the simple Keynesian theory. Somewhat surprisingly, the simple quantity theory comes even closer to describing experience for the United Kingdom than for the United States. The later chapters show that this result too reflects the idiosyncrasy of the United States interwar years.

The simple quantity theory does not deserve the denigration that it has received in recent decades. It is a surprisingly good first approximation and clearly recommends itself as a better starting point for a more sophisticated analysis than the simple Keynesian theory. That more sophisticated analysis reveals the existence of a stable demand function for money covering the whole of the period we examine. The major variables that have affected the real quantity of money have, with one exception, apparently been the same in the two countries. The exception is the increasing financial sophistication in the United States monetary system relative to the United Kingdom system before the early 1900s. Presumably the degree of financial sophistication has continued to play a role in the United States and has been relevant in the United Kingdom all along, but, since it seems to have been affecting both countries to roughly the same extent, we have been unable to identify it.

For the rest, the basic forces that we have identified as affecting the real quantity of money demanded throughout the period have been the level of real per capita income, the difference between the nominal yields on money and on other nominal-value assets, and the nominal yield on physical assets—which we have been able to proxy successfully by the rate of change of nominal income. In addition, two forces were operative for part of the period: (1) after both of the major wars, it took time for the quantity of money demanded to adjust to the drastic change in circumstances; (2) the Great Depression in the United States and the stagnation in the United Kingdom from the mid-1920s until World War II in both countries produced a temporary upward shift in the quantity of money demanded for given values of the other variables—a shift we interpret as reflecting a widespread perception that there was greater economic uncertainty to which a high desired level of liquidity was one response.

With one exception, the basic forces affecting demand in the United Kingdom and the United States had roughly the same quantitative impact in the two countries. The exception is the elasticity of real per capita money balances with respect to real per capita income. That elasticity was somewhat higher than unity in the United States, about 1.1, and somewhat lower than unity in the United Kingdom, about 0.9. For yields, we estimate that a one percentage point (*not* 1 percent) change in the differential yield on money would produce something more than a 9 percent (not percentage point) change in the quantity of money demanded; a one percentage point change in our proxy for the nominal yield on physical assets would produce something more than a 0.04 percent change in the quantity of money demanded. However, these estimates are less securely grounded and subject to a wider margin of error than the estimated income elasticities.

Not only are the basic forces affecting the quantity of money demanded, and their quantitative effects, largely the same in the two countries, but the single statistical equation that we estimate from data for the two countries combined leaves about the same residual variation to be explained in the United States and the United Kingdom by omitted variables or statistical error—about 5 percent for the level of money demanded, about 1.5 percentage points for the rate of change of the quantity of money demanded.

12.4 Common Financial System

The two countries are clearly part of a common financial system, in which monetary variables—prices, interest rates, nominal incomes, stocks of money—are constrained to keep largely in step except as changes in exchange rates alter the number of units of one country's currency equivalent to one unit of the other country's currency. Within the unified financial system, there is much room for divergence of physical magnitudes—for example, there is only a loose link between the two countries in the movements of real per capita income (chap. 7).

Even with respect to financial magnitudes, the unification is far from complete. We have indirectly been able to examine this issue—to see how well, for example, the "law of one price" holds—by estimating year-by-year over the whole of our period the number of United States dollars that had the same purchasing power as one British pound—the purchasing-power-parity exchange rate. If the "law of one price" were perfectly satisfied, the purchasing-power-parity exchange rate would equal the market rate. In fact, it does not do so but fluctuates around the market rate. Before the early 1930s, the purchasing-power-parity rate stayed within plus or minus 10 percent of the market rate—a reasonable approximation to the law of one price. After the early 1930s, the variation was much wider, ranging from 10 percent below to 60 percent above. Government intervention in the exchange market since the 1930s has been more potent in disunifying the markets than improvements in transportation and communication have been in unifying them (sec. 6.8).

12.5 Dynamic Effects on Nominal Income

A stable demand function for real money balances means that an autonomous change in either nominal money or nominal income will have to be accompanied by a corresponding change in the other variable, or in variables entering into the demand function for money, in order to equate the desired quantity of money balances with the quantity available to be held. The parallelism in the temporal patterns of nominal money and nominal income means that the adjustment comes about primarily through the other nominal magnitude rather than through the yields or other variables entering into the demand function for money. Given stability of money demand, variability in conditions of money supply, and similar parallelism for the whole of the period, it is appropriate to regard the observed fluctuations in the two nominal magnitudes as reflecting primarily an influence running from money to income. The process is two-way, not unidirectional, so there undoubtedly has also been a feedback from income to money, yet the element that gives consistency to the century as a whole is the influence from money to income.[4]

---

4. Note that this says nothing about "endogeneity" or "exogeneity." Even for the gold standard period, when the quantity of money is an endogenous variable, the parallel fluctuations in nominal money and income can reflect primarily an influence running from money to income.

Accordingly, in chapters 8 and 9, we have examined the temporal pattern of response to changes in the quantity of money—in chapter 8, the response of nominal income; in chapter 9, of prices and output separately—with special reference to giving empirical content to the dynamic patterns in chapter 2. Though not inconsistent with the suggestions in that chapter, the empirical results do not enable us to specify those hypotheses at all precisely.

The response of nominal income to changes in the nominal quantity of money is generally cyclical, distributed over a long period, and sharply damped in amplitude. The cumulative effect is consistent with theoretical expectation: a sustained one percentage point increase in the rate of monetary growth ultimately produces a one percentage point increase in the rate of nominal income growth. However, we have been unable to pin down at all precisely the magnitude of the transitory effects to be expected en route to this long-term result.

12.6 Dynamic Effects on Prices and Output

The response of prices, like that of nominal income, is generally cyclical, distributed over a long period, and sharply damped in amplitude. Except only for the United States interwar period, the ultimate effect of monetary change is absorbed by prices. There is no persistent effect on output. Indeed, for the United Kingdom we have not been able to isolate even transitory effects on output. The change in United Kingdom output from cycle phase to cycle phase behaves like a strictly random series—white noise in the jargon of stochastic series. That is not true for the United States, but the output effects are smaller and less consistent over time than the price effects—again with the conspicuous exception of the interwar period.

12.7 Interest Rates

According to the simple Keynesian theory, changes in the quantity of money would be reflected first in changes in the opposite direction in interest rates, which in turn would affect investment and, through investment, nominal income. The implied inverse relation between changes in the quantity of money and in interest rates, widely taken for granted as recently as the mid-1960s, by now has been thoroughly discredited by the simultaneous upward trends of the past several decades in the quantity of money, nominal income, inflation, and interest rates. One result has been an explosion of economic research into the relation between prices and interest rates, research inspired largely by the seminal contributions of Irving Fisher and secondarily by some comments of Keynes in the *Treatise on Money*, which preceded the *General Theory* and out of which the *General Theory* developed.

By now there is general agreement on the theory of the relation between money and interest rates (sec. 10.1). The theoretical relation is complex, so that our empirical analysis, based on that theory, offers a rich understanding of particular episodes but does not yield any simple empirical generalization enabling an observer to predict the effects of monetary change on interest rates.

Our empirical analysis is devoted primarily to two related themes: the relation between yields on nominal and on physical assets and the effect of the level and rate of change of prices on interest rates.

For the century we cover as a whole, nominal yields on nominal assets roughly equal our proxy for nominal yields on physical assets, averaging about 4.5 percent for the United States, about 4 percent for the United Kingdom; short-term nominal assets yielded somewhat less on the average, long-term nominal assets somewhat more, in line with the widespread belief that liquidity commands a premium. The equality between yields on nominal assets and our proxy for physical assets is evidence in favor of the validity of our proxy as well as testimony to the existence of effective arbitrage between different categories of assets over long periods.

The real yield—the excess of the nominal yield over the average rate of inflation—averaged about 3 percent for the United States, about 1.25 percent for the United Kingdom. The excess of the United States yield over the United Kingdom yield is greater for real than for nominal yields because United Kingdom prices rose on the average more rapidly than United States prices, a difference that was reflected almost precisely in the average behavior of the exchange rate.

Arbitrage roughly equated yields on nominal and physical assets for the century as a whole but not for shorter periods—there is little correlation between the phase-to-phase movements of yields on nominal and physical assets. During periods of rising prices, physical assets provided higher yields than nominal assets; during periods of falling prices they provided lower yields. As between such periods, nominal yields were much stabler for nominal than for physical assets; real yields were much less stable. The conclusion is inescapable: for the greater part, inflation and deflation were not accurately anticipated and therefore were not reflected in the terms on which nominal assets were acquired: lenders did not succeed in protecting themselves against having their real returns eroded by inflation; borrowers did not succeed in protecting themselves against having their real interest payments increased by deflation.

The greater stability of the real yield on physical assets than on nominal assets does not reflect greater foresight by their holders. It reflects the absence of advance contractual arrangements. Yields on physical assets are realized mostly as a difference between receipts from the physical assets and costs (other than the return on physical capital) of acquiring those receipts. Inflation and deflation affect both receipts and costs. A measure of automatic indexing, as it were, stabilizes the real return on physical assets.

The importance of *anticipations* as opposed to *realizations* is highlighted by one particularly instructive episode. That episode is the transition from the fear that the United States would go off the gold standard, produced by the free silver movement before 1896, to confidence in the maintenance of the gold standard following McKinley's election in 1896. From 1873 to 1896, the short-term interest rate in the United States was slightly *higher* on the average than it was from 1896 to 1914, although prices on the average were falling by nearly 2 percent a year before 1896 and rising by nearly 2 percent a year after 1896. In the United Kingdom, by contrast, the short-term interest rate was slightly *lower* on the average before than after 1896. The United States rate averaged about 2.5 percentage points higher than the United Kingdom rate before 1896, less than 1.5 percentage points higher than the United Kingdom rates after 1896.

These seemingly paradoxical results are readily explicable. Before 1896, the political strength of the free silver movement made it entirely reasonable for farsighted investors to anticipate inflation. The fact turned out to be deflation; the anticipation was inflation. The investors proved to be wrong—but there was no way anyone could know that in advance, no evidence that would have in advance contradicted a personal probability judgment that the probability of inflation was decidedly greater than 50 percent. After 1896, the *fact* was inflation; the anticipation was stability or deflation. The shift in anticipations reduced the differential between United Kingdom and United States interest rates: investors in the United Kingdom presumably shared the fears of those in the United States and hence were reluctant to lend in the United States before 1896 except at a premium that compensated them for the possibility of a devaluation of the dollar relative to the pound. After 1896 this premium was no longer necessary; the remaining excess simply reflected the premium required to compensate for investing abroad rather than at home—a differential to be expected between a capital-importing country, such as the United States then was, and a capital-exporting country, such as the United Kingdom then was. After World War I, the United States too became a capital exporter and, while the real yield in the United States remained higher than in the United Kingdom, the excess declined by about one percentage point. Nominal yields became higher in the United Kingdom than in the United States, reflecting the depreciation of the pound relative to the dollar.

12.8 Rational Expectations

The free silver episode is especially instructive with respect to the proper interpretation of the recently popular theory of rational expectations. In applying this idea, it is common to proceed on two assumptions: (1) that participants in whatever market is considered have "correct" estimates of the probability distribution of outcomes (itself something that is difficult or impossible to define objectively), so that on the average anticipations are correct; and (2) that errors of forecast in successive time units are uncorrelated. This episode brings out sharply the difficulty of giving a precise meaning to the first assumption, and the ambiguity of "time unit" for the second assumption. For that episode, the relevant time unit is about twenty years—so that averaging out may take a long time. Our analysis gives one example: the real yield on nominal assets matches the real yield on physical assets only for the whole century our data cover.

The formalization in the theory of rational expectations of the ancient idea that economic actors use available information intelligently in judging future possibilities is an important and valuable development. But it is not the open sesame to unraveling the riddle of dynamic change that some of its more enthusiastic proponents make it out to be.

12.9 Fisher and Gibson

Irving Fisher was an early and sophisticated user of the basic idea of rational expectations. His expectation (in 1896) that nominal interest rates would be relatively high during periods of rising prices and relatively low during periods of falling prices was based on the view that lenders and borrowers seek to anticipate price movements and allow for them in the interest rates they are willing to accept or to pay. His examination of empirical evidence persuaded him that there was an effect in this direction but that it was very much damped—the conclusion that we too have reached on the basis of experience for a much longer period. He suggested an explanation in terms of the slowness with which participants adapted their anticipations to experience, leading to an appearance that interest rates vary with the price *level* rather than the rate of price change.

At about the same time, Knut Wicksell was impressed by the same empirical observation that prices and interest rates apparently moved together—the observation that Keynes later termed the Gibson paradox—and suggested an explanation in terms of the slowness with which banks adapted their anticipations to changes in the productivity of physical capital. Keynes offered a variant of this explanation for the same phenomenon more than two decades later.

Our interest in the effect of monetary change on interest rates naturally led us to examine the relation between the level and rate of change of prices and interest rates, because the effect of monetary change on prices is a major channel through which monetary change affects interest rates. Our examination of the evidence confirms the doubts expressed by Frederick Macaulay more than forty years ago about the generality of the Gibson phenomenon. It does not exist over very long periods. It frequently does not exist over short periods. In particular, it is present before World War I in both the United States and the United Kingdom, though apparently, according to studies by Gerald Dwyer, not in some other countries. There are traces of it in the interwar period, almost none in the post–World War II period. The major change in price level from before to after World War I leaves no reflection at all in the level of interest rates. In short, there has at times been a Gibson phenomenon; there is no Gibson paradox.

Wicksell's and Keynes's suggested explanation of the Gibson phenomenon is clearly contradicted by the evidence and can definitely be rejected. Fisher's explanation is not, though it must be modified from his final (1930) version, in which he regarded participants as forming their anticipations of future price change as a very long weighted average of past price change. The modifications are, first, that the period of averaging is much shorter than Fisher estimated it to be, though still lengthy—something like six to nine years rather than the much longer period he estimated—and, second, that participants also take into account other relevant episodic evidence, such as the free silver movement.

A sharp break has apparently occurred in recent years in the relation between price change and interest rates in both the United States and the United Kingdom. Since about the mid-sixties, a close relation between interest rates and the rate of price change has emerged for the first time in the century we study. Gibson has been replaced by the original Fisher. Nominal returns have become more variable than real returns; nominal returns on nominal assets are as variable as nominal returns on physical assets. Lenders and borrowers apparently have been able to predict price changes more accurately and to adjust the terms of lending and borrowing accordingly.

This break has been noted by other investigators. Like Benjamin Klein, we are inclined to attribute the break to a belated and gradual recognition by market participants of the drastic change in the monetary system from a largely specie standard to a fiduciary standard. One caveat is in order: the extent of the shift may have been exaggerated by the failure to allow for the effect of taxes on the real yield from nominal assets during an inflationary period. This is a complex issue that is far from settled. In any event, whether the shift in pattern proves permanent or temporary is likely to depend on future developments in the monetary system and on the future course of inflation.

12.10 Long Swings

Our final substantive chapter (chap. 11) applies our findings to a fairly extensive body of research on long swings in economic activity. This research has examined swings in economic activity of a decidedly longer duration than business cycles, swings that encompass several business cycles. Investigators have documented such swings for the United States in many physical magnitudes for roughly the century our study covers. They have been asserted to exist but not comparably documented for the United Kingdom, as well as other countries.

Some investigators have maintained that these swings reflect a self-generating cyclical process of longer duration than the ordinary business cycle and have offered a series of hypotheses about the economic forces producing them.

It is a remarkable testament to the extent to which the Keynesian revolution dominated economic research during the period when the initial research on long swings was done that no investigator we have been able to uncover paid more than the most casual attention to the behavior of the quantity of money or nominal income during the asserted long swings or to the role that monetary phenomena might play. The investigators restricted themselves to "real" phenomena in the sense of physical magnitudes—an extreme example of the widespread view that "money does not matter." More recently, there has been a welcome recognition by some leading investigators of long swings of the necessity of incorporating monetary magnitudes into their analysis.

Our data demonstrate that Hamlet has been left out of most long-swing research. The swings isolated in the physical magnitudes have their counterpart in the nominal magnitudes. More important, the swings in the nominal magnitudes are wider in amplitude and more clearly marked than in the physical magnitudes. No explanation of long swings is acceptable that does not account for the monetary phenomena.

The observed swings may reflect a self-generating cyclical mechanism, as some investigators have claimed, or they may represent the smoothing, by the economic process or statistical procedures, of episodic disturbances. Our data strongly support the episodic interpretation.

Long-swing research is a clear example of a branch of economics that has been "shunted . . . on to a wrong line": masses of sophisticated statistical data and economic analysis; many useful empirical results, yet its basic theoretical generalizations null and void thanks to a shuttered vision.

References

Abramovitz, Moses. 1956. *Resource and output trends in the United States since 1870.* NBER Occasional Paper 52. New York: NBER. Reprinted from *American Economic Review* 46 (May): 5–23.

———. 1959. Statement. United States. Congress. Joint Economic Committee. *Hearings on employment, growth, and price levels.* Part 2. *Historical and comparative rates of production, productivity and prices.* 86th Cong., 1st sess., 10 April, 411-66, Washington, D.C.: Government Printing Office.

———. 1961. The nature and significance of Kuznets cycles. *Economic Development and Cultural Change* 9 (April): 225–48.

———. 1964. *Evidences of long swings in aggregate construction since the Civil War.* NBER Occasional Paper 90. New York: NBER.

———. 1973. The monetary side of long swings in U.S. economic growth. Memorandum no. 146. Stanford University Center for Research in Economic Growth.

Akerlof, George A. 1979. The case against conservative macroeconomics: An inaugural lecture. *Economica* 46 (August): 219–37.

Allais, Maurice. 1965. Réformulation de la théorie quantitative de la monnaie. *Bulletin Sedeis*, no. 928, suppl. Société d'Etudes et de Documentation Economiques Industrielles et Sociales. Paris.

———. 1966. A restatement of the quantity theory of money. *American Economic Review* 56 (December): 1123–57.

———. 1969. Growth and inflation. *Journal of Money, Credit and Banking* 1 (August): 355–426.

———. 1972. Forgetfulness and interest. *Journal of Money, Credit and Banking* 4 (February): 40–71.

Allen, Stuart D., and Hafer, R. W. "Money Demand and the Term

Structure of Interest Rates: Some Consistent Estimates." Unpublished paper, University of North Carolina at Greensboro and Federal Reserve Bank of Saint Louis, 1981.

Argarwala, R.; Drinkwater, J.; Khosla, S. D.; and McMenomy, J. 1972. A neoclassical approach to the determination of prices and wages. *Economica*, n.s., 39 (August): 250–63.

Asakuri, Kokishi, and Nishiyama, Chiaki, eds. 1974. *A monetary analysis and history of the Japanese economy, 1868–1970*. Tokyo: Sobunsha.

Auerbach, Robert. 1969. The income effects of the government deficit. Ph.D. diss., University of Chicago.

Auerbach, Robert, and Moses, R. 1974. "The Phillips curve and all that": A comment. *Scottish Journal of Political Economy* 21 (November): 299–301.

Barro, Robert J. 1977. Unanticipated money growth and unemployment in the United States. *American Economic Review* 67 (March): 101–15.

———. 1978. Unanticipated money, output, and the price level in the United States. *Journal of Political Economy* 86 (August): 549–80.

Barro, Robert J., and Fischer, Stanley. 1976. Recent developments in monetary theory. *Journal of Monetary Economics* 2 (April): 133–67.

Barro, Robert J., and Rush, Mark. 1980. Unanticipated money and economic activity. In *Rational expectations and economic policy*, ed. Stanley Fischer. Chicago: University of Chicago Press.

Baumol, William J. 1952. The transactions demand for cash: An inventory theoretic approach. *Quarterly Journal of Economics* 66 (November): 545–56.

Bilson, John F. O., and Hale, R. Stephen. "Further Evidence on the Term Structure of Interest Rates and the Demand for Money." Unpublished report no. 8001, Center for Mathematical Studies in Business and Economics, University of Chicago, 1980.

Bird, R. C.; Desai, M. J.; Enzler, J. J.; and Taubman, P. J. 1965. "Kuznets cycles" in growth rates: The meaning. *International Economic Review* 6 (May): 229–39.

Black, Fischer. 1972. Active and passive monetary policy in a neoclassical model. *Journal of Finance* 27 (September): 801–4.

Black, Harold. 1975. The relative importance of determinants of the money supply: The British case. *Journal of Monetary Economics* 1 (April): 251–64.

Blackaby, F. T. 1978. Incomes policy. In *British economic policy, 1960-74*, ed. F. T. Blackaby. Cambridge: Cambridge University Press for National Institute of Economic and Social Research.

Bordo, Michael, D. 1972. The effects of the sources of change in the money supply on the level of economic activity. Ph.D. diss., University of Chicago.

———. 1981. The U.K. money supply, 1870–1914. *Research in Economic History* 6:107–25.

Bordo, Michael D., and Jonung, Lars. 1981. The long-run behavior of income velocity of money in five advanced countries, 1870–1975: An institutional approach. *Economic Inquiry* 19 (January):96–116.

Brainard, William. 1967. *Financial institutions and a theory of monetary control.* Cowles Foundation Monograph 21. New York: Wiley.

Brittan, Samuel, and Lilley, Peter. 1977. *The delusion of incomes policy.* London: M. T. Smith.

Brock, W. A. 1974. Money and growth: The case of long-run perfect foresight. *International Economic Review* 15 (October): 750–77.

Brunner, Karl. 1970. The "monetarist revolution" in monetary theory. *Weltwirtschaftliches Archiv* 105 (1): 1–30.

Brunner, Karl; Cukierman, Alex; and Meltzer, Allan H. 1980. Stagflation, persistent unemployment, and the permanence of economic shocks. *Journal of Monetary Economics* 6 (October): 467–92.

———. 1980. Money and economic activity, inventories and business cycles. Unpublished. University of Rochester Graduate School of Management, GPB-80-81.

Brunner, Karl, and Meltzer, Allan H. 1963. Predicting velocity: Implications for theory and policy. *Journal of Finance* 18 (May): 319–54.

Burger, Albert E. 1971. *The money supply process.* Belmont, Calif.: Wadsworth.

———. 1972. Money stock control. In *Controlling monetary aggregates II: The implementation,* pp. 33–55. Conference series no. 9. Boston: Federal Reserve Bank of Boston.

Burns, Arthur F. 1934. *Production trends in the United States since 1870.* New York: NBER.

Burns, Arthur F., and Mitchell, W. C. 1946. *Measuring business cycles.* New York: NBER.

Cagan, Phillip. 1956. The monetary dynamics of hyperinflation. *Studies in the quantity theory of money,* ed. Milton Friedman. Chicago: University of Chicago Press.

———. 1965. *Determinants and effects of changes in the stock of money, 1875–1960.* New York: Columbia University Press for NBER.

———. 1969. A study of liquidity premiums on federal and municipal government securities. In *Essays on interest rates,* vol. 1, ed. P. Cagan and J. Guttentag. New York: NBER.

———. 1972. *The channels of monetary effects on interest rates.* New York: NBER.

———. 1975. Changes in the recession behavior of wholesale prices in the 1920s and post-World War II. *Explorations in Economic Research 2* (winter): 54–104.

Cairnes, J. H. 1873. Essays toward a solution of the gold question. In *Essays in political economy.* London: Macmillan.

Carlson, John A. 1977a. Short-term interest rates as predictors of inflation: Comment. *American Economic Review* 67 (June): 469–75.

———. 1977b. A study of price forecasts. *Annals of Economic and Social Measurement* 6 (1): 27–56.

———. 1979. Expected inflation and interest rates. *Economic Inquiry* 17 (October): 597–608.

Carlson, John A., and Frew, James R. 1980. Money demand regressions with the rate of return on money: A methodological critique. *Journal of Political Economy* 88 (June): 598–607.

Carlson, John A., and Parkin, J. M. 1975. Inflation expectations. *Economica* 42 (February): 123–38.

Carr, Jack, and Darby, Michael R. 1981. The role of money supply shocks in the short-run demand for money. *Journal of Monetary Economics* 8 (September): 183–99.

Carr, Jack; Pesando, James E.; and Smith, Lawrence B. 1976. Tax effects, price expectations and the nominal rate of interest. *Economic Inquiry* 14 (June): 259–69.

Cass, David; Okuno, Masahiro; and Zilcha, Itzhak. 1980. The role of money in supporting the Pareto optimality of competitive equilibrium in consumption loan type models. In *Models of monetary economies*, ed. John H. Kareken and Neil Wallace. Minneapolis: Federal Reserve Bank of Minneapolis.

Chandavarkar, Anand G. 1977. Monetization of developing economies. *IMF Staff Papers* 24 (November): 665–721.

Chow, Gregory C. 1966. On the long-run and short-run demand for money. *Journal of Political Economy* 74 (April): 111–31.

Christensen, Laurits R., and Jorgenson, Dale W. 1973. U.S. income, saving, and wealth, 1929–1969. *Review of Income and Wealth* 19 (December): 329–62.

Clapham, Sir John. 1945. *The Bank of England, 1694–1914*. Cambridge: Cambridge University Press.

Connolly, M., and Taylor, D. 1976a. Adjustment to devaluation with money and nontraded goods. *Journal of International Economics* 6 (August): 289–98.

———. 1976b. Testing the monetary approach to devaluation in developing countries. *Journal of Political Economy* 84, part 1 (August): 849–59.

Courchene, T. J. 1969. An analysis of the Canadian money supply, 1925–34. *Journal of Political Economy* 77 (May/June): 363–91.

Crouch, R. L. 1967. A model of the United Kingdom's monetary sector. *Econometrica* 35 (July–October): 398–418.

Cukierman, Alex. 1977. A test of expectational processes using information from the capital market—the Israeli case. *International Economic Review* 18 (October): 737–53.

Cukierman, Alex, and Wachtel, Paul. 1979. Differential inflationary expectations and the variability of the rate of inflation: Theory and evidence. *American Economic Review* 69 (September): 595–609.

Culbertson, John M. 1964. United States monetary history: Its implications for monetary theory. *National Banking Review* 1 (March): 372–75.

Darby, Michael R. 1975. The financial and tax effects of monetary policy on interest rates. *Economic Inquiry* 13 (June): 266–76.

———. 1976. Price and wage controls: Further evidence. In *The economics of price and wage controls*, ed. Karl Brunner, and Allan H. Meltzer. Carnegie-Rochester Conference Series on Public Policy, vol. 2. Amsterdam: North-Holland.

Davis, Lance E., and Hughes, Jonathan R. T. 1960. A dollar-sterling exchange, 1803–95. *Economic History Review* vol. 8, table A-2.

Deane, Phyllis. 1968. New estimates of gross national product for the United Kingdom, 1830–1914. *Review of Income and Wealth* 6: 104–7.

Deane, Phyllis, and Cole, W. A. 1962. *British economic growth, 1888–1959: Trends and structure*. Cambridge: Cambridge University Press.

Deaver, John V. 1970. The Chilean inflation and the demand for money. In *Varieties of monetary experience*, ed. David Meiselman. Chicago: University of Chicago Press.

Defris, L. V., and Williams, R. A. 1979. Quantitative versus qualitative measures of price expectations. *Economic Letters* 2 (2): 169–73.

De Menil, G., and Bhalla, S. S. 1975. Direct measurement of popular price expectations. *American Economic Review* 65 (March): 169–80.

Demery, D., and Duck, N. 1978. The behavior of nominal interest rates in the U.K., 1961–73. *Economica* 45 (February): 23–37.

Dow, J. C. R. 1964. *The management of the British economy, 1945–60*. Cambridge: Cambridge University Press.

Drakatos, C. 1963. Leading indicators for the British economy. *National Institute Economic Review*, no. 24 (May), p. 43.

Durand, David. 1942. *Basic yields of corporate bonds, 1900–1942*. Technical Paper 3. New York: NBER.

Dwyer, Gerald P., Jr. 1979. An explanation of the Gibson paradox. Ph.D. diss., University of Chicago.

Easterlin, Richard A. 1962. *The American baby boom in historical perspective*. NBER Occasional Paper 79. New York: NBER.

———. 1968. *Population, labor force, and long swings in economic growth*. New York: NBER.

Elliott, J. Walter. 1977. Measuring the expected real rate of interest: An exploration of macroeconomic alternatives. *American Economic Review* 67 (June): 429–43.

Fabricant, Solomon. 1972. The "recession" of 1969–1970. In *The business cycle today*, ed. Victor Zarnowitz. NBER Fiftieth Anniversary Colloquim I. New York: NBER.

Fama, Eugene. 1975. Short-term interest rates as predictors of inflation. *American Economic Review* 65 (June): 269–82.

———. 1976. Inflation uncertainty and expected return on Treasury bills. *Journal of Political Economy* 84 (June): 427–48.

———. 1977. Interest rates and inflation: The message in the entrails. *American Economic Review* 67 (June): 487–96.

Fand, David I. 1967. Some implications of money supply analysis. *American Economic Association Papers and Proceedings* 57 (May): 380–400.

Feige, Edgar L. 1964. *The demand for liquid assets: A temporal cross-section analysis.* Englewood Cliffs, N.J.: Prentice-Hall.

———. 1974. Alternative temporal cross-section specifications of the demand for demand deposits. In *Issues in monetary economics,* ed. Harry G. Johnson and A. R. Nobay. London: Oxford University Press.

Feige, Edgar L., and Pearce, Douglas K. 1974. The causality relationship between money and income: A time series approach. Unpublished paper. University of Wisconsin Department of Economics.

———. 1976*a*. Inflation and incomes policy: An application of time series models. In *The economics of price and wage controls,* ed. Karl Brunner and Allan H. Meltzer. Carnegie-Rochester Conference Series on Public Policy, vol. 2. Amsterdam: North-Holland.

———. 1976*b*. Economically rational expectations: Are innovations in the rate of inflation independent of innovations in measures of monetary and fiscal policy? *Journal of Political Economy* 84 (June): 499–522.

Feinstein, Charles H. 1972. *National income, expenditure, and output of the United Kingdom, 1855–1965.* Cambridge: Cambridge University Press.

Feldman, S. J. 1974. The formation of price expectations and the nominal rate of interest: Is Fisher right? Federal Reserve Bank of New York Research Paper no. 7416 (July).

Feldstein, Martin. 1976. Inflation, income taxes, and the rate of interest: A theoretical analysis. *American Economic Review* 66 (December): 809–30.

Fisher, Douglas. 1970. The instruments of monetary policy and the generalized tradeoff function for Britain, 1955–1968. *Manchester School of Economics and Social Studies* 38 (September): 209–22.

Fisher, Franklin M. 1966. *The identification problem in econometrics.* New York: McGraw-Hill.

Fisher, Irving. 1896. *Appreciation and interest.* Cambridge, Mass.: American Economic Association.

———. 1907. *The rate of interest.* New York: Macmillan.

———. 1911. *The purchasing power of money.* New York: Macmillan. Rev. ed. 1920. 2d rev. ed. 1922. Reprinted New York: Kelley, 1963.

———. 1919. Money, prices, credit, and banking. *American Economic Review* 9 (June): 407–9.

———. 1926. A statistical relation between unemployment and price changes. *International Labour Review* 6 (June): 785–92. Reprinted

1973, *Journal of Political Economy* 81 (March/April): 496–502.

———. 1930. *The theory of interest*. New York: Macmillan.

Foster, John. Interest rates and inflation expectations: The British experience. *Oxford Bulletin of Economics and Statistics* 41 (May): 145–64.

Frenkel, Jacob A. 1975. Inflation and the formation of expectations. *Journal of Monetary Economics* 1 (October): 403–21.

———. 1976. Adjustment mechanisms and the monetary approach to the balance of payments. In *Recent issues in international monetary economics*, ed. E. Classin, and P. Salin. Amsterdam: North-Holland.

———. 1977. The forward exchange rate, expectations, and the demand for money: The German hyperinflation. *American Economic Review* 67 (September) 653–70.

Frenkel, Jacob A., and Johnson, Harry J. 1976. The monetary approach to the balance of payments: Essential concepts and historical origins. In *The monetary approach to the balance of payments*, ed. J. Frenkel and H. Johnson. Toronto: University of Toronto Press.

Frickey, Edwin. 1947. *Production in the United States, 1860–1914*. Cambridge: Harvard University Press.

Friedman, Benjamin M. 1978. Stability and rationality in models of hyperinflation. *International Economic Review* 19 (February): 45–64.

———. 1979. Optimal expectations and the extreme information assumptions of "rational expectations" macromodels. *Journal of Monetary Economics* 5 (January): 23–42.

Friedman, Milton. 1955. Leon Walras and his economic system. *American Economic Review* 45 (December): 900–909.

———. 1956. The quantity theory of money—a restatement. In *Studies in the quantity theory of money*, ed. M. Friedman. University of Chicago Press. Reprinted in M. Friedman, *The optimum quantity of money and other essays*. Chicago: Aldine, 1969.

———. 1957. *A theory of the consumption function*. Princeton: Princeton University Press for NBER.

———. 1958. The supply of money and changes in prices and output. In *The relationship of prices to economic stability and growth*, ed. United States Congress, Joint Economic Committee. Reprinted in Friedman (1969).

———. 1959. The demand for money: Some theoretical and empirical results. *Journal of Political Economy* 67 (August): 327–51. Reprinted as NBER Occasional Paper 68. New York: NBER. Reprinted in Friedman (1969).

———. 1961. The lag in effect of monetary policy. *Journal of Political Economy* 69 (October): 447–66. Reprinted in Friedman (1969).

———. 1962a. *The interpolation of time series by related series*. Technical Paper 16. New York: NBER.

———. 1962b. *Price theory*. Chicago: Aldine. 2d ed. 1976.

————. 1964. The monetary studies of the National Bureau. In *The National Bureau enters its forty-fifth year.* 44th Annual Report. New York: NBER. Reprinted in Friedman (1969).

————. 1966. Interest rates and the demand for money. *Journal of Law and Economics* 9 (October): 71–85. Reprinted in Friedman (1969).

————. 1967. The monetary theory and policy of Henry Simons. *Journal of Law and Economics* 10 (October): 1–13. Reprinted in Friedman (1969).

————. 1968a. The role of monetary policy. *American Economic Review* 58 (March): 1–17. Reprinted in Friedman (1969).

————. 1968b. Factors affecting the level of interest rates. In *Proceedings of the 1968 conference on savings and residential financing.* Chicago: United States Savings and Loan League.

————. 1968c. Money: Quantity theory. *International encyclopedia of the social sciences*, Vol. 10. New York: Macmillan and Free Press.

————. 1969. *The optimum quantity of money and other essays.* Chicago: Aldine.

————. 1970a. A theoretical framework for monetary analysis. *Journal of Political Economy* 78 (March/April): 193–238.

————. 1970b. *The counter-revolution in monetary theory.* Institute of Economic Affairs for the Wincott Foundation. Occasional Paper 33. London: Tonbridge.

————. 1971. A monetary theory of nominal income. *Journal of Political Economy* 79 (March/April): 323–37.

————. 1974. Comments on the critics. In *Milton Friedman's monetary framework*, ed. Robert J. Gordon. Chicago: University of Chicago Press.

————. 1975. Comment: The rediscovery of money. *American Economic Review Papers and Proceedings* 65 (May): 176–78.

————. 1977a. Inflation and unemployment (Nobel lecture). *Journal of Political Economy* 85 (June): 451–72.

————. 1977b. Time perspective in the demand for money. *Scandinavian Journal of Economics* 79 (4): 397–416.

Friedman, Milton, and Meiselman, David. 1963. The relative stability of monetary velocity and the investment multiplier in the United States, 1897–1958. In *Stabilization policies*, ed. Commission on Money and Credit. Englewood Cliffs, N.J.: Prentice-Hall.

Friedman, Milton, and Schwartz, Anna J. 1963a. Money and business cycles. *Review of Economics and Statistics* 45, no. 1, part 2 (February): 32–64. Reprinted in Friedman (1969).

————. 1963b. *A monetary history of the United States, 1867–1960.* Princeton: Princeton University Press for NBER.

————. 1970. *Monetary statistics of the United States.* New York: Columbia University Press for NBER.

Gallman, Robert E. 1966. Gross national product in the United States, 1834–1909. In *Output, employment, and productivity in the United States after 1800.* Studies in Income and Wealth, no. 30. Princeton: Princeton University Press for NBER.

Gandolfi, Arthur E. 1976. Taxation and the "Fisher effect." *Journal of Finance* 31 (December): 1375–86.

Gandolfi, Arthur E., and Lothian, James R. 1977. Did monetary forces cause the Great Depression? *Journal of Money, Credit and Banking* 9 (November): 679–91.

Garbade, Kenneth, and Wachtel, Paul. 1978. Time variation in the relationship between inflation and interest rates. *Journal of Monetary Economics* 4 (November): 755–65.

Gibson, William E. 1970. Price-expectations effects on interest rates. *Journal of Finance* 25 (March): 19–34.

———. 1972. Interest rates and inflationary expectations. *American Economic Review* 62 (December): 854–65.

Gibson, William E., and Kaufman, George G. 1968. The sensitivity of interest rates to changes in money and income. *Journal of Political Economy* 76 (May/June): 472–78.

Goldfeld, Stephen M. 1966. *Commercial bank behavior and economic activity.* Amsterdam: North-Holland.

———. 1973. The demand for money revisited. *Brookings Papers on Economic Activity*, no. 3, pp. 577–646.

Goodhart, Charles A. E. 1972. *The business of banking, 1891–1914.* London School of Economics Research Monographs. London: Weidenfeld and Nicolson.

Goodhart, Charles A. E., and Crockett, A. D. 1970. The importance of money. *Quarterly Bulletin, Bank of England* 10 (June): 159–98.

Gordon, Robert J. 1971. Inflation in recession and recovery. *Brookings Papers on Economic Activity*, no. 1, pp. 145–48.

———. 1973. Interest rates and prices in the long run: A comment. *Journal of Money, Credit and Banking* 5, no. 1, part 2 (February): 460–65.

———, ed. 1974. *Milton Friedman's monetary framework: A debate with his critics.* Chicago: University of Chicago Press.

———. 1975. Alternative responses of policy to external supply shocks. *Brookings Papers on Economic Activity*, no. 1, pp. 183–206.

———. 1976. Recent developments in the theory of inflation and unemployment. *Journal of Monetary Economics* 2 (April): 185–219.

———. 1980. A consistent characterization of a near-century of price behavior. *American Economic Review Papers and Proceedings* 70 (May): 243–49.

Gottlieb, Manuel M. 1964. *Estimates of residential building, United States, 1840–1939.* Technical Paper 17. New York: NBER.

————. 1976. *Long swings in urban development*. New York: NBER.

Gould, J. P., and Nelson, C. R. 1974. The stochastic structure of the velocity of money. *American Economic Review* 65 (June): 405–18.

Gramley, Lyle, and Chase, Samuel B., Jr. 1965. Time deposits in monetary analysis. *Federal Reserve Bulletin* 51 (October): 1380–1406. Reprinted in Karl Brunner, ed. *Targets and indicators of monetary policy*. San Francisco: Chandler, 1969.

Grassman, Sven. 1980. Long-term trends in openness of national economies. *Oxford Economic Papers* 32 (March): 123–33.

Gray, Jo Anna. 1978. On indexation and contract length. *Journal of Political Economy* 86 (February): 1–18.

Great Britain, Central Statistical Office. 1964. *Method of construction and calculation of the index of retail prices*. Studies in Official Statistics, no. 6. London: HMSO.

Great Britain, Central Office of Information. 1979. *Britain 1979: An official handbook*. London: HMSO.

Griffiths, Brian. 1973. The development of restrictive practices in the U.K. monetary system. *Manchester School of Economics and Social Studies* 41 (March): 3–18.

Grossman, Herschel. 1972. Was Keynes a "Keynesian"? A Review Article. *Journal of Economic Literature* 10 (March): 26–30.

Gupta, Suraj. 1964. Expected rate of change of prices and rates of interest. Ph.D. diss., University of Chicago.

Gurley, John G., and Shaw, Edward S. 1959. *Money in a theory of finance*. Washington, D.C.: Brookings Institution.

Haberler, Gottfried. 1941. *Prosperity and depression*. 3d ed. Geneva: League of Nations.

Hamburger, Michael J. 1977. The demand for money in an open economy: Germany and the United Kingdom. *Journal of Monetary Economics* 3 (January): 25–40.

Hansen, Alvin. 1957. *The American economy*. New York: McGraw-Hill.

Harkness, J. P. 1968. A spectral-analytic test of the long-swing hypothesis in Canada. *Review of Economics and Statistics* 50 (November): 429-36.

Harley, C. Knick. 1977. The interest rate and prices in Britain, 1873–1913: A study of the Gibson paradox. *Explorations in Economic History* 14 (February): 169–89.

Hatanaka, M., and Howrey, E. P. 1969. Low frequency variation in economic time series. *Kyklos* 22 (3): 752–63.

Hay, K. A. J. 1967. Money and cycles in post confederation Canada. *Journal of Political Economy* 75 (June): 262–73.

Heller, H. Robert. 1965. The demand for money: The evidence from the short-run data. *Quarterly Journal of Economics* 79 (May): 291–303.

Heller, H. Robert, and Khan, Mohsin S. 1979. The demand for money and the term structure of interest rates. *Journal of Political Economy* 87 (February): 109–29.

Helliweill, John, and Maxwell, Tom. 1974. Monetary interdependence of Canada and the United States under alternative exchange rate systems. In *National monetary policies and the international financial system*, ed. Robert Z. Aliber. Chicago: University of Chicago Press.

Hess, Patrick, and Bicksler, James J. 1975. Capital asset prices versus time series models as predictors of inflation. *Journal of Financial Economics* 2 (December): 341–60.

Hester, Donald, and Tobin, James, eds. 1967. *Financial markets and economic activity*. Cowles Foundation Monograph 21. New York: Wiley.

Holden, K., and Peel, D. A. 1977. An empirical investigation of inflationary expectations. *Oxford Bulletin of Economics and Statistics* 39 (November): 291–99.

Holmes, A. B., and Kwast, M. L. 1979. Interest rates and inflationary expectations: Tests for structural changes, 1952–1976. *Journal of Finance* 34 (June): 732–41.

Holzman, Franklyn D., and Bronfenbrenner, Martin. 1963. Survey of inflation theory. *American Economic Review* 53 (September): 593–661.

Homer, Sidney. 1963. *A history of interest rates*. New Brunswick, N.J.: Rutgers University Press.

Howrey, E. P. 1968. A spectrum analysis of the long-swing hypothesis. *International Economic Review* 9 (June): 228–52.

Hume, David. 1752. *Political discourses*. Edinburgh: Fleming.

Ibbotson, R. G., and Sinquefield, R. A. 1976. Stocks, bonds, bills, and inflation: Year-by-year historical returns (1926–1974). *Journal of Business* 49 (January): 11–47.

Ibrahim, I. B., and Williams, R. M. 1978*a*. The Fisher relationship under different monetary standards. *Journal of Money, Credit and Banking* 10 (August): 363–70.

———. 1978*b*. Price unpredictability and monetary standards: A comment on Klein's measure of price uncertainty. *Economic Inquiry* 16 (July): 431–37.

Jenkins, Glenn P. 1971. The role of the United States money stock in a model of the Canadian economy. Paper given at the Money and Banking Workshop at the University of Chicago (April).

Jevons, William Stanley. 1871. *The theory of political economy*. 2d ed. 1879. London: Macmillan.

———. 1884. *Investigations in currency and finance*. 2d ed. 1909. London: Macmillan.

Johnson, Harry G. 1961. *The General Theory* after twenty-five years. *American Economic Association Papers and Proceedings* 51(May): 1–17.

———. 1967*a*. The neo-classical one-sector growth model: A geometrical exposition and extension to a monetary economy. In *Essays in monetary economics*. London: Allen and Unwin.

―――. 1967*b*. Neutrality of money in growth models: A reply. *Economica*, n.s., 34 (February): 73–74.

Johnson, Harry G., and associates, eds. 1972. The supply of money. Section 3. In *Readings in British monetary economics*. Oxford: Clarendon Press.

Johnson, Karen. 1977. Inflation and interest rates: Recent evidence. Discussion Paper no. 10. Stanford Workshop on the Microeconomics of Inflation (May).

Jonung, Lars. 1975. Money and prices in Sweden, 1732–1972. In *Inflation in the world economy*, ed. J. M. Parkin and G. Zis. Manchester: Manchester University Press.

Juster, F. Thomas, and Wachtel, Paul. 1972. Inflation and the consumer. *Brookings Papers on Economic Activity*, no. 1, pp. 71–121.

Kantor, Brian. 1979. Rational expectations and economic thought. *Journal of Economic Literature* 17 (December): 1422–41.

Kareken, John H., and Wallace, Neil, eds. 1980. *Models of monetary economies*. Minneapolis: Federal Reserve Bank of Minneapolis.

Katona, George; Mandell, Lewis; and Schmiedeskamp, Jay. 1971. *1970 survey of consumer finances*. Survey Research Center, Institute for Social Research. Ann Arbor: University of Michigan.

Kendrick, John W. 1961. *Productivity trends in the United States*. Princeton: Princeton University Press for NBER.

Kessel, Reuben. 1965. *The cyclical behavior of the term structure of interest rates*. Occasional Paper 91. New York: NBER.

Keynes, John Maynard. 1923. *A tract on monetary reform*. London: Macmillan. Reprinted in 1971, Royal Economic Society.

―――. 1930. *A treatise on money*. Vol. 2. London: Macmillan. Reprinted in 1971, Royal Economic Society.

―――. 1936. *The general theory of employment, interest, and money*. London: Macmillan. Reprinted in 1973, Royal Economic Society.

―――. 1946. The balance of payments of the United States. *Economic Journal* 56 (June): 172–87.

Klein, Benjamin. 1970. The payment of interest on commercial bank deposits and the price of money: A study of the demand for money. Ph.D. diss., University of Chicago.

―――. 1975. Our new monetary standard: The measurement and effects of price uncertainty, 1880–1973. *Economic Inquiry* 13 (April): 461–84.

―――. 1977. The demand for quality-adjusted cash balances: Price uncertainty in the U.S. demand for money function. *Journal of Political Economy* 85 (August): 691–715.

―――. 1978. The measurement of long- and short-term price uncertainty: A moving regression analysis. *Economic Inquiry* 16 (July): 438–52.

Klein, John J. 1956. German money and prices, 1932–44. In *Studies in the quantity theory of money*, ed. M. Friedman. Chicago: University of Chicago Press.

———. 1960. Price-level and money-denomination movements. *Journal of Political Economy* 68 (August): 369–78.

Klein, Phillip A. 1976. Postwar growth cycles in the United Kingdom: An interim report. *Explorations in Economic Research* 3, no. 1 (winter): 110.

Klotz, Benjamin P. 1973. Oscillatory growth in three nations. *Journal of the American Statistical Association* 60 (August): 562–67.

Konig, H. Demand function, short-run and long-run function, and the distributed lag. *Zeitschrift für die Gesamte Staatswissenschaft* (February): 124 ff.

Koopmans, T. C. 1953. Identification problems in model construction. In *Studies in econometric method*, ed. W. C. Hood and T. C. Koopmans. Cowles Commission Monograph no. 14. New York: Wiley.

Koyck, L. M. 1954. *Distributed lags and investment analysis*. Amsterdam: North-Holland.

Kravis, Irving B.; Heston, Alan W.; and Summers, Robert. 1978. Real GDP *per capita* for more than one hundred countries. *Economic Journal* 88 (June): 215–42.

Kuznets, Simon. 1952. Long-term changes in the national income of the United States of America since 1870. In *Income and wealth in the United States, trends and structure*. Income and Wealth, series 2. Cambridge: Bowes and Bowes.

———. 1956. Quantitative aspects of the economic growth of nations. 1. Levels and variability of rates of growth. *Economic Development and Cultural Change* 5 (October): 1–94.

———. 1958. Long swings in the growth of population and related economic variables. *Proceedings of the American Philosophical Society* 102 (February): 25–52.

———. 1961. *Capital in the American economy: Its formation and financing*. Princeton: Princeton University Press for NBER.

———. 1965. *Economic growth and structure*. New York: Norton.

———. 1971. *Economic growth of nations*. Cambridge: Harvard University Press.

Lahiri, Kajal. 1976. Inflationary expectations: Their formation and interest rate effects. *American Economic Review* 66 (March): 124–31.

Lahiri, Kajal, and Lee, Jungsoo. 1979. Tests of rational expectations and the Fisher effect. *Southern Economic Journal* 46 (October): 413–24.

Laidler, David. 1971. The influence of money on economic activity: A survey of some current problems. In *Monetary theory and policy in the 1970s*, ed. G. Clayton, J. C. Gilbert and R. Sedgwick. London: Oxford University Press.

———. 1980. Monetarism: An interpretation and an assessment. University of Western Ontario Centre for the Study of International Economic Relations, Working Paper no. 8010 (July).

Laurent, Robert. 1969. Currency transfers by denominations. Ph.D. diss., University of Chicago.

Lebergott, Stanley. 1964. *Manpower in economic growth*. New York: McGraw-Hill.

Lefton, Norman. 1972. The demand for real cash balances and the expected permanent and contemporaneous rates of change of prices. Ph.D. diss., University of Chicago.

Leijonhufvud, Axel. 1968. *On Keynesian economics and the economics of Keynes*. London: Oxford University Press.

———. 1974. Keynes' employment function. *History of Political Economy* 6: 158–74.

Levi, Maurice D., and Makin, John H. 1979. Fisher, Phillips, Friedman, and the measured impact of inflation on interest. *Journal of Finance* 34 (March): 35–52.

Lothian, James R. 1976. The demand for high-powered money. *American Economic Review* 66 (March): 56–68.

Lucas, Robert E., Jr. 1972. Econometric testing of the natural rate hypothesis. In *The econometrics of price determination conference*, ed. Otto Eckstein. Washington, D.C.: Board of Governors of the Federal Reserve System and Social Science Research Council.

———. 1973. Some international evidence on output-inflation tradeoffs. *American Economic Review* 63 (June): 326–34.

———. 1976. Econometric policy evaluation: A critique. In *The Phillips curve and labor markets*, ed. Karl Brunner and Allan H. Meltzer. Carnegie-Rochester Conference Series on Public Policy, vol. 1. Amsterdam: North-Holland.

McCallum, Bennett T., ed. 1980. Rational expectations: A seminar sponsored by the American Enterprise Institute. *Journal of Money, Credit and Banking*, 12 part 2 (November): 691–836.

Macaulay, Frederick R. 1938. *The movements of interest rates, bond yields and stock prices in the United States since 1856*. New York: NBER.

McCloskey, Donald N., and Zecher, J. Richard. 1976. How the gold standard worked, 1880–1913. In *The monetary approach to the balance of payments*, ed. J. A. Frenkel and H. G. Johnson. London: George Allen and Unwin.

McGuire, Timothy W. 1976. On estimating the effects of controls. In *The economics of price and wage controls*, ed. Karl Brunner and Allan H. Meltzer. Carnegie-Rochester Conference Series on Public Policy, vol. 2. Amsterdam: North-Holland.

Marshall, Alfred. 1926. *Official papers*. London: Macmillan.

Martin, P. W. 1924. *The flaw in the price system*. London: King.

Marty, Alvin. 1968. The optimal rate of growth of money. *Journal of Political Economy* 76, part 2 (July/August): 860–73.

Matthews, R. C. O. 1969. Postwar business cycles in the United Kingdom. In *Is the business cycle obsolete?* ed. Martin Bronfenbrenner. New York: Wiley.

Meiselman, David, ed. 1970. *Varieties of monetary experience.* Chicago: University of Chicago Press.

Meltzer, Allan H. 1959. The behavior of the French money supply: 1938–54. *Journal of Political Economy* 67 (June): 275–91.

———. 1963. The demand for money: The evidence from the time series. *Journal of Political Economy* 71 (June): 219–46.

———. 1965. Monetary theory and monetary history. *Schweizerische Zeitschrift für Volkswirtschaft und Statistik* 101, no. 4 (December): 404–22.

Melvin, Michael. 1981. Competitive interest payments and the demand for money: Economic forces or spurious correlation? Unpublished paper, January, Arizona State University.

Mill, John Stuart. 1844. Review of books by Thomas Tooke and R. Torrens. *Westminster Review* 41 (June): 579–93.

———. 1848. *Principles of political economy.* London: Parker, Son and Bourn. 5th ed. 1862.

Mills, Terry C., and Wood, Geoffrey E. 1978. Money-income relationships and the exchange rate regime. *Federal Reserve Bank of Saint Louis Review* 60 (August): 22–27.

Mishkin, Frederic S. 1981. Monetary policy and long-term interest rates: An efficient markets approach. *Journal of Monetary Economics* 7 (January): 29–55.

Mitchell, B. R., and Deane, Phyllis. 1962. *Abstract of British historical statistics.* Cambridge: Cambridge University Press.

Mitchell, Wesley C. 1908. *Gold, prices, and wages under the greenback standard.* Berkeley: University of California Press.

———. 1927. *Business cycles.* New York: NBER.

Modigliani, Franco, and Sutch, Richard. 1966. Innovations in interest rate policy. *American Economic Review Papers and Proceedings* 56 (May): 178–97.

Moggridge, D. E. 1971. British controls on long-term capital movements, 1924–1931. In ed. Donald N. McCloskey. *Essays on a mature economy: Britain after 1840.* Princeton: Princeton University Press.

Moore, Geoffrey H., ed. 1961. *Business cycle indicators*: Vol. 1. *Contributions to the analysis of current business conditions.* Princeton: Princeton University Press for NBER.

———. 1980. *Business cycles, inflation, and forecasting.* Cambridge, Mass.: Ballinger for NBER.

Morgenstern, Oskar. 1959. *International financial transactions and busi-*

ness cycles. Studies in Business Cycles, no. 8. Princeton: Princeton University Press for NBER.

Mullineaux, Donald J. 1980. Unemployment, industrial production, and inflation uncertainty in the United States. *Review of Economics and Statistics* 62 (May): 163–69.

Mundell, Robert. 1963. Inflation and real interest. *Journal of Political Economy* 71 (June): 280–83.

Muth, John F. 1961. Rational expectations and the theory of price movements. *Econometrica* 29 (July): 313–35.

Nelson, Charles R., and Schwert, G. William. 1977. Short-term interest rates as predictors of inflation: On testing the hypothesis that the real rate of interest is constant. *American Economic Review* 67 (June): 478–86.

Nerlove, Marc. 1958. *Distributed lags and demand analysis*. Agriculture Handbook no. 141. Washington, D.C.: Department of Agriculture.

Nishimura, Shizuya. 1973. The growth of the stock of money in the U.K., 1870–1913. Unpublished paper. Hosei University, Tokyo.

Nobay, A. R. 1972. A model of the United Kingdom monetary authorities' behaviour, 1958–1969. Paper presented at Money Study Group Conference (February).

O'Dea, D. J. 1975. *Cyclical indicators for the postwar British economy*. Cambridge: Cambridge University Press for National Institute of Economic and Social Research.

O.E.C.D. 1970, 1975. *Economic surveys: United Kingdom*. Paris: OECD Publications.

Okhawa, Kayushi, and Rosovsky, Henry. 1973. *Japanese economic growth: Trend acceleration in the twentieth century*. Studies of Economic Growth in Industrialized Countries. Stanford, Calif.: Stanford University Press.

Okun, Arthur M. 1963. Money and business cycles: A comment. *Review of Economics and Statistics* 45, suppl. (1), part 2 (February): 72–77.

O'Leary, P. J., and Lewis, W. Arthur. 1955. Secular swings in production and trade, 1870–1913. *Manchester School of Economics and Social Studies* 23 (May): 113–52. Reprinted in R. A. Gordon and L. R. Klein eds., [American Economic Association] *Readings in business cycles*. Homewood, Ill.: Irwin, 1965.

Patinkin, Don. 1948. Price flexibility and full employment. *American Economic Review* 38 (September): 543–64. Revised and reprinted in F. A. Lutz and L. W. Mints, [American Economic Association] *Readings in monetary theory*. Homewood, Ill.: Irwin, 1951.

———. 1972. On the short-run non-neutrality of money in the quantity theory. *Banca Nazionale del Lavoro Quarterly Review* 100 (March): 3–22.

———. 1974. Friedman on the quantity theory and Keynesian economics. In *Milton Friedman's monetary framework*, ed. Robert J. Gordon. Chicago: University of Chicago Press.

Pesando, James E. 1975. A note on the rationality of the Livingston price expectations. *Journal of Political Economy* 83 (August): 849–58.

Phillips, A. W. 1958. The relation between unemployment and the rate of change of money wage rates in the United Kingdom, 1861–1957. *Economica* 25 (November): 283–99.

Pigou, Arthur C. 1917. The value of money. *Quarterly Journal of Economics* 32 (November): 38–65. Reprinted in F. A. Lutz and L. W. Mints, [American Economic Association] *Readings in monetary theory*. Homewood, Ill.: Irwin, 1951.

———. 1947. Economic progress in a stable environment. *Economica*, n.s., 14 (August): 180–88.

Pollard, Sidney. 1962. *The development of the British economy, 1914–1950*. London: E. Arnold.

Poole, William. 1974. Book review of Phillip Cagan, *The channels of monetary effects of interest rates*. *Journal of Political Economy* 82 (May/June): 665–68.

Presnell, L. S. 1968. Gold reserves, banking reserves, and the banking crisis of 1890. In *Essays in money and banking in honour of R. S. Sayers*, ed. C. R. Whittlsey and J. S. G. Wilson. Oxford: Clarendon Press.

Pyle, David H. 1972. Observed price expectations and interest rates. *Review of Economics and Statistics* 54 (August): 275–81.

[Radcliffe] Committee on the Working of the Monetary System. 1959. *Report*. Cmd. 827. London: HMSO.

Rasche, Robert H. 1972. A review of empirical studies of the money supply mechanism. *Federal Reserve Bank of Saint Louis Review* 54 (July): 11–19.

Robbins, Lionel. 1934. *The great depression*. London: Macmillan.

Roll, Richard. 1972. Interest rates on monetary assets and commodity price changes. *Journal of Finance* 27 (May): 251–78.

Rutledge, John. 1974. *A monetarist model of inflationary expectations*. Cambridge, Mass.: Lexington.

———. 1977. Irving Fisher and autoregressive expectations. *American Economic Review Papers and Proceedings* 67 (February): 200–205.

Sachs, Jeffrey. 1980. The changing cyclical behavior of wages and prices. *American Economic Review* 70 (March): 78–90.

Santomero, A. M., and Seater, J. J. 1978. The inflation-unemployment trade-off: A critique of the literature. *Journal of Economic Literature* 16 (June): 499–544.

Sargent, Thomas. 1971. A note on the "accelerationist" controversy. *Journal of Money, Credit and Banking* 3 (August): 721–25.

———. 1972. Anticipated inflation and the nominal rate of interest. *Quarterly Journal of Economics* 86 (May): 212–25.

———. 1973*a*. Interest rates and prices in the long run: A study of the Gibson paradox. *Journal of Money, Credit and Banking* 5, no. 1, part 2 (February): 383–449.

———. 1973*b*. "Rational" expectations, the real rate of interest, and the "natural" rate of unemployment. *Brookings Papers on Economic Activity*, no. 2, pp. 429–72.

———. 1976. Interest rates and expected inflation: A selective summary of recent research. *Explorations in Economic Research* 3, no. 3 (summer): 303–25.

———. 1977. The demand for money during hyperinflations under rational expectations: I. *International Economic Review* 18 (February): 59–82.

Sargent, Thomas, and Wallace, Neil. 1973*a*. Rational expectations and the dynamics of hyperinflation. *International Economic Review* 14 (June): 328–50.

———. 1973*b*. The stability of models of money and growth with perfect foresight. *Econometrica* 41 (November): 1043–48.

Saul, S. B. 1969. *The myth of the great depression, 1873–1896*. London: Macmillan.

Sayers, R. S. 1960. Monetary thought and monetary policy in England. *Economic Journal* 70 (December): 710–24.

Scadding, John L. 1974. Monetary growth and aggregate savings. Ph.D. diss., University of Chicago.

Schwartz, Anna J. 1981. Understanding 1929–1933. In *The great depression revisited*, ed. Karl Brunner. Boston: Martinus Nijhoff.

Shapiro, Edward. 1976. Fluctuations in prices and output in the United Kingdom, 1921–71. *Economic Journal* 86 (December): 746–58.

Sheppard, David K. 1971. *The growth and role of U.K. financial institutions, 1880–1962*. London: Methuen.

Shiller, Robert J. 1972. Rational expectations and the structure of interest rates. Ph.D. diss., Massachusetts Institute of Technology.

———. 1978. Rational expectations and the dynamic structure of macroeconomic models: A critical review. *Journal of Monetary Economics* 4 (January): 1–44.

Shiller, Robert J., and Siegel, Jeremy J. 1977. The Gibson paradox and historical movements in real interest rates. *Journal of Political Economy* 85 (October): 891–907.

Siegel, Jeremy J. 1975. The correlation between interest and prices: Explanations of the Gibson paradox. Unpublished paper, University of Pennsylvania.

Sijben, J. J. 1980. *Rational expectations and monetary policy*. Germantown, Md.: Sijthoff and Noordhoff.

Sims, Christopher A. 1972. Money, income, and causality. *American Economic Review* 62 (September): 540–52.

Smith, Adam. 1930 [1776]. *The wealth of nations*. Cannan ed. London: Methuen.

Snyder, Carl. 1934. On the statistical relation of trade, credit, and prices. *Review of International Statistical Institute* 2 (October): 278–91.

Solow, Robert M. 1968. Recent controversy in the theory of inflation: An eclectic view. In *Inflation: Its causes, consequences, and control*, ed. Stephen W. Rousseas. Proceedings of a symposium held at New York University, 31 January. Wilton, Conn.: Calvin K. Kazanjian Economics Foundation.

———. 1969. *Price expectations and the behavior of the price level*. Manchester: Manchester University Press.

Soper, John C. 1975. Myth and reality in economic time series: The long swing revisited. *Southern Economic Journal* 41 (April): 570–79.

Stein, Jerome L. 1966. Money and capacity growth. *Journal of Political Economy* 74 (October): 451–65.

Stokes, Houston H. and Neuberger, Hugh. 1979. A note on the stochastic structure of the velocity of money: Some reservations. *American Economist* 23 (fall): 62–4.

Tanzi, Vito. 1975. Inflation, indexation, and interest income taxation. *Banca Nazionale del Lavoro Quarterly Review* 111 (December): 319–28.

———. 1977. Inflation and the incidence of income taxes on interest income: Some results for the United States, 1973–74. *IMF Staff Papers* 24 (July): 200–213.

———. 1980. Inflationary expectations, economic activity, taxes, and interest rates. *American Economic Review* 70 (March): 12–21.

Tawney, R. H. 1943. The abolition of economic controls, 1918–21. *Economic History Review* 13 (1–2): 1–30.

Taylor, Dean G. 1972. The effects of monetary growth on the interest rate. Ph.D. diss., University of Chicago.

———. 1976. Friedman's dynamic models: Empirical tests. *Journal of Monetary Economics* 2 (November): 531–38.

Temin, Peter. 1976. *Did monetary forces cause the great depression?* New York: Norton.

Thomas, Brinley. 1954. *Migration and economic growth*. Cambridge: Cambridge University Press. 2d ed. 1973.

Thornton, Henry. 1939. [1802]. *An enquiry into the nature and effects of the paper credit of Great Britain; Evidence given before the Committees of Secrecy of the two houses of Parliament on the Bank of England, March and April 1797; Some manuscript notes; and speeches on the Bullion Report*, May 1811. Ed. F. A. von Hayek, London: Allen and Unwin.

Tobin, James. 1947. Money wage rates and employment. In *The new economics*, ed. Seymour Harris. New York: Knopf.

————. 1956. The interest-elasticity of transactions demand for cash. *Review of Economics and Statistics* 38 (August): 241–47.

————. 1958. Liquidity preference as behavior towards risk. *Review of Economic Studies* 25 (February): 65–86.

————. 1965*a*. The monetary interpretation of history. *American Economic Review* 55 (June): 464–85.

————. 1965*b*. Money and economic growth. *Econometrica* 33 (October): 671–84.

————. 1974. Friedman's theoretical framework. In *Milton Friedman's monetary framework: A debate with his critics*, ed. Robert J. Gordon. Chicago: University of Chicago Press.

————. 1978. Monetary policies and the economy: The transmission mechanism. *Southern Economic Journal* 44 (January): 421–31.

Tobin, James, and Brainard, William C. 1967. Financial intermediaries and the effectiveness of monetary controls. In *Financial markets and economic activity*. Cowles Foundation Monograph 21. New York: Wiley.

————. 1968. Pitfalls in financial model building. *American Economic Review Papers and Proceedings* 58 (May): 99–122.

Toribio, Juan. 1970. On the monetary effects of repressed inflation. Ph.D. diss., University of Chicago.

Tucker, Donald P. 1966. Dynamic income adjustment to money supply changes. *American Economic Review* 56 (June): 433–49.

Turnovsky, Stephen J. 1970. Empirical evidence on the formation of price expectations. *Journal of the American Statistical Association* 65 (December): 144–54.

————. 1972. The expectations hypothesis and the aggregate wage equation: Some empirical evidence for Canada. *Economica* 39 (February): 1–17.

————. 1974. On the role of inflationary expectations in a short-run macro-economic model. *Economic Journal* 84 (June): 317–37.

Turnovsky, Stephen J., and Wachter, Michael L. 1972. A test of the "expectations hypothesis" using directly observed wages and price expectations. *Review of Economics and Statistics* 54 (February): 47–54.

United States Department of Commerce, Bureau of the Census. 1975. *Historical statistics of the United States, colonial times to 1970.* Bicentennial ed. Washington, D.C.: Government Printing Office.

United States Department of Commerce, Bureau of the Census. 1976, 1979. *Statistical abstract of the United States.* Washington, D.C.: Government Printing Office.

United States Department of Commerce, Bureau of Economic Analysis. 1973. *Long-term economic growth, 1860–1970.* Washington, D.C.: Government Printing Office.

United States Department of Labor, Bureau of Labor Statistics. 1966. *Handbook of methods of surveys and studies*. Bulletin no. 1458. Washington, D.C.: Government Printing Office.

Van Horne, James. 1965. Interest-rate risk and the term structure of interest rates. *Journal of Political Economy* 73 (August): 344–51.

Viner, Jacob. 1924. *Canada's Balance of International Indebtedness, 1900–1913*. Cambridge: Harvard University Press.

Wachtel, Paul. 1977. Survey measures of expected inflation and their potential usefulness. *Analysis of inflation, 1965–1974*, Joel Popkin. In Studies in Income and Wealth, no. 42. Cambridge, Mass.: Ballinger for NBER.

Wallace, Neil. 1980. The overlapping generations model of fiat money. In *Models of monetary economies*, ed. John H. Kareken and Neil Wallace. Minneapolis: Federal Reserve Bank of Minneapolis.

Walters, A. A. 1970. A survey of empirical evidence. In *Money in Britain, 1959–1969*, ed. David R. Croome and Harry G. Johnson. London: Oxford University Press.

———. 1971. *Money in boom and slump*. 3d ed. Hobart Paper 44. London: Institute of Economic Analysis.

Warren, George F., and Pearson, Frank A. 1933. *Prices*. New York: Wiley.

Wicksell, Knut. 1907. The influence of the rate of interest on prices. *Economic Journal* 17 (June): 213–20.

Wold, Herman. 1949. Statistical estimation of economic relationships. *Econometrica* 17, suppl. (July): 1–22.

Wold, Herman, and Strotz, R. H. 1960. Recursive vs. non-recursive systems: An attempt at synthesis. *Econometrica* 28 (April): 417–27.

Wonnacott, Paul. 1965. *The Canadian dollar, 1948–1962*. Toronto: University of Toronto Press.

Working, E. J. 1927. What do statistical "demand curves" show? *Quarterly Journal of Economics* 41 (February): 212–35.

Yohe, William P., and Karnosky, Denis S. 1969. Interest rates and price level changes, 1952–69. *Federal Reserve Bank of St. Louis Review* 51 (December): 19–36.

Zecher, J. Richard. 1970. An evaluation of four econometric models of the financial sector. *Federal Reserve Bank of Cleveland, Economic Papers*, dissertation series no. 1 (January).

Author Index

Subject Index